Asian Americans and the Law

Asian Americans and the Law

Cases and Materials

Denny Chin
LAWRENCE W. PIERCE DISTINGUISHED JURIST IN RESIDENCE
CO-DIRECTOR OF THE CENTER ON ASIAN AMERICANS AND THE LAW
FORDHAM UNIVERSITY SCHOOL OF LAW

UNITED STATES CIRCUIT JUDGE FOR THE UNITED STATES COURT
OF APPEALS FOR THE SECOND CIRCUIT

Thomas H. Lee
LEITNER FAMILY PROFESSOR OF INTERNATIONAL LAW
CO-DIRECTOR OF THE CENTER ON ASIAN AMERICANS AND THE LAW
FORDHAM UNIVERSITY SCHOOL OF LAW

CAROLINA ACADEMIC PRESS
Durham, North Carolina

ISBN 978-1-5310-3186-2
e-ISBN 978-1-5310-3187-9
LCCN 2025948639

Carolina Academic Press
700 Kent Street
Durham, NC 27701
(919) 489-7486
www.caplaw.com

Printed in the United States of America

Dedicated to
the laborers, laundrymen, cooks,
and the others
who fought injustice

Contents

Foreword xiii

Introduction xvii

UNIT ONE
ARRIVAL, EXCLUSION, AND CITIZENSHIP

Chapter 1 · Arrival 5
1. Constitutional and Statutory Provisions 6
   United States Constitution, Article I 7
   An Act to establish an uniform Rule of Naturalization, First Congress of the United States 7
   United States Constitution, Amendment XIV 8
   Act of July 14, 1870 8
   Notes 8
2. The Case of the 22 Lewd Chinese Women 10
   Chy Lung v. Freeman 11
   Notes 14

Chapter 2 · Exclusion 19
1. The Chinese Exclusion Laws 19
   Chinese Exclusion Act of 1882 (excerpt) 20
2. The Chinese Exclusion Cases 22
   Chae Chan Ping v. United States 22
   Notes 32
3. The Travel Ban 37
   Trump v. Hawaii 38
   Notes 62

Chapter 3 · Citizenship 65
1. Birthright Citizenship 65
   United States v. Wong Kim Ark 67
   Notes 79

2. Naturalization 83
In re Ah Yup 84
Notes 87
Ozawa v. United States 89
Notes 94
United States v. Thind 95
Notes 100

UNIT TWO
HISTORICAL DISCRIMINATION

Chapter 4 · Early Violence and Expulsions **111**
1. Los Angeles—1871 111
2. San Francisco—1877 115
3. Eureka, California—1885 117
4. Rock Springs, Wyoming Territory—1885 118
5. Seattle, Washington—1886 119
6. Hells Canyon, Oregon—1887 121
7. Bellingham, Washington—1907 123
8. Watsonville, California—1930 124
Notes 125

Chapter 5 · State Regulation **127**
1. The Pigtail Ordinance Case 127
Ho Ah Kow v. Nunan 127
Notes 135
2. The Chinese Laundry Case 136
Yick Wo v. Hopkins 137
Notes 140
3. The Bubonic Plague Cases 143
Notes 144
4. The Administration of Justice 146
People v. Hall 147
Notes 148
People v. Washington 149
Notes 158
5. Anti-Miscegenation 159
Roldan v. Los Angeles County 160
Notes 164
6. Education 171
Tape v. Hurley 172
Notes 174

Gong Lum v. Rice 174
Notes 178
7. The Bar Admission Cases 184
In re Hong Yen Chang 185
Notes 186
In re Hong Yen Chang on Admission 186
Notes 190
8. Japanese "Alien" Economic Cases 191
A. Pawnbroking 191
Asakura v. City of Seattle 191
Notes 194
B. The Land Law Case 194
Oyama v. California 195
Notes 203

UNIT THREE
INTERNMENT AND REDRESS

Chapter 6 · The Japanese Internment Cases **213**
Hirabayashi v. United States 214
Notes 227
Yasui v. United States 228
Notes 229
Korematsu v. United States 231
Notes 245
Ex parte Endo 246
Notes 250
Trump v. Hawaii 256
Notes 256

Chapter 7 · The Draft Resisters **259**
United States v. Fujii 260
Fujii v. United States 264
Notes 266

Chapter 8 · The Coram Nobis Cases **271**
Korematsu v. United States 271
Notes 279
Hirabayashi v. United States 281
Notes 293

Chapter 9 · Redress and Reparation **295**
Notes 298

UNIT FOUR
CONTEMPORARY ISSUES

Chapter 10 · Spies 303
1. The Tokyo Rose Case 306
   Toguri D'Aquino v. United States 308
   Notes 313
2. *United States v. Wen Ho Lee* 315
   Notes 320
3. Asians in the U.S. Military and the MAVNI Litigation 321
   Tiwari v. Mattis 323
   Notes 330

Chapter 11 · Employment 333
1. The Alaskan Cannery Case 333
   Atonio v. Wards Cove Packing Co. 336
   Atonio v. Wards Cove Packing Co. 337
   Wards Cove Packing Co. v. Atonio 338
   Notes 346
2. The Bamboo Ceiling 347
3. Intersectionalism 351

Chapter 12 · The Model Minority 353

Chapter 13 · Education 357
   Students for Fair Admissions, Inc. v. President and Fellows of Harvard College 359
   Notes 369

Chapter 14 · The Administration of Justice 373
1. *People v. Chol Soo Lee* 373
   In re Chol Soo Lee 377
2. *People v. Abacus Federal Savings Bank* 377
3. Police Officer Peter Liang 378
4. Prosecutorial Discretion and Immunity 380
5. Private Danny Chen 383

Chapter 15 · Contemporary Violence 385
1. 9/11 and the Global Pandemic 385
2. The Vietnamese Fishermen 387
   Vietnamese Fishermen's Ass'n v. Texas Knights of the Ku Klux Klan 388
   Notes 398
3. The Vincent Chin Case 400
   United States v. Ebens 401
   Notes 411

Conclusion 415

Table of Cases 417

Index 421

Foreword

Why a book on Asian Americans and the Law? Until recently, the number of persons of Asian descent in this country has been miniscule: less than 0.2% of the American population until the late 1950s. Only 114,189 people claimed Asian descent in the 1900 census. The numbers grew after changes in the federal immigration laws starting in the 1950s, but they did not exceed 1% until the 1970s. Even as recently as 2020, Asian Americans comprised only 7.2% of this country's population—some 24 million people.

But despite their historically small numbers, Asian Americans have been at the center of a remarkable array of landmark legal controversies. Subjected to discriminatory laws and ordinances at the state and federal levels, denial of American citizenship and its rights, governmental action to keep them out and drive them back to Asia, and acts of outright hostility and violence, Asian Americans pushed back, often taking the fight to the courts. In response to restrictive immigration laws enacted specifically to stem the influx of Chinese laborers into California and other western states, the Chinese filed thousands of petitions for writs of habeas corpus in the federal courts. And during World War II, when military orders uprooted some 120,000 Japanese Americans, two-thirds of them American citizens, from their homes on the West Coast and sent them to concentration camps in isolated areas of the country, Japanese Americans challenged the orders all the way to the Supreme Court of the United States. There are myriad other examples of injustice, many of which are not well known or have long been forgotten, but there were also scores of lawsuits brought to vindicate the rights that had been violated.

Why did episodes of antagonism and resentment against persons of Asian descent in the United States recur? What were the discriminatory legal measures and how and why were they adopted? How did they come to be litigated in the courts? Who were the persons of Asian descent who brought lawsuits to challenge the discriminatory laws? And how did the courts respond? These questions are the subject of this book.

The focus of many of the cases was the Constitution of the United States. Among those drawn to the United States by the promise of liberty and equality enshrined in the Constitution were persons of Asian descent who came in search of better futures, initially perhaps as sojourners but later as American citizens. When they encountered hatred, violence, and discrimination, even though they were individuals of limited means, they looked to the Constitution and the courts, where they were represented by skilled lawyers who asserted creative and innovative legal theories and arguments. Their stories, the challenges they faced, and their experiences with the courts teach us much about the Constitution and what the rule of law means in this country. Those lessons continue to be relevant today.

As discussed in more detail in the Introduction, this book is organized into four units: (1) immigration and citizenship; (2) historical discrimination; (3) internment; and (4) contemporary topics in Asian Americans and the Law. Immigration and internment are the topics most familiar to American law students and the public in general, but they are typically not the subject of sustained attention in American casebooks and courses. Some of the landmark cases in our book's historical and contemporary units—like *Yick Wo v. Hopkins* and *SFFA v. Harvard*—figure prominently in the U.S. constitutional law canon and may also be featured in casebooks and courses on race and the law. In this book, they are set out in the context of larger social and legal trends that involve Asian Americans but impact all Americans. One theme that emerges from this review of Asian American interactions with law and legal institutions over time is that history does indeed repeat itself.

The methodology of the book relies principally on cases (edited for length) chosen with an eye for their use as the central focal point for class discussions. Other legal materials (e.g., the Constitution, statutes, ordinances) are also featured, along with case filings and other primary source documents. Units and Chapters are prefaced and punctuated with organizing thoughts and principles. The Notes following principal cases discuss related cases, provide context as needed, suggest pertinent secondary literature, and also raise questions based on the holdings of the principal cases and future subjects for investigation or research. We have also included photographs, political cartoons, illustrations, and exhibits to help make the cases come alive and to visualize the people involved. Our subject is ultimately grounded in the stories of real people and their interactions with law and legal institutions. Although the primary audience for this book are law students and lawyers, college and secondary-school students and general readers with an interest in Asian American studies or U.S. constitutional law and history will also find the book useful and accessible.

The book grows out of materials that we compiled and edited for a course on Asian Americans and the Law that we first taught at Fordham Law School in 2017. Those materials drew inspiration from a series of historic trial reenactments developed and presented by a team from the Asian American Bar Association of New York. The book also builds upon the path-breaking scholarship of pioneers who led the way, at a time when there was little interest in Asian American history. We have since taught the course multiple times at Fordham and also at Columbia, Harvard, and Yale law schools. We are grateful to the now hundreds of students whose discussions, comments, reactions, and research papers informed and enriched our understanding of the subject. We are also greatly appreciative of the colleagues who used our materials to teach Asian Americans and the Law.

In 2021, we established our Center on Asian Americans and the Law at Fordham Law School, and we acknowledge and deeply appreciate the support of former Dean Matthew Diller and current Dean Joseph Landau. The Center's coordinator, Danielle Kim, has been enormously helpful as we put together the book. Many DC law clerks helped with the development of the Center, our syllabus, and the book, in particular Chloe Bartholomew, Angie Cui, Jamel Gross-Cassel, and Norah Senftleber, who assisted with proofreading and indexing.

Finally, the book would not have been possible without the loving support of our families, especially our partners in life and love, Kathy Hirata Chin and Alexandra Lee.

Denny Chin and Thomas H. Lee
New York, New York
January 1, 2026

Introduction

The history of Asian America is a history reflected in laws and cases. The earliest U.S. legal texts addressing persons of Asian descent were U.S. treaties and California state laws and municipal ordinances dealing with Chinese migrant workers who arrived in the American West in significant numbers after the 1849 Gold Rush. The Chinese were welcome at first as a source of cheap labor, particularly by employers in the mining and railroad industries. But as resentment and prejudice supplanted initial good feelings, the Chinese were subject to discriminatory regulations starting at the local level and culminating in federal statutes excluding Chinese laborers from entering the United States. These statutes were at odds with China-U.S. treaties of amity and commerce that sought to put the two nations on an equal, mutually advantageous footing.

The Chinese brought suits to challenge these restrictive and discriminatory laws and ordinances. They pooled funds and, with the support of U.S. businesses that valued access to Chinese laborers, hired top U.S. lawyers to litigate their interests. The plaintiffs won some of these cases, including a suit brought in U.S. federal court against California laws used to exclude entry by categories of undesired foreigners as applied to Chinese women. It was a Pyrrhic victory, however, as Congress passed a series of increasingly restrictive federal statutes to control the entry of Chinese laborers into the United States. The Supreme Court upheld these statutes, despite the fact that the most restrictive of them blatantly contradicted the terms of applicable U.S.-China bilateral treaties of amity and commerce.

Related to laws controlling entry of Chinese and other Asian migrants into the United States were laws limiting persons who could obtain U.S. citizenship after birth. Until the mid-twentieth century, persons of Asian descent born outside the United States could not be naturalized as citizens under U.S. federal naturalization statutes. It did not matter if such persons of Asian descent had lived in the United States for decades, had fully assimilated to American culture, or even served in the U.S. armed forces. The Supreme Court repeatedly upheld these restrictive naturalization statutes. One bright spot, however, was the Supreme Court's decision in *United States v. Wong Kim Ark*, 169 U.S. 649 (1898). The Court there interpreted the Fourteenth Amendment to ordain that the San-Francisco-born child of Chinese subjects who were domiciled in California was a citizen of the United States by birth, regardless of the status and political allegiance of his parents. Unit One covers these laws and judicial decisions relating to entry, exclusion, and citizenship.

Unit Two addresses various instances of discriminatory laws and actions over more than a century of U.S. history and judicial decisions in which they were challenged. Again, the Asian-American litigants achieved some notable successes in the courts. The courts were often the only recourse for Americans of Asian descent, as foreign-born Asian Americans were not entitled to the political rights of citizenship for most of the Nation's history. Indeed, the fact that residents of Hawaii were predominantly Asian and Pacific Islander was a primary reason why it was denied statehood until 1959, despite the fact that it had been a U.S. territory since 1898.

Resentment and discriminatory acts against Asians in America took many forms. In the 1870s and 1880s, before and after the enactment of the federal exclusion acts, violence against Chinese erupted across California and other western states, where they were present in significant numbers. Asians were also broadly targeted by discriminatory local laws. San Francisco, in particular, enacted ordinances that were applied overwhelmingly against Chinese and other Asians in various matters including hairstyles, laundry houses, and vaccinations. Chinese and then Japanese Americans brought lawsuits that successfully invalidated all three of these specific ordinances. But challenges to other state and local laws alleged to be discriminatory against Asians in the administration of justice, marriage, education, bar admission, and land ownership were not as successful.

Unit Three covers laws and litigation related to the internment of persons of Japanese descent, including U.S. citizens, during World War II. It was a dark chapter in the history of the United States, including with respect to the rule of law, given the Supreme Court's acquiescence in the internment and related policies. Decades later, however, all three branches of the federal government acknowledged their errors in acquiescing in a military policy of forced exclusion, removal, and internment of Japanese-American U.S. citizens in concentration camps because of their race in blatant violation of their constitutional rights. Congress, in particular, authorized reparations. But is it so clear that the United States has evolved to a point that a similar episode will not recur in the near future? And how can we ensure that the rule of law will protect against such recurrence?

Unit Four deals with a range of contemporary issues involving Asian Americans and the Law, and it is accordingly the largest section. We begin with espionage cases implicating Americans of Japanese, Chinese, and other Asian descent. We revisit some of the issues addressed in the earlier units, including the administration of justice, education, and violence, as the issues have evolved with the passage of time but still remain.

Asian Americans and the Law

UNIT ONE

Arrival, Exclusion, and Citizenship

With the exception of indigenous Americans who had inhabited the North American continent for tens of thousands of years, the United States "is a nation of immigrants and their descendants." *Mojica v. Reno*, 970 F. Supp. 130, 143 (E.D.N.Y. 1997) (Weinstein, *J.*). Europeans established the first permanent settlements in the territory of the United States just over four centuries ago, in the early 1600s. In its infancy, the United States welcomed the arrival of new immigrants, as the newcomers provided much-needed labor and helped to fuel westward expansion, often in the face of native American resistance. *See* Lucy E. Salyer, *Laws Harsh as Tigers: Chinese Immigrants and the Shaping of Modern Immigration Law* 2–3 (1995). There was a presumption, however, that the immigrants would be White and of European descent. The American founders' desire to welcome able and ambitious White Europeans coexisted with their acceptance of Black race-based slavery, particularly in the southern states where enslaved labor dominated the economy. The prospect of significant immigration from Asia was so remote and unimaginable that it was not an issue when the United States was established.

The first Asians to settle for extended periods in the United States—Chinese arriving in California in the mid-nineteenth century—were "greeted with a mixture of enthusiasm and curiosity. They were few in number and seemed a harmless and exotic addition to the cosmopolitan mass of humanity that was gathering in Northern California in the wake of discovery of gold at Sutter's Mill." Charles J. McClain, *In Search of Equality: The Chinese Struggle against Discrimination in Nineteenth-Century America* 9 (1994). In a January 1852 address to the California legislature, John McDougal, the second governor of the state, referred to the Chinese as "one of the most worthy classes of our newly adopted citizens." John Mack Faragher, *California: An American History* 229 (2022). The reaction to the Chinese, however, would quickly change as their numbers grew. Governor John Bigler, who succeeded McDougal, urged the legislature to exclude "'Chinese cheap labor' that would drive down the wages of White workers," even as he acknowledged that such exclusion ran against the United States' "'long cherished' policy of welcoming 'the oppressed of all nations.'" *Id.* at 229–30. Hostility to the Chinese led not only to exclusionary policies, but also to myriad discriminatory laws and regulations at the state and then federal levels, blatant bigotry, and rampant acts of violence and murder against the Chinese. As other Asian groups arrived in the United States, they too would face attempts to exclude, discriminatory laws, and widespread instances of race-based bigotry and violence.

We begin our study of Asian Americans and the Law with the arrival of the first Asians in America, the enactment of federal Chinese exclusion laws, and the question what it means to be a citizen of the United States.

Chapter 1
Arrival

The first Asians to land in North America were sailors who arrived in the eighteenth century, decades before the United States declared independence from Great Britain. In 1750, a small group of Filipino sailors landed in what would later become Louisiana, then a French possession.[1] In fact, South and East Asian sailors were common among the crews of European and American sailing ships from the late seventeenth century onward, in large part due to the imperial expansion of the European powers and their East India companies in Asia. These sailors of Asian ethnicity were often called "lascars," derived from the Urdu word "lashkar" meaning an army or camp.[2] In 1785, one such lashkar, named "Sick Keesar," filed an official "memorial" of grievances on behalf of himself and 34 other sailors "from Bengal and China in East India" to the Supreme Executive Council of Pennsylvania in Philadelphia, then led by Benjamin Franklin. The memorial explained that Kessar and the other Asian sailors had been crewed to an American merchantman but were effectively stranded in Baltimore by their employer who refused to pay for their way back. The Council appropriated funds for their subsistence, and, with the support of officials in Maryland and Pennsylvania, the Asian sailors returned to Asia.[3] The episode, only two years before the Constitutional Convention, was the first example of how persons of Asian descent advocated on their behalf in the legal institutions of the United States.

Chinese who were not seamen also began arriving in the United States in the early nineteenth century. Even earlier, in 1788, 50 Chinese men, including carpenters and blacksmiths, were part of Captain John Meares's fur trading post on the Nootka Sound in what is now the Province of British Columbia in Canada.[4] By 1848, however, there were only approximately 325 Chinese (all men)—in the United States. Within just a few years, the numbers jumped dramatically, with some 20,000 Chinese arriving in San Francisco in 1852 alone, when the population of the entire city was only about

1. Gary Y. Okihiro, *The Columbia Guide to Asian American History* xv, 178 (2001); Sucheng Chan, *Asian Americans: An Interpretive History* 25 (1991); Asian Nation, *The First Asian Americans*, *available at* www.asian-nation.org/first.shtml.

2. R.L. Brunhouse, *Lascars in Pennsylvania: A Side-Light on the China Trade*, 7 Pa. History: J. Mid-Atlantic Studies 20–30 (Jan. 1940).

3. *See id.*

4. Gunther Barth, *Bitter Strength: A History of the Chinese in the United States, 1850–1870*, 185 (1964).

36,000 people. The vast majority of this earliest substantial wave of Asians and Pacific Islanders to come to the United States were Chinese male migrant workers, trafficked by foreign labor importers and Chinese middlemen. *See* Barth, supra, at 50–76 (describing different types of Chinese workers and how they were transported from China to the United States). Some came to escape the Taiping Rebellion in China, some dreamed of making a fortune in the California Gold Rush, and others came to work on building out railroads, including the first transcontinental railroad, or on southern plantations after the Civil War.[5]

Other Asian groups followed the Chinese to the United States, seeking work and opportunity. After U.S. Navy Commodore Matthew Perry "opened" Japan to U.S. trade relations, the Japanese started emigrating to the United States in the mid-to-late 1800s. Japanese migrants mostly went to Hawaii, to work as laborers on sugar plantations.[6] As Korea became a Japanese protectorate (1905) and then colony (1910), Korean migrants followed their Japanese predecessors to work in Hawaii, and some eventually made it to the western continental United States. When the Philippines became a U.S. territory in 1898 under the terms of the Treaty of Paris to end the United States' war with Spain, Filipino workers started arriving in the United States in significant numbers. And, starting in the second half of the nineteenth century, workers from India, then a part of the British empire, came to British possessions in the Americas, including Canada, from which some migrated across the border into the U.S. Pacific Northwest.

We will start our discussion of laws relevant to the admission of foreign persons into the United States and the process by which they may become citizens (called naturalization) with relevant provisions in the Constitution and federal naturalization statutes, starting with the first enactment in 1790. We turn then to the case of the 22 Lewd Chinese Women—*Chy Lung v. Freeman*—the first major Supreme Court decision implicating Asian Americans, which the Court decided in favor of the Chinese claimants.

1. Constitutional and Statutory Provisions

The Constitution, which was drafted between May and September 1787 and ratified by the requisite number of States in June 1788, contains two provisions relevant to Congress's power to regulate the entry of persons into the United States and the

5. McClain, at 1–2; Okihiro, at xiii–xiv; George Anthony Peffer, *If They Don't Bring Their Women Here: Chinese Female Immigration Before Exclusion* 121 (1999); Immigration in America (Sept. 22, 2011).

6. Library of Congress, Immigration: Japanese, *available at* www.loc.gov/teachers/ classroommaterials/presentationsandactivities/presentations/immigration/japanese. html.

process by which a foreigner may be "naturalized" as a U.S. citizen. Congress passed its first naturalization statute in 1790. It was amended several times, including in 1870, after the Civil War. The Fourteenth Amendment, ratified in 1868, is also relevant to the rights of foreign persons who have entered the United States. Here are these constitutional and statutory provisions in chronological order:

United States Constitution, Article I

Section 8: The Congress shall have Power . . . To establish an uniform Rule of Naturalization.

Section 9: The Migration or Importation of such Persons as any of the States now existing shall think proper to admit, shall not be prohibited by the Congress prior to the Year one thousand eight hundred and eight, but a Tax or duty may be imposed on such Importation, not exceeding ten dollars for each Person.

An Act to establish an uniform Rule of Naturalization

First Congress of the United States

March 26, 1790, 1 Stat. 104, 104-05

Section 1. *Be it enacted by the Senate and House of Representatives of the United States of America in Congress assembled,* That any alien, being a free white person, who shall have resided within the limits and under the jurisdiction of the United States for the term of two years, may be admitted to become a citizen thereof, on application to any common law court of record, in any one of the states wherein he shall have resided for the term of one year at least, and making proof to the satisfaction of such court, that he is a person of good character, and taking the oath or affirmation prescribed by law, to support the constitution of the United States . . . ; and thereupon such person shall be considered as a citizen of the United States. And the children of such persons so naturalized, dwelling within the United States, being under the age of twenty-one years at the time of such naturalization, shall also be considered as citizens of the United States. And the children of citizens of the United States that may be born beyond sea, or out of the limits of the United States, shall be considered as natural born citizens: *Provided,* That the right of citizenship shall not descend to persons whose fathers have never been resident in the United States.

United States Constitution, Amendment XIV,

§ 1 (1868)

All persons born or naturalized in the United States, and subject to the jurisdiction thereof, are citizens of the United States and of the State wherein they reside. No State shall make or enforce any law which shall abridge the privileges or immunities of citizens of the United States; nor shall any State deprive any person of life, liberty, or property, without due process of law; nor deny to any person within its jurisdiction the equal protection of the laws.

Act of July 14, 1870

§ 7, 16 Statutes at Large 254, 256

And be it further enacted, That the naturalization laws are hereby extended to aliens of African nativity and to persons of African descent.

Notes

1. Why do you think the original Constitution vested Congress with the power to establish "an uniform Rule of Naturalization?" Does it necessarily preempt the respective states' own power to pass laws relating to the admission of foreigners? Why do you think the Constitution does not provide Congress with an explicit Article I, Section 8 power over immigration, that is, the regulation of the entry of foreign persons into the United States? Is such power implicit in Congress's Article I, Section 8 power to "regulate Commerce with foreign nations, and among the several States, and with the Indian Tribes," which immediately precedes the Naturalization Power?

2. In *The Federalist Papers*, John Jay, the first Chief Justice of the United States, the first foreign minister of the United States, and a governor of New York, emphasized the common ancestry, language, religion, and culture of the American people as a significant benefit to the foundation of the United States.[7] Do you agree that

7. *See* John Jay, Federalist No. 2, *Concerning Dangers from Foreign Force and Influence for the Independent Journal* (1787) ("With equal pleasure I have as often taken notice that Providence has been pleased to give this one connected country to one united people—a people descended from the same ancestors, speaking the same language, professing the same religion, attached to the same principles of government, very similar in their manners and customs, and who, by their joint counsels, arms, and efforts, fighting side by side throughout a long and bloody war, have nobly established general liberty and independence.").

homogeneity is advantageous to nation-building? Did there come a time when some leaders and citizens of the United States embraced racial, cultural, and religious diversity—the antithesis of Jay's homogeneity—as beneficial to nation-building? When? How was this acceptance of diversity consistent with the long history of race-based slavery in the United States and the continuation of race-based segregation in the Jim Crow era, well into the late twentieth century? How significantly have things changed, that is, has multiracial diversity fully displaced the opposite view expressed by Jay that racial and cultural homogeneity are a source of strength for the United States? To what extent is assimilation of different racial groups—rather than celebration of differences—a preferable end state for a strong Nation?

3. The First Naturalization Act of 1790 applied only to "free white persons." Why was the adjective "free" used when Black persons were the only enslaved persons? Even if "yellow" or "brown" persons were not contemplated when the First Congress enacted the statute, shouldn't the plain words of the text have been interpreted to exclude them? The general federal naturalization statutes—laws providing for the process by which foreigners can become citizens—had some enduring form of race qualification until 1952. The current U.S. statutes are codified at 8 U.S.C. § 1401 et seq.

4. If Congress has the power to "establish an uniform rule of Naturalization," why does the First Naturalization Act appear to authorize state courts to accept naturalization applications? Do you think that this allowance in the First Naturalization Act is constitutional? Why were courts given the function of naturalizing U.S. citizens?

5. Consider the "natural born citizen" provision of the 1790 Act. What do you think is the significance of the residency requirement for fathers? Specifically, why does the statute say that for children of citizens born outside of the United States, "the right of citizenship shall not descend to persons whose fathers have never been resident in the United States?"

6. The "natural born citizen" provision of the 1790 Act has assumed great importance in constitutional interpretation of the Article II requirement that a person must be a "natural born Citizen" to be eligible to be President of the United States. Recall that the issue arose prominently in the 2016 presidential campaign. *See* Thomas Lee, *Is Ted Cruz a "Natural Born Citizen"? Not If You're a Constitutional Originalist*, L.A. Times, Jan. 10, 2016, *available at* http://www.latimes.com/opinion/op-ed/la-oe-lee-is-ted-cruz-eligible-to-be-president-20160110-story.html. *See also* Thomas H. Lee, *Natural Born Citizen*, 67 Am. Univ. L. Rev. 327 (2017). How exactly are the original 1790 Naturalization Act and its successors relevant to this Founding-era constitutional provision regarding eligibility to be the President? Does "natural born citizen," when used in the Constitution, mean any person who is entitled to U.S. citizenship upon birth? What about the children of persons who

have entered the United States without visas or official permission? If Congress were to enact a statute that provided that any person born in the United States to Chinese-national parents in the United States on a temporary basis (e.g., tourists and students) are not "natural born citizens" eligible to be President, would the statute be unconstitutional? If the answer is yes, under which constitutional provision: the Article II Natural Born Citizen Clause, the Fourteenth Amendment Citizenship Clause, Fifth Amendment Equal Protection, or some other basis? *See* Chapter 3 *infra* on citizenship.

7. Other important immigration statutes include:

    - the Immigration Act of 1917, also known as the Asiatic Barred Zone Act, which restricted the entry of "undesirables" into the country, including individuals from much of Asia and the Pacific Islands;
    - the Immigration Act of 1924, also known as the Johnson-Reed Act, which limited the number of immigrants allowed entry into the United States through a quota system based on nationality; it excluded immigrants from Asia; and
    - the Immigration and Nationality Act of 1965, also known as the Hart-Celler Act, which abolished the national origin quota system and created categories of preferences for admission; however, it continued caps on per-country and total immigration.

---

2. The Case of the 22 Lewd Chinese Women

Almost all of the thousands of Chinese arrivals in California and the West Coast in the first decades after the Gold Rush were men. The first case involving Chinese migrants to reach the U.S. Supreme Court (in 1875), however, involved Chinese women. *Chy Lung v. Freeman*, otherwise known as the Case of the 22 Lewd Chinese Women, involved a challenge in federal court to a California statute authorizing a local official to detain and deport 22 Chinese women who arrived in San Francisco Bay on a ship from Hong Kong, on the view that they were sex workers. Consequently, although prostitution was lawful in San Francisco, the Chinese women were detained for deportation on the basis that each was a "lewd or debauched woman" subject to exclusion under the California law.

Chy Lung v. Freeman

92 U.S. 275 (1875)

Justice MILLER delivered the opinion of the court.

... The plaintiff in error was a passenger on a vessel from China, being a subject of the Emperor of China, and is held a prisoner because the owner or master of the vessel who brought her over refused to give a bond in the sum of $500 in gold, conditioned to indemnify all the counties, towns, and cities of California against liability for her support or maintenance for two years.

... The statute of California, unlike those of New York and Louisiana, does not require a bond for *all* passengers landing from a foreign country, but only for classes of passengers specifically described, among which are 'lewd and debauched women,' to which class it is alleged plaintiff belongs.

The plaintiff, with some twenty other women, on the arrival of the steamer 'Japan' from China, was singled out by the Commissioner of Immigration, an officer of the State of California, as belonging to that class, and the master of the vessel required to give the bond prescribed by law before he permitted them to land. This he refused to do, and detained them on board. They sued out a writ of *habeas corpus*, which by regular proceedings resulted in their committal, by order of the Supreme Court of the State, to the custody of the sheriff of the county and city of San Francisco, to await the return of the 'Japan,' which had left the port pending the progress of the case; the order being to remand them to that vessel on her return, to be removed from the State.

All of plaintiff's companions were released from the custody of the sheriff on a writ of *habeas corpus* issued by Mr. Justice Field of this court. But plaintiff by a writ of error brings the judgment of the Supreme Court of California to this court, for the purpose, as we suppose, of testing the constitutionality of the act under which she is held a prisoner. We regret very much, that, while the Attorney-General of the United States has deemed the matter of such importance as to argue it in person, there has been no argument in behalf of the State of California, the Commissioner of Immigration, or the Sheriff of San Francisco, in support of the authority by which plaintiff is held a prisoner; nor have we been furnished even with a brief in support of the statute of that State.

It is a most extraordinary statute. It provides that the Commissioner of Immigration is 'to satisfy himself whether or not any passenger who shall arrive in the State by vessels from any foreign port or place (who is not a citizen of the United States) is lunatic, idiotic, deaf, dumb, blind, crippled, or infirm, and is not accompanied by relatives who are able and willing to support him, or is likely to become a public charge, or has been a pauper in any other country, or is from sickness or disease (existing either at the time of sailing from the port of departure or at the time of his arrival in the State) a public charge, or likely soon to become so, or is a convicted criminal, or a lewd or debauched woman;' and no such person shall be permitted to land from the vessel, unless the master or owner or consignee shall give a separate bond in each case, conditioned to save harmless every county, city, and town of the State against any expense incurred for the relief, support, or care of such person for two years thereafter.

The commissioner is authorized to charge the sum of seventy-five cents for every examination of a passenger made by him; which sum he may collect of the master, owner, or consignee, or of the vessel by attachment. The bonds are to be prepared by the commissioner, and two sureties are required to each bond, and, for preparing the bond, the commissioner is allowed to charge and collect a fee of three dollars; and for each oath administered to a surety, concerning his sufficiency as such, he may charge one dollar. It is expressly provided that there shall be a separate bond for each passenger; that there shall be two sureties on each bond, and that the same sureties must not be on more than one bond; and they must in all cases be residents of the State.

If the ship-master or owner prefers, he may commute for these bonds by paying such a sum of money as the commissioner may in each case think proper to exact; and, after retaining twenty per cent of the commutation-money for his services, the commissioner is required once a month to deposit the balance with the Treasurer of the State....

It is hardly possible to conceive a statute more skillfully framed, to place in the hands of a single man the power to prevent entirely vessels engaged in a foreign trade, say with China, from carrying passengers, or to compel them to submit to systematic extortion of the grossest kind.

The commissioner has but to go aboard a vessel filled with passengers ignorant of our language and our laws, and without trial or hearing or evidence, but from the external appearances of persons with whose former habits he is unfamiliar, to point with his finger to twenty, as in this case, or a hundred if he chooses, and say to the master, 'These are idiots, these are paupers, these are convicted criminals, these are lewd women, and these others are debauched women. I have here a hundred blank forms of bonds, printed. I require you to fill me up and sign each of these for $500 in gold, and that you furnish me two hundred different men, residents of this State, and of sufficient means, as sureties on these bonds. I charge you five dollars in each case for preparing the bond and swearing your sureties; and I charge you seventy-five cents each for examining these passengers, and all others you have on board. If you don't do this, you are forbidden to land your passengers under a heavy penalty. But I have the power to commute with you for all this for any sum I may choose to take in cash. I am open to an offer; for you must remember that twenty per cent of all I can get out of you goes into my own pocket, and the remainder into the treasury of California.'

If, as we have endeavored to show in the opinion in the preceding cases, we are at liberty to look to the effect of a statute for the test of its constitutionality, the argument need go no further. But we have thus far only considered the effect of the statute on the owner of the vessel. As regards the passengers, sect. 2963 declares that consuls, ministers, agents, or other public functionaries, of any foreign government, arriving in this State in their *official capacity*, are exempt from the provisions of this chapter.

All other passengers are subject to the order of the Commissioner of Immigration. Individual foreigners, however distinguished at home for their social, their literary, or their political character, are helpless in the presence of this potent commissioner. Such a person may offer to furnish any amount of surety on his own bond, or deposit any sum of money; but the law of California takes no note of him. It is the master, owner, or consignee of the vessel alone whose bond can be accepted; and so a silly, an obstinate, or a wicked commissioner may bring disgrace upon the whole country, the enmity of a powerful nation, or the loss of an equally powerful friend.

While the occurrence of the hypothetical case just stated may be highly improbable, we venture the assertion, that, if citizens of our own government were treated by any foreign nation as subjects of the Emperor of China have been actually treated under this law, no administration could withstand the call for a demand on such government for redress.

Or, if this plaintiff and her twenty companions had been subjects of the Queen of Great Britain, can any one doubt that this matter would have been the subject of international inquiry, if not of a direct claim for redress? Upon whom would such a claim be made? Not upon the State of California; for, by our Constitution, she can hold no exterior relations with other nations. It would be made upon the government of the United States. If that government should get into a difficulty which would lead to war, or to suspension of intercourse, would California alone suffer, or all the Union? If we should conclude that a pecuniary indemnity was proper as a satisfaction for the injury, would California pay it, or the Federal government? If that government has forbidden the States to hold negotiations with any foreign nations, or to declare war, and has taken the whole subject of these relations upon herself, has the Constitution, which provides for this, done so foolish a thing as to leave it in the power of the States to pass laws whose enforcement renders the general government liable to just reclamations which it must answer, while it does not prohibit to the States the acts for which it is held responsible?

The Constitution of the United States is no such instrument. The passage of laws which concern the admission of citizens and subjects of foreign nations to our shores belongs to Congress, and not to the States. It has the power to regulate commerce with foreign nations: the responsibility for the character of those regulations, and for the manner of their execution, belongs solely to the national government. If it be otherwise, a single State can, at her pleasure, embroil us in disastrous quarrels with other nations.

We are not called upon by this statute to decide for or against the right of a State, in the absence of legislation by Congress, to protect herself by necessary and proper laws against paupers and convicted criminals from abroad; nor to lay down the definite limit of such right, if it exist[s]. Such a right can only arise from a vital necessity for its exercise, and cannot be carried beyond the scope of that necessity. When a State statute, limited to provisions necessary and appropriate to that object alone, shall, in a proper controversy, come before us, it will be time enough to decide that question.

The statute of California goes so far beyond what is necessary, or even appropriate, for this purpose, as to be wholly without any sound definition of the right under which it is supposed to be justified. Its manifest purpose, as we have already said, is, not to obtain indemnity, but money.

The amount to be taken is left in every case to the discretion of an officer, whose cupidity is stimulated by a reward of one fifth of all he can obtain. The money, when paid, does not go to any fund for the benefit of immigrants, but is paid into the general treasury of the State, and devoted to the use of all her indigent citizens. The blind, or the deaf, or the dumb passenger is subject to contribution, whether he be a rich man or a pauper. The patriot, seeking out shores after an unsuccessful struggle against despotism in Europe or Asia, may be kept out because there his resistance has been adjudged a crime. The woman whose error has been repaired by a happy marriage and numerous children, and whose loving husband brings her with his wealth to a new home, may be told she must pay a round sum before she can land, because it is alleged that she was debauched by her husband before marriage. Whether a young woman's manners are such as to justify the commissioner in calling her lewd may be made to depend on the sum she will pay for the privilege of landing in San Francisco.

It is idle to pursue the criticism. In any view which we can take of this statute, it is in conflict with the Constitution of the United States, and therefore void.

Judgment reversed, and the case remanded, with directions to make an order discharging the prisoner from custody.

Notes

1. The decision refers to 21 Chinese women ("plaintiff and her twenty companions") but in fact there were 22 women involved in the case. *See* McClain, at 55 (the case came to be called "The Case of the Twenty-two Chinese Women"); *Chinese Women Arrested: A Furore in Chinadom in Reference to the Matter*, Daily Alta, Aug. 26, 1874 (reporting 22 women arrested); *The Twenty-Two Chinese Maidens: Undeniable Evidence of Their Immoral Tendencies*, Daily Alta, Aug. 28, 1874.

2. Why did the State of California enact this statute? Was it a reasonable application of a state's police powers?

3. Although *Chy Lung v. Freeman* was the first case involving Chinese migrants transported to the United States to reach the Supreme Court, libels (the admiralty law term for complaints) were filed as early as 1854 in the U.S. District Court in San Francisco for forfeiture of ships transporting passengers in excess of limits specified in relevant legislation of seagoing passenger vessels. Barth, *Bitter Strength*, at 72–74. Furthermore, during the Civil War, the Republican-controlled Congress enacted "An Act to Prohibit the Coolie Trade by American Citizens in American Vessels" to block Southerners from replacing Black enslaved persons

with Chinese coolie laborers. Section 1 of the statute provided that "no citizen or citizens of the United States, or foreigner coming into or residing within the same, shall build, equip, load, or otherwise prepare, any ship or vessel... registered... in the United States... for the purpose of procuring from China... the inhabitants or subjects of China, known as 'coolies'... to be disposed of, or sold, or transferred, for any term of years or for any time whatever, as servants or apprentices, or to be held to service or labor." What Article I power was Congress exercising in enacting the Coolie Trade Prohibition Act?

4. Is *Chy Lung v. Freeman* relevant to any recent immigration controversy? What about the State of Arizona's efforts to address the influx of undocumented foreigners when it believed the federal government was taking inadequate steps to address the issue? *See Arizona v. United States*, 567 U.S. 387 (2012). Imagine that a statute today vested similarly broad discretion in a state health commissioner to quarantine and deny entry based on the global threat of a powerful, deadly virus, such as Ebola or COVID-19. Do you think the Supreme Court today would strike down the statute as beyond the state's police power? Should a state be able to take matters in its own hands with respect to regulating the entry of foreigners into the state whom the state's legislature has deemed undesirable in the absence of any relevant federal regulation or failure to enforce federal laws? And what about the recent conflicts between the State of Texas and the federal government over the influx of migrants? *See, e.g.*, Arelis R. Hernandez and Nick Miroff, *Texas Blocks Feds from Rio Grande Park in New Escalation at Border*, Wash. Post, Jan. 12, 2024; *see also United States v. Iowa*, No. 24-2265, 2025 WL 287401 (8th Cir. Jan. 24, 2025) (affirming issuance of preliminary injunction against enforcement of Iowa statute criminalizing presence within its border of aliens who illegally reentered the United States and ordering their return to their country of origin, and citing *Chy Lung v. Freeman*).

5. Why was the California statute void, in the view of the U.S. Supreme Court? Was it a matter of federalism (i.e., interfering with Congress's and the national government's power over foreign commerce), or a matter of due process (i.e., limitless discretion to the commissioner to harass and extort foreign inbound passengers and captain), or a matter of equal protection (i.e., distinguishing between Chinese women and women from other countries, under the terms of applicable bilateral treaties of amity and commerce between the United States and the women's countries of origin)? The writ of habeas corpus is predicated on judicial review of the legality of a person's detention. To what extent would you say the Supreme Court's decision was grounded in a genuine concern for the well-being of the Chinese women detained? What other motivations do you imagine were at play behind the Court's decision?

6. The trial in state court regarding the application of the California law was held in San Francisco, starting on August 26, 1874, just two days after the ship arrived in San Francisco. A trial transcript exists. Among the witnesses were the captain

of the ship, a police officer, several of the women, and an Episcopalian minister. Why would an Episcopalian minister be qualified to testify in this case?

7. The women were represented by Leander Quint, a prominent San Francisco attorney and former judge. How do you think the women were able to retain such top-flight counsel? It is possible, perhaps even likely, that the costs of litigating the case were borne by financial backers of commercial sex traffickers, in modern parlance. How does that likely fact affect your perception of the importance and significance of the Supreme Court's decision?

8. Here is an excerpt from the trial court's decision:

   Judge MORRISON:

   > Are they lewd women? There is no positive proof that they are. The evidence is purely circumstantial. [A number] testified that they were married and the husbands had written them to come. It was a matter of surprise to the Court that these husbands did not appear....
   >
   > The lover has not come to claim the sweetheart, the mother to claim the daughter, the husband the wife. Have the women come here with good purpose? Reverend Gibson testifies that women of the prostitute class are known by their dress—wide sleeves and gaudy garments. When the counsel for the petitioners made the examination, these women were dressed exactly as he described. As a rule, married women do not dress in gaudy colors. It is a very rare thing for married women to be sent from China abroad without any escort. It is said the law presumes chastity, but the evidence in this case is the most unfavorable to the petitioners. Reverend Gibson says that there are some 2,000 Chinese women in California, and only 100 are married. Only forty odd marriage licenses were issued since May 1872 to Chinese persons. That overthrows the chastity presumption altogether. Many of these people say they were here before, and have friends here. Not one witness has been called to testify on their behalf.
   >
   > What, then, can the Court believe but that these women are unchaste? Believing, as I do, that they are here for purposes of prostitution, and that they come within the certain class designated by this law, I deem it my duty to remand them to the custody from which they were taken. Such, then, is my decision.

   In re Chy Lung (Dist. Ct., 4th Jud. Dist. San Francisco, Cal. Aug. 29, 1874), *published in A Righteous Decision: Judge Morrison Orders the Chinese Courtesans to Be Taken Back to China*, S.F. Chronicle, at 5, Aug. 30, 1874 (edited). As outdated as the judge's statement may seem today, was the judge correct to take evidence and make these findings about whether these women were indeed "lewd" women as the law specified? If the critical question is whether these women were sex workers or "picture brides," isn't it probative that "husbands" and "friends" did not show up to testify and otherwise provide support to the women?

9. The taking and transportation of young women for sex work—in many instances against their will but also sometimes with the consent of guardians—was unfortunately as common in economically depressed circumstances then as it is now. Thousands of young Chinese women and girls were victimized and trafficked into the United States in the nineteenth century. Human trafficking, including of countless Asian women, is still a significant problem today.[8] Even if the California laws were discriminatory, why does it matter if the ultimate outcome was deterring the international human trafficking of Chinese sex workers into the United States?

10. The 22 Chinese women in *Chy Lung* prevailed in the litigation, but what do you think became of them once they got their freedom? Should it have mattered to the legal challenge to the state law whether they were transported with or without their consent?

11. One of the ironies of the decision is that it led to the passage of stricter federal legislation. The Court struck down California's effort to regulate, but its ruling contributed to pressure on Congress to act in its stead, which it did by passing the exclusion laws that were progressively more restrictive than California's invalidated statute. In light of this development, would it have been better as a strategic matter not to have challenged the California law to preempt agitation for anti-Chinese legislation at the national level?

Figure 1.1 ***View of a young woman looking out a wire mesh window in a Chinese brothel door.*** **San Francisco (ca. 1880). California State Library.**

---

8. *See generally* Kerry Abrams, *Polygamy, Prostitution, and the Federalization of Immigration Law*, 105 Colum. L. Rev. 64 (2005); Lucie Cheng Hirata, *Free, Indentured, Enslaved: Chinese Prostitutes in Nineteenth-Century America*, 5 Signs 3 (Autumn 1979); McClain, at 55–56; *see also* Anne Anlin Cheng, *Ornamentalism* 16–46 (2019). *See also* Jenny Tinghui Zhang, *Four Treasures of the Sky* (2022) (historical novel about a young girl kidnapped in China and smuggled to America, set against the backdrop of the Chinese Exclusion Act and anti-Chinese hostility in the American West in the 1880s).

12. The Thirteenth Amendment to the U.S. Constitution, which was ratified on December 6, 1865 to end slavery, provides: "Neither slavery nor involuntary servitude, except as a punishment for crime whereof the party shall have been duly convicted, shall exist within the United States, or any place subject to their jurisdiction." In 1900, 15-year-old Ah Sou was sold by her foster mother in China to a man who brought her to America to Port Townsend in the State of Washington. He forced her into prostitution. After several years of beatings and abuse, she managed to escape and took refuge in the Chinese Women's Home of the Presbyterian Church in Portland. With the cooperation of the man who originally kidnapped her, however, the immigration authorities apprehended her and commenced deportation proceedings. Calling the case "unique and perplexing" and relying on the Thirteenth Amendment's prohibition against slavery, a federal district judge ordered her released from custody, concluding that "[t]he effort which [Ah Sou] has made to escape from thraldom and to rise from her condition of degradation entitles her to humane consideration." *United States v. Ah Sou*, 132 F. 878, 879–80 (D. Wash. 1904). The Ninth Circuit reversed, rejecting the argument that the Thirteenth Amendment provided a basis for relief and holding that "we regret that the law is so written that it does not permit us, as we view it, to yield to the humane considerations which actuated the court below." *United States v. Ah Sou*, 138 F. 775, 778 (9th Cir. 1905). Do the facts of Ah Sou's plight amount to "slavery" or "involuntary servitude" as those words are used in the Thirteenth Amendment? Even if so, what is the proper remedy? Does the Thirteenth Amendment preclude immigration authorities from deporting her back to her home country where she was sold to her tormentor? Does it entitle her to the remedy of settling permanently in the country into which she was trafficked as a sex worker? On what basis? Should the law have provided a remedy for what appeared to be a grievous wrong? Should the appellate court have deferred to the adjudication and remedial order of the district judge who heard the case?

Chapter 2
Exclusion

1. The Chinese Exclusion Laws

On May 6, 1882, President Arthur signed into law a bill titled "Act to Execute Certain Treaty Stipulations Relating to Chinese." This was the first of the so-called Chinese Exclusion Acts—and the first federal immigration statute to single out an ethnic group by name for discriminatory treatment. (Recall that the 1870 Naturalization Act had expanded naturalization rights limited to "free white persons" to "aliens of African nativity and to persons of African descent.") The Act suspended the immigration of Chinese laborers into the United States for 10 years. In light of a treaty entered into with China in 1880, the Act also provided that Chinese laborers who were in the United States when the treaty was signed had the right to remain in the country and to travel back and forth from the country at will. The Act further provided that those laborers who had the right to leave and return could obtain proof of their travel to and from China in the form of certificates of identification from certain U.S. customs officials. Chinese who were not laborers, e.g., merchants and students, could enter the United States if they had a certificate from the Chinese government identifying them as such. Finally, the Act prohibited any state or federal court from admitting any Chinese person to citizenship, which was superfluous in light of the continuing "free white person" provision as modified by the 1870 Naturalization Act to include "aliens of African nativity and to persons of African descent."

The Chinese Exclusion Act was amended (and its prohibitions extended) several times, and it would not be repealed until 1943. *See generally* McClain, chaps. 6–8; Salyer, at 37. In 1888, China and the United States signed a new treaty that prohibited the immigration or reentry of Chinese laborers for 20 years, with certain exceptions. The Chinese government had second thoughts and refused to ratify the treaty, but in the meantime, Congress passed legislation (the Scott Act) to implement the treaty's terms. The bill was signed into law by President Cleveland on October 1, 1888. The law forbade any Chinese laborer then in the United States to leave, for example, to visit China, and then return to the United States. McClain, at 192–93.

Figure 2.1 ***Poster announcing the democratic passage of the Chinese Exclusion Act*** **(ca. 1882). Royal BC Museum and Archives.**

CHINESE EXCLUSION ACT of 1882 (excerpt)

An Act to execute certain treaty stipulations relating to Chinese.

Whereas in the opinion of the Government of the United States the coming of Chinese laborers to this country endangers the good order of certain localities within the territory thereof: Therefore,

Be it enacted by the Senate and House of Representatives of the United States of America in Congress assembled, That from and after the expiration of ninety days next after the passage of this act, and until the expiration of 10 years next after the passage of this act, the coming of Chinese laborers to the United States be, and the same is hereby, suspended; and during such suspension it shall not be lawful for any Chinese laborer to come, or having so come after the expiration of said ninety days to remain within the United States.

SEC. 2. That the master of any vessel who shall knowingly bring within the United States on such vessel, and land or permit to be landed, any Chinese laborer, from any foreign port or place, shall be deemed guilty of a misdemeanor, and on conviction thereof shall be punished by a fine of not more than five hundred dollars for each and every such Chinese laborer so brought, and may be also imprisoned for a term not exceeding one year.

SEC. 3. That the two foregoing sections shall not apply to Chinese laborers who were in the United States on the seventeenth day of November, eighteen hundred and

Figure 2.2 ***The magic washer, manufactured by Geo. Dee, Dixon, Illinois. The Chinese must go*** **(ca. 1886). Library of Congress, Prints and Photographs Division, Washington, D.C.**

eighty, or who shall have come into the same before the expiration of ninety days next after the passage of this act, and who shall produce to such master before going on board such vessel, and shall produce to the collector of the port in the United States at which such vessel shall arrive, the evidence hereinafter in this act required of his being one of the laborers in this section mentioned; nor shall the two foregoing sections apply to the case of any master whose vessel, being bound to a port not within the United States, shall come within the jurisdiction of the United States by reason of being in distress or in stress of weather, or touching at any port of the United States on its voyage to any foreign port or place: Provided, That all Chinese laborers brought on such vessel shall depart with the vessel on leaving port.

2. The Chinese Exclusion Cases

Chinese laborers and trade associations acting on their behalf brought numerous lawsuits challenging the Exclusion Acts, particularly given their tension with ratified United States-China bilateral treaties. One case was brought by Chae Chan Ping, a Chinese laborer who returned to San Francisco from a visit to China just seven days after the Scott Act of 1888 was passed, foreclosing such return. Salyer, at 22.

Chae Chan Ping v. United States

130 U.S. 581 (1889)

FIELD, J.

This case comes before us on appeal from an order of the circuit court of the United States for the Northern district of California, refusing to release the appellant, on a writ of *habeas corpus*, from his alleged unlawful detention by Capt. Walker, master of the steam-ship Belgic, lying within the harbor of San Francisco. The appellant is a subject of the emperor of China, and a laborer by occupation. He resided at San Francisco, Cal., following his occupation, from some time in 1875 until June 2, 1887, when he left for China on the steam-ship Gaelic, having in his possession a certificate in terms entitling him to return to the United States, bearing date on that day, duly issued to him by the collector of customs of the port of San Francisco, pursuant to the provisions of section 4 of the restriction act of May 6, 1882, as amended by the act of July 5, 1884, (22 St. p. 59, c. 126; 23 St. p. 115, c. 220).

On the 7th of September, 1888, the appellant, on his return to California, sailed from Hong Kong in the steam-ship Belgic, which arrived within the port of San Francisco on the 8th of October following. On his arrival he presented to the proper custom-house officers his certificate, and demanded permission to land. The collector of the port refused the permit, solely on the ground that under the act of congress approved October 1, 1888, supplementary to the restriction acts of 1882 and 1884, the certificate had been annulled, and his right to land abrogated, and he had been thereby forbidden again to enter the United States. 25 St. p. 504, c. 1064. The captain of the steam-ship, therefore, detained the appellant on board the steamer.

Thereupon a petition on his behalf was presented to the circuit court of the United States for the Northern district of California, alleging that he was unlawfully restrained of his liberty, and praying that a writ of *habeas corpus* might be issued directed to the master of the steam-ship, commanding him to have the body of the appellant, with the cause of his detention, before the court at a time and place designated, to do and receive what might there be considered in the premises. A writ was accordingly issued, and in obedience to it the body of the appellant was produced before the court. Upon the hearing which followed, the court, after finding the facts substantially as stated, held as conclusions of law that the appellant was not entitled to enter the United States, and was not unlawfully restrained of his liberty, and ordered that he be remanded to the custody of the master of the steam-ship from which he had been taken under the writ. From this order an appeal was taken to this court.

The appeal involves a consideration of the validity of the act of congress of October 1, 1888, prohibiting Chinese laborers from entering the United States who had departed before its passage, having a certificate issued under the act of 1882 as amended by the act of 1884, granting them permission to return. The validity of the act is assailed as being in effect an expulsion from the country of Chinese laborers, in violation of existing treaties between the United States and the government of China, and of rights vested in them under the laws of congress.

... The first treaty between the United States and the empire of China was concluded on the 3d of July, 1844, and ratified in December of the following year. 8 Stat. 592. Previous to that time there had been an extensive commerce between the two nations, that to China being confined to a single port. It was not, however, attended by any serious disturbances between our people there and the Chinese.

In August, 1842, as the result of a war between England and China, a treaty was concluded stipulating for peace and friendship between them, and, among other things, that British subjects, with their families and establishments, should be allowed to reside for the purpose of carrying on mercantile pursuits at the five principal ports of the empire. 6 Hert. Treaties, 221. Actuated by a desire to establish by treaty friendly relations between the United States and the Chinese empire, and to secure to our people the same commercial privileges which had been thus conceded to British subjects, congress placed at the disposal of the president the means to enable him to establish future commercial relations between the two countries, 'on terms of national equal reciprocity.' Act March, 1843, c. 90, (5 Stat. 624).

A mission was accordingly sent by him to China, at the head of which was placed Mr. Caleb Cushing, a gentleman of large experience in public affairs. He found the Chinese government ready to concede by treaty to the United States all that had been reluctantly yielded to England through compulsion. As the result of his negotiations, the treaty of 1844 was concluded. It stipulated, among other things, that there should be a 'perfect, permanent, and universal peace, and a sincere and cordial amity,' between the two nations; that the five principal ports of the empire should be opened to the citizens of the United States, who should be permitted to reside with their families and trade there, and to proceed with their vessels and merchandise to and from any foreign port and either of said five ports; and while peaceably attending to their affairs should receive the protection of the Chinese authorities. Senate Document No. 138, 28th Cong. 2d Sess.

The treaty between England and China did not have the effect of securing permanent peace and friendship between those countries. British subjects in China were often subjected, not only to the violence of mobs, but to insults and outrages from local authorities of the country, which led to retaliatory measures for the punishment of the aggressors. To such an extent were these measures carried, and such resistance offered to them, that in 1856 the two countries were in open war. England then determined with the co-operation of France, between which countries there seemed to be perfect accord, to secure from the government of China, among other things, a recognition of the right of other powers to be represented there by accredited ministers, an extension of commercial intercourse with that country, and stipulations for religious freedom to all foreigners there, and for the suppression of piracy. England requested of the president the concurrence and active co-operation of the United States similar to that which France had accorded, and to authorize our naval and political authorities to act in concert with the allied forces. As this proposition involved a participation in existing hostilities, the request could not be acceded to, and the secretary of state in his communication to the English government explained that the war-making power of the United States was not vested in the president, but in congress, and that he had no authority, therefore, to order aggressive hostilities to be undertaken.

But as the rights of citizens of the United States might be seriously affected by the results of existing hostilities, and commercial intercourse between the United States and China be disturbed, it was deemed advisable to send to China a minister plenipotentiary to represent our government, and watch our interests there. Accordingly, Mr. William B. Reed, of Philadelphia, was appointed such minister, and instructed, while abstaining from any direct interference, to aid by peaceful cooperation the objects the allied forces were seeking to accomplish. Senate Document No. 47, 35th Cong. 1st Sess. Through him a new treaty was negotiated with the Chinese government. It was concluded in June, 1858, and ratified in August of the following year. 12 St. 1023. It reiterated the pledges of peace and friendship between the two nations, renewed the promise of protection to all citizens of the United States in China peaceably attending to their affairs, and stipulated for security to Christians in the profession of their religion.

Neither the treaty of 1844 nor that of 1858 touched upon the migration and emigration of the citizens and subjects of the two nations, respectively, from one country to the other. But in 1868 a great change in the relations of the two nations was made in that respect. In that year a mission from China, composed of distinguished functionaries of that empire, came to the United States with the professed object of establishing closer relations between the two countries and their peoples. At its head was placed Mr. Anson Burlingame, an eminent citizen of the United States, who had at one time represented this country as commissioner to China. He resigned his office under our government to accept the position tendered to him by the Chinese government. The mission was hailed in the United States as the harbinger of a new era in the history of China, as the opening up to free intercourse with other nations and peoples a country that for ages had been isolated and closed against foreigners, who were allowed to have intercourse and to trade with the Chinese only at a few designated places; and the belief was general, and confidently expressed, that great benefits would follow to the world generally, and especially to the United States.

On its arrival in Washington, additional articles to the treaty of 1858 were agreed upon, which gave expression to the general desire that the two nations and their peoples should be drawn closer together. The new articles, eight in number, were agreed to on the 28th of July, 1868, and ratifications of them were exchanged at Peking in November of the following year. 16 St. 739....

But notwithstanding these strong expressions of friendship and good will, and the desire they evince for free intercourse, events were transpiring on the Pacific coast which soon dissipated the anticipations indulged as to the benefits to follow the immigration of Chinese to this country. The previous treaties of 1844 and 1858 were confined principally to mutual declarations of peace and friendship, and to stipulations for commercial intercourse at certain ports in China, and for protection to our citizens while peaceably attending to their affairs. It was not until the additional articles of 1868 were adopted that any public declaration was made by the two nations that there were advantages in the free migration and emigration of their citizens and subjects, respectively, from one country to the other, and stipulations given that each should enjoy in the country of the other, with respect to travel or residence, the 'privileges, immunities, and exemptions' enjoyed by citizens or subjects of the most favored nation.

Whatever modifications have since been made to these general provisions have been caused by a well-founded apprehension—from the experience of years—that a limitation to the immigration of certain classes from China was essential to the peace of the community on the Pacific coast, and possibly to the preservation of our civilization there. A few words on this point may not be deemed inappropriate here, they being confined to matters of public notoriety, which have frequently been brought to the attention of congress. Report of Committee of H. R. No. 872, 46th Cong. 2d Sess.

The discovery of gold in California in 1848, as is well known, was followed by a large immigration thither from all parts of the world, attracted not only by the hope of gain from the mines, but from the great prices paid for all kinds of labor. The news of the discovery penetrated China, and laborers came from there in great numbers, a few with their own means, but by far the greater number under contract with employers, for whose benefit they worked. These laborers readily secured employment, and, as domestic servants, and in various kinds of outdoor work, proved to be exceedingly useful. For some years little opposition was made to them, except when they sought to work in the mines, but, as their numbers increased, they began to engage in various mechanical pursuits and trades, and thus came in competition with our artisans and mechanics, as well as our laborers in the field.

The competition steadily increased as the laborers came in crowds on each steamer that arrived from China, or Hong Kong, an adjacent English port. They were generally industrious and frugal. Not being accompanied by families, except in rare instances, their expenses were small; and they were content with the simplest fare, such as would not suffice for our laborers and artisans. The competition between them and our people was for this reason altogether in their favor, and the consequent irritation, proportionately deep and bitter, was followed, in many cases, by open conflicts, to the great disturbance of the public peace. The differences of race added greatly to the difficulties of the situation.

Notwithstanding the favorable provisions of the new articles of the treaty of 1868, by which all the privileges, immunities, and exemptions were extended to subjects of China in the United States which were accorded to citizens or subjects of the most favored nation, they remained strangers in the land, residing apart by themselves, and adhering to the customs and usages of their own country. It seemed impossible for them to assimilate with our people, or to make any change in their habits or modes of living. As they grew in numbers each year the people of the coast saw, or believed they saw, in the facility of immigration, and in the crowded millions of China, where population presses upon the means of subsistence, great danger that at no distant day that portion of our country would be overrun by them, unless prompt action was taken to restrict their immigration. The people there accordingly petitioned earnestly for protective legislation.

In December, 1878, the convention which framed the present constitution of California, being in session, took this subject up, and memorialized congress upon it, setting forth, in substance, that the presence of Chinese laborers had a baneful effect upon the material interests of the state, and upon public morals; that their immigration was in numbers approaching the character of an Oriental invasion, and was a menace to our civilization; that the discontent from this cause was not confined to any political party, or to any class or nationality, but was well nigh universal; that they retained the habits and customs of their own country, and in fact constituted a Chinese settlement within the state, without any interest in our country or its institutions; and praying congress to take measures to prevent their further immigration. This memorial was presented to congress in February, 1879.

So urgent and constant were the prayers for relief against existing and anticipated evils, both from the public authorities of the Pacific coast and from private individuals, that congress was impelled to act on the subject. Many persons, however, both in and out of congress, were of opinion that, so long as the treaty remained unmodified, legislation restricting immigration would be a breach of faith with China. A statute was accordingly passed appropriating money to send commissioners to China to act with our minister there in negotiating and concluding by treaty a settlement of such matters of interest between the two governments as might be confided to them. 21 St. p. 133, c. 88. Such commissioners were appointed, and as the result of their negotiations the supplementary treaty of November 17, 1880, was concluded and ratified in May of the following year. 22 St. 826. It declares in its first article that

> Whenever, in the opinion of the government of the United States, the coming of Chinese laborers to the United States, or their residence therein, affects or threatens to affect the interests of that country, or to endanger the good order of the said country or of any locality within the territory thereof, the government of China agrees that the government of the United States may regulate, limit, or suspend such coming or residence, but may not absolutely prohibit it. The limitation or suspension shall be reasonable, and shall apply only to Chinese who may go to the United States as laborers, other classes not being included in the limitations. Legislation taken in regard to Chinese laborers will be of such a character only as is necessary to enforce the regulation, limitation, or suspension of immigration, and immigrants shall not be subject to personal maltreatment or abuse.
>
> In its second article it declares that
>
> Chinese subjects, whether proceeding to the United States as teachers, students, merchants, or from curiosity, together with their body and household servants, and Chinese laborers who are now in the United States, shall be allowed to go and come of their own free will and accord, and shall be accorded all the rights, privileges, immunities, and exemptions which are accorded to the citizens and subjects of the most favored nation.'

The government of China thus agreed that, notwithstanding the stipulations of former treaties, the United States might regulate, limit, or suspend the coming of Chinese laborers, or their residence therein, without absolutely forbidding it, whenever in their opinion the interests of the country, or of any part of it, might require such action. Legislation for such regulation, limitation, or suspension was intrusted to the discretion of our government, with the condition that it should only be such as might be necessary for that purpose, and that the immigrants should not be maltreated or abused. On the 6th of May, 1882, an act of congress was approved, to carry this supplementary treaty into effect. 22 St. 58, c. 126. It is entitled 'An act to execute certain treaty stipulations relating to Chinese.'

Its first section declares that after 90 days from the passage of the act, and for the period of 10 years from its date, the coming of Chinese laborers to the United States is suspended, and that it shall be unlawful for any such laborer to come, or, having come, to remain within the United States. The second makes it a misdemeanor, punishable by fine, to which imprisonment may be added, for the master of any vessel knowingly to bring within the United States from a foreign country, and land, any such Chinese laborer. The third provides that those two sections shall not apply to Chinese laborers who were in the United States November 17, 1880, or who shall come within 90 days after the passage of the act. The fourth declares that, for the purpose of identifying the laborers who were here on the 17th of November, 1880, or who should come within the 90 days mentioned, and to furnish them with 'the proper evidence' of their right to go from and come to the United States, the 'collector of customs of the district from which any such Chinese laborer shall depart from the United States shall, in person or by deputy, go on board each vessel having on board any such Chinese laborer and cleared or about to sail from his district for a foreign port, and on such vessel make a list of all such Chinese laborers, which shall be entered in registry books to be kept for that purpose, in which shall be stated the name, age, occupation, last place of residence, physical marks or peculiarities, and all facts necessary for the identification of each of such Chinese laborers, which books shall be safely kept in the custom-house;' and each laborer thus departing shall be entitled to receive, from the collector or his deputy, a certificate containing such particulars, corresponding with the registry, as may serve to identify him. 'The certificate herein provided for,' says the section, 'shall entitle the Chinese laborer to whom the same is issued to return to and reenter the United States upon producing and delivering the same to the collector of customs of the district at which such Chinese laborer shall seek to re-enter.'

The enforcement of this act with respect to laborers who were in the United States on November 17, 1880, was attended with great embarrassment, from the suspicious nature, in many instances, of the testimony offered to establish the residence of the parties, arising from the loose notions entertained by the witnesses of the obligation of an oath. This fact led to a desire for further legislation restricting the evidence receivable, and the amendatory act of July 5, 1884, was accordingly passed. 23 Stat. 115, c. 220. The committee of the house of representatives on foreign affairs, to whom the original bill was referred, in reporting it, recommending its passage, stated that there had been such manifold evasions, as well as attempted evasions, of the act of 1882, that it had failed to meet the demands which called it into existence. Report in H. R. No. 614, 48th Cong. 1st Sess. To obviate the difficulties attending its enforcement, the amendatory act of 1884 declared that the certificate which the laborer must obtain 'shall be the only evidence permissible to establish his right of reentry' into the United States. This act was held by this court not to require the certificate from laborers who were in the United States on the 17th of November, 1880, who had departed out of the country before May 6, 1882, and remained out until after July 5, 1884. Chew Heong v. U. S., 112 U. S. 536. The same difficulties and embarrassments continued with respect to the proof of their former residence. Parties were able to pass successfully the required examination as to their residence before November 17, 1880, who, it was generally believed, had never visited our shores.

To prevent the possibility of the policy of excluding Chinese laborers being evaded, the act of October 1, 1888, the validity of which is the subject of consideration in this case, was passed. It is entitled 'An act a supplement to an act entitled 'An act to execute certain treaty stipulations relating to Chinese,' approved the 6th day of May, eighteen hundred and eighty-two.' 25 St. p. 504, c. 1064. It is as follows:

> Be it enacted by the senate and house of representatives of the United States of America, in congress assembled, that from and after the passage of this act it shall be unlawful for any Chinese laborer who shall at any time heretofore have been, or who may now or hereafter be, a resident within the United States, and who shall have departed, or shall depart, therefrom, and shall not have returned before the passage of this act, to return to or remain the United States.
>
> Sec. 2. That no certificates of identity provided for in the fourth and fifth sections of the act to which this is a supplement shall hereafter be issued; and every certificate heretofore issued in pursuance thereof is hereby declared void and of no effect, and the Chinese laborer claiming admission by virtue thereof shall not be permitted to enter the United States....

The validity of this act, as already mentioned, is assailed, as being in effect an expulsion from the country of Chinese laborers, in violation of existing treaties between the United States and the government of China, and of rights vested in them under the laws of congress. The objection that the act is in conflict with the treaties was earnestly pressed in the court below, and the answer to it constitutes the principal part of its opinion. 36 Fed. Rep. 431. Here the objection made is that the act of 1888 impairs a right vested under the treaty of 1880, as a law of the United States, and the statutes of 1882 and of 1884 passed in execution of it. It must be conceded that the act of 1888 is in contravention of express stipulations of the treaty of 1868, and of the supplemental treaty of 1880, but it is not on that account invalid, or to be restricted in its enforcement. The treaties were of no greater legal obligation than the act of congress.

By the constitution, laws made in pursuance thereof, and treaties made under the authority of the United States, are both declared to be the supreme law of the land, and no paramount authority is given to one over the other. A treaty, it is true, is in its nature a contract between nations, and is often merely promissory in its character, requiring legislation to carry its stipulations into effect. Such legislation will be open to future repeal or amendment. If the treaty operates by its own force, and relates to a subject within the power of congress, it can be deemed in that particular only the equivalent of a legislative act, to be repealed or modified at the pleasure of congress. In either case the last expression of the sovereign will must control.

The effect of legislation upon conflicting treaty stipulations was elaborately considered in the Head-Money Cases, and it was there adjudged 'that, so far as a treaty made by the United States with any foreign nation can become the subject of judicial cognizance in the courts of this country, it is subject to such acts as congress may pass for its enforcement, modification, or repeal.' 112 U. S. 580, 599. This doctrine was affirmed and followed in Whitney v. Robertson, 124 U. S. 190, 195. It will not be presumed that the legislative department of the government will lightly pass laws which are in conflict with the treaties of the country; but that circumstances may arise which would not only justify the government in disregarding their stipulations, but demand in the interests of the country that it should do so, there can be no question.

Unexpected events may call for a change in the policy of the country. Neglect or violation of stipulations on the part of the other contracting party may require corresponding action on our part. When a reciprocal engagement is not carried out by one of the contracting parties, the other may also decline to keep the corresponding engagement....

The question whether our government is justified in disregarding its engagements with another nation is not one for the determination of the courts.... This court is not a censor of the morals of other departments of the government; it is not invested with any authority to pass judgment upon the motives of their conduct. When once it is established that congress possesses the power to pass an act, our province ends with its construction and its application to cases as they are presented for determination....

There being nothing in the treaties between China and the United States to impair the validity of the act of congress of October 1, 1888, was it on any other ground beyond the competency of congress to pass it? If so, it must be because it was not within the power of congress to prohibit Chinese laborers who had at the time departed from the United States, or should subsequently depart, from returning to the United States. Those laborers are not citizens of the United States; they are aliens. That the government of the United States, through the action of the legislative department, can exclude aliens from its territory is a proposition which we do not think open to controversy. Jurisdiction over its own territory to that extent is an incident of every independent nation. It is a part of its independence. If it could not exclude aliens it would be to that extent subject to the control of another power. As said by this court in the case of The Exchange, 7 Cranch, 116, 136, speaking by Chief Justice MARSHALL:

> The jurisdiction of the nation within its own territory is necessarily exclusive and absolute. It is susceptible of no limitation not imposed by itself. Any restriction upon it, deriving validity from an external source, would imply a diminution of its sovereignty to the extent of the restriction, and an investment of that sovereignty to the same extent in that power which could impose such restriction. All exceptions, therefore, to the full and complete power of a nation within its own territories, must be traced up to the consent of the nation itself. They can flow from no other legitimate source.

While under our constitution and form of government the great mass of local matters is controlled by local authorities, the United States, in their relation to foreign countries and their subjects or citizens, are one nation, invested with powers which belong to independent nations, the exercise of which can be invoked for the maintenance of its absolute independence and security throughout its entire territory. The powers to declare war, make treaties, suppress insurrection, repel invasion, regulate foreign commerce, secure republican governments to the states, and admit subjects of other nations to citizenship, are all sovereign powers, restricted in their exercise only by the constitution itself and considerations of public policy and justice which control, more or less, the conduct of all civilized nations....

The control of local matters being left to local authorities, and national matters being entrusted to the government of the Union, the problem of free institutions existing over a widely extended country, having different climates and varied interests, has been happily solved. For local interests the several states of the Union exist, but for national purposes, embracing our relations with foreign nations, we are but one people, one nation, one power. To preserve its independence, and give security against foreign aggression and encroachment, is the highest duty of every nation, and to attain these ends nearly all other considerations are to be subordinated. It matters not in what form such aggression and encroachment come, whether from the foreign nation acting in its national character, or from vast hordes of its people crowding in upon us. The government, possessing the powers which are to be exercised for protection and security, is clothed with authority to determine the occasion on which the powers shall be called forth; and its determinations, so far as the subjects affected are concerned, are necessarily conclusive upon all its departments and officers. If, therefore, the government of the United States, through its legislative department, considers the presence of foreigners of a different race in this country, who will not assimilate with us, to be dangerous to its peace and security, their exclusion is not to be stayed because at the time there are no actual hostilities with the nation of which the foreigners are subjects. The existence of war would render the necessity of the proceeding only more obvious and pressing. The same necessity, in a less pressing degree, may arise when war does not exist, and the same authority which adjudges the necessity in one case must also determine it in the other. In both cases its determination is conclusive upon the judiciary. If the government of the country of which the foreigners excluded are subjects is dissatisfied with this action, it can make complaint to the executive head of our government, or resort to any other measure which, in its judgment, its interests or dignity may demand; and there lies its only remedy....

The power of exclusion of foreigners being an incident of sovereignty belonging to the government of the United States as a part of those sovereign powers delegated by the constitution, the right to its exercise at any time when, in the judgment of the government, the interests of the country require it, cannot be granted away or restrained on behalf of any one. The powers of government are delegated in trust to the United States, and are incapable of transfer to any other parties. They cannot be abandoned or surrendered. Nor can their exercise be hampered, when needed for the public good, by any considerations of private interest. The exercise of these public trusts is not the subject of barter or contract. Whatever license, therefore, Chinese laborers may have obtained, previous to the act of October 1, 1888, to return to the United States after their departure, is held at the will of the government, revocable at any time, at its pleasure.

Whether a proper consideration by our government of its previous laws, or a proper respect for the nation whose subjects are affected by its action, ought to have qualified its inhibition, and made it applicable only to persons departing from the country after the passage of the act, are not questions for judicial determination. If there be any just ground of complaint on the part of China, it must be made to the political department of our government, which is alone competent to act upon the subject. The rights and interests created by a treaty, which have become so vested that its expiration or abrogation will not destroy or impair them, are such as are connected with and lie in property capable of sale and transfer, or other disposition, not such as are personal and untransferable in their character....

Order affirmed.

Notes

1. How do you think Chinese laborers could continue to come into the United States after Congress passed the Exclusion Act of 1882, section 14 of which was excerpted above? The truth is that despite anti-Chinese sentiment among working-class Americans who resented the large numbers of Chinese willing to work dangerous jobs for low wages, U.S. businesses wanted and needed the continuous supply of cheap labor from China (and later Japan, Korea, and the Philippines). Thus, the exclusion acts were in reality a much more complicated affair that permitted the migration of Chinese laborers while prohibiting their acquisition of citizenship.

Figure 2.3 ***Judge Stephen Johnson Field, Appointed to the Supreme Court by Lincoln in 1863*** **(photo ca. 1875). Library of Congress Prints and Photographs Division, Washington, D.C.**

2. Justice Stephen Field, the author of *Chae Chan Ping*, was a member of an East Coast minister's family and a New York lawyer who moved to California during the Gold Rush of 1849. He built a law practice in California and was Chief Justice of the California Supreme Court before he was nominated to join the U.S. Supreme Court in 1863 by President Abraham Lincoln. Field authored the majority opinion in *Chae Chan Ping*, with its anti-Chinese overtones and its upholding of the federal government's plenary power to restrict entry of Chinese laborers despite "most favored nation" treaty provisions compelling equal treatment with the nationals of other foreign countries. At the same time, he authored or joined decisions that struck down disembarkation bond statutes (a writ of habeas corpus in *Chy Lung v. Freeman*) and upheld Chinese claims of denial of equal protection in the application of facially neutral local ordinances in California regarding hair length (*Ho Ah Kow v. Nunan*) and building safety. Are the two positions reconcilable? If so, how?

3. The following passage is in the opinion:

   > [The Chinese] remained strangers in the land, residing apart by themselves, and adhering to the customs and usages of their own country. It seemed impossible for them to assimilate with our people, or to make any change in their habits or modes of living. As they grew in numbers each year the people of the coast saw, or believed they saw, in the facility of immigration, and in the crowded millions of China, where population presses upon the means of subsistence, great danger that at no distant day that portion of our country would be overrun by them, unless prompt action was taken to restrict their immigration. The people there accordingly petitioned earnestly for protective legislation....

   To what extent do you think the capacity or willingness of a particular immigrant group to assimilate into American mores and society is a relevant factor in the legal analysis of a law enacted to exclude the group from entry into the United States? Federal naturalization statutes from 1790 until 1965 contained explicit or implicit national-origin restrictions—doesn't that suggest that national-origin-based exclusion was surely lawful at the time *Chae Chan Ping* was decided? Are some of the themes Justice Field expressed still relevant, long after the extinction of the Exclusion Acts?

4. *Chae Chan Ping* is well-known today to stand for two propositions: (1) the federal government's plenary powers over immigration, i.e., the entry of foreigners into the United States; and (2) the "later in time" rule, namely the principle that a later enacted statute can repeal a treaty provision regulating the same matter. What, according to Justice Field, is the legal basis of Congress's power to exclude foreigners from U.S. territory? Is there any limitation to Congress's power? In terms of the later-in-time rule, is it compelled by the Supremacy Clause of the Constitution or any other provision in the Constitution? If so, what is the basis for the rule?

5. *Chae Chan Ping* is still being cited. *See, e.g., Sun Valley Orchards, LLC v. U.S. Dep't of Justice*, 148 F.4th 121, 130 (3d Cir. 2025) (citing *Chae Chan Ping* and plenary power doctrine and noting limitations on doctrine); *United States v. Texas*, 97 F.4th 268 (5th Cir. 2024) (denying motion by Texas for stay pending appeal of district court's preliminary injunction barring enforcement of Texas statute criminalizing certain immigration offenses by noncitizens); *Raouf v. U.S. Dep't of State*, 702 F. Supp. 3d 19, 25 (D.N.H. 2023) (citing *Chae Chan Ping* in context of consular nonreviewability); *Brackeen v. Haaland*, 994 F.3d 249, 453 n.10 (5th Cir. 2021) (Costa, *J.*, concurring) (citing *Chae Chan Ping* and observing that "[t]he Supreme Court has recognized the extraordinary breadth of federal power in another area where Congress wields plenary power: immigration"); *Tineo v. Attorney General United States of America*, 937 F.3d 200, 216 (3d Cir. 2019) (describing *Chae Chan Ping* as condoning "even the most blatant discrimination"); *Int'l Refugee Assistance Project v. Trump*, 883 F.3d 233, 331 (4th Cir. 2018) (Wynn, J., concurring); *Hawaii v. Trump*, 878 F.3d 662, 695 n.22 (9th Cir. 2017), *rev'd and remanded*, 138 S. Ct. 2382 (2018); *Castro v. U.S. Dep't of Homeland Security*, 835 F.3d 422, 440 (3d Cir. 2016). How does the case continue to be relevant? To the extent that the decision stands for the plenary power of Congress over immigration, is it still good law?

6. *Chae Chan Ping* is an early example of "impact litigation," a case brought not just to address individual harm but to effect broader societal change. Although he was just a Chinese laborer, Chae Chan Ping was represented by "a 'Dream Team' of elite lawyers of the day," including prominent Supreme Court practitioners. *See* Gabriel J. Chin, *Chae Chan Ping and Fong Yue Ting: The Origins of Plenary Power* 5–6 (May 19, 2005), https://papers.ssrn.com/sol3/papers.cfm?abstract_id=722681&download=yes. These lawyers did not work pro bono and were not what we would today consider public interest lawyers; instead, they were fee-charging lawyers who "represented trusts and railroads more often than humble toilers like their Chinese clients." *Id.* at 6. How do you think Chinese immigrants like Chae Chan Ping, a mere laborer, were able to retain these distinguished lawyers?

7. Chae Chan Ping was expelled from the United States in 1889, "[b]ut his ghost haunts American immigration law, and the U.S. Supreme Court, more than 125 years later." Garrett Epps, *The Ghost of Chae Chan Ping*, The Atlantic, Jan. 20, 2018, https://www.theatlantic.com/politics/archive/2018/01/ghost-haunting-immigration/551015/. The Supreme Court's language in *Chae Chan Ping* gave the federal government broad power over who will be admitted to this country and arguably supported the proposition "that Congress can do anything it wants in immigration, Constitution be damned." *Id.* Have there been any changes in immigration law that might suggest otherwise?

8. The Geary Act was enacted in 1892. It extended Chinese exclusion for another 10 years. It also required all Chinese laborers in the United States to obtain a

certificate of residence—any Chinese laborer found without one was presumed to be present illegally and was subject to arrest and deportation. The failure to obtain a certificate could be excused—but only through the testimony of White witnesses. *See* McClain, at 202–03. Three Chinese laborers challenged the constitutionality of the law. Two intentionally refused to register so that they could bring legal challenges. The third applied for and was denied the requisite certificate. Their cases were consolidated in the Supreme Court in *Fong Yue Ting v. United States*, 149 U.S. 698 (1893). *See generally* McClain, at 201–13. Relying on *Chae Chan Ping*, the Court upheld the constitutionality of the Geary Act, concluding that:

> The right of a nation to expel or deport foreigners who have not been naturalized, or taken any steps towards becoming citizens of the country, rests upon the same grounds, and is as absolute and unqualified, as the right to prohibit and prevent their entrance into the country....
>
> The power of congress, therefore, to expel, like the power to exclude, aliens, or any specified class of aliens, from the country, may be exercised entirely through executive officers; or congress may call in the aid of the judiciary to ascertain any contested facts on which an alien's right to be in the country has been made by congress to depend.
>
> Congress, having the right, as it may see fit, to expel aliens of a particular class, or to permit them to remain, has undoubtedly the right to provide a system of registration and identification of the members of that class within the country, and to take all proper means to carry out the system which it provides....
>
> After some years' experience under that treaty, the government of the United States was brought to the opinion that the presence within our territory of large numbers of Chinese laborers, of a distinct race and religion, remaining strangers in the land, residing apart by themselves, tenaciously adhering to the customs and usages of their own country, unfamiliar with our institutions, and apparently incapable of assimilating with our people, might endanger good order, and be injurious to the public interests, and therefore requested and obtained from China a modification of the treaty....
>
> The question whether, and upon what conditions, these aliens shall be permitted to remain within the United States being one to be determined by the political departments of the government, the judicial department cannot properly express an opinion upon the wisdom, the policy, or the justice of the measures enacted by congress in the exercise of the powers confided to it by the constitution over this subject.

Fong Yue Ting, 149 U.S. at 707, 713–14, 717, 731.

9. The Court in *Fong Yue Ting* seemed to suggest that foreigners who "had not taken any steps toward becoming citizens of the country" could not be heard to complain and could be expelled or deported for any reason. Could the three Chinese laborers have applied to be naturalized as U.S. citizens? To what extent is it relevant that each congressional enactment of Chinese migrant labor registration followed after a more permissive certificate system that proved unworkable? Do you think it would or should change the legal analysis if the draconian provisions of the 1892 Geary Act had been passed right away in 1880, despite the expansive language of the 1868 Burlingame Treaty?

10. Justice Field, who wrote the majority opinion in *Chae Chan Ping*, dissented in *Fong Yue Ting*. He reasoned that between legislation for the exclusion of Chinese persons—that is, to prevent them from entering the country—"and legislation for the deportation of those who have acquired a residence in the country under a treaty with China, there is a wide and essential difference. The power of the government to exclude foreigners from this country—that is, to prevent them from entering it—whenever the public interests, in its judgment, require such exclusion, has been repeatedly asserted by the legislative and executive branches of our government, and never denied; but its power to deport from the country persons lawfully domiciled therein by its consent, and engaged in the ordinary pursuits of life, has never been asserted by the legislative or executive branches, except for crime, or as an act of war, in view of existing or anticipated hostilities." Is Field persuasive in drawing a distinction of constitutional significance between the political branches' plenary power to exclude foreigners from the power to deport them? How is this distinction relevant today? If the distinction is to be accepted, doesn't it give a perverse incentive for non-citizens to evade U.S. immigration authorities and enter the country unlawfully?

11. On June 18, 2012, the House of Representatives passed a resolution expressing regret for the passage of laws that adversely affected the Chinese in the United States, including the Chinese Exclusion Act. The House resolution was sponsored by Judy Chu, the first Chinese-American woman elected to Congress. She stated as follows:

    > [This] expression of regret... is for my grandfather and for all Chinese Americans... who were told for six decades by the U.S. Government that the land of the free wasn't open to them. We must finally and formally acknowledge these ugly laws that were incompatible with America's founding principles.
    >
    > We must express the sincere regret that Chinese-Americans deserve. By doing so, we will acknowledge that discrimination has no place in our society, and we will reaffirm our strong commitment to preserving the civil rights and constitutional protections for all people of every color, every race, and from every background.

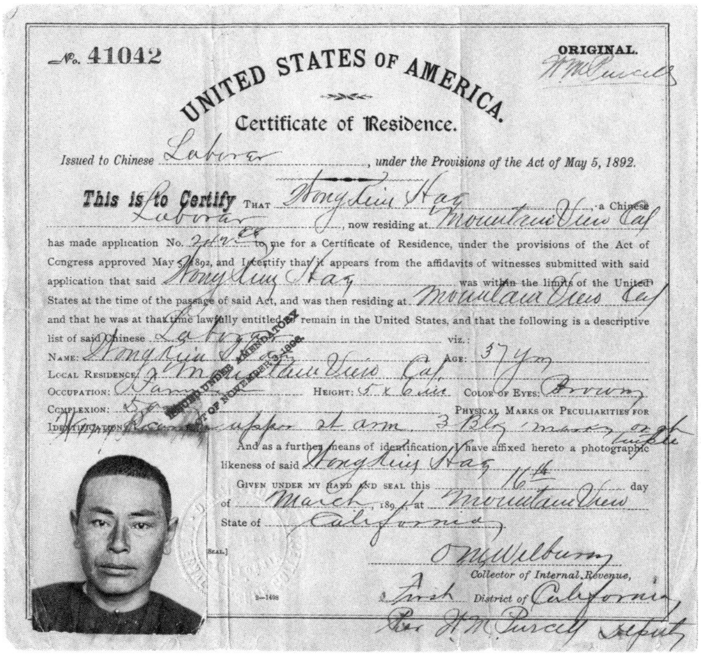
No. 41042 ORIGINAL.

UNITED STATES OF AMERICA.

Certificate of Residence.

Issued to Chinese Laborer, under the Provisions of the Act of May 5, 1892.

This is to Certify THAT Wong Kin Hay, a Chinese Laborer, now residing at Mountain View Cal has made application No. ... to me for a Certificate of Residence, under the provisions of the Act of Congress approved May 5, 1892, and I certify that it appears from the affidavits of witnesses submitted with said application that said Wong Kin Hay was within the limits of the United States at the time of the passage of said Act, and was then residing at Mountain View Cal and that he was at that time lawfully entitled to remain in the United States, and that the following is a descriptive list of said Chinese Laborer viz.:

NAME: Wong Kin Hay AGE: 37 yrs

LOCAL RESIDENCE: Mountain View Cal.

OCCUPATION: Farmer HEIGHT: 5 ft 6 in COLOR OF EYES: Brown

COMPLEXION: ... PHYSICAL MARKS OR PECULIARITIES FOR IDENTIFICATION: ...

And as a further means of identification I have affixed hereto a photographic likeness of said Wong Kin Hay.

GIVEN UNDER MY HAND AND SEAL this 16th day of March 189_, at Mountain View State of California.

[SEAL.]

O. M. Welburn Collector of Internal Revenue, First District of California. Per H. M. Purcell Deputy

Figure 2.4 ***A certificate of residence required by the Geary Act. Certificate of residence for Wong Kin Hay, farmer, age 37 years, of Mountain View, California* (ca. 1890). California Historical Society.**

Remarks by Rep. Judy Chu on H.R. 683 expressing regret for Chinese Exclusion Laws, June 18, 2012, https://www.c-span.org/video/?c4668317/rep-judy-chu-resolution-regret-chinese-exclusion-act.

12. The Immigration Act of 1917, also known as the Asiatic Barred Zone Act, prohibited immigration from most Asian countries, but not Japan. In 1924, with the passage of the Johnson-Reed Act, Congress adopted a quota system, based on national origin, limiting the number of immigrants allowed entry into the country. It also barred the entry of those "ineligible for naturalization." The 1924 law thus had the effect of barring all Asians from entering, including the Japanese. The quota system was not abolished until 1965. *See* National Archives, Restricting Immigration from Asian and the Pacific, 1870s to 1950s, https://www.archives.gov/research/aapi/immigration.

3. The Travel Ban

The issue of closing the United States' borders to certain foreign persons raised by the Exclusion Acts and *Chae Chan Ping* continues to the present day. One week after taking office in 2016, President Donald Trump issued an executive order suspending

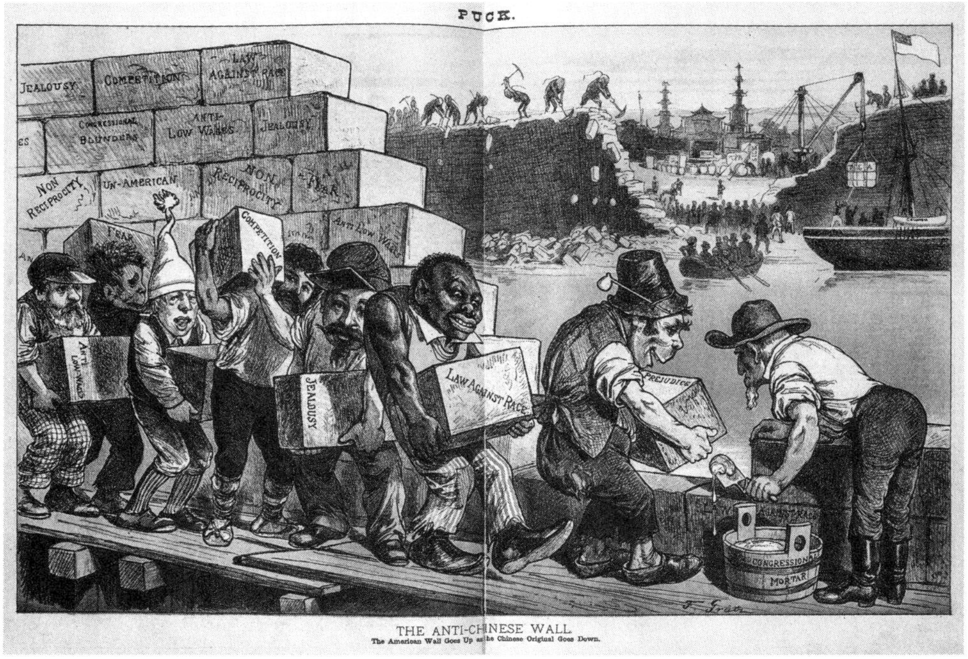

Figure 2.5 ***The anti-Chinese wall—the American wall goes up as the Chinese original goes down.*** **F. Grätz (1882), Library of Congress, Prints and Photographs Division, Washington, D.C.**

the entry of nationals from seven predominantly Muslim countries. Litigation quickly followed, and the President issued two more iterations of the executive order, which became known as the "Travel Ban" or, in some circles, the "Muslim Ban," although the orders purported to "suspend," not to end, entry. On June 26, 2018, the Supreme Court upheld the executive order.

Trump v. Hawaii

138 S. Ct. 2392 (2018)

ROBERTS, C.J.:

Under the Immigration and Nationality Act, foreign nationals seeking entry into the United States undergo a vetting process to ensure that they satisfy the numerous requirements for admission. The Act also vests the President with authority to restrict the entry of aliens whenever he finds that their entry "would be detrimental to the interests of the United States." 8 U.S.C. § 1182(f). Relying on that delegation, the President concluded that it was necessary to impose entry restrictions on nationals of countries that do not share adequate information for an informed entry determination, or that otherwise present national security risks. Presidential Proclamation No. 9645, 82 Fed. Reg. 45161 (2017) (Proclamation). The plaintiffs in this litigation, respondents here, challenged the application of those entry restrictions to certain aliens abroad. We now decide whether the President had authority under the Act to issue the Proclamation, and whether the policy violates the Establishment Clause of the First Amendment.

I

A

Shortly after taking office, President Trump signed Executive Order No. 13769, Protecting the Nation From Foreign Terrorist Entry Into the United States. 82 Fed. Reg. 8977 (2017) (EO–1). EO–1 directed the Secretary of Homeland Security to conduct a review to examine the adequacy of information provided by foreign governments about their nationals seeking to enter the United States. § 3(a). Pending that review, the order suspended for 90 days the entry of foreign nationals from seven countries—Iran, Iraq, Libya, Somalia, Sudan, Syria, and Yemen—that had been previously identified by Congress or prior administrations as posing heightened terrorism risks. § 3(c). The District Court for the Western District of Washington entered a temporary restraining order blocking the entry restrictions, and the Court of Appeals for the Ninth Circuit denied the Government's request to stay that order. *Washington v. Trump,* 847 F.3d 1151 (2017) (*per curiam*).

In response, the President revoked EO–1, replacing it with Executive Order No. 13780, which again directed a worldwide review. 82 Fed. Reg. 13209 (2017) (EO–2). Citing investigative burdens on agencies and the need to diminish the risk that dangerous individuals would enter without adequate vetting, EO–2 also temporarily restricted the entry (with case-by-case waivers) of foreign nationals from six of the countries covered by EO–1: Iran, Libya, Somalia, Sudan, Syria, and Yemen. §§ 2(c), 3(a). The order explained that those countries had been selected because each "is a state sponsor of terrorism, has been significantly compromised by terrorist organizations, or contains active conflict zones." § 1(d). The entry restriction was to stay in effect for 90 days, pending completion of the worldwide review.

These interim measures were immediately challenged in court. The District Courts for the Districts of Maryland and Hawaii entered nationwide preliminary injunctions barring enforcement of the entry suspension, and the respective Courts of Appeals upheld those injunctions, albeit on different grounds. *International Refugee Assistance Project (IRAP) v. Trump,* 857 F.3d 554 (C.A.4 2017); *Hawaii v. Trump,* 859 F.3d 741 (C.A.9 2017) (*per curiam*). This Court granted certiorari and stayed the injunctions—allowing the entry suspension to go into effect—with respect to foreign nationals who lacked a "credible claim of a bona fide relationship" with a person or entity in the United States. *Trump v. IRAP,* 582 U.S.——,——, 137 S. Ct. 2080, 2088 (2017) (*per curiam*). The temporary restrictions in EO–2 expired before this Court took any action, and we vacated the lower court decisions as moot. *Trump v. IRAP,* 583 U.S.——, 138 S. Ct. 353 (2017); *Trump v. Hawaii,* 583 U.S.——, 138 S. Ct. 377 (2017).

On September 24, 2017, after completion of the worldwide review, the President issued the Proclamation before us—Proclamation No. 9645, Enhancing Vetting Capabilities and Processes for Detecting Attempted Entry Into the United States by

Terrorists or Other Public–Safety Threats. 82 Fed. Reg. 45161. The Proclamation (as its title indicates) sought to improve vetting procedures by identifying ongoing deficiencies in the information needed to assess whether nationals of particular countries present "public safety threats." § 1(a). To further that purpose, the Proclamation placed entry restrictions on the nationals of eight foreign states whose systems for managing and sharing information about their nationals the President deemed inadequate.

The Proclamation described how foreign states were selected for inclusion based on the review undertaken pursuant to EO–2. As part of that review, the Department of Homeland Security (DHS), in consultation with the State Department and several intelligence agencies, developed a "baseline" for the information required from foreign governments to confirm the identity of individuals seeking entry into the United States, and to determine whether those individuals pose a security threat. § 1(c). The baseline included three components. The first, "identity-management information," focused on whether a foreign government ensures the integrity of travel documents by issuing electronic passports, reporting lost or stolen passports, and making available additional identity-related information. Second, the agencies considered the extent to which the country discloses information on criminal history and suspected terrorist links, provides travel document exemplars, and facilitates the U.S. Government's receipt of information about airline passengers and crews traveling to the United States. Finally, the agencies weighed various indicators of national security risk, including whether the foreign state is a known or potential terrorist safe haven and whether it regularly declines to receive returning nationals following final orders of removal from the United States. *Ibid.*

DHS collected and evaluated data regarding all foreign governments. § 1(d). It identified 16 countries as having deficient information-sharing practices and presenting national security concerns, and another 31 countries as "at risk" of similarly failing to meet the baseline. § 1(e). The State Department then undertook diplomatic efforts over a 50–day period to encourage all foreign governments to improve their practices. § 1(f). As a result of that effort, numerous countries provided DHS with travel document exemplars and agreed to share information on known or suspected terrorists.

Following the 50–day period, the Acting Secretary of Homeland Security concluded that eight countries—Chad, Iran, Iraq, Libya, North Korea, Syria, Venezuela, and Yemen—remained deficient in terms of their risk profile and willingness to provide requested information. The Acting Secretary recommended that the President impose entry restrictions on certain nationals from all of those countries except Iraq. §§ 1(g), (h). She also concluded that although Somalia generally satisfied the information-sharing component of the baseline standards, its "identity-management deficiencies" and "significant terrorist presence" presented special circumstances justifying additional limitations. She therefore recommended entry limitations for certain nationals of that country. § 1(i). As for Iraq, the Acting Secretary found that entry limitations on its nationals were not warranted given the close cooperative relationship between the U.S. and Iraqi Governments and Iraq's commitment to combating ISIS. § 1(g).

After consulting with multiple Cabinet members and other officials, the President adopted the Acting Secretary's recommendations and issued the Proclamation. Invoking his authority under 8 U.S.C. §§ 1182(f) and 1185(a), the President determined that certain entry restrictions were necessary to "prevent the entry of those foreign nationals about whom the United States Government lacks sufficient information"; "elicit improved identity-management and information-sharing protocols and practices from foreign governments"; and otherwise "advance [the] foreign policy, national security, and counterterrorism objectives" of the United States. Proclamation § 1(h). The President explained that these restrictions would be the "most likely to encourage cooperation" while "protect[ing] the United States until such time as improvements occur." *Ibid.*

The Proclamation imposed a range of restrictions that vary based on the "distinct circumstances" in each of the eight countries. *Ibid.* For countries that do not cooperate with the United States in identifying security risks (Iran, North Korea, and Syria), the Proclamation suspends entry of all nationals, except for Iranians seeking nonimmigrant student and exchange-visitor visas. §§ 2(b)(ii), (d)(ii), (e)(ii). For countries that have information-sharing deficiencies but are nonetheless "valuable counterterrorism partner[s]" (Chad, Libya, and Yemen), it restricts entry of nationals seeking immigrant visas and nonimmigrant business or tourist visas. §§ 2(a)(i), (c)(i), (g)(i). Because Somalia generally satisfies the baseline standards but was found to present special risk factors, the Proclamation suspends entry of nationals seeking immigrant visas and requires additional scrutiny of nationals seeking nonimmigrant visas. § 2(h)(ii). And for Venezuela, which refuses to cooperate in information sharing but for which alternative means are available to identify its nationals, the Proclamation limits entry only of certain government officials and their family members on nonimmigrant business or tourist visas. § 2(f)(ii).

The Proclamation exempts lawful permanent residents and foreign nationals who have been granted asylum. § 3(b). It also provides for case-by-case waivers when a foreign national demonstrates undue hardship, and that his entry is in the national interest and would not pose a threat to public safety. § 3(c)(i) .... The Proclamation further directs DHS to assess on a continuing basis whether entry restrictions should be modified or continued, and to report to the President every 180 days. § 4. Upon completion of the first such review period, the President, on the recommendation of the Secretary of Homeland Security, determined that Chad had sufficiently improved its practices, and he accordingly lifted restrictions on its nationals. Presidential Proclamation No. 9723, 83 Fed. Reg. 15937 (2018).

B

Plaintiffs in this case are the State of Hawaii, three individuals (Dr. Ismail Elshikh, John Doe # 1, and John Doe # 2), and the Muslim Association of Hawaii. The State operates the University of Hawaii system, which recruits students and faculty from the designated countries. The three individual plaintiffs are U.S. citizens or lawful permanent residents who have relatives from Iran, Syria, and Yemen applying for immigrant or nonimmigrant visas. The Association is a nonprofit organization that operates a mosque in Hawaii.

Plaintiffs challenged the Proclamation—except as applied to North Korea and Venezuela—on several grounds. As relevant here, they argued that the Proclamation contravenes provisions in the Immigration and Nationality Act (INA), 66 Stat. 187, as amended. Plaintiffs further claimed that the Proclamation violates the Establishment Clause of the First Amendment, because it was motivated not by concerns pertaining to national security but by animus toward Islam.

The District Court granted a nationwide preliminary injunction barring enforcement of the entry restrictions. The court concluded that the Proclamation violated two provisions of the INA: § 1182(f), because the President did not make sufficient findings that the entry of the covered foreign nationals would be detrimental to the national interest, and § 1152(a)(1)(A), because the policy discriminates against immigrant visa applicants on the basis of nationality. 265 F.Supp.3d 1140, 1155–1159 (Haw. 2017). The Government requested expedited briefing and sought a stay pending appeal. The Court of Appeals for the Ninth Circuit granted a partial stay, permitting enforcement of the Proclamation with respect to foreign nationals who lack a bona fide relationship with the United States. This Court then stayed the injunction in full pending disposition of the Government's appeal. 583 U.S.——,——S.Ct.——(2017).

The Court of Appeals affirmed. The court first held that the Proclamation exceeds the President's authority under § 1182(f). In its view, that provision authorizes only a "temporary" suspension of entry in response to "exigencies" that "Congress would be ill-equipped to address." 878 F.3d 662, 684, 688 (2017). The court further reasoned that the Proclamation "conflicts with the INA's finely reticulated regulatory scheme" by addressing "matters of immigration already passed upon by Congress." *Id.*, at 685, 690. The Ninth Circuit then turned to § 1152(a)(1)(A) and determined that the entry restrictions also contravene the prohibition on nationality-based discrimination in the issuance of immigrant visas. The court did not reach plaintiffs' Establishment Clause claim.

We granted certiorari. 583 U.S.——, 138 S.Ct. 923 (2018)....

III

The INA establishes numerous grounds on which an alien abroad may be inadmissible to the United States and ineligible for a visa. *See, e.g.*, 8 U.S.C. §§ 1182(a)(1) (health-related grounds), (a)(2) (criminal history), (a)(3)(B) (terrorist activities), (a)(3)(C) (foreign policy grounds). Congress has also delegated to the President authority to suspend or restrict the entry of aliens in certain circumstances. The principal source of that authority, § 1182(f), enables the President to "suspend the entry of all aliens or any class of aliens" whenever he "finds" that their entry "would be detrimental to the interests of the United States."

Plaintiffs argue that the Proclamation is not a valid exercise of the President's authority under the INA. In their view, § 1182(f) confers only a residual power to temporarily halt the entry of a discrete group of aliens engaged in harmful conduct. They also assert that the Proclamation violates another provision of the INA—8 U.S.C. § 1152(a)(1)(A)—because it discriminates on the basis of nationality in the issuance of immigrant visas.

By its plain language, § 1182(f) grants the President broad discretion to suspend the entry of aliens into the United States. The President lawfully exercised that discretion based on his findings—following a worldwide, multi-agency review—that entry of the covered aliens would be detrimental to the national interest. And plaintiffs' attempts to identify a conflict with other provisions in the INA, and their appeal to the statute's purposes and legislative history, fail to overcome the clear statutory language.

A

The text of § 1182(f) states:

> "Whenever the President finds that the entry of any aliens or of any class of aliens into the United States would be detrimental to the interests of the United States, he may by proclamation, and for such period as he shall deem necessary, suspend the entry of all aliens or any class of aliens as immigrants or nonimmigrants, or impose on the entry of aliens any restrictions he may deem to be appropriate."

By its terms, § 1182(f) exudes deference to the President in every clause. It entrusts to the President the decisions whether and when to suspend entry ("[w]henever [he] finds that the entry" of aliens "would be detrimental" to the national interest); whose entry to suspend ("all aliens or any class of aliens"); for how long ("for such period as he shall deem necessary"); and on what conditions ("any restrictions he may deem to be appropriate"). It is therefore unsurprising that we have previously observed that § 1182(f) vests the President with "ample power" to impose entry restrictions in addition to those elsewhere enumerated in the INA. *Sale,* 509 U.S., at 187 (finding it "perfectly clear" that the President could "establish a naval blockade" to prevent illegal migrants from entering the United States); *see also Abourezk v. Reagan,* 785 F.2d 1043, 1049, n. 2 (C.A.D.C. 1986) (describing the "sweeping proclamation power" in § 1182(f) as enabling the President to supplement the other grounds of inadmissibility in the INA).

The Proclamation falls well within this comprehensive delegation. The sole prerequisite set forth in § 1182(f) is that the President "find[ ]" that the entry of the covered aliens "would be detrimental to the interests of the United States." The President has undoubtedly fulfilled that requirement here. He first ordered DHS and other agencies to conduct a comprehensive evaluation of every single country's compliance with the information and risk assessment baseline. The President then issued a Proclamation setting forth extensive findings describing how deficiencies in the practices of select foreign governments—several of which are state sponsors of terrorism—deprive the Government of "sufficient information to assess the risks [those countries' nationals] pose to the United States." Proclamation § 1(h)(i). Based on that review, the President found that it was in the national interest to restrict entry of aliens who could not be vetted with adequate information—both to protect national security and public safety, and to induce improvement by their home countries. The Proclamation therefore "craft[ed] … country-specific restrictions that would be most likely to encourage cooperation given each country's distinct circumstances," while securing the Nation "until such time as improvements occur." *Ibid.*…

In short, the language of § 1182(f) is clear, and the Proclamation does not exceed any textual limit on the President's authority.

B

Confronted with this "facially broad grant of power," 878 F.3d, at 688, plaintiffs focus their attention on statutory structure and legislative purpose. They seek support in, first, the immigration scheme reflected in the INA as a whole, and, second, the legislative history of § 1182(f) and historical practice. Neither argument justifies departing from the clear text of the statute.

1

Plaintiffs' structural argument starts with the premise that § 1182(f) does not give the President authority to countermand Congress's considered policy judgments. The President, they say, may supplement the INA, but he cannot supplant it. And in their view, the Proclamation falls in the latter category because Congress has already specified a two-part solution to the problem of aliens seeking entry from countries that do not share sufficient information with the United States. First, Congress designed an individualized vetting system that places the burden on the alien to prove his admissibility. *See* § 1361. Second, instead of banning the entry of nationals from particular countries, Congress sought to encourage information sharing through a Visa Waiver Program offering fast-track admission for countries that cooperate with the United States. *See* § 1187.

We may assume that § 1182(f) does not allow the President to expressly override particular provisions of the INA. But plaintiffs have not identified any conflict between the statute and the Proclamation that would implicitly bar the President from addressing deficiencies in the Nation's vetting system.

To the contrary, the Proclamation supports Congress's individualized approach for determining admissibility. The INA sets forth various inadmissibility grounds based on connections to terrorism and criminal history, but those provisions can only work when the consular officer has sufficient (and sufficiently reliable) information to make that determination. The Proclamation promotes the effectiveness of the vetting process by helping to ensure the availability of such information.

Plaintiffs suggest that the entry restrictions are unnecessary because consular officers can simply deny visas in individual cases when an alien fails to carry his burden of proving admissibility—for example, by failing to produce certified records regarding his criminal history. Brief for Respondents 48. But that misses the point: A critical finding of the Proclamation is that the failure of certain countries to provide reliable information prevents the Government from accurately determining whether an alien is inadmissible or poses a threat. Proclamation § 1(h). Unless consular officers are expected to apply categorical rules and deny entry from those countries across the board, fraudulent or unreliable documentation may thwart their review in individual cases. And at any rate, the INA certainly does not *require* that systemic problems such as the lack of reliable information be addressed only in a progression of case-by-case admissibility determinations. One of the key objectives of the Proclamation is to encourage foreign governments to improve their practices, thus facilitating the Government's vetting process overall. *Ibid.*...

Because plaintiffs do not point to any contradiction with another provision of the INA, the President has not exceeded his authority under § 1182(f)....

C

Plaintiffs' final statutory argument is that the President's entry suspension violates § 1152(a)(1)(A), which provides that "no person shall... be discriminated against in the issuance of an immigrant visa because of the person's race, sex, nationality, place of birth, or place of residence." They contend that we should interpret the provision as prohibiting nationality-based discrimination throughout the *entire* immigration process, despite the reference in § 1152(a)(1)(A) to the act of visa issuance alone. Specifically, plaintiffs argue that § 1152(a)(1)(A) applies to the predicate question of a visa applicant's eligibility for admission and the subsequent question whether the holder of a visa may in fact enter the country. Any other conclusion, they say, would allow the President to circumvent the protections against discrimination enshrined in § 1152(a)(1)(A).

As an initial matter, this argument challenges only the validity of the entry restrictions on *immigrant* travel. Section 1152(a)(1)(A) is expressly limited to the issuance of "immigrant visa[s]" while § 1182(f) allows the President to suspend entry of "immigrants or nonimmigrants." At a minimum, then, plaintiffs' reading would not affect any of the limitations on nonimmigrant travel in the Proclamation.

In any event, we reject plaintiffs' interpretation because it ignores the basic distinction between admissibility determinations and visa issuance that runs throughout the INA. Section 1182 defines the pool of individuals who are admissible to the United States. Its restrictions come into play at two points in the process of gaining entry (or admission) into the United States. First, any alien who is inadmissible under § 1182 (based on, for example, health risks, criminal history, or foreign policy consequences) is screened out as "ineligible to receive a visa." 8 U.S.C. § 1201(g). Second, even if a consular officer issues a visa, entry into the United States is not guaranteed. As every visa application explains, a visa does not entitle an alien to enter the United States "if, upon arrival," an immigration officer determines that the applicant is "inadmissible under this chapter, or any other provision of law"—including § 1182(f). § 1201(h).

Sections 1182(f) and 1152(a)(1)(A) thus operate in different spheres: § 1182(f) defines the universe of aliens who are admissible into the United States (and therefore eligible to receive a visa). Once § 1182 sets the boundaries of admissibility into the United States, § 1152(a)(1)(A) prohibits discrimination in the allocation of immigrant visas based on nationality and other traits. The distinction between admissibility—to which § 1152(a)(1)(A) does not apply—and visa issuance—to which it does—is apparent from the text of the provision, which specifies only that its protections apply to the "issuance" of "immigrant visa[s]," without mentioning admissibility or entry. Had Congress instead intended in § 1152(a)(1)(A) to constrain the President's power to determine who may enter the country, it could easily have chosen language directed to that end. *See, e.g.*, §§ 1182(a)(3)(C)(ii), (iii) (providing that certain aliens "*shall not be excludable or subject to restrictions or conditions on entry*... because of the alien's past, current, or expected beliefs, statements, or associations" (emphasis added)). "The fact that [Congress] did not adopt [a] readily available and apparent alternative strongly supports" the conclusion that § 1152(a)(1)(A) does not limit the President's delegated authority under § 1182(f). *Knight v. Commissioner*, 552 U.S. 181, 188 (2008).

Common sense and historical practice confirm as much. Section 1152(a)(1)(A) has never been treated as a constraint on the criteria for admissibility in § 1182. Presidents have repeatedly exercised their authority to suspend entry on the basis of nationality. As noted, President Reagan relied on § 1182(f) to suspend entry "as immigrants by all Cuban nationals," subject to exceptions. Proclamation No. 5517, 51 Fed. Reg. 30470 (1986). Likewise, President Carter invoked § 1185(a)(1) to deny and revoke visas to all Iranian nationals. *See* Exec. Order No. 12172, 3 C.F.R. 461 (1979), as amended by Exec. Order No. 12206, 3 C.F.R. 249 (1980); Public Papers of the Presidents, Jimmy Carter, Sanctions Against Iran, Vol. 1, Apr. 7, 1980, pp. 611–612 (1980); see also n. 1, *supra*.

On plaintiffs' reading, those orders were beyond the President's authority. The entry restrictions in the Proclamation on North Korea (which plaintiffs do not challenge in this litigation) would also be unlawful. Nor would the President be permitted to suspend entry from particular foreign states in response to an epidemic confined to a single region, or a verified terrorist threat involving nationals of a specific foreign nation, or even if the United States were on the brink of war....

IV

A

We now turn to plaintiffs' claim that the Proclamation was issued for the unconstitutional purpose of excluding Muslims. Because we have an obligation to assure ourselves of jurisdiction under Article III, we begin by addressing the question whether plaintiffs have standing to bring their constitutional challenge.

Federal courts have authority under the Constitution to decide legal questions only in the course of resolving "Cases" or "Controversies." Art. III, § 2. One of the essential elements of a legal case or controversy is that the plaintiffs have standing to sue. Standing requires more than just a "keen interest in the issue." *Hollingsworth v. Perry*, 570 U.S. 693, 700 (2013). It requires allegations—and, eventually, proof—that the plaintiff "personal[ly]" suffered a concrete and particularized injury in connection with the conduct about which he complains. *Spokeo, Inc. v. Robins,* 578 U.S.——,——, 136 S. Ct. 1540, 1547–1548 (2016). In a case arising from an alleged violation of the Establishment Clause, a plaintiff must show, as in other cases, that he is "directly affected by the laws and practices against which [his] complaints are directed." *School Dist. of Abington Township v. Schempp,* 374 U.S. 203, 224 (1963). That is an issue here because the entry restrictions apply not to plaintiffs themselves but to others seeking to enter the United States.

Plaintiffs first argue that they have standing on the ground that the Proclamation "establishes a disfavored faith" and violates "their own right to be free from federal [religious] establishments." Brief for Respondents 27–28 (emphasis deleted). They describe such injury as "spiritual and dignitary." *Id.,* at 29.

We need not decide whether the claimed dignitary interest establishes an adequate ground for standing. The three individual plaintiffs assert another, more concrete injury: the alleged real-world effect that the Proclamation has had in keeping them separated from certain relatives who seek to enter the country. *See ibid.*; *Town of Chester v. Laroe Estates, Inc.,* 581 U.S.——,——, 137 S.Ct. 1645, 1651 (2017) ("At least one plaintiff must have standing to seek each form of relief requested in the complaint."). We agree that a person's interest in being united with his relatives is sufficiently concrete and particularized to form the basis of an Article III injury in fact. This Court has previously considered the merits of claims asserted by United States citizens regarding violations of their personal rights allegedly caused by the Government's exclusion of particular foreign nationals. *See Kerry v. Din,* 576 U.S.——,——, 135 S.Ct. 2128,——(2015) (plurality opinion); *id.,* at——, 135 S. Ct., at 2139 (KENNEDY, J., concurring in judgment); *Kleindienst v. Mandel,* 408 U.S. 753, 762 (1972). Likewise, one of our prior stay orders in this litigation recognized that an American individual who has "a bona fide relationship with a particular person seeking to enter the country… can legitimately claim concrete hardship if that person is excluded." *Trump v. IRAP,* 582 U.S., at——, 137 S.Ct., at 2089….

B

The First Amendment provides, in part, that "Congress shall make no law respecting an establishment of religion, or prohibiting the free exercise thereof." Our cases recognize that "[t]he clearest command of the Establishment Clause is that one religious denomination cannot be officially preferred over another." *Larson v. Valente,* 456 U.S. 228, 244 (1982). Plaintiffs believe that the Proclamation violates this prohibition by singling out Muslims for disfavored treatment. The entry suspension, they contend, operates as a "religious gerrymander," in part because most of the countries covered by the Proclamation have Muslim-majority populations. And in their view, deviations from the information-sharing baseline criteria suggest that the results of the multi-agency review were "foreordained." Relying on Establishment Clause precedents concerning laws and policies applied domestically, plaintiffs allege that the primary purpose of the Proclamation was religious animus and that the President's stated concerns about vetting protocols and national security were but pretexts for discriminating against Muslims. Brief for Respondents 69–73.

At the heart of plaintiffs' case is a series of statements by the President and his advisers casting doubt on the official objective of the Proclamation. For example, while a candidate on the campaign trail, the President published a "Statement on Preventing Muslim Immigration" that called for a "total and complete shutdown of Muslims entering the United States until our country's representatives can figure out what is going on." App. 158. That statement remained on his campaign website until May 2017. *Id.,* at 130–131. Then-candidate Trump also stated that "Islam hates us" and asserted that the United States was "having problems with Muslims coming into the country." *Id.,* at 120–121, 159. Shortly after being elected, when asked whether violence in Europe had affected his plans to "ban Muslim immigration," the President replied, "You know my plans. All along, I've been proven to be right." *Id.,* at 123.

One week after his inauguration, the President issued EO–1. In a television interview, one of the President's campaign advisers explained that when the President "first announced it, he said, 'Muslim ban.' He called me up. He said, 'Put a commission together. Show me the right way to do it legally.'" *Id.,* at 125. The adviser said he assembled a group of Members of Congress and lawyers that "focused on, instead of religion, danger.... [The order] is based on places where there [is] substantial evidence that people are sending terrorists into our country." *Id.,* at 229.

Plaintiffs also note that after issuing EO–2 to replace EO–1, the President expressed regret that his prior order had been "watered down" and called for a "much tougher version" of his "Travel Ban." Shortly before the release of the Proclamation, he stated that the "travel ban... should be far larger, tougher, and more specific," but "stupidly that would not be politically correct." *Id.,* at 132–133. More recently, on November 29, 2017, the President retweeted links to three anti-Muslim propaganda videos. In response to questions about those videos, the President's deputy press secretary denied that the President thinks Muslims are a threat to the United States, explaining that "the President has been talking about these security issues for years now, from the campaign trail to the White House" and "has addressed these issues with the travel order that he issued earlier this year and the companion proclamation." *IRAP v. Trump,* 883 F.3d 233, 267 (C.A.4 2018).

The President of the United States possesses an extraordinary power to speak to his fellow citizens and on their behalf. Our Presidents have frequently used that power to espouse the principles of religious freedom and tolerance on which this Nation was founded. In 1790 George Washington reassured the Hebrew Congregation of Newport, Rhode Island that "happily the Government of the United States... gives to bigotry no sanction, to persecution no assistance [and] requires only that they who live under its protection should demean themselves as good citizens." 6 Papers of George Washington 285 (D. Twohig ed. 1996). President Eisenhower, at the opening of the Islamic Center of Washington, similarly pledged to a Muslim audience that "America would fight with her whole strength for your right to have here your own church," declaring that "[t]his concept is indeed a part of America." Public Papers of the Presidents, Dwight D. Eisenhower, June 28, 1957, p. 509 (1957). And just days after the attacks of September 11, 2001, President George W. Bush returned to the same Islamic Center to implore his fellow Americans—Muslims and non-Muslims alike—to remember during their time of grief that "[t]he face of terror is not the true faith of Islam," and that America is "a great country because we share the same values of respect and dignity and human worth." Public Papers of the Presidents, George W. Bush, Vol. 2, Sept. 17, 2001, p. 1121 (2001). Yet it cannot be denied that the Federal Government and the Presidents who have carried its laws into effect have—from the Nation's earliest days—performed unevenly in living up to those inspiring words.

Plaintiffs argue that this President's words strike at fundamental standards of respect and tolerance, in violation of our constitutional tradition. But the issue before us is not whether to denounce the statements. It is instead the significance of those statements in reviewing a Presidential directive, neutral on its face, addressing a matter within the core of executive responsibility. In doing so, we must consider not only the statements of a particular President, but also the authority of the Presidency itself.

The case before us differs in numerous respects from the conventional Establishment Clause claim. Unlike the typical suit involving religious displays or school prayer, plaintiffs seek to invalidate a national security directive regulating the entry of aliens abroad. Their claim accordingly raises a number of delicate issues regarding the scope of the constitutional right and the manner of proof. The Proclamation, moreover, is facially neutral toward religion. Plaintiffs therefore ask the Court to probe the sincerity of the stated justifications for the policy by reference to extrinsic statements—many of which were made before the President took the oath of office. These various aspects of plaintiffs' challenge inform our standard of review.

C

For more than a century, this Court has recognized that the admission and exclusion of foreign nationals is a "fundamental sovereign attribute exercised by the Government's political departments largely immune from judicial control." *Fiallo v. Bell,* 430 U.S. 787, 792 (1977); *see Harisiades v. Shaughnessy,* 342 U.S. 580, 588–589 (1952) ("[A]ny policy toward aliens is vitally and intricately interwoven with contemporaneous policies in regard to the conduct of foreign relations [and] the war power."). Because decisions in these matters may implicate "relations with foreign powers," or involve "classifications defined in the light of changing political and economic circumstances," such judgments "are frequently of a character more appropriate to either the Legislature or the Executive." *Mathews v. Diaz,* 426 U.S. 67, 81 (1976).

Nonetheless, although foreign nationals seeking admission have no constitutional right to entry, this Court has engaged in a circumscribed judicial inquiry when the denial of a visa allegedly burdens the constitutional rights of a U.S. citizen. In *Kleindienst v. Mandel,* the Attorney General denied admission to a Belgian journalist and self-described "revolutionary Marxist," Ernest Mandel, who had been invited to speak at a conference at Stanford University. 408 U.S., at 756–757. The professors who wished to hear Mandel speak challenged that decision under the First Amendment, and we acknowledged that their constitutional "right to receive information" was implicated. *Id.,* at 764–765. But we limited our review to whether the Executive gave a "facially legitimate and bona fide" reason for its action. *Id.,* at 769. Given the authority of the political branches over admission, we held that "when the Executive exercises this [delegated] power negatively on the basis of a facially legitimate and bona fide reason, the courts will neither look behind the exercise of that discretion, nor test it by balancing its justification" against the asserted constitutional interests of U.S. citizens. *Id.* at 770....

Mandel's narrow standard of review "has particular force" in admission and immigration cases that overlap with "the area of national security." *Din,* 576 U.S., at——, 135 S.Ct., at 2140 (KENNEDY, J., concurring in judgment). For one, "[j]udicial inquiry into the national-security realm raises concerns for the separation of powers" by intruding on the President's constitutional responsibilities in the area of foreign affairs. *Ziglar v. Abbasi,* 582 U.S.——,——, 137 S. Ct. 1843, 1861 (2017) (internal quotation marks omitted). For another, "when it comes to collecting evidence and drawing inferences" on questions of national security, "the lack of competence on the part of the courts is marked." *Humanitarian Law Project,* 561 U.S., at 345.

The upshot of our cases in this context is clear: "Any rule of constitutional law that would inhibit the flexibility" of the President "to respond to changing world conditions should be adopted only with the greatest caution," and our inquiry into matters of entry and national security is highly constrained. *Mathews,* 426 U.S., at 81–82. We need not define the precise contours of that inquiry in this case. A conventional application of *Mandel,* asking only whether the policy is facially legitimate and bona fide, would put an end to our review. But the Government has suggested that it may be appropriate here for the inquiry to extend beyond the facial neutrality of the order. *See* Tr. of Oral Arg. 16–17, 25–27 (describing *Mandel* as "the starting point" of the analysis). For our purposes today, we assume that we may look behind the face of the Proclamation to the extent of applying rational basis review. That standard of review considers whether the entry policy is plausibly related to the Government's stated objective to protect the country and improve vetting processes. *See Railroad Retirement Bd. v. Fritz,* 449 U.S. 166, 179 (1980). As a result, we may consider plaintiffs' extrinsic evidence, but will uphold the policy so long as it can reasonably be understood to result from a justification independent of unconstitutional grounds.

D

Given the standard of review, it should come as no surprise that the Court hardly ever strikes down a policy as illegitimate under rational basis scrutiny. On the few occasions where we have done so, a common thread has been that the laws at issue lack any purpose other than a "bare... desire to harm a politically unpopular group." *Department of Agriculture v. Moreno,* 413 U.S. 528, 534 (1973). In one case, we invalidated a local zoning ordinance that required a special permit for group homes for the intellectually disabled, but not for other facilities such as fraternity houses or hospitals. We did so on the ground that the city's stated concerns about (among other things) "legal responsibility" and "crowded conditions" rested on "an irrational prejudice" against the intellectually disabled. *Cleburne v. Cleburne Living Center, Inc.*, 473 U.S. 432, 448–450 (1985) (internal quotation marks omitted). And in another case, this Court overturned a state constitutional amendment that denied gays and lesbians access to the protection of antidiscrimination laws. The amendment, we held, was "divorced from any factual context from which we could discern a relationship to legitimate state interests," and "its sheer breadth [was] so discontinuous with the reasons offered for it" that the initiative seemed "inexplicable by anything but animus." *Romer v. Evans,* 517 U.S. 620, 632, 635 (1996).

The Proclamation does not fit this pattern. It cannot be said that it is impossible to "discern a relationship to legitimate state interests" or that the policy is "inexplicable by anything but animus." Indeed, the dissent can only attempt to argue otherwise by refusing to apply anything resembling rational basis review. But because there is persuasive evidence that the entry suspension has a legitimate grounding in national security concerns, quite apart from any religious hostility, we must accept that independent justification.

The Proclamation is expressly premised on legitimate purposes: preventing entry of nationals who cannot be adequately vetted and inducing other nations to improve their practices. The text says nothing about religion. Plaintiffs and the dissent nonetheless emphasize that five of the seven nations currently included in the Proclamation have Muslim-majority populations. Yet that fact alone does not support an inference of religious hostility, given that the policy covers just 8% of the world's Muslim population and is limited to countries that were previously designated by Congress or prior administrations as posing national security risks. *See* 8 U.S.C. § 1187(a)(12)(A) (identifying Syria and state sponsors of terrorism such as Iran as "countr[ies] or area[s] of concern" for purposes of administering the Visa Waiver Program); Dept. of Homeland Security, DHS Announces Further Travel Restrictions for the Visa Waiver Program (Feb. 18, 2016) (designating Libya, Somalia, and Yemen as additional countries of concern); see also *Rajah,* 544 F.3d, at 433, n. 3 (describing how nonimmigrant aliens from Iran, Libya, Somalia, Syria, and Yemen were covered by the National Security Entry–Exit Registration System).

The Proclamation, moreover, reflects the results of a worldwide review process undertaken by multiple Cabinet officials and their agencies. Plaintiffs seek to discredit the findings of the review, pointing to deviations from the review's baseline criteria resulting in the inclusion of Somalia and omission of Iraq. But as the Proclamation explains, in each case the determinations were justified by the distinct conditions in each country. Although Somalia generally satisfies the information-sharing component of the baseline criteria, it "stands apart... in the degree to which [it] lacks command and control of its territory." Proclamation § 2(h)(i). As for Iraq, the Secretary of Homeland Security determined that entry restrictions were not warranted in light of the close cooperative relationship between the U.S. and Iraqi Governments and the country's key role in combating terrorism in the region. § 1(g). It is, in any event, difficult to see how exempting one of the largest predominantly Muslim countries in the region from coverage under the Proclamation can be cited as evidence of animus toward Muslims....

More fundamentally, plaintiffs and the dissent challenge the entry suspension based on their perception of its effectiveness and wisdom. They suggest that the policy is overbroad and does little to serve national security interests. But we cannot substitute our own assessment for the Executive's predictive judgments on such matters, all of which "are delicate, complex, and involve large elements of prophecy." *Chicago & Southern Air Lines, Inc. v. Waterman S.S. Corp.*, 333 U.S. 103, 111 (1948); *see also Regan v. Wald,* 468 U.S. 222, 242–243 (1984) (declining invitation to conduct an "independent foreign policy analysis"). While we of course "do not defer to the Government's reading of the First Amendment," the Executive's evaluation of the underlying facts is entitled to appropriate weight, particularly in the context of litigation involving "sensitive and weighty interests of national security and foreign affairs." *Humanitarian Law Project,* 561 U.S., at 33–34....

* * *

Under these circumstances, the Government has set forth a sufficient national security justification to survive rational basis review. We express no view on the soundness of the policy. We simply hold today that plaintiffs have not demonstrated a likelihood of success on the merits of their constitutional claim.

V

Because plaintiffs have not shown that they are likely to succeed on the merits of their claims, we reverse the grant of the preliminary injunction as an abuse of discretion. *Winter v. Natural Resources Defense Council, Inc.*, 555 U.S. 7, 32 (2008). The case now returns to the lower courts for such further proceedings as may be appropriate. Our disposition of the case makes it unnecessary to consider the propriety of the nationwide scope of the injunction issued by the District Court.

The judgment of the Court of Appeals is reversed, and the case is remanded for further proceedings consistent with this opinion.

It is so ordered.

Justice Sotomayor, with whom Justice Ginsburg joins, dissenting:

The United States of America is a Nation built upon the promise of religious liberty. Our Founders honored that core promise by embedding the principle of religious neutrality in the First Amendment. The Court's decision today fails to safeguard that fundamental principle. It leaves undisturbed a policy first advertised openly and unequivocally as a "total and complete shutdown of Muslims entering the United States" because the policy now masquerades behind a facade of national-security concerns. But this repackaging does little to cleanse Presidential Proclamation No. 9645 of the appearance of discrimination that the President's words have created. Based on the evidence in the record, a reasonable observer would conclude that the Proclamation was motivated by anti-Muslim animus. That alone suffices to show that plaintiffs are likely to succeed on the merits of their Establishment Clause claim. The majority holds otherwise by ignoring the facts, misconstruing our legal precedent, and turning a blind eye to the pain and suffering the Proclamation inflicts upon countless families and individuals, many of whom are United States citizens. Because that troubling result runs contrary to the Constitution and our precedent, I dissent.

I

Plaintiffs challenge the Proclamation on various grounds, both statutory and constitutional. Ordinarily, when a case can be decided on purely statutory grounds, we strive to follow a "prudential rule of avoiding constitutional questions." *Zobrest v. Catalina Foothills School Dist.*, 509 U.S. 1, 8 (1993). But that rule of thumb is far from categorical, and it has limited application where, as here, the constitutional question proves far simpler than the statutory one. Whatever the merits of plaintiffs' complex statutory claims, the Proclamation must be enjoined for a more fundamental reason: It runs afoul of the Establishment Clause's guarantee of religious neutrality.

A

The Establishment Clause forbids government policies "respecting an establishment of religion." U.S. Const., Amdt. 1. The "clearest command" of the Establishment Clause is that the Government cannot favor or disfavor one religion over another. *Larson v. Valente,* 456 U.S. 228, 244 (1982); *Church of Lukumi Babalu Aye, Inc. v. Hialeah,* 508 U.S. 520, 532 (1993) ("[T]he First Amendment forbids an official purpose to disapprove of a particular religion") .... Consistent with that clear command, this Court has long acknowledged that governmental actions that favor one religion "inevitabl[y]" foster "the hatred, disrespect and even contempt of those who [hold] contrary beliefs." *Engel v. Vitale,* 370 U.S. 421, 431 (1962). That is so, this Court has held, because such acts send messages to members of minority faiths " 'that they are outsiders, not full members of the political community.'" *Santa Fe Independent School Dist. v. Doe,* 530 U.S. 290, 309 (2000). To guard against this serious harm, the Framers mandated a strict "principle of denominational neutrality." *Larson,* 456 U.S., at 246 ....

"When the government acts with the ostensible and predominant purpose" of disfavoring a particular religion, "it violates that central Establishment Clause value of official religious neutrality, there being no neutrality when the government's ostensible object is to take sides." *McCreary County v. American Civil Liberties Union of Ky.*, 545 U.S. 844, 860 (2005). To determine whether plaintiffs have proved an Establishment Clause violation, the Court asks whether a reasonable observer would view the government action as enacted for the purpose of disfavoring a religion. *See id.*, at 862, 866, 125 S. Ct. 2722; accord, *Town of Greece v. Galloway,* 572 U.S.——,——, 134 S. Ct. 1811, 1825 (2014) (plurality opinion).

In answering that question, this Court has generally considered the text of the government policy, its operation, and any available evidence regarding "the historical background of the decision under challenge, the specific series of events leading to the enactment or official policy in question, and the legislative or administrative history, including contemporaneous statements made by" the decisionmaker. *Lukumi,* 508 U.S., at 540 (opinion of KENNEDY, J.); *McCreary,* 545 U.S., at 862 (courts must evaluate "text, legislative history, and implementation . . . , or comparable official act" (internal quotation marks omitted)). At the same time, however, courts must take care not to engage in "any judicial psychoanalysis of a drafter's heart of hearts." *Id.,* at 862.

B

1

Although the majority briefly recounts a few of the statements and background events that form the basis of plaintiffs' constitutional challenge, *ante,* at 2417–2418, that highly abridged account does not tell even half of the story. *See* Brief for The Roderick & Solange MacArthur Justice Center as *Amicus Curiae* 5–31 (outlining President Trump's public statements expressing animus toward Islam). The full record paints a far more harrowing picture, from which a reasonable observer would readily conclude that the Proclamation was motivated by hostility and animus toward the Muslim faith.

During his Presidential campaign, then-candidate Donald Trump pledged that, if elected, he would ban Muslims from entering the United States. Specifically, on December 7, 2015, he issued a formal statement "calling for a total and complete shutdown of Muslims entering the United States." App. 119. That statement, which remained on his campaign website until May 2017 (several months into his Presidency), read in full:

> "Donald J. Trump is calling for a total and complete shutdown of Muslims entering the United States until our country's representatives can figure out what is going on. According to Pew Research, among others, there is great hatred towards Americans by large segments of the Muslim population. Most recently, a poll from the Center for Security Policy released data showing '25% of those polled agreed that violence against Americans here in the United States is justified as a part of the global jihad' and 51% of those polled 'agreed that Muslims in America should have the choice of being governed according to Shariah.' Shariah authorizes such atrocities as murder against nonbelievers who won't convert, beheadings and more unthinkable acts that pose great harm to Americans, especially women.
>
> "Mr. Trum[p] stated, 'Without looking at the various polling data, it is obvious to anybody the hatred is beyond comprehension. Where this hatred comes from and why we will have to determine. Until we are able to determine and understand this problem and the dangerous threat it poses, our

> country cannot be the victims of the horrendous attacks by people that believe only in Jihad, and have no sense of reason or respect of human life. If I win the election for President, we are going to Make America Great Again.'—Donald J. Trump." *Id.*, at 158 ....

On December 8, 2015, Trump justified his proposal during a television interview by noting that President Franklin D. Roosevelt "did the same thing" with respect to the internment of Japanese Americans during World War II. *Id.*, at 120. In January 2016, during a Republican primary debate, Trump was asked whether he wanted to "rethink [his] position" on "banning Muslims from entering the country." *Ibid.* He answered, "No." *Ibid.* A month later, at a rally in South Carolina, Trump told an apocryphal story about United States General John J. Pershing killing a large group of Muslim insurgents in the Philippines with bullets dipped in pigs' blood in the early 1900's. *Id.*, at 163–164. In March 2016, he expressed his belief that "Islam hates us.... [W]e can't allow people coming into this country who have this hatred of the United States... [a]nd of people that are not Muslim." *Id.*, at 120–121. That same month, Trump asserted that "[w]e're having problems with the Muslims, and we're having problems with Muslims coming into the country." *Id.*, at 121. He therefore called for surveillance of mosques in the United States, blaming terrorist attacks on Muslims' lack of "assimilation" and their commitment to "sharia law." *Ibid.*; *id.*, at 164. A day later, he opined that Muslims "do not respect us at all" and "don't respect a lot of the things that are happening throughout not only our country, but they don't respect other things." *Ibid.*

As Trump's presidential campaign progressed, he began to describe his policy proposal in slightly different terms. In June 2016, for instance, he characterized the policy proposal as a suspension of immigration from countries "where there's a proven history of terrorism." *Id.*, at 121. He also described the proposal as rooted in the need to stop "importing radical Islamic terrorism to the West through a failed immigration system." *Id.*, at 121–122. Asked in July 2016 whether he was "pull[ing] back from" his pledged Muslim ban, Trump responded, "I actually don't think it's a rollback. In fact, you could say it's an expansion." *Id.*, at 122–123. He then explained that he used different terminology because "[p]eople were so upset when [he] used the word Muslim." *Id.*, at 123.

A month before the 2016 election, Trump reiterated that his proposed "Muslim ban" had "morphed into a[n] extreme vetting from certain areas of the world." *Ibid.* Then, on December 21, 2016, President-elect Trump was asked whether he would "rethink" his previous "plans to create a Muslim registry or ban Muslim immigration." *Ibid.* He replied: "You know my plans. All along, I've proven to be right." *Ibid.*

On January 27, 2017, one week after taking office, President Trump signed Executive Order No. 13769, 82 Fed. Reg. 8977 (2017) (EO–1), entitled "Protecting the Nation From Foreign Terrorist Entry Into the United States." As he signed it, President Trump read the title, looked up, and said "We all know what that means." App. 124. That same day, President Trump explained to the media that, under EO–1,

Christians would be given priority for entry as refugees into the United States. In particular, he bemoaned the fact that in the past, "[i]f you were a Muslim [refugee from Syria] you could come in, but if you were a Christian, it was almost impossible." *Id.,* at 125. Considering that past policy "very unfair," President Trump explained that EO–1 was designed "to help" the Christians in Syria. *Ibid.* The following day, one of President Trump's key advisers candidly drew the connection between EO–1 and the "Muslim ban" that the President had pledged to implement if elected. *Ibid.* According to that adviser, "[W]hen [Donald Trump] first announced it, he said, 'Muslim ban.' He called me up. He said, 'Put a commission together. Show me the right way to do it legally.'" *Ibid.*...

While litigation over EO–2 was ongoing, President Trump repeatedly made statements alluding to a desire to keep Muslims out of the country. For instance, he said at a rally of his supporters that EO–2 was just a "watered down version of the first one" and had been "tailor[ed]" at the behest of "the lawyers." App. 131. He further added that he would prefer "to go back to the first [executive order] and go all the way" and reiterated his belief that it was "very hard" for Muslims to assimilate into Western culture. *Id.,* at 131–132. During a rally in April 2017, President Trump recited the lyrics to a song called "The Snake," a song about a woman who nurses a sick snake back to health but then is attacked by the snake, as a warning about Syrian refugees entering the country. *Id.,* at 132, 163. And in June 2017, the President stated on Twitter that the Justice Department had submitted a "watered down, politically correct version" of the "original Travel Ban" "to S[upreme] C [ourt]." *Id.,* at 132. The President went on to tweet: "People, the lawyers and the courts can call it whatever they want, but I am calling it what we need and what it is, a TRAVEL BAN!" *Id.,* at 132–133. He added: "That's right, we need a TRAVEL BAN for certain DANGEROUS countries, not some politically correct term that won't help us protect our people!" *Id.,* at 133. Then, on August 17, 2017, President Trump issued yet another tweet about Islam, once more referencing the story about General Pershing's massacre of Muslims in the Philippines: "Study what General Pershing... did to terrorists when caught. There was no more Radical Islamic Terror for 35 years!" *IRAP v. Trump,* 883 F.3d 233, 267 (C.A.4 2018) (*IRAP II*) (en banc) (alterations in original).

In September 2017, President Trump tweeted that "[t]he travel ban into the United States should be far larger, tougher and more specific—but stupidly, that would not be politically correct!" App. 133. Later that month, on September 24, 2017, President Trump issued Presidential Proclamation No. 9645, 82 Fed. Reg. 45161 (2017) (Proclamation), which restricts entry of certain nationals from six Muslim-majority countries. On November 29, 2017, President Trump "retweeted" three anti-Muslim videos, entitled "Muslim Destroys a Statue of Virgin Mary!", "Islamist mob pushes teenage boy off roof and beats him to death!", and "Muslim migrant beats up Dutch boy on crutches!" *IRAP II,* 883 F.3d, at 267. Those videos were initially tweeted by a British political party whose mission is to oppose "all alien and destructive politic [al] or religious doctrines, including... Islam." *Ibid.* When asked about these videos, the White House Deputy Press Secretary connected them to the Proclamation, responding that the "President has been talking about these security issues for years now, from the campaign trail to the White House" and "has addressed these issues with the travel order that he issued earlier this year and the companion proclamation." *Ibid.*

2

As the majority correctly notes, "the issue before us is not whether to denounce" these offensive statements. *Ante,* at 2418. Rather, the dispositive and narrow question here is whether a reasonable observer, presented with all "openly available data," the text and "historical context" of the Proclamation, and the "specific sequence of events" leading to it, would conclude that the primary purpose of the Proclamation is to disfavor Islam and its adherents by excluding them from the country. *See McCreary,* 545 U.S., at 862–863. The answer is unquestionably yes.

Taking all the relevant evidence together, a reasonable observer would conclude that the Proclamation was driven primarily by anti-Muslim animus, rather than by the Government's asserted national-security justifications. Even before being sworn into office, then-candidate Trump stated that "Islam hates us," App. 399, warned that "[w]e're having problems with the Muslims, and we're having problems with Muslims coming into the country," *id.,* at 121, promised to enact a "total and complete shutdown of Muslims entering the United States," *id.,* at 119, and instructed one of his advisers to find a "lega[l]" way to enact a Muslim ban, *id.,* at 125. The President continued to make similar statements well after his inauguration, as detailed above, *see supra,* at 2436–2438.

Moreover, despite several opportunities to do so, President Trump has never disavowed any of his prior statements about Islam. Instead, he has continued to make remarks that a reasonable observer would view as an unrelenting attack on the Muslim religion and its followers. Given President Trump's failure to correct the reasonable perception of his apparent hostility toward the Islamic faith, it is unsurprising that the President's lawyers have, at every step in the lower courts, failed in their attempts to launder the Proclamation of its discriminatory taint. *See United States v. Fordice,* 505 U.S. 717, 746–747 (1992) ("[G]iven an initially tainted policy, it is eminently reasonable to make the [Government] bear the risk of nonpersuasion with respect to intent at some future time, both because the [Government] has created the dispute through its own prior unlawful conduct, and because discriminatory intent does tend to persist through time" (citation omitted)). Notably, the Court recently found less pervasive official expressions of hostility and the failure to disavow them to be constitutionally significant. *Cf. Masterpiece Cakeshop, Ltd. v. Colorado Civil Rights Comm'n,* 584 U.S.——,——, 138 S. Ct. 1719, 1732 (2018) ("The official expressions of hostility to religion in some of the commissioners' comments—comments that were not disavowed at the Commission or by the State at any point in the proceedings that led to the affirmance of the order—were inconsistent with what the Free Exercise Clause requires"). It should find the same here.

Ultimately, what began as a policy explicitly "calling for a total and complete shutdown of Muslims entering the United States" has since morphed into a "Proclamation" putatively based on national-security concerns. But this new window dressing cannot conceal an unassailable fact: the words of the President and his advisers create the strong perception that the Proclamation is contaminated by impermissible discriminatory animus against Islam and its followers.

II

Rather than defend the President's problematic statements, the Government urges this Court to set them aside and defer to the President on issues related to immigration and national security. The majority accepts that invitation and incorrectly applies a watered-down legal standard in an effort to short circuit plaintiffs' Establishment Clause claim.

The majority begins its constitutional analysis by noting that this Court, at times, "has engaged in a circumscribed judicial inquiry when the denial of a visa allegedly burdens the constitutional rights of a U.S. citizen." *Ante,* at 2419 (citing *Kleindienst v. Mandel,* 408 U.S. 753 (1972)). As the majority notes, *Mandel* held that when the Executive Branch provides "a facially legitimate and bona fide reason" for denying a visa, "courts will neither look behind the exercise of that discretion, nor test it by balancing its justification." *Id.,* at 770. In his controlling concurrence in *Kerry v. Din,* 576 U.S.——, 135 S. Ct. 2128 (2015), Justice KENNEDY applied *Mandel* 's holding and elaborated that courts can "'look behind' the Government's exclusion of" a foreign national if there is "an affirmative showing of bad faith on the part of the consular officer who denied [the] visa." *Din,* 576 U.S., at——, 135 S. Ct., at 2141 (opinion concurring in judgment). The extent to which *Mandel* and *Din* apply at all to this case is unsettled, and there is good reason to think they do not....

In light of the Government's suggestion "that it may be appropriate here for the inquiry to extend beyond the facial neutrality of the order," the majority rightly declines to apply *Mandel* 's "narrow standard of review" and "assume [s] that we may look behind the face of the Proclamation." *Ante,* at 2420. In doing so, however, the Court, without explanation or precedential support, limits its review of the Proclamation to rational-basis scrutiny. *Ibid.* That approach is perplexing, given that in other Establishment Clause cases, including those involving claims of religious animus or discrimination, this Court has applied a more stringent standard of review. *See, e.g., McCreary,* 545 U.S., at 860–863; *Larson,* 456 U.S., at 246; *Presbyterian Church in U.S. v. Mary Elizabeth Blue Hull Memorial Presbyterian Church,* 393 U.S. 440, 449–452 (1969); *see also Colorado Christian Univ. v. Weaver,* 534 F.3d 1245, 1266 (C.A.10 2008) (McConnell, J.) (noting that, under Supreme Court precedent, laws "involving discrimination on the basis of religion, including interdenominational discrimination, are subject to heightened scrutiny whether they arise under the Free Exercise Clause, the Establishment Clause, or the Equal Protection Clause" (citations omitted)). As explained above, the Proclamation is plainly unconstitutional under that heightened standard. *See supra,* at 2438–2440.

But even under rational-basis review, the Proclamation must fall. That is so because the Proclamation is "'divorced from any factual context from which we could discern a relationship to legitimate state interests,' and 'its sheer breadth [is] so discontinuous with the reasons offered for it'" that the policy is "inexplicable by anything but animus." *Ante,* at 2420 (quoting *Romer v. Evans,* 517 U.S. 620, 632, 635 (1996)); *see also Cleburne v. Cleburne Living Center, Inc.*, 473 U.S. 432, 448 (1985) (recognizing that classifications predicated on discriminatory animus can never be legitimate because the Government has no legitimate interest in exploiting "mere negative attitudes, or fear" toward a disfavored group). The President's statements, which the majority utterly fails to address in its legal analysis, strongly support the conclusion that the Proclamation was issued to express hostility toward Muslims and exclude them from the country. Given the overwhelming record evidence of anti-Muslim animus, it simply cannot be said that the Proclamation has a legitimate basis. *IRAP II,* 883 F.3d, at 352 (Harris, J., concurring) (explaining that the Proclamation contravenes the bedrock principle "that the government may not act on the basis of *animus* toward a disfavored religious minority" (emphasis in original))....

Beyond that, Congress has already addressed the national-security concerns supposedly undergirding the Proclamation through an "extensive and complex" framework governing "immigration and alien status." *Arizona v. United States,* 567 U.S. 387, 395 (2012). The Immigration and Nationality Act sets forth, in painstaking detail, a reticulated scheme regulating the admission of individuals to the United States. Generally, admission to the United States requires a valid visa or other travel document. 8 U.S.C. §§1181, 1182(a)(7)(A)(i)(I), 1182(a)(7)(B)(i)(II). To obtain a visa, an applicant must produce "certified cop[ies]" of documents proving her identity, background, and criminal history. §§1202(b), 1202(d). An applicant also must undergo an in-person interview with a State Department consular officer. §§1201(a)(1), 1202(h)(1), 22 CFR §§42.62(a)-(b) (2017); *see also* 8 U.S.C. §§1202(h)(2)(D), 1202(h)(2)(F) (requiring in-person interview if the individual "is a national of a country officially designated by the Secretary of State as a state sponsor of terrorism" or is "a member of a group or section that... poses a security threat to the United States"). "Any alien who... has engaged in a terrorist activity," "incited terrorist activity," or been a representative, member, or endorser of a terrorist organization, or who "is likely to engage after entry in any terrorist activity," §1182(a)(3)(B), or who has committed one or more of the many crimes enumerated in the statute is inadmissible and therefore ineligible to receive a visa. *See* §1182(a)(2)(A) (crime of moral turpitude or drug offense); §1182(a)(2)(C) (drug trafficking or benefiting from a relative who recently trafficked drugs); §1182(a)(2)(D) (prostitution or "unlawful commercialized vice"); §1182(a)(2)(H) (human trafficking); §1182(a)(3) ("Security and related grounds").

In addition to vetting rigorously any individuals seeking admission to the United States, the Government also rigorously vets the information-sharing and identity-management systems of other countries, as evidenced by the Visa Waiver Program, which permits certain nationals from a select group of countries to skip the ordinary visa-application process. *See* §1187. To determine which countries are eligible for the Visa Waiver Program, the Government considers whether they can satisfy numerous criteria—*e.g.*, using electronic, fraud-resistant passports, § 1187(a)(3)(B), 24–hour reporting of lost or stolen passports, § 1187(c)(2)(D), and not providing a safe haven for terrorists, § 1187(a)(12)(D)(iii). The Secretary of Homeland Security, in consultation with the Secretary of State, also must determine that a country's inclusion in the program will not compromise "the law enforcement and security interests of the United States." § 1187(c)(2)(C). Eligibility for the program is reassessed on an annual basis. *See* § 1187(a)(12)(D)(iii), 1187(c)(12)(A). As a result of a recent review, for example, the Executive decided in 2016 to remove from the program dual nationals of Iraq, Syria, Iran, and Sudan. *See* Brief for Former National Security Officials as *Amici Curiae* 27.

Put simply, Congress has already erected a statutory scheme that fulfills the putative national-security interests the Government now puts forth to justify the Proclamation. Tellingly, the Government remains wholly unable to articulate any credible national-security interest that would go unaddressed by the current statutory scheme absent the Proclamation. The Government also offers no evidence that this current vetting scheme, which involves a highly searching consideration of individuals required to obtain visas for entry into the United States and a highly searching consideration of which countries are eligible for inclusion in the Visa Waiver Program, is inadequate to achieve the Proclamation's proclaimed objectives of "preventing entry of nationals who cannot be adequately vetted and inducing other nations to improve their [vetting and information-sharing] practices." *Ante*, at 2421....

In sum, none of the features of the Proclamation highlighted by the majority supports the Government's claim that the Proclamation is genuinely and primarily rooted in a legitimate national-security interest. What the unrebutted evidence actually shows is that a reasonable observer would conclude, quite easily, that the primary purpose and function of the Proclamation is to disfavor Islam by banning Muslims from entering our country.

III

As the foregoing analysis makes clear, plaintiffs are likely to succeed on the merits of their Establishment Clause claim. To obtain a preliminary injunction, however, plaintiffs must also show that they are "likely to suffer irreparable harm in the absence of preliminary relief," that "the balance of equities tips in [their] favor," and that "an injunction is in the public interest." *Winter v. Natural Resources Defense Council, Inc.*, 555 U.S. 7, 20 (2008). Plaintiffs readily clear those remaining hurdles.

First, plaintiffs have shown a likelihood of irreparable harm in the absence of an injunction. As the District Court found, plaintiffs have adduced substantial evidence showing that the Proclamation will result in "a multitude of harms that are not compensable with monetary damages and that are irreparable—among them, prolonged separation from family members, constraints to recruiting and retaining students and faculty members to foster diversity and quality within the University community, and the diminished membership of the [Muslim] Association." 265 F.Supp.3d 1140, 1159 (Haw.2017).

Second, plaintiffs have demonstrated that the balance of the equities tips in their favor. Against plaintiffs' concrete allegations of serious harm, the Government advances only nebulous national-security concerns. Although national security is unquestionably an issue of paramount public importance, it is not "a talisman" that the Government can use "to ward off inconvenient claims—a 'label' used to 'cover a multitude of sins.'" *Ziglar v. Abbasi,* 582 U.S.——,——, 137 S. Ct. 1843, 1862 (2017). That is especially true here, because, as noted, the Government's other statutory tools, including the existing rigorous individualized vetting process, already address the Proclamation's purported national-security concerns. *See supra,* at 2443–2445.

Finally, plaintiffs and their *amici* have convincingly established that "an injunction is in the public interest." *Winter,* 555 U.S., at 20. As explained by the scores of *amici* who have filed briefs in support of plaintiffs, the Proclamation has deleterious effects on our higher education system; national security; healthcare; artistic culture; and the Nation's technology industry and overall economy. Accordingly, the Court of Appeals correctly affirmed, in part, the District Court's preliminary injunction.

IV

The First Amendment stands as a bulwark against official religious prejudice and embodies our Nation's deep commitment to religious plurality and tolerance. That constitutional promise is why, "[f]or centuries now, people have come to this country from every corner of the world to share in the blessing of religious freedom." *Town of Greece v. Galloway,* 572 U.S., at——, 134 S. Ct., at 1841 (KAGAN, J., dissenting). Instead of vindicating those principles, today's decision tosses them aside. In holding that the First Amendment gives way to an executive policy that a reasonable observer would view as motivated by animus against Muslims, the majority opinion upends this Court's precedent, repeats tragic mistakes of the past, and denies countless individuals the fundamental right of religious liberty.

Just weeks ago, the Court rendered its decision in *Masterpiece Cakeshop,* 584 U.S.——, 138 S. Ct. 1719,——L.Ed.2d——, which applied the bedrock principles of religious neutrality and tolerance in considering a First Amendment challenge to government action. See *id.,* at——, 138 S. Ct., at 1731 ("The Constitution 'commits government itself to religious tolerance, and upon even slight suspicion that proposals for state intervention stem from animosity to religion or distrust of its practices, all officials must pause to remember their own high duty to the Constitution and to the rights it secures.'" (quoting *Lukumi,* 508 U.S., at 547, 113 S.Ct. 2217)); *Masterpiece,* 584 U.S., at——, 138 S. Ct., at 1732 (KAGAN, J., concurring) ("[S]tate actors cannot show hostility to religious views; rather, they must give those views 'neutral and respectful consideration."). Those principles should apply equally here. In both instances, the question is whether a government actor exhibited tolerance and neutrality in reaching a decision that affects individuals' fundamental religious freedom. But unlike in *Masterpiece,* where a state civil rights commission was found to have acted without "the neutrality that the Free Exercise Clause requires," *id.,* at——, 138 S. Ct., at 1731, the government actors in this case will not be held accountable for breaching the First Amendment's guarantee of religious neutrality and tolerance. Unlike in *Masterpiece*, where the majority considered the state commissioners' statements about religion to be persuasive evidence of unconstitutional government action, *id.*, at—, 138 S. Ct., at 1728–1730, the majority here completely sets aside the President's charged statements about Muslims as irrelevant. That holding erodes the foundational principles of religious tolerance that the Court elsewhere has so emphatically protected, and it tells members of minority religions in our country "that they are outsiders, not full members of the political community." *Santa Fe*, 530 U.S., at 309, 120 S. Ct. 2266....

Our Constitution demands, and our country deserves, a Judiciary willing to hold the coordinate branches to account when they defy our most sacred legal commitments. Because the Court's decision today has failed in that respect, with profound regret, I dissent.

Notes

1. The vote was 5–4, with Justices Kennedy, Thomas, Alito, and Gorsuch joining Chief Justice Roberts in his majority opinion. Justices Kennedy and Thomas filed concurring opinions. Justice Sotomayor's dissent was joined by Justice Ginsberg. Justice Breyer also filed a dissenting opinion, joined by Justice Kagan.

2. The Court took the opportunity to overrule *Korematsu v. United States*, 323 U.S. 214 (1944). We have omitted the discussions of *Korematsu* from the excerpts of the majority opinion and Justice Sotomayor's dissent above, as we will discuss this aspect of the Court's ruling in Unit 3.

3. How is the Proclamation similar to or different from the prior exclusion laws? If exclusion of foreigners from entry into the United States based on national origin or race is constitutional, why not exclusions on the basis of religion? And is it relevant that Great Britain, around the time of the Founding, discriminated against Catholic immigration while favoring the immigration of continental Protestants?

4. What was the Court's reasoning with respect to, first, the statutory argument, and second, the constitutional challenge? With respect to the statutory argument, is the travel ban distinguishable from President Reagan's qualified restrictions on Cubans, President Carter's on Iranians after the hostage crisis, and multiple presidents' restrictions on the entry of North Koreans? Why did the dissent disagree with the majority on the constitutional challenge?

5. Did the Proclamation discriminate on the basis of race or religion? Does the decision stand for the proposition that the federal government can, in the immigration context (or at least in *this* immigration context), discriminate on the basis

of race or religion? Did the majority agree with the plaintiffs' contention that the Proclamation discriminated against Muslims? Do you think that religious animus played any role in the Administration's decision to issue the travel ban? To what extent was national security a genuine concern? Could both factors have been a consideration?

6. The Court did not cite *Chae Chan Ping*, but was the plenary power doctrine a factor here?

7. What standard of review did the Court apply? What is the appropriate standard of review? *See generally First Amendment—Establishment Clause—Judicial Review of Pretext—* Trump v. Hawaii, 132 Harv. L. Rev. 327 (2018).

8. The Court held that plaintiffs had standing to challenge the Proclamation. What was the basis for its standing ruling?

9. Should it be relevant to the legal analysis that the Proclamation represented the third attempt at a travel ban? If so, how does it cut—in favor of legality or against legality, and why? Did the Administration present a "moving target," and, if so, what is the significance, if any?

10. On January 20, 2021, the day he was inaugurated, President Joe Biden issued his own executive Proclamation, revoking President Trump's Proclamation, ending the travel ban, and declaring:

    > The United States was built on a foundation of religious freedom and tolerance, a principle enshrined in the United States Constitution. Nevertheless, the previous administration enacted a number of Executive Orders and Presidential Proclamations that prevented certain individuals from entering the United States—first from primarily Muslim countries, and later, from largely African countries. Those actions are a stain on our national conscience and are inconsistent with our long history of welcoming people of all faiths and no faith at all.
    >
    > Beyond contravening our values, these Executive Orders and Proclamations have undermined our national security. They have jeopardized our global network of alliances and partnerships and are a moral blight that has dulled the power of our example the world over. And they have separated loved ones, inflicting pain that will ripple for years to come. They are just plain wrong.
    >
    > Make no mistake, where there are threats to our Nation, we will address them. Where there are opportunities to strengthen information-sharing with partners, we will pursue them. And when visa applicants request entry to the United States, we will apply a rigorous, individualized vetting system. But we will not turn our backs on our values with discriminatory bans on entry into the United States.

White House, Briefing Room, *Proclamation on Ending Discriminatory Bans on Entry to the United States* (2021), https://www.whitehouse.gov/briefing-room/presidential-actions/2021/01/20/proclamation-ending-discriminatory-bans-on-entry-to-the-united-states/.

11. Does President Biden's revocation of his predecessor's Proclamation on his first day in office mean that the Supreme Court was wrong to uphold it as permissible under the relevant statutes and the Establishment Clause? Shouldn't Biden have had to make findings of non-threat to confirm that his revocation is consistent with U.S. national interests, given his predecessor's contrary findings of threat?

12. Is it consistent with the rule of law that one president issued a travel ban a few days after assuming office and then his successor revoked the final version of that ban which the Supreme Court had upheld as lawful a few days after taking office? Isn't that merely the consequence of a shift of political parties in a national election? Why should the President, as opposed to Congress, have the power to choose to prohibit entry into the United States of persons from certain countries for reasons of national security? If we accept the validity of some unilateral presidential power to do this, how should courts ensure that presidential actions are really about national security rather than some other illegitimate reasons?

13. The Court did not resolve the issue of the appropriateness of a nationwide injunction in the Travel Ban case. Recently, however, in litigation over President Trump's 2025 executive order on birthright citizenship, the Supreme Court substantially limited the ability of federal courts to issue universal or nationwide injunctions. *See Trump v. CASA, Inc.*, 606 U.S. 831 (2025). We discuss this issue in Chapter 3.

Chapter 3
Citizenship

1. Birthright Citizenship

Section One of the Fourteenth Amendment provides that "[a]ll persons born or naturalized in the United States, and subject to the jurisdiction thereof, are citizens of the United States and of the State wherein they reside."

On January 20, 2025, shortly after being sworn in to his second term as President, Donald Trump issued an executive order titled "Protecting the Meaning and Value of American Citizenship," purporting to end birthright citizenship for two categories of persons born in the United States whose fathers are not U.S. citizens or lawful permanent residents at the person's time of birth: "when that person's mother was unlawfully present in the United States" or "when that person's mother's presence in the United States was lawful but temporary." *See* White House, *Protecting the Meaning and Value of American Citizenship* (Jan. 20, 2025), *available at* https://www.whitehouse.gov/presidential-actions/2025/01/protecting-the-meaning-and-value-of-american-citizenship/. Most scholars have condemned the American Citizenship Order as an indefensible interpretation of the U.S. Constitution, and lawsuits were quickly filed challenging the Order in federal district courts across the country. So far, the plaintiffs have prevailed; the lower courts have preliminarily enjoined enforcement of the executive order.

President Trump articulated the policy reasons behind the Order a decade prior to its issuance when he was first campaigning for the presidency. In 2015, then-candidate Donald Trump observed:

> A woman gets pregnant. She's nine months, she walks across the border, she has the baby in the United States, and we take care of the baby for 85 years.... I don't think so.[1]

In 2023, an estimated 225,000 to 250,000 babies were born to unauthorized immigrant parents in the United States, amounting to almost seven percent of the 3.6

1. *See* Pamela Constable, *For Illegal Aliens with Babies, the Anchor Pulls in Many Directions*, Wash. Post, Sept. 15, 2015, *available at* https://www.fosterglobal.com/blog/for-illegal-immigrants-with-babies-the-anchor-pulls-in-many-directions.

million births in the United States that year.[2] "Birth tourism" also has become a phenomenon—foreigners coming to the United States legally, for example, on tourist visas, and giving birth here to U.S. citizen babies.[3] Based on limited data, it is estimated that some 33,000 pregnant tourists give birth in the United States every year.[4]

In 2020, the State Department revised regulations to provide that applications for nonimmigrant visas would be denied for individuals believed to be traveling for the primary purpose of giving birth in the United States to obtain U.S. citizenship for the child. U.S. Dep't of State, *Birth Tourism Update*, Travel.State.Gov (Jan. 23, 2020), *available at* https://travel.state.gov/content/travel/en/us-visas/visa-information-resources/visas-news-archive/20200123_birth-tourism-update.html. U.S. Customs and Border Protection advised in 2024:

> Although there are no specific regulations prohibiting pregnant foreign nationals from entering the United States, entry is allowed or denied at the discretion of the admitting U.S. Customs and Border Patrol Protection (CBP) Officer. If the CBP officer determines that you are likely to become a ward of the government (meaning that the government must provide medical care because you do not have medical coverage), you can be denied entry.

Knowledge Article, CBP.gov (Mar. 29, 2024), *available at* https://www.help.cbp.gov/s/article/ Article1838?language=en_US. The political backlash has resulted in a growing interest in eliminating birthright citizenship for children of undocumented or temporarily present foreigners, which culminated in Trump's 2025 Order.

By 1882, when the Chinese Exclusion Act was passed, there were 300,000 Chinese people in California—10% of the state's population. The overwhelming majority were laborers who had come to the United States after the Gold Rush of 1849, and particularly after the Burlingame Treaty of 1868. A few of those laborers were married and had children born on U.S. soil. Wong Kim Ark was a Chinese laborer born in 1873 in San Francisco to Chinese-born parents, who returned to China in 1890. Wong had lived in California all his life but went to China in 1890 and returned later that year. In 1894, Wong again took a trip to China, but this time he was denied reentry when he returned to California in 1895, on the basis of the Chinese Exclusion Acts.

---

2. Jason Richwine and Steven A. Camorata, *Births to Illegal Immigrants and Long-Term Temporary Visitors*, Center for Immigrant Studies, Feb. 14, 2025, *available at* https://cis.org/Richwine/Births-Illegal-Immigrants-and-LongTerm-Temporary-Visitors.

3. Matt Sheehan, *Born in the USA: Why Chinese "Birth Tourism" Is Booming in California*, Huffington Post, May 1, 2015, *available at* https://www.huffpost.com/entry/china-us-birth-tourism_n_7187180 *see also* AP, *"Birth tourism" organizer jailed over scheme to bring pregnant Chinese women to US*, CNN.com, Jan. 27, 2025, *available at* https://www.cnn.com/2025/01/27/us/woman-sentenced-chinese-birth-tourism-intl-hnk.

4. *Birth Tourism: Facts and Recommendations*, Center for Immigration Studies, Jan. 23, 2020, *available at* https://cis.org/CIS/Birth-Tourism-Facts-and-Recommendations.

United States v. Wong Kim Ark

169 U.S. 649 (1898)

MR. JUSTICE GRAY, after stating the case, delivered the opinion of the Court.

* * *

It is conceded that, if [Wong Kim Ark] is a citizen of the United States, the acts of Congress, known as the Chinese Exclusion Acts, prohibiting persons of the Chinese race, and especially Chinese laborers, from coming into the United States, do not and cannot apply to him.

The question presented by the record is whether a child born in the United States, of parents of Chinese descent, who at the time of his birth are subjects of the Emperor of China, but have a permanent domicil[e] and residence in the United States, and are there carrying on business, and are not employed in any diplomatic or official capacity under the Emperor of China, becomes at the time of his birth a citizen of the United States, by virtue of the first clause of the Fourteenth Amendment of the [C]onstitution," All persons born or naturalized in the United States, and subject to the jurisdiction thereof, are citizens of the United States and of the State wherein they reside."

* * *

The Constitution nowhere defines the meaning of these words, either by way of inclusion or of exclusion.... In this, as in other respects, it must be interpreted in the light of the common law, the principles and history of which were familiarly known to the framers of the Constitution....

Figure 3.1 ***Identification Photograph on Affidavit, "In the Matter of Wong Kim Ark, Native Born Citizen of the United States."*** **Filed with the Immigration Service in San Francisco prior to his May 19, 1894, departure on the Steamer "China." National Archives.**

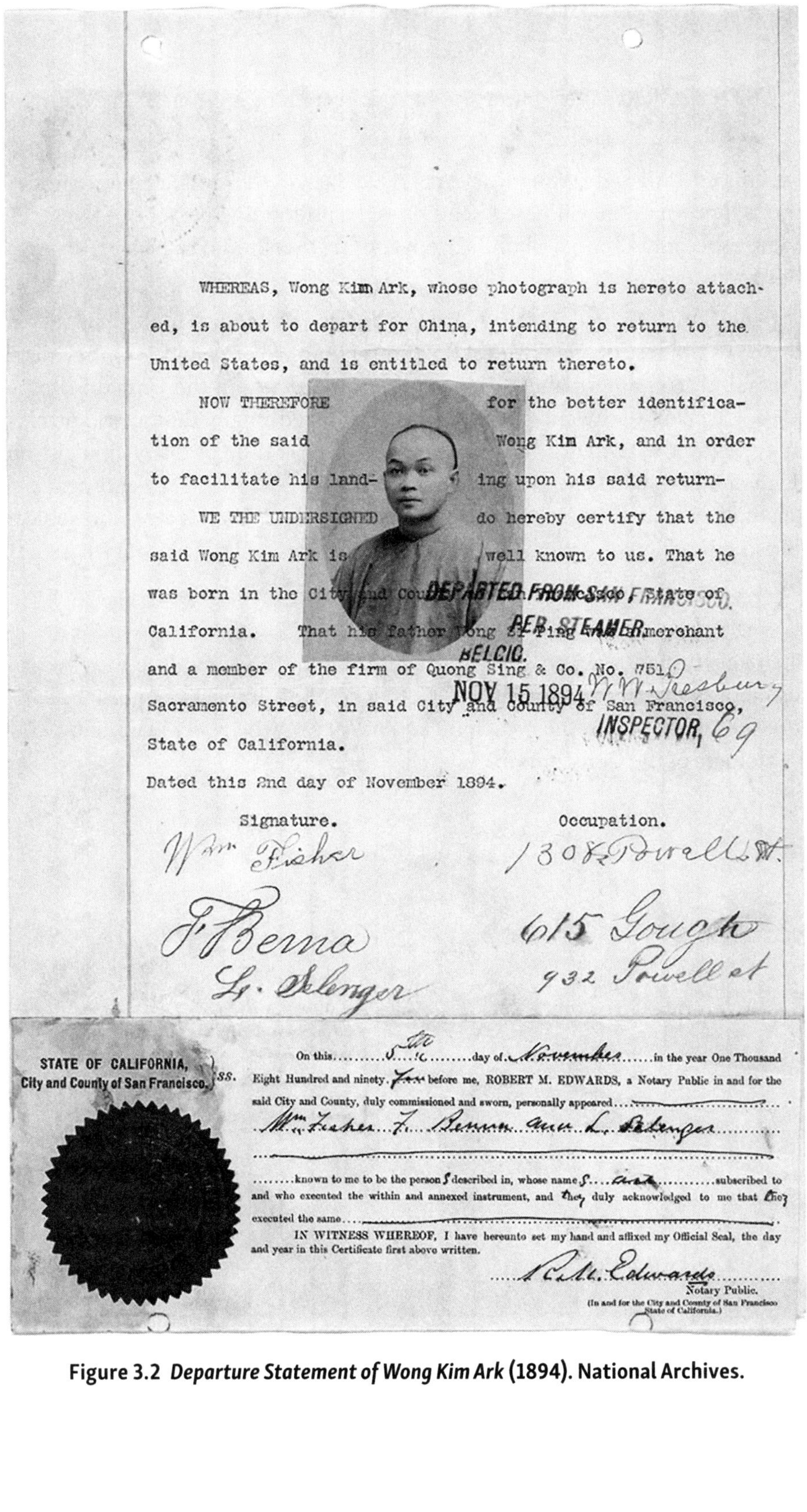

WHEREAS, Wong Kim Ark, whose photograph is hereto attached, is about to depart for China, intending to return to the United States, and is entitled to return thereto.

NOW THEREFORE for the better identification of the said Wong Kim Ark, and in order to facilitate his landing upon his said return—

WE THE UNDERSIGNED do hereby certify that the said Wong Kim Ark is well known to us. That he was born in the City and County of San Francisco, State of California. That his father Wong Si Ping was a merchant and a member of the firm of Quong Sing & Co. No. 751 Sacramento Street, in said City and County of San Francisco, State of California.

DEPARTED FROM SAN FRANCISCO, PER STEAMER BELGIC. NOV 15 1894 INSPECTOR, C9

Dated this 2nd day of November 1894.

Signature.	Occupation.
Wm Fisher	1308½ Powell St.
F. Berna	615 Gough
L. Selenger	932 Powell st

STATE OF CALIFORNIA, City and County of San Francisco, } SS.

On this 5th day of November in the year One Thousand Eight Hundred and ninety four before me, ROBERT M. EDWARDS, a Notary Public in and for the said City and County, duly commissioned and sworn, personally appeared Wm Fisher F. Berna and L. Selenger known to me to be the persons described in, whose names are subscribed to and who executed the within and annexed instrument, and they duly acknowledged to me that they executed the same.

IN WITNESS WHEREOF, I have hereunto set my hand and affixed my Official Seal, the day and year in this Certificate first above written.

R. M. Edwards
Notary Public.
(In and for the City and County of San Francisco State of California.)

Figure 3.2 ***Departure Statement of Wong Kim Ark*** **(1894). National Archives.**

The fundamental principle of the common law with regard to English nationality was birth within the allegiance, also called "ligealty," "obedience," "faith" or "power," of the King. The principle embraced all persons born within the King's allegiance and subject to his protection. Such allegiance and protection were mutual—as expressed in the maxim, *protectio trahit subjectionem, et subjectio protectionem*—and were not restricted to natural-born subjects and naturalized subjects, or to those who had taken an oath of allegiance; but were predicable of aliens in amity, so long as they were within the kingdom. Children, born in England, of such aliens, were therefore natural-born subjects. But the children, born within the realm, of foreign ambassadors, or the children of alien enemies, born during and within their hostile occupation of part of the King's dominions, were not natural-born subjects, because [they were] not born within the allegiance, the obedience, or the power, or, as would be said at this day, within the jurisdiction, of the King....

Lord Chief Justice Cockburn . . . said:

> By the common law of England, every person born within the dominions of the Crown, no matter whether of English or of foreign parents, and, in the latter case, whether the parents were settled or merely temporarily sojourning, in the country, was an English subject; save only the children of foreign ambassadors (who were excepted because their fathers carried their own nationality with them), or a child born to a foreigner during the hostile occupation of any part of the territories of England. No effect appears to have been given to descent as a source of nationality....

It thus clearly appears that by the law of England for the last three centuries, beginning before the settlement of this country, and continuing to the present day, aliens, while residing in the dominions possessed by the Crown of England, were within the allegiance, the obedience, the faith or loyalty, the protection, the power, the jurisdiction of the English Sovereign; and therefore every child born in England of alien parents was a natural-born subject, unless the child of an ambassador or other diplomatic agent of a foreign State, or of an alien enemy in hostile occupation of the place where the child was born....

The same rule was in force in all the English Colonies upon this continent down to the time of the Declaration of Independence, and in the United States afterwards, and continued to prevail under the Constitution as originally established.

. . .

Nothing is better settled at the common law than the doctrine that the children, even of aliens, born in a country, while the parents are resident there under the protection of the government, and owing a temporary allegiance thereto, are subjects by birth....

It was contended by one of the learned counsel for the United States that the rule of the Roman law, by which the citizenship of the child followed that of the parent, was the true rule of international law, as now recognized in most civilized countries, and had superseded the rule of the common law, depending on birth within the realm, originally founded on feudal considerations.

But at the time of the adoption of the Constitution of the United States in 1789, and long before, it would seem to have been the rule in Europe generally, as it certainly was in France, that, as said by Pothier, "citizens, true and native-born citizens, are those who are born within the extent of the dominion of France," and "mere birth within the realm gives the rights of a native-born citizen, independently of the origin of the father or mother, and of their domicil[e];" and children born in a foreign country, of a French father who had not established his domicil[e] there nor given up the intention of returning, were also deemed Frenchmen, as Laurent says, by "a favor, a sort of fiction," and Calvo, "by a sort of fiction of exterritoriality, considered as born in France, and therefore invested with French nationality." . . .

The general principle of citizenship by birth within French territory prevailed until after the French Revolution, and was affirmed in successive constitutions, from the one adopted by the Constituent Assembly in 1791 to that of the French Republic in 1799. . . . The Code Napoleon of 1807 changed the law of France and adopted, instead of the rule of country of birth, *jus soli,* the rule of descent or blood, *jus sanguinis,* as the leading principle; but an eminent commentator has observed that the framers of that code "appear not to have wholly freed themselves from the ancient rule of France, or rather, indeed, ancient rule of Europe . . . according to which nationality had always been, in former times, determined by the place of birth." 1 Demolombe Cours de Code Napoleon, (4th ed.) no. 146. . . .

There is, therefore, little ground for the theory that, at the time of the adoption of the Fourteenth Amendment of the Constitution of the United States, there was any settled and definite rule of international law, generally recognized by civilized nations, inconsistent with the ancient rule of citizenship by birth within the dominion.

Nor can it be doubted that it is the inherent right of every independent nation to determine for itself, and according to its own constitution and laws, what classes of persons shall be entitled to its citizenship.

Both in England and in the United States, indeed, statutes have been passed, at various times enacting that certain issue born abroad of English subjects, or of American citizens, respectively, should inherit, to some extent at least, the rights of their parents. But those statutes applied only to cases coming within their purport, and they have never been considered, in either country, as affecting the citizenship of persons born within its dominion. . . .

By the Constitution of the United States, Congress was empowered "to establish an uniform rule of naturalization." In the exercise of this power, Congress, by successive acts, beginning with the act entitled "An act to establish an uniform rule of naturalization," passed at the second session of the First Congress under the Constitution, has made provision for the admission to citizenship of three principal classes of persons: First. Aliens, having resided for a certain time "within the limits and under the jurisdiction of the United States," and naturalized individually by proceedings in a court of record. Second. Children of persons so naturalized, "dwelling within the United States, and being under the age of twenty-one years at the time of such naturalization." Third. Foreign-born children of American citizens, coming within the definitions prescribed by Congress....

It thus clearly appears that, during the half century intervening between 1802 and 1855, there was no legislation whatever for the citizenship of children born abroad, during that period, of American parents who had not become citizens of the United States before the act of 1802; and that the act of 1855, like every other act of Congress upon the subject, has, by express proviso, restricted the right of citizenship, thereby conferred upon foreign-born children of American citizens, to those children themselves, unless they became residents of the United States. Here is nothing to countenance the theory that a general rule of citizenship by blood or descent has displaced in this country the fundamental rule of citizenship by birth within its sovereignty....

Passing by questions once earnestly controverted, but finally put at rest by the Fourteenth Amendment of the Constitution, it is beyond doubt that, before the enactment of the Civil Rights Act of 1866 or the adoption of the Constitutional Amendment, all white persons, at least, born within the sovereignty of the United States, whether children of citizens or of foreigners, excepting only children of ambassadors or public ministers of a foreign government, were native-born citizens of the United States....

In the fore front, both of the Fourteenth Amendment of the Constitution and of the Civil Rights Act of 1866, the fundamental principle of citizenship by birth within the dominion was reaffirmed in the most explicit and comprehensive terms.

The Civil Rights Act, passed at the first session of the Thirty-ninth Congress, began by enacting that

> all persons born in the United States, and not subject to any foreign power, excluding Indians not taxed, are hereby declared to be citizens of the United States; and such citizens, of every race and color, without regard to any previous condition of slavery or involuntary servitude, except as a punishment for crime whereof the party shall have been duly convicted, shall have the same right, in every State and Territory in the United States, to make and enforce contracts, to sue, be parties and give evidence, to inherit, purchase, lease, sell, hold and convey real and personal property, and to full and equal benefit of all laws and proceedings for the security of person and property, as is enjoyed by white citizens, and shall be subject to like punishment, pains and penalties, and to none other, any law, statute, ordinance, regulation or custom, to the contrary notwithstanding.

Act of April 9, 1866, c. 31, § 1; 14 Stat. 27.

The same Congress, shortly afterwards, evidently thinking it unwise, and perhaps unsafe, to leave so important a declaration of rights to depend upon an ordinary act of legislation, which might be repealed by any subsequent Congress, framed the

Fourteenth Amendment of the Constitution, and, on June 16, 1866, by joint resolution proposed it to the legislatures of the several States; and on July 28, 1868, the Secretary of State issued a proclamation showing it to have been ratified by the legislatures of the requisite number of States. 14 Stat. 358; 1 Stat. 708.

The first section of the Fourteenth Amendment of the Constitution begins with the words,

> All persons born or naturalized in the United States, and subject to the jurisdiction thereof, are citizens of the United States and of the State wherein they reside.

As appears upon the face of the amendment, as well as from the history of the times, this was not intended to impose any new restrictions upon citizenship, or to prevent any persons from becoming citizens by the fact of birth within the United States who would thereby have become citizens according to the law existing before its adoption. It is declaratory in form, and enabling and extending in effect. Its main purpose doubtless was, as has been often recognized by this court, to establish the citizenship of free negroes, which had been denied in the opinion delivered by Chief Justice Taney in *Dred Scott v. Sandford*, (1857) 19 How. 393; and to put it beyond doubt that all blacks, as well as whites, born or naturalized within the jurisdiction of the United States, are citizens of the United States. *The Slaughterhouse Cases* (1873), 16 Wall. 36, 73.... But the opening words, "All persons born," are general, not to say universal, restricted only by place and jurisdiction, and not by color or race—as was clearly recognized in all the opinions delivered in *The Slaughterhouse Cases,* above cited.

In those cases, the point adjudged was that a statute of Louisiana, granting to a particular corporation the exclusive right for twenty-five years to have and maintain slaughterhouses within a certain district including the City of New Orleans, requiring all cattle intended for sale or slaughter in that district to be brought to the yards and slaughterhouses of the grantee, authorizing all butchers to slaughter their cattle there, and empowering the grantee to exact a reasonable fee for each animal slaughtered, was within the police powers of the State, and not in conflict with the Thirteenth Amendment of the Constitution as creating an involuntary servitude, nor with the Fourteenth Amendment as abridging the privileges or immunities of citizens of the United States, or as depriving persons of their liberty or property without due process of law, or as denying to them the equal protection of the laws.

MR. JUSTICE MILLER, delivering the opinion of the majority of the court, after observing that the Thirteenth, Fourteenth and Fifteenth Articles of Amendment of the Constitution were all addressed to the grievances of the negro race, and were designed to remedy them, continued as follows:

> We do not say that no one else but the negro can share in this protection. Both the language and spirit of these Articles are to have their fair and just weight in any question of construction. Undoubtedly, while negro slavery

> alone was in the mind of the Congress which proposed the Thirteenth Article, it forbids any other kind of slavery, now or hereafter. If Mexican peonage or the Chinese coolie labor system shall develop slavery of the Mexican or Chinese race within our territory, this Amendment may safely be trusted to make it void. And so if other rights are assailed by the States, which properly and necessarily fall within the protection of these Articles, that protection will apply, though the party interested may not be of African descent.

16 Wall. 72. And in treating of the first clause of the Fourteenth Amendment, he said:

> The distinction between citizenship of the United States and citizenship of a State is clearly recognized and established. Not only may a man be a citizen of the United States without being a citizen of a State, but an important element is necessary to convert the former into the latter. He must reside within the State to make him a citizen of it, but it is only necessary that he should be born or naturalized in the United States to be a citizen of the Union.

16 Wall. 73, 74....

By the Civil Rights Act of 1866, "all persons born in the United States, and not subject to any foreign power, excluding Indians not taxed," were declared to be citizens of the United States. In the light of the law as previously established, and of the history of the times, it can hardly be doubted that the words of that act, "not subject to any foreign power," were not intended to exclude any children born in this country from the citizenship which would theretofore have been their birthright; or, for instance, for the first time in our history, to deny the right of citizenship to native-born children of foreign white parents not in the diplomatic service of their own country, nor in hostile occupation of part of our territory. But any possible doubt in this regard was removed when the negative words of the Civil Rights Act, "not subject to any foreign power," gave way, in the Fourteenth Amendment of the Constitution, to the affirmative words, "subject to the jurisdiction of the United States."

This sentence of the Fourteenth Amendment is declaratory of existing rights, and affirmative of existing law, as to each of the qualifications therein expressed—"born in the United States," "naturalized in the United States," and "subject to the jurisdiction thereof"—in short, as to everything relating to the acquisition of citizenship by facts occurring within the limits of the United States. But it has not touched the acquisition of citizenship by being born abroad of American parents; and has left that subject to be regulated, as it had always been, by Congress, in the exercise of the power conferred by the Constitution to establish an uniform rule of naturalization....

The foregoing considerations and authorities irresistibly lead us to these conclusions: the Fourteenth Amendment affirms the ancient and fundamental rule of citizenship by birth within the territory, in the allegiance and under the protection of the country, including all children here born of resident aliens, with the exceptions or qualifications (as old as the rule itself) of children of foreign sovereigns or their ministers, or born on foreign public ships, or of enemies within and during a hostile occupation of part of our territory, and with the single additional exception of children of members of the Indian tribes owing direct allegiance to their several tribes. The Amendment, in clear words and in manifest intent, includes the children born, within the territory of the United States, of all other persons, of whatever race or color, domiciled within the United States. Every citizen or subject of another country, while domiciled here, is within the allegiance and the protection, and consequently subject to the jurisdiction, of the United States....

To hold that the Fourteenth Amendment of the Constitution excludes from citizenship the children, born in the United States, of citizens or subjects of other countries, would be to deny citizenship to thousands of persons of English, Scotch, Irish, German or other European parentage, who have always been considered and treated as citizens of the United States....

Whatever considerations, in the absence of a controlling provision of the Constitution, might influence the legislative or the executive branch of the Government to decline to admit persons of the Chinese race to the status of citizens of the United States, there are none that can constrain or permit the judiciary to refuse to give full effect to the peremptory and explicit language of the Fourteenth Amendment, which declares and ordains that "All persons born or naturalized in the United States, and subject to the jurisdiction thereof, are citizens of the United States."

Chinese persons, born out of the United States, remaining subjects of the Emperor of China, and not having become citizens of the United States, are entitled to the protection of and owe allegiance to the United States so long as they are permitted by the United States to reside here; and are "subject to the jurisdiction thereof" in the same sense as all other aliens residing in the United States. *Yick Wo v. Hopkins* (1886), 118 U.S. 356; *Law Ow Bew v. United States,* 144 U.S. 47, 61, 62; *Fong Yue Ting v. United States* (1893), 149 U.S. 698, 724; *Lem Moon Sing v. United States* (1893),158 U.S. 538, 547; *Wong Wing v. United States* (1896), 163 U.S. 228, 238....

Upon the facts agreed in this case, the American citizenship which Wong Kim Ark acquired by birth within the United States has not been lost or taken away by anything happening since his birth. No doubt he might himself, after coming of age, renounce this citizenship, and become a citizen of the country of his parents, or of any other country; for by our law, as solemnly declared by Congress, "the right of expatriation is a natural and inherent right of all people," and "any declaration, instruction, opinion, order or direction of any officer of the United States which denies, restricts, impairs or questions the right of expatriation, is declared inconsistent with the fundamental principles of the Republic." Rev. Stat. § 1999, reenacting act of July 27, 1868, c. 249, § 1; 15 Stat. 223, 224.

Whether any act of himself, or of his parents during his minority, could have the same effect, is at least doubtful. But it would be out of place to pursue that inquiry; inasmuch as it is expressly agreed that his residence has always been in the United States, and not elsewhere; that each of his temporary visits to China, the one for some months when he was about seventeen years old, and the other for something like a year about the time of his coming of age, was made with the intention of returning, and was followed by his actual return, to the United States; and "that said Wong Kim Ark has not, either by himself or his parents acting for him, ever renounced his allegiance to the United States, and that he has never done or committed any act or thing to exclude him therefrom."

The evident intention, and the necessary effect, of the submission of this case to the decision of the court upon the facts agreed by the parties, were to present for determination the single question stated at the beginning of this opinion, namely, whether a child born in the United States, of parent of Chinese descent, who, at the time of his birth, are subjects of the Emperor of China, but have a permanent domicile and residence in the United States, and are there carrying on business, and are not employed in any diplomatic or official capacity under the Emperor of China, becomes at the time of his birth a citizen of the United States. For the reasons above stated, this court is of opinion that the question must be answered in the affirmative.

Order affirmed.

MR. CHIEF JUSTICE FULLER, with whom concurred MR. JUSTICE HARLAN, dissenting.

I cannot concur in the opinion and judgment of the court in this case.

The proposition is that a child born in this country of parents who were not citizens of the United States, and under the laws of their own country and of the United States could not become such—as was the fact from the beginning of the Government in respect of the class of aliens to which the parents in this instance belonged—is, from the moment of his birth a citizen of the United States, by virtue of the first clause of the Fourteenth Amendment, any act of Congress to the contrary notwithstanding.

The argument is, that although the Constitution prior to that amendment nowhere attempted to define the words "citizens of the United States" and "natural-born citizen" as used therein, yet that it must be interpreted in the light of the English common law rule which made the place of birth the criterion of nationality; that that rule was in force in all the English colonies upon this continent down to the time of the Declaration of Independence, and in the United States afterwards, and continued to prevail under the Constitution as originally established; and "that before the enactment of the Civil Rights Act of 1866 and the adoption of the Constitutional Amendment, all white persons, at least, born within the sovereignty of the United States, whether children of citizens or of foreigners, excepting only children of ambassadors or public ministers of a foreign Government, were native-born citizens of the United States.

Thus the Fourteenth Amendment is held to be merely declaratory except that it brings all persons, irrespective of color, within the scope of the alleged rule, and puts that rule beyond the control of the legislative power.

If the conclusion of the majority opinion is correct, then the children of citizens of the United States, who have been born abroad since July 8, 1868, when the amendment was declared ratified, were, and are, aliens, unless they have, or shall on attaining majority, become citizens by naturalization in the United States; and no statutory provision to the contrary is of any force or effect. And children who are aliens by descent, but born on our soil, are exempted from the exercise of the power to exclude or to expel aliens, or any class of aliens, so often maintained by this court, an exemption apparently disregarded by the acts in respect of the exclusion of persons of Chinese descent.

The English common law rule, which it is insisted was in force after the Declaration of Independence, was that "every person born within the dominions of the Crown, no matter whether of English or of foreign parents, and, in the latter case, whether the parents were settled or merely temporarily sojourning in the country, was an English subject; save only the children of foreign ambassadors (who were excepted because their fathers carried their own nationality with them) or a child born to a foreigner during the hostile occupation of any part of the territories of England." Cockburn on Nationality 7. The tie which bound the child to the Crown was indissoluble. The nationality of his parents had no bearing on his nationality. Though born during a temporary stay of a few days, the child was irretrievably a British subject. Hall on Foreign Jurisdiction, etc., § 1.

The rule was the outcome of the connection in feudalism between the individual and the soil on which he lived, and the allegiance due was that of liegemen to their liege lord. It was not local and temporary as was the obedience to the laws owed by aliens within the dominions of the Crown, but permanent and indissoluble, and not to be cancelled by any change of time or place or circumstances.

And it is this rule, pure and simple, which it is asserted determined citizenship of the United States during the entire period prior to the passage of the act of April 9, 1866, and the ratification of the Fourteenth Amendment, and governed the meaning of the words "citizen of the United States" and "natural-born citizen" used in the Constitution as originally framed and adopted....

"The true bond which connects the child with the body politic is not the matter of an inanimate piece of land, but the moral relations of his parentage.... The place of birth produces no change in the rule that children follow the condition of their fathers, for it is not naturally the place of birth that gives rights, but extraction.... "

The framers of the Constitution were familiar with the distinctions between the Roman law and the feudal law, between obligations based on territoriality and those based on the personal and invisible character of origin, and there is nothing to show that, in the matter of nationality they intended to adhere to principles derived from regal government, which they had just assisted in overthrowing. Manifestly, when the sovereignty of the Crown was thrown off and an independent government established, every rule of the common law and every statute of England obtaining in the Colonies, in derogation of the principles on which the new government was founded, was abrogated....

"By the Thirteenth Amendment of the Constitution slavery was prohibited. The main object of the opening sentence of the Fourteenth Amendment was to settle the question, upon which there had been a difference of opinion throughout the country and in this court, as to the citizenship of free negroes, *Scott v. Sandford,* 19 How. 393; and to put it beyond doubt that all persons, white or black, and whether formerly slaves or not, born or naturalized in the United States, and *owing no allegiance to any alien power,* should be citizens of the United States, and of the State in which they reside. *Slaughterhouse Cases,* 16 Wall. 36, 73; *Strauder v. West Virginia,* 100 U.S. 303, 306.

"This section contemplates two sources of citizenship, and two sources only: birth and naturalization. The persons declared to be citizens are 'all persons born or naturalized in the United States, and subject to the jurisdiction thereof.' The evident meaning of these last words is, not merely subject in some respect or degree to the jurisdiction of the United States, but *completely subject to their political jurisdiction,* and *owing them direct and immediate allegiance.* And the words relate to the time of birth in the one case, as they do to the time of naturalization in the other. *Persons not thus subject to the jurisdiction of the United States at the time of birth* cannot become so afterwards, except by being naturalized, either individually, as by proceedings under the naturalization acts, or collectively, as by the force of a treaty by which foreign territory is acquired."

To be "completely subject" to the political jurisdiction of the United States is to be in no respect or degree subject to the political jurisdiction of any other government. Now I take it that the children of aliens, whose parents have not only not renounced their allegiance to their native country, but are forbidden by its system of government, as well as by its positive laws, from doing so, and are not permitted to acquire another citizenship by the laws of the country into which they come, must necessarily remain themselves subject to the same sovereignty as their parents, and cannot, in the nature of things, be, any more than their parents, completely subject to the jurisdiction of such other country.

Generally speaking, I understand the subjects of the Emperor of China—that ancient Empire, with its history of thousands of years and its unbroken continuity in belief, traditions and government, in spite of revolutions and changes of dynasty—to be bound to him by every conception of duty and by every principle of their religion, of which filial piety is the first and greatest commandment; and formerly, perhaps still, their penal laws denounced the severest penalties on those who renounced their country and allegiance, and their abettors; and, in effect, held the relatives at home of Chinese in foreign lands as hostages for their loyalty. And whatever concession may have been made by treaty in the direction of admitting the right of expatriation in some sense, they seem in the United States to have remained pilgrims and sojourners as all their fathers were. 149 U.S. 717. At all events, they have never been allowed by our laws to acquire our nationality, and, except in sporadic instances, do not appear ever to have desired to do so.

The Fourteenth Amendment was not designed to accord citizenship to persons so situated and to cut off the legislative power from dealing with the subject....

Was it intended thereby that children of aliens should, by virtue of being born in the United States, be entitled on attaining majority to vote irrespective of the treaties and laws of the United States in regard to such aliens?

In providing that persons born or naturalized in the United States, and subject to the jurisdiction thereof, are citizens, the Fourteenth Amendment undoubtedly had particular reference to securing citizenship to the members of the colored race, whose servile status had been obliterated by the Thirteenth Amendment and who had been born in the United States, but were not and never had been subject to any foreign power. They were not aliens (and even if they could be so regarded, this operated as a collective naturalization) and their political status could not be affected by any change of the laws for the naturalization of individuals.

Nobody can deny that the question of citizenship in a nation is of the most vital importance. It is a precious heritage, as well as an inestimable acquisition; and I cannot think that any safeguard surrounding it was intended to be thrown down by the amendment....

These considerations lead to the conclusion that the rule in respect of citizenship of the United States prior to the Fourteenth Amendment differed from the English common law rule in vital particulars, and, among others, in that it did not recognize allegiance as indelible, and in that it did recognize an essential difference between birth during temporary, and birth during permanent, residence. If children born in the United States were deemed presumptively and generally citizens, this was not so when they were born of aliens whose residence was merely temporary, either in fact, or in point of law.

Did the Fourteenth Amendment impose the original English common law rule as a rigid rule on this country?

Did the amendment operate to abridge the treaty-making power, or the power to establish an uniform rule of naturalization?

I insist that it cannot be maintained that this Government is unable through the action of the President, concurred in by the Senate, to make a treaty with a foreign government providing that the subjects of that government, although allowed to enter the United States, shall not be made citizens thereof, and that their children shall not become such citizens by reason of being born therein.

A treaty couched in those precise terms would not be incompatible with the Fourteenth Amendment, unless it be held that that amendment has abridged the treaty-making power.

Nor would a naturalization law excepting persons of a certain race and their children be invalid, unless the amendment has abridged the power of naturalization. This cannot apply to our colored fellow-citizens, who never were aliens—were never beyond the jurisdiction of the United States....

By the convention of March 17, 1894, it was agreed "that Chinese laborers or Chinese of any other class, either permanently or temporarily residing within the United

States, shall have for the protection of their persons and property all rights that are given by the laws of the United States to citizens of the most favored nation, excepting the right to become naturalized citizens."

These treaties show that neither Government desired such change nor assented thereto. Indeed, if the naturalization laws of the United States had provided for the naturalization of Chinese persons, China manifestly would not have been obliged to recognize that her subjects had changed their allegiance thereby. But our laws do not so provide, and, on the contrary, are in entire harmony with the treaties.

I think it follows that the children of Chinese born in this country do not, *ipso facto,* become citizens of the United States unless the Fourteenth Amendment overrides both treaty and statute. Does it bear that construction; or rather is it not the proper construction that all persons born in the United States of parents permanently residing here and susceptible of becoming citizens, and not prevented therefrom by treaty or statute, are citizens, and not otherwise....

In other words, the Fourteenth Amendment does not exclude from citizenship by birth children born in the United States of parents permanently located therein, and who might themselves become citizens; nor, on the other hand, does it arbitrarily make citizens of children born in the United States of parents who, according to the will of their native government and of this Government, are and must remain aliens.

Tested by this rule, Wong Kim Ark never became and is not a citizen of the United States, and the order of the District Court should be reversed.

Notes

1. The fundamental disagreement between the six-justice majority and the two-justice dissent (one justice did not participate in the case) was the baseline rule of U.S. citizenship and how the enactment of the Fourteenth Amendment changed it. For the majority, the rule was *jus soli*—citizenship was based on birth on U.S. soil, which was the common law rule in England since feudal times. The dissent thought the baseline should be *jus sanguinis*, or citizenship by parentage, which was the rule on the European continent in the nineteenth century. Which argument did you find more persuasive? Could the United States have adopted both rules, that is, persons born within the United States are U.S. citizens, as are persons born to U.S. citizens abroad? Would the acceptance of both rules have been more consistent with the fact that the United States at its Founding and through its early decades was desirous of encouraging immigration, particularly from Europe, for labor and settlement? *See* Thomas H. Lee, *"Natural Born Citizen,"* 60 Am. U. L. Rev. 327, 335 (2017) ("Early Americans, desirous of increasing the immigration of ambitious Europeans and of encouraging American merchants to go and trade with Europe, adopted both" *jus soli* and *jus sanguinis.*).

2. What is the argument that the Fourteenth Amendment did not apply to the children of Chinese nationals born within the United States? How is the language of the Civil Rights Act of 1866 relevant to interpretation of the Fourteenth Amendment's citizenship clause?

3. In light of the statistics discussed in the introduction above about so-called anchor babies and birth tourism, do you think it makes sense today for the United States to continue to adhere to the *jus soli* rule? Is it relevant that many other countries that share the English common law tradition, including the United Kingdom itself, do not presently give citizenship to babies born to foreigners who are temporarily in the country, such as tourists and students?

4. Both the majority and dissenting opinions focused on the history of citizenship at the Founding and the enactment of the Civil Rights Act of 1866 and the Fourteenth Amendment. The Supreme Court justices did not disparage the Chinese and engaged in lawyerly analysis of the relevant question. One of the briefs for the U.S. government, however, took a different approach:

    > For the most persuasive reasons we have refused citizenship to Chinese subjects; and yet, as to their offspring, who are just as obnoxious, and to whom the same reasons for exclusion apply with equal force, we are told that we must accept them as fellow-citizens, and that, too, because of the mere accident of birth. There certainly should be some honor and dignity in American citizenship that would be sacred from the foul and corrupting taint of a debasing alienage. Are Chinese children born in this country to share with the descendants of the patriots of the American Revolution the exalted qualification of being eligible to the Presidency of the nation, conferred by the Constitution in recognition of the importance and dignity of citizenship by birth? If so, then verily there has been a most degenerate departure from the patriotic ideals of our forefathers; and surely in that case American citizenship is not worth having.

    Brief for the United States at 34, *United States v. Wong Kim Ark*, 169 U.S. 649 (1898). What do you think of the notion that "American citizenship is not worth having" if "Chinese children born in this country" are deemed U.S. citizens?

5. Whatever the contemporary ramifications, the decision in *Wong Kim Ark* brought with it many complications. How were Chinese laborers born in the United States who left and sought to return like Wong supposed to prove that they were U.S. citizens? Many, like Wong, traveled with one or more affidavits from White persons who testified to having known them and the circumstances of their birth. From an enforcement perspective, the possibility that some Chinese laborers could be U.S. citizens complicated enforcement of immigration and other laws that were keyed to Chinese nationals. This complication was a contributing factor to the ultimate creation of a federal centralized immigration service in 1906.

6. For good discussions of Wong Kim Ark's story and interviews of his great-granddaughter and great-grandson, *see* Fred Barbash, *Donald Trump Meet Wong Kim Ark, the Chinese American Cook Who Is the Father of Birthright Citizenship*, Wash. Post, Aug. 31, 2015, *and* David Nakamura, *His Great-Grandfather Enshrined Birthright Citizenship. Norman Wong Is Trying to Save It,* Wash. Post, May 13, 2025.

7. The issue of birthright citizenship was raised some years before *Wong Kim Ark* in the little-known case of Look Tin Sing (sometimes referred to as Look Tin Eli), who was born in 1870 in the back of his father's store in Mendocino, California. When Look was nine years old, his father sent him back to China to learn the Chinese language and culture. He tried to return to the United States in 1884, when he was 14, but he was denied reentry—the Chinese Exclusion Act had been signed into law two years earlier. Although his father was a merchant, Look did not have the necessary paperwork to reenter. He sued, successfully arguing that he was an American citizen because he was born in this country. Justice Field wrote the decision for the Circuit Court, which would later be cited by the Supreme Court in *Wong Kim Ark*. *See In re Look Tin Sing, on Habeas Corpus*, 21 F. 905 (Cir. Ct. D. Calif. 1884).

8. President Trump's January 20, 2025 Executive Order provided in part:

   > Section 1. Purpose. The privilege of United States citizenship is a priceless and profound gift. The Fourteenth Amendment states: "All persons born or naturalized in the United States, and subject to the jurisdiction thereof, are citizens of the United States and of the State wherein they reside." That provision rightly repudiated the Supreme Court of the United States's shameful decision in *Dred Scott v. Sandford*, 60 U.S. (19 How.) 393 (1857), which misinterpreted the Constitution as permanently excluding people of African descent from eligibility for United States citizenship solely based on their race.
   >
   > But the Fourteenth Amendment has never been interpreted to extend citizenship universally to everyone born within the United States. The Fourteenth Amendment has always excluded from birthright citizenship persons who were born in the United States but not "subject to the jurisdiction thereof." Consistent with this understanding, the Congress has further specified through legislation that "a person born in the United States, and subject to the jurisdiction thereof" is a national and citizen of the United States at birth, 8 U.S.C. 1401, generally mirroring the Fourteenth Amendment's text.
   >
   > Among the categories of individuals born in the United States and not subject to the jurisdiction thereof, the privilege of United States citizenship does not automatically extend to persons born in the United States:

> (1) when that person's mother was unlawfully present in the United States and the father was not a United States citizen or lawful permanent resident at the time of said person's birth, or (2) when that person's mother's presence in the United States at the time of said person's birth was lawful but temporary (such as, but not limited to, visiting the United States under the auspices of the Visa Waiver Program or visiting on a student, work, or tourist visa) and the father was not a United States citizen or lawful permanent resident at the time of said person's birth.
>
> Sec. 2. Policy. (a) It is the policy of the United States that no department or agency of the United States government shall issue documents recognizing United States citizenship, or accept documents issued by State, local, or other governments or authorities purporting to recognize United States citizenship, to persons: (1) when that person's mother was unlawfully present in the United States and the person's father was not a United States citizen or lawful permanent resident at the time of said person's birth, or (2) when that person's mother's presence in the United States was lawful but temporary, and the person's father was not a United States citizen or lawful permanent resident at the time of said person's birth.
>
> (b) Subsection (a) of this section shall apply only to persons who are born within the United States after 30 days from the date of this order....

Are the Executive Order's restrictions on citizenship by birth within the United States consistent with the text and context of the Fourteenth Amendment? Are they consistent with the facts and holding of *Wong Kim Ark*, which involved the child of Chinese subjects who were domiciled in the United States at the time of their child's birth, unlike noncitizens present in the United States under temporary visas like tourists or students? How relevant is it that the Executive Order would bring the United States more into line with the birthright citizenship rules of other liberal democracies? Regardless of whether one believes the Executive Order is a permissible interpretation of the Fourteenth Amendment Citizenship Clause, does the President have the constitutional power to change American birthright citizenship by Executive Order, bypassing Congress? Under which provision of the Constitution?

9. On January 23, 2025, just days after the executive order was issued, a federal judge in Seattle temporarily blocked the executive order. *See Washington v. Trump*, No. C25-0127-JCC, 2025 WL 272198 (W.D. Wash. Jan. 23, 2025); Mike Baker and Mattathies Schwartz, *Judge Temporarily Block's Trump's Plan to End Birthright Citizenship*, N.Y. Times, Jan. 26, 2025. Other cases were filed as well, with nationwide injunctions blocking enforcement of the executive order, and eventually three cases were consolidated in the Supreme Court. On June 27, 2025, the Supreme Court granted the government's applications for a partial stay of the preliminary injunctions entered by district courts enjoining the Trump

Administration's executive order restricting birthright citizenship. *Trump v. CASA, Inc.*, 606 U.S. 831 (2025). The Court left open the possibility that plaintiffs could bring class actions to seek nationwide relief and it did not resolve the question of the constitutionality of the Executive Order as its decision was limited to the scope of relief. Justice Sotomayor dissented, stating that "absent cumbersome class-action litigation, courts cannot completely enjoin even such plainly unlawful policies unless doing so is necessary to afford the formal parties complete relief." *Id.* (Sotomayor, *J.*, dissenting).

10. Shortly after the Supreme Court issued its opinion, immigrants' rights advocates filed a nationwide class-action lawsuit in the District of New Hampshire, challenging the executive order. Complaint at 1, *Barbara v. Trump*, No. 25-cv-244 (D.N.H. June 27, 2025) (alleging violations of the Fourteenth Amendment, 8 U.S.C. § 1401, and the Administrative Procedure Act, and seeking to preliminarily and permanently enjoin the government from enforcing the executive order). The New Hampshire federal district court provisionally granted class certification. In the District of Maryland, a similar suit was filed on February 19, 2025, and on June 27, 2025, the plaintiffs sought an emergency order for class certification. *See* Plaintiffs' Motion for Class Certification at 1, *CASA, Inc. v. Trump*, No. 25-cv-201 (D. Md. June 27, 2025); Laura Romero, *Federal Judge Asks DOJ to Clarify How Birthright Citizenship Order Will Be Implemented*, ABC News (June 30, 2025), https://abcnews.go.com/US/federal-judge-asks-doj-clarify-birthright-citizenship-order/story?id=123350646. Finally, a suit was filed in the District of Columbia also seeking to enjoin the enforcement of the executive order. On July 1, 2025, plaintiffs filed an amended complaint seeking class certification following the Supreme Court's decision in *Trump v. CASA*. Amended Complaint at 1, *OCA—Asian Pacific American Advocates v. Rubio*, No. 25-cv-287 (D.D.C. July 1, 2025). In September 2025, the government filed two petitions for certiorari in the Supreme Court seeking review of the question on the merits. On December 5, 2025, the Supreme Court granted certiorari in the *Barbara* case.

2. Naturalization

To be naturalized as a U.S. citizen under the first five federal naturalization statutes (of 1790, 1795, 1798, 1802, and 1855), one had to be "a free white person." The 1870 Naturalization Act, passed after the Civil War, extended naturalization to "aliens of African nativity and persons of African descent."

Enforcement of the standard, however, was at first diffuse and uneven, because there was no centralized federal immigration and naturalization service until 1906.

Instead, federal and state courts had to determine which foreigners who applied for citizenship were "free white persons" as the relevant statute required. A California federal judge in 1878 held that a "native Chinaman" named Ah Yup was not a "free white person" because he was "of the Mongolian race" and was not White.

In re Ah Yup

1 F. Cas. 223 (Cir. Ct. D. Cal. 1878)

SAWYER, Circuit Judge.

Ah Yup, a native and citizen of the empire of China, of the Mongolian race, presented a petition in writing, praying that he be permitted to make proof of the facts alleged, and upon satisfactory proof being made, and his taking the oath required in such cases, he be admitted as a citizen of the United States. The petition stated all the qualifications required by the statute to entitle the petitioner to be naturalized, provided the statute authorizes the naturalization of a native of China of the Mongolian race. The petitioner was represented by B. S. Brooks, a counsellor of this court. This being the first application made by a native Chinaman for naturalization, the members of the bar were requested by the court to make such suggestions as amici curiae as occurred to them upon either side of the question; whereupon S. Heydenfeldt, Jr., argued the case very fully in opposition to the application. Suggestions were also made by other members of the bar present. The only question is, whether the statute authorizes the naturalization of a native of China of the Mongolian race.

In all the acts of congress relating to the naturalization of aliens, from that of April 14, 1802, down to the Revised Statutes, the language has been 'that any alien, being a free white person, may be admitted to become a citizen,' etc. After the adoption of the thirteenth and fourteenth amendments to the national constitution; the former prohibiting slavery, and the latter declaring who shall be citizens, congress in the act of July 14, 1870, amending the naturalization laws, added the following provision: 'That the naturalization laws are hereby extended to aliens of African nativity, and to persons of African descent.' 16 Stat. 256, § 7. Upon the revision of the statutes, the revisors, probably inadvertently, as congress did not contemplate a change in the laws in force, omitted the words 'white persons;' section 2165 of the Revised Statutes, being the section conferring the right, reading: 'An alien may be admitted to become a citizen,' etc., etc. The provision relating to Africans of the act of 1870, is carried into the Revised Statutes in a separate section, which reads as follows: 'The provisions of this title shall apply to aliens of African nativity, and to persons of African descent.' Section 2169. This section was amended by the 'act to correct errors and to supply omissions in the Revised Statutes of the United States,' of February 18, 1875, so as to read: 'The provisions of this title shall apply to aliens being free white persons, and to aliens of African nativity, and to persons of African descent.' Rev. St. (1st Ed.) p. 1435; 18 Stat. 318. And so the statute now stands.

The questions are: 1. Is a person of the Mongolian race a 'white person' within the meaning of the statute? 2. Do these provisions exclude all but white persons and persons of African nativity or African descent[?]

Words in a statute, other than technical terms, should be taken in their ordinary sense. The words 'white person,' as well argued by petitioner's counsel, taken in a strictly literal sense, constitute a very indefinite description of a class of persons, where none can be said to be literally white, and those called white may be found of every shade from the lightest blonde to the most swarthy brunette. But these words in this country, at least, have undoubtedly acquired a well settled meaning in common popular speech, and they are constantly used in the sense so acquired in the literature of the country, as well as in common parlance. As ordinarily used everywhere in the United States, one would scarcely fail to understand that the party employing the words 'white person' would intend a person of the Caucasian race.

In speaking of the various classifications of races, Webster in his dictionary says, 'The common classification is that of Blumenbach, who makes five. 1. The Caucasian, or white race, to which belong the greater part of the European nations and those of Western Asia; 2. The Mongolian, or yellow race, occupying Tartary, China, Japan, etc.; 3. The Ethiopian or Negro (black) race, occupying all Africa, except the north; 4. The American, or red race, containing the Indians of North and South America; and, 5. The Malay, or Brown race, occupying the islands of the Indian Archipelago,' etc. This division was adopted from Buffon, with some changes in names, and is founded on the combined characteristics of complexion, hair and skull. Linnaeus makes four divisions, founded on the color of the skin: '1. European, whitish; 2. American, coppery; 3. Asiatic, tawny; and, 4. African, black.' Cuvier makes three: Caucasian, Mongol, and Negro. Others make many more, but no one includes the white, or Caucasian, with the Mongolian or yellow race; and no one of those classifications recognizing color as one of the distinguishing characteristics includes the Mongolian in the white or whitish race.' See New American Cyclopedia, tit. 'Ethnology.'

Neither in popular language, in literature, nor in scientific nomenclature, do we ordinarily, if ever, find the words 'white person' used in a sense so comprehensive as to include an individual of the Mongolian race. Yet, in all, color, notwithstanding its indefiniteness as a word of description, is made an important factor in the basis adopted for the distinction and classification of races. I am not aware that the term 'white person,' as used in the statutes as they have stood from 1802 till the late revision, was ever supposed to include a Mongolian. While I find nothing in the history of the country, in common or scientific usage, or in legislative proceedings, to indicate that congress intended to include in the term 'white person' any other than an individual of the Caucasian race, I do find much in the proceedings of congress to show that it was universally understood in that body, in its recent legislation, that it excluded Mongolians. At the time of the amendment, in 1870, extending the naturalization laws to the African race, Mr. Summer made repeated and strenuous efforts to strike the word 'white' from the naturalization laws, or to accomplish the same object by other language. It was opposed on the sole ground that the effect would be to authorize the admission of Chinese to citizenship. Every senator, who spoke upon the subject, assumed that they were then excluded by the term 'white person,' and that the amendment would admit them, and the amendment was advocated on the one hand, and opposed on the other, upon that single idea. Senator Morton, in the course of the discussion said: 'This amendment involves the whole Chinese problem. * * * The country has just awakened to the question and to the enormous magnitude of the question, involving a possible immigration of many millions, involving another civilization; involving labor problems that no intellect can solve without study and time. Are you now prepared to settle the Chinese problem, thus in advance inviting that immigration?' Congressional Globe, pt. 6, 1869–70, p. 5122. Senator Sumner replied: 'Senators undertake to disturb us in our judgment by reminding us of the possibility of large numbers swarming from China; but the answer to all this is very obvious and very simple. If the Chinese come here they will come for citizenship, or merely for labor. If they come for citizenship then in this desire to they give a pledge of loyalty to our institutions, and where is the peril in such vows? They are peaceful and industrious; how can their citizenship be the occasion of solicitude?' Id. 5155.

Many other senators spoke pro and con on the question, this being the point of the contest, and these extracts being fair examples of the opposing opinions. Id. 5121–5177. It was finally defeated, and the amendment cited, extending the right of naturalization to the African only, was adopted. It is clear, from these proceedings that congress retained the word 'white' in the naturalization laws for the sole purpose of excluding the Chinese from the right of naturalization. Again, when it was found that the term 'white person' had been omitted in the Revised Statutes it was restored by the act passed 'to correct errors and to supply omissions' in the Revised Statutes before cited. Upon reporting this bill, Mr. Poland, chairman of the committee, explained the various amendments correcting the errors, and upon the amendment to insert the words 'being free white persons,' said: 'The original naturalization laws only extended to free white persons.... '

A very few years since [in 1870] Mr. Sumner, of Massachusetts, then in the senate, moved to strike out the word 'white' from the naturalization laws, and it was objected to on the ground that that would authorize the naturalization of that class of Asiatic immigrants that are so plentiful on the Pacific coast. After considerable debate, instead of striking out the word 'white,' it was provided that the naturalization laws should extend to Africans, and persons of African descent.' After explaining the omission in the Revised Statutes he adds: 'The member of our committee who had this chapter on the naturalization laws to examine as a sub-committee, failed to notice this change in the law, or it would have been brought before the house when the revision was adopted.' Congressional Record, vol. 4, pt. 2, Sess. 1875, p. 1081. Upon this report the amendment was made as it now stands in the statute. Thus, whatever latitudinarian construction might otherwise have been given to the term 'white person,' it is entirely clear that congress intended by this legislation to exclude Mongolians from the right of naturalization. I am, therefore, of the opinion that a native of China, of the Mongolian race, is not a white person within the meaning of the act of congress.

The second question is answered in the discussion of the first. The amendment is intended to limit the operation of the provision as it then stood in the Revised Statutes. It would have been more appropriately inserted in section 2165, than where it is found in section 2169. But the purpose is clear. It was certainly intended to have some operation, or it would not have been adopted. The purpose undoubtedly was to restore the law to the condition in which it stood before the revision, and to exclude the Chinese. It was intended to exclude some classes, and as all white aliens and those of the African race are entitled to naturalization under other words, it is difficult to perceive whom it could exclude unless it be the Chinese. It follows that the petition must be denied, and it is so ordered.

Notes

1. Why do you think the 1870 statute referred to both "aliens of African nativity" and "persons of African descent?" Wouldn't "persons of African descent" have sufficed to include any descendent of enslaved persons within the United States? Did this mean that any immigrant from an African country could be naturalized as a U.S. citizen? Particularly if the intent of the statute was to effectuate the citizenship clause of the Fourteenth Amendment, then why did it not suffice to only say "persons of African descent?"

2. Why do you think that the circuit judge referred so extensively to legislative history rather than the plain meaning of the statutory words "free white persons" as set forth in the revised statute of 1875? Do you agree with his conclusion that the sole reason for retaining "free white person" was specifically to exclude Chinese persons from naturalizing as U.S. citizens? If so, then how is the naturalization statute reconciled with the holding in *Wong Kim Ark*, according citizenship to a Chinese person born in the United States even though his parents could never become citizens?

3. In 1921, a federal judge in Missouri held that Easurk Emsen Charr, "a native of Korea" and a student at Park College who served in the U.S. Army and was honorably discharged, was not eligible to be naturalized:

   > The petitioner is a Korean, admittedly of the Mongol family. Whatever their precise shade of color may be defined to be, they are confessedly not white persons, either in fact or in accordance with common understanding, and they are about as far removed from Europe and the Mediterranean Sea as could well be imagined.

   In re Easurk Emsen Charr, 273 F. 207, 210 (W.D. Mo. 1921). *Cf. In re Halladjian*, 174 F. 834 (Cir. Ct. D. Mass. 1909) (granting petitions of four Armenians for naturalization, concluding that Armenians are "white persons," even though born in Asia).

4. What about individuals of mixed blood, that is, individuals who were part White? A federal judge in Oregon held in 1880 that a Canadian man born to a White father and a Native American mother was not a "free white person." *In re Camille*, 6 F. 256 (Cir. Ct. D. Or. 1880). For cases involving individuals who were half Asian and half White, *see In re Young*, 198 F. 715 (W.D. Wash. 1912), and *In re Knight*, 171 F. 299 (E.D.N.Y. 1909).

5. In 1882, when Congress passed the first Chinese exclusion act, it included a provision declaring that "hereafter no State court or court of the United States shall admit Chinese to citizenship." Why was this explicit prohibition necessary given the "free white person" specification in the 1870 naturalization statute?

6. What about the Japanese? Some lower courts had apparently held that they were "free white persons" and granted U.S. citizenship. How do you think that the Japanese litigants argued their case and managed to win in the district courts? The Supreme Court in 1922 held otherwise. A former U.S. Attorney General, George Wickersham (the "Wickersham" of the law firm Cadwalader, Wickersham & Taft) argued the case for the Japanese man, Takao Ozawa, at the Supreme Court. His two main arguments were: (1) the Japanese race was part of the Aryan race, not the Mongoloid race like the Chinese; and (2) an assimilated, civilized gentleman like Ozawa was a "free white person," not the type of lower-class laborers that the words in the statute were meant to restrict. Recall that, with respect to the second argument, the Chinese Exclusion Act did not apply to students, academics, diplomats, and, presumably, those Chinese wealthy enough to travel to the United States as tourists. The Supreme Court held, however, that "free white person" meant a member of the Caucasian race under then-cutting-edge social science.

7. Around the same time, Bhagat Singh Thind, who was born in India but had served in the U.S. military during World War I, was able to obtain U.S. citizenship—twice. The first time the U.S. district court in Washington reversed its decision to grant him citizenship after the U.S. government intervened. The second time, the U.S. district court in Oregon granted Thind's petition and then rejected the government's petition to cancel his citizenship. The government appealed to the court of appeals, which certified the question to the U.S. Supreme Court. Thind argued that as a high caste Indian, he was a member of the Caucasian race. In 1923, the Supreme Court held that "free white person" in the naturalization statutes meant not only members of the Caucasian race but also what ordinary people would take the words to mean. In 1952, Congress amended the immigration laws to provide that "[t]he right of a person to become a naturalized citizen of the United States shall not be denied or abridged because of race or sex." *See* Ian F. Haney López, *White by Law: The Legal Construction of Race* 33 & n.44 (2006) (quoting Immigration & Nationality Act of 1952, ch. 2, § 311, 66 Stat. 239). The amendment did little to increase the entry into the United States of Asian immigrants who could avail

themselves of the new naturalization statute, however, as the substantial exclusion of Asians through the country-of-origin quota system was not relaxed until 1965. *Id.* at 33 & n.45.

Ozawa v. United States

260 U.S. 178 (1922)

MR. JUSTICE SUTHERLAND delivered the opinion of the Court.

The appellant is a person of the Japanese race born in Japan. He applied, on October 16, 1914, to the United States District Court for the Territory of Hawaii to be admitted as a citizen of the United States. His petition was opposed by the United States District Attorney for the District of Hawaii. Including the period of his residence in Hawaii, appellant had continuously resided in the United States for twenty years. He was a graduate of the Berkeley, California, High School, had been nearly three years a student in the University of California, had educated his children in American schools; his family had attended American churches and he had maintained the use of the English language in his home. That he was well qualified by character and education for citizenship is conceded.

The District Court of Hawaii, however, held that, having been born in Japan and being of the Japanese race, he was not eligible to naturalization under § 2169 of the Revised Statutes, and denied the petition. Thereupon the appellant brought the cause to the Circuit Court of Appeals for the Ninth Circuit and that court has certified the following questions, upon which it desires to be instructed:

"1. Is the Act of June 29, 1906 (34 Stats. at Large, Part. I, Page 596), providing 'for a uniform rule for the naturalization of aliens' complete in itself, or is it limited by Section 2169 of the Revised Statutes of the United States?

"2. Is one who is of the Japanese race and born in Japan eligible to citizenship under the naturalization laws?

"3. If said act of June 29, 1906, is limited by Section 2169 and naturalization is limited to aliens being free white persons and to aliens of African nativity and to persons of African descent, is one of the Japanese race, born in Japan, under any circumstances eligible to naturalization?"

These questions for purposes of discussion may be briefly restated:

1. Is the Naturalization Act of June 29, 1906 (Comp. St. § 4351 et seq.), limited by the provisions of § 2169 of the Revised Statutes of the United States?

2. If so limited, is the appellant eligible to naturalization under that section?

First. Section 2169 is found in Title XXX of the Revised Statutes, under the heading "Naturalization," and reads as follows:

> "The provisions of this Title shall apply to aliens, being free white persons and to aliens of African nativity and to persons of African descent."

The Act of June 29, 1906, entitled "An Act To establish a Bureau of Immigration and Naturalization, and to provide for a uniform rule for the naturalization of aliens throughout the United States," consists of thirty-one sections and deals primarily with the subject of procedure. There is nothing in the circumstances leading up to or accompanying the passage of the act which suggests that any modification of § 2169, or of its application, was contemplated....

It is the duty of this Court to give effect to the intent of Congress. Primarily this intent is ascertained by giving the words their natural significance, but if this leads to an unreasonable result plainly at variance with the policy of the legislation as a whole, we must examine the matter further. We may then look to the reason of the enactment and inquire into its antecedent history and give it effect in accordance with its design and purpose, sacrificing, if necessary, the literal meaning in order that the purpose may not fail. See *Holy Trinity Church* v. *United States*, 143 U. S. 457; *Heydenfeldt* v. *Daney Gold Mining Co.*, 93 U. S. 634, 638. We are asked to conclude that Congress, without the consideration or recommendation of any committee, without a suggestion as to the effect, or a word of debate as to the desirability, of so fundamental a change, nevertheless, by failing to alter the identifying words of § 2169, which section we may assume was continued for some serious purpose, has radically modified a statute always theretofore maintained and considered as of great importance. It is inconceivable that a rule in force from the beginning of the Government, a part of our history as well as our law, welded into the structure of our national polity by a century of legislative and administrative acts and judicial decisions, would have been deprived of its force in such dubious and casual fashion. We are, therefore, constrained to hold that the Act of 1906 is limited by the provisions of § 2169 of the Revised Statutes.

Second. This brings us to inquire whether, under § 2169, the appellant is eligible to naturalization. The language of the naturalization laws from 1790 to 1870 had been uniformly such as to deny the privilege of naturalization to an alien unless he came within the description "free white person." By § 7 of the Act of July 14, 1870 c. 254, 16 Stat. 254, 256, the naturalization laws were "extended to aliens of African nativity and to persons of African descent." Section 2169 of the Revised Statutes, as already pointed out, restricts the privilege to the same classes of persons, viz: "to aliens [being free white persons, and to aliens] of African nativity and to persons of African descent." It is true that in the first edition of the Revised Statutes of 1873 the words in brackets, "being free white persons, and to aliens" were omitted, but this was clearly an error of the compilers and was corrected by the subsequent legislation of 1875 (c. 80, 18 Stat. 316, 318). Is appellant, therefore, a "free white person," within the meaning of that phrase as found in the statute?

On behalf of the appellant it is urged that we should give to this phrase the meaning which it had in the minds of its original framers in 1790 and that it was employed by them for the sole purpose of excluding the black or African race and the Indians then inhabiting this country. It may be true that those two races were alone thought of as

Figure 3.3 *Portrait of Takao Ozawa*, 1916.
Gift of the Takeya Family, Japanese American National Museum.

Figure 3.4 *Photograph of Bhagat Singh Thind in his U.S. Army Uniform, 1918.*
Thind enlisted in the U.S. Army and trained at Camp Lewis, Washington.

being excluded, but to say that they were the only ones within the intent of the statute would be to ignore the affirmative form of the legislation. The provision is not that Negroes and Indians shall be *excluded*, but it is, in effect, that only free white persons shall be *included*. The intention was to confer the privilege of citizenship upon that class of persons whom the fathers knew as white, and to deny it to all who could not be so classified. It is not enough to say that the framers did not have in mind the brown or yellow races of Asia. It is necessary to go farther and be able to say that had these particular races been suggested the language of the act would have been so varied as to include them within its privileges....

If it be assumed that the opinion of the framers was that the only persons who would fall outside the designation "white" were Negroes and Indians, this would go no farther than to demonstrate their lack of sufficient information to enable them to foresee precisely who would be excluded by that term in the subsequent administration of the statute. It is not important in construing their words to consider the extent of their ethnological knowledge or whether they thought that under the statute the only persons who would be denied naturalization would be Negroes and Indians. It is sufficient to ascertain whom they intended to include and having ascertained that it follows, as a necessary corollary, that all others are to be excluded.

The question then is, Who are comprehended within the phrase "free white persons?" Undoubtedly the word "free" was originally used in recognition of the fact that slavery then existed and that some white persons occupied that status. The word, however, has long since ceased to have any practical significance and may now be disregarded.

We have been furnished with elaborate briefs in which the meaning of the words "white person" is discussed with ability and at length, both from the standpoint of judicial decision and from that of the science of ethnology. It does not seem to us necessary, however, to follow counsel in their extensive researches in these fields. It is sufficient to note the fact that these decisions are, in substance, to the effect that the words import a racial and not an individual test, and with this conclusion, fortified as it is by reason and authority, we entirely agree. Manifestly, the test afforded by the mere color of the skin of each individual is impracticable as that differs greatly among persons of the same race, even among Anglo-Saxons, ranging by imperceptible gradations from the fair blond to the swarthy brunette, the latter being darker than many of the lighter hued persons of the brown or yellow races. Hence to adopt the color test alone would result in a confused overlapping of races and a gradual merging of one into the other, without any practical line of separation. Beginning with the decision of Circuit Judge Sawyer, in *In Re Ah Yup*, 5 Sawy. 155 (1878), the federal and state courts, in an almost unbroken line, have held the words "white person" were meant to indicate only a person of what is popularly known as the Caucasian race. Among these decisions, see for example: *In re Camille*, 6 Fed. 256; *In re Saito*, 62 Fed. 126; *In re Nian*, 6 Utah, 259; *In re Kumagai* 163 Fed. 922; *In re Yamashita*, 30 Wash. 234, 237; *In re Ellis* 179 Fed. 1002; *In re Mozumdar* 207 Fed. 115, 117; *In re Singh* 257 Fed. 209,

211–212; and *In re Charr* 273 Fed. 207. With the conclusion reached in these several decisions we see no reason to differ. Moreover, that conclusion has become so well established by judicial and executive concurrence and legislative acquiescence that we should not at this late day feel at liberty to disturb it, in the absence of reasons far more cogent than any that have been suggested....

The determination that the words "white person" are synonymous with the words "a person of the Caucasian race" simplifies the problem, although it does not entirely dispose of it. Controversies have arisen and will no doubt arise again in respect of the proper classification of individuals in border line cases. The effect of the conclusion that the words "white person" mean a Caucasian is not to establish a sharp line of demarcation between those who are entitled and those who are not entitled to naturalization, but rather a zone of more or less debatable ground outside of which, upon the one hand, are those clearly eligible, and outside of which, upon the other hand, are those clearly ineligible for citizenship. Individual cases falling within this zone must be determined as they arise from time to time by what this court has called, in another connection (*Davidson v. New Orleans*, 96 U. S. 97, 104) "the gradual process of judicial inclusion and exclusion."

The appellant, in the case now under consideration, however, is clearly of a race which is not Caucasian and therefore belongs entirely outside the zone on the negative side. A large number of the federal and state courts have so decided and we find no reported case definitely to the contrary. These decisions are sustained by numerous scientific authorities, which we do not deem it necessary to review. We think these decisions are right and so hold.

The briefs filed on behalf of appellant refer in complimentary terms to the culture and enlightenment of the Japanese people, and with this estimate we have no reason to disagree; but these are matters which cannot enter into our consideration of the questions here at issue. We have no function in the matter other than to ascertain the will of Congress and declare it. Of course there is not implied—either in the legislation or in our interpretation of it—any suggestion of individual unworthiness or racial inferiority. These considerations are in no manner involved.

The questions submitted are, therefore, answered as follows:

Question No. 1. The Act of June 29, 1906, is not complete in itself but is limited by § 2169 of the Revised Statutes of the United States.

Question No. 2. No.

Question No. 3. No.

It will be so certified.

Notes

1. Is it implausible, as the Court suggests, that, as a matter of statutory interpretation, the words "free white person" should be understood to refer to a free person who has the physical appearance and manner, the cultural sensibilities, the civilized mien, and the language ability of a White European "gentleman" or "lady?" What are the arguments the Court accepted for rejecting this interpretation? Do you agree that the word "free" is essentially surplusage as Justice Sutherland suggests? If so, would it be possible to argue that "White" is also a word that does not have the same meaning that it did in 1790? And why is the original meaning of the word in 1790 relevant at all, as opposed to 1870?

2. Takao Ozawa was born in Japan in 1875. At the age of 19, he relocated to San Francisco. He graduated from Berkeley High School in Berkeley, California, studied at the University of California for nearly three years until it closed after the earthquake in 1906, and then moved to Hawaii. There he worked as a sales clerk at one of the Big Five sugar companies in Honolulu for 23 years.

   In 1870, a few years before Ozawa's birth, there were apparently only 55 Japanese people living in the United States, compared to about 60,000 Chinese people. *See* Dep't of Commerce, Bureau of Census, *Chinese and Japanese in the United States—1910*, table 6 (1914), *available at* https://www2.census.gov/prod2/decennial/documents/ 03322287no71-80ch6.pdf. By 1900, the number of Japanese people had risen to almost 25,000. *Id.* By the time Ozawa moved to Hawaii, anti-Japanese sentiment was regularly featured in the press in California, with story after story claiming that the Japanese were trying to take over the United States. By 1913, the number of Japanese people in the United States rose to over 70,000, with more than half living in California. Japanese land ownership also increased, leading the state legislature to pass the Alien Land Act in 1913, restricting land ownership by Japanese individuals. *See* Chapter 5 *supra*.

   Ozawa filed his declaration of intent to naturalize in 1902 while still a resident of California, and filed his petition for naturalization on October 16, 1914, the day his American-born daughter turned two. Commentators subsequently described Ozawa as "a paragon of an assimilated Japanese immigrant," noting that he was fully qualified for citizenship given his years of residency, his personal character, and his English fluency. Ozawa presented his own petition to the United States District Court for the Territory of Hawaii, writing out in composition books his legal briefs for submission to the Court. Ozawa argued that skin color was not the key. Rather, he contended that the intent of Congress in using the term "free white person" was to make a person's character, not a person's race, relevant for purposes of naturalization.

   Ozawa's efforts were not successful. In 1926, he opened Kaimuki Dry Goods, a store that remained in the family and was eventually run by his granddaughter.

He lived out his days in Hawaii, raising four daughters and one son, and died in 1936. His son George Yoshio Ozawa served in the U.S. military in World War II and died, as a U.S. citizen, in Italy, fighting for the country his father had so proudly adopted as his own.[5]

United States v. Thind

261 U.S. 204 (1923)

MR. JUSTICE SUTHERLAND delivered the opinion of the Court.

This cause is here upon a certificate from the Circuit Court of Appeals, requesting the instruction of this Court in respect of the following questions:

"1. Is a high caste Hindu, of full Indian blood, born at Amrit Sar, Punjab, India, a white person within the meaning of section 2169, Revised Statutes?

"2. Does the Act of February 5, 1917 (39 Stat. 875, section 3) disqualify from naturalization as citizens those Hindus, now barred by that act, who had lawfully entered the United States prior to the passage of said act?"

The appellee was granted a certificate of citizenship by the District Court of the United States for the District of Oregon, over the objection of the naturalization examiner for the United States. A bill in equity was then filed by the United States, seeking a cancellation of the certificate on the ground that the appellee was not a white person and therefore not lawfully entitled to naturalization. The District Court, on motion, dismissed the bill (268 Fed. 683), and an appeal was taken to the Circuit Court of Appeals. No question is made in respect of the individual qualifications of the appellee. The sole question is whether he falls within the class designated by Congress as eligible.

Section 2169, Revised Statutes, provides that the provisions of the Naturalization Act "shall apply to aliens, being free white persons, and to aliens of African nativity and to persons of African descent."

If the applicant is a white person, within the meaning of this section, he is entitled to naturalization; otherwise not. In *Ozawa v. United States*, 260 U. S. 178, we had occasion to consider the application of these words to the case of a cultivated Japanese and were constrained to hold that he was not within their meaning. As there pointed out, the provision is not that any particular class of persons shall be excluded, but it is, in effect, that only white persons shall be included within the privilege of the statute.

---

5. *See* Devon W. Carbado, *Yellow by Law*, 97 Calif. L. Rev. 633 (2009); M. Browning Carrott, *Prejudice Goes to Court: The Japanese & the Supreme Court in the 1920s*, California History, 62:2, 122–138 (1983); Ian Haney-Lopez, *White by Law: The Legal Construction of Race* 56–61 (2006); Yuji Ichioka, *The Early Japanese Immigrant Quest for Citizenship: The Background of the 1922* Ozawa *Case*, 4 AmerAsia 1 (1977).

"The intention was to confer the privilege of citizenship upon that class of persons whom the fathers knew as white, and to deny it to all who could not be so classified. It is not enough to say that the framers did not have in mind the brown or yellow races of Asia. It is necessary to go farther and be able to say that had these particular races been suggested the language of the act would have been so varied as to include them within its privileges,"—(p. 195) citing *Dartmouth College v. Woodward*, 4 Wheat. 518, 644. Following a long line of decisions of the lower federal courts, we held that the words imported a racial and not an individual test and were meant to indicate only persons of what is *popularly* known as the Caucasian race.

But, as there pointed out, the conclusion that the phrase "white persons" and the word "Caucasian" are synonymous does not end the matter. It enabled us to dispose of the problem as it was there presented, since the applicant for citizenship clearly fell outside the zone of debatable ground on the negative side; but the decision still left the question to be dealt with, in doubtful and different cases, by the "process of judicial inclusion and exclusion." Mere ability on the part of an applicant for naturalization to establish a line of descent from a Caucasian ancestor will not *ipso facto* and necessarily conclude the inquiry. 'Caucasian" is a conventional word of much flexibility, as a study of the literature dealing with racial questions will disclose, and while it and the words "white persons" are treated as synonymous for the purposes of that case, they are not of identical meaning—*idem per idem*.

In the endeavor to ascertain the meaning of the statute we must not fail to keep in mind that it does not employ the word "Caucasian," but the words "white persons," and these are words of common speech and not of scientific origin. The word "Caucasian," not only was employed in the law but was probably wholly unfamiliar to the original framers of the statute in 1790. When we employ it we do so as an aid to the ascertainment of the legislative intent and not as an invariable substitute for the statutory words. Indeed, as used in the science of ethnology, the connotation of the word is by no means clear and the use of it in its scientific sense as an equivalent for the words of the statute, other considerations aside, would simply mean the substitution of one perplexity for another. But in this country, during the last half century especially, the word by common usage has acquired a popular meaning, not clearly defined to be sure, but sufficiently so to enable us to say that its popular as distinguished from its scientific application is of appreciably narrower scope. It is in the popular sense of the word, therefore, that we employ is as an aid to the construction of the statute, for it would be obviously illogical to convert words of common speech used in a statute into words of scientific terminology when neither the latter nor the science for whose purposes they were coined was within the contemplation of the framers of the statute or of the people for whom it was framed. The words of the statute are to be interpreted in accordance with the understanding of the common man from whose vocabulary they were taken. See *Maillard v. Lawrence*, 16 How. 251, 261.

They imply, as we have said, a racial test; but the term "race" is one which, for the practical purposes of the statute, must be applied to a group of living persons *now* possessing in common the requisite characteristics, not to groups of persons who are supposed to be or really are descended from some remote, common ancestor, but who, whether they both resemble him to a greater or less extent, have, at any rate, ceased altogether to resemble one another. It may be true that the blond Scandinavian and the brown Hindu have a common ancestor in the dim reaches of antiquity, but the average man knows perfectly well that there are unmistakable and profound differences between them today; and it is not impossible, if that common ancestor could be materialized in the flesh, we should discover that he was himself sufficiently differentiated from both of his descendants to preclude his racial classification with either. The question for determination is not, therefore, whether by the speculative processes of ethnological reasoning we may present a probability to the scientific mind that they have the same origin, but whether we can satisfy the common understanding that they are now the same or sufficiently the same to justify the interpreters of a statute—written in the words of common speech, for common understanding, by unscientific men—in classifying them together in the statutory category as white persons. In 1790 the Adamite theory of creation—which gave a common ancestor to all mankind—was generally accepted, and it is not at all probable that it was intended by the legislators of that day to submit the question of the application of the words "white persons" to the mere test of an indefinitely remote common ancestry, without regard to the extent of the subsequent divergence of the various branches from such common ancestry or from one another.

The eligibility of this applicant for citizenship is based on the sole fact that he is of high caste Hindu stock, born in Punjab, one of the extreme northwestern districts of India, and classified by certain scientific authorities as of the Caucasian or Aryan race. The Aryan theory as a racial basis seems to be discredited by most, if not all, modern writers on the subject of ethnology. A review of their contentions would serve no useful purpose. It is enough to refer to the works of Deniker (Races of Man, 317), Keane (Man, Past and Present, 445-6), and Huxley (Man's Place in Nature, 278) and to the Dictionary of Races, Senate Document No. 662, 61st Cong., 3d sess. 1910–1911, p. 17.

The term "Aryan" has to do with linguistic and not at all with physical characteristics, and it would seem reasonably clear that mere resemblance in language, indicating a common linguistic root buried in remotely ancient soil, is altogether inadequate to prove common racial origin. There is, and can be, no assurance that the so-called Aryan language was not spoken by a variety of races living in proximity to one another. Our own history has witnessed the adoption of the English tongue by millions of Negroes, whose descendants can never be classified racially with the descendants of white persons notwithstanding both may speak a common root language.

The word "Caucasian" is in scarcely better repute. It is at best a conventional term, with an altogether fortuitous origin, which under scientific manipulation, has come to include far more than the unscientific mind suspects. According to Keane, for example (The World's Peoples, 24, 28, 307, *et seq.*) it includes not only the Hindu, but some of the Polynesians, (that is, the Maori, Tahitians, Samoans, Hawaiians and others), the Hamites of Africa, upon the ground of the Caucasic cast of their features, though in color they range from brown to black. We venture to think that the average well informed white American would learn with some degree of astonishment that the race to which he belongs is made up of such heterogeneous elements.

The various authorities are in irreconcilable disagreement as to what constitutes a proper racial division. For instance, Blumenbach has five races; Keane following Linnaeus, four; Deniker, twenty-nine. The explanation probably is that "the innumerable varieties of mankind run into one another by insensible degrees," and to arrange them in sharply bounded divisions is an undertaking of such uncertainty that common agreement is practically impossible.

It may be, therefore, that a given group cannot be properly assigned to any of the enumerated grand racial divisions. The type may have been so changed by intermixture of blood as to justify an intermediate classification. Something very like this has actually taken place in India. Thus, in Hindustan and Berar there was such an intermixture of the "Aryan" invader with the dark skinned Dravidian.

In the Punjab and Rajputana, while the invaders seem to have met with more success in the effort to preserve their racial purity, intermarriages did occur producing an intermingling of the two and destroying to a greater or less degree the purity of the "Aryan" blood. The rules of caste, while calculated to prevent this intermixture, seem not to have been entirely successful.

It does not seem necessary to pursue the matter of scientific classification further. We are unable to agree with the District Court, or with other lower federal courts, in the conclusion that a native Hindu is eligible for naturalization under § 2169. The words of familiar speech, which were used by the original framers of the law, were intended to include only the type of man whom they knew as white. The immigration of that day was almost exclusively from the British Isles and Northwestern Europe, whence they and their forebears had come. When they extended the privilege of American citizenship to "any alien being a free white person" it was these immigrants—bone of their bone and flesh of their flesh—and their kind whom they must have had affirmatively in mind. The succeeding years brought immigrants from Eastern, Southern and Middle Europe, among them the Slavs and the dark-eyed, swarthy people of Alpine and Mediterranean stock, and these were received as unquestionably akin to those already here and readily amalgamated with them. It was the descendants of these, and other immigrants of like origin, who constituted the white population of the country when § 2169, reenacting the naturalization test of 1790, was adopted; and there is no reason to doubt with like intent and meaning.

What, if any, people of primarily Asiatic stock come within the words of the section we do not deem it necessary now to decide. There is much in the origin and historic development of the statute to suggest that no Asiatic whatever was included. The debates in Congress, during the consideration of the subject in 1870 and 1875, are persuasively of this character. In 1873, for example, the words "free white persons" were unintentionally omitted from the compilation of the Revised Statutes. This omission was supplied in 1875 by the act to correct errors and supply omissions. C. 80, 17 Stat. 318. When this act was under consideration by Congress efforts were made to strike out the words quoted, and it was insisted upon the one hand and conceded upon the other, that the effect of their retention was to exclude Asiatics generally from citizenship. While what was said upon that occasion, to be sure, furnishes no basis for judicial construction of the statute, it is, nevertheless, an important historic incident, which may not be altogether ignored in the search for the true meaning of words which are themselves historic. That question, however, may well be left for final determination until the details have been more completely disclosed by the consideration of particular cases, as they from time to time arise. The words of the statute, it must be conceded, do not readily yield to exact interpretation, and it is probably better to leave them as they are than to risk undue extension or undue limitation of their meaning by any general paraphrase at this time.

What we now hold is that the words "free white persons" are words of common speech, to be interpreted in accordance with the understanding of the common man, synonymous with the word "Caucasian" only as that word is popularly understood. As so understood and used, whatever may be the speculations of the ethnologist, it does not include the body of people to whom the appellee belongs. It is a matter of familiar observation and knowledge that the physical group characteristics of the Hindus render them readily distinguishable from the various groups of persons in this country commonly recognized as white. The children of English, French, German, Italian, Scandinavian, and other European parentage, quickly merge into the mass of our population and lose the distinctive hallmarks of their European origin. On the other hand, it cannot be doubted that the children born in this country of Hindu parents would retain indefinitely the clear evidence of their ancestry. It is very far from our thought to suggest the slightest question of racial superiority or inferiority. What we suggest is merely racial difference, and it is of such character and extent that the great body of our people instinctively recognize it and reject the thought of assimilation.

It is not without significance in this connection that Congress, by the Act of February 5, 1917, c. 29, § 3, 39 Stat. 874, has now excluded from admission into this country all natives of Asia within designated limits of latitude and longitude, including the whole of India. This not only constitutes conclusive evidence of the congressional attitude of opposition to Asiatic immigration generally, but is persuasive of a similar attitude toward Asiatic naturalization as well, since it is not likely that Congress would be willing to accept as citizens a class of persons whom it rejects as immigrants.

It follows that a negative answer must be given to the first question, which disposes of the case and renders an answer to the second question unnecessary, and it will be so certified.

Answer to question No. 1, No.

Notes

1. Thind was born in 1892, in northern India in Amritsar, Punjab, "the holy city" of the Sikh religion. He attended Khalsa College in India but moved to the United States at the age of 21 to pursue an education in an American university. He arrived in Seattle, Washington, in 1913, and worked in the lumber mills of Astoria, Oregon. On July 22, 1918, while still a subject of British India (India became an independent nation in 1947), he joined the U.S. Army to fight in World War I. A few months later, he was promoted to Acting Sergeant.

   Thind filed a petition to be an American citizen, in part because he wanted to be a lawyer and citizenship was required to become a licensed member of the bar in Washington state, as was true for all the states at the time. On December 9, 1918, a U.S. district judge in Washington granted his petition for U.S. citizenship. He was sworn in as a U.S. citizen, while wearing his uniform as a soldier in the U.S. Army. But just four days later, his citizenship was revoked, as the Bureau of Naturalization opposed his naturalization and the court overturned its prior decision.

   Undeterred, Thind tried again. In May 1919, he petitioned for citizenship in a U.S. district court in Oregon. In November 1920, the court granted the petition, without addressing the question of whether Thind was a "free white person." Thind was naturalized. One month later, however, the U.S. government filed a bill in equity to cancel Thind's citizenship. The Oregon District Court disagreed with the government, holding that Thind was entitled to be naturalized. The government appealed to the Ninth Circuit, which certified the question directly to the Supreme Court—whether a high caste Hindu of full Indian blood was a White person within the meaning of the statute.

   For Asian Indians, the Supreme Court decision in *Thind* was devastating: Asian Indians who had previously been naturalized, and had believed their status to be secure, were stripped of their citizenship. More than 65 Asian Indians were denaturalized between 1923 and 1927 in the wake of *Thind*. Among them was Vaishno Das Bagai, who had lived with his family in the United States since 1915, and had become a citizen. He died by suicide, and in his suicide note, he wrote as follows:

   > But they now come to me and say, I am no longer an American citizen.... What have I made of myself and my children? We cannot exercise our rights, we cannot leave this country. Humility and insults, who is responsible for all of this? ... Obstacles this way, blockades that way, and the bridges burnt behind.

   Rani Bagai, *Bridges Burnt Behind*, Angel Island Immigration Station Foundation (2021), https://www.immigrant-voices.aiisf.org/stories-by-author/876-bridges-burnt-behind-the-story-of-vaishno-das-bagai/.

   As for Thind, his U.S. citizenship was revoked. In 1935, however, Congress passed a law allowing citizenship to U.S. veterans of World War I. Thind was eligible under the new law and he took the oath of citizenship in 1936 in New York. By that time, he had completed his Ph.D. and was delivering lectures in metaphysics. Soon after, he was ordained a minister, and then met and married Vivian Davies, a White woman, in Ohio in 1940. He went on to become a revered spiritual leader and wrote many religious books. Thind was working on additional books when he died on September 15, 1967.[6]

2. Thind must have been confident when he went to the Supreme Court. He had won below and the reasoning of the Supreme Court's decision relying on a pseudo-scientific definition of White in *Ozawa* supported his position, as he was Caucasian. How did Justice Sutherland, who also wrote the majority opinion in *Ozawa,* distinguish that case in holding that Thind was not a free White person under the statute? Is Sutherland's distinction persuasive as a matter of statutory interpretation, of which Sutherland was widely acknowledged as the master at the time? The federal government took an extremely aggressive position, petitioning to cancel Thind's citizenship after it was initially granted and then appealing to the Ninth Circuit and then the Supreme Court after Thind won in the District Court. Why do you think that the government made the effort to nullify Thind's win, particularly given the long-settled rule that there is no issue or claim preclusion against the government, with the consequence that no one else could use Thind's win as binding precedent in a subsequent case?

3. In the Supreme Court, Thind argued that he was born a member of a high Hindu caste, a caste regarded as being descendants of the Aryan race. As Aryans were Caucasian, Thind argued, he was White. Thind also maintained that he was of pure blood, and that there was no chance he was of mixed blood. He wrote:

    > Bhagat Singh Thind is a high caste Hindu of full Indian blood, born at Amritsar, Punjab, India. Being a high caste Indian and having no intermixture of Dravidian or other alien blood, and coming from the Punjab, one of the most northwestern provinces of India, the original home of the Aryan conquerors, unless all the historical, ethnological and philological authorities cited in this brief are disregarded it must be held that Bhagat Singh Thind belongs to the Caucasian or white race. If Bhagat Singh Thind is not a free white person then no Hindu can claim citizenship in this country. His high caste and pure Aryan blood make of him a full-fledged Caucasian according to all the well-reasoned authorities.
    >
    > This particular Hindu is a high class man in every respect, a veteran of the late war and a volunteer, who received high commendation from his

---

6. *See generally* Haney-Lopez, at 61–65; Carbado. *See also* Jasmine K. Singh, *Everything I'm Not Made Me Everything I Am: The Racialization of Sikhs in the United States*, 14 Asian Pac. Am. L.J. 54 (2008-2009); John Tehranian, *Performing Whiteness: Naturalization Litigation and the Construction of Racial Identity in America*, 109 Yale L.J. 817 (2000); Amin Vafa, *The Fight to Be American: Military Naturalization and Asian Citizenship*, 17 Asian Am. L.J. 119 (2010).

> superior officers for his distinguished services. His personal desirability is therefore apparent and as a general proposition a man who fights for the flag should be entitled to come under the flag....

Brief of Respondent at 28–29, *United States v. Bhagat Singh Thind*, 261 U.S. 204 (1923). What do you think of the arguments that Thind made essentially underlining his noble birth, "pure Aryan blood," and high social status to state a claim to U.S. citizenship? Why did they fail? Relatedly, what do you think of Ozawa's argument that he was not Chinese? And how do we decide a person's race?

4. Thind was not actually Hindu; rather, he was a Sikh. *See* Vikramdeep Johal, *Sikh Soldier Who Fought Racial US Laws*, The Tribune, Feb. 26, 2018, http://www.tribuneindia.com/news/nation/sikh-soldier-who-fought-racial-us-laws/549822.html. Although most Hindus and Sikhs come from the Punjab region of India, Hinduism and Sikhism are different religions, not racial groups, and it is unlikely that a Sikh would have made the argument that Thind's lawyers made. *See* Sukhmandir Khalsa, *10 Ways That Sikhism Differs from Hinduism: A Comparison of Beliefs, Faith, and Practices*, ThoughtCo. (June 3, 2017), https://www.thoughtco.com/ways-that-sikhism-differs-from-hinduism-2992955 ("Sikhs are not Hindus. Sikhism rejects many aspects of Hinduism."). Do you think that Thind's lawyers knew that he was a Sikh and not Hindu or even comprehended the difference? Assuming that they did, would it have been unethical or improper for Thind's counsel to make representations to the court that he was Hindu when he was not? What if, as was likely the case in line with popular conceptions at the time, most people believed all Indians were Hindus?

5. Takao Ozawa had taken a somewhat different approach. He submitted handwritten arguments, in composition books, to the United States District Court for the Territory of Hawaii and explained as follows:

> For the sake of clearness, I will use an illustration. Whenever we speak of white eggs, we mean the eggs having white shells. However the term "white" does not indicate any quality of eggs. It only designates the color of eggs. On the other hand, when we speak of "fresh white eggs," we mean newly laid eggs. A white egg may or may not be fresh. But a fresh white egg must always be fresh, that is, of good quality. Hence the term fresh white eggs indicate[s] the good quality of eggs.
>
> Similarly, in the expression "white person," the word "white" designates the color of the person, but not quality. On the other hand, the term "free" indicates the good quality of the person....

Hand-written arguments of Petitioner, *In re Takao Ozawa*, at 12–13, filed in U.S. Dist. Ct., Territory of Hawaii, May 29, 1915. He submitted a "second brief," also pro se, that stated:

> In name, General Benedict Arnold was an American, but at heart he was a Traitor. In name, I am not an American, but at heart I am a true

> American. I set forth the following facts that will sufficiently prove this. (1) I did not report my name, my marriage, or the names of my children to the Japanese Consulate in Honolulu; notwithstanding all Japanese subjects are requested to do so. These matters were reported to the American government. (2) I do not have any connection with any Japanese churches or schools, or any Japanese organizations here or elsewhere. (3) I am sending my children to an American Church in place of a Japanese one. (4) Most of the time I use the American (English) language at home, so that my children cannot speak the Japanese language. (5) I educated myself in American Schools for nearly eleven years by supporting myself. (6) I ex-communicated myself from my brothers and sisters, all living in Japan, for nearly seventeen (17) years. (7) I have lived continuously within the United States for over twenty one years. (8) I chose as my wife, one educated in American Schools here, instead of one educated in Japan. (9) I have steadily prepared to return the kindness which our Uncle Sam has extended me; that is, the United States gave me a good, free education for nearly eleven years. It is this education which enables me to support my family; so it is my honest hope to do something good to the United States before I bid a farewell to this world.

Second Brief of Petitioner, *In re Takao Ozawa* (filing date unclear, circa 1915 or 1916). Ozawa apparently went to great lengths to try to make himself an American. What do you think of his cultural assimilation approach as compared to Thind's race and status arguments? Which argument strategy do you think would have seemed more persuasive in 1922 and 1923? Which do you think are more persuasive today?

6. Two years after *Thind* was handed down, the Supreme Court decided *Toyota v. United States*, 268 U.S. 402 (1925). Hidemitsu Toyota was born in Japan but emigrated to the United States in 1913 and served in the U.S. Coast Guard from 1913 to 1923. In 1921, Toyota successfully petitioned for U.S. citizenship in U.S. federal district court in Massachusetts, and the government sought to invalidate it. He petitioned on the basis of a different statute than the general "free white person" naturalization act, namely, a 1919 statute that provided for U.S. citizenship for "any alien" serving in the U.S. armed services under prescribed conditions that Toyota met. The Supreme Court held that the more specific 1919 statute did not create an exception to the general naturalization act. Although *Ozawa* and *Thind* were unanimous decisions of the Supreme Court (authored by noted statutory interpretation expert Justice George Sutherland), Chief Justice William Howard Taft dissented without opinion from Justice Pierce Butler's opinion for the Court, which the other seven justices joined. Why do you think Taft, who had been President of the United States and U.S. governor of the Philippines when it was a U.S. territory, dissented? As a matter of statutory interpretation, do you think that the later-enacted military service statute's provision for "any alien" should override the naturalization act, which was originally enacted in 1790?

7. Step back for a second. What does it mean that Congress used its Article I power to "establish an uniform Rule of Naturalization" for 162 years that required an applicant to be a "free white person" to be naturalized a citizen of the United States? What did a person's race have to do with citizenship, whether in the late eighteenth century or the early twentieth century? Congress dropped the requirement in 1952, but would it be constitutional if a Congress in the future were to reconstitute it? Even today, some countries like Japan have laws that connect race to citizenship and do not automatically give birthright citizenship to the children born of foreign residents of the country. How might such race-based citizenship and naturalization laws be defended today? Should the citizenship law of other countries, especially industrialized democracies like Japan, influence U.S. citizenship law?

8. Many federal judges will tell you that one of the most rewarding things they do is to swear in new U.S. citizens in naturalization proceedings. How has our review of the history of Asian Americans and access to U.S. citizenship changed, if at all, your view of the meaning of being a citizen of the United States? What rights and obligations do you think citizenship entails or should entail? Does a Japanese-American U.S. citizen owe an obligation of loyalty, even to the extent of mandatory military service in World War II, if the federal government is engaged in systematic discrimination against persons of Japanese descent, including family members and U.S. citizens?

In our consideration of the arrival of Asians to the United States, the exclusion laws, and the question of citizenship, a number of themes emerge—initial curiosity supplanted by hostility toward Chinese laborers as economic competitors, the role of the media, the use of immigrants and immigration to mobilize voters, the impact of U.S.-Asia international relations on the treatment of people of Asian descent in the United States, the role of lawyers, and the willingness of Asians to look to the courts to challenge what they perceived to be unlawful actions and to protect their rights in the absence of meaningful access to political process. We also saw constitutional principles in action, and as the courts confronted difficult questions, we saw the tension that often arose between these principles and popular opinion.

Hostility toward immigrants has not been confined solely to Asians in the history of the United States. In the nineteenth century, notably, Irish, Italian, and other immigrants from South, Central, and Eastern Europe were subjects of scorn and prejudice. Countless numbers of laborers also migrated from Mexico into the United States. All of them were perceived as economic threats. But no other foreign migrants resulted in congressional statutes excluding their entry. What motivated the particular hostility and racism toward the Chinese and other Asian groups? Was it the perception that they could not be assimilated into a predominantly White citizenry as readily as persons from European descent groups? Part of the answer, of course, was economic competition. But was there more? Most of the early Asian arrivals were unskilled laborers. How much of a threat did they really pose? In recent years, we've seen a rise in racism and hostility toward immigrants, not just in this country but in others as well. What is motivating this antagonism? William Wan and Sarah Kaplan, *Why Are People Still Racist? What Science Says About America's Race Problem*, Wash. Post, Aug. 14, 2017 (quoting one psychologist as saying: "In some ways, it's super simple. People learn to be whatever their society and culture teaches them. We often assume that it takes parents actively teaching their kids for them to be racist. The truth is that unless parents actively teach kids not to be racists, they will be," said Jennifer Richeson, a Yale University social psychologist. "This is not the product of some deep-seated, evil heart that is cultivated. It comes from the environment, the air all around us."). Are the dynamics similar to what we saw in the late nineteenth century? Are they different?[7]

In the next unit, we consider other forms of historical discrimination against Asian Americans, including acts of violence and state legislation intended to drive Asian Americans back to the Far East.

7. *See also, e.g.*, Maureen A. Craig et al., *Racial and Political Dynamics of an Approaching "Majority-Minority in the United States*, Annals of American Academy, XX, at 3–4 (2018) ("exposure to these anticipated changes [increasing racial and ethnic diversity] results in increased feelings of anxiety and negative affect among white Americans"; "cultural threats in response to the declining white majority also engender racially exclusionary sentiments"); Gerard Kleinpenning and Louk Hagendoorn, *Forms of Racism and the Cumulative Dimension of Ethnic Attitudes*, 56 Soc. Psych. Q. 21, 22 (1993) ("racism as a philosophy [has] two important components: a belief in the innate quality of interethnic differences and a belief in the superiority of one's own race").

UNIT TWO

Historical Discrimination

In Unit One, we considered the immigration of Asians to the United States, and specifically their arrival, subsequent exclusion, and ability to be and become citizens of this country. We turn next to the treatment of the early Asian Americans. As we will see, the immigration and naturalization laws were not the only means by which the states and the federal government discriminated against Asian Americans.

Asians began immigrating to the United States in significant numbers in the mid-nineteenth century, when the Gold Rush drew the Chinese to California. They quickly became a source of cheap labor, generating resentment on the part of organized labor in particular. Politicians capitalized on anti-Asian sentiment, and the press fanned the flames by publishing anti-Asian stories and editorials.[1]

In 1851, John Bigler was elected the third Governor of the new state of California and he was the first to serve two terms. But he won his first election by fewer than 500 votes, and he faced a tough battle for reelection in 1853. He seized on "the specter of Chinese coolies" and used "anticoolieism" as a racist trope and political tool to win

1. *See generally* Charles J. McClain, *In Search of Equality: The Chinese Struggle against Discrimination in Nineteenth-Century America* 9–13 (1994); Erika Lee, *The Making of Asian America: A History* 29–33, 59–108 (2015); Lucy E. Salyer, *Laws as Harsh as Tigers: Chinese Immigrants and the Shaping of Modern Immigration Law* 7–17 (1995).

Figure II.1 ***The Yellow Terror in All His Glory*. Editorial Cartoon (1889).**

reelection. Mae Ngai, *The Chinese Question: The Gold Rushes and Global Politics* 79–87 (2021). In April 1852, Bigler delivered a message to the state legislature, urging control of Chinese immigration:

> The subject which I deem it my duty to present for your consideration . . . is the present wholesale importation into this country of immigrants from the Asiatic quarter of the globe. . . . [T]o enhance the prosperity and to preserve the tranquility of the State, measures must be adopted to check this tide of Asiatic immigration, and to prevent the exportation by them of the precious metals which they dig up from our soil without charge, and without assuming any of the obligations imposed upon citizens. I allude, particularly, to a class of Asiatics known as "Coolies."
>
> Under the impulse of gold, with its talismanic powers, vast numbers of the Chinese are immigrating hither, not, however, to avail themselves of the blessings of a free Government. They do not seek our land as "the asylum for the oppressed of all nations." They have no desire to become American citizens. They come instead to acquire a certain amount of the precious metals, and then to return to their native country.[2]

In May 1852, the California Legislature passed a law—the Foreign Miners' License Tax—imposing a licensing tax on foreign miners. The law was aimed primarily at the

---

2. Gov. John Bigler, *Message on Chinese Immigration* (April 23, 1852), *available at* http://global.oup.com/us/companion.websites/fdscontent/uscompanion/us/static/companion.websites/9780199338863/whittington_updata/ch_5_bigler_message_on_chinese_immigration.pdf.

Chinese. McClain, at 10–13. Other taxes and other discriminatory laws followed. In 1862, the California state legislature imposed a "Chinese Police Tax" with the passage of a law titled "An Act to protect Free White Labor against competition with Chinese Coolie Labor, and to Discourage the Immigration of the Chinese into the State of California." *See Lin Sing v. Washburn*, 20 Cal. 534 (1862). The act levied a tax of $2.50 per month on all Chinese residing in the state, except for those operating businesses or those with mining licenses, and those in the production of sugar, rice, coffee, or tea. The California Supreme Court struck down the law, holding that it violated the U.S. Constitution because the power to regulate foreign commerce belonged to the federal government and not to the states. 20 Cal. at 564–65, 580.

In the aftermath of *Lin Sing*, the City of San Francisco passed ordinances imposing restrictions such as minimum space requirements in housing and limits on the length of hair for men who were in prison. Other laws followed, regulating, for example, the operation of laundries, owning or farming land, and practicing law. While the laws (or at least some of them) were neutral on their face, they were directed at the Chinese. The haircut ordinance, for instance, was aimed at Chinese men, most of whom kept a long queue of hair as was required of Chinese subjects of the Qing dynasty.

Why the hostility? The first arrivals of Chinese in California were greeted warmly; they were treated as a curiosity and were seen to be hard workers. McClain, at 9. But that changed quickly. An observer remarked in 1898:

> As a class, [the Chinese] were harmless, peaceful and exceedingly industrious; but, as they were remarkably economical and spent little or none of their earnings except for the necessities of life and this chiefly to merchants of their own nationality, they soon began to provoke the prejudice and ill-will of those who could not see any value in their labor to the country.

McClain, at 9–10 (quoting Thomas Hittell, *History of California* 4:99 (1898)). In other words, "they worked too hard (often for less pay than others were willing to accept), saved too much, and spent too little." McClain, at 10. Of course, there was an element of racism—the Chinese looked different and behaved in unfamiliar ways, and, consequently, the conventional view was that they could not be assimilated into American society at large.[3]

The Chinese did not sit back quietly, and they were surprisingly litigious. They pooled funds to pay for political and legal representation. As early as 1860, Chinese laborers in California sought to retain a lobbyist to oppose anti-Chinese legislation. And with each new discriminatory law, they filed lawsuits. Indeed, between 1880 and

---

3. Lee, *The Making of Asian America,* at 90 ("Americans were first introduced to the Chinese through reports from traders, diplomats, and missionaries in China. Their portrayals of Chinese as heathen, crafty, and dishonest 'marginal members of the human race' quickly set Chinese apart. At first seen as exotic curiosities from a distant land, Chinese immigrants came to be viewed as threats, especially as their numbers increased throughout the Gold Rush period and other changes in the United States helped shape ideas about race and what it meant to be American.").

1900, Chinese litigants brought some 20 appeals to the Supreme Court. McClain, at 3. They formed family and trade associations that helped finance the litigations.

After the Chinese Exclusion Act was passed in 1882, the number of Chinese entering the United States dropped significantly.[4] As the number of Chinese decreased, the number of Japanese in the United States increased. When the Japanese government permitted its citizens to emigrate for the first time in 1880, many headed to America. While only a few hundred Japanese immigrants entered before the 1880s, by 1910 the number had grown to more than 152,000 and by 1920 to more than 220,000. *See* Hing, at 53–54 & Table 4; *see also* Dep't of Commerce, Bureau of Census, *Chinese and Japanese in the United States—1910*, table 6 (1914), *available at* https://www2.census.gov/ prod2/decennial/documents/03322287no71-80ch6.pdf. The number of Japanese in the United States was so alarming to U.S. leaders that President Roosevelt negotiated a "Gentlemen's Agreement" in 1907 with the Japanese foreign minister to impose voluntary restrictions on Japanese coming to America (including Koreans—Korea became a Japanese protectorate in 1905 and was formally annexed by Japan in 1910). The Agreement diminished the number of Japanese emigrants, but many still made the journey through the territory of Hawaii, from which many eventually continued to the West Coast for economic opportunities. Early in the twentieth century, Japanese immigrants became one of California's major sources of agricultural labor. The Japanese soon encountered the same resentment previously directed toward the Chinese. *See generally* Hing, at 53–60; Erika Lee, *At America's Gates: Chinese Immigration During the Exclusion Area, 1882–1943* 246 (2003); Eric K. Yamamoto et al., *Race, Rights and Reparation: Law and the Japanese American Internment* 24–27 (2013).

Historical discrimination against Asian Americans took many forms. We consider, in Chapter 4, early violence and expulsions and, in Chapter 5, state restrictions with respect to (1) pigtails, (2) laundries, (3) the bubonic plague, (4) testimony, (5) marriage, (6) education, (7) the practice of law, and (8) economic opportunities, including the ownership of land.

4. While 39,000 Chinese entered the United States in 1882, the number dropped to 279 in 1884 and only 10 in 1888. Bill Ong Hing, *Making and Remaking Asian America Through Immigration Policy, 1850–1990* 47 (1993). The Chinese population in the United States in 1880 was 105,465; by 1920 it had dropped to 85,202. Hing, at 48 & Table 3.

Chapter 4
Early Violence and Expulsions

The Chinese at first and eventually other Asian Americans were subjected to repeated episodes of mob violence in the nineteenth and early twentieth centuries. There were also expulsions of entire Asian-American populations from numerous communities across the country. In 1885 and 1886, at least 168 communities in the West drove out all their Chinese residents. When juxtaposed with the Exclusion Acts of increasing severity, it seems that there was widespread sentiment in the United States to drive out Chinese laborers in communities in which they were present in numbers. *See* Beth Lew-Williams, *The Chinese Must Go: Violence, Exclusion, and the Making of the Alien in America* 1 (2018). As we summarize some of the key episodes, consider why the mob violence occurred and the response or non-response of local and state authorities in the states, as well as the federal authorities when the violence occurred in federal territories. *See generally* Denny Chin and Kathy Hirata Chin, *"Kung Flu": A History of Hostility and Violence Against Asian Americans*, 90 Fordham L. Rev. 1889 (2022).

1. Los Angeles—1871

One of the earliest large-scale incidents of violence against Asians took place in Los Angeles on October 24, 1871. The Los Angeles riots were sparked by the death of a White man caught in the crossfire during a gunfight between rival Chinese gangs in a particularly notorious part of the city filled with bars, gambling dens, and bordellos. A local mob systematically rounded up and attacked every Chinese male it could find in the area. At least 15 Chinese males were tortured and hanged; one was a 15-year-old who had arrived from China only a week earlier. Several others were fatally shot, bringing the total killed to at least 18. *See* Scott Zesch, *The Chinatown War: Chinese Los Angeles and the Massacre of 1871* 136–44, 153 (2012); *Many Others Wounded and Killed—In All Twenty-one Dead*, Daily Alta California, Oct. 26, 1871. More recently, a reporter examined the historical record of the massacre and noted that the violence was indiscriminate, with respect to both perpetrators and victims:

> Of all the Chinese in Los Angeles, Dr. Gene Tong was probably the most eminent and beloved among both his countrymen and Americans. He could have made much more money hanging his shingle in the American

"HOODLUMS" PELTING CHINESE EMIGRANTS ON THEIR ARRIVAL AT SAN FRANCISCO.

Figure 4.1 ***The Chinese Massacre of 1871*****. Engraving by George Augustus Sala (1885).**

part of town. But Tong stayed in the Alley, dispensing both traditional and modern cures from a small shop in the decrepit Coronel Building.

As Tong was dragged along the street, he tried to strike a bargain with his captors. He could pay a ransom, he said. He had $3,000 in gold in his shop. He had a diamond wedding ring. They could have it all.

Instead of negotiating, one of his captors shot him in the mouth to silence him. Then they hanged him, first cutting off his finger to steal the ring.

The next morning, the citizens of Los Angeles filed past the town's jail building to view the bodies of the dead laid out in double rows. There were 17. It was the largest mass lynching in American history.

When word of the massacre reached the outside world, the reaction was universal horror. In the East, citizens asked what sorts of ghouls had taken up residence on the West Coast. Turning its gaze from heathen lands, the Methodist Conference started raising funds for missionary work in Los Angeles.

Frontier apologists blamed the massacre on the "dregs" of California society, an assortment of thugs and highwaymen who slouched into town every fall from the mines in the north and the lawless Mexican territory to the south.

> "American hoodlum and Mexican greaser, Irish tramp and French communist all joined to murder and dispatch the foe," wrote poet and historian A.J. Wilson.
>
> The truth was different. While the looting and murder were carried out mostly by hoodlums, the deeds required the tacit approval and occasional intervention of the town's elite. What's more, the vast majority of those responsible could not have escaped punishment without a legal cover-up.[1]

Twenty-five indictments were returned, but only 10 men went to trial. The prosecutors faced significant hurdles. Given the frenzied nature of the rioting, it was difficult to determine who did what to whom. *See* Zesch, at 188. Moreover, a California statute prohibited Chinese witnesses from testifying against any White person; the statute was upheld in 1854 when the California Supreme Court decided in *People v. Hall* that Chinese testimony was inadmissible against a "free white citizen" charged with murdering a Chinese victim. *People v. Hall*, 4 Cal. 399 (1854). *See* Chapter 5 *infra*.

In the face of these difficulties, the prosecutors focused on the murder of the well-regarded Dr. Tong. The first defendant to go to trial was Curley Crenshaw, a 22-year-old man of Irish descent, a drifter known to have a "reputation of the worst sort." Zesch, at 193–94; *see also* Daily Alta California, Feb. 19, 1871. He was charged as an accessory to the murder of Dr. Tong. A bystander testified that Crenshaw told him he had "killed three Chinamen." Zesch, at 193–94; *see also* Daily Alta California, Feb. 19, 1871.

The jury found Crenshaw guilty of manslaughter. In a second trial, nine other rioters were tried together as accessories to the murder of Dr. Tong. On March 27, 1872, the jury found two defendants not guilty, but convicted the remaining seven defendants of manslaughter. Zesch, at 195.

Crenshaw was sentenced to three years' imprisonment and the other seven defendants were given sentences ranging from two to six years. Zesch, at 201–02. On appeal, however, the California Supreme Court reversed the convictions, concluding in a terse decision issued May 21, 1873, as follows:

> The indictment in this case is fatally defective in that it fails to allege that Chee Long Tong [Dr. Tong] was murdered. The charge attempted against the defendants is that they were accessories before the fact to the crime of murder. It is alleged that the defendants did stand by, aid, abet, assist, advise, counsel, and encourage one John Doe and one Richard Roe to feloniously, unlawfully, willfully, deliberately, premeditatedly, and of their malice aforethought, one Chee Long Tong to kill and murder. Admitting that the defendants did all these things, still it does not follow by necessary legal

1. John Johnson, Jr., *How Los Angeles Covered Up the Massacre of 17 Chinese*, LA Weekly, March 10, 2011, http://www.laweekly.com/news/how-los-angeles-covered-up-the-massacre-of-17-chinese-2169478.

Figure 4.2 ***The anti-Chinese riot in Denver, Colorado, on October 31st. Chinese being beaten and property destroyed by large mob, 1880.*** **Library of Congress.**

conclusion that after all any person was actually murdered. It is the settled rule of criminal pleading that in an indictment against a person intended to be charged as an accessory before the fact in the crime of murder, every allegation is necessary which would be necessary had the indictment been against the principal felons themselves.

Unless, therefore, it can be maintained that an indictment against a principal for the crime of murder would be sufficient, even though it did not appear that the death of the party assaulted had ensued, it is difficult to see how the indictment here is to be sustained. The authorities are uniform that in either case it is indispensable that it appear by the indictment that death has resulted from the assault and wounding charged.

Judgment reversed and remittitur to issue forthwith.

People v. Crenshaw, 46 Cal. 65, 65–66 (1873) (*per curiam*). In summary, the California court held that because there was no specific allegation that Dr. Tong was murdered, the indictment was "fatally defective" and the convictions ought to be reversed. As formalistic as it seems, ensuring that indictments specifically plead each fact serves an important notice-giving function to criminal defendants. However, the defendants were not retried, nor were any charges brought with respect to any of the other victims. As a consequence, no one was held accountable for the murder of 18 (or more) Chinese Americans. *See also Fong Yuen Ling v. Mayor & Common Council of City of Los Angeles*, 47 Cal. 531 (1874) (upholding jury verdict in favor of City of Los Angeles and rejecting claims of Chinese businesses for property damaged during riots caused by October 1871 rioting).

2. San Francisco—1877

A severe economic depression starting in 1873 sparked westward migration within the United States. California, along with the Pacific states of Oregon and Washington, and the newly emerging Rocky Mountain metropolis of Denver were the principal destinations. The Western states, however, were not immune from the effects of the financial and economic dislocations experienced in the Eastern states.

By 1877, the City of San Francisco was wracked by severe unemployment and resultant unrest. The Workingmen's Party of the United States, a new pro-labor organization (which later became the Socialist Labor Party of America), called a meeting on July 23, 1877, on sandlots near the newly constructed San Francisco City Hall. The meeting, which was attended by about 8,000 people, started peaceably enough, without explicit mention of Chinese immigrants. But then the tone of the meeting changed:

> Everything was orderly until an anti-coolie procession pushed its way into the audience and insisted that the speakers say something about the Chinese. This was refused and thereupon the crowd which had gathered on the outskirts of the meeting attacked a passing Chinaman and started the cry, "On to Chinatown.'"[2]

Mass violence ensued. Two days of rioting resulted in four Chinese deaths and more than $100,000 of property damage. Twenty Chinese-owned laundries were burned down; the Chinese Methodist Mission's windows were smashed by rocks. It took the combined efforts of the police, state militia, and several hundred members of a citizens' "vigilance committee" also known as the "Pick Handle Brigade"—each

2. Selig Perlman, *The Anti-Chinese Agitation in California*, in John R. Commons et al., 2 *History of Labour in the United States* 253 (1918).

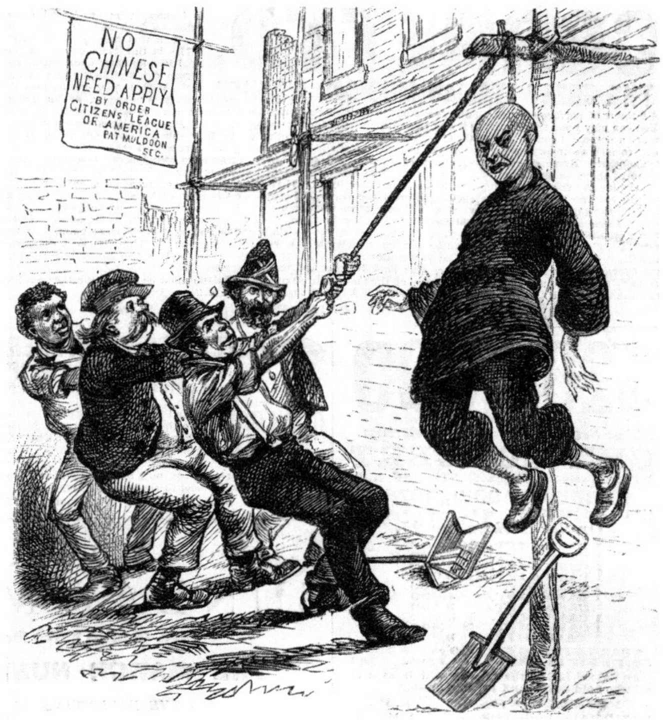

Figure 4.3 *The Argument of Nationality*. Lithograph from the 1880s.

Figure 4.4 *Chinese? No! No! No!* Handbill, Tacoma, WA, July 23, 1892. Washington State Historical Society, Tacoma.

member was armed with a hickory pickaxe handle—to restore peace. Denis Kearney, an Irish immigrant, was mobilized to political consciousness by his participation in the Brigade. He sought entry into the national Workingmen's Party but was denied, and so started a new organization, the Workingmen's Trade and Labor Union of San Francisco. This Union, which changed its name to the Workingmen's Party of California in October 1877 with Kearney as president, coined the slogan "The Chinaman Must Go!" and played a leading role in agitating for state and federal anti-Chinese legislation. Indeed, Winfield Scott Hancock, the Democratic candidate for President in the 1880 election, campaigned on a promise to pass Chinese exclusion legislation. These efforts eventually succeeded, with the passage of the Chinese Exclusion Act of 1882.

3. Eureka, California—1885

The passage of the Chinese Exclusion laws did not end violence against Chinese who were already in the United States. Indeed, the 1880s were the apex of anti-Chinese violence, mostly in the West but also in New Orleans, which, owing to its importance as a commercial center, had a large and diverse population. Chinese communities were attacked and millions of dollars in property damage was sustained in Alaska, California, Colorado, Oregon, South Dakota, and other states and territories.

On February 5, 1885, after a White man was killed in the crossfire between two Chinese men (an incident eerily similar to the start of the Los Angeles riots 14 years earlier), violence erupted in the city of Eureka, California. All the Chinese residents—300 or more—were expelled, as they were put on two steamships and taken to San Francisco. Eventually, 52 former residents of Eureka's Chinatown sued the city for damages. The claims were dismissed on the theory that the Chinese lacked standing because they had never been landowners. The tactics employed became known as the "Eureka Plan," and were replicated in other communities in the West as a "nonviolent" way to rid a community of unwanted individuals.[3] Still, the lawsuit served a purpose, as it sent a message that the Chinese were not going to go away easily. Moreover, the lawsuit showed a great deal of ingenuity, as the Chinese brought what was essentially a collective action to impose liability on a municipality for failing to control a mob long before such lawsuits became popular.

---

3. *See* Keith Easthouse, *The Chinese Expulsion: Looking Back on a Dark Episode*, North Coast Weekly Journal, 2003, *available at* https://www.northcoastjournal.com/022703/ cover0227.html; Hector Alejandro Arzate, *Chinese Immigrants Were Forced Out of Eureka in 1885—Here's How Locals Are Making That History Known*, KQED (Oct. 15, 2021), https://www.kqed.org/news/11891987/chinese-immigrants-were-forced-out-of-eureka-in-1885-heres-how-locals-are-making-that-history-known.

Figure 4.5 ***The massacre of the Chinese at Rock Springs, Wyoming*****. Drawn by T. de Thulstrup from photographs by Lieutenant C.A. Booth, Seventh United States Infantry. Library of Congress.**

4. Rock Springs, Wyoming Territory—1885

The deadliest attack against Chinese workers took place at the Rock Springs mines in the Wyoming Territory. The Union Pacific Railroad had been employing Chinese laborers at its mines there since 1875, when it used them to break a strike of White miners. On September 2, 1885, 150 armed White men launched a full-scale attack on the Chinese community, resulting in 28 deaths, 15 wounded, and property damage of nearly $150,000. *See generally Whites Massacre Chinese in Wyoming Territory*, History.com (2009), *available at* http://www.history.com/this-day-in-history/whites-massacre-chinese-in-wyoming-territory; Daryl Worthington, *The Rock Springs Massacre*, New Historian, Sept. 1, 2015, *available at* http://www.newhistorian.com/the-rock-springs-massacre/4733/.

The governor of the Wyoming Territory, Francis Warren, telegraphed U.S. President Grover Cleveland, requesting federal troops to quell the violence. There were reports that the several hundred surviving Chinese, who had fled the violence, had regrouped nearby and had armed themselves to exact revenge. Cleveland sent the requested federal troops under orders to prevent disruption to the U.S. mail. Thus, the troop did not have explicit orders to protect the Chinese, who were entitled to safety of their persons and property under the Burlingame Treaty of 1868.

Chinese diplomatic pressure invoking the Treaty, seconded by the State Department, prompted Cleveland to revise his orders to include protection of the Chinese "at points of threatened or actual violence." A battalion of U.S. army infantry escorted the surviving Chinese back into Rock Springs, setting a precedent for the deployment of federal troops to protect the Chinese from violence in the Wyoming Territory. No White miner complicit in the murders was tried or punished. The United States paid $150,000 to the Chinese government as compensation, although it is unclear whether these amounts were paid out to individual Chinese victims. Federal troops stayed in the area for another 14 years after the massacre to keep the peace.

5. Seattle, Washington—1886

The next flashpoint in the wave of anti-Chinese violence occurred in Seattle, Washington (then a U.S. territory like Wyoming), from February 6–9, 1886.[4] Angry White "committees" affiliated with the Seattle chapter of the Knights of Labor, a pro-labor group, mobilized to expel all Chinese immigrants from the city. These immigrants (about 3,000) had taken urban labor jobs (in addition to mining and railroad construction) at pay, hours, and conditions that White workers, many represented by unions, were simply unwilling to accept. Furthermore, these laborers were remitting a significant part of their earnings back to China. White workers viewed the Chinese as "semi-slaves" of the big companies, like the railroads.

On the morning of February 7, multiple Knights of Labor "committees" forced their way into Chinese homes in Seattle's Chinatown and ordered the terrified inhabitants to pack and book passage on the steamship *Queen of the Pacific*, which was scheduled to sail at 1:00 p.m. The committees arranged wagons to pick up bags and haul them to the steamship's slip. About 350 Chinese were rounded up and led to the port. Some of the Chinese beseeched the local sheriff, John McGraw, to intercede. Undermanned and perhaps sympathetic to the Knights of Labor, McGraw simply ordered his deputies to prevent violence to the hapless Chinese on their forced march to the pier. When the mob ignored the territorial governor's order to disperse, he ordered the deployment of the territorial militia and wired President Cleveland for federal troops.

4. *See generally* Phil Dougherty, *Mobs Forcibly Expel Most of Seattle's Chinese Residents Beginning on February 7, 1886*, History Link (Nov. 17, 2013), *available at* http://www.historylink.org/File/2745; *Anti-Chinese Riot in Seattle*, Harper's Weekly, Mar. 6, 1888, *available at* http://immigrants.harpweek.com/ChineseAmericans/Items/ Item095L.htm; Lenore Ziontz, *The Anti-Chinese Riots in Seattle*, 6 Pacific Nw. Forum 28 (1981), *available at* http://www.narhist.ewu.edu/pnf/articles/s1/vi-2/anti-chinese/anti-chinese.html; Doug Chin, *Seattle's Anti-Chinese Riot—February 7, 1886: The Day Seattle Imploded*, Int'l Exam'r, Feb. 7, 2016, https://iexaminer.org/seattles-anti-chinese-race-riotfebruary-7-1886-the-day-seattle-imploded/ [https://perma.cc/Z4M3-5YVU].

Figure 4.6 ***The Seattle Anti-Chinese Riot. West Shore Magazine*** **(1886). Oregon Historical Society.**

The rioters, however, were significantly short of the funds needed to book passage for all 350 Chinese back to China—only 97 fares were paid. The Chief Justice for the Washington Territory, Roger Greene, thereupon received a petition from an aggrieved Chinese businessman for help and issued a writ of habeas corpus to the captain of the *Queen* requiring him to produce the 97 Chinese held "in custody" before the court on the next morning, February 8. At midnight, Sheriff McGraw, backed by the territorial militia, blocked attempts by the mob to put the remaining 253 Chinese without passage on a train to Tacoma.

The next morning, McGraw disembarked the 97 Chinese who had spent the night on the *Queen of the Pacific* and brought them before Justice Greene as directed. When mobs tried to block the way, eight Knights of Labor leaders were arrested. In court, Greene instructed the Chinese brought before him that they had a legal right to remain in the city and promised them federal protection if they chose to stay. Only 16 of the group stayed; the other 81 returned to the ship. By this time, the Knights of

Labor had collected sufficient funds to book passages for 115 more Chinese aboard the *Queen*. It was agreed that the 150 other Chinese would be shipped aboard the next steamship bound for China once funding was arranged.

The mobs, however, attacked McGraw, his deputies, and the state militia as they sought to return the 150 Chinese back to their homes. In the scuffle that ensued, shots were fired, resulting in serious injury to two militia members and three rioters. Governor Squire declared martial law because of the crisis, believing McGraw and his deputies and the militia incapable of keeping the peace. But when U.S. Army elements arrived in Seattle two days later, on February 10, the situation had already calmed down, and Squire lifted martial law two weeks later on February 23, 1886. Most of the federal troops were then withdrawn; but two army companies remained in Seattle for four months after the riots.

As with the Rock Spring massacre, the Chinese government protested and argued treaty violations to the U.S. State Department. Congress ended up appropriating $276,619.15 to the Chinese government for all damage done to Chinese nationals during this period (including not only the Seattle riot but other incidents), but, again, the individual victims themselves were not directly compensated. And, in a troubling pattern, although 13 men were tried in court, no one was convicted.

Many of the more than 2,000 Chinese in Seattle voluntarily decided to repatriate to China in the wake of the riots. The Chinese government commissioned fact-finding enquiries and tried to secure compensation for destroyed property. But the U.S. government pleaded the limitation of federalism with respect to violence in the states, and even when the federal government had jurisdiction as in the territories of Wyoming and Washington, federal officials were loath to declare martial law and vigorously bring offenders to justice. In fact, some embittered Chinese officials thought that the best way to prevent future harm to Chinese was to stop emigration altogether, just as the Chinese Exclusion Acts were designed to do.

6. Hells Canyon, Oregon—1887

In terms of death toll, the bloodiest violence against Chinese in this period took place in Hells Canyon, Oregon, beginning on May 25, 1887. A gang of seven horse thieves shot and killed 10 to 13 Chinese miners (the precise number is unclear). The next day, the gang killed eight more Chinese miners who had arrived in the camp by boat. The gang then proceeded to a second camp nearby, where they killed 13 more. The horse thieves thus killed at least 31 and as many as 34 Chinese miners, stole their gold, burned their camps, and threw their bodies into the Snake River.

The authorities in Wallowa County began a public investigation in fall 1887 after the discovery of the decomposed bodies of several of the victims in Hells Canyon.

Figure 4.7 *Hobson's Choice—You Can Go, or Stay. Puck Magazine* (1886).

The horse thieves were eventually charged with murder, but three fled and were never caught. One turned state's evidence and was not charged. In a two-day trial that concluded on September 1, 1888, the other three were found not guilty.[5]

In 2005, the site was renamed Chinese Massacre Cove, and in 2012 a memorial was installed. *See Chinese Massacre Memorial Planned in Hells Canyon in June*, Northwest Asian Weekly, Nov. 29, 2011, http://nwasianweekly.com/2011/11/chinese-massacre-memorial-planned-in-hells-canyon-in-june.

5. Associated Press, *Files Found in Oregon Detail Massacre of Chinese*, N.Y. Times, Aug. 20, 1995; R. Gregory Nokes, *"A Most Daring Outrage": Murders at Chinese Massacre Cove, 1887*, History Cooperative, https://historycooperative.org/journal/a-most-daring-outrage-murders-at-chinese-massacre-cove-1887/; R. Gregory Nokes, *A Most Daring Outrage: Murders at Massacre Cove, 1887*, Oregon History Quarterly, Jan. 28, 2006, *available at* https://web.archive.org/web/20070128140548/http://www.historycooperative.org/journals/ohq/107.3/nokes.html. *See also* R. Gregory Nokes, *Massacred for Gold: The Chinese in Hells Canyon* (2009); Dana Hand, *Deep Creek* (2010) (novel inspired by events at Hells Canyon).

7. Bellingham, Washington—1907

On September 4, 1907, in Bellingham, Washington, a mob of 500 White men, including members of the Asiatic Exclusion League, attacked the homes of South Asian Indians, many of whom worked at local lumber mills. Although called Hindus by the media in the vernacular of the day, they were mostly Sikhs. The cry "Drive out the Hindus" was heard throughout the city. *See Mob Drives Out Hindus*, N.Y. Times, Sept. 6, 1907, at 1. The mob threw the Sikh workers into the streets, beat them, and stole their valuables. The local police, likely in tacit cooperation with the mobs, herded the Indian immigrants into City Hall, ostensibly for their own safety. More than 100 Indians left Washington state the next day for British Columbia; six Indians were hospitalized; 400 were held in the Bellingham Jail under "protective custody." Five men were arrested for the rioting, but they were released and in the end no one was prosecuted. *See* David Cahn, *The 1907 Bellingham Riots in Historical Context*, Seattle C.R. & Lab. Hist. Project, https://depts.washington.edu/civilr/bham_history.htm.

The local newspapers weighed in on the riots. While they did not approve of the violence, they expressed satisfaction with the end result of expulsion.[6] There were editorials in, for example, the *Bellingham Herald* and the *Seattle Morning Times*:

> **BELLINGHAM HERALD**: The Hindu is not a good citizen. . . . It would require centuries to assimilate him, and this country need not take the trouble. Our racial burdens are already heavy enough to bear.[7]
>
> **MORNING TIMES:** [The matter is] not a question of race, but of wages; not a question of men, but modes of life; not a matter of nations, but of habits of life. . . . When men who require meat to eat and real beds to sleep in are ousted from their employment to make room for vegetarians who can find the bliss of sleep in some filthy corner, it is rather difficult to say at what limit indignation ceases to be righteous.[8]

On September 4, 2007, 100 years later, local officials in Whatcom County and the City of Bellingham proclaimed a "Day of Healing and Reconciliation" to acknowledge the "anti-Sikh and anti-East Indian riots."[9]

---

6. *See id.*
7. *Id.* (quoting *Bellingham Herald*).
8. Cahn, *supra* note 128 (quoting Gerald N. Hallberg, *Bellingham, Washington's Anti-Hindu Riot*, Nw. Mosaics 150–51 (1973) (quoting *Seattle Morning Times*), https://depts.washington.edu/civilr/bham_history.htm.
9. Joint Proclamation, dated Aug. 14, 2007, *available at* www.cob.org/Documents/ articles/day-of-healing-proclamation.pdf. *See generally* Univ. of Washington, *1907 Bellingham Riots*, Seattle Civil Rights & Labor History Project, *available at* depts.washington.edu/civilr/bham_intro.htm. The Bellingham riots were part of a series of riots that became known as "the 1907 Pacific Coast Race Riots." These extended beyond the United States. On September 7, 1907, a crowd of approximately 10,000

8. Watsonville, California—1930

For five days beginning on January 19, 1930, mobs of White people—at times as many as 500—attacked Filipino men in and around Watsonville, California. The rioting was motivated by fears that Filipino laborers were bringing down wages and mixing with White women. A few days earlier, on January 10, 1930, D.W. Rohrbach, a justice of the peace and a leader of the Northern Monterey County Chamber of Commerce, had issued a resolution condemning the Filipinos:

> For a wage that a white man cannot exist on, the Filipinos will take the job and, through their clannish, low standard mode of housing and feeding, practiced among them, will soon be well clothed, and strutting about like a peacock and endeavoring to attract the eyes of the young American and Mexican girls. Fifteen Filipinos will live in a room or two, sleeping on the floor and contenting themselves with squatting on the floors and eating fish and rice. The same group will form a club and buy a partnership in a classy automobile and attired like Solomon in all his glory, will roll along the highways. Marriages among white and Filipinos soon will be common, and if the present state of affairs continues there will be 40,000 half-breeds in the State of California before 10 years have passed. We do not advocate violence but we do feel that the United States should give the Filipinos their liberty and send those unwelcome inhabitants from our shores so that the whites who have inherited this country for themselves and their offspring, might live.[10]

A dance hall where Filipino men could dance with White women was burned down—ostensibly to "rescue" the women. Dozens of Filipino farmhands were injured and 22-year-old Fermin Tobera was killed as he slept in a bunkhouse at a nearby farm. No one was arrested for the murder of Tobera, but eight young men eventually pleaded guilty to rioting—they were sentenced to probation or 30 days in jail.[11]

---

people gathered in Vancouver to support an anti-Asian parade, and the group marched into Chinese and Japanese communities, attacking buildings occupied by Chinese and Japanese immigrants. *See* Erika Lee, *Hemispheric Orientalism and the 1907 Pacific Race Riots*, 33 Amerasia J. 19 (2019), *available at* https://www.tandfonline.com /doi/abs/10.17953/amer.33.2.y263745731125524?journalCode=ramj20.

10. *See* Estella Habal, *Radical Violence in the Fields: Anti-Filipino Riot in Watsonville* at 2 (San Francisco St. Univ. 1991) (pdf) (quoting Rohrbach's statement as published in *Evening Pajaronian*, Jan. 11, 1930).

11. Michael P. Showalter, *The Watsonville Anti-Filipino Riot of 1930: A Reconsideration of Fermin Tobera's Murder*, 71 S. Cal. Q. 341, 345 (1989), *citing People of California v. Edward Fry, et al.*, at 38–39, 40–41; Equal Justice Initiative, *White Mobs Attack Filipino Farmworkers in Watsonville, California*, https://calendar.eji.org/racial-injustice/jan/19.

Notes

1. There were perhaps 100,000 persons of Asian descent in the United States in the 1880s when these historical acts of mob violence occurred—less than 0.2 % of the total population of the country. Why, given these small numbers, do you think that there was such an epidemic of anti-Chinese and other anti-Asian mob violence? Was there a genuine fear that hordes of Asians would overrun the country? Do you think the extent and nature of the violence differed appreciably as compared to violence against other groups (such as Irish Catholic immigrants in the nineteenth century) over the years? Was the violence against the Chinese and other early Asian arrivals different?

2. Political theorists since Thomas Hobbes have justified government to save human beings from the state of nature where violence is endemic as human beings resort to self-help. But too often in history, as with Black Americans in the Jim Crow South, Jews in Nazi Germany, and Asian Americans in the late nineteenth and early twentieth centuries, the relevant governments did not intervene forcefully to prevent or punish violence directed at minority groups. But is it reasonable to expect action by governments in the face of society-wide bias or prejudice against the targeted minority groups? Is there a meaningful line between government complicity and inaction?

3. The Chinese government filed diplomatic protests with the U.S. State Department, especially toward the end of the nineteenth century as it became more experienced in the ways of the Western world order. The State Department, concerned about the safety of U.S. citizens in China (mostly missionaries and merchants), particularly during the time of the Boxer rebellion, made efforts but did not try hard, pleading the affirmative defense of federalism. Congress provided some compensation, as we saw. What explains what the national government did and did not do? How about the territorial governments, where the federal government had broader authority?

4. One impediment to bringing the assailants to justice was the difficulty of proof, particularly given the chaotic circumstances of the rioting and the absence of modern technology such as video and cell phone cameras. Moreover, as we will discuss in the next chapter, at one point there were laws barring Chinese witnesses from testifying against Whites. Consider the riots and massacres discussed above and how difficult it was to obtain a conviction if the only available witnesses were Chinese.

5. We will return to the topic of violence against Asians in America in Unit 4, where we will consider the iconic Vincent Chin case and violence against Asian Americans in a more contemporary context. As we do, keep in mind how modern race-based crimes and the governmental reactions to them have evolved since the historical episodes recounted in this Unit.

Chapter 5
State Regulation

1. The Pigtail Ordinance Case

By 1870, the Chinese population in San Francisco had grown substantially, as many Chinese found it desirable to settle in the city with its greater opportunities for employment and small business enterprise. Not surprisingly, resentment and hostility toward the Chinese grew and San Francisco city officials began passing ordinances targeting the Chinese. One ordinance the city board passed in 1870 prohibited the use of poles to carry laundry and packages on city sidewalks. Ostensibly neutral, it plainly targeted the Chinese practice of carrying such goods on poles. Another ordinance regulated the amount of cubic space (500 cubic feet, e.g., 5 feet width × 10 feet height × 10 feet length) that could be inhabited by one person, which disproportionately impacted overcrowded Chinese-laborer dwellings in Chinatown. When many Chinese went to jail rather than pay the fine for violating the cubic air ordinance, the city passed another ordinance in 1873 regulating the length of hair in prisons. Prisoners with hair that was longer than the prescribed length were to have their hair cut. Ho Ah Kow had his queue cut off while in county jail and sued the sheriff personally for damages in federal court. *See* McClain, at 43–44, 73–76.

Ho Ah Kow v. Nunan

12 F. Cas. 252 (Cir. Ct. D. Cal. 1879)

Field, Circuit Justice:

The plaintiff is a subject of the emperor of China, and the present action is brought to recover damages for his alleged maltreatment by the defendant, a citizen of the state of California and the sheriff of the city and county of San Francisco. The maltreatment consisted in having wantonly and maliciously cut off the queue of the plaintiff, a queue being worn by all Chinamen, and its deprivation being regarded by them as degrading and as entailing future suffering.

It appears that in April, 1876, the legislature of California passed an act "concerning lodging-houses and sleeping apartments within the limits of incorporated cities," declaring, among other things, that any person found sleeping or lodging in a room or an apartment containing less than five hundred cubic feet of space in the clear for each person occupying it, should be deemed guilty of a misdemeanor, and on conviction thereof be punished by a fine of not less than ten or more than fifty dollars, or imprisonment in the county jail, or by both such fine and imprisonment. Sess. Laws 1875–76, p. 759. Under this act the plaintiff, in April 1878, was convicted and sentenced to pay a fine of ten dollars, or in default of such payment to be imprisoned five days in the county jail. Failing to pay the fine, he was imprisoned. The defendant, as sheriff of the city and county, had charge of the jail, and during the imprisonment of the plaintiff cut off his queue, as alleged. The complaint avers that it is the custom of Chinamen to shave the hair from the front of the head and to wear the remainder of it braided into a queue; that the deprivation of the queue is regarded by them as a mark of disgrace, and is attended, according to their religious faith, with misfortune and suffering after death; that the defendant knew of this custom and religious faith of the Chinese, and knew also that the plaintiff venerated the custom and held the faith; yet, in disregard of his rights, inflicted the injury complained of; and that the plaintiff has, in consequence of it, suffered great mental anguish, been disgraced in the eyes of his friends and relatives, and ostracized from association with his countrymen; and that hence he has been damaged to the amount of ten thousand dollars.

Two defenses to the action are set up by the defendant; the second one being a justification of his conduct under an ordinance of the city and county of San Francisco. It is upon the sufficiency of the latter defense that the case is before us. The ordinance

PACIFIC CHIVALRY.
Encouragement to Chinese Immigration.

Figure 5.1 ***Pacific Chivalry*****. Drawing by Thomas Nast,** ***Harper's Weekly*** **(August 7, 1869).**

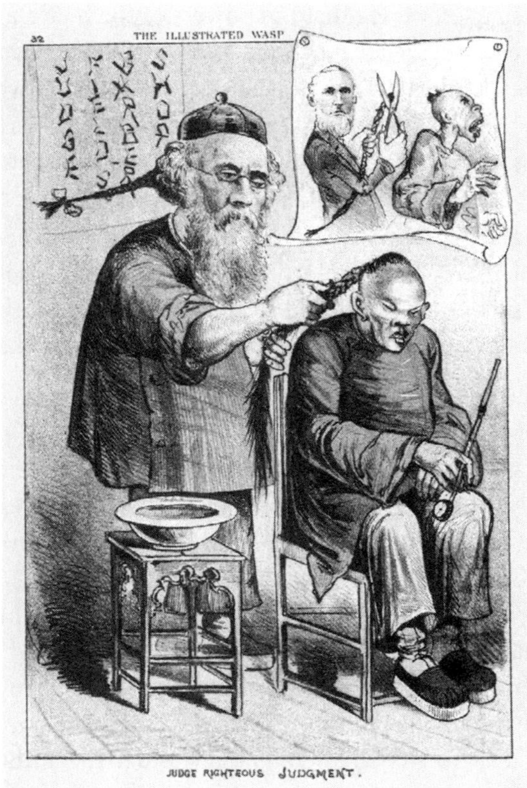

Figure 5.2 ***Judge Righteous Judgment. The Illustrated Wasp*** **(1879–1880). A depiction of Justice Stephen Field—after his ruling in *Ho Ah Kow v. Nunan*—in Chinese garb with a queue, in his "Barber Shop," braiding the hair of a Chinese man. On the wall is a drawing of Sheriff Nunan cutting the queue off another Chinese man.**

referred to was passed on the fourteenth of June 1876, and it declares that every male person imprisoned in the county jail, under the judgment of any court having jurisdiction in criminal cases in the city and county, shall immediately upon his arrival at the jail have the hair of his head "cut or clipped to an uniform length of one inch from the scalp thereof," and it is made the duty of the sheriff to have this provision enforced. Under this ordinance the defendant cut off the queue of the plaintiff.

The validity of this ordinance is denied by the plaintiff on two grounds: 1. That it exceeds the authority of the board of supervisors, the body in which the legislative power of the city and county is vested; and, 2. That it is special legislation imposing a degrading and cruel punishment upon a class of persons who are entitled, alike with all other persons within the jurisdiction of the United States, to the equal protection of the laws. We are of opinion that both these positions are well taken.

The board of supervisors is limited in its authority by the act consolidating the government of the city and county. It can do nothing unless warrant be found for it there, or in a subsequent statute of the state. As with all other municipal bodies, its charter—here the consolidation act—is the source and measure of its powers.

In looking at this charter, we see that the powers of the board and the subjects upon which they are to operate are all specified. The board has no general powers, and its special power to determine the fines, forfeitures and penalties which may be incurred is limited. . . . [W]hen a penalty other than that of fine or forfeiture is imposed, it must, by the terms of the act, be in the form of imprisonment. It can take no other form. . . . . No one, for example, would pretend that the board could for any breach of a municipal regulation or any violation of the consolidation act, declare that a man should be deprived of his right to vote, or to testify, or to sit on a jury, or that he should be punished with stripes, or be ducked in a pond, or be paraded through the streets, or be seated in a pillory, or have his ears cropped or his head shaved.

The cutting off the hair of every male person within an inch of his scalp, on his arrival at the jail, was not intended and cannot be maintained as a measure of discipline or as a sanitary regulation. The act by itself has no tendency to promote discipline, and can only be a measure of health in exceptional cases. Had the ordinance contemplated a mere sanitary regulation it would have been limited to such cases and made applicable to females as well as to males, and to persons awaiting trial as well as to persons under conviction. The close cutting of the hair which is practiced upon inmates of the state penitentiary, like dressing them in striped clothing, is partly to distinguish them from others, and thus prevent their escape and facilitate their recapture. They are measures of precaution, as well as parts of a general system of treatment prescribed by the directors of the penitentiary under the authority of the state, for parties convicted of and imprisoned for felonies. Nothing of the kind is prescribed or would be tolerated with respect to persons confined in a county jail for simple misdemeanors, most of which are not of a very grave character. For the discipline or detention of the plaintiff in this case, who had the option of paying a fine of ten dollars, or of being imprisoned for five days, no such clipping of the hair was required. It was done to add to the severity of his punishment.

But even if the proceeding could be regarded as a measure of discipline or as a sanitary regulation, the conclusion would not help the defendant, for the board of supervisors had no authority to prescribe the discipline to which persons convicted under the laws of the state should be subjected, or to determine what special sanitary regulations should be enforced with respect to their persons. That is a matter which the legislature had not seen fit to entrust to the wisdom and judgment of that body. . . .

The claim, however, put forth that the measure was prescribed as one of health is notoriously a mere pretense. A treatment to which disgrace is attached, and which is not adopted as a means of security against the escape of the prisoner, but merely to aggravate the severity of his confinement, can only be regarded as a punishment additional to that fixed by the sentence. If adopted in consequence of the sentence it is punishment in addition to that imposed by the court; if adopted without regard to the sentence it is wanton cruelty.

In the present case, the plaintiff was not convicted of any breach of a municipal regulation, nor of violating any provision of the consolidation act. The punishment which the supervisors undertook to add to the fine imposed by the court was without semblance of authority. The legislature had not conferred upon them the right to change or add to the punishments which it deemed sufficient for offenses; nor had it bestowed upon them the right to impose in any case a punishment of the character inflicted in this case. They could no more direct that the queue of the plaintiff should be cut off than that the punishments mentioned should be inflicted. Nor could they order the hair of any one, Mongolian or other person, to be clipped within an inch of his scalp. That measure was beyond their power.

The second objection to the ordinance in question is equally conclusive. It is special legislation on the part of the supervisors against a class of persons who, under the constitution and laws of the United States, are entitled to the equal protection of the laws. The ordinance was intended only for the Chinese in San Francisco. This was avowed by the supervisors on its passage, and was so understood by everyone. The ordinance is known in the community as the "Queue Ordinance," being so designated from its purpose to reach the queues of the Chinese, and it is not enforced against any other persons. The reason advanced for its adoption, and now urged for its continuance, is that only the dread of the loss of his queue will induce a Chinaman to pay his fine. That is to say, in order to enforce the payment of a fine imposed upon him, it is necessary that torture should be superadded to imprisonment. Then, it is said, the Chinaman will not accept the alternative, which the law allows, of working out his fine by his imprisonment, and the state or county will be saved the expense of keeping him during the imprisonment. Probably the bastinado, or the knout, or the thumbscrew, or the rack, would accomplish the same end; and no doubt the Chinaman would prefer either of these modes of torture to that which entails upon him disgrace among his countrymen and carries with it the constant dread of misfortune and suffering after death. It is not creditable to the humanity and civilization of our people, much less to their Christianity, that an ordinance of this character was possible.

The class character of this legislation is none the less manifest because of the general terms in which it is expressed. The statements of supervisors in debate on the passage of the ordinance cannot, it is true, be resorted to for the purpose of explaining the meaning of the terms used; but they can be resorted to for the purpose of ascertaining the general object of the legislation proposed, and the mischiefs sought to be remedied. Besides, we cannot shut our eyes to matters of public notoriety and general cognizance. When we take our seats on the bench we are not struck with blindness, and forbidden to know as judges what we see as men; and where an ordinance, though general in its terms, only operates upon a special race, sect or class, it being universally understood that it is to be enforced only against that race, sect or class, we may justly conclude that it was the intention of the body adopting it that it should only have such operation, and treat it accordingly. We may take notice of the limitation given to the general terms of an ordinance by its practical construction as a fact in its history, as we do in some cases that a law has practically become obsolete. If this were not so, the most important provisions of the constitution, intended for the security of personal rights, would, by the general terms of an enactment, often be evaded and practically annulled. *Brown v. Piper*, 91 U. S. 42; *Ohio Life Ins. & Trust Co. v. Debolt*, 16 How. [57 U. S.] 435; *Scott v. Sandford*, 19 How. [60 U. S.] 407. The complaint in this case shows that the ordinance acts with special severity upon Chinese prisoners, inflicting upon them suffering altogether disproportionate to what would be endured by other prisoners if enforced against them. Upon the Chinese prisoners its enforcement operates as "a cruel and unusual punishment."

Many illustrations might be given where ordinances, general in their terms, would operate only upon a special class, or upon a class, with exceptional severity, and thus incur the odium and be subject to the legal objection of intended hostile legislation against them. We have, for instance, in our community a large number of Jews. They are a highly intellectual race, and are generally obedient to the laws of the country. But, as is well known, they have peculiar opinions with respect to the use of certain articles of food, which they cannot be forced to disregard without extreme pain and suffering. They look, for example, upon the eating of pork with loathing. It is an offense against their religion, and is associated in their minds with uncleanness and impurity. Now, if they should in some quarter of the city overcrowd their dwellings and thus become amenable, like the Chinese, to the act concerning lodging-houses and sleeping apartments, an ordinance of the supervisors requiring that all prisoners confined in the county jail should be fed on pork would be seen by everyone to be leveled at them; and, notwithstanding its general terms, would be regarded as a special law in its purpose and operation.

During various periods of English history, legislation, general in its character, has often been enacted with the avowed purpose of imposing special burdens and restrictions upon Catholics; but that legislation has since been regarded as not less odious and obnoxious to animadversion than if the persons at whom it was aimed had been particularly designated.

But in our country hostile and discriminating legislation by a state against persons of any class, sect, creed or nation, in whatever form it may be expressed, is forbidden by the fourteenth amendment of the constitution. That amendment in its first section declares who are citizens of the United States, and then enacts that no state shall make or enforce any law which shall abridge their privileges and immunities. It further declares that no state shall deprive any person (dropping the distinctive term citizen) of life, liberty or property, without due process of law, nor deny to any person the equal protection of the laws. This inhibition upon the state applies to all the instrumentalities and agencies employed in the administration of its government, to its executive, legislative and judicial departments, and to the subordinate legislative bodies of counties and cities. And the equality of protection thus assured to every one whilst within the United States, from whatever country he may have come, or of whatever race or color he may be, implies not only that the courts of the country shall be open to him on the same terms as to all others for the security of his person or property, the prevention or redress of wrongs and the enforcement of contracts; but that no charges or burdens shall be laid upon him which are not equally borne by others, and that in the administration of criminal justice he shall suffer for his offenses no greater or different punishment.

Since the adoption of the fourteenth amendment, congress has legislated for the purpose of carrying out its provisions in accordance with these views. The Revised Statutes reenacting provisions of law passed in 1870 declare that "all persons within the jurisdiction of the United States shall have the same right in every state and territory to make and enforce contracts, to sue, be parties, give evidence, and to the full and equal benefit of all laws and proceedings for the security of persons and property as is enjoyed by white citizens, and shall be subject to like punishment, pains, penalties, taxes, licenses and exactions of every kind, and to no other." Section 1977. They also declare that "every person who, under color of any statute, ordinance, regulation, custom or usage of any state or territory, subjects, or causes to be subjected, any citizen of the United States, or other person within the jurisdiction thereof, to the deprivation of any rights, privileges or immunities secured by the constitution and laws, shall be liable to the party injured in an action at law, suit in equity or other proper proceeding for redress." Section 1979.

It is certainly something in which a citizen of the United States may feel a generous pride that the government of his country extends protection to all persons within its jurisdiction; and that every blow aimed at any of them, however humble, come from what quarter it may, is "caught upon the broad shield of our blessed constitution and our equal laws."

We are aware of the general feeling—amounting to positive hostility—prevailing in California against the Chinese, which would prevent their further immigration hither and expel from the state those already here. Their dissimilarity in physical characteristics, in language, manners and religion would seem, from past experience, to prevent the possibility of their assimilation with our people. And thoughtful persons, looking at the millions which crowd the opposite shores of the Pacific, and the possibility at no distant day of their pouring over in vast hordes among us, giving rise to fierce antagonisms of race, hope that some way may be devised to prevent their further immigration. We feel the force and importance of these considerations; but the remedy for the apprehended evil is to be sought from the general government, where, except in certain special cases, all power over the subject lies. To that government belong exclusively the treaty-making power and the power to regulate commerce with foreign nations, which includes intercourse as well as traffic, and, with the exceptions presently mentioned, the power to prescribe the conditions of immigration or importation of persons. The state in these particulars, with those exceptions, is powerless, and nothing is gained by the attempted assertion of a control which can never be admitted. The state may exclude from its limits paupers and convicts of other countries, persons incurably diseased, and others likely to become a burden upon its resources. It may also exclude persons whose presence would be dangerous to its established institutions. But there its power ends. Whatever is done by way of exclusion beyond this must come from the general government. That government alone can determine what aliens shall be permitted to land within the United States and upon what conditions they shall be permitted to remain; whether they shall be restricted in business transactions to such as appertain to foreign commerce, as is practically the case with our people in China, or whether they shall be allowed to engage in all pursuits equally with citizens. For restrictions necessary or desirable in these matters, the appeal must be made to the general government; and it is not believed that the appeal will ultimately be disregarded. Be that as it may, nothing can be accomplished in that direction by hostile and spiteful legislation on the part of the state, or of its municipal bodies, like the ordinance in question—legislation which is unworthy of a brave and manly people. Against such legislation it will always be the duty of the judiciary to declare and enforce the paramount law of the nation.

The plaintiff must have judgment on the demurrer to the defendant's plea of justification; and it is so ordered.

Figure 5.3 ***Out of the Frying Pan, Into the Fire. The Illustrated Wasp*** **(March 2, 1878). The cartoon lambasts Sheriff Nunan for placing Chinese men arrested for violating the Cubic Air Law.**

Notes

1. As noted earlier, two San Francisco ordinances were involved in the *Ho Ah Kow* case: one imposing minimum space requirements on "lodging-houses and sleeping apartments," and the other requiring every male prisoner in the county jail to have his hair "cut or clipped to an uniform length of one inch from the scalp thereof." Are there rational justifications for these ordinances? What is the connection between the two ordinances?

2. The first ordinance was the Cubic Air Ordinance, or Lodging House Law, passed in San Francisco in 1870 ostensibly to prevent unsafe, overcrowded conditions in tenements. Once again, however, this was a law targeting the Chinese, who often lived in very cramped quarters, to make them feel so unwelcome they would want to return to China. In one night-time raid on a Chinese lodging house, for example, the authorities arrested 56 lodgers in one fell swoop. The law was enacted at the urging of officers of the "Anti-Coolie Association." Like Ho Ah Kow, many Chinese refused or were unable to pay the fine, and this led to overcrowding in the prisons. The Pigtail Ordinance was enacted to address this issue—to deter the Chinese from ignoring the Cubic Air Ordinance. *See generally* McClain, at 65–73.

3. Justice Field wrote: "The ordinance was intended only for the Chinese in San Francisco. This was avowed by the supervisors on its passage, *and was so understood by everyone*." Can a court take judicial notice of what is "understood by everyone?" Perhaps certain facts such as the capital of the United States is Washington DC or that the earth is round. But was it justifiable for the court to assume without any factual proof that everyone knew that these ordinances were enacted specifically to make life difficult for the Chinese?

4. Justice Stephen J. Field was appointed by Abraham Lincoln in 1863 to a newly created tenth seat on the Supreme Court. He heard the *Ho Ah Kow* case sitting as the Circuit Justice. He used colorful language and discussed not just discrimination against the Chinese but also discrimination against Jews and Catholics. He had, however, a mixed record on racial issues: recall that he wrote the majority opinion in *Chae Chan Ping* and that he was in the majority in *Plessy v. Ferguson*. What was motivating him here to strike down the ordinances?

5. *Ho Ah Kow* is surely one of the most important of the early decisions involving Asian Americans. *See* McClain, at 76 ("*Ho Ah Kow*'s significance for the future struggles of the Chinese can hardly be exaggerated."). A Chinese laborer had the courage to sue a sheriff personally for money damages—in 1879, long before civil rights cases became popular. His victory led to the recognition that: (a) the Equal Protection Clause applied not just to citizens, but to noncitizens as well, and (b) facially neutral laws could violate the Constitution if unfairly applied.

6. The modern-day equivalent of the *Ho Ah Kow* case is a civil rights suit for damages brought pursuant to 42 U.S.C. § 1983 against someone acting under color of law. A common modern-day defense to such a case is qualified immunity, which provides that a government official acting under color of law is liable for violating a plaintiff's rights only where the rights were clearly established. Do you think Sheriff Nunan could have successfully asserted a qualified immunity defense?

7. In recent years, challenges have been brought to requirements in prison systems, the military, police forces, and schools with respect to hair length and facial hair. Is *Ho Ah Kow* of any relevance to these modern cases? What, do you think, were the legal grounds for these modern-day hair-regulation challenges?

---

2. The Chinese Laundry Case

One of the most important decisions in constitutional law is *Yick Wo v. Hopkins*, decided by the Supreme Court in 1886. It involved two cases, brought by Chinese laundrymen who operated their laundries in wooden buildings.

Figure 5.4 ***The Coming Man Washing, Drying, Sprinkling and Ironing Clothes. Leslie's Illustrated Newspaper*** **(May 14, 1870).**

Yick Wo v. Hopkins

118 U.S. 356 (1886)

MATTHEWS, Justice: . . .

We are . . . constrained, at the outset, to differ from the supreme court of California upon the real meaning of the ordinances in question. That court considered these ordinances as vesting in the board of supervisors a not unusual discretion in granting or withholding their assent to the use of wooden buildings as laundries, to be exercised in reference to the circumstances of each case, with a view to the protection of the public against the dangers of fire. We are not able to concur in that interpretation of the power conferred upon the supervisors. There is nothing in the ordinances which points to such a regulation of the business of keeping and conducting laundries. They seem intended to confer, and actually to confer, not a discretion to be exercised upon a consideration of the circumstances of each case, but a naked and arbitrary power to give or withhold consent, not only as to places, but as to persons; so that, if an applicant for such consent, being in every way a competent and qualified person, and having complied with every reasonable condition demanded by any public interest, should, failing to obtain the requisite consent of the supervisors to the prosecution of his business, apply for redress by the judicial process of *mandamus* to require the supervisors to consider and act upon his case, it would be a sufficient answer for them to say that the law had conferred upon them authority to withhold their assent, without reason and without responsibility. The power given to them is not confided to their discretion in the legal sense of that term, but is granted to their mere will. It is purely arbitrary, and acknowledges neither guidance nor restraint.

This erroneous view of the ordinances in question led the supreme court of California into the further error of holding that they were justified by the decisions of this court in the cases of *Barbier* v. *Connelly*, 113 U. S. 27, and *Soon Hing* v. *Crowley*, 113 U. S. 703. In both of these cases the ordinance involved was simply a prohibition to carry on the washing and ironing of clothes in public laundries and wash houses, within certain prescribed limits of the city and county of San Francisco, from 10 o'clock at night until 6 o'clock in the morning of the following day. This provision was held to be purely a police regulation, within the competency of any municipality possessed of the ordinary powers belonging to such bodies, a necessary measure of precaution in a city composed largely of wooden buildings, like San Francisco, in the application of which there was no invidious discrimination against anyone within the prescribed limits; all persons engaged in the same business being treated alike, and subject to the same restrictions, and entitled to the same privileges, under similar conditions. For these reasons that ordinance was adjudged not to be within the prohibitions of the fourteenth amendment to the constitution of the United States, which, it was said in the first case cited, "undoubtedly intended, not only that there should be no arbitrary deprivation of life or liberty, or arbitrary spoliation of property, but that equal protection and security should be given to all under like circumstances in the enjoyment of their personal and civil rights; that all persons should be equally entitled to pursue their happiness, and acquire and enjoy property; that they should have like access to the courts of the country for the protection of their persons and property, the prevention and redress of wrongs, and the enforcement of contracts; that no impediment should be interposed to the pursuits of any one, except as applied to the same pursuits by others under like circumstances; that no greater burdens should be laid upon one than are laid upon others in the same calling and condition; and that, in the administration of criminal justice, no different or higher punishment should be imposed upon one than such as is prescribed to all for like offenses.... Class legislation, discriminating against some and favoring others, is prohibited; but legislation which, in carrying out a public purpose, is limited in its application, if, within the sphere of its operation, it affects alike all persons similarly situated, is not within the amendment."

The ordinance drawn in question in the present case is of a very different character. It does not prescribe a rule and conditions, for the regulation of the use of property for laundry purposes, to which all similarly situated may conform. It allows, without restriction, the use for such purposes of buildings of brick or stone; but, as to wooden buildings, constituting nearly all those in previous use, it divides the owners or occupiers into two classes, not having respect to their personal character and qualifications for the business, nor the situation and nature and adaptation of the buildings themselves, but merely by an arbitrary line, on one side of which are those who are permitted to pursue their industry by the mere will and consent of the supervisors, and on the other those from whom that consent is withheld, at their mere will and pleasure. And both classes are alike only in this: that they are tenants at will, under the supervisors, of their means of living. The ordinance, therefore, also differs from the not unusual case where discretion is lodged by law in public officers or bodies to grant or withhold licenses to keep taverns, or places for the sale of spirituous liquors, and the like, when one of the conditions is that the applicant shall be a fit person for the exercise of the privilege, because in such cases the fact of fitness is submitted to the judgment of the officer, and calls for the exercise of a discretion of a judicial nature.

The rights of the petitioners, as affected by the proceedings of which they complain, are not less because they are aliens and subjects of the emperor of China. By the third article of the treaty between this government and that of China, concluded November 17, 1880 (22 St. 827), it is stipulated: "If Chinese laborers, or Chinese of any other class, now either permanently or temporarily residing in the territory of the United States, meet with ill treatment at the hands of any other persons, the government of the United States will exert all its powers to devise measures for their protection, and to secure to them the same rights, privileges, immunities, and exemptions as may be enjoyed by the citizens or subjects of the most favored nation, and to which they are entitled by treaty." The fourteenth amendment to the constitution is not confined to the protection of citizens. It says: "Nor shall any state deprive any person of life, liberty, or property without due process of law; nor deny to any person within its jurisdiction the equal protection of the laws." These provisions are universal in their application, to all persons within the territorial jurisdiction, without regard to any differences of race, of color, or of nationality; and the equal protection of the laws is a pledge of the protection of equal laws. It is accordingly enacted by section 1977 of the Revised Statutes that "all persons within the jurisdiction of the United States shall have the same right, in every state and territory, to make and enforce contracts, to sue, be parties, give evidence, and to the full and equal benefit of all laws and proceedings for the security of persons and property as is enjoyed by white citizens, and shall be subject to like punishment, pains, penalties, taxes, licenses, and exactions of every kind, and to no other." The questions we have to consider and decide in these cases, therefore, are to be treated as involving the rights of every citizen of the United States equally with those of the strangers and aliens who now invoke the jurisdiction of the court.

It is contended on the part of the petitioners that the ordinances for violations of which they are severally sentenced to imprisonment are void on their face, as being within the prohibitions of the fourteenth amendment, and, in the alternative, if not so, that they are void by reason of their administration, operating unequally, so as to punish in the present petitioners what is permitted to others as lawful, without any distinction of circumstances, an unjust and illegal discrimination, it is claimed, which, though not made expressly by the ordinances, is made possible by them.

When we consider the nature and the theory of our institutions of government, the principles upon which they are supposed to rest, and review the history of their development, we are constrained to conclude that they do not mean to leave room for the play and action of purely personal and arbitrary power. Sovereignty itself is, of course, not subject to law, for it is the author and source of law; but in our system, while sovereign powers are delegated to the agencies of government, sovereignty itself remains with the people, by whom and for whom all government exists and acts. And the law is the definition and limitation of power. It is, indeed, quite true that there must always be lodged somewhere, and in some person or body, the authority of final decision; and in many cases of mere administration, the responsibility is purely political, no appeal lying except to the ultimate tribunal of the public judgment, exercised either in the pressure of opinion, or by means of the suffrage. But the fundamental rights to life, liberty, and the pursuit of happiness, considered as individual possessions, are secured by those maxims of constitutional law which are the monuments showing the victorious progress of the race in securing to men the blessings of civilization under the reign of just and equal laws, so that, in the famous language of the Massachusetts bill of rights, the government of the commonwealth "may be a government of laws and not of men." For the very idea that one man may be compelled to hold his life, or the means of living, or any material right essential to the enjoyment of life, at the mere will of another, seems to be intolerable in any country where freedom prevails, as being the essence of slavery itself. . . .

In the present cases, we are not obliged to reason from the probable to the actual, and pass upon the validity of the ordinances complained of, as tried merely by the opportunities which their terms afford, of unequal and unjust discrimination in their administration; for the cases present the ordinances in actual operation, and the facts shown establish an administration directed so exclusively against a particular class of persons as to warrant and require the conclusion that, whatever may have been the intent of the ordinances as adopted, they are applied by the public authorities charged with their administration, and thus representing the state itself, with a mind so unequal and oppressive as to amount to a practical denial by the state of that equal protection of the laws which is secured to the petitioners, as to all other persons, by the broad and benign provisions of the fourteenth amendment to the constitution of the United States. Though the law itself be fair on its face, and impartial in appearance, yet, if it is applied and administered by public authority with an evil eye and an unequal hand, so as practically to make unjust and illegal discriminations between persons in similar circumstances, material to their rights, the denial of equal justice is still within the prohibition of the constitution. This principle of interpretation has been sanctioned by this court in *Henderson* v. *Mayor of New York*, 92 U. S. 259; *Chy Lung* v. *Freeman*, 92 U. S. 275; *Ex parte Virginia*, 100 U. S. 339; *Neal* v. *Delaware*, 103 U.S. 370; and *Soon Hing* v. *Crowley*, 113 U. S. 703.

The present cases, as shown by the facts disclosed in the record, are within this class. It appears that both petitioners have complied with every requisite deemed by the law, or by the public officers charged with its administration, necessary for the protection of neighboring property from fire, or as a precaution against injury to the public health. No reason whatever, except the will of the supervisors, is assigned why they should not be permitted to carry on, in the accustomed manner, their harmless and useful occupation, on which they depend for a livelihood; and while this consent of the supervisors is withheld from them, and from 200 others who have also petitioned, all of whom happen to be Chinese subjects, 80 others, not Chinese subjects, are permitted to carry on the same business under similar conditions. The fact of this discrimination is admitted. No reason for it is shown, and the conclusion cannot be resisted that no reason for it exists except hostility to the race and nationality to which the petitioners belong, and which, in the eye of the law, is not justified. The discrimination is therefore illegal, and the public administration which enforces it is a denial of the equal protection of the laws, and a violation of the fourteenth amendment of the constitution. The imprisonment of the petitioners is therefore illegal, and they must be discharged. To this end the judgment of the supreme court of California in the *Case of Yick Wo*, and that of the circuit court of the United States for the district of California in the *Case of Wo Lee*, are severally reversed, and the cases remanded, each to the proper court, with directions to discharge the petitioners from custody and imprisonment.

Notes

1. *Yick Wo v. Hopkins* involved two cases: one was an appeal from the Supreme Court of California and the other was an appeal from the United States Circuit Court for the District of California. Both involved Chinese immigrants—Yick Wo and Wo

Lee—who operated laundries in wooden buildings. In 1880, the City of San Francisco enacted an ordinance that provided:

> Section 1. It shall be unlawful, from and after the passage of this order, for any person or persons to establish, maintain, or carry on a laundry, within the corporate limits of the city and county of San Francisco, without having first obtained the consent of the board of supervisors, except the same be located in a building constructed either of brick or stone.

Yick Wo had operated his laundry for 22 years and Wo Lee had operated his laundry for 25 years, and they continued to do so after the board of supervisors denied their applications for relief from the ordinance. The ordinance also contained a provision prohibiting scaffolding on rooftops, a common feature of Chinese laundries, which used the scaffolding for drying clothing. The ordinance was a criminal statute, and petitioners were arrested and convicted. They challenged their convictions on equal protection grounds—the board of supervisors had denied the applications for consent of all 200 Chinese and granted all but one of the applications of 80 non-Chinese. Can you think of a legitimate reason why the authorities might have enforced the ordinance in such a discriminatory manner? What was the Court's principal reasoning for ruling as it did? To what extent was a treaty that the United States had with China a factor in the Court's decision?

2. The Court's opinion states that "80 others, not Chinese subjects, are permitted to carry on the same business under similar conditions." 118 U.S. at 374. In fact, one of the 80 was denied a permit—a woman, Mrs. Mary Meagles. *Id.* at 359 (recitation of facts). Was it a coincidence that the only denial of an application from a non-Chinese was one submitted by a woman?

3. The Court noted at the outset that it was interpreting the ordinance differently from the California Supreme Court. But this was a *local* ordinance, granting local authorities discretion in the exercise of police powers; the Supreme Court is the arbiter of the final meaning of federal law, not of state laws. On what basis, then, could the Court reach a different conclusion as to the "real meaning" of the ordinance?

4. *Yick Wo v. Hopkins* was the most prominent of a series of "Laundry Cases." In the 1880s, Chinese laundries became the target of public sinophobic sentiment and legislative measures. Some claimed that "the Chinese were as a race careless in the use of fire" and would cause insurance rates to rise. McClain, at 99. Indeed, on February 5, 1880, there was a fire in a Chinese laundry in San Francisco, and 10 laundry workers were killed as a result. *Id.* at 100. To what extent were these concerns genuine?

5. The petitioners' lawyers were hired by the Tung Hing Tong, a trade association that eventually became "the defender of Chinese laundrymen against threats from the Caucasian world." McClain, at 47–48, 115. In its brief, the state attacked the trade association:

What the Tung Hing Tong Does. . . .

> Do we know that there are in San Francisco a large number, to wit, 3,000 foreigners, who have created a Tung Hing Tong association, which exercises legislative, executive and judicial power in this city and county in opposition to the lawful authorities. . . .
>
> That it has employed, and now employs at very great expense, some of the most distinguished, fertile and powerful members of the bar of San Francisco to defend its members when charged with violating the regulations of the municipal government of San Francisco. That it does not admit American citizens to membership, and that it owes no allegiance to the laws of the land. . . .
>
> That the Tung Hing Tong represents 300 laundries employing 3,000 people and controlling nearly a quarter of a million of capital, paying annually for rent, license, gas and water, $180,000. That its power of taxation is unlimited. The industry of its members so untiring that they are "willing to work as many hours a day as nature will permit," . . . "by relays of help the whole twenty-four hours of each day continuously, Sundays included."

Yick Wo v. Hopkins, Points and authorities for defendant and respondent, at 17–18. What was the state complaining about here? How was the trade association able to hire these high-priced lawyers?

6. The result in *Yick Wo. v. Hopkins* seems surprising in the contemporaneous context of virulent anti-Chinese sentiment in California and the West Coast and the recent passage of the first of the Exclusion Acts at the federal level. From a socioeconomic perspective, why do you think the Supreme Court might have ruled the way it did? What is the significance of *Yick Wo v. Hopkins* to modern U.S. constitutional law?

7. There was a little-known companion case to *Yick Wo v. Hopkins*. Before the Supreme Court issued its opinion in *Hopkins*, Yick Wo sued Patrick Crowley, the Chief of Police of San Francisco, on behalf of himself and 250 other Chinese laundrymen, seeking to enjoin Crowley and his subordinates from enforcing the laundry ordinance. Yick Wo argued that Crowley had arrested many Chinese laundry owners for violating the ordinance while permitting White laundry owners to operate in wooden buildings. The court denied the injunction, holding that the federal court did not have authority to restrain state court proceedings. Y*ick Wo v. Crowley*, 26 F. 207 (C.C.D. Cal. 1886). Nonetheless, this was a bold and creative effort by Yick Wo and his lawyers to fight discrimination.

3. The Bubonic Plague Cases

Like the Cubic Air and Pigtail Ordinances discussed earlier, the laundry ordinance was ostensibly directed at public health and safety. There were other similar regulations purporting to address health concerns but motivated by questionable race-based factors. In 1900, for example, the San Francisco board of health adopted a resolution "requiring the inoculation of all the Chinese residents" of the city and county of San Francisco with a "serum known as 'Haffkine Prophylactic,'" before they could leave the city, to address purported concerns over the bubonic plague. *Wong Wai v. Williamson*, 103 F. 1, 2–3 (Cir. Ct. N.D. Cal. 1900). Citing *Ho Ah Kow* (the Pigtail Ordinance case), the court issued an injunction enjoining the defendants from enforcing the regulation. The court noted as follows:

> It appears that there are about 25,000 Chinese residents in the City of San Francisco.... The city has a population of about 350,000, but the restriction does not apply to any of the inhabitants other than Chinese or Asiatics, and the inhabitants other than Chinese or Asiatics are permitted to depart from and return to the city without being subject to the inoculation imposed upon the Chinese inhabitants....
>
> [T]he regulations ... are directed against the Asiatic race exclusively, and by name. There is no pretense that previous residence, habits, exposure to disease, method of living, or physical condition has anything to do with their classification as subject to the regulations. They are denied the privilege of traveling from one place to another, except upon conditions not enforced against any other class of people; and this privilege is denied, it appears, to Chinese persons born in the United States as well as to those born elsewhere....

Id. at 6, 9.

In what was arguably the first pan-Asian effort to seek relief in U.S. courts, Wong Wai was joined in a separate but coordinated lawsuit by three Japanese Americans who lived in San Francisco who were denied passage on the ferry from San Francisco to Oakland because they did not have proof of inoculation. *Obata v. Williamson*, No. 12938 (C.C.N.D. Cal.). The separate lawsuit was not litigated to a final decision because Wong Wai won his case.

In addition to the forced inoculation of Asians measure, the San Francisco board of health adopted another resolution imposing a quarantine on individuals within a particular district in San Francisco—what was essentially Chinatown—again ostensibly because of concerns about the spread of the bubonic plague. *Jew Ho v. Williamson*, 103 F. 10, 12 (Cir. Ct. N.D. Cal. 1900). The court held that "this quarantine discriminates against the Chinese population of this city, and in favor of the people of other races." *Id.* at 23. The court described how the quarantine was carried out only as to the Chinese:

> [W]hile the board of supervisors has quarantined a district bounded by streets, the operation of the quarantine is such as to run along in the rear of certain houses, and that certain houses are excluded, while others are included; that, for instance, upon Stockton street, in the block numbered from 900 to 1,000, there are two places belonging to persons of another race, and these persons and places are excluded from this quarantine, although the Chinese similarly situated are included, and although the quarantine, in terms, is imposed upon all the persons within the blocks bounded by such streets. The evidence here is clear that this is made to operate against the Chinese population only, and the reason given for it is that the Chinese may communicate the disease from one to the other. That explanation, in the judgment of the court, is not sufficient. It is, in effect, a discrimination, and it is the discrimination that has been frequently called to the attention of the federal courts where matters of this character have arisen with respect to Chinese.

Id.

Citing *Chy Lung v. Freeman* and *Yick Wo v. Hopkins*, the court concluded: "this ordinance is invalid and cannot be maintained, that it is contrary to the provisions of the fourteenth amendment of the constitution of the United States." *Id.* at 24. The court granted an injunction prohibiting the Board of Health from enforcing the resolution.

Notes

1. At the turn of the twentieth century, there was indeed a worldwide fear of a bubonic plague pandemic, and general opinion and evidence indicated a Chinese origin. For instance, the British Crown issued a medal to members of its armed forces who assisted in battling an outbreak of the bubonic plague in Hong Kong in 1894. On March 6, 1900, San Francisco health officials examined the body of a Chinese man at a "coffin shop" and suspected the plague. The authorities quickly took action—imposing the quarantine and inoculation requirements described above.[1] What parallels, if any, are there to the circumstances of the recent COVID-19 pandemic? If state and local governments had required inoculation of a certain racial minority based on evidence indicating that those groups were not voluntarily

1. *See* Katie Dowd, *San Francisco's Bubonic Plague Epidemic Has Eerie Parallels to Modern Day*, SFGate, Apr. 10, 2020, https://www.sfgate.com/sfhistory/article/San-Francisco-Chinatown-plague-1900s-15188267.php [https://perma.cc/WD5M-BAJ6]; Julia Flynn Siler, *Inside San Francisco's Plague-Ravaged Chinatown, c. 1900: A City on the Edge*, Literary Hub (May 15, 2019), https://lithub.com/inside-san-franciscos-plagueravaged-chinatown-c-1900/ [https://perma.cc/96DU-YNMZ].

getting vaccinated, could these bubonic plague precedents be deployed to challenge such required vaccinations?

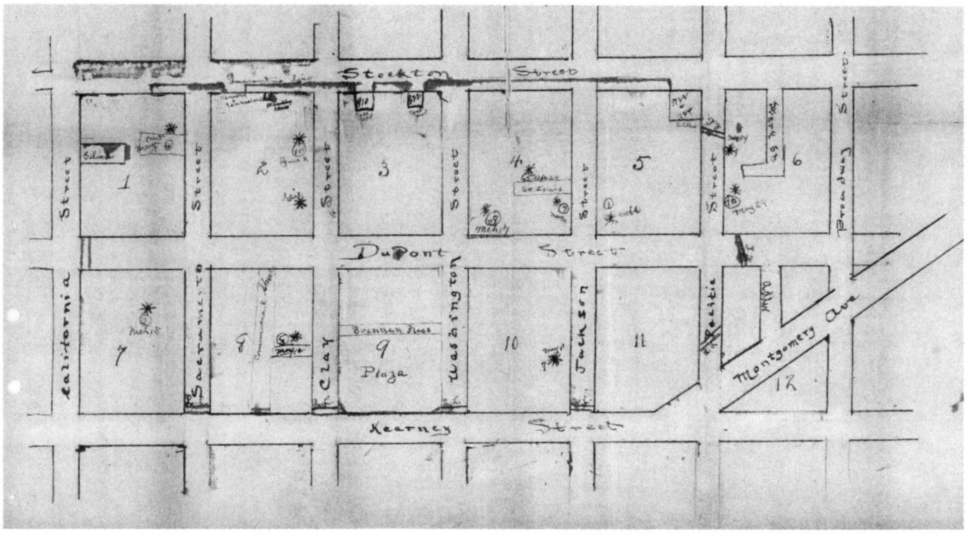

Figure 5.5 ***Map showing quarantine of Chinatown.*** **Used as exhibit in court proceedings; note two residences on Stockton Street carved out from quarantine.** ***Wong Wai v. Williamson*****, 103 F. 1 (Cir. Ct. N.D. Cal. 1900).**

2. The authorities cordoned off an entire section of the city—but only after all White persons who could be found were escorted out. *See* McClain, at 236; Dowd, *supra* ("[W]hite residents and visitors had been escorted out the night before."). A single case of the bubonic plague was discovered in Chinatown, White persons were escorted out, a quarantine was imposed (with carve-outs for certain properties used by non-Chinese), and all Chinese and Asiatics were required to be inoculated with an experimental vaccine if they wanted to leave the county and return. Putting all of these measures together, can you frame a plausible argument that they were reasonable government measures? Consider a modern, exotic deadly virus like Ebola, of suspected African origin. Could we imagine such actions being taken today in the modern United States?

3. Do you think that local officials would have taken the same actions if the case of the bubonic plague had been discovered in a White neighborhood? Consider that the authorities waited two years to begin trapping and killing rats in Chinatown, even though this was understood under the scientific authorities of the time to be the most effective way to fight the plague. *See* McClain, 275–76. In 1907, there was a second outbreak of the bubonic plague in the Bay area—in White communities. The authorities acted quickly, trapping and exterminating rats, without considering, apparently, whether to impose a quarantine or to require inoculations. *See id.* at 276.

4. The "outbreak" of the plague in San Francisco in 1900 lasted for several years. The final toll, as of February 1904, was 121 cases and 113 deaths, the vast majority of whom were Chinese. *See* McClain, at 276; Dowd, *supra* ("The epidemic's official death toll is 119, but it's impossible to know if more cases were hidden, covered up or never discovered."). Contrast those numbers to the number of cases and deaths in the COVID-19 pandemic nationwide. And then compare and contrast the bubonic-plague measures with controversial COVID policies like cutting off travel to and from foreign countries, particularly those suspected of having originated the virus or having high concentrations of diseased persons; compulsory masking in public; requiring vaccinations as a condition of returning to work; and individual quarantines of persons infected or exposed to infected persons. To what extent do you think race is still a factor in how governments, particularly in the United States, respond to infectious diseases even today?

---

4. The Administration of Justice

We turn next to state regulation of the right of early Asian Americans to testify in court proceedings. In 1850, the California legislature passed a statute that provided that "[n]o Black, or Mulatto person, or Indian" was permitted to testify "against a White man." Act of Apr. 16, 1850, ch. 125, § 14. Taking into consideration the fact that the law of evidence in the Anglo-American common-law tradition is inextricably linked to the principle that a jury of one's peers is the ultimate finder of fact, is there a plausibly legitimate reason for such a law precluding non-White persons from providing testimony in judicial proceedings, particularly criminal prosecutions, in which the defendant is White? The statute, however, made no reference to the Chinese. So could a Chinese person testify against a White man? The California Supreme Court was presented with this question in 1854.

People v. Hall

4 Cal. 399 (1854)

Figure 5.6 ***Hon. Hugh C. Murray, late Chief Justice of the Supreme Court, State of California.*** **San Francisco, California: Lith. print of L. Nagel, 1857.**

MURRAY, Chief Judge:

We are of the opinion that the words "White," "Negro," "Mulatto," "Indian," and "Black person," wherever they occur in our Constitution and laws, must be taken in their generic sense, and that, even admitting the Indian of this Continent is not of the Mongolian type, that the words "Black person," in the 14th section must be taken as contradistinguished from White, and necessarily excludes all races other than the Caucasian.

We have carefully considered all the consequences resulting from a different rule of construction, and are satisfied that even in a doubtful case we would be impelled to this decision on grounds of public policy.

The same rule which would admit them to testify, would admit them to all the equal rights of citizenship, and we might soon see them at the polls, in the jury box, upon the bench, and in our legislative halls.

This is not a speculation which exists in the excited and over-heated imagination of the patriot and statesman, but it is an actual and present danger.

The anomalous spectacle of a distinct people, living in our community, recognizing no laws of this State except through necessity, bringing with them their prejudices and national feuds, in which they indulge in open violation of law; whose mendacity is proverbial; a race of people whom nature has marked as inferior, and who are incapable of progress or intellectual development beyond a certain point, as their history has shown; differing in language, opinions, color, and physical conformation; between whom and ourselves nature has placed an impassable difference, is now presented, and for them is claimed, not only the right to swear away the life of a citizen, but the further privilege of participating with us in administering the affairs of our Government.

These facts were before the Legislature that framed this Act, and have been known as matters of public history to every subsequent Legislature.

There can be no doubt as to the intention of the Legislature, and that if it had ever been anticipated that this class of people were not embraced in the prohibition, then such specific words would have been employed as would have put the matter beyond any possible controversy.

For these reasons, we are of opinion that the testimony was inadmissible.

Notes

1. Hall and two others came across a camp of Chinese miners. Looking for gold to steal, they beat up one Chinese miner. As the miner tried to run away, another Chinese miner tried to help. Hall shot and killed the second miner. There was a criminal trial, which raised issues such as the translating of Chinese testimony and an oath for Chinese witnesses ("cutting off a chicken's head or burning paper, or something of that kind, [to] 'swear' a Chinaman"). *See* Stephen Lee, *The Opinion That Silenced Non-White People*, medium.com (May 26, 2020), *available at* https://stephenchahnlee.medium.com/the-opinion-that-silenced-non-white-people-f0db146fe56c. The jury convicted Hall, but the California Supreme Court reversed, holding that the testimony of the Chinese witnesses was inadmissible. Hall was set free; without the Chinese testimony, there was insufficient evidence to sustain the conviction.

2. Several years later the California legislature amended the statute to explicitly extend the ban on testimony to "Mongolian" and "Chinese" witnesses.

3. As a consequence of *People v. Hall*, Chinese victims of crimes could not testify against White assailants. But could they testify against Black defendants after the passage of the Reconstruction constitutional amendments granting Black persons

equal rights to White persons? In *People v. Washington*, in the words of the Court, a "mulatto" was charged with robbing a "Chinaman." The only witnesses were Chinese. Although the statute's words only barred testimony against a White man, the defendant argued that it should be applied to him as well in light of the Civil War amendments to the federal Constitution.

People v. Washington

36 Cal. 658 (1869)

RHODES, J.:

The defendant was indicted for the crime of robbery. The person alleged to have been robbed was a Chinaman named Ah Wang. The indictment was found exclusively upon the testimony of Chinese witnesses, and for that reason counsel for the defendant moved to set it aside. Thereupon, . . . it was stipulated between the District Attorney and counsel for the defendant, that the defendant was a mulatto, born within the United States, and not subject to any foreign power; that all the evidence in the case known to the District Attorney was the testimony of Chinese witnesses, who were born without the United States and within the Chinese Empire. In view of these facts the indictment was set aside, and the defendant discharged.

The case presents for our consideration the fourteenth section of the statute of this State in relation to crimes and punishments, which provides that "no Indian or person having one half or more of Indian blood, or Mongolian, or Chinese, shall be permitted to give evidence in favor or against any white person," as affected by the adoption of the Thirteenth Amendment to the Federal Constitution, which provides that "neither slavery nor involuntary servitude, except as punishment for crime, whereof the party shall have been duly convicted shall exist within the United States, or any place subject to their jurisdiction," and that "Congress shall have power to enforce this Article by appropriate legislation;" and the first section of the Act of Congress passed in pursuance thereof, entitled "An Act to protect all persons in the United States in their civil rights, and furnish the means of their vindication," which provides that "all persons born in the United States and not subject to any foreign power, excluding Indians not taxed, are hereby declared to be citizens of the United States; and such citizens, of every race and color, without regard to any previous condition of slavery or involuntary servitude, except as a punishment for crime, whereof the party shall have been duly convicted, shall have the same right, in every State or Territory of the United States, to make and enforce contracts, to sue, be parties and give evidence, to inherit, purchase, lease, sell, hold and convey real and personal property, and to full and equal benefit of all laws and proceedings for the security of person and property as is enjoyed by white citizens, shall be subject to like punishment, pains and penalties, and to none other, any law, statute, ordinance, regulation or custom to the contrary notwithstanding." (13 U. S. Stats, at Large, pp. 774, 775; 14 U. S. Stats. at Large, p. 27.)

In view of the foregoing constitutional and statutory provisions, we are asked to determine whether the Act of Congress of the 9th of April, 1866, commonly called the "Civil Rights Bill," so far as it bears upon the question before us, was repugnant to the Constitution of the United States as it read prior to the adoption of the Fourteenth Amendment; and if not, what has been its effect upon the fourteenth section of the statute of this State in relation to crimes and punishments?

We regret that we are called upon to decide so important a question without any argument on the part of the defendant.

The nature and objects of the Act first claim our attention. The Attorney General claims "that it at least only extended and only could extend to the *political* rights of white persons and negroes, and no further." A slight examination of the Act would readily show this position to be untenable. The title of the Act is, "An Act to protect all persons in the United States in their *civil rights,* and furnish the means of their vindication." . . .

The absolute rights of persons have no necessary connection with the establishment or management of Government. Females, infants, the Chinese and Indians are entitled to the benefit of the writ of *habeas corpus,* may sue, contract, hold property, etc., but it is preposterous to assert that the possession of those rights implies the possession of the elective franchise, or the right to discharge the duties of a public office. Did the Act in fact confer political rights, all the other provisions of the Act were unnecessary and useless, for the ballot is the safeguard of civil as well as political rights. In the same section certain rights are secured to those who are declared to be citizens of the United States. It is provided that they shall have "the same right in every State and Territory in the United States to make and enforce contracts, to sue, be parties, to *give evidence,* to inherit, purchase, lease, sell, hold and convey real and personal property, and to *full and equal benefit of all laws and proceedings for the security of person and property as is enjoyed by white citizens,* and shall be subject to like punishment, pains, and penalties, and to none other, any law, statute, ordinance, regulation, or custom to the contrary notwithstanding." Most of the rights here enumerated are such as are enjoyed by aliens as well as citizens, and, indeed, all the residents of the United States, except those laboring under the disabilities growing out of the condition of slavery. But some of the rights mentioned go beyond that line, as the right to inherit property, to give evidence, the right to the full and equal benefit of all laws for the security of person and property as is enjoyed by white citizens; and it is claimed that the regulation of these and the like matters belongs to the several States. If it be admitted that this was true before the adoption of the Thirteenth Amendment to the Constitution of the United States, yet upon the adoption of that amendment legislation of the character of the Civil Rights Bill became appropriate; and in order to confer full authority therefor, the second section of the amendment was adopted, which provides that "Congress shall have power to enforce this Article by appropriate legislation." At common law one of the usual divisions of persons was into the comprehensive titles of aliens and native born subjects. The term *citizen* is now nearly synonymous with that of *subject* at common law. But under our system of government there was a third class, the persons of which it was composed being neither aliens nor citizens. "Indians not taxed," and slaves, composed the main portion of this class. As most of the persons of African descent within the United States were introduced as slaves, or were the descendants of slaves, they were not regarded in some of the States as citizens, and in the midst of the great political conflicts which preceded the civil war, the Supreme Court of the United States (some of the Justices dissenting) held that a negro was not a citizen of the United States, and consequently could not sue in their Courts. (*Dred Scott v. Sandford,* 19 How. 393.) Persons of that race were, in several of the States, subject to disabilities, restrictions, and penalties to which white persons were not liable, and others were being added by laws enacted for that purpose.

The object of the adoption of the first section of the Thirteenth Amendment to the Constitution was not only to effect the emancipation of all persons then held in slavery, but also to forever thereafter deprive both Congress and the respective States of any and all power to reduce either the persons so emancipated or any others within the jurisdiction of the United States to the condition of slavery or involuntary servitude, except as a punishment for crime, whereof the party shall have been duly convicted. And the object of the second section was to enable Congress, by appropriate legislation, to secure the persons so emancipated, as well as all others, while within the jurisdiction of the United States, in the full enjoyment of that personal liberty contemplated in the first section or, in other words, the Thirteenth Amendment was at least intended to make all men born in the United States, without reference to color, equal before the law with respect to *personal liberty,* one of the absolute rights of man, and to give Congress power to pass any and all laws necessary and proper to accomplish that end. Undoubtedly, to secure *personal freedom* to all within the purview of its provisions, was the first great and leading object of the Thirteenth Amendment. *Personal security,* and the right to acquire and enjoy private property—and these cover the remaining elements of one's civil rights—would certainly seem to be powerful auxiliaries to the maintenance of *personal liberty.* The continued enjoyment of *personal liberty* cannot well be assured without the enjoyment of *personal security.* And the right to acquire and enjoy private property would seem to be necessary to give that independence and freedom from want essential to the full enjoyment of personal liberty. Whatever, therefore, tends to maintain and assure to a person personal security, and to protect him in the acquisition and enjoyment of private property, would seem to aid in the maintenance of his personal liberty. Congress doubtless took this view in passing the Civil Rights Bill, and extended its provisions to these auxiliary and cognate rights. But it is still apparent that the great and leading object was the maintenance of the persons provided for in their *personal liberty,* and it is *in this aspect only* that we are now called upon to consider it. . . .

In the administration of justice the subject of evidence occupies a large space. It is the means by which the judicial branch of the Government is informed of the violation of that personal liberty which this amendment of the Constitution guarantees to all persons within the jurisdiction of the Federal Government, and whereby it is enabled to perceive the wrong and apply the proper remedy for enforcing the right. It is ordinarily the proper function of the legislative department of Governments to prescribe rules as to the production and competency of evidence. It would seem, as a general proposition, that a rule of evidence which is best adapted to elicit the truth, facilitate the administration of justice, and protect personal liberty as to one class of persons, ought to be the best adapted to accomplish the same end as to all living under the protection of the same Government. At all events, the establishment of different rules as to the competency of evidence applicable to different classes of persons may tend to the advantage of one class and to the oppression and encroachment upon the personal liberty of another. For example, it is not difficult to perceive, if the individuals of the entire class likely to be reduced to the condition of involuntary servitude are excluded from testifying against the class likely to attempt to deprive them of their liberty, or in any matter arising between the two classes, while the other class is at full liberty to testify in such cases, that the strong tendency of such a rule of evidence would be to obstruct the operation of the amendment in question, and overthrow that personal liberty guaranteed by it; and it would seem to be self-evident that a law providing that the same rule of evidence should apply to both parties, placing the class likely to be reduced to servitude upon an equal footing with the other in respect to the right to testify as to the encroachment upon their personal liberty, would strongly conduce to the enforcement of this constitutional provision. So, a law which, while it would not permit a class of persons deemed unworthy to testify against a white person in a matter where such white person's personal liberty is concerned, would yet allow them to testify against a black person in a similar case, would discriminate against the personal liberty of the latter, and also tend to obstruct, as to him, an equal enforcement of the amendment in question. Such discriminations might well tend to affect the security of that personal liberty which the amendment to the Constitution guarantees to all. This being so, it seems clear to us that under the provision in question Congress is fully authorized to judge of the necessity of legislation upon the subject, and, if found necessary, to prescribe that all alike, black and white, shall be entitled to "give evidence"; and further, that the rules of evidence shall apply equally to all alike, in order that all may, in the language of the Civil Rights Act, have the "full and equal benefit of all laws and proceedings for the security of person," etc. This provision prescribing a uniform rule of evidence with reference to all classes embraced in the broad terms of the amendment, necessarily bears directly upon the great right of personal liberty which its adoption was expressly designed to secure. To secure the enforcement of this provision was the leading object of the Civil Rights Act, and this precise provision is the only one the constitutionality of which is involved in this case, or upon which we now express any opinion. If such legislation is not "appropriate" to enforce the provision for personal liberty in question, we are at a loss to know what would be appropriate....

Our conclusion is that the portion of the Civil Rights Act now in question—and we are not called upon to consider any other—was not repugnant to the Constitution of the United States as it read prior to the adoption of the Fourteenth Amendment, and that its effect was to put all persons, irrespective of race and color, born within the United States and not subject to any foreign power, excluding Indians not taxed, upon an equality before the laws of this State in respect to their personal liberty and that the fourteenth section of the statute of this State in relation to crimes and punishments, so far as it discriminates against persons on the score of race or color, born within the United States and not subject to any foreign power, excluding Indians not taxed, has, by the force and effect of the Civil Rights Act, become null and void. . . .

Judgment affirmed.

MR. JUSTICE CROCKETT delivered the following dissenting opinion, in which MR. JUSTICE SPRAGUE concurred:

Being unable to agree with the majority of the Court, in the conclusions at which they have arrived in this case, I propose to state the reasons which have influenced my judgment.

Section fourteen of the statute of this State, concerning crimes and punishments, provides that "no Indian or person having one half or more of Indian blood, or Mongolian or Chinese, shall be permitted to give evidence in favor or against any white person."

The defendant in this case is a negro, born within the United States, and is accused in the indictment of robbing a Chinaman; and it was proposed at the trial to support the indictment solely by the testimony of Chinamen born within the Chinese Empire. The Court below ruled out the evidence on the ground that the testimony of a Chinaman was not admissible against a negro, under the conditions stated, and the propriety of this ruling is the only question presented on the appeal.

The statute only disqualifies Indians, Mongolians and Chinese from testifying for or against *"any white person."* It was never doubted that they were competent to testify for or against each other, and it has been the uniform practice of the Courts of this State to admit such testimony without any question of its propriety, so far as I am advised. Nor do I understand the majority of the Court as maintaining the contrary, except upon the grounds that by the Thirteenth Amendment of the Federal Constitution and the Act of Congress of April 9th, 1866, generally known as the Civil Rights Bill, the statute of this State, before quoted, has been in so far superseded or modified as to place the negro, born in the United States, in respect to all his civil rights, on the same footing with the white man; and assuming this to be his *status,* the argument is, that inasmuch as a foreign born Chinaman cannot, under our statute, testify against a white person, *ergo,* he cannot testify against a native born negro, who, by the Act of Congress, is endowed with precisely the same civil rights that appertain to white persons. . . .

It may be safely assumed as a political and legal axiom, maintained by the Courts through an unbroken series of decisions, and by eminent statesmen of all shades of opinion, that the Government of the United States is one of limited and enumerated powers, and that Congress can exercise no powers except those expressly granted in the Constitution, and such others as "shall be necessary and proper for carrying into execution the foregoing powers, and all other powers vested by this Constitution in the Government of the United States, or any department or officer thereof." (Art. I, Sec. 8, subdivision 19.) It is quite as well established by the same weight of authority, that the several States in their sovereign capacity retain all the mass of powers which a sovereign State can exercise, which are not, either expressly or by necessary implication, granted to the Federal Government.... Prior to the adoption of the Thirteenth Amendment, it was conceded on all sides that each State had the exclusive right to prescribe by its own Constitution and laws who should or should not be entitled to make and enforce contracts, sue and be sued, and give evidence in its Courts, inherit, purchase, lease, sell, hold and convey property, and to define the punishment, pains and penalties to be inflicted on any violator of its laws, subject, however, to the limitation contained in Article IV, section two of the Constitution, which provides that "the citizens of each State shall be entitled to all privileges and immunities of citizens in the several States."

Subject only to this limitation, it has been the practice from the earliest period of our existence as a nation, for each State, by its Constitution and laws, to exercise these powers unquestioned, often discriminating between classes of its own citizens, as its views of public policy dictated. The proceedings and debates of the Convention which framed the Constitution render it morally certain that the States which were represented in that august body would not have conceded to the Federal Government the power to interfere in such vital questions of their internal policy as those relating to the making and enforcement of contracts, the prosecution and conduct of suits in their Courts, the law of inheritance, the tenure of property, and the punishment of crime. These embraced the most important functions to be exercised by any Government for the protection of private rights and the preservation of public order. Deny to a Government the right to regulate, at its absolute discretion, the laws of inheritance, the tenure of property, the conduct of suits in its Courts, and the punishment of crime, and but little will remain which will be worth preserving. At an early period after the adoption of the Constitution, fears were entertained that there might, in the future, grow up such a latitude of construction as gradually to abridge the power of the States over their internal policy, and to absorb in the Federal Government important powers reserved to the States. Consequently, in 1789, only two years after the adoption of the Constitution, Congress proposed ten amendments to it, which were afterward duly ratified, and now form a part of that instrument. The tenth amendment is in these words, to wit: "The powers not delegated to the United States by the Constitution, nor prohibited by it to the States, are reserved to the States respectively or to the people."...

If this bill be a valid enactment, no State has the power to prohibit marriages between native born negro men and white women; because marriage is, in law, only a civil contract, and the bill provides that all persons born in the United States and not subject to any foreign power, excluding Indians not taxed, are citizens, and that such citizens, *of every race and color,* shall have the same right to make and enforce contracts as is enjoyed by white persons. Marriage being in law only a civil contract, and every unmarried white man of lawful age having the right to marry a white woman, it follows as a logical sequence that every native born black man is entitled to the same right, if the Civil Rights Bill be a valid law; and that, too, in defiance of any State law to the contrary. It may also happen that a State may be influenced by considerations of public policy to deny to certain races or classes the right to inherit, purchase, or hold real estate. The State of California, for example, with a view to discourage emigration from China or Japan, might see fit to deny to the descendants of those races born in this State the right to inherit, hold, or transmit real estate; but though the strongest considerations of State policy might dictate this course, all State laws enacted for that purpose would be void if the Civil Rights Bill be valid. So, too, there may be in a State a degraded, brutal, and vicious race, peculiarly addicted to crime and vice, and demanding more stringent regulations for their government than are required for the general mass of citizens; but the Civil Rights Bill forbids any discrimination, and the State would be powerless to protect itself against a great and perhaps growing evil. So, too, in perhaps every State of the Union, minors and married women, on grounds of public policy, are disabled by law from making valid contracts; but if Congress should decide that these restrictions are restraints on the state of freedom established by the Thirteenth Amendment, they might supersede all State laws on the subject, and this would be deemed to be "appropriate legislation" under the second section. Illustrations might be multiplied almost indefinitely to show that the Civil Rights Bill withdraws from the States a mass of powers essential to the maintenance of order and the administration of local government, and which the wise men who framed the Constitution jealously withheld from the Federal Government, conceding to it only such powers as were deemed essential to the proper conduct of national affairs, but reserving to the States the mass of powers pertaining to the administration of local government. Amongst these none were of so great importance as the right to regulate contracts, the administration of justice, the tenures of property, and the punishment of crime. The Civil Rights Bill infringes upon the power of the States over these subjects in many important particulars, and the theory on which it is founded is so repugnant to that on which the Constitution was originally based, that it should not be upheld on a doubtful construction merely. Nothing short of the most explicit language in an amendment to the Constitution would justify legislation so entirely subversive of the theory on which the Government was originally founded.

But if it be true that the second section of the Thirteenth Amendment was adopted only to enable Congress to secure to those whose condition was changed from that of slavery to freedom, the full benefit and protection of the laws enjoyed by white persons, then it evidently can have no application to this case, inasmuch as it does not appear from the record that the defendant ever was a slave; but if the purpose of the amendment was to make all men born within the United States equal before the law in respect to their *civil* rights, it has utterly failed to indicate that purpose. The last proposition is not a correlative of the first. To secure to those whose condition was changed from that of slavery to freedom the full benefit and protection of the laws enjoyed by white persons, would apply only to the class of emancipated slaves;

but to make all men born within the United States equal before the law, in respect to their *civil* rights, is a wholly different proposition, and of much wider scope. If the latter be the true purpose of the Civil Rights Bill, as it undoubtedly is, it follows of necessity that it was not designed simply to secure to slaves who were emancipated by the Thirteenth Amendment the full benefit and protection of the laws enjoyed by white persons, but also to operate upon those who never were slaves; as, for example, upon the descendants of Chinese, Malays or Japanese, born within the United States. If this be the purpose and scope of the Act, it is an attempt on the part of Congress, under the plea of legislation, designed to enforce the prohibition of slavery or involuntary servitude, contained in the Thirteenth Amendment, to supersede all State legislation on an important class of subjects, which do not, in any sense, fall within the purview of the Thirteenth Amendment. I do not perceive what necessary or even remote relation there is between the prohibition of slavery and the proposition that a son of Chinese parents, born within the United States, shall have the same right to inherit, purchase, sell, lease, hold and convey property as is enjoyed by white persons; or the proposition involved in this case, to wit: that because a Chinaman is prohibited by law from testifying against a white person, therefore he shall not testify against a colored person who never was a slave; or the proposition that because a white man has the lawful right to make a contract of marriage with a white woman, every colored man born within the United States shall have the right to contract marriage with a white woman, in defiance of any State law to the contrary. If all these propositions, and numerous others of a similar character, come within the purview of the Thirteenth Amendment, it is not difficult to demonstrate that, under the pretext of enforcing the prohibition of slavery by "appropriate legislation," Congress might practically absorb all the powers of the State Governments, in matters pertaining purely to the administration of local affairs. It might decide that discriminating taxes imposed by a State on its own citizens, though warranted by its Constitution, or the establishment of separate schools for white and colored children, or the enforcement of laws for the observance of the Sabbath by Chinese or Japanese residents, or police regulations intended to preserve order amongst a certain vicious class of the community, such as Chinese prostitutes or gamblers, or health regulations, applicable alone to a degraded class of colored population, all tended to infringe upon the prohibition of slavery contained in the Thirteenth Amendment, and were therefore void. Congress, it is claimed, is the sole judge of what is "appropriate legislation" to accomplish the end contemplated in the Thirteenth Amendment; and if the Civil Rights Bill be maintained by the Courts as a valid exercise of the constitutional powers of Congress, it is quite evident that the division of power between the State and Federal Governments, as originally established by the Constitution, has been abrogated by the Thirteenth Amendment; and instead of a National Government to administer purely national affairs, and State Governments to administer the local affairs of the several States, the power of local administration has been practically transferred to the Federal Government, and the State Governments have been emasculated of the chief portion of the mass of powers reserved to them originally.

All that Congress was authorized to do was to see that the prohibition of slavery was not infringed. But, instead of this, it has undertaken to define, not only the civil rights of emancipated slaves, but of all other persons born within the United States not subject to any foreign power, except Indians not taxed. This is done on the plea that, inasmuch as the Thirteenth Amendment establishes a condition of universal freedom in the United States, all legislation is appropriate to enforce that result, which secures to all persons the rights of freemen. If by the term "the rights of freemen" is to be understood the right not to be held in slavery or involuntary servitude, the proposition is sound; but if the term "rights of freemen" is intended to include all the social and civil rights which men enjoy under a free form of government, then it follows from this interpretation that Congress, by virtue of the second section of the amendment, may supersede all State laws on all subjects affecting the social or civil *status* of every individual citizen of the United States; and this would practically withdraw from the State Governments all that mass of powers by which they have hitherto defined the rights, duties and obligations of their citizens toward each other and to the State. It would practically annihilate the power of the State over its own citizens and within its own territory, and transfer to the Federal Government the authority to exercise the most important functions pertaining to a local government. In my opinion the Thirteenth Amendment contemplated nothing of the kind.

Nor can it escape observation that the same argument which attempts to uphold the Civil Rights Bill, if carried to its legitimate conclusion, would concede to Congress the right to regulate the ballot in the several States. If Congress has the power to enact this bill on the plea that in order to enable a freeman to maintain his freedom, it is necessary to secure to him the right to make and enforce contracts, sue and be sued, testify in Courts, inherit, purchase, lease, sell, hold, and convey real and personal property, it would seem to follow as a logical result that it also has the power to confer upon him the ballot, as one of the most potent methods of maintaining his freedom. If it be "appropriate legislation" under the Thirteenth Amendment to confer upon all native born persons in the United States the civil rights which are enumerated as a legitimate method of maintaining their freedom, why withhold from them the ballot, the most potent of all methods? It cannot be denied that it is competent for Congress to regulate the ballot in every State, provided it has the constitutional power to pass the Civil Rights Bill. If it can confer civil rights as a means of securing freedom, why not political rights for the same purpose?

We should thus see concentrated in the Federal Government the power not only to regulate the local affairs of every State, but also to define who should be entitled to the ballot. The Federal Government would no longer be a Government of limited and enumerated powers; and the State Governments would scarcely retain a remnant of the mass of powers so jealously withheld by them when the Constitution was adopted. . . .

In my opinion the judgment ought to be reversed.

Notes

1. The California Supreme Court affirmed the dismissal of the indictment based on the Civil Rights Act of 1866: if White persons could exclude testimony of the Chinese, then a Black person was entitled to do so as well. But what about the rights of Chinese under the Fourteenth Amendment?

2. One of the key issues was whether the Civil Rights Act of 1866 was unconstitutional. The majority held it was not. What did the dissent conclude? How is it that a state court was opining on the constitutionality of a federal statute? The 1866 Act was eventually codified as 42 U.S.C. § 1981.

3. The dissent raised the concern that if indeed the 1866 Civil Rights Act was valid, "no State has the power to prohibit marriages between native born negro men and white women." This was in 1869. Wasn't the dissent accurate in its prediction of the likely consequences of the majority's holding? We will discuss anti-miscegenation in the next section.

4. Soon after *Washington*, the California Supreme Court considered the case of a White man who was convicted of robbing a Chinese man based on the testimony of the victim; the trial court had allowed the testimony to create a test case. The Court set aside the conviction and ordered a new trial, concluding that the statute banning Chinese testimony was lawful. The court opined that "the law provides for the Chinaman the same protection against threatened violence as for the white man.... If a white man be robbed by a white man, the fact cannot be established by Chinese testimony; and yet it may frequently happen that the fact cannot be proven in any other way. The same is true of a robbery committed upon a Chinaman by a white man." *People v. Brady*, 40 Cal. 198, 208 (1870); *see* McClain, at 34–36. The point appears to be that, when the only witness to a crime committed by a White person is Chinese, the victim cannot get justice against the perpetrator regardless of whether the victim is White or Chinese. Isn't that in fact true? What is troubling about this reasoning?

5. What did this mean for Chinese victims of criminal conduct by White (or Black) assailants? What was the reasoning behind the ban on Chinese testimony against Whites? *See* Gabriel J. Chin, *"A Chinaman's Chance" in Court: Asian Pacific Americans and Racial Rules of Evidence*, 3 U.C. Irvine L. Rev. 965, 970–71 (2013) (reviewing cases finding Chinese testimony to be unreliable as a general matter).

6. The California state legislature eliminated the ban on Chinese testimony in both civil and criminal proceedings in 1872. McClain, at 42 & n.224.

7. On the federal level, as discussed in Unit One, the Geary Act, which was enacted in 1892, imposed restrictions on the ability of Chinese laborers to remain in the United States. It also required a Chinese person in deportation proceedings to prove his immigration status through the testimony of White witnesses.

5. Anti-Miscegenation

In 1661, the General Assembly of Maryland, then an English colony, enacted the first anti-miscegenation law in what would become the United States.[2] It did not explicitly prohibit marriage between Whites and Blacks—rather, it declared any White woman who married a Black man to be a slave as well as the couple's children. For the next two centuries, state anti-miscegenation laws declared "illegal" and "void" or "voidable" marriage between Whites and Blacks or "mulattoes," or between Whites and "colored persons" or "persons of color," sometimes specifying that Native Americans were included. Some of these laws defined the proscribed category of non-White persons to encompass those with mixed blood—for instance, any one with one-sixteenth non-White blood "in their veins." *See generally Perez v. Sharp*, 32 Cal. 2d 711, 746–48 (1948) (Shenk, *J.*, dissenting) (providing "a short history of miscegenetic marriage laws").

In 1850, California, upon becoming a state, passed a law declaring that "All marriages of white persons with negroes or mulattoes are declared to be illegal and void."[3] In subsequent years, with the influx of Chinese laborers into the state, the vast majority of whom were male, the California legislature in 1880 passed a law prohibiting the issuance of licenses to marriages between "white persons" and "Mongolians."[4] As Japanese immigration increased in the late nineteenth and early twentieth centuries, the "Mongolian" characterization was extended to them. Finally, in 1905, the California legislature expanded the prohibition even further: "All marriages of white persons with negroes, Mongolians, or mulattoes are illegal and void."[5]

After the United States acquired the Philippines in the Spanish-American War, Filipinos, availing themselves of their newfound status as U.S. nationals, started coming to the continental United States in significant numbers. By 1930, there were estimated to be about 30,000 Filipinos in California, most of them male, and 15,000 more in the other Pacific states. Given the dramatic gender imbalance, as Filipino men dated and married White women, the legal question soon arose whether Filipinos were "Mongolians" under the 1905 California amended statute, and, consequently, whether a marriage between a Filipino and a White person was "illegal and void."

---

2. Edward Byron Reuter, *Race Mixture: Studies in Intermarriage and Miscegenation* (1969); Note, *Constitutionality of Anti-Miscegenation Statutes,* 58 Yale L.J. 472, 480–82 (1949).

3. Act Regulating Marriages, ch. 140, 1850 Cal. Stat. 494 (codified as Cal. Code § 35(1853)). *See generally* Rachel F. Moran, *Love with a Proper Stranger: What Anti-Miscegenation Laws Can Tell Us About the Meaning of Race, Sex, and Marriage*, 32 Hofstra L. Rev. 1663 (2004).

4. *See* 1880 Cal Stat. Ch. 41, Sec. 1, p. 3.

5. Cal. Civ. Code § 60 (1906).

Roldan v. Los Angeles County

129 Cal. App. 267
(Cal. Ct. App. 1933)

ARCHBALD, Justice:

Solvador Roldan[6] applied to the county clerk of Los Angeles County for a license to wed a woman of Caucasian descent and was refused such license. On a hearing of his application before the superior court for a writ to compel the issuance thereof he was found to be a "Filipino," viz., "an Illocano, born in the Philippine Islands of Filipino progenitors in whose blood was co-mingled a strain of Spanish," and not a Mongolian. From a judgment making the alternative writ of mandate permanent the defendants have appealed.

Section 69 of the Civil Code, relating to marriage licenses, was amended in 1880 to prohibit the issuance of a license authorizing the marriage of a white person "with a . . . Mongolian." Section 60 of the Civil Code was amended in 1905 by adding "Mongolians" to the classes whose marriage with a "white" was made "illegal and void." The sole question involved in this appeal is whether or not the legislature in 1880 and 1905 meant to include Filipinos in its use of the word "Mongolian."

We find no dissent to the statement that the Filipino is included among the Malays, although since the time of Huxley, at least, there has been some question among ethnologists as to whether the five grand subdivisions of the races of mankind, as classified by Blumenbach, is the proper classification or whether the Malays are to be included among the "Mongoloid" group and as a branch of the Mongolian family. We are not, however, interested in what the best scientific thought of the day was, but in what was the common use of the word "Mongolian" in California at the time of the enactment of the legislation above mentioned.

The case of *Ah Yup*, decided by Judge Sawyer of the United States Circuit Court, District of California, in 1878, contains this information: "In speaking of the various classifications of races, Webster in his dictionary says [italics ours]: 'The *common* classification is that of Blumenbach, who makes five: (1) the Caucasian, or white race, . . . (2) the Mongolian, or yellow race, occupying Tartary, China, Japan, etc., (3) the Ethiopian or negro (black) race, . . . (4) the American, or red race, . . . and (5) the Malay, or brown race, occupying the Indian Archipelago.'" . . . The Standard Dictionary of 1911 gives the following definition of a Mongolian: "(1) A Mongol. (2) By extension a Chinaman: In Blumenbach's system any one of the yellow peoples of China." The New American Cyclopaedia (1863) defines "Mongolian Race" as "one of the great ethnological divisions of mankind," and the article thereon continues:

---

6. The opinion spells Roldan's first name as "Solvador." An article recently co-authored by his son, however, spells it as "Salvador." *See* Susie Ling with Bryan Roldan, *One Love Story Behind Marriage Rights: The Roldan Family*, EastWind (July 20, 2022), *available at* https://eastwindezine.com/one-love-story-behind-marriage-rights-the-roldan-family/.

"Dr. Pickering, in 'The Races of Men', includes the American Indians among the Mongolians ... By most writers, however, the American Indians are held to be a distinct race, and the term Mongolian is restricted chiefly to the following nations: the Mongols proper, the Mantchoos, Coreans, Chinese, Thibetans, Anamites, Burmese, Siamese, Japanese, Samoyeds, Koriaks, Ourals, Ostiaks, Kamchatdales, Finns, Laplanders, Esquimaux and the various tribes inhabiting Toorkistan or Independent Tartary, who are commonly called Tartars by Europeans." Ogilvie's Imperial Dictionary of the English Language (1884), under "Mongol, Mongolian," says: "An epithet sometimes employed to the whole class of Turanian tongues, sometimes restricted to that group spoken by the Kalmucks and other tribes from Thibet to China.—Mongolian race, the second in Blumenbach's classification of the races of mankind. It corresponded very closely with the modern Turanian division." This dictionary also defines "Malay" as "belonging or relating to the Malays or to their country.—Malay race, one of the five principal divisions of mankind according to Blumenbach." In the "Reports of the Immigration Commission" of the United States (1911), vol. 5, "Dictionary of Races or Peoples," p. 94, under "Malay, Malaysian or Brown Race," appears the following, the italics being ours:

> "One of the five grand divisions of mankind as *commonly* classified since the time of Blumenbach, but the most disputable one in the view of recent ethnologists. Many consider it to be a branch of the Mongolian race, but such admit, at least, that it is the most divergent great branch of the latter." And on page 97 of the same volume, under "Mongolian, etc.", we read: "Many ethnologists so define 'Mongolian' as to include the entire American and Malay races."

We think we have quoted enough to show that, regardless of the fine points of the argument from the ethnologist's standpoint, the early classification of Blumenbach left its impression on the writers from his day to 1905, at least, so that his classification is spoken of as the one "commonly" used; and we venture to think that in the recollection of those whose early schooling was anywhere in the period from 1850 to 1905 his classification of the races into the five divisions, the white, black, yellow, red and brown, still persists.

From 1862 to 1885 the history of California is replete with legislation to curb the so-called "Chinese invasion," and as we read we are impressed with the fact that the terms "Asiatics," "Coolies" and "Mongolians" meant "Chinese" to the people who discussed and legislated on the problem, or at most that they only extended in their thought to natives of China and the inhabitants of adjacent countries having the same characteristics. It appears from the report in 1878 to the state senate of its "Special Committee on Chinese Immigration" that the mass of the immigration complained of came from the "port of Hong Kong" (p. 64), and that of the Chinese then here "you would not find one in a thousand—probably one in five thousand—but that came from Kwang-Tung, the province of which Canton is capital" (p. 70). In the same volume (p. 265) is an article by H.W. Clement, a member of the San Francisco bar,

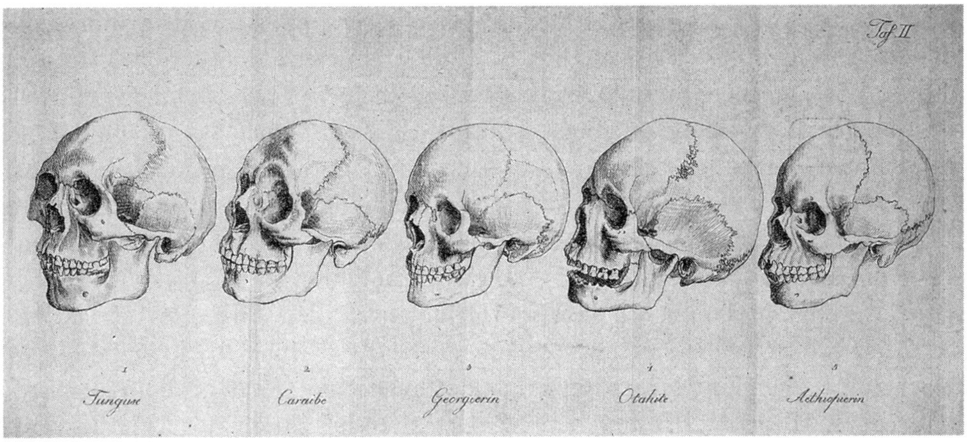

Figure 5.7 ***Five skulls labelled Tungusae, Caribaei, Feminae Georgianae, O-taheitae, and Aethiopissae, presumably serving as specimens for Blumenbach's Mongolian, American, Caucasian, Malayan, and Aethiopian races*** **(ca. 1795).**

entitled "Caucasian vs. Mongolian," in which he speaks of the Americans as the sons of Japheth in possession of America; that "seized with an insane desire to revisit the old homestead," and finding it surrounded by the "Chinese Wall," they battered it down, "but from out the breach swarmed one hundred fifty thousand of the three hundred millions of overcrowded humanity within, who threaten to overrun us. . . . We find by our twenty-five years of acquaintance with them . . . that the . . . changeless life of 'Shem' and his descendants from Asia has shaped their character . . . and determined their race, and we call them Mongolians. . . . The conflicting rights, prejudices and interests of those two races in California constitutes the Chinese problem."

In the "Debates and Proceedings of the Constitutional Convention of the State of California" (1878-79), speaking on the report of the "Committee on Chinese" relative to articles proposed affecting those nationals, Mr. John F. Miller says: "They [certain church people opposing restrictions] would Mongolize this land in a vain attempt to bring the Chinese to a knowledge . . ." (vol. 1, p. 633). Mr. Charles C. O'Donnell (p. 647): "If you expect to wipe out crime you must wipe out the presence of the Mongolian in our midst." We could quote an infinite number of similar statements, all of which point to the fact that the speakers were using the term "Mongolian" in the sense of the problem that they were discussing, viz., the Chinese problem, and that it only applied to that people, including possibly the inhabitants of contiguous countries of the same characteristics. Mr. Burt, not liking the designations "Mongolian race" and "persons not eligible to become citizens," in some of the proposed articles, said (p. 652): "We mean Chinese, and why not come out squarely and say so." The report of the committee, instead of using the words "Chinese or Mongolian" now appearing in section 2, article XIX of the Constitution, used the words "foreigners who are not eligible for citizenship," and Mr. N.G. Wyatt, a member from Monterey County, moved to amend the section by inserting in place of such words the words "Chinese or Mongolian," because of the uncertainty of the original language. Some courts apparently having admitted Chinese to citizenship while some denied them that privilege, Mr. Wyatt said (vol. 2, p. 681): "I want it amended so as to apply, *eo nomine,* to the class it is intended to affect." Mr. Barnes made a similar objection to the language used by the committee, saying (p. 687): "If we mean Chinamen, why not say Chinamen or Mongolian?"

Mr. John S. Hager, who moved to amend section 5 of the proposed article by prohibiting any resident or foreigner ineligible to citizenship from owning property in the state after 1880, said (vol. 3, p. 1429): "That applies to all classes of foreigners who are ineligible to become citizens. It also gives them sufficient notice." Mr. C.V. Stuart then inquired: "Will that apply to any but Chinese in fact?" Mr. Hager replied: "I think there are some others." The lone voice in the convention that objected to the use of the word "Mongolian" was that of James J. Ayers, who said (vol. 2, p. 717): "The term Mongolian does not apply exclusively to the Chinese. It is a generic type of the human family, and some of the leading authorities on ethnology have divided the species into three classes: Mongolian, Caucasian and Negro. Some of them claim that the word Mongol embraces the American Indian." He then added: "We all know that we mean Chinamen, and why not say Chinamen?" That the Malay race was not in the thoughts of any in the convention as being included in the designations used is clearly shown from the speech of Mr. James M. Shafter against the proposed amendment prohibiting the employment of Chinese by public officers and making a candidate for office ineligible who employed or had employed them within three months previously. After stating that such provision was the equivalent to debarring Chinese from employment (vol. 2, p. 676), he declared: "I have had in my employment natives of most European countries, of the isles of the sea, including the Cannibal Islands of the south Pacific. Why do you not exclude the Kanakas, the Fiji, the Malay or the criminal from Australia? No reason against the Chinaman but presses with greater force against these people." Apparently no one challenged this statement, which implied that the Malay, at least, was not included in the designation "Mongolian"; and we can draw but one conclusion from the debates, and that is that such an idea was not present in the minds of the members of the convention.

Much more could be shown but we think we have set down sufficient to indicate that in 1880, in a group that would compare very favorably with the average legislature, there was no thought of applying the name Mongolian to a Malay; that the word was used to designate the class of residents whose presence caused the problem at which all the legislation was directed, viz., the Chinese, and possibly contiguous peoples of like characteristics; that the *common* classification of the races was Blumenbach's, which made the "Malay" one of the five grand subdivisions, i.e., the "brown race," and that such classification persisted until after section 60 of the Civil Code was amended in 1905 to make it consistent with section 69 of the same code. As counsel for appellants have well pointed out, this is not a social question before us, as that was decided by the legislature at the time the code was amended; and if the common thought of to-day is different from what it was at such time, the matter is one that addresses itself to the legislature and not to the courts.

Judgment affirmed.

Works, P.J., and Craig, J., concurred.

Seawell, J., Preston, J., and Thompson, J., dissented.

Notes

1. The decision was 3–3—thus an affirmance because the tie vote meant the trial court's decision would stand. The discussion brings to mind the Supreme Court's decisions in *Ozawa* and *Thind*, which we read in Unit One. The court here held that Filipinos were Malays and not Mongolians, and that, as commonly used, the word Mongolian meant Chinese—and that was what the legislature intended. Would you characterize the court's opinion as textualist, purposivist, or a blend of both approaches to statutory interpretation?

2. Roldan tried to distance himself from the Chinese to win his case, which is the same tactic adopted by Ozawa and Thind. Indeed, the very concept of "Asian American" did not come into broad usage until the second half of the twentieth century. Why do you think that Asian-American self-identification and identity did not emerge until that time, given the centuries-old history of the presence of persons of Asian descent in the United States? Consider, by contrast, the much longer provenance of a Black American identity regardless of country of origin. Why the difference? How about Hispanic ethnicity?

3. Three months after the decision in *Roldan*, the California legislature amended the anti-miscegenation statute by adding "members of the Malay race" to the list of persons with whom marriage to a White person was declared to be "illegal and void." The statute purported to affect all such marriages retroactively, including, presumably, Roldan's. Several other states followed suit, including Maryland in 1935, even though there were very few Filipinos in the state. What inference can you draw from the fact that a state would change its miscegenation law to address cases that were unlikely to arise? What was the rationale behind anti-miscegenation laws in general? Was it purely racial animus against the disfavored persons who were prohibited from marrying White persons?

4. Salvador Roldan and Marjorie Rogers were both immigrants who came to this country in the 1920s—he from the Philippines and she from England. They met on tennis courts in Pasadena, California, and fell in love, and by 1931 they wanted to get married. They were married in April 1933, shortly after the appellate court's decision. Although their marriage was voided by the amendment to the statute, they persevered, had two children, and lived together in a mixed neighborhood in East Pasadena. On August 6, 2016, the California state assembly formally apologized to the Roldan family and honored Salvador and Marjorie for their

commitment to civil rights. *See* Susie Ling with Bryan Roldan, *One Love Story Behind Marriage Rights: The Roldan Family*, EastWind (July 20, 2022), *available at* https://eastwindezine.com/one-love-story-behind-marriage-rights-the-roldan-family/.

Figure 5.8 ***Marjorie Rogers and Salvador Roldan*** **(1931). Pasadena Digital History Collaborative. Photo courtesy of Bryan Roldan.**

5. The U.S. acquisition of the Philippines in 1898 resulted in an increase in the number of Filipinos emigrating to Hawaii and the mainland United States. As noted earlier, the overwhelming majority of the Filipino immigrants were men, who found some comfort in dance halls and gambling resorts. *See* Leti Volpp, *American Mestizo: Filipinos and Antimiscegenation Laws in California*, 33 U.C. Davis L. Rev. 795, 803–08 (2000). A number of Filipino men married White women, and the expansion of the California anti-miscegenation statute placed these marriages in jeopardy. *See Scores of Marriages Here Declared to Be Illegal*, San Diego Evening Tribune, Feb. 28, 1925.

6. Anti-miscegenation laws presented a host of complicated legal questions. What was the difference between a law that prohibited the granting of a marriage license to a forbidden couple and a law that made such marriages illegal and

void? Some statutes specified that such marriages were unlawful and "voidable"—what's the difference between void and voidable? What if a proscribed mixed-race couple went to another state, for instance, New Mexico, where there was no applicable anti-miscegenation statute? Would California have to honor that marriage under the Full Faith and Credit Clause of the Constitution? (The California Assembly and Senate passed a resolution requesting the State of Utah to ban marriages between Whites and Malays, which it did in 1939; Arizona, Nevada, South Dakota, and Wyoming already had such laws on the books.) What would be the status of a child born to a forbidden marriage? Would he or she be deemed illegitimate?

7. Public awareness of the Filipino miscegenation issue was piqued by a sensational murder case in 1925 involving Timothy Yatko, a Filipino waiter, who stabbed a White man he discovered with his estranged wife, Lola Butler. Yatko had originally met Butler when she was a "taxi dance" girl at a dance hall where Filipino men would go to dance with women, mostly White, at 10 cents a dance. *See generally* Carlos Bulosan, *America Is in the Heart* (1946); Volpp, 33 U.C. Davis L. Rev. at 805–08. Butler left Yatko and took up with the murder victim, Harry Kidder, a piano player. The prosecution sought to use Butler as a witness against her estranged husband, but was prevented from doing so by the spousal privilege. The state made the argument that the marriage was "illegal and void" because Yatko was a Mongolian and that therefore the privilege did not apply. The prosecution prevailed in getting Butler's testimony in, and Yatko was convicted and sentenced to life imprisonment at San Quentin state penitentiary.

8. In 1934, Congress passed the Tydings-McDuffie Act, which promised the Philippines independence. The Act contributed to a dramatic decline in Philippine immigration, which was a principal purpose for its enactment. Shortly thereafter, Pearl Harbor and World War II ensued. The social changes triggered by the war, including the important role played in the fight by non-White persons both in the United States and abroad, occasioned reexamination of anti-miscegenation laws, including the California version.

9. In 1948, the California Supreme Court decided *Perez v. Sharp*, 32 Cal. 2d 711 (Cal. 1948), striking down the California anti-miscegenation statute in a case involving a White woman and a Black man. The decision was apparently the first in the country to hold a race restriction on marriage unconstitutional. At a time when popular opinion overwhelmingly disapproved of interracial marriage, three California justices concluded that the ban violated the Due Process and Equal Protection clauses of the U.S. Constitution and a fourth justice concurred in the judgment on the ground that the statute violated the plaintiffs' right to freedom of religion. The vagueness of the California statute was an additional concern. The dissent argued for deference to the state legislature and noted that 30 states had anti-miscegenation laws and that numerous scientific articles argued that interracial marriage was unhealthy and undesirable. 32 Cal. 2d at 747.

Figure 5.9 ***Timothy Yatko in the Los Angeles courtroom*** **(1925). UCLA Library Special Collections.**

10. The *Perez* decision preceded *Loving v. Virginia* by 19 years. In *Loving*, decided in 1967, the Supreme Court struck down all laws prohibiting interracial marriage. *Loving v. Virginia*, 388 U.S. 1 (1967). Mildred Jeter was African American and also of Native American ancestry. She married Richard Loving, a White man, in Washington, D.C. They returned to their home in Virginia. Based on an anonymous tip, the police raided their home and found them sleeping in bed. They were arrested and eventually pleaded guilty to "cohabiting as man and wife, against the peace and dignity of the Commonwealth," in violation of Virginia's anti-miscegenation law. The Supreme Court reversed unanimously, holding:

    There can be no question but that Virginia's miscegenation statutes rest solely upon distinctions drawn according to race. The statutes proscribe generally accepted conduct if engaged in by members of different races. Over the years, this Court has consistently repudiated "[d]istinctions between citizens solely because of their ancestry" as being "odious to a free people whose institutions are founded upon the doctrine of equality." *Hirabayashi v. United States,* 320 U.S. 81, 100 (1943). At the very least, the Equal Protection Clause demands that racial classifications, especially suspect in criminal statutes, be subjected to the "most rigid

> scrutiny," *Korematsu v. United States,* 323 U.S. 214, 216 (1944), and, if they are ever to be upheld, they must be shown to be necessary to the accomplishment of some permissible state objective, independent of the racial discrimination which it was the object of the Fourteenth Amendment to eliminate. . . .
>
> There is patently no legitimate overriding purpose independent of invidious racial discrimination which justifies this classification. The fact that Virginia prohibits only interracial marriages involving white persons demonstrates that the racial classifications must stand on their own justification, as measures designed to maintain White Supremacy. We have consistently denied the constitutionality of measures which restrict the rights of citizens on account of race. There can be no doubt that restricting the freedom to marry solely because of racial classifications violates the central meaning of the Equal Protection Clause. . . .
>
> These statutes also deprive the Lovings of liberty without due process of law in violation of the Due Process Clause of the Fourteenth Amendment. The freedom to marry has long been recognized as one of the vital personal rights essential to the orderly pursuit of happiness by free men. Marriage is one of the "basic civil rights of man," fundamental to our very existence and survival. *Skinner v. Oklahoma,* 316 U.S. 535, 541 (1942). . . . To deny this fundamental freedom on so unsupportable a basis as the racial classifications embodied in these statutes, classifications so directly subversive of the principle of equality at the heart of the Fourteenth Amendment, is surely to deprive all the State's citizens of liberty without due process of law. . . .

11. The Japanese American Citizens League submitted an amicus brief in support of the Lovings. A Japanese-American attorney—William Marutani—was permitted to argue, and he focused on the impact of the Virginia law on Japanese Americans. Marutani would eventually become a judge in the Court of Common Pleas in Philadelphia, the first Asian-American judge on the East Coast. *See* David Muto, *An Unsung Hero in the Story of Interracial Marriage*, New Yorker, Nov. 17, 2016.

12. The majority opinions in both *Perez* and *Loving* rely on the Fourteenth Amendment Due Process and Equal Protection Clauses to strike down the relevant state anti-miscegenation laws. How does the reasoning for the unconstitutionality of anti-miscegenation statutes differ as between the two Clauses? Which is more persuasive to you? Which do you think has greater potential to be used to challenge other laws regulating marriage?

13. Some years before *Loving*, the Supreme Court had the opportunity to address the Virginia anti-miscegenation statute in a case involving a White woman, Ruby Lamberth, and a Chinese man, Ham Say Naim, in Norfolk, Virginia. They

were married in North Carolina, which banned only marriage between Whites and Blacks, and then returned to live in Virginia. Eventually, however, they fell apart—and Ruby sued to annul the marriage, arguing that it was illegal for them to have married in the first place. Denise M. Watson, *Before* Loving v. Virginia, *There Was* Naim v. Naim *in Norfolk to Challenge the State's Race Laws*, The Virginian-Pilot, Dec. 10, 2016, *available at* https://www.pilotonline.com/history/article_58459574-0ba6-5ecc-b2f3-6b8a23f7e02a.html. The Virginia courts agreed, holding the marriage void, relying on the right of states to prevent the "corruption of the races." *Naim v. Naim*, 197 Va. 80 (1955), *adhered to*, 197 Va. 734 (1956). The U.S. Supreme Court's appellate jurisdiction over cases decided by state supreme courts against federal constitutional rights at the time was mandatory. And yet, the Supreme Court declined to hear the case—a move that was heavily criticized by federal courts scholars who espoused the dogma that a court must exercise the jurisdiction Congress has given it by statute. *Naim v. Naim*, 250 U.S. 985 (1956). Some have suggested that the Court did not hear the case because it believed the country was not ready to accept mixed marriages. Does that seem plausible to you, and, if so, is "the country's not ready yet for mixed marriage" a legitimate ground for Supreme Court justices to adopt a questionable way to wiggle out of mandatory jurisdiction? And do you think the fact that *Naim v. Naim* involved an Asian-White marriage as opposed to a Black-White marriage made a difference in the Court's decision to wait? Do you think it mattered that in *Naim* the woman was White whereas in *Loving* the woman was Black? And what about the procedural posture of the initial case—a White woman suing to get out of an unhappy marriage, as opposed to *Loving*, which involved a criminal statute?

14. If there is any domain of human activity in which the courts have recognized the states' police power as paramount, it is family law. Even today, U.S. federal courts apply abstention doctrines that generally avoid adjudicating U.S. family law issues. How do you explain the willingness, then, of the California State Supreme Court in 1948 and the U.S. Supreme Court in 1967 to issue decisions affirming a federal constitutional constraint on the right of states to regulate marriage?

15. After World War II, tens of thousands of Japanese women married American G.I.s and returned with them to live in America. *See* Kathryn Tolbert, *The Untold Stories of Japanese War Brides*, Wash. Post, Sept. 22, 2016, *available at* https://www.washingtonpost.com/sf/national/2016/09/22/from-hiroko-to-susie-the-untold-stories-of-japanese-war-brides/?utm_term=.6c4e5b3fb173. In 1945, Congress passed what became known as the War Brides Act to facilitate the admission of spouses of members of the U.S. Armed Forces into the United States as non-quota immigrants. Rose Cuison Villazor, *The Other Loving: Uncovering the Federal Government's Racial Regulation of Marriage*, 86 N.Y.U. L. Rev. 1361, 1381–82 (2011). In *Bonham v. Bouiss*, 161 F.2d 678 (9th Cir. 1947), however, the Ninth Circuit held that Helene Bouiss, a woman who met and eventually married an American serviceman she met in Japan, was not admissible because she was half Japanese.

Figure 5.10 ***Airmen and Their Japanese Dates "Do" the Town Together. Visiting the Local Points of Interest in Tachikawa in May 1952.*** **National Archives.**

Id. at 679 ("Since we conclude that appellee is not eligible to citizenship by reason of her Japanese blood, she is not admissible as a non-quota immigrant . . ., unless [the War Brides Act] has somehow removed that bar to her entry. . . . We cannot agree with that contention."). What is the court referring to when it said that the appellee was not eligible for citizenship because of her Japanese blood? Eventually, additional legislation helped ease the admission of women of Asian origin as spouses or fiancés of American servicemen. *See, e.g.*, Alien Fiancées and Fiancés Act of 1946, Pub. L. 79-471, 60 Stat. 339 (1946). Indeed, in 1948, Bouiss was admitted pursuant to one of these amendments to the War Brides Act. *See* Christina Ponsa, *Love and War*, Jotwell (April 6, 2012), https://legalhist.jotwell.com/love-and-war/.

16. The early marriage equality cases brought by Asian Americans helped pave the way for what was apparently the first same-sex marriage case to be tried in the United States. The case was *Baehr v. Lewin*, and it was brought nearly a quarter of a century before the United States Supreme Court held, in *Obergefell v. Hodges*, that the Fourteenth Amendment guaranteed same-sex couples the right to marry. *See Obergefell v. Hodges*, 576 U.S. 644 (2015); *Baehr v. Lewin*, 852 P.2d 44 (Ha. 1993); *Baehr v. Miike*, Civ. No. 91-1394, 1996 WL 694235 (Cir. Ct. Haw.

Dec. 3, 1996). The case arose in Hawaii, and three of the six plaintiffs were Asian American, as were several of the judges. The Hawaii Supreme Court held that "sex" was a "suspect category" under the Hawaii constitution and that therefore the Hawaii statute limiting marriage to a marriage between a man and a woman was subject to strict scrutiny. *Baehr v. Lewin*, 852 P.2d at 67. On remand, the Circuit Court (the trial court) held that the state had failed to carry its burden of proving a compelling state interest for the bar on same-sex marriages and it held the statute unconstitutional. *Baehr v. Miike*, 1996 WL 694235 at *19–21. While the decision was on appeal back to the Hawaii Supreme Court, the Hawaii legislature proposed a constitutional amendment and on November 3, 1998, 69% of the voters in Hawaii chose to ratify the proposal, which gave the legislature the power to limit marriage to opposite-sex couples. On December 9, 1999, the Hawaii Supreme Court reversed the judgment of the Circuit Court, declaring that the constitutional amendment had rendered the plaintiffs' complaint moot. The case was remanded for entry of judgment in favor of the state. *Baehr v. Miike*, No. 20371, 1999 WL 35643448 (Haw. Dec. 9, 1999). Despite the constitutional amendment, the *Baehr* decision still played a significant role in the marriage equality movement, and, indeed, the Supreme Court cited it in *Obergefell*. 576 U.S. at 662.

---

6. Education

Related to the freedom to marry is the freedom of parents to teach their children the skills and knowledge to thrive in society, and to raise their children according to their values, norms, and culture. In modern times, schools and universities, some funded by the government, and others by private actors such as religious groups, cultural associations, or private organizations, play the principal role in education.

Asian immigrants to the United States had additional reasons to be particularly concerned about education. First, China, Korea, and—to a lesser extent—Japan, were ancient social and political orders that venerated the scholar-official selected through a competitive examination for the ostensible purpose of favoring merit over birth. The highest mark of social prestige and political power in those East Asian countries was passing the highest civil service examination, which meant a position in the government. In China for a millennium and in Korea for several centuries, the civil service examination was required to enter the ranks of officialdom and to ascend to the highest positions in government. To a great extent, Asians in the United States carried with them the veneration of education and the belief that it was central to personal, social, and political success. Second, Asian parents sought to preserve and pass on their cultures to their children. Juxtaposed to the desire to assimilate and to be accepted in the United States was the desire to preserve their cultural identity and language, which differed so dramatically from their European counterparts dominant in the

United States. The importance of education to Asian immigrants led, unsurprisingly, to litigation in the U.S. courts.

We consider two cases: one decided by the California Supreme Court and one by the United States Supreme Court.

Figure 5.11 ***Joseph, Emily, Mamie, Frank, and Mary Tape*** **(ca. 1884–85).**

Tape v. Hurley

66 Cal. 473 (1885)

SHARPSTEIN, J.

The main question in this case is whether a child between six and twenty-one years of age, of Chinese parentage, but who was born and has always lived in the city and county of San Francisco, is entitled to admission in the public school of the district in which she resides. The language of the Code is as follows:

> 'Every school, unless otherwise provided by law, must be open for the admission of all children between six and twenty-one years of age residing in the district; and the board of trustees, or city board of education,

> have power to admit adults and children not residing in the district whenever good reasons exist therefor. Trustees shall have the power to exclude children of filthy or vicious habits, or children suffering from contagious or infectious diseases.' Pol. Code, § 1667.

That is the latest legislative expression on the subject, and was passed as late as 1880. Prior to that time the first clause of the section read: 'Every school, unless otherwise provided by special statute, must be open for the admission of all *white* children between five and twenty-one years of age, residing in the district.'

As amended, the cause is broad enough to include all children who are not precluded from entering a public school by some provision of law. And we are not aware of any law which forbids the entrance of children of any race or nationality. The legislature not only declares who shall be admitted, but also who may be excluded, and it does not authorize the exclusion of any one on the ground upon which alone the exclusion of the respondent here is sought to be justified. The vicious, the filthy, and those having contagious or infectious diseases may be excluded, without regard to their race, color, or nationality. This law must be construed as any other would be construed. 'Where a law is plain and unambiguous, whether it be expressed in general or limited terms, *the legislature should be intended to mean what they have plainly expressed*, and consequently no room is left for construction.' *U. S.* v. *Fisher*, 2 Cranch, 358, 399. 'When the law is clear and explicit, and its provisions are susceptible of but one interpretation, its consequences, if evil, can only be avoided by a change of the law itself, to be effected by legislative and not judicial action.' *Bosley* v. *Mattingly*, 14 B. Mon. 72. This rule is never controverted or doubted, although perhaps sometimes lost sight of. In this case, if effect be given to the intention of the legislature, as indicated by the clear and unambiguous language used by them, respondent here has the same right to enter a public school that any other child has. It is not alleged that she is vicious or filthy, or that she has a contagious or infectious disease. As the legislature has not denied to the children of any race or nationality the right to enter our public schools, the question whether it might have done so does not arise in this case.

We think the superintendent of schools was improperly joined as a defendant in this action, and that the court properly dismissed the action as to the board of education. In *Ward* v. *Flood*, 48 Cal. 36, the action was against the teacher alone. That it was properly brought seems to have been conceded. The board of education has power 'to make, establish, and enforce all necessary and proper rules and regulations *not contrary to law*,' and none other. St. 1871–72, p. 846. Teachers cannot justify a violation of law on the ground that a resolution of the board of education required them to do so.

The judgment must be modified so as to make the writ run against the defendant Hurley alone. In other respects, it is affirmed.

Notes

1. The child in question was Mamie Tape, who was eight years old when she was denied admission to a "white school" because she was Chinese. Her parents were Mary Tape and Joseph Tape, immigrants from China who worked hard and became "archetypal members of the first Chinese American middle class." Mae Ngai, *The Lucky Ones* ix (2010). They wanted to send Mamie to the public school in their neighborhood in San Francisco. In September 1884, Mary took Mamie to the Spring Valley Primary School, but the principal, Jennie Hurley, turned her away. *Id.* 43–44. The Tapes hired a lawyer (William Gibson, son of the former missionary Otis Gibson) and filed suit, *Tape v. Hurley*.
2. What was the basis of the Court's decision? Did it rule on equal protection or other constitutional grounds?
3. The Tapes' victory was short-lived. The school board persuaded the California legislature to authorize separate schools for "children of Chinese and Mongolian descent." The school board was prepared to educate Chinese children, but in segregated schools. It thereafter opened the Chinese Primary School in Chinatown. Although the Tapes preferred to send Mamie and her younger brother to a White school, their further efforts to do so were rebuffed. When the Chinese Primary School opened in April 1885, the two Tape children were the first to arrive. Ngai, at 54–56.

Gong Lum v. Rice

275 U.S. 78 (1927)

TAFT, Chief Justice:

This was a petition for mandamus filed in the state circuit court of Mississippi for the First judicial district of Bolivar County. Gong Lum is a resident of Mississippi, resides in the Rosedale Consolidated High School District, and is the father of Martha Lum. He is engaged in the mercantile business. Neither he nor she was connected with the consular service, or any other service, of the government of China, or any other government at the time of her birth.

She was nine years old when the petition was filed, having been born January 21, 1915, and she sued by her next friend, Chew How, who is a native-born citizen of the United States and the State of Mississippi. The petition alleged that she was of good moral character, between the ages of 5 and 21 years, and that, as she was such a citizen and an educable child, it became her father's duty under the law to send her to school; that she desired to attend the Rosedale Consolidated High School; that, at the opening of the school, she appeared as a pupil, but at the noon recess she was notified by the superintendent that she would not be allowed to return to the school; that an order had been issued by the board of trustees, who are made defendants, excluding her from attending the school solely on the ground that she was of Chinese descent, and not a member of the white or Caucasian race, and that their order had been made in pursuance to instructions from the State Superintendent of Education of Mississippi, who is also made a defendant. The petitioners further show that there is no school maintained in the district for the education of children of Chinese descent, and none established in Bolivar County where she could attend.

The Constitution of Mississippi requires that there shall be a county common school fund, made up of poll taxes from the various counties, to be retained in the counties where the same is collected, and a state common school fund to be taken from the general fund in the state treasury, which together shall be sufficient to maintain a common school for a term of four months in each scholastic year, but that any county or separate school district may levy an additional tax to maintain schools for a longer time than a term of four months, and that the said common school fund shall be distributed among the several counties and separate school districts in proportion to the number of educable children in each, to be collected from the data in the office of the State Superintendent of Education in the manner prescribed by law; that the legislature encourage by all suitable means the promotion of intellectual, scientific, moral, and agricultural improvement by the establishment of a uniform system of free public schools by taxation or otherwise, for all children between the ages of 5 and 21 years, and, as soon as practicable, establish schools of higher grade.

The petition alleged that, in obedience to this mandate of the constitution, the legislature has provided for the establishment and for the payment of the expenses of the Rosedale Consolidated High School, and that the plaintiff, Gong Lum, the petitioner's father, is a taxpayer and helps to support and maintain the school; that Martha Lum is an educable child, is entitled to attend the school as a pupil, and that this is the only school conducted in the district available for her as a pupil; that the right to attend it is a valuable right; that she is not a member of the colored race, nor is she of mixed blood, but that she is pure Chinese; that she is, by the action of the board of trustees and the state superintendent, discriminated against directly, and denied her right to be a member of the Rosedale school; that the school authorities have no discretion under the law as to her admission as a pupil in the school, but that they continue without authority of law to deny her the right to attend it as a pupil. For these reasons, the writ of mandamus is prayed for against the defendants, commanding them and each of them to desist from discriminating against her on account of her race or ancestry, and to give her the same rights and privileges that other educable children between the ages of 5 and 21 are granted in the Rosedale Consolidated High School.

The petition was demurred to by the defendants on the ground, among others, that the bill showed on its face that plaintiff is a member of the Mongolian or yellow race, and therefore not entitled to attend the schools provided by law in the State of Mississippi for children of the white or Caucasian race. The trial court overruled the demurrer and ordered that a writ of mandamus issue to the defendants as prayed in the petition.

The defendants then appealed to the Supreme Court of Mississippi, which heard the case. *Rice v. Gong Lum,* 139 Miss. 760. In its opinion, it directed its attention to the proper construction of § 207 of the state constitution of 1890, which provides: "Separate schools shall be maintained for children of the white and colored races." The court held that this provision of the constitution divided the educable children into those of the pure white or Caucasian race, on the one hand, and the brown, yellow, and black races, on the other, and therefore that Martha Lum, of the Mongolian or yellow race, could not insist on being classed with the whites under this constitutional division. The court said:

> "The legislature is not compelled to provide separate schools for each of the colored races, and unless and until it does provide such schools, and provide for segregation of the other races, such races are entitled to have the benefit of the colored public schools. Under our statutes, a colored public school exists in every county and in some convenient district, in which every colored child is entitled to obtain an education. These schools are within the reach of all the children of the state, and the plaintiff does not show by her petition that she applied for admission to such schools. On the contrary, the petitioner takes the position that, because there are no separate public schools for Mongolians, she is entitled to enter the white public schools in preference to the colored public schools. . . . "
>
> "If the plaintiff desires, she may attend the colored public schools of her district, or, if she does not so desire, she may go to a private school. The compulsory school law of this state does not require the attendance at a public school, and a parent under the decisions of the Supreme Court of the United States has a right to educate his child in a private school if he so desires. But plaintiff is not entitled to attend a white public school."

As we have seen, the plaintiffs aver that the Rosedale Consolidated High School is the only school conducted in that district available for Martha Lum as a pupil. They also aver that there is no school maintained in the district of Bolivar County for the education of Chinese children, and none in the county. How are these averments to be reconciled with the statement of the state supreme court that colored schools are maintained in every county by virtue of the constitution? This seems to be explained, in the language of the state supreme court, as follows:

> "By statute it is provided that all the territory of each county of the state shall be divided into school districts separately for the white and colored races—that is to say, the whole territory is to be divided into white school districts, and then a new division of the county for colored school districts. . . ."

We must assume, then, that there are school districts for colored children in Bolivar County, but that no colored school is within the limits of the Rosedale Consolidated High School District. This is not inconsistent with there being at a place outside of that district and in a different district, a colored school which the plaintiff Martha Lum may conveniently attend. If so, she is not denied, under the existing school system, the right to attend and enjoy the privileges of a common school education in a colored school. If it were otherwise, the petition should have contained an allegation showing it. Had the petition alleged specifically that there was no colored school in Martha Lum's neighborhood to which she could conveniently go, a different question would have been presented, and this without regard to the state supreme court's construction of the state constitution as limiting the white schools provided for the education of children of the white or Caucasian race. But we do not find the petition to present such a situation.

The case then reduces itself to the question whether a state can be said to afford to a child of Chinese ancestry, born in this country and a citizen of the United States, the equal protection of the laws by giving her the opportunity for a common school education in a school which receives only colored children of the brown, yellow, or black races.

The right and power of the state to regulate the method of providing for the education of its youth at public expense is clear. In *Cumming v. Richmond County Board of Education,* 175 U. S. 528, 545, persons of color sued the board of education to enjoin it from maintaining a high school for white children without providing a similar school for colored children, which had existed and had been discontinued. Mr. Justice Harlan, in delivering the opinion of the Court, said:

> "Under the circumstances disclosed, we cannot say that this action of the state court was, within the meaning of the Fourteenth Amendment, a denial by the state to the plaintiffs and to those associated with them of the equal protection of the laws, or of any privileges belonging to them as citizens of the United States. We may add that, while all admit that the benefits and burdens of public taxation must be shared by citizens without discrimination against any class on account of their race, the education of the people in schools maintained by state taxation is a matter belonging to the respective states, and any interference on the part of federal authority with the management of such schools cannot be justified, except in the case of a clear and unmistakable disregard of rights secured by the supreme law of the land."

The question here is whether a Chinese citizen of the United States is denied equal protection of the laws when he is classed among the colored races and furnished facilities for education equal to that offered to all, whether white, brown, yellow, or black. Were this a new question, it would call for very full argument and consideration; but we think that it is the same question which has been many times decided to be within the constitutional power of the state legislature to settle, without intervention of the federal courts under the federal Constitution. *Citations omitted*; *Wong Him v. Callahan,* 119 F. 381.

In *Plessy v. Ferguson,* 163 U. S. 537, 544-545, in upholding the validity under the Fourteenth Amendment of a statute of Louisiana requiring the separation of the white and colored races in railway coaches, a more difficult question than this, this Court, speaking of permitted race separation, said:

> "The most common instance of this is connected with the establishment of separate schools for white and colored children, which has been held to be a valid exercise of the legislative power even by courts of states where the political rights of the colored race have been longest and most earnestly enforced."

The case of *Roberts v. City of Boston, supra,* in which Chief Justice Shaw, of the Supreme Judicial Court of Massachusetts, announced the opinion of that court upholding the separation of colored and white schools under a state constitutional injunction of equal protection, the same as the Fourteenth Amendment, was then referred to, and this Court continued:

> "Similar laws have been enacted by Congress under its general power of legislation over the District of Columbia, Rev.Stat.D.C. §§281, 282, 283, 310, 319, as well as by the legislatures of many of the states, and have been generally, if not uniformly, sustained by the courts"—citing many of the cases above named.

Most of the cases cited arose, it is true, over the establishment of separate schools as between white pupils and black pupils, but we cannot think that the question is any different, or that any different result can be reached, assuming the cases above cited to be rightly decided, where the issue is as between white pupils and the pupils of the yellow races. The decision is within the discretion of the state in regulating its public schools, and does not conflict with the Fourteenth Amendment.

The judgment of the Supreme Court of Mississippi is *Affirmed.*

Notes

1. The Court, of course, relied on its decision in *Plessy v. Ferguson*, 163 U.S. 537 (1896). While Justice Harlan dissented in *Plessy*, concluding that the state of Louisiana was inconsistent in its treatment of "the personal liberty of citizens, white and black," and was "hostile to both the spirit and letter of the Constitution of the United States," *id.* at 563, he made the following observations about the Chinese:

   > There is a race so different from our own that we do not permit those belonging to it to become citizens of the United States. Persons belonging

> to it are, with few exceptions, absolutely excluded from our country. I allude to the Chinese race. But, by the statute in question, a Chinaman can ride in the same passenger coach with white citizens of the United States, while citizens of the black race in Louisiana, many of whom, perhaps, risked their lives for the preservation of the Union, who are entitled, by law, to participate in the political control of the state and nation, who are not excluded, by law or by reason of their race, from public stations of any kind, and who have all the legal rights that belong to white citizens, are yet declared to be criminals, liable to imprisonment, if they ride in a public coach occupied by citizens of the white race. It is scarcely just to say that a colored citizen should not object to occupying a public coach assigned to his own race. He does not object, nor, perhaps, would he object to separate coaches for his race if his rights under the law were recognized. But he does object, and he ought never to cease objecting, that citizens of the white and black races can be adjudged criminals because they sit, or claim the right to sit, in the same public coach on a public highway.

Id. at 562. What was Justice Harlan saying here? Why was he invoking the Chinese? How do these observations square with his declaration that "[o]ur constitution is color-blind?" *Id.* at 559. *See generally* Gabriel J. Chin, *The* Plessy *Myth: Justice Harlan and the Chinese Cases*, 82 Iowa L. Rev. 151 (1996).

2. Martha Lum was the daughter of Gong Lum, a Chinese immigrant who had prospered in Rosedale, Mississippi, as a grocer. The Lum family was one of a number of Chinese families in the Mississippi Delta who successfully operated grocery stores in the early 1900s. How did this come about? Consider in this respect the Anti-Coolie Labor Act of 1863. *See* G. Edward White, *The Lost Episode of* Gong Lum v. Rice, 18 Green Bag 2d 191 (2015).

3. Martha and her sister Berda were initially able to enroll in the Rosedale Consolidated School, and they spent the 1923–1924 school year there. They were placed in a classroom for third- and fourth-grade students. There were five Chinese kids in the school that year. Martha, who was nine years old at the time, was one of the top students in her class. At the start of the next school year, however, Martha, Berda, and the two other Chinese kids who were in the school were summoned to the principal's office and told that they were no longer welcome because they were "colored," and the school was only for White children. The four Chinese kids were sent home.

4. One Chinese resident of the Mississippi Delta in the 1920s offered this explanation for why Martha Lum was turned away from the "white school":

> By law, the Chinese weren't allowed to go to the Bok Guey [white] schools, but . . . some went anyway. If you lived in a small town and you mixed with the Bok Guey, . . . they would let the Chinese go to their schools 'cause they don't know no better. But as soon as . . . somebody said [a

Figure 5.12 ***The two Lum sisters were admitted to a school in Rosedale, Mississippi, which did not enforce the law restricting White schools to Caucasians. Three other Chinese children attended the school.*** **Photo taken in 1924. Delta State University Archives & Museum.**

> child] was colored, she's Chinese, then you have to be dismissed. . . . [T]hat's what happened to Mrs. Gong Lum.

White, 18 Green Bag 2d at 197 (quoting Robert Seto Quan, *Lotus Among the Magnolias: The Mississippi Chinese* 46 (1982)). This suggests that some Whites were willing to accept the Chinese until they came to believe the Chinese were "colored." What does this tell us?

5. To this day, there is a community of Chinese Americans in Mississippi, many of whom are descendants of the grocery store owners. *See* James Estrin, *Neither Black nor White in the Mississippi Delta*, N.Y. Times, March 13, 2018.

6. Martha Lum was born in the United States and therefore a U.S. citizen. The Court held that, nonetheless, she was not denied equal protection by a law that required her to attend a school for "colored children of the brown, yellow, or black races." What was the Court's reasoning? How can the decision be reconciled with some of the Court's other, earlier equal protection decisions?

7. In *Farrington v. Tokushige*, decided the same year as *Gong Lum v. Rice*, the Supreme Court considered a law passed by the Territory of Hawaii requiring schools to obtain a permit, adhere to a comprehensive set of rules, and pay certain fees to teach foreign languages. 273 U.S. 284 (1927). The Court unanimously held that the law violated the due process clause of the Fifth Amendment:

> There are one hundred and sixty-three foreign language schools in the territory. Nine are conducted in the Korean language, seven in the Chinese, and the remainder in the Japanese. Respondents are members of

> numerous voluntary unincorporated associations conducting foreign language schools for instruction of Japanese children. These are owned, maintained, and conducted by upwards of 5,000 persons, the property used in connection therewith is worth $250,000, the enrolled pupils number 20,000, and 300 teachers are employed. These schools receive no aid from public funds. All children residing within the territory are required to attend some public or equivalent school, and practically all who go to foreign language schools also attend public or such private schools. It is affirmed by counsel for petitioners that Japanese pupils in the public and equivalent private schools increased from 1,320 in 1900 to 19,354 in 1920, and that, out of a total of 65,369 pupils of all races on December 31, 1924, 30,487 were Japanese. . . .
>
> [T]he School Act and the measures adopted thereunder go far beyond mere regulation of privately supported schools, where children obtain instruction deemed valuable by their parents and which is not obviously in conflict with any public interest. They give affirmative direction concerning the intimate and essential details of such schools, intrust their control to public officers, and deny both owners and patrons reasonable choice and discretion in respect of teachers, curriculum, and textbooks. Enforcement of the Act probably would destroy most if not all of them, and certainly it would deprive parents of fair opportunity to procure for their children instruction which they think important, and we cannot say is harmful. The Japanese parent has the right to direct the education of his own child without unreasonable restrictions; the Constitution protects him as well as those who speak another tongue.

273 U.S. at 290–91, 298. The *Tokushige* Court concluded that the Hawaii territorial government law deprived the liberty and property of school owners and the parents and children who patronized them without due process. In so doing, the Court relied on a line of Fourteenth Amendment substantive due process precedents affirming the right of parents to educate their children in their native languages and parochial schools, despite state English-language-only and mandatory public education laws respectively. *See id.* at 299 (citing *Meyer v. Nebraska*, 262 U.S. 404 (1923)); *Bartels v. Iowa*, 262 U.S. 404 (1923); *Pierce v. Soc'y of Sisters*, 268 U.S. 510 (1925). How can one reconcile the Supreme Court's decision in *Gong Lum v. Rice* denying Chinese parents a constitutional right to send their child to a White public school with its simultaneous decision in *Farrington v. Tokushige* affording Japanese parents a constitutional right to educate their children at Japanese language schools without comprehensive regulation by the local government?

8. Twenty-seven years after *Gong Lum* and *Farrington*, the Supreme Court handed down its monumental decision in *Brown v. Board of Education*, 347 U.S. 483 (1954). The *Brown* Court held that "separate educational facilities are inherently unequal" with respect to public elementary schools, in violation of the Fourteenth

Amendment's Equal Protection Clause. In practical terms, that holding overruled *Plessy v. Ferguson*, which had upheld the constitutionality of "separate but equal" public facilities for Black and White persons. *Brown* had enormous consequences for U.S. society at large, including the growing Asian American population, but it did not specify a concrete plan for how desegregation was to be effected. In a follow-up case, the Supreme Court broadly directed that states and localities desegregate their schools "with all deliberate speed." *Brown v. Board of Education* (*Brown II*), 394 U.S. 294 (1955).

9. San Francisco proved to be a focal point of *Brown*'s impact on Asian Americans. In *Johnson v. San Francisco Unified School District*, 339 F. Supp. 1315 (N.D. Cal. 1971), parents of Black children in the San Francisco Unified School District sued to desegregate the district's public schools based on the Supreme Court decision in *Brown*. The district court held that "[f]or a long period of time there has been and there now is *de jure* segregation in the San Francisco public elementary schools.... This segregation must be eradicated forthwith." 339 F. Supp. at 1323. The district court thus approved plans submitted by the San Francisco school system to desegregate the schools.

A major part of the plans was the breakup of Chinatown schools that were overwhelmingly populated by Chinese American children, a consequence of *Tape v. Hurley* and the decades-old California statutes enacted to overturn it. Until they were repealed in 1947, Sections 8003 and 8004 of the California Education Code had provided that:

> The governing board of any school district may establish separate schools for Indian children... and for children of Chinese, Japanese, or Mongolian parentage. When separate schools are established for Indian children or children of Chinese, Japanese, or Mongolian parentage, the Indian children or children of Chinese, Japanese, or Mongolian parentage shall not be admitted into any other school.

1947 Cal. Stats., chap. 737, §§ 1–2.

Parents with students in three schools with large supermajorities of children of Chinese descent (1,074 of 1,111 total students—96.7%; 456 of 482—94.6%; 230 of 289—79.6%) sued to enjoin the plan. They did not want their children bused or otherwise assigned out of neighborhood schools that had robust bilingual English-Chinese programs and Asian-inclusive cultures and communities. The district court denied the class's motion to enjoin the comprehensive desegregation plan, and the Ninth Circuit twice denied motions for a stay of the district court's ruling. Likewise, when the parents sought a stay in the U.S. Supreme Court, Justice Douglas denied the request, writing:

> It is not for me to approve or disapprove the plans; that is a matter that goes to the merits, and the appeal has not been heard. The plan, however, has earmarks of a thoughtful plan, at least measured by some of

> the thoughtful concerns of the Chinese community. The District Court ruled:
>
> "Bilingual classes are not proscribed. They may be provided in any manner which does not create, maintain or foster segregation.
>
> "There is no prohibition of courses teaching the cultural background and heritages of various racial and ethnic groups. While such courses may have particular appeal to members of the particular racial or ethnic group whose background and heritage is being studied, it would seem to be highly desirable that this understanding be shared with those of other racial and ethnic backgrounds."

Guey Heung Lee v. Johnson, 404 U.S. 1215, 1217 (1971) (Douglas, *J.*) (quoting *Johnson v. San Francisco Unified School District*, 339 F. Supp. 1315, 1322 (N.D. Cal. 1971)). Should courts view a minority racial group's voluntary desire to maintain public schools (or colleges) with supermajorities of the group to allow for an inclusive and multicultural community focused on the group as beyond the purview of *Brown*'s mandate to desegregate? If courts should not do so, as the district court, appellate court, and circuit justice holdings in *Lee v. Johnson* imply, then what are the implications for government sponsorship or funding of historically Black colleges and universities (HBCUs)? Is *Lee v. Johnson* in tension with *Farrington v. Tokushige* upholding the constitutional rights of parents to educate their children in their native language and culture?

10. The concern of Chinese-American parents for bilingual education resulted in an important victory at the Supreme Court three years later in *Lau v. Nichols*, 414 U.S. 563 (1974). Kinney Kinmon Lau and 20 other Chinese-American students brought a class action against the San Francisco Unified School District, arguing that the failure of the school system to provide some 1,800 students with supplemental instruction to improve their English language proficiency violated their rights. (The school district provided such supplemental instruction to approximately 1,000 of the 2,856 non-English-speaking Chinese students in the school system.) The plaintiffs relied on the Equal Protection Clause of the Fourteenth Amendment as well as Title VI of the Civil Rights Act of 1964, 42 U.S.C. § 2000d *et seq*. The district court had denied relief and the Ninth Circuit affirmed, both initially and upon rehearing the case *en banc*.

    The school district argued that its policies were not discriminatory because it offered the same instruction to all students regardless of national origin. In other words, the school district's position was that it was not the district's fault that some students were not proficient in English. The Supreme Court unanimously reversed, with Justice Douglas writing for the Court. He noted that California law provided that "English shall be the basic instruction in all schools," it was "'the policy of the state' to insure 'the mastery of English by all pupils in the schools,'" and no student could graduate from grade 12 who did not meet the standards for English proficiency. 414 U.S. at 565 (citations omitted). He then concluded:

> Under these state-imposed standards there is no equality of treatment merely by providing students with the same facilities, textbooks, teachers, and curriculum; for students who do not understand English are effectively foreclosed from any meaningful education.
>
> Basic English skills are at the very core of what these public schools teach. Imposition of a requirement that, before a child can effectively participate in the educational program, he must have already acquired those basic skills is to make a mockery of public education. We know that those who do not understand English are certain to find their classroom experiences wholly incomprehensible and in no way meaningful.

414 U.S. at 566. The Court relied solely on § 601 of Title VI and did not reach the constitutional claim. But if the Court had reached the equal protection constitutional claim, how should it have ruled, particularly in light of *Brown*, the holding in *Lee v. Johnson*, the arguments that had been rejected in *Lee v. Johnson*, the holdings in *Farrington v. Tokushige*, and the Fourteenth Amendment Due Process Clause precedents?

---

7. The Bar Admission Cases

We turn next to a topic dear to the hearts of law students: admission to the bar. We look at two decisions: one filed in 1890 and one filed 125 years later, in 2015.

Figure 5.13 ***Hong Yen Chang*. Studio portrait (ca. 1890). The Huntington Library, San Marino, California.**

In re Hong Yen Chang

84 Cal. 163 (1890)

FOX, J.

Motion made in due form for the admission of Hong Yen Chang to practice as an attorney and counselor of this court, and his moral character duly vouched for. Upon the motion there is exhibited to us a license admitting him to practice as an attorney and counselor at law in all the courts of the state of New York, issued by the supreme court of that state at a general term held at the city of Poughkeepsie, May 17, 1888; also a certificate of naturalization issued by the court of common pleas of the city of New York, November 11, 1887.

Title 30 of the Revised Statutes of the United States provides for the naturalization of aliens. The first section of that title (section 2165) reads: "An alien may be admitted to become a citizen of the United States," etc.; and that and subsequent sections provide how, and the conditions of such admission. As the statute originally stood, there was no express language to indicate a limitation upon the class of aliens who might be so admitted; but by "An act to correct errors and supply omissions in the Revised Statutes of the United States," passed February 18, 1875, this provision was amended so as to limit the right of naturalization to "aliens, being free white persons, and to aliens of African nativity, and to persons of African descent." Under this statute it was held by the federal courts that persons of the Mongolian race are not entitled to be admitted as citizens of the United States. In re *Ah Yup*, 5 Sawy, 155; In re *Look Tin Sing*, 21 Fed. Rep. 905. We have no doubt about the correctness of this ruling. Then, by section 14 of the act of May 6, 1882, (22 St. U. S. p. 61), courts are expressly forbidden to issue certificates of naturalization to any native of China. Under the constitutions of the United States, congress alone has the power to determine who shall and who shall not be entitled to the privileges of the naturalization laws. We are therefore of opinion that the certificate of naturalization presented in this case was issued without authority of law, and is void; it being conceded that the holder of it is a person of Mongolian nativity. Only those who are citizens of the United States, or who have bona fide declared their intention to become such in the manner provided by law (and we hold that this requires that they shall be persons eligible to become such, as well as to have declared their intention) are entitled to be admitted to practice as attorneys and counselors of this court, on presentation of license to practice in the highest court of a sister state. Code Civil Proc. § 279. Holding, as we do, that the applicant is not a citizen of the United States, and is not eligible under the law to become such, the motion must be denied.

So ordered.

Notes

1. How do you think Hong Yen Chang obtained a bar license in New York?
2. Once again, the 1790 naturalization statute comes into play, as Hong Yen Chang's application was denied because he was not a "free white person" and therefore was not eligible to be naturalized. Was there a citizenship requirement in New York to be admitted to the bar? It may be helpful to recall that both state and federal courts could naturalize citizens of the United States at the time, albeit pursuant to uniform rules passed by Congress.

In re Hong Yen Chang on Admission

60 Cal. 4th 1169 (2015)

THE COURT.

We grant Hong Yen Chang posthumous admission as an attorney and counselor at law in all courts of the state of California.

Hong Yen Chang, a native of China, came to this country in 1872 as part of an educational program to teach Chinese youth about the West. (Farkas, Bury My Bones in America (1998) p. 87 (Farkas).) Chang graduated from the Philips Academy in Andover, Massachusetts, in 1879 and earned his undergraduate degree at Yale. (*Id.* at pp. 87, 89, 93.) He went on to graduate from Columbia Law School in 1886. (*Id.* at p. 90.) He applied for admission to the New York Bar, but despite a "high marking" and unanimous recommendation from the bar examiners, he was turned down by the state supreme court in 1887 because he was not a citizen. (*In and About the City: Naturalizing a Chinaman. Hong Yen Chang's Struggles to be Admitted to the Bar,* N.Y. Times (Nov. 19, 1887) p. 8.) That same year, a New York judge issued Chang a certificate of naturalization. (*Ibid.*) After the New York Legislature passed a law allowing him to reapply for bar admission, Chang was admitted in 1888, becoming "the only regularly admitted Chinese lawyer in this country." (*A Chinese Lawyer: Hong Yen Chang and a Colored Student Admitted to the Bar,* N.Y. Times (May 18, 1888) p. 1.)

Chang then relocated to California, "where he planned to serve the large Chinese community of San Francisco." (Farkas, *supra,* at p. 90.) When he moved for admission to the California bar, this court observed that his motion was "made in due form" and "his moral character duly vouched for." (*In re Hong Yen Chang* (1890) 84 Cal. 163, 164.) At the time, however, a California statute provided that only United States citizens or persons "who have *bona fide* declared their intention to become such in the manner provided by law" could gain admission upon presentation of a license to practice law from another state. (*Id.* at p. 165, citing Code Civ. Proc., former § 279, enacted 1872 and repealed by Stats. 1931, ch. 861, § 2, p. 1762.) This court held that the statute "requires that they shall be persons eligible to become [citizens], as well as to have declared their intention." (*In re Hong Yen Chang,* at p. 165.) Observing that "courts are expressly forbidden to issue certificates of naturalization to any native of China" under the federal Chinese Exclusion Act (Act of May 6, 1882, 47th Cong., ch. 126, § 14, 22 Stat. 58, 61), we determined that the certificate of naturalization Chang had obtained in New York "was issued without authority of law, and is void, it being conceded that the holder of it is a person of Mongolian nativity." (*In re Hong Yen Chang,* at pp. 164–165.) The court concluded: "Holding, as we do, that the applicant is not a citizen of the United States, and is not eligible under the law to become such, the motion must be denied." (*Id.* at p. 165.)

Understanding the significance of our two-page decision denying Chang admission to the bar requires a candid reckoning with a sordid chapter of our state and national history. (See McClain, In Search of Equality: The Chinese Struggle Against Discrimination in Nineteenth-Century America (1994) (McClain); Takaki, Strangers from a Different Shore: A History of Asian Americans (1989) pp. 79–131.) The general outline of this history is recounted in *Chae Chan Ping v. United States* (1889) 130 U.S. 581 (*Chae Chan Ping*), which upheld the Chinese Exclusion Act against various legal challenges one year before our decision in *In re Hong Yen Chang.* Reflecting then prevalent sensibilities, a unanimous high court said:

> "The discovery of gold in California in 1848, as is well known, was followed by a large immigration thither from all parts of the world, attracted not only by the hope of gain from the mines, but from the great prices paid for all kinds of labor. The news of the discovery penetrated China, and laborers came from there in great numbers, a few with their own means, but by far the greater number under contract with employers, for whose benefit they worked. These laborers readily secured employment, and, as domestic servants, and in various kinds of outdoor work, proved to be exceedingly useful. For some years little opposition was made to them, except when they sought to work in the mines, but, as their numbers increased, they began to engage in various mechanical pursuits and trades, and thus came in competition with our artisans and mechanics, as well as our laborers in the field. The competition steadily increased as the laborers came in crowds on each steamer that arrived from China, or Hong Kong, an adjacent English port. They were generally industrious and frugal. Not being accompanied by families, except in rare instances, their expenses were small; and they were content with the simplest fare, such as would not suffice for our laborers and artisans. The competition between them and our people was for this reason altogether in their favor, and the consequent irritation, proportionately deep and bitter, was followed, in many cases, by open conflicts, to the great disturbance of the public peace.
>
> "The differences of race added greatly to the difficulties of the situation.... [T]hey remained strangers in the land, residing apart by themselves, and

> adhering to the customs and usages of their own country. It seemed impossible for them to assimilate with our people, or to make any change in their habits or modes of living. As they grew in numbers each year the people of the coast saw, or believed they saw, in the facility of immigration, and in the crowded millions of China, where population presses upon the means of subsistence, great danger that at no distant day that portion of our country would be overrun by them, unless prompt action was taken to restrict their immigration. The people there accordingly petitioned earnestly for protective legislation." (*Chae Chan Ping, supra,* 130 U.S. at pp. 594–595.)

Hostility toward Chinese labor, together with cultural tensions and xenophobia, prompted the California Legislature to enact a raft of laws designed to disadvantage Chinese immigrants. (See, e.g., Stats. 1880, ch. 116, § 1, p. 123 [establishing commercial fishing ban for "aliens incapable of becoming electors of this State"]; Pen .Code, former §§ 178, 179, added by Amends. to Codes 1880, ch. 3, §§ 1, 2, pp. 1, 2 [imposing criminal liability on corporations that employed Chinese workers]; Stats. 1862, ch. 339, § 1, p. 462 [creating "the Chinese Police Tax" in order "to protect Free White Labor against competition with Chinese Coolie Labor, and to discourage the Immigration of the Chinese into the State of California"]; Stats. 1855, ch. 174, § 1, p. 216 [imposing license tax on each foreigner who was "ineligible to become a citizen"].) Many of the era's discriminatory laws and government actions were upheld by this court. (See, e.g., *Mott v. Cline* (1927) 200 Cal. 434; *In re Yick Wo* (1885) 68 Cal. 294, revd. *sub nom. Yick Wo v. Hopkins* (1886) 118 U.S. 356; *Ex parte Ah Fook* (1874) 49 Cal. 402, revd. *sub nom. Chy Lung v. Freeman* (1875) 92 U.S. 275; *People v. Brady* (1870) 40 Cal. 198; *People v. Hall* (1854) 4 Cal. 399, 404–405; *People v. Naglee* (1850) 1 Cal. 232.)

Anti-Chinese sentiment was a major impetus for the California Constitutional Convention of 1879. (See McClain, *supra,* at pp. 79–81 [describing the influence of the California's Workingmen's Party led by Dennis Kearney, whose slogan was "The Chinese Must Go!"].) As ratified by the electorate in 1879, the California Constitution denied the right to vote to any "native of China" alongside any "idiot, insane person, or person convicted" of various crimes. (Cal. Const., art. II, § 1 as ratified 1879.) It also included an entire article titled "Chinese," directing the Legislature to enact laws to combat "the burdens and evils" posed by Chinese immigrants, including laws "to impose conditions upon which persons may reside in the State, and to provide the means and mode of their removal from the State." (*Id.,* art. XIX, § 1 as ratified 1879.) The article specifically prohibited any corporation or government entity from "employ[ing] directly or indirectly, in any capacity, any Chinese or Mongolian," and directed the Legislature to "pass such laws as may be necessary to enforce this provision." (*Id.,* art. XIX, § 2 as ratified 1879.)

When the Legislature convened in 1880, it took up its new constitutional duties "with enthusiasm" in a session that "prove[d] to be the most Sinophobic in the state's history." (McClain, *supra,* at p. 83; see *id.* at pp. 83–93 [discussing anti-Chinese laws enacted in 1880]; see *In re Ah Chong* (C.C.D.Cal.1880) 2 F. 733, 733–734 [same].) The laws enacted that session included "An Act to prohibit the issuance of licenses to aliens not eligible to become electors of the State of California," which provided that "[n]o license to transact any business or occupation shall be granted or issued by the State, or any county or city, or city and county, or town, or any municipal corporation, to any alien not eligible to become an elector of this State." (Stats. 1880, ch. 51, § 1, p. 39.)

The 1879 Constitution also directed the Legislature to "provide the necessary legislation to prohibit the introduction into this State of Chinese" going forward and to "discourage their immigration by all the means within its power." (Cal. Const., art. XIX, § 4, as ratified in 1879.) This provision continued the state's decades-long policy of opposing Chinese immigration. . . .

The United States Supreme Court, in upholding the Chinese Exclusion Act, observed that California's advocacy played a key role in motivating Congress to pass the law. . . . This was the historical context in which this court denied Chang admission to the bar.

More than a century later, the legal and policy underpinnings of our 1890 decision have been discredited. In 1972, this court unanimously held it was "constitutionally indefensible" to forbid noncitizens to practice law, calling such a ban "the lingering vestige of a xenophobic attitude" that "should now be allowed to join those anachronistic classifications among the crumbled pedestals of history." (*Raffaelli v. Committee of Bar Examiners* (1972) 7 Cal.3d 288, 291, 101 Cal.Rptr. 896, 496 P.2d 1264.) One year later, the high court reached the same conclusion. (*In re Griffiths* (1973) 413 U.S. 717.) In 2013, our Legislature passed a law making undocumented immigrants eligible for admission to the State Bar. (Bus. & Prof.Code, § 6064, subd. (b).) We thereafter granted admission to an undocumented immigrant who had been brought to the United States as a child, put himself through college and law school, passed the California bar exam, and met the requirement of good moral character. (*In re Garcia* (2014) 58 Cal.4th 440, 466.) We said "the fact that an undocumented immigrant is present in the United States without lawful authorization does not itself involve moral turpitude or demonstrate moral unfitness so as to justify exclusion from the State Bar, or prevent the individual from taking an oath promising faithfully to discharge the duty to support the Constitution and laws of the United States and California." (*Id.* at p. 460.)

In addition, Congress repealed the Chinese Exclusion Act in 1943 (Act of Dec. 17, 1943, Pub.L. No. 78–199, 57 Stat. 600), and both Houses of Congress have recently expressed regret for the act and similar laws discriminating against Chinese immigrants (H.Res. No. 683, 112th Cong., 2d Sess. (2012); Sen.Res. No. 201, 112th Cong., 1st Sess. (2011).) The anti-Chinese provisions of the California Constitution were repealed in 1952. (Cal. Const., former art. XIX, repealed by initiative, Prop. 14, Gen. Elec. (Nov. 4, 1952).) In 2014, our Legislature adopted a resolution acknowledging California's history of discrimination against its Chinese population. (Sen. Joint Res. No. 23, Stats. 2014 (2013–2014 Reg. Sess.) res. ch. 134.) Among its findings, the resolution observed that "California's stance against the Chinese community influenced the promotion and passage of the federal Chinese Exclusion Act"; that "California lobbied Congress for years to strictly prohibit immigration from China"; and that "[t]he Chinese Exclusion Act set the precedent for racist foreign and national policy that led to broader exclusion laws and fostered an environment of racism that quickly led to the Jim Crow laws of the 1880s." (*Ibid.*) While commending Congress on its recent resolutions expressing regret for the Chinese Exclusion Act, the resolution called on Congress to issue "a formal apology for the legalized governmental mistreatment marked by the Chinese Exclusion Act." (*Ibid.*)

In light of these developments, it is past time to acknowledge that the discriminatory exclusion of Chang from the State Bar of California was a grievous wrong. It denied Chang equal protection of the laws; apart from his citizenship, he was by all accounts qualified for admission to the bar. It was also a blow to countless others who, like Chang, aspired to become a lawyer only to have their dream deferred on account of their race, alienage, or nationality. And it was a loss to our communities and to society as a whole, which denied itself the full talents of its people and the important benefits of a diverse legal profession.

More than a century later, Chang's descendants and the Asian Pacific American Law Students Association at the University of California, Davis School of Law have sought to right this wrong. Even if we cannot undo history, we can acknowledge it and, in so doing, accord a full measure of recognition to Chang's pathbreaking efforts to become the first lawyer of Chinese descent in the United States. The people and the courts of California were denied Chang's services as a lawyer. But we need not be denied his example as a pioneer for a more inclusive legal profession. In granting Hong Yen Chang posthumous admission to the California Bar, we affirm his rightful place among the ranks of persons deemed qualified to serve as an attorney and counselor at law in the courts of California.

Notes

1. The petition for Hong Yen Chang's posthumous admission was brought by students at UC Davis Law School, under the supervision of Professor Gabriel "Jack" Chin, with pro bono assistance by the law firm Munger, Tolles & Olson. *See* Maura Dolan, *Chinese Immigrant, Denied Law License in 1890, Gets One Posthumously*, L.A. Times, March 16, 2015, http://www.latimes.com/local/lanow/la-me-ln-chinese-lawyer-20150316-story.html. The project began in 2011, when Professor Chin asked his students to see if they could find a way to overturn the Court's 1890 decision. *See also* Li Chen, *Pioneers in the Fight for the Inclusion of Chinese Students in American Legal Education and Legal Profession*, 22 Asian Am. L.J. 5 (2015).

2. In 2015, when the petition was granted, the California Supreme Court was a particularly diverse court. Three of the seven justices, including the Chief Justice, were

Asian American, one was Latino, and one was African American. Is diversity on the bench important, and if so, why? If "justice is blind," why should the race of the judge matter?

3. What was to be gained by granting the petition and admitting Hong Yen Chang posthumously? Isn't it a case of too little, too late?

8. Japanese "Alien" Economic Cases

We consider two cases involving economic restrictions on the Japanese based on alienage: pawnbroking and land ownership.

A. Pawnbroking

Asakura v. City of Seattle

265 U.S. 332 (1924)

Justice BUTLER:

Plaintiff in error is a subject of the emperor of Japan, and since 1904 has resided in Seattle, Wash. Since July, 1915, he has been engaged in business there as a pawnbroker. The city passed an ordinance, which took effect July 2, 1921, regulating the business of pawnbroker. . . . It makes it unlawful for any person to engage in the business unless he shall have a license, and the ordinance provides "that no such license shall be granted unless the applicant be a citizen of the United States." Violations of the ordinance are punishable by fine or imprisonment or both. Plaintiff in error brought this suit in the superior court of King county, Wash., against the city, its comptroller, and chief of police, to restrain them from enforcing the ordinance against him. He attacked the ordinance on the ground that it violates the treaty between the United States and the empire of Japan, proclaimed April 5, 1911 (37 Stat. 1504); violates the Constitution of the state of Washington, and also the due process and equal protection clauses of the Fourteenth Amendment of the Constitution of the United States. He declared his willingness to comply with any valid ordinance relating to the business of pawnbroker. It was shown that he had about $5,000 invested in his business, which would be broken up and destroyed by the enforcement of the ordinance. The superior court granted the relief prayed. On appeal, the Supreme Court of the state held the ordinance valid and reversed the decree. The case is here on writ of error. . . .

Does the ordinance violate the treaty? Plaintiff in error invokes and relies upon the following provisions:

> "The citizens or subjects of each of the high contracting parties shall have liberty to enter, travel and reside in the territories of the other to carry on trade, wholesale and retail, to own or lease and occupy houses, manufactories, warehouses and shops, to employ agents of their choice, to lease land for residential and commercial purposes, and generally to do anything incident to or necessary for trade upon the same terms as native citizens or subjects, submitting themselves to the laws and regulations there established. . . . The citizens or subjects of each . . . shall receive, in the territories of the other, the most constant protection and security of their persons and property. . . ." Article 1.

A treaty made under the authority of the United States—"shall be the supreme law of the land; and the judges in every state shall be bound thereby, anything in the Constitution or laws of any state to the contrary notwithstanding." Constitution, art. 6, § 2.

The treaty-making power of the United States is not limited by any express provision of the Constitution, and, though it does not extend "so far as to authorize what the Constitution forbids," it does extend to all proper subjects of negotiation between our government and other nations. *Geofroy v. Riggs*, 133 U. S. 258, 266; *In re Ross*, 140 U. S. 453, 463. The treaty was made to strengthen friendly relations between the two nations. As to the things covered by it, the provision quoted establishes the rule of equality between Japanese subjects while in this country and native citizens. Treaties for the protection of citizens of one country residing in the territory of another are numerous, and make for good understanding between nations. The treaty is binding within the state of Washington. *Baldwin v. Franks*, 120 U. S. 678, 682, 683 The rule of equality established by it cannot be rendered nugatory in any part of the United States by municipal ordinances or state laws. It stands on the same footing of supremacy as do the provisions of the Constitution and laws of the United States. It operates of itself without the aid of any legislation, state or national; and it will be applied and given authoritative effect by the courts. *Foster v. Neilson*, 2 Pet. 253, 314; *Head Money Cases*, 112 U. S. 580, 598; *Chew Heong v. United States*, 112 U. S. 536, 540, 5 Sup. Ct. 255, 28 L. Ed. 770; *Whitney v. Robertson*, 124 U. S. 190, 194 ; *Maiorano v. Baltimore & Ohio R. R. Co.*, 213 U. S. 268, 272.

The purpose of the ordinance complained of is to regulate, not to prohibit, the business of pawnbroker. But it makes it impossible for aliens to carry on the business. It need not be considered whether the state, if it sees fit, may forbid and destroy the business generally. Such a law would apply equally to aliens and citizens, and no question of conflict with the treaty would arise. The grievance here alleged is that plaintiff in error, in violation of the treaty, is denied equal opportunity.

It remains to be considered whether the business of pawnbroker is "trade" within the meaning of the treaty. Treaties are to be construed in a broad and liberal spirit, and, when two constructions are possible, one restrictive of rights that may be claimed under it and the other favorable to them, the latter is to be preferred.

Hauenstein v. Lynham, 100 U. S. 483, 487; *Geofroy v. Riggs*, supra, 271 (10 Sup. Ct. 295); *Tucker v. Alexandroff*, 183 U. S. 424, 437. The ordinance defines "pawnbroker" to "mean and include every person whose business or occupation it is to take and receive by way of pledge, pawn or exchange, goods, wares or merchandise, or any kind of personal property whatever, for the repayment or security of any money loaned thereon, or to loan money on deposit or personal property," and defines "pawnshop" to "mean and include every place at which the business of pawnbroker is carried on." The language of the treaty is comprehensive. The phrase "to carry on trade" is broad. That it is not to be given a restricted meaning is plain. The clauses, "to . . . own or lease . . . shops, . . . to lease land . . . for . . . commercial purposes, and generally to do anything incident to or necessary for trade," and "shall receive . . . the most constant protection and security of their . . . property, . . ." all go to show the intention of the parties that the citizens or subjects of either shall have liberty in the territory of the other to engage in all kinds and classes of business that are or reasonably may be embraced within the meaning of the word "trade" as used in the treaty.

By definition contained in the ordinance, pawnbrokers are regarded as carrying on a "business." A feature of it is the lending of money upon the pledge or pawn of personal property which, in case of default, may be sold to pay the debt. While the amounts of the loans made in that business are relatively small and the character of property pledged as security is different, the transactions are similar to loans made by banks on collateral security. The business of lending money on portable securities has been carried on for centuries. In most of the countries of Europe, the pledge system is carried on by governmental agencies; in some of them the business is also carried on by private parties. In England, as in the United States, the private pledge system prevails. In this country, the practice of pledging personal property for loans dates back to early colonial times, and pawnshops have been regulated by state laws for more than a century. We have found no state legislation abolishing or forbidding the business. Most, if not all, of the states provide for licensing pawnbrokers and authorize regulation by municipalities. While regulation has been found necessary in the public interest, the business is not on that account to be excluded from the trade and commerce referred to in the treaty. Many worthy occupations and lines of legitimate business are regulated by state and federal laws for the protection of the public against fraudulent and dishonest practices. There is nothing in the character of the business of pawnbroker which requires it to be excluded from the field covered by the above-quoted provision, and it must be held that such business is "trade" within the meaning of the treaty. The ordinance violates the treaty. The question in the present case relates solely to Japanese subjects who have been admitted to this country. We do not pass upon the right of admission or the construction of the treaty in this respect, as that question is not before us and would require consideration of other matters with which it is not now necessary to deal. We need not consider other grounds upon which it is attacked.

Decree reversed.

Notes

1. Pawnbroking—the lending of money "upon the pledge or pawn of personal property"—has been in existence for as long as people have found themselves in need of fast cash. Pawn shops existed in China some 3,000 years ago, and pawn brokers operated in ancient Greece and Rome as well. *Pawning Through the Ages*, history.com, https://www.history.com/shows/pawn-stars/articles/pawning-through-the-ages#:~:text=More%20than%203%2C000%20years%20ago,short%2Dterm%20credit%20to%20peasants.&text=These%20rules%20were%20relaxed%20in,temporary%20aid%20to%20the%20poor (2021). Pawnbroking was and remains a form of credit, particularly for people of insubstantial means and on the fringes of society. Is pawnbroking a "trade" in the sense that it might be referred to in a bilateral treaty of amity and commerce?

2. Do you think that Asakura, the pawnbroker, was a Japanese businessman who was carrying on business in the United States or that he was someone who had emigrated to the United States and had made his home in Seattle? A pawnbroker of Japanese descent, who was not a U.S. citizen, was able to persuade the Court to enforce a treaty and strike down a municipal ordinance—in 1924. Does that surprise you? If so, why? How can this decision be reconciled with, for example, *Chae Chan Ping*? And how can it be reconciled with *Ozawa*, which declared a man of Japanese descent not a "free white person" for purposes of the U.S. naturalization statute a mere two years before this case was decided? What lessons do you draw about characterizing Japanese as "aliens" from the juxtaposition of these cases? Were there any advantages to the status?

B. The Land Law Case

While the vast majority of the early Chinese immigrants were male, the early Japanese arrivals were able to bring their families with them. The Japanese were adept at farming and many were determined to become independent farmers. They quickly became California's major source of agricultural labor. The number of farms operated by Japanese in California grew from 1,147 in 1890 to 41,356 in 1910. The number of acres owned by Japanese spiked from 2,442 in 1905 to 26,707 in 1913, and the number of acres leased or contracted by Japanese more than quadrupled, from 59,416 in 1905 to 254,980 in 1913. Mark Brilliant, *The Color of America Has Changed* 34 (2012); Hing, at 28–30, 59.

The success of the Japanese led to agitation against them, including in the form of legalized discrimination. Perhaps the "most pervasive and pernicious" of these laws were the Alien Land Laws, which barred aliens "ineligible for citizenship" from owning or leasing land. Brilliant, at 30. The first efforts to enact an alien land law in California were made in 1909, but the first law was not enacted until 1913. It was thereafter amended several times. The 1920 version was unsuccessfully challenged. *See Porterfield v. Webb*, 263 U.S. 225 (1923). In 1944, however, the California Attorney General brought an action against Kajiro and Kohide Oyama to escheat—or seize for the State—eight acres of land they had purchased, in two parcels, in San Diego County in the name of their son Fred, who was six and nine years old, respectively, when each parcel was purchased.

Oyama v. California

332 U.S. 633 (1948)

VINSON, Chief Justice:

Petitioners challenge the constitutionality of California's Alien Land Law as it has been applied in this case to effect an escheat of two small parcels of agricultural land. One of the petitioners is Fred Oyama, a minor American citizen in whose name title was taken. The other is his father and guardian, Kajiro Oyama, a Japanese citizen not eligible for naturalization, who paid the purchase price.

Petitioners press three attacks on the Alien Land Law as it has been applied in this case: first, that it deprives Fred Oyama of the equal protection of the laws and of his privileges as an American citizen; secondly, that it denies Kajiro Oyama equal protection of the laws; and, thirdly, that it contravenes the due process clause by sanctioning a taking of property after expiration of the applicable limitations period. Proper foundation for these claims has been laid in the proceedings below. . . .

In broad outline, the Alien Land Law forbids aliens ineligible for American citizenship to acquire, own, occupy, lease, or transfer agricultural land. It also provides that any property acquired in violation of the statute shall escheat as of the date of acquisition and that the same result shall follow any transfer made with "intent to prevent, evade or avoid" escheat. In addition, that intent is presumed, prima facie, whenever an ineligible alien pays the consideration for a transfer to a citizen or eligible alien.

The first of the two parcels in question, consisting of six acres of agricultural land in southern California, was purchased in 1934, when Fred Oyama was six years old. Kajiro Oyama paid the $4,000 consideration, and the seller executed a deed to Fred. The deed was duly recorded.

Some six months later, the father petitioned the Superior Court for San Diego County to be appointed Fred's guardian, stating that Fred owned the six acres. After a hearing, the court found the allegations of the petition true and Kajiro Oyama "a competent and proper person" to be appointed Fred's guardian. The appointment was then ordered, and the father posted the necessary bond. . . .

The second parcel, an adjoining two acres, was acquired in 1937, when Fred was nine years old. It was sold by the guardian of another minor, and the court supervising that guardianship confirmed the sale "to Fred Oyama" as highest bidder at a publicly advertised sale. A copy of the court's order was recorded. Fred's father again paid the purchase price, $1,500.

From the time of the two transfers until the date of trial, however, Kajiro Oyama did not file the annual reports which the Alien Land Law requires of all guardians of agricultural land belonging to minor children of ineligible aliens.

In 1942, Fred and his family were evacuated from the Pacific Coast along with all other persons of Japanese descent. And in 1944, when Fred was sixteen and still forbidden to return home, the State filed a petition to declare an escheat of the two parcels on the ground that the conveyances in 1934 and 1937 had been with intent to violate and evade the Alien Land Law. At the trial the only witness, other than a court official testifying to records showing the facts set forth above, was one John Kurfurst, who had been left in charge of the land at the time of the evacuation. He testified that the Oyama family once lived on the land but had not occupied it for several years before the evacuation. After the evacuation, Kurfurst and those to whom he rented the property drew checks to Fred Oyama for the rentals (less expenses), and Kurfurst transmitted them to Fred Oyama through the War Relocation Authority. The canceled checks were returned endorsed "Fred Oyama," and no evidence was offered to prove that the signatures were not by the son. Moreover, the receipts issued by the War Relocation Authority for the funds transmitted by Kurfurst were for the account of Fred Oyama, and Kurfurst identified a letter signed "Fred Oyama" directing him to turn the property over to a local bank for management.

On direct examination by the State's Attorney, however, Kurfurst also testified that he knew the father as "Fred," but he added that he had never heard the father refer to himself by that name. In addition, he testified on cross-examination that he had once heard the father say, "Someday the boy will have a good piece of property because that is going to be valuable." He also admitted that he knew "the father was running the boy's business" and that "the property belonged to the boy and to June Kushino" (Fred's cousin, an American citizen). . . .

From this evidence the trial court found as facts that the father had had the beneficial use of the land and that the transfers were subterfuges effected with intent to prevent, evade or avoid escheat. Accordingly, the court entered its conclusion of law that the parcels had vested in the State as of the date of the attempted transfers in 1934 and 1937.

The trial court filed no written opinion but indicated orally that its findings were based primarily on four inferences: (1) the statutory presumption that any conveyance is with "intent to prevent, evade or avoid" escheat if an ineligible alien pays the consideration; (2) an inference of similar intent from the mere fact that the conveyances ran to a minor child; (3) an inference of lack of bona fides at the time of the original transactions from the fact that the father thereafter failed to file annual guardianship reports; and (4) an inference from the father's failure to testify that his testimony would have been adverse to his son's cause. No countervailing inference was warranted by the exhibits in Fred's name, the judge said, "because there are many instances where there is little in a name."

In holding the trial court's findings of intent fully justified by the evidence, the Supreme Court of California pointed to the same four inferences. It also ruled that California could constitutionally exclude ineligible aliens from any interest in agricultural land, and that Fred Oyama was deprived of no constitutional guarantees since the land had passed to the State without ever vesting in him.

We agree with petitioners' first contention, that the Alien Land Law, as applied in this case, deprives Fred Oyama of the equal protection of California's laws and of his privileges as an American citizen. In our view of the case, the State has discriminated against Fred Oyama; the discrimination is based solely on his parents' country of origin; and there is absent the compelling justification which would be needed to sustain discrimination of that nature.

By federal statute, enacted before the Fourteenth Amendment but vindicated by it, the states must accord to all citizens the right to take and hold real property. California, of course, recognizes both this right and the fact that infancy does not incapacitate a minor from holding realty. It is also established under California law that ineligible aliens may arrange gifts of agricultural land to their citizen children. Likewise, when a minor citizen does become the owner of agricultural land, by gift or otherwise, his father may be appointed guardian of the estate, whether the father be a citizen, an eligible alien, or an ineligible alien. And, once appointed, a guardian is entitled to have custody of the estate and to manage and husband it for the ward's benefit. To that extent Fred Oyama is ostensibly on a par with minors of different lineage.

At this point, however, the road forks. The California law points in one direction for minor citizens like Fred Oyama, whose parents cannot be naturalized, and in another for all other children—for minor citizens whose parents are either citizens or eligible aliens, and even for minors who are themselves aliens though eligible for naturalization.

In the first place, for most minors California has the customary rule that where a parent pays for a conveyance to his child there is a presumption that a gift is intended; there is no presumption of a resulting trust, no presumption that the minor takes the land for the benefit of his parent. When a gift is thus presumed and the deed is recorded in the child's name, the recording suffices for delivery, and, absent evidence that the gift is disadvantageous, acceptance is also presumed. Thus the burden of proving that there was in fact no completed bona fide gift falls to him who would attack its validity. Fred Oyama, on the other hand, faced at the outset the necessity of overcoming a statutory presumption that conveyances financed by his father and recorded in Fred's name were not gifts at all. Something very akin to a resulting trust was presumed and, at least prima facie, Fred was presumed to hold title for the benefit of his parent.

In the second place, when it came to rebutting this statutory presumption, Fred Oyama ran into other obstacles which, so far as we can ascertain, do not beset the path of most minor donees in California.

Thus the California courts said that the very fact that the transfer put the land beyond the father's power to deal with it directly—to deed it away, to borrow money on it, and to make free disposition of it in any other way—showed that the transfer was not complete, that it was merely colorable. The fact that the father attached no strings to the transfer was taken to indicate that he meant, in effect, to acquire the beneficial ownership himself. The California law purports to permit citizen sons to take gifts of agricultural land from their fathers, regardless of the fathers' nationality. Yet, as indicated by this case, if the father is ineligible for citizenship, facts which would usually be considered indicia of the son's ownership are used to make that ownership suspect; if the father is not an ineligible alien, however, the same facts would be evidence that a completed gift was intended.

Furthermore, Fred Oyama had to counter evidence that his father was remiss in his duties as guardian. Acts subsequent to a transfer may, of course, be relevant to indicate a transferor's intent at the time of the transfer. In this case the trial court itself had reservations as to the evidentiary value of the father's omissions; with these we agree, especially because there was some reason to believe reports were not required of him until 1943, and he had been excluded from the state from 1942 on. More important to the issue of equal protection, however, our attention has been called to no other case in which the penalty for a guardian's derelictions has fallen on any one but the guardian. At any time the court supervising the guardianship could have demanded the annual accounts and, if appropriate, could have removed Kajiro Oyama as guardian; severe punishment could also have been meted out. The whole theory of guardianships is to protect the ward during his period of incapacity to protect himself. In Fred Oyama's case, however, the father's deeds were visited on the son; the ward became the guarantor of his guardian's conduct.

The cumulative effect, we believe, was clearly to discriminate against Fred Oyama. He was saddled with an onerous burden of proof which need not be borne by California children generally. The statutory presumption and the two ancillary inferences, which would not be used against most children, were given such probative value as to prevail in the face of a deed entered in the public records, four court orders recognizing Fred Oyama as the owner of the land, several newspaper notices to the same effect, and testimony that business transactions regarding the land were generally understood to be on his behalf. In short, Fred Oyama lost his gift, irretrievably and without compensation, solely because of the extraordinary obstacles which the State set before him.

The only basis for this discrimination against an American citizen, moreover, was the fact that his father was Japanese and not American, Russian, Chinese, or English. But for that fact alone, Fred Oyama, now a little over a year from majority, would be the undisputed owner of the eight acres in question.

The State argues that racial descent is not the basis for whatever discrimination has taken place. The argument is that the same statutory presumption of fraud would apply alike to any person taking agricultural land paid for by Kajiro Oyama, whether the recipient was Fred Oyama or a stranger of entirely different ancestry. We do not know how realistic it is to suppose that Kajiro Oyama would attempt gifts of land to other than his close relatives. But in any event, the State's argument ignores the fact that the generally applicable California law treats conveyances to the transferor's children differently from conveyances to strangers. Whenever a Chinese or English parent, to take an example, pays a third party to deed land to a stranger, a resulting trust is presumed to arise, and the stranger is presumed to hold the land for the benefit of the person paying the consideration; when the Alien Land Law applies a similar presumption to a like transfer by Kajiro Oyama to a stranger, it appears merely to reiterate the generally applicable law of resulting trusts. When, on the other hand, the same Chinese or English father uses his own funds to buy land in his citizen son's name, an indefeasible title is presumed to vest in the boy; but when Kajiro Oyama arranges a similar transfer to Fred Oyama, the Alien Land Law interposes a presumption just to the contrary. Thus, as between the citizen children of a Chinese or English father and the citizen children of a Japanese father, there is discrimination; as between strangers taking from the same transferors, there appears to be none. . . .

There remains the question of whether discrimination between citizens on the basis of their racial descent, as revealed in this case, is justifiable. Here we start with the proposition that only the most exceptional circumstances can excuse discrimination on that basis in the face of the equal protection clause and a federal statute giving all citizens the right to own land. In *Hirabayashi v. United States* this Court sustained a war measure which involved restrictions against citizens of Japanese descent. But the Court recognized that, as a general rule, "Distinctions between citizens solely because of their ancestry are by their very nature odious to a free people whose institutions are founded upon the doctrine of equality." . . .

Since the view we take of petitioners' first contention requires reversal of the decision below, we do not reach their other contentions: that the Alien Land Law denies ineligible aliens the equal protection of the laws, and that failure to apply any limitations period to escheat actions under that law takes property without due process of law.

Reversed.

Murphy, Justice, concurring, with Justice Rutledge joining:

To me the controlling issue in this case is whether the California Alien Land Law on its face is consistent with the Constitution of the United States. Can a state prohibit all aliens ineligible for American citizenship from acquiring, owning, occupying, enjoying, leasing or transferring agricultural land? Does such a prohibition square with the language of the Fourteenth Amendment that no state shall "deny to any person within its jurisdiction the equal protection of the laws?"

The negative answer to those queries is dictated by the uncompromising opposition of the Constitution to racism, whatever cloak or disguise it may assume. The California statute in question, as I view it, is nothing more than an outright racial discrimination. As such, it deserves constitutional condemnation. And since the very core of the statute is so defective, I consider it necessary to give voice to that fact even though I join in the opinion of the Court.

In its argument before us, California has disclaimed any implication that the Alien Land Law is racist in its origin, purpose or effect. Reference is made to the fact that nowhere in the statute is there a single mention of race, color, creed or place of birth or allegiance as a determinant of who may not own or hold farm land. The discrimination established by the statute is said to be entirely innocent of the use of such factors, being grounded solely upon the reasonable distinctions created by Congress in its naturalization laws. However, an examination of the circumstances surrounding the original enactment of this law in 1913, St.1913, p. 206, its reenactment in 1920 and its subsequent application reveals quite a different story.

The California Alien Land Law was spawned of the great anti-Oriental virus which, at an early date, infected many persons in that state. The history of this anti-Oriental agitation is not one that does credit to a nation that prides itself, at least historically, on being the friendly haven of the tired and the oppressed of other lands. Beginning in 1850, with the arrival of substantial numbers of Chinese immigrants, racial prejudices and discriminations began to mount. Much of the opposition to these Chinese came from trade unionists, who feared economic competition, and from politicians, who sought union support. Other groups also shared in this opposition. Various laws and ordinances were enacted for the purpose of discouraging the immigrants and dramatizing the native dissatisfaction. Individual Chinese were subjected to many acts of violence. Eventually, Congress responded to this popular agitation and adopted Chinese exclusion laws.

It was not until 1900 that Japanese began to arrive in California in large numbers. By that time the repressive measures directed at the Chinese had achieved much of their desired effect; the Chinese population had materially decreased and the antipathy of the Americans was on the decline. But the arrival of the Japanese fanned anew the flames of anti-Oriental prejudice. History then began to repeat itself. White workers resented the new influx, a resentment which readily lent itself to political exploitation. Demands were made that Japanese immigration be limited or prohibited entirely. Numerous acts of violence were perpetrated against Japanese businessmen and workers, combined with private economic sanctions designed to drive them out of business. Charges of espionage, unassimilativeness, clannishness and corruption of young children were made against these "Mongolian invaders." Campaigns were organized to secure segregated schools and to preserve 'America for the Americans.'

Indeed, so loud did this anti-Japanese clamor become that the Japanese Government made formal protests to the United States. President Theodore Roosevelt thereupon investigated and intervened in the California situation. He was able to secure a slight amelioration. Further negotiations with the Japanese Government resulted in a so-called "gentlemen's agreement," whereby the Japanese Government agreed to limit passports to the United States to nonlaborers and to others who had already established certain business and personal interests in this country.

But the agitation did not die and anti-Japanese measures continued to be proposed in wholesale fashion. The first anti-Japanese land bills were introduced in the California legislature in 1907, but the combined efforts of President Roosevelt and Governor Gillett prevented their passage. At least seventeen anti-Japanese bills were introduced in the 1909 session, including another land bill. President Roosevelt again intervened. This time he succeeded in having the land bill amended to apply to all aliens, as a result of which the bill was defeated; he was also instrumental in preventing the passage of a school segregation bill. The flood of anti-Japanese proposals continued in the 1911 session, at which more than twenty such measures were introduced. Among them, of course, was still another alien land bill. It provided that 'no alien who is not eligible to citizenship' should hold real property in California. The prospects for the passage of this bill seemed good, for by this time all political parties in the state had anti-Japanese planks in their platforms. But Presidential intervention was once again successful and the bill died in committee.

In 1913, however, nothing could stop the passage of the original version of what is now the Alien Land Law. This measure, though limited to agricultural lands, represented the first official act of discrimination aimed at the Japanese. Many Japanese were engaged in agricultural pursuits in 1913 and they constituted a substantial segment of the California farm labor supply. From 1900 to 1910, Japanese-controlled farms in California had increased from 4,698 acres to 99,254 acres. The agricultural situation thus offered a fruitful target for the anti-Japanese forces, who had been balked in their attempts to secure a ban on all Japanese immigration and to outlaw Japanese acquisition and enjoyment of residential and commercial property. In this new endeavor they were eminently successful. Secretary of State Bryan, acting on behalf of President Wilson, made a personal appearance in California to plead for caution, but his request was ignored as the legislators voted overwhelmingly in favor of the bill. This 1913 law denied 'aliens ineligible to citizenship' the privilege of buying land for agricultural purposes in California, and allowed them to lease land for such purposes for no more than three years. . . .

The more basic purpose of the statute was to irritate the Japanese, to make economic life in California as uncomfortable and unprofitable for them as legally possible. It was thus but a step in the long campaign to discourage the Japanese from entering California and to drive out those who were already there. . . .

That fact has been further demonstrated by the subsequent enforcement of the Alien Land Law. At least 79 escheat actions have been instituted by the state since the statute became effective. Of these 79 proceedings, 4 involved Hindus, 2 involved Chinese and the remaining 73 involved Japanese. Curiously enough, 59 of the 73 Japanese cases were begun by the state subsequent to Pearl Harbor, during the period when the hysteria generated by World War II magnified the opportunities for effective anti-Japanese propaganda. Vigorous enforcement of the Alien Land Law has been but one of the cruel discriminatory actions which have marked this nation's treatment since 1941 of those residents who chanced to be of Japanese origin.

The Alien Land Law, in short, was designed to effectuate a purely racial discrimination, to prohibit a Japanese alien from owning or using agricultural land solely because he is a Japanese alien. It is rooted deeply in racial, economic and social antagonisms. The question confronting us is whether such a statute, viewed against the background of racism, can mount the hurdle of the equal protection clause of the Fourteenth Amendment. Can a state disregard in this manner the historic ideal that those within the borders of this nation are not to be denied rights and privileges because they are of a particular race? I say that it cannot.

The equal protection clause is too clear to admit of any other conclusion. It provides that no state shall "deny to any person within its jurisdiction the equal protection of the laws." The words "any person" have sufficient scope to include resident aliens, whether eligible for citizenship or not. *Yick Wo v. Hopkins*, 118 U.S. 356 ; *Truax v. Raich*, 239 U.S. 33 , L.R.A. 1916D, 545, Ann.Cas. 1917B, 283. Hence Japanese aliens ineligible for citizenship must be accorded equal protection. And the laws as to which equal protection must be given certainly include those protecting the right to engage in common occupations like farming, *Yick Wo v. Hopkins*, supra, and those pertaining to the use and ownership of agricultural lands, *Buchanan v. Warley*, 245 U.S. 60 , L.R.A. 1918C, 210, Ann.Cas. 1918A, 1201. The concept of equal protection, however, may in rare cases permit a state to single out a class of persons, such as ineligible aliens, for distinctive treatment. The crucial test in these exceptional instances is whether there is a rational basis for the particular kind of discrimination involved. Are the characteristics of the class such as to provide a rational justification for the difference in treatment?

Such a rational basis is completely lacking where, as here, the discrimination stems directly from racial hatred and intolerance. The Constitution of the United States, as I read it, embodies the highest political ideals of which man is capable. It insists that our government, whether state or federal, shall respect and observe the dignity of each individual, whatever may be the name of his race, the color of his skin or the nature of his beliefs. It thus renders irrational, as a justification for discrimination, those factors which reflect racial animosity. Yet the history of the Alien Land Law shows beyond all doubt that factors of that nature make up the foundation upon which rests the discrimination established therein. And such factors are at once evident when the legal, social and economic considerations advanced in support of the discrimination are subjected to rigid scrutiny....

Unquestionably there were and are cultural, linguistic and racial differences between Japanese aliens and native Americans not of Japanese origin or ancestry. The physical characteristics of the Japanese, their different customs and habits, their past connections with Japan, their unique family relationships, their Oriental religion, and their extreme efficiency all contributed to the social and economic conflicts which unfortunately developed. But the crucial mistake that was made, the mistake that made the attitude of many Americans one of intolerance and bigotry, was the quick assumption that these differences were all racial and unchangeable. From that mistake it was an easy step to charge that the Japanese race was undesirable and that all Japanese persons were inassimilable. And from that mistake flowed the many proposals to deal with the social and economic conflicts on a group or racial basis. It was just such a proposal that became the Alien Land Law.

Hence the basic vice, the constitutional infirmity, of the Alien Land Law is that its discrimination rests upon an unreal racial foundation. It assumes that there is some racial characteristic, common to all Japanese aliens, that makes them unfit to own or use agricultural land in California. There is no such characteristic. None has even been suggested. The arguments in support of the statute make no attempt whatever to discover any true racial factor. They merely represent social and economic antagonisms which have been translated into false racial terms. As such, they cannot form the rationalization necessary to conform the statute to the requirements of the equal protection clause of the Fourteenth Amendment. Accordingly, I believe that the prior decisions of this Court giving sanction to this attempt to legalize racism should be overruled....

And so in origin, purpose, administration and effect, the Alien Land Law does violence to the high ideals of the Constitution of the United States and the Charter of the United Nations. It is an unhappy facsimile, a disheartening reminder, of the racial policy pursued by those forces of evil whose destruction recently necessitated a devastating war. It is racism in one of its most malignant forms. Fortunately, the majority of the inhabitants of the United States, and the majority of those in California, reject racism and all of its implications. They recognize that under our Constitution all persons are entitled to the equal protection of the laws without regard to their racial ancestry. Human liberty is in too great a peril today to warrant ignoring that principle in this case. For that reason I believe that the penalty of unconstitutionality should be imposed upon the Alien Land Law.

Notes

1. The Court issued five opinions: the majority opinion, two concurring opinions, and two dissents. Like Justice Murphy, Justice Black (with Justice Douglas joining) agreed with the result but would have reversed on the broader ground that the California statute discriminated not just against citizens but against "people of Japanese origin residing in this country." Justices Reed and Jackson wrote dissents, with Justice Burton joining Justice Reed's dissenting opinion. Chief Justice Vinson's opinion for the majority observed that "[t]he only basis for this discrimination against an American citizen ... was the fact that his father was Japanese and not American, Russian, Chinese, or English. But for that fact alone, Fred Oyama, now a little over a year from majority, would be the undisputed owner of the eight acres in question." Why would there have been a different result if Fred's father was Chinese, not Japanese? How is that different result consistent with the history

of anti-Chinese sentiment in California, which was of longer standing than anti-Japanese prejudice in California? It may be helpful to know that the Exclusion Acts were repealed in 1943 and replaced with a quota of authorized Chinese immigrants; however, the quota was a mere 105 persons annually. Why were the Exclusion Acts repealed? Can a quota of 105 really mean progress?

2. We again see a law that is neutral on its face applied in a discriminatory fashion. The California Alien Land Law was first enacted in 1913, but it was not vigorously enforced for some years. In the three decades prior to 1942, only 14 escheat actions were brought in California; between 1942 and 1947, however, the California Attorney General brought 59 escheat actions, all against persons of Japanese ancestry. Brilliant, at 38. What sparked the greater interest on the part of the state?

3. How do you decide legislative intent? One way, of course, is to consider what the legislators said when debating a proposed law. Justice Murphy dropped a footnote in his concurrence quoting two assemblymen who supported the passage of the Alien Land Law:

   > "I would rather every foot of California was in its native wilderness than to be cursed by the foot of these yellow invaders, who are a curse to the country, a menace to our institutions, and destructive of every principle of Americanism. I want no aliens, white, red, black or yellow, to own a foot of land in the State of California." Another assemblyman said that he intensely and unalterably hated the Japanese, whom he characterized as "a bandy-legged bagaboo, miserable craven Simian, degenerated rotten little devil."

   332 U.S. at 653 n.4 (quoting Ichihashi, *Japanese in the United States* 262 (1932) (quoting San Francisco Chronicle, Feb. 3, 1909)). In a 1944 poll, 65% of Los Angeles residents favored a constitutional amendment for the deportation of all Japanese from the country and forbidding further immigration. *See* Brilliant, at 31. To be fair, laws against alien ownership of real property have a long pedigree in in English common law, which, of course, was the law of a feudal island kingdom where land was scarce and significant ownership of it was reserved for the aristocracy. But why were the alien land laws revived in California where land was more abundant? And what explains the 1944 Los Angeles public poll results? Do you think that there are continuing themes to the modern revival of alien land laws in certain states justified on the basis of national security threats posed by Chinese land ownership, particularly near U.S. military bases and other sensitive sites? Why does it seem that, as a historical matter, not all foreign enemies have sparked U.S. popular movements against land ownership?

4. Professor Randall Kennedy has written that "[t]he opinions [of the Supreme Court] that condemn racist practices in America with the most candor, care, thoroughness, and passion are those written by Associate Justice Frank Murphy, an unjustly neglected jurist." Randall Kennedy, *Justice Murphy's Concurrence in*

Oyama v. California: *Cussing Out Racism*, 74 Tex. L. Rev. 1245, 1245 (1995–1996). His "favorite of Murphy's stentorian objections to racist law" is Justice Murphy's concurring opinion in *Oyama*. We provided only a brief excerpt above, but it is worth reading the entire concurrence. In what other cases did Justice Murphy express similar sentiments? Why do you think Justice Murphy was so passionate about majority discrimination against racial minority groups? Is it relevant that he was an Irish American and appointed by President Franklin Delano Roosevelt to replace Justice Pierce Butler in the "Catholic seat" on the Supreme Court at the time? Butler, on the other hand, had been a very conservative justice, one of the "Four Horsemen" who sparked Roosevelt's Court-packing plan. Murphy, a lifelong bachelor who lived for four decades with a male companion, was dogged by rumors while he was alive and afterward that he was homosexual, although he was engaged to be married to a woman at the time of his untimely death at age 59. Regardless of the truth of these rumors, do you think sexual orientation or religion should be relevant to presidential appointment of federal judges?

5. The Oyamas, who lived in San Diego County, were not interned after President Roosevelt signed Executive Order 9066. Kajiro Oyama took advantage of an opportunity to lease farmland in Utah, and he moved his family there before internment was imposed. He loaded his farming tools in a railroad box car and brought four other families with his own during the brief period allowed for "voluntary evacuation." It was in Utah that Fred—then 17 years old—was served with the escheat papers. *See generally* Rose Cuison Villazor, *Rediscovering* Oyama v. California: *At the Intersection of Property, Race, and Citizenship*, 87 Wash. U. L. Rev. 979 (2010); Onell R. Soto, *Equal-Rights Gains Have Local Roots*, San Diego Union-Tribune, Sept. 21, 2008, *available at* http://legacy.sandiegouniontribune.com/uniontrib/20080921/ news_1n21land.html; Brilliant, at 31–34, 56–57.

6. The Oyamas were not the only Japanese family subjected to the Alien Land Laws. In 1946, Akira Iwamura wrote a letter to the *Los Angeles Times*:

> I am Ex-Sgt. Akira Iwamura, 26, and I'm puzzled. My brother and I came out of the Army to find an alien land law suit to escheat my farm and evict the family from my home.
>
> Your newspaper and the magazines and newsreels told about the 442nd Infantry Regiment made up of Japanese Americans. They praised its combat record and said the terrific casualties suffered bought the right to fair play for us and our families.
>
> My brother Cecil is 24 but his black hair is now streaked with gray. He sweated it out and got wounded in the 442nd as they fought in Italy. In the battle for Germany he aided in the "rescue of the Lost Battalion."
>
> While my brother was in the European hot spots I was in the South Pacific with the Nisei intelligence. We both thought we were fighting to keep our family and home safe....

> I came home and read the alien land law court summons to take away my farm. I read the arguments for Proposition 15 to strengthen the alien land law. They sound like criminal indictments. Why are we hounded like outlaws?
>
> Many in our outfits died to prove Americanism is in the heart; looks and nationality don't count. My folks have lived here for 40 years under the present law which bars them from citizenship. We were born in Fresno County, but because my folks happen to come from Japan my farm and home are being taken away from me.
>
> Why does California with its alien land law keep kicking us in the teeth? . . . .

Ex-Sgt. Akira Iwamura Is Puzzled, Letter to Editor, L.A. Times, Oct. 14, 1946; *see* Brilliant at 42.

7. The Court did not strike down the California Alien Land law; what exactly was the outcome of the Supreme Court's decision? Could the California legislature have amended the law and kept it? How exactly? Regardless, what impact do you think the ruling had on the Oyamas and other Japanese families in California and elsewhere?

8. Alien land laws have seen a resurgence in recent years. The Committee of 100 has reported that, as of July 22, 2024, 32 states as well as Congress were considering bills restricting property ownership by foreign entities or individuals, including 71 bills prohibiting Chinese nationals from purchasing or owning property. Comm. of 100, *Federal and State Bills Restricting Property Ownership by Foreign Entities* (2024), *available at* https://www.committee100.org/our-work/federal-and-state-bills-prohibiting-property-ownership-by-foreign-individuals-and-entities/. In 2023, Chinese nationals sued to bar enforcement of the Florida law. The district court denied plaintiffs' motion for a preliminary injunction, *Yifan Shen v. Simpson*, 687 F. Supp. 3d 1219 (N.D. Fla. 2023), but in February 2024 the Eleventh Circuit granted in part plaintiffs' motion for a preliminary injunction pending appeal. *See* Reuters, *US Court Blocks Florida Law Barring Chinese Citizens From Owning Property*, U.S. News & World Report, Feb. 2, 2024, *available at* https://www.usnews.com/news/world/articles/2024-02-02/us-court-blocks-florida-law-barring-chinese-citizens-from-owning-property#:~:text=Lawmakers%20in%20several%20Republican%2Dled,economy%20and%20international%20trade%20rules%22; *see also* Samantha Delouya, *"They're Treating Us Like We're Spies": Florida Property Ban Has Chinese Citizens Fuming*, CNN.com (June 17, 2024), *available at* https://www.cnn.com/2024/06/17/homes/florida-law-bans-chinese-citizens-buying-homes/index.html. The Eleventh Circuit panel relied on federal preemption rationale, just as in *Chy Lung v. Freeman*, on U.S. national security grounds. Does the federal preemption rationale seem persuasive to you? What about state police powers over land within its state borders, particularly in light of the common-law tradition that

anchors much of U.S. real property law (although, interestingly, not as much in California given its Spanish influence).

9. There have been restrictions on the ability of the Chinese and other Asian Americans to purchase or own land for years, including in the form of restrictive covenants in deeds. In 1892, in *Gandolfo v. Hartman*, a California court held that a covenant in a deed barring the renting or conveyance of any part of a parcel of property to "a Chinaman or Chinamen" was "absolutely void" as violating the Fourteenth Amendment and the United States' treaty obligations with China. 49 F. 181 (Cir. Ct. S.D. Cal. 1892). *See generally* Mary Szto, *From Exclusion to Exclusivity: Chinese American Property Ownership and Discrimination in Historical Perspective*, 25 J. Transnat'l Law 33, 81–82 (2015–16) (discussing, *inter alia*, restrictive covenant cases brought by Tom Amer, a Chinese American, and Jin Kim, a Korean American). *See generally Shelley v. Kraemer*, 334 U.S. 1 (1948) (holding that states could not enforce private agreements restricting the use or occupancy of real property to White persons). The prevalence of restrictive covenants in deeds in Southern California undoubtedly led to the creation of "Little Tokyos." And as the Japanese were forced to move out by internment, they were largely replaced by African Americans and other non-White migrants.

In this Unit's readings, we saw the myriad forms of discrimination against the early Asian Americans and their efforts to fight back. Some of the efforts succeeded and some did not—but all helped set the stage for future battles for the vindication of constitutional rights and civil liberties. We saw the themes that first emerged in the readings on arrival, exclusion, and citizenship—the application to Asian Americans of laws neutral on their face, the difficulties Asian Americans faced in seeking vindication of their rights, the willingness of Asian Americans to challenge unfairness, the role of trade and family associations, the rise of groups such as the Anti-Coolie Association and the Asiatic Exclusion League, the impact of economic competition, the influence of the media, and the interplay among the courts, legislators, and other politicians.

In Unit Three, we turn to the internment of Japanese Americans during World War II—the mass relocation, without individualized suspicion or opportunity to be heard, of some 120,000 individuals, two-thirds of them United States citizens, and the subsequent efforts to seek redress and reparations.

UNIT THREE

Internment and Redress

On December 7, 1941, Japan attacked Pearl Harbor. Congress declared war on Japan the next day. On February 19, 1942, President Franklin D. Roosevelt signed Executive Order 9066, giving the Secretary of War authority "to prescribe military areas... from which any or all persons may be excluded."

The Executive Order did not specifically refer to the Japanese, but Lt. General John DeWitt, Commander of the Western Defense Command, issued a series of military orders that eventually led to the internment of nearly 120,000 Japanese Americans, two-thirds of whom were United States citizens. This was done without any individualized hearings or factual findings or evidence of individual dangerousness. Although Italian and German nationals were interned, no similar mass-scale internment program was instituted for U.S. citizens of Italian or German descent in the Western Defense Command or otherwise in the United States.

Why were Japanese Americans on the West Coast singled out for these extreme wartime measures? Japan, of course, did engage in a surprise attack on the United States, but there were other factors as well, including the historical racism that we have seen and a presumption that the Japanese remained loyal to Japan and could not be assimilated into American society. Another was economic pressure. As the Japanese prospered in farming on the West Coast, resentment built—the Alien Land Laws were a "prelude to internment." *See* Keith Aoki, *No Right to Own?: The Early Twentieth-Century "Alien Land Laws" as a Prelude to Internment*, 19 B.C. Third World L.J. 37 (1998). The United States also became concerned about conflict with Japan long before Pearl Harbor. In the 1930s, the FBI compiled a list of Japanese resident aliens deemed to be suspicious, including "aliens who led cultural or assistance organizations."[1] The FBI, the Department of Justice, and the War Department were conducting investigations of purported Japanese espionage and developing contingency plans well before war was declared. Yamamoto et al. at 85–86.

Figure III.1 ***Members of the Mochida Family Awaiting Evacuation*** **(1942). Photo by Dorothea Lange. National Archives.**

And then war broke out. As the Commission on Wartime Relocation and Internment of Civilians concluded:

> War inflamed many passions in the country. On the West Coast it rekindled the fears and prejudices of long years of anti-Asian agitation carried on by organized interest groups. Decades of discrimination against immigrants from Japan and public hostility toward Americans of Japanese descent fueled outraged shock at the Pearl Harbor attack and impotent anger against the Japanese as they swept through the Philippines and down the Malay

---

1. Comm'n on Wartime Relocation and Internment of Civilians, *Personal Justice Denied: Report of the Comm'n on Wartime Relocation and Internment of Civilians* 54 (1982–83) ("*Personal Justice Denied*"); *see generally* Eric K. Yamamoto et al., *Race, Rights and Reparation: Law and the Japanese American Internment* 85 & n.220 (2d ed. 2013).

> Peninsula to Singapore. Reports of American battlefield deaths lit sparks in one community after another up and down the West Coast, where fear of invasion was very real. In significant measure, the evacuation decision was ignited by the fire of those emotions, especially in California.

Personal Justice Denied at 28.

Figure III.2 ***Six-year-old Mamoru Takeuchi waits with family to be taken to relocation center*** **(1942). Photo by Dorothea Lange. National Archives.**

First, we consider the four Japanese American "internment" cases: *Hirabayashi*, *Yasui*, *Korematsu*, and *Endo*. As we shall see, the cases involved different aspects of the treatment of Japanese Americans during World War II. Second, we take a look at the little-known story of the Japanese-American draft resisters—Nisei who were drafted to fight for the United States but who refused to report because they and their families were imprisoned in internment camps. Third, we review the *coram nobis* cases—the efforts years later by Fred Korematsu, Gordon Hirabayashi, and Minoru Yasui to set aside their convictions. Finally, we consider the redress and reparations movement and the efforts to seek relief for the internees generally.

Figure III.3 *Richard Kobayashi, farmer, Manzanar Relocation Center* (1943). Photo by Ansel Adams. Library of Congress.

Figure III.4 *Persons of Japanese ancestry arrive at the Santa Anita Assembly center from San Pedro, California* (1942). Photo by Clem Albers. National Archives.

Chapter 6

The Japanese Internment Cases

Four U.S. citizens of Japanese descent challenged the military orders. Minoru Yasui and Gordon Hirabayashi brought challenges soon after the military orders took effect. They were arrested for violating the curfew that required individuals of Japanese descent to remain in their homes from 8:00 p.m. to 6:00 a.m. Fred Korematsu was arrested for remaining in San Leandro, California, after military orders directed the exclusion of "all alien Japanese, all alien Germans, all alien Italians, and *all persons of Japanese ancestry*" from the area, and challenged the legality of the military orders in that context. Unlike the others, Mitsuye Endo brought her challenge after she was interned; she filed a petition for a writ of habeas corpus after she reported to the Tanforan assembly center. Her petition squarely presented the issue of the legality of her internment.

Figure 6.1 ***Portrait of Gordon K. Hirabayashi, Seattle*** **(July 1, 1944). Photo by Art French. *Seattle Post-Intelligencer* Collection.**

Hirabayashi v. United States

320 U.S. 81 (1943)

MR. CHIEF JUSTICE STONE delivered the opinion of the Court.

Appellant, an American citizen of Japanese ancestry, was convicted in the district court of violating the Act of Congress of March 21, 1942, 56 Stat. 173, 18 U.S.C. § 97a, which makes it a misdemeanor knowingly to disregard restrictions made applicable by a military commander to persons in a military area prescribed by him as such, all as authorized by an Executive Order of the President.

The questions for our decision are whether the particular restriction violated, namely that all persons of Japanese ancestry residing in such an area be within their place of residence daily between the hours of 8:00 p.m. and 6:00 a.m., was adopted by the military commander in the exercise of an unconstitutional delegation by Congress of its legislative power, and whether the restriction unconstitutionally discriminated between citizens of Japanese ancestry and those of other ancestries in violation of the Fifth Amendment.

The indictment is in two counts. The second charges that appellant, being a person of Japanese ancestry, had on a specified date, contrary to a restriction promulgated by the military commander of the Western Defense Command, Fourth Army, failed to remain in his place of residence in the designated military area between the hours of 8:00 o'clock p.m. and 6:00 a.m. The first count charges that appellant, on May 11 and 12, 1942, had, contrary to a Civilian Exclusion Order issued by the military commander, failed to report to the Civil Control Station within the designated area, it appearing that appellant's required presence there was a preliminary step to the exclusion from that area of persons of Japanese ancestry.

By demurrer and plea in abatement, which the court overruled, appellant asserted that the indictment should be dismissed because he was an American citizen who had never been a subject of and had never borne allegiance to the Empire of Japan, and also because the Act of March 21, 1942, was an unconstitutional delegation of Congressional power. On the trial to a jury it appeared that appellant was born in Seattle in 1918, of Japanese parents who had come from Japan to the United States, and who had never afterward returned to Japan; that he was educated in the Washington public schools and at the time of his arrest was a senior in the University of Washington; that he had never been in Japan or had any association with Japanese residing there.

The evidence showed that appellant had failed to report to the Civil Control Station on May 11 or May 12, 1942, as directed, to register for evacuation from the military area. He admitted failure to do so, and stated it had at all times been his belief that he would be waiving his rights as an American citizen by so doing. The evidence also showed that for like reason he was away from his place of residence after 8:00 p.m. on May 9, 1942. The jury returned a verdict of guilty on both counts and appellant was sentenced to imprisonment for a term of three months on each, the sentences to run concurrently.

On appeal the Court of Appeals for the Ninth Circuit certified to us questions of law upon which it desired instructions for the decision of the case. See § 239 of the Judicial Code as amended, 28 U.S.C. § 346, 28 U.S.C. § 346. Acting under the authority conferred upon us by that section we ordered that the entire record be certified to this Court so that we might proceed to a decision of the matter in controversy in the same manner as if it had been brought here by appeal. Since the sentences of three months each imposed by the district court on the two counts were ordered to run concurrently, it will be unnecessary to consider questions raised with respect to the first count if we find that the conviction on the second count, for violation of the curfew order, must be sustained. Brooks v. United States, 267 U.S. 432, 441; Gorin v. United States, 312 U.S. 19, 33.

The curfew order which appellant violated, and to which the sanction prescribed by the Act of Congress has been deemed to attach, purported to be issued pursuant to an Executive Order of the President. In passing upon the authority of the military commander to make and execute the order, it becomes necessary to consider in some detail the official action which preceded or accompanied the order and from which it derives its purported authority.

On December 8, 1941, one day after the bombing of Pearl Harbor by a Japanese air force, Congress declared war against Japan. 55 Stat. 795, 50 U.S.C. Appendix, preceding section 1 note. On February 19, 1942, the President promulgated Executive Order No. 9066. 7 Federal Register 1407. The Order recited that 'the successful prosecution of the war requires every possible protection against espionage and against sabotage to national-defense material, national-defense premises, and national-defense utilities as defined in Section 4, Act of April 20, 1918, 40 Stat. 533, as amended by the Act of November 30, 1940, 54 Stat. 1220, and the Act of August 21, 1941, 55 Stat. 655 (50 U.S.C. § 104)'. By virtue of the authority vested in him as President and as Commander in Chief of the Army and Navy, the President purported to 'authorize and direct the Secretary of War, and the Military Commanders whom he may from time to time designate, whenever he or any designated Commander deems such action necessary or desirable, to prescribe military areas in such places and of such extent as he or the appropriate Military Commander may determine, from which any or all persons may be excluded, and with respect to which, the right of any person to enter, remain in, or leave shall be subject to whatever restrictions the Secretary of War or the appropriate Military Commander may impose in his discretion.'

On February 20, 1942, the Secretary of War designated Lt. General J. L. DeWitt as Military Commander of the Western Defense Command, comprising the Pacific Coast states and some others, to carry out there the duties prescribed by Executive Order No. 9066. On March 2, 1942, General DeWitt promulgated Public Proclamation No. 1. 7 Federal Register 2320. The proclamation recited that the entire Pacific Coast 'by its geographical location is particularly subject to attack, to attempted invasion by the armed forces of nations with which the United States is now at war, and, in connection therewith, is subject to espionage and acts of sabotage, thereby requiring the adoption of military measures necessary to establish safeguards against such enemy operations'. It stated that 'the present situation requires as a matter of military necessity the establishment in the territory embraced by the Western Defense Command of Military Areas and Zones thereof'; it specified and designated as military areas certain areas within the Western Defense Command; and it declared that 'such persons or classes of persons as the situation may require' would, by subsequent proclamation, be excluded from certain of these areas, but might be permitted to enter or remain in certain others, under regulations and restrictions to be later prescribed. Among the military areas so designated by Public Proclamation No. 1 was Military Area No. 1, which embraced, besides the southern part of Arizona, all the coastal regions of the three Pacific Coast states, including the City of Seattle, Washington, where appellant resided....

Congress, by the Act of March 21, 1942, 18 U.S.C. § 97a, provided: 'That whoever shall enter, remain in, leave, or commit any act in any military area or military zone prescribed, under the authority of an Executive order of the President, by the Secretary of War, or by any military commander designated by the Secretary of War, contrary to the restrictions applicable to any such area or zone or contrary to the order of the Secretary of War or any such military commander, shall, if it appears that he knew or should have known of the existence and extent of the restrictions or order and that his act was in violation thereof, be guilty of a misdemeanor and upon conviction shall be liable' to fine or imprisonment, or both.

Three days later, on March 24, 1942, General DeWitt issued Public Proclamation No. 3. 7 Federal Register 2543. After referring to the previous designation of military areas by Public Proclamations No. 1 and 2, it recited that '... the present situation within these Military Areas and Zones requires as a matter of military necessity the establishment of certain regulations pertaining to all enemy aliens and all persons of Japanese ancestry within said Military Areas and Zones....' It accordingly declared and established that from and after March 27, 1942, 'all alien Japanese, all alien Germans, all alien Italians, and all persons of Japanese ancestry residing or being within the geographical limits of Military Area No. 1 ... shall be within their place of residence between the hours of 8:00 P.M. and 6:00 A.M., which period is hereinafter referred to as the hours of curfew'. It also imposed certain other restrictions on persons of Japanese ancestry, and provided that any person violating the regulations would be subject to the criminal penalties provided by the Act of Congress of March 21, 1942.

Beginning on March 24, 1942, the military commander issued a series of Civilian Exclusion Orders pursuant to the provisions of Public Proclamation No. 1. Each such order related to a specified area within the territory of his command. The order applicable to appellant was Civilian Exclusion Order No. 57 of May 10, 1942. 7 Federal Register 3725. It directed that from and after 12:00 noon, May 16, 1942, all persons of Japanese ancestry, both alien and non-alien, be excluded from a specified portion of Military Area No. 1 in Seattle, including appellant's place of residence, and it required a member of each family, and each individual living alone, affected by the order to report on May 11 or May 12 to a designated Civil Control Station in Seattle. Meanwhile the military commander had issued Public Proclamation No. 4 of March 27, 1942, which recited the necessity of providing for the orderly evacuation and resettlement of Japanese within the area, and prohibited all alien Japanese and all persons of Japanese ancestry from leaving the military area until future orders should permit. 7 Federal Register 2601.

Appellant does not deny that he knowingly failed to obey the curfew order as charged in the second count of the indictment, or that the order was authorized by the terms of Executive Order No. 9066, or that the challenged Act of Congress purports to punish with criminal penalties disobedience of such an order. His contentions are only that Congress unconstitutionally delegated its legislative power to the military commander by authorizing him to impose the challenged regulation, and that, even if the regulation were in other respects lawfully authorized, the Fifth Amendment prohibits the discrimination made between citizens of Japanese descent and those of other ancestry....

The Chairman of the Senate Military Affairs Committee explained on the floor of the Senate that the purpose of the proposed legislation was to provide means of enforcement of curfew orders and other military orders made pursuant to Executive Order No. 9066. He read General DeWitt's Public Proclamation No. 1, and statements from newspaper reports that 'evacuation of the first Japanese aliens and American-born Japanese' was about to begin. He also stated to the Senate that 'reasons for suspected widespread fifth-column activity among Japanese' were to be found in the system of dual citizenship which Japan deemed applicable to American-born Japanese, and in the propaganda disseminated by Japanese consuls, Buddhist priests and other leaders, among American-born children of Japanese. Such was stated to be the explanation of the contemplated evacuation from the Pacific Coast area of persons of Japanese ancestry, citizens as well as aliens. 88 Cong.Rec. 2722-2726; see also pp. 2729, 2730. Congress also had before it the Preliminary Report of a House Committee investigating national defense migration, of March 19, 1942, which approved the provisions of Executive Order No. 9066, and which recommended the evacuation, from military areas established under the Order, of all persons of Japanese ancestry, including citizens. H.R. Rep. No. 1911, 77th Cong., 2d Sess....

The conclusion is inescapable that Congress, by the Act of March 21, 1942, ratified and confirmed Executive Order No. 9066.... And so far as it lawfully could, Congress authorized and implemented such curfew orders as the commanding officer should promulgate pursuant to the Executive Order of the President. The question then is not one of Congressional power to delegate to the President the promulgation of the Executive Order, but whether, acting in cooperation, Congress and the Executive have constitutional authority to impose the curfew restriction here complained of. We must consider also whether, acting together, Congress and the Executive could leave it to the designated military commander to appraise the relevant conditions and on the basis of that appraisal to say whether, under the circumstances, the time and place were appropriate for the promulgation of the curfew order and whether the order itself was an appropriate means of carrying out the Executive Order for the 'protection against espionage and against sabotage' to national defense materials, premises and utilities. For reasons presently to be stated, we conclude that it was within the constitutional power of Congress and the executive arm of the Government to prescribe this curfew order for the period under consideration and that its promulgation by the military commander involved no unlawful delegation of legislative power.

Executive Order No. 9066, promulgated in time of war for the declared purpose of prosecuting the war by protecting national defense resources from sabotage and espionage, and the Act of March 21, 1942, ratifying and confirming the Executive Order, were each an exercise of the power to wage war conferred on the Congress and on the President, as Commander in Chief of the armed forces, by Articles I and II of the Constitution. See Ex parte Quirin, 317 U.S. 1, 25, 26. We have no occasion to consider whether the President, acting alone, could lawfully have made the curfew order in question, or have authorized others to make it. For the President's action has the support of the Act of Congress, and we are immediately concerned with the question whether it is within the constitutional power of the national government, through the joint action of Congress and the Executive, to impose this restriction as an emergency war measure. The exercise of that power here involves no question of martial law or trial by military tribunal. Cf. Ex parte Milligan, 4 Wall. 2; Ex parte Quirin, supra. Appellant has been tried and convicted in the civil courts and has been subjected to penalties prescribed by Congress for the acts committed.

The war power of the national government is 'the power to wage war successfully'. See Charles Evans Hughes, War Powers Under the Constitution, 42 A.B.A.Rep. 232, 238. It extends to every matter and activity so related to war as substantially to affect its conduct and progress. The power is not restricted to the winning of victories in the field and the repulse of enemy forces. It embraces every phase of the national defense, including the protection of war materials and the members of the armed forces from injury and from the dangers which attend the rise, prosecution and progress of war.... Since the Constitution commits to the Executive and to Congress the exercise of the war power in all the vicissitudes and conditions of warfare, it has necessarily given them wide scope for the exercise of judgment and discretion in determining the nature and extent of the threatened injury or danger and in the selection of the means for resisting it. Ex parte Quirin, supra, 317 U.S. 28, 29; cf. Prize Cases, supra, 2 Black 670; Martin v. Mott, 12 Wheat. 19, 29. Where, as they did here, the conditions call for the exercise of judgment and discretion and for the choice of means by those branches of the Government on which the Constitution has placed the responsibility of war-making, it is not for any court to sit in review of the wisdom of their action or substitute its judgment for theirs.

The actions taken must be appraised in the light of the conditions with which the President and Congress were confronted in the early months of 1942, many of which since disclosed, were then peculiarly within the knowledge of the military authorities.

On December 7, 1941, the Japanese air forces had attacked the United States Naval Base at Pearl Harbor without warning, at the very hour when Japanese diplomatic representatives were conducting negotiations with our State Department ostensibly for the peaceful settlement of differences between the two countries. Simultaneously or nearly so, the Japanese attacked Malaysia, Hong Kong, the Philippines, and Wake and Midway Islands. On the following day their army invaded Thailand. Shortly afterwards they sank two British battleships. On December 13th, Guam was taken. On December 24th and 25th they captured Wake Island and occupied Hong Kong. On January 2, 1942, Manila fell, and on February 10th Singapore, Britain's great naval base in the East, was taken. On February 27th the battle for the Java Sea resulted in a disastrous naval defeat to the United Nations. By the 9th of March Japanese forces had established control over the Netherlands East Indies; Rangoon and Burma were occupied; Bataan and Corregidor were under attack.

Although the results of the attack on Pearl Harbor were not fully disclosed until much later, it was known that the damage was extensive, and that the Japanese by their successes had gained a naval superiority over our forces in the Pacific which might enable them to seize Pearl Harbor, our largest naval base and the last stronghold of defense lying between Japan and the west coast. That reasonably prudent men charged with the responsibility of our national defense had ample ground for concluding that they must face the danger of invasion, take measures against it, and in making the choice of measures consider our internal situation, cannot be doubted.

The challenged orders were defense measures for the avowed purpose of safeguarding the military area in question, at a time of threatened air raids and invasion by the Japanese forces, from the danger of sabotage and espionage. As the curfew was made applicable to citizens residing in the area only if they were of Japanese ancestry, our inquiry must be whether in the light of all the facts and circumstances there was any substantial basis for the conclusion, in which Congress and the military commander united, that the curfew as applied was a protective measure necessary to meet the threat of sabotage and espionage which would substantially affect the war effort and which might reasonably be expected to aid a threatened enemy invasion. The alternative which appellant insists must be accepted is for the military authorities to impose the curfew on all citizens within the military area, or on none. In a case of threatened danger requiring prompt action, it is a choice between inflicting obviously needless hardship on the many, or sitting passive and unresisting in the presence of the threat. We think that constitutional government, in time of war, is not so powerless and does not compel so hard a choice if those charged with the responsibility of our national defense have reasonable ground for believing that the threat is real.

When the orders were promulgated there was a vast concentration, within Military Areas No. 1 and 2, of installations and facilities for the production of military equipment, especially ships and airplanes. Important Army and Navy bases were located in California and Washington. Approximately one-fourth of the total value of the major aircraft contracts then let by Government procurement officers were to be performed in the State of California. California ranked second, and Washington fifth, of all the states of the Union with respect to the value of shipbuilding contracts to be performed.

In the critical days of March, 1942, the danger to our war production by sabotage and espionage in this area seems obvious. The German invasion of the Western European countries had given ample warning to the world of the menace of the 'fifth column.' Espionage by persons in sympathy with the Japanese Government had been found to have been particularly effective in the surprise attack on Pearl Harbor. At a time of threatened Japanese attack upon this country, the nature of our inhabitants' attachments to the Japanese enemy was consequently a matter of grave concern. Of the 126,000 persons of Japanese descent in the United States, citizens and non-citizens, approximately 112,000 resided in California, Oregon and Washington at the time of the adoption of the military regulations. Of these approximately two-thirds are citizens [] born in the United States. Not only did the great majority of such persons reside within the Pacific Coast states but they were concentrated in or near three of the large cities, Seattle, Portland and Los Angeles, all in Military Area No. 1.

There is support for the view that social, economic and political conditions which have prevailed since the close of the last century, when the Japanese began to come to this country in substantial numbers, have intensified their solidarity and have in large measure prevented their assimilation as an integral part of the white population. In addition, large numbers of children of Japanese parentage are sent to Japanese language schools outside the regular hours of public schools in the locality. Some of these schools are generally believed to be sources of Japanese nationalistic propaganda, cultivating allegiance to Japan. Considerable numbers, estimated to be approximately 10,000, of American-born children of Japanese parentage have been sent to Japan for all or a part of their education.

Congress and the Executive, including the military commander, could have attributed special significance, in its bearing on the loyalties of persons of Japanese descent, to the maintenance by Japan of its system of dual citizenship. Children born in the United States of Japanese alien parents, and especially those children born before December 1, 1924, are under many circumstances deemed, by Japanese law, to be citizens of Japan. No official census of those whom Japan regards as having thus retained Japanese citizenship is available, but there is ground for the belief that the number is large.

The large number of resident alien Japanese, approximately one-third of all Japanese inhabitants of the country, are of mature years and occupy positions of influence in Japanese communities. The association of influential Japanese residents with Japanese Consulates has been deemed a ready means for the dissemination of propaganda and for the maintenance of the influence of the Japanese Government with the Japanese population in this country.

As a result of all these conditions affecting the life of the Japanese, both aliens and citizens, in the Pacific Coast area, there has been relatively little social intercourse between them and the white population. The restrictions, both practical and legal, affecting the privileges and opportunities afforded to persons of Japanese extraction residing in the United States, have been sources of irritation and may well have tended to increase their isolation, and in many instances their attachments to Japan and its institutions.

Viewing these data in all their aspects, Congress and the Executive could reasonably have concluded that these conditions have encouraged the continued attachment of members of this group to Japan and Japanese institutions. These are only some of the many considerations which those charged with the responsibility for the national defense could take into account in determining the nature and extent of the danger of espionage and sabotage, in the event of invasion or air raid attack. The extent of that danger could be definitely known only after the event and after it was too late to meet it. Whatever views we may entertain regarding the loyalty to this country of the citizens of Japanese ancestry, we cannot reject as unfounded the judgment of the military authorities and of Congress that there were disloyal members of that population, whose number and strength could not be precisely and quickly ascertained. We cannot say that the war-making branches of the Government did not have ground for believing that in a critical hour such persons could not readily be isolated and separately dealt with, and constituted a menace to the national defense and safety, which demanded that prompt and adequate measures be taken to guard against it.

Appellant does not deny that, given the danger, a curfew was an appropriate measure against sabotage. It is an obvious protection against the perpetration of sabotage most readily committed during the hours of darkness. If it was an appropriate exercise of the war power its validity is not impaired because it has restricted the citizen's liberty. Like every military control of the population of a dangerous zone in war time, it necessarily involves some infringement of individual liberty, just as does the police establishment of fire lines during a fire, or the confinement of people to their houses during an air raid alarm—neither of which could be thought to be an infringement of constitutional right. Like them, the validity of the restraints of the curfew order depends on all the conditions which obtain at the time the curfew is imposed and which support the order imposing it.

But appellant insists that the exercise of the power is inappropriate and unconstitutional because it discriminates against citizens of Japanese ancestry, in violation of the Fifth Amendment. The Fifth Amendment contains no equal protection clause and it restrains only such discriminatory legislation by Congress as amounts to a denial of due process. Detroit Bank v. United States, 317 U.S. 329, 337, 338, and cases cited. Congress may hit at a particular danger where it is seen, without providing for others which are not so evident or so urgent. Keokee Consol. Coke Co. v. Taylor, 234 U.S. 224, 227.

Distinctions between citizens solely because of their ancestry are by their very nature odious to a free people whose institutions are founded upon the doctrine of equality. For that reason, legislative classification or discrimination based on race alone has often been held to be a denial of equal protection. Yick Wo v. Hopkins, 118

U.S. 356; Yu Cong Eng v. Trinidad, 271 U.S. 500; Hill v. Texas, 316 U.S. 400. We may assume that these considerations would be controlling here were it not for the fact that the danger of espionage and sabotage, in time of war and of threatened invasion, calls upon the military authorities to scrutinize every relevant fact bearing on the loyalty of populations in the danger areas. Because racial discriminations are in most circumstances irrelevant and therefore prohibited, it by no means follows that, in dealing with the perils of war, Congress and the Executive are wholly precluded from taking into account those facts and circumstances which are relevant to measures for our national defense and for the successful prosecution of the war, and which may in fact place citizens of one ancestry in a different category from others. 'We must never forget, that it is a constitution we are expounding', 'a constitution intended to endure for ages to come, and, consequently, to be adapted to the various crises of human affairs'. McCulloch v. Maryland, 4 Wheat. 316, 407, 415. The adoption by Government, in the crisis of war and of threatened invasion, of measures for the public safety, based upon the recognition of facts and circumstances which indicate that a group of one national extraction may menace that safety more than others, is not wholly beyond the limits of the Constitution and is not to be condemned merely because in other and in most circumstances racial distinctions are irrelevant. Cf. State of Ohio ex rel. Clarke v. Deckebach, 274 U.S. 392, and cases cited.

Here the aim of Congress and the Executive was the protection against sabotage of war materials and utilities in areas thought to be in danger of Japanese invasion and air attack. We have stated in detail facts and circumstances with respect to the American citizens of Japanese ancestry residing on the Pacific Coast which support the judgment of the war-waging branches of the Government that some restrictive measure was urgent. We cannot say that these facts and circumstances, considered in the particular war setting, could afford no ground for differentiating citizens of Japanese ancestry from other groups in the United States. The fact alone that attack on our shores was threatened by Japan rather than another enemy power set these citizens apart from others who have no particular associations with Japan.

Our investigation here does not go beyond the inquiry whether, in the light of all the relevant circumstances preceding and attending their promulgation, the challenged orders and statute afforded a reasonable basis for the action taken in imposing the curfew. We cannot close our eyes to the fact, demonstrated by experience, that in time of war residents having ethnic affiliations with an invading enemy may be a greater source of danger than those of a different ancestry. Nor can we deny that Congress, and the military authorities acting with its authorization, have constitutional power to appraise the danger in the light of facts of public notoriety. We need not now attempt to define the ultimate boundaries of the war power. We decide only the issue as we have defined it—we decide only that the curfew order as applied, and at the time it was applied, was within the boundaries of the war power. In this case it is enough that circumstances within the knowledge of those charged with the responsibility for maintaining the national defense afforded a rational basis for the decision which they made. Whether we would have made it is irrelevant....

The military commander's appraisal of facts in the light of the authorized standard, and the inferences which he drew from those facts, involved the exercise of his informed judgment. But as we have seen, those facts, and the inferences which could be rationally drawn from them, support the judgment of the military commander, that the danger of espionage and sabotage to our military resources was imminent, and that the curfew order was an appropriate measure to meet it.

Where, as in the present case, the standard set up for the guidance of the military commander, and the action taken and the reasons for it, are in fact recorded in the military orders, so that Congress, the courts and the public are assured that the orders, in the judgment of the commander, conform to the standards approved by the President and Congress, there is no failure in the performance of the legislative function. Opp Cotton Mills v. Administrator, 312 U.S. 126, 142-146, and cases cited. The essentials of that function are the determination by Congress of the legislative policy and its approval of a rule of conduct to carry that policy into execution. The very necessities which attend the conduct of military operations in time of war in this instance as in many others preclude Congress from holding committee meetings to determine whether there is danger, before it enacts legislation to combat the danger.

The Constitution as a continuously operating charter of government does not demand the impossible or the impractical. The essentials of the legislative function are preserved when Congress authorizes a statutory command to become operative, upon ascertainment of a basic conclusion of fact by a designated representative of the Government. Cf. The Aurora, 7 Cranch 382, 3 L.Ed. 378; United States v. Chemical Foundation, 272 U.S. 1, 12. The present statute, which authorized curfew orders to be made pursuant to Executive Order No. 9066 for the protection of war resources from espionage and sabotage, satisfies those requirements. Under the Executive Order the basic facts, determined by the military commander in the light of knowledge then available, were whether that danger existed and whether a curfew order was an appropriate means of minimizing the danger. Since his findings to that effect were, as we have said, not without adequate support, the legislative function was performed and the sanction of the statute attached to violations of the curfew order. It is unnecessary to consider whether or to what extent such findings would support orders differing from the curfew order.

The conviction under the second count is without constitutional infirmity. Hence we have no occasion to review the conviction on the first count since, as already stated, the sentences on the two counts are to run concurrently and conviction on the second is sufficient to sustain the sentence. For this reason also it is unnecessary to consider the Government's argument that compliance with the order to report at the Civilian Control Station did not necessarily entail confinement in a relocation center.

AFFIRMED.

MR. JUSTICE DOUGLAS concurring.

While I concur in the result and agree substantially with the opinion of the Court, I wish to add a few words to indicate what for me is the narrow ground of decision.

After the disastrous bombing of Pearl Harbor the military had a grave problem on its hands. The threat of Japanese invasion of the west coast was not fanciful but real. The presence of many thousands of aliens and citizens of Japanese ancestry in or near to the key points along that coast line aroused special concern in those charged with the defense of the country. They believed that not only among aliens but also among citizens of Japanese ancestry there were those who would give aid and comfort to the Japanese invader and act as a fifth column before and during an invasion. If the military are right in their belief that among citizens of Japanese ancestry there was an actual or incipient fifth column, we were indeed faced with the imminent threat of a dire emergency. We must credit the military with as much good faith in that belief as we would any other public official acting pursuant to his duties. We cannot possibly know all the facts which lay behind that decision. Some of them may have been as intangible and as imponderable as the factors which influence personal or business decisions in daily life. The point is that we cannot sit in judgment on the military requirements of that hour. Where the orders under the present Act have some relation to 'protection against espionage and against sabotage', our task is at an end.

Much of the argument assumes that as a matter of policy it might have been wiser for the military to have dealt with these people on an individual basis and through the process of investigation and hearings separated those who were loyal from those who were not. But the wisdom or expediency of the decision which was made is not for us to review. Nor are we warranted where national survival is at stake in insisting that those orders should not have been applied to anyone without some evidence of his disloyalty. The orders as applied to the petitioner are not to be tested by the substantial evidence rule. Peacetime procedures do not necessarily fit wartime needs. It is said that if citizens of Japanese ancestry were generally disloyal, treatment on a group basis might be justified. But there is no difference in power when the number of those who are finally shown to be disloyal or suspect is reduced to a small per cent. The sorting process might indeed be as time-consuming whether those who were disloyal or suspect constituted nine or ninety-nine per cent. And the pinch of the order on the loyal citizens would be as great in any case. But where the peril is great and the time is short, temporary treatment on a group basis may be the only practicable expedient whatever the ultimate percentage of those who are detained for cause. Nor should the military be required to wait until espionage or sabotage becomes effective before it moves....

Since we cannot override the military judgment which lay behind these orders, it seems to me necessary to concede that the army had the power to deal temporarily with these people on a group basis. Petitioner therefore was not justified in disobeying the orders.

But I think it important to emphasize that we are dealing here with a problem of loyalty not assimilation. Loyalty is a matter of mind and of heart not of race. That indeed is the history of America. Moreover, guilt is personal under our constitutional system. Detention for reasonable cause is one thing. Detention on account of ancestry is another....

MR. JUSTICE MURPHY, concurring.

It is not to be doubted that the action taken by the military commander in pursuance of the authority conferred upon him was taken in complete good faith and in the firm conviction that it was required by considerations of public safety and military security. Neither is it doubted that the Congress and the Executive working together may generally employ such measures as are necessary and appropriate to provide for the common defense and to wage war 'with all the force necessary to make it effective.' United States v. Macintosh, 283 U.S. 605, 622, 51 S.Ct. 570, 574, 75 L.Ed. 1302. This includes authority to exercise measures of control over persons and property which would not in all cases be permissible in normal times.

It does not follow, however, that the broad guaranties of the Bill of Rights and other provisions of the Constitution protecting essential liberties are suspended by the mere existence of a state of war. It has been frequently stated and recognized by this Court that the war power, like the other great substantive powers of government, is subject to the limitations of the Constitution. See Ex parte Milligan, 4 Wall. 2; Hamilton v. Kentucky Distilleries Co., 251 U.S. 146, 156; Home Building & Loan Association v. Blaisdell, 290 U.S. 398, 426, 54 S.Ct. 231, 235. We give great deference to the judgment of the Congress and of the military authorities as to what is necessary in the effective prosecution of the war, but we can never forget that there are constitutional boundaries which it is our duty to uphold. It would not be supposed, for instance, that public elections could be suspended or that the prerogatives of the courts could be set aside, or that persons not charged with offenses against the law of war (see Ex parte Quirin, 317 U.S. 1) could be deprived of due process of law and the benefits of trial by jury, in the absence of a valid declaration of martial law. Cf. Ex parte Milligan, supra.

Distinctions based on color and ancestry are utterly inconsistent with our traditions and ideals. They are at variance with the principles for which we are now waging war. We cannot close our eyes to the fact that for centuries the Old World has been torn by racial and religious conflicts and has suffered the worst kind of anguish because of inequality of treatment for different groups. There was one law for one and a different law for another. Nothing is written more firmly into our law than the compact of the Plymouth voyagers to have just and equal laws. To say that any group cannot be assimilated is to admit that the great American experiment has failed, that our way of life has failed when confronted with the normal attachment of certain groups to the lands of their forefathers. As a nation we embrace many groups, some of them among the oldest settlements in our midst, which have isolated themselves for religious and cultural reasons.

Today is the first time, so far as I am aware, that we have sustained a substantial restriction of the personal liberty of citizens of the United States based upon the accident of race or ancestry. Under the curfew order here challenged no less than 70,000 American citizens have been placed under a special ban and deprived of their liberty because of their particular racial inheritance. In this sense it bears a melancholy resemblance to the treatment accorded to members of the Jewish race in Germany and in other parts of Europe. The result is the creation in this country of two classes of citizens for the purposes of a critical and perilous hour—to sanction discrimination between groups of United States citizens on the basis of ancestry. In my opinion this goes to the very brink of constitutional power.

Except under conditions of great emergency a regulation of this kind applicable solely to citizens of a particular racial extraction would not be regarded as in accord with the requirement of due process of law contained in the Fifth Amendment. We have consistently held that attempts to apply regulatory action to particular groups solely on the basis of racial distinction or classification is not in accordance with due process of law as prescribed by the Fifth and Fourteenth Amendments. Cf. Yick Wo. v. Hopkins, 118 U.S. 356, 369; Yu Con Eng v. Trinidad, 271 U.S. 500, 524-528....

In view, however, of the critical military situation which prevailed on the Pacific Coast area in the spring of 1942, and the urgent necessity of taking prompt and effective action to secure defense installations and military operations against the risk of sabotage and espionage, the military authorities should not be required to conform to standards of regulatory action appropriate to normal times. Because of the damage wrought by the Japanese at Pearl Harbor and the availability of new weapons and new techniques with greater capacity for speed and deception in offensive operations, the immediate possibility of an attempt at invasion somewhere along the Pacific Coast had to be reckoned with. However desirable such a procedure might have been, the military authorities could have reasonably concluded at the time that determinations as to the loyalty and dependability of individual members of the large and widely scattered group of persons of Japanese extraction on the West Coast could not be made without delay that might have had tragic consequences. Modern war does not always wait for the observance of procedural requirements that are considered essential and appropriate under normal conditions. Accordingly I think that the military arm, confronted with the peril of imminent enemy attack and acting under the authority conferred by the Congress, made an allowable judgment at the time the curfew restriction was imposed. Whether such a restriction is valid today is another matter.

In voting for affirmance of the judgment I do not wish to be understood as intimating that the military authorities in time of war are subject to no restraints whatsoever, or that they are free to impose any restrictions they may choose on the rights and liberties of individual citizens or groups of citizens in those places which may be designated as 'military areas'. While this Court sits, it has the inescapable duty of seeing that the mandates of the Constitution are obeyed. That duty exists in time of war as well as in time of peace, and in its performance we must not forget that few indeed have been the invasions upon essential liberties which have not been accompanied by pleas of urgent necessity advanced in good faith by responsible men. Cf. Mr. Justice Brandeis concurring in Whitney v. California, 274 U.S. 357, 372.

Nor do I mean to intimate that citizens of a particular racial group whose freedom may be curtailed within an area threatened with attack should be generally prevented from leaving the area and going at large in other areas that are not in danger of attack and where special precautions are not needed. Their status as citizens, though subject to requirements of national security and military necessity, should at all times be accorded the fullest consideration and respect. When the danger is past, the restrictions imposed on them should be promptly removed and their freedom of action fully restored.

Notes

1. *Hirabayashi* was decided unanimously; all nine justices agreed that the conviction should be affirmed. Justices Douglas, Murphy, and Rutledge filed concurring opinions.

2. The majority recognized that "[d]istinctions between citizens solely because of their ancestry are by their very nature odious to a free people whose institutions are founded upon the doctrine of equality." Yet, in affirming, it upheld a distinction between citizens based on Japanese ancestry. What was the Court's reasoning? Why did it distinguish between Japanese-American citizens and other American citizens of German and Italian descent?

3. What level of scrutiny did the Court apply to the government's justification for its actions? Was this the appropriate level of scrutiny?

4. What did Justice Douglas mean by the following statement in his concurring opinion? "I think it important to emphasize that we are dealing here with a problem of loyalty not assimilation. Loyalty is a matter of mind and of heart not of race. That indeed is the history of America." Does his distinction between loyalty and assimilation hold up in light of the policy to detain only Japanese Americans and not German or Italian Americans?

5. Gordon Hirabayashi was born in 1918 in Auburn, Washington, a town about 20 miles south of Seattle. His father, a Japanese immigrant, ran a roadside fruit market. He entered the University of Washington in Seattle in 1937, but his family's financial circumstances forced him to take some time off to work, as a houseboy and farmhand. He was 24 years old and still a senior when the military curfew for Japanese Americans became effective in March 1942. He belonged to a number of religious organizations, and registered for the draft but was granted conscientious objector status. He complied with the curfew for some weeks before he decided to resist in May 1942. As he later recalled to Professor Peter Irons:

   > I was expected like every citizen to obey the law, and I did.... There were twelve of us living in the YMCA dorm, and they all became my volunteer time keepers—"Hey, it's five minutes to eight, Gordy"—and I'd dash back from the library or the coffeeshop. One of the times I stopped and said, "Why the hell am I running back? Am I American or not? Why am I running back and nobody else is?"

Peter Irons, *Justice At War: The Story of the Japanese American Internment Cases* 89–90 (1993). What if the curfew had been limited to all men of Asian appearance between the ages of 18 and 35. Do you think that such a hypothetical curfew would have been constitutionally unassailable? What if the curfew had applied to all persons?

6. What differences and similarities do you see between Executive Order 9066 and President Trump's "Travel Ban" executive order?

7. The same day that it decided *Hirabayashi*, the Court handed down its decision in *Yasui v. United States*. Like *Hirabayashi*, *Yasui* involved the curfew—the requirement that Japanese Americans in designated areas be within their residences between 8:00 p.m. and 6:00 a.m. Neither case involved the issues of exclusion or internment.

Yasui v. United States

320 U.S. 115 (1943)

MR. CHIEF JUSTICE STONE delivered the opinion of the Court.

This is a companion case to Hirabayashi v. United States, 320 U.S. 81, decided this day.

The case comes here on certificate of the Court of Appeals for the Ninth Circuit, certifying to us questions of law upon which it desires instructions for the decision of the case. § 239 of the Judicial Code as amended, 28 U.S.C. § 346. Acting under that section we ordered the entire record to be certified to this Court so that we might proceed to a decision, as if the case had been brought here by appeal.

Appellant, an American-born person of Japanese ancestry, was convicted in the district court of an offense defined by the Act of March 21, 1942, 56 Stat. 173, 18 U.S.C. § 97a. The indictment charged him with violation, on March 28, 1942, of a curfew order made applicable to Portland, Oregon, by Public Proclamation No. 3, issued by Lt. General J. L. DeWitt on March 24, 1942. 7 Federal Register 2543. The validity of the curfew was considered in the Hirabayashi case, and this case presents the same issues as the conviction on Count 2 of the indictment in that case. From the evidence it appeared that appellant was born in Oregon in 1916 of alien parents; that when he was eight years old he spent a summer in Japan; that he attended the public schools in Oregon, and also, for about three years, a Japanese language school; that he later attended the University of Oregon, from which he received A.B. and LL.B degrees; that he was a member of the bar of Oregon, and a second lieutenant in the Army of the United States, Infantry Reserve; that he had been employed by the Japanese Consulate in Chicago, but had resigned on December 8, 1941, and immediately offered his services to the military authorities; that he had discussed with an agent of the Federal Bureau of Investigation the advisability of testing the constitutionality of the curfew;

and that when he violated the curfew order he requested that he be arrested so that he could test its constitutionality.

The district court ruled that the Act of March 21, 1942, was unconstitutional as applied to American citizens, but held that appellant, by reason of his course of conduct, must be deemed to have renounced his American citizenship. The Government does not undertake to support the conviction on that ground, since no such issue was tendered by the Government, although appellant testified at the trial that he had not renounced his citizenship. Since we hold, as in the Hirabayashi case, that the curfew order was valid as applied to citizens, it follows that appellant's citizenship was not relevant to the issue tendered by the Government and the conviction must be sustained for the reasons stated in the Hirabayashi case.

But as the sentence of one year's imprisonment—the maximum permitted by the statute—was imposed after the finding that appellant was not a citizen, and as the Government states that it has not and does not now controvert his citizenship, the case is an appropriate one for resentence in the light of these circumstances. See Husty v. United States, 282 U.S. 694, 703. The conviction will be sustained but the judgment will be vacated and the cause remanded to the district court for resentence of appellant, and to afford that court opportunity to strike its findings as to appellant's loss of United States citizenship.

SO ORDERED.

Notes

1. The Court's decision in *Yasui* was brief because it was a companion decision to *Hirabayashi*.

2. Minoru Yasui was the first person to challenge the military orders. He was a lawyer in Portland, Oregon. On March 28, 1942, the first day the curfew took effect, Yasui broke the curfew by walking the streets after 8:00 p.m., trying to get arrested. When he did not succeed, he finally went to the police station to turn himself in. For his actions, he eventually spent nine months in difficult conditions in solitary confinement.

   Yasui had been unable to find a job as a lawyer after his graduation from law school in 1939. He found work as an attaché at the Japanese consulate in Chicago. The day after the attack on Pearl Harbor, he resigned his position at the consulate and returned to Oregon. He was a member of the U.S. Army Reserves and reported to Fort Vancouver for duty but was ordered off the base because of his race. He returned to Fort Vancouver eight times to try to serve but was rebuffed each time. Irons at 81–83.

   The trial court found Yasui guilty. It ruled that the curfew order, as applied to American citizens of Japanese descent, was unconstitutional. At the same time,

Figure 6.2 ***Portrait of Minoru Yasui*** **(1946). National Portrait Gallery, Smithsonian. Gift in loving memory of Minoru and True Yasui Institution.**

however, it found that Yasui had renounced his American citizenship because, as an employee of the Japanese consulate, he was a "propaganda agent" for Japan who chose "allegiance to the Emperor of Japan." Because the curfew order could be lawfully applied to aliens, and because Yasui had forfeited his American citizenship, the trial court reasoned, he was guilty.

Before the Supreme Court, the government did not even try to defend the trial court's determination that Yasui had renounced his citizenship, and the Court reversed that finding. But the Court also reversed the trial court on the constitutional question, holding that the military orders could be applied to American citizens of Japanese ancestry. Hence, it upheld the conviction, and remanded only for resentencing.

Korematsu v. United States

323 U.S. 214 (1944)

MR. JUSTICE BLACK delivered the opinion of the Court.

The petitioner, an American citizen of Japanese descent, was convicted in a federal district court for remaining in San Leandro, California, a 'Military Area', contrary to Civilian Exclusion Order No. 34 of the Commanding General of the Western Command, U.S. Army, which directed that after May 9, 1942, all persons of Japanese ancestry should be excluded from that area. No question was raised as to petitioner's loyalty to the United States. The Circuit Court of Appeals affirmed, and the importance of the constitutional question involved caused us to grant certiorari.

It should be noted, to begin with, that all legal restrictions which curtail the civil rights of a single racial group are immediately suspect. That is not to say that all such restrictions are unconstitutional. It is to say that courts must subject them to the most rigid scrutiny. Pressing public necessity may sometimes justify the existence of such restrictions; racial antagonism never can.

In the instant case prosecution of the petitioner was begun by information charging violation of an Act of Congress, of March 21, 1942, 56 Stat. 173, 18 U.S.C. § 97a, which provides that

> " ... whoever shall enter, remain in, leave, or commit any act in any military area or military zone prescribed, under the authority of an Executive order of the President, by the Secretary of War, or by any military commander designated by the Secretary of War, contrary to the restrictions applicable to any such area or zone or contrary to the order of the Secretary of War or any such military commander, shall, if it appears that he knew or should have known of the existence and extent of the restrictions or order and that his act was in violation thereof, be guilty of a misdemeanor and upon conviction shall be liable to a fine of not to exceed $5,000 or to imprisonment for not more than one year, or both, for each offense."

Exclusion Order No. 34, which the petitioner knowingly and admittedly violated was one of a number of military orders and proclamations, all of which were substantially based upon Executive Order No. 9066, 7 Fed.Reg. 1407. That order, issued after we were at war with Japan, declared that "the successful prosecution of the war requires every possible protection against espionage and against sabotage to national-defense material, national-defense premises, and national-defense utilities.... "

One of the series of orders and proclamations, a curfew order, which like the exclusion order here was promulgated pursuant to Executive Order 9066, subjected all persons of Japanese ancestry in prescribed West Coast military areas to remain in their residences from 8 p.m. to 6 a.m. As is the case with the exclusion order here, that prior curfew order was designed as a "protection against espionage and against sabotage." In Kiyoshi Hirabayashi v. United States, 320 U.S. 81, we sustained a conviction obtained

Figure 6.3 ***Fred Toyosaburo Korematsu*** **(1940). Courtesy of the Fred T. Korematsu Institute.**

for violation of the curfew order. The Hirabayashi conviction and this one thus rest on the same 1942 Congressional Act and the same basic executive and military orders, all of which orders were aimed at the twin dangers of espionage and sabotage.

The 1942 Act was attacked in the Hirabayashi case as an unconstitutional delegation of power; it was contended that the curfew order and other orders on which it rested were beyond the war powers of the Congress, the military authorities and of the President, as Commander in Chief of the Army; and finally that to apply the curfew order against none but citizens of Japanese ancestry amounted to a constitutionally prohibited discrimination solely on account of race. To these questions, we gave the serious consideration which their importance justified. We upheld the curfew order as an exercise of the power of the government to take steps necessary to prevent espionage and sabotage in an area threatened by Japanese attack.

In the light of the principles we announced in the Hirabayashi case, we are unable to conclude that it was beyond the war power of Congress and the Executive to exclude those of Japanese ancestry from the West Coast war area at the time they did. True, exclusion from the area in which one's home is located is a far greater deprivation than constant confinement to the home from 8 p.m. to 6 a.m. Nothing short of apprehension by the proper military authorities of the gravest imminent danger to the public safety can constitutionally justify either. But exclusion from a threatened area, no less than curfew, has a definite and close relationship to the prevention of espionage and sabotage. The military authorities, charged with the primary responsibility of defending our shores, concluded that curfew provided inadequate protection and ordered exclusion. They did so, as pointed out in our Hirabayashi opinion, in accordance with Congressional authority to the military to say who should, and who should not, remain in the threatened areas.

In this case the petitioner challenges the assumptions upon which we rested our conclusions in the Hirabayashi case. He also urges that by May 1942, when Order No. 34 was promulgated, all danger of Japanese invasion of the West Coast had disappeared. After careful consideration of these contentions we are compelled to reject them.

Here, as in the Hirabayashi case, supra, 320 U.S. at page 99, "...we cannot reject as unfounded the judgment of the military authorities and of Congress that there were disloyal members of that population, whose number and strength could not be precisely and quickly ascertained. We cannot say that the war-making branches of the Government did not have ground for believing that in a critical hour such persons could not readily be isolated and separately dealt with, and constituted a menace to the national defense and safety, which demanded that prompt and adequate measures be taken to guard against it."

Like curfew, exclusion of those of Japanese origin was deemed necessary because of the presence of an unascertained number of disloyal members of the group, most of whom we have no doubt were loyal to this country. It was because we could not reject the finding of the military authorities that it was impossible to bring about an immediate segregation of the disloyal from the loyal that we sustained the validity of the curfew order as applying to the whole group. In the instant case, temporary exclusion of the entire group was rested by the military on the same ground. The judgment that exclusion of the whole group was for the same reason a military imperative answers the contention that the exclusion was in the nature of group punishment based on antagonism to those of Japanese origin. That there were members of the group who retained loyalties to Japan has been confirmed by investigations made subsequent to the exclusion. Approximately five thousand American citizens of Japanese ancestry refused to swear unqualified allegiance to the United States and to renounce allegiance to the Japanese Emperor, and several thousand evacuees requested repatriation to Japan.

We uphold the exclusion order as of the time it was made and when the petitioner violated it. Cf. Chastleton Corporation v. Sinclair, 264 U.S. 543, 547; Block v. Hirsh, 256 U.S. 135, 154, 155. In doing so, we are not unmindful of the hardships imposed by it upon a large group of American citizens. Cf. Ex parte Kumezo Kawato, 317 U.S. 69, 73. But hardships are part of war, and war is an aggregation of hardships. All citizens alike, both in and out of uniform, feel the impact of war in greater or lesser measure.

Citizenship has its responsibilities as well as its privileges, and in time of war the burden is always heavier. Compulsory exclusion of large groups of citizens from their homes, except under circumstances of direst emergency and peril, is inconsistent with our basic governmental institutions. But when under conditions of modern warfare our shores are threatened by hostile forces, the power to protect must be commensurate with the threatened danger.

It is argued that on May 30, 1942, the date the petitioner was charged with remaining in the prohibited area, there were conflicting orders outstanding, forbidding him both to leave the area and to remain there. Of course, a person cannot be convicted for doing the very thing which it is a crime to fail to do. But the outstanding orders here contained no such contradictory commands.

There was an order issued March 27, 1942, which prohibited petitioner and others of Japanese ancestry from leaving the area, but its effect was specifically limited in time "until and to the extent that a future proclamation or order should so permit or direct." 7 Fed.Reg. 2601. That 'future order', the one for violation of which petitioner was convicted, was issued May 3, 1942, and it did 'direct' exclusion from the area of all persons of Japanese ancestry, before 12 o'clock noon, May 9; furthermore it contained a warning that all such persons found in the prohibited area would be liable to punishment under the March 21, 1942 Act of Congress. Consequently, the only order in effect touching the petitioner's being in the area on May 30, 1942, the date specified in the information against him, was the May 3 order which prohibited his remaining there, and it was that same order, which he stipulated in his trial that he had violated, knowing of its existence. There is therefore no basis for the argument that on May 30, 1942, he was subject to punishment, under the March 27 and May 3rd orders, whether he remained in or left the area.

It does appear, however, that on May 9, the effective date of the exclusion order, the military authorities had already determined that the evacuation should be effected by assembling together and placing under guard all those of Japanese ancestry, at central points, designated as 'assembly centers', in order "to insure the orderly evacuation and resettlement of Japanese voluntarily migrating from military area No. 1 to restrict and regulate such migration." Public Proclamation No. 4, 7 Fed.Reg. 2601. And on May 19, 1942, eleven days before the time petitioner was charged with unlawfully remaining in the area, Civilian Restrictive Order No. 1, 8 Fed.Reg. 982, provided for detention of those of Japanese ancestry in assembly or relocation centers. It is now argued that the validity of the exclusion order cannot be considered apart from the orders requiring him, after departure from the area, to report and to remain in an assembly or relocation center. The contention is that we must treat these separate orders as one and inseparable; that, for this reason, if detention in the assembly or relocation center would have illegally deprived the petitioner of his liberty, the exclusion order and his conviction under it cannot stand.

We are thus being asked to pass at this time upon the whole subsequent detention program in both assembly and relocation centers, although the only issues framed at the trial related to petitioner's remaining in the prohibited area in violation of the exclusion order. Had petitioner here left the prohibited area and gone to an assembly center we cannot say either as a matter of fact or law, that his presence in that center would have resulted in his detention in a relocation center. Some who did report to the assembly center were not sent to relocation centers, but were released upon condition that they remain outside the prohibited zone until the military orders were modified or lifted. This illustrates that they pose different problems and may be governed by different principles. The lawfulness of one does not necessarily determine the lawfulness of the others. This is made clear when we analyze the requirements of the separate provisions of the separate orders. These separate requirements were that those of Japanese ancestry (1) depart from the area; (2) report to and temporarily remain in an assembly center; (3) go under military control to a relocation center there to remain for an indeterminate period until released conditionally or unconditionally by the military authorities. Each of these requirements, it will be noted, imposed distinct duties in connection with the separate steps in a complete evacuation program. Had Congress directly incorporated into one Act the language of these separate orders, and provided sanctions for their violations, disobedience of any one would have constituted a separate offense. Cf. Blockburger v. United States, 284 U.S. 299, 304. There is no reason why violations of these orders, insofar as they were promulgated pursuant to congressional enactment, should not be treated as separate offenses.

The Endo case (Ex parte Mitsuye Endo) 323 U.S. 283, graphically illustrates the difference between the validity of an order to exclude and the validity of a detention order after exclusion has been effected.

Since the petitioner has not been convicted of failing to report or to remain in an assembly or relocation center, we cannot in this case determine the validity of those separate provisions of the order. It is sufficient here for us to pass upon the order which petitioner violated. To do more would be to go beyond the issues raised, and to decide momentous questions not contained within the framework of the pleadings or the evidence in this case. It will be time enough to decide the serious constitutional issues which petitioner seeks to raise when an assembly or relocation order is applied or is certain to be applied to him, and we have its terms before us.

Some of the members of the Court are of the view that evacuation and detention in an Assembly Center were inseparable. After May 3, 1942, the date of Exclusion Order No. 34, Korematsu was under compulsion to leave the area not as he would choose but via an Assembly Center. The Assembly Center was conceived as a part of the machinery for group evacuation. The power to exclude includes the power to do it by force if necessary. And any forcible measure must necessarily entail some degree of detention or restraint whatever method of removal is selected. But whichever view is taken, it results in holding that the order under which petitioner was convicted was valid.

It is said that we are dealing here with the case of imprisonment of a citizen in a concentration camp solely because of his ancestry, without evidence or inquiry concerning his loyalty and good disposition towards the United States. Our task would be simple, our duty clear, were this a case involving the imprisonment of a loyal citizen in a concentration camp because of racial prejudice. Regardless of the true nature of the assembly and relocation centers—and we deem it unjustifiable to call them concentration camps with all the ugly connotations that term implies—we are dealing specifically with nothing but an exclusion order. To cast this case into outlines of racial prejudice, without reference to the real military dangers which were presented, merely confuses the issue.

Korematsu was not excluded from the Military Area because of hostility to him or his race. He was excluded because we are at war with the Japanese Empire, because the properly constituted military authorities feared an invasion of our West Coast and felt constrained to take proper security measures, because they decided that the military urgency of the situation demanded that all citizens of Japanese ancestry be segregated from the West Coast temporarily, and finally, because Congress, reposing its confidence in this time of war in our military leaders—as inevitably it must—determined that they should have the power to do just this. There was evidence of disloyalty on the part of some, the military authorities considered that the need for action was great, and time was short. We cannot—by availing ourselves of the calm perspective of hindsight—now say that at that time these actions were unjustified.

AFFIRMED....

MR. JUSTICE ROBERTS.

I dissent, because I think the indisputable facts exhibit a clear violation of Constitutional rights.

This is not a case of keeping people off the streets at night as was Kiyoshi Hirabayashi v. United States, 320 U.S. 81, nor a case of temporary exclusion of a citizen from an area for his own safety or that of the community, nor a case of offering him an opportunity to go temporarily out of an area where his presence might cause danger to himself or to his fellows. On the contrary, it is the case of convicting a citizen as a punishment for not submitting to imprisonment in a concentration camp, based on his ancestry, and solely because of his ancestry, without evidence or inquiry concerning his loyalty and good disposition towards the United States. If this be a correct statement of the facts disclosed by this record, and facts of which we take judicial notice, I need hardly labor the conclusion that Constitutional rights have been violated.

The Government's argument, and the opinion of the court, in my judgment, erroneously divide that which is single and indivisible and thus make the case appear as if the petitioner violated a Military Order, sanctioned by Act of Congress, which excluded him from his home, by refusing voluntarily to leave and, so, knowingly and intentionally, defying the order and the Act of Congress.

The petitioner, a resident of San Leandro, Alameda County, California, is a native of the United States of Japanese ancestry who, according to the uncontradicted evidence, is a loyal citizen of the nation....

The predicament in which the petitioner thus found himself was this: He was forbidden, by Military Order, to leave the zone in which he lived; he was forbidden, by Military Order, after a date fixed, to be found within that zone unless he were in an Assembly Center located in that zone. General DeWitt's report to the Secretary of War concerning the program of evacuation and relocation of Japanese makes it entirely clear, if it were necessary to refer to that document—and, in the light of the above recitation, I think it is not—that an Assembly Center was a euphemism for a prison. No person within such a center was permitted to leave except by Military Order.

In the dilemma that he dare not remain in his home, or voluntarily leave the area, without incurring criminal penalties, and that the only way he could avoid punishment was to go to an Assembly Center and submit himself to military imprisonment, the petitioner did nothing....

...The liberty of every American citizen freely to come and to go must frequently, in the face of sudden danger, be temporarily limited or suspended. The civil authorities must often resort to the expedient of excluding citizens temporarily from a locality. The drawing of fire lines in the case of a conflagration, the removal of persons from the area where a pestilence has broken out, are familiar examples. If the exclusion worked by Exclusion Order No. 34 were of that nature the Hirabayashi case would be authority for sustaining it. But the facts above recited, and those set forth in Ex parte Mitsuye Endo, supra, show that the exclusion was but a part of an over-all plan for forceable detention. This case cannot, therefore, be decided on any such narrow ground as the possible validity of a Temporary Exclusion Order under which the residents of an area are given an opportunity to leave and go elsewhere in their native land outside the boundaries of a military area. To make the case turn on any such assumption is to shut our eyes to reality....

We cannot shut our eyes to the fact that had the petitioner attempted to violate Proclamation No. 4 and leave the military area in which he lived he would have been arrested and tried and convicted for violation of Proclamation No. 4. The two conflicting orders, one which commanded him to stay and the other which commanded him to go, were nothing but a cleverly devised trap to accomplish the real purpose of the military authority, which was to lock him up in a concentration camp. The only course by which the petitioner could avoid arrest and prosecution was to go to that camp according to instructions to be given him when he reported at a Civil Control Center. We know that is the fact. Why should we set up a figmentary and artificial situation instead of addressing ourselves to the actualities of the case?

These stark realities are met by the suggestion that it is lawful to compel an American citizen to submit to illegal imprisonment on the assumption that he might, after going to the Assembly Center, apply for his discharge by suing out a writ of habeas corpus, as was done in the Endo case, supra. The answer, of course, is that where he was subject to two conflicting laws he was not bound, in order to escape violation of one or the other, to surrender his liberty for any period. Nor will it do to say that the detention was a necessary part of the process of evacuation, and so we are here concerned only with the validity of the latter.

Again it is a new doctrine of constitutional law that one indicted for disobedience to an unconstitutional statute may not defend on the ground of the invalidity of the statute but must obey it though he knows it is no law and, after he has suffered the disgrace of conviction and lost his liberty by sentence, then, and not before, seek, from within prison walls, to test the validity of the law....

I would reverse the judgment of conviction.

MR. JUSTICE MURPHY, dissenting.

This exclusion of "all persons of Japanese ancestry, both alien and non-alien," from the Pacific Coast area on a plea of military necessity in the absence of martial law ought not to be approved. Such exclusion goes over "the very brink of constitutional power" and falls into the ugly abyss of racism.

In dealing with matters relating to the prosecution and progress of a war, we must accord great respect and consideration to the judgments of the military authorities who are on the scene and who have full knowledge of the military facts. The scope of their discretion must, as a matter of necessity and common sense, be wide. And their judgments ought not to be overruled lightly by those whose training and duties ill-equip them to deal intelligently with matters so vital to the physical security of the nation.

At the same time, however, it is essential that there be definite limits to military discretion, especially where martial law has not been declared. Individuals must not be left impoverished of their constitutional rights on a plea of military necessity that has neither substance nor support. Thus, like other claims conflicting with the asserted constitutional rights of the individual, the military claim must subject itself to the judicial process of having its reasonableness determined and its conflicts with other interests reconciled. "What are the allowable limits of military discretion, and whether or not they have been overstepped in a particular case, are judicial questions." Sterling v. Constantin, 287 U.S. 378, 401.

The judicial test of whether the Government, on a plea of military necessity, can validly deprive an individual of any of his constitutional rights is whether the deprivation is reasonably related to a public danger that is so 'immediate, imminent, and impending' as not to admit of delay and not to permit the intervention of ordinary constitutional processes to alleviate the danger. United States v. Russell, 13 Wall. 623, 627, 628; Mitchell v. Harmony, 13 How. 115, 134, 135; Raymond v. Thomas, 91 U.S. 712, 716. Civilian Exclusion Order No. 34, banishing from a prescribed area of the Pacific Coast "all persons of Japanese ancestry, both alien and non-alien," clearly does not meet that test. Being an obvious racial discrimination, the order deprives all those within its scope of the equal protection of the laws as guaranteed by the Fifth Amendment. It further deprives these individuals of their constitutional rights to live and work where they will, to establish a home where they choose and to move about freely. In excommunicating them without benefit of hearings, this order also deprives them of all their constitutional rights to procedural due process. Yet no reasonable relation to an 'immediate, imminent, and impending' public danger is evident to support this racial restriction which is one of the most sweeping and complete deprivations of constitutional rights in the history of this nation in the absence of martial law.

It must be conceded that the military and naval situation in the spring of 1942 was such as to generate a very real fear of invasion of the Pacific Coast, accompanied by fears of sabotage and espionage in that area. The military command was therefore justified in adopting all reasonable means necessary to combat these dangers. In adjudging the military action taken in light of the then apparent dangers, we must not erect too high or too meticulous standards; it is necessary only that the action have some reasonable relation to the removal of the dangers of invasion, sabotage and espionage. But the exclusion, either temporarily or permanently, of all persons with Japanese blood in their veins has no such reasonable relation. And that relation is lacking because the exclusion order necessarily must rely for its reasonableness upon the assumption that all persons of Japanese ancestry may have a dangerous tendency to commit sabotage and espionage and to aid our Japanese enemy in other ways. It is difficult to believe that reason, logic or experience could be marshalled in support of such an assumption.

That this forced exclusion was the result in good measure of this erroneous assumption of racial guilt rather than bona fide military necessity is evidenced by the Commanding General's Final Report on the evacuation from the Pacific Coast area. In it he refers to all individuals of Japanese descent as 'subversive,' as belonging to 'an enemy race' whose 'racial strains are undiluted,' and as constituting "over 112,000 potential enemies... at large today" along the Pacific Coast. In support of this blanket condemnation of all persons of Japanese descent, however, no reliable evidence is cited to show that such individuals were generally disloyal, or had generally so conducted themselves in this area as to constitute a special menace to defense installations or war industries, or had otherwise by their behavior furnished reasonable ground for their exclusion as a group.

Justification for the exclusion is sought, instead, mainly upon questionable racial and sociological grounds not ordinarily within the realm of expert military judgment, supplemented by certain semi-military conclusions drawn from an unwarranted use of circumstantial evidence. Individuals of Japanese ancestry are condemned because they are said to be "a large, unassimilated, tightly knit racial group, bound to an enemy nation by strong ties of race, culture, custom and religion." They are claimed to be given to 'emperor worshipping ceremonies' and to 'dual citizenship.' Japanese language schools and allegedly pro-Japanese organizations are cited as evidence of possible group disloyalty, together with facts as to certain persons being educated and residing at length in Japan. It is intimated that many of these individuals deliberately resided 'adjacent to strategic points,' thus enabling them "to carry into execution a tremendous program of sabotage on a mass scale should any considerable number of them have been inclined to do so." The need for protective custody is also asserted. The report refers without identity to 'numerous incidents of violence' as well as to other admittedly unverified or cumulative incidents. From this, plus certain other events not shown to have been connected with the Japanese Americans, it is concluded that the "situation was fraught with danger to the Japanese population itself" and that the general public "was ready to take matters into its own hands." Finally, it is intimated, though not directly charged or proved, that persons of Japanese ancestry were responsible for three minor isolated shellings and bombings of the Pacific Coast area, as well as for unidentified radio transmissions and night signalling.

The main reasons relied upon by those responsible for the forced evacuation, therefore, do not prove a reasonable relation between the group characteristics of Japanese Americans and the dangers of invasion, sabotage and espionage. The reasons appear, instead, to be largely an accumulation of much of the misinformation, half-truths and insinuations that for years have been directed against Japanese Americans by people with racial and economic prejudices—the same people who have been among the foremost advocates of the evacuation. A military judgment based upon such racial and sociological considerations is not entitled to the great weight ordinarily given the judgments based upon strictly military considerations. Especially is this so when every charge relative to race, religion, culture, geographical location, and legal and economic status has been substantially discredited by independent studies made by experts in these matters.

The military necessity which is essential to the validity of the evacuation order thus resolves itself into a few intimations that certain individuals actively aided the enemy, from which it is inferred that the entire group of Japanese Americans could not be trusted to be or remain loyal to the United States. No one denies, of course, that there were some disloyal persons of Japanese descent on the Pacific Coast who did all in their power to aid their ancestral land. Similar disloyal activities have been engaged in by many persons of German, Italian and even more pioneer stock in our country. But to infer that examples of individual disloyalty prove group disloyalty and justify discriminatory action against the entire group is to deny that under our system of law individual guilt is the sole basis for deprivation of rights. Moreover, this inference, which is at the very heart of the evacuation orders, has been used in support of the abhorrent and despicable treatment of minority groups by the dictatorial tyrannies which this nation is now pledged to destroy. To give constitutional sanction to that inference in this case, however well-intentioned may have been the military command on the Pacific Coast, is to adopt one of the cruelest of the rationales used by our enemies to destroy the dignity of the individual and to encourage and open the door to discriminatory actions against other minority groups in the passions of tomorrow.

No adequate reason is given for the failure to treat these Japanese Americans on an individual basis by holding investigations and hearings to separate the loyal from the disloyal, as was done in the case of persons of German and Italian ancestry. See House Report No. 2124 (77th Cong., 2d Sess.) 247-52. It is asserted merely that the loyalties of this group "were unknown and time was of the essence." Yet nearly four months elapsed after Pearl Harbor before the first exclusion order was issued; nearly eight months went by until the last order was issued; and the last of these 'subversive' persons was not actually removed until almost eleven months had elapsed. Leisure and deliberation seem to have been more of the essence than speed. And the fact that conditions were not such as to warrant a declaration of martial law adds strength to the belief that the factors of time and military necessity were not as urgent as they have been represented to be.

Moreover, there was no adequate proof that the Federal Bureau of Investigation and the military and naval intelligence services did not have the espionage and sabotage situation well in hand during this long period. Nor is there any denial of the fact that not one person of Japanese ancestry was accused or convicted of espionage or sabotage after Pearl Harbor while they were still free, a fact which is some evidence of the loyalty of the vast majority of these individuals and of the effectiveness of the established methods of combatting these evils. It seems incredible that under these circumstances it would have been impossible to hold loyalty hearings for the mere 112,000 persons involved—or at least for the 70,000 American citizens—especially when a large part of this number represented children and elderly men and women. Any inconvenience that may have accompanied an attempt to conform to procedural due process cannot be said to justify violations of constitutional rights of individuals.

I dissent, therefore, from this legalization of racism. Racial discrimination in any form and in any degree has no justifiable part whatever in our democratic way of life. It is unattractive in any setting but it is utterly revolting among a free people who have embraced the principles set forth in the Constitution of the United States. All residents of this nation are kin in some way by blood or culture to a foreign land. Yet they are primarily and necessarily a part of the new and distinct civilization of the United States. They must accordingly be treated at all times as the heirs of the American experiment and as entitled to all the rights and freedoms guaranteed by the Constitution.

MR. JUSTICE JACKSON, dissenting.

Korematsu was born on our soil, of parents born in Japan. The Constitution makes him a citizen of the United States by nativity and a citizen of California by residence. No claim is made that he is not loyal to this country. There is no suggestion that apart from the matter involved here he is not law-abiding and well disposed. Korematsu, however, has been convicted of an act not commonly a crime. It consists merely of being present in the state whereof he is a citizen, near the place where he was born, and where all his life he has lived.

Even more unusual is the series of military orders which made this conduct a crime. They forbid such a one to remain, and they also forbid him to leave. They were so drawn that the only way Korematsu could avoid violation was to give himself up to the military authority. This meant submission to custody, examination, and transportation out of the territory, to be followed by indeterminate confinement in detention camps.

A citizen's presence in the locality, however, was made a crime only if his parents were of Japanese birth. Had Korematsu been one of four—the others being, say, a German alien enemy, an Italian alien enemy, and a citizen of American-born ancestors, convicted of treason but out on parole—only Korematsu's presence would have violated the order. The difference between their innocence and his crime would result, not from anything he did, said, or thought, different than they, but only in that he was born of different racial stock.

Now, if any fundamental assumption underlies our system, it is that guilt is personal and not inheritable. Even if all of one's antecedents had been convicted of treason, the Constitution forbids its penalties to be visited upon him, for it provides that "no Attainder of Treason shall work Corruption of Blood, or Forfeiture except during the Life of the Person attained." Article 3, § 3, cl. 2. But here is an attempt to make an otherwise innocent act a crime merely because this prisoner is the son of parents as to whom he had no choice, and belongs to a race from which there is no way to resign. If Congress in peace-time legislation should enact such a criminal law, I should suppose this Court would refuse to enforce it.

But the 'law' which this prisoner is convicted of disregarding is not found in an act of Congress, but in a military order. Neither the Act of Congress nor the Executive Order of the President, nor both together, would afford a basis for this conviction. It rests on the orders of General DeWitt. And it is said that if the military commander had reasonable military grounds for promulgating the orders, they are constitutional and become law, and the Court is required to enforce them. There are several reasons why I cannot subscribe to this doctrine.

It would be impracticable and dangerous idealism to expect or insist that each specific military command in an area of probable operations will conform to conventional tests of constitutionality. When an area is so beset that it must be put under military control at all, the paramount consideration is that its measures be successful, rather than legal. The armed services must protect a society, not merely its Constitution. The very essence of the military job is to marshal physical force, to remove every obstacle to its effectiveness, to give it every strategic advantage. Defense measures will not, and often should not, be held within the limits that bind civil authority in peace. No court can require such a commander in such circumstances to act as a reasonable man; he may be unreasonably cautious and exacting. Perhaps he should be. But a commander in temporarily focusing the life of a community on defense is carrying out a military program; he is not making law in the sense the courts know the term. He issues orders, and they may have a certain authority as military commands, although they may be very bad as constitutional law.

But if we cannot confine military expedients by the Constitution, neither would I distort the Constitution to approve all that the military may deem expedient. This is what the Court appears to be doing, whether consciously or not. I cannot say, from any evidence before me, that the orders of General DeWitt were not reasonably expedient military precautions, nor could I say that they were. But even if they were permissible military procedures, I deny that it follows that they are constitutional. If, as the Court holds, it does follow, then we may as well say that any military order will be constitutional and have done with it.

The limitation under which courts always will labor in examining the necessity for a military order are illustrated by this case. How does the Court know that these orders have a reasonable basis in necessity? No evidence whatever on that subject has been taken by this or any other court. There is sharp controversy as to the credibility of the DeWitt report. So the Court, having no real evidence before it, has no choice but to accept General DeWitt's own unsworn, self-serving statement, untested by any cross-examination, that what he did was reasonable. And thus it will always be when courts try to look into the reasonableness of a military order.

In the very nature of things military decisions are not susceptible of intelligent judicial appraisal. They do not pretend to rest on evidence, but are made on information that often would not be admissible and on assumptions that could not be proved. Information in support of an order could not be disclosed to courts without danger that it would reach the enemy. Neither can courts act on communications made in confidence. Hence courts can never have any real alternative to accepting the mere declaration of the authority that issued the order that it was reasonably necessary from a military viewpoint.

Much is said of the danger to liberty from the Army program for deporting and detaining these citizens of Japanese extraction. But a judicial construction of the due process clause that will sustain this order is a far more subtle blow to liberty than the promulgation of the order itself. A military order, however unconstitutional, is not apt to last longer than the military emergency. Even during that period a succeeding commander may revoke it all. But once a judicial opinion rationalizes such an order to show that it conforms to the Constitution, or rather rationalizes the Constitution to show that the Constitution sanctions such an order, the Court for all time has validated the principle of racial discrimination in criminal procedure and of transplanting American citizens. The principle then lies about like a loaded weapon ready for the hand of any authority that can bring forward a plausible claim of an urgent need. Every repetition imbeds that principle more deeply in our law and thinking and expands it to new purposes. All who observe the work of courts are familiar with what Judge Cardozo described as "the tendency of a principle to expand itself to the limit of its logic." A military commander may overstep the bounds of constitutionality, and it is an incident. But if we review and approve, that passing incident becomes the doctrine of the Constitution. There it has a generative power of its own, and all that it creates will be in its own image. Nothing better illustrates this danger than does the Court's opinion in this case.

It argues that we are bound to uphold the conviction of Korematsu because we upheld one in Kiyoshi Hirabayashi v. United States, 320 U.S. 81, 63 S.Ct. 1375, 87 L. Ed. 1774, when we sustained these orders in so far as they applied a curfew requirement to a citizen of Japanese ancestry. I think we should learn something from that experience.

In that case we were urged to consider only that curfew feature, that being all that technically was involved, because it was the only count necessary to sustain Hirabayashi's conviction and sentence. We yielded, and the Chief Justice guarded the opinion as carefully as language will do. He said: "Our investigation here does not go beyond the inquiry whether, in the light of all the relevant circumstances preceding and attending their promulgation, the challenged orders and statute *afforded a reasonable basis for the action taken in imposing the curfew.*" 320 U.S. at page 101. "We decide only the issue as we have defined it—we decide only that the curfew order as applied, and at the time it was applied, was within the boundaries of the war power." 320 U.S. at page 102. And again: "It is unnecessary to consider whether or to what extent *such findings would support orders differing from the curfew order.*" 320 U.S. at page 105. (Italics supplied.) However, in spite of our limiting words we did validate a discrimination of the basis of ancestry for mild and temporary deprivation of liberty. Now the principle of racial discrimination is pushed from support of mild measures to very harsh ones, and from temporary deprivations to indeterminate ones. And the precedent which it is said requires us to do so is Hirabayashi. The Court is now saying that in Hirabayashi we did decide the very things we there said we were not deciding. Because we said that these citizens could be made to stay in their homes during the hours of dark, it is said we must require them to leave home entirely; and if that, we are told they may also be taken into custody for deportation; and if that, it is argued they may also be held for some undetermined time in detention camps. How far the principle of this case would be extended before plausible reasons would play out, I do not know.

I should hold that a civil court cannot be made to enforce an order which violates constitutional limitations even if it is a reasonable exercise of military authority. The courts can exercise only the judicial power, can apply only law, and must abide by the Constitution, or they cease to be civil courts and become instruments of military policy.

Of course the existence of a military power resting on force, so vagrant, so centralized, so necessarily heedless of the individual, is an inherent threat to liberty. But I would not lead people to rely on this Court for a review that seems to me wholly delusive. The military reasonableness of these orders can only be determined by military superiors. If the people ever let command of the war power fall into irresponsible and unscrupulous hands, the courts wield no power equal to its restraint. The chief restraint upon those who command the physical forces of the country, in the future as in the past, must be their responsibility to the political judgments of their contemporaries and to the moral judgments of history.

My duties as a justice as I see them do not require me to make a military judgment as to whether General DeWitt's evacuation and detention program was a reasonable military necessity. I do not suggest that the courts should have attempted to interfere with the Army in carrying out its task. But I do not think they may be asked to execute a military expedient that has no place in law under the Constitution. I would reverse the judgment and discharge the prisoner.

Notes

1. Fred Korematsu was born in the United States and eventually became a welder in the shipyards of San Francisco Bay. He was 22 years old when he was arrested on May 30, 1942, in San Leandro, California. He had remained behind—to be with his White girlfriend—after his family reported to the Tanforan assembly center (a converted race track). He was turned over to the FBI, tried, and convicted. *See* Irons at 93–96. Unlike Hirabayashi and Yasui, Korematsu did not set out to present a test case. Nonetheless, he pressed his challenge to the lawfulness of the military orders to the Supreme Court and, as we shall see, continued to press that challenge decades later.

2. Did the majority hold the government to a different standard when the deprivation inflicted upon U.S. citizens of Japanese descent was detention, as opposed to a curfew or exclusion from a designated military area?

3. The majority opinion was authored by Justice Hugo Black, a former Senator from Alabama—and a former member of the Ku Klux Klan. *See* Thad Morgan, *How an Ex-KKK Member Made His Way Onto the U.S. Supreme Court*, History.com (Oct. 2018), *available at* https://www.history.com/news/kkk-supreme-court-hugo-black-fdr. Is it surprising to you that a former KKK member was appointed by President Franklin Delano Roosevelt to the Supreme Court? Interestingly, Justice Black was a key member of the Warren Court's liberal bloc advancing the cause of civil rights for minorities. How do you think his future rulings in favor of civil rights, particularly First Amendment rights, are connected—if at all—to his deference to the government's forced internment of Japanese-American U.S. citizens in *Korematsu*?

4. In the footnotes in his concurrence, Justice Murphy addressed a couple of issues of interest. First, the question of birthright citizenship:

   > The charge of 'dual citizenship' springs from a misunderstanding of the simple fact that Japan in the past used the doctrine of jus sanguinis, as she had a right to do under international law, and claimed as her citizens all persons born of Japanese nationals wherever located. Japan has greatly modified this doctrine, however, by allowing all Japanese born in the United States to renounce any claim of dual citizenship and by releasing her claim as to all born in the United States after 1925....

   Second, Justice Murphy considered voluntary comments made by Lt. General DeWitt in assessing the actual purpose behind the government's actions:

   > Further evidence of the Commanding General's attitude toward individuals of Japanese ancestry is revealed in his voluntary testimony on April 13, 1943, in San Francisco before the House Naval Affairs Subcommittee to Investigate Congested Areas, Part 3, pp. 739-40 (78th Cong., 1st Sess.):

> "I don't want any of them (persons of Japanese ancestry) here. They are a dangerous element. There is no way to determine their loyalty. The west coast contains too many vital installations essential to the defense of the country to allow any Japanese on this coast.... The danger of the Japanese was, and is now—if they are permitted to come back—espionage and sabotage. It makes no difference whether he is an American citizen, he is still a Japanese. American citizenship does not necessarily determine loyalty.... But we must worry about the Japanese all the time until he is wiped off the map. Sabotage and espionage will make problems as long as he is allowed in this area.... "

One of the issues in the litigation over President Trump's 2017 Travel Ban was whether the courts could consider, in determining the intent behind issuing the Travel Ban, comments candidate Trump had made during the presidential campaign. Are the two sets of comments distinguishable?

5. One of the most quoted lines from Justice Jackson's dissent is his "loaded weapon" comment—that once the Court adopts "a judicial construction of the due process clause" that strikes a "blow to liberty," "[t]he principle then lies about like a loaded weapon ready for the hand of any authority that can bring forward a plausible claim of an urgent need." What did he mean by this?

Ex parte Endo

323 U.S. 283 (1944)

MR. JUSTICE DOUGLAS delivered the opinion of the Court....

Mitsuye Endo, hereinafter designated as the appellant, is an American citizen of Japanese ancestry. She was evacuated from Sacramento, California, in 1942, pursuant to certain military orders which we will presently discuss, and was removed to the Tule Lake War Relocation Center located at Newell, Modoc County, California. In July, 1942, she filed a petition for a writ of habeas corpus in the District Court of the United States for the Northern District of California, asking that she be discharged and restored to liberty. That petition was denied by the District Court in July, 1943, and an appeal was perfected to the Circuit Court of Appeals in August, 1943. Shortly thereafter appellant was transferred from the Tule Lake Relocation Center to the Central Utah Relocation Center located at Topaz, Utah, where she is presently detained....

The program of the War Relocation Authority is said to have three main features: (1) the maintenance of Relocation Centers as interim places of residence for evacuees; (2) the segregation of loyal from disloyal evacuees; (3) the continued detention of the disloyal and so far as possible the relocation of the loyal in selected communities. In connection with the latter phase of its work the War Relocation Authority established a procedure for obtaining leave from Relocation Centers. That procedure, so far as indefinite leave is concerned, presently provides as follows:

Application for leave clearance is required. An investigation of the applicant is made for the purpose of ascertaining 'the probable effect upon the war program and upon the public peace and security of issuing indefinite leave' to the applicant. The grant of leave clearance does not authorize departure from the Relocation Center. Application for indefinite leave must also be made. Indefinite leave may be granted under 14 specified conditions. For example, it may be granted (1) where the applicant proposes to accept an employment offer or an offer of support that has been investigated and approved by the Authority; or (2) where the applicant does not intend to work but has 'adequate financial resources to take care of himself' and a Relocation Officer has investigated and approved 'public sentiment at his proposed destination', or (3) where the applicant has made arrangements to live at a hotel or in a private home approved by a Relocation Officer while arranging for employment; or (4) where the applicant proposes to accept employment by a federal or local governmental agency; or (5) where the applicant is going to live with designated classes of relatives.

But even if an applicant meets those requirements, no leave will issue when the proposed place of residence or employment is within a locality where it has been ascertained that 'community sentiment is unfavorable' or when the applicant plans to go to an area which has been closed by the Authority to the issuance of indefinite leave. Nor will such leave issue if the area where the applicant plans to reside or work is one which has not been cleared for relocation. Moreover, the applicant agrees to give the Authority prompt notice of any change of employment or residence. And the indefinite leave which is granted does not permit entry into a prohibited military area, including those from which these people were evacuated.

Mitsuye Endo made application for leave clearance on February 19, 1943, after the petition was filed in the District Court. Leave clearance was granted her on August 16, 1943. But she made no application for indefinite leave.

Her petition for a writ of habeas corpus alleges that she is a loyal and law-abiding citizen of the United States, that no charge has been made against her, that she is being unlawfully detained, and that she is confined in the Relocation Center under armed guard and held there against her will.

It is conceded by the Department of Justice and by the War Relocation Authority that appellant is a loyal and law-abiding citizen. They make no claim that she is detained on any charge or that she is even suspected of disloyalty. Moreover, they do not contend that she may be held any longer in the Relocation Center. They concede that it is beyond the power of the War Relocation Authority to detain citizens against whom no charges of disloyalty or subversiveness have been made for a period longer than that necessary to separate the loyal from the disloyal and to provide the necessary guidance for relocation. But they maintain that detention for an additional period after leave clearance has been granted is an essential step in the evacuation program....

Figure 6.4 ***Mitsuye Endo at the Central Utah Relocation Center*** **(1942). National Archives.**

First. We are of the view that Mitsuye Endo should be given her liberty. In reaching that conclusion we do not come to the underlying constitutional issues which have been argued. For we conclude that, whatever power the War Relocation Authority may have to detain other classes of citizens, it has no authority to subject citizens who are concededly loyal to its leave procedure.

It should be noted at the outset that we do not have here a question such as was presented in Ex parte Milligan, 4 Wall. 2, or in Ex parte Quirin, 317 U.S. 1, where the jurisdiction of military tribunals to try persons according to the law of war was challenged in habeas corpus proceedings. Mitsuye Endo is detained by a civilian agency, the War Relocation Authority, not by the military. Moreover, the evacuation program was not left exclusively to the military; the Authority was given a large measure of responsibility for its execution and Congress made its enforcement subject to civil penalties by the Act of March 21, 1942. Accordingly, no questions of military law are involved....

A citizen who is concededly loyal presents no problem of espionage or sabotage. Loyalty is a matter of the heart and mind not of race, creed, or color. He who is loyal is by definition not a spy or a saboteur. When the power to detain is derived from the power to protect the war effort against espionage and sabotage, detention which has no relationship to that objective is unauthorized.

Nor may the power to detain an admittedly loyal citizen or to grant him a conditional release be implied as a useful or convenient step in the evacuation program, whatever authority might be implied in case of those whose loyalty was not conceded or established. If we assume (as we do) that the original evacuation was justified, its lawful character was derived from the fact that it was an espionage and sabotage measure, not that there was community hostility to this group of American citizens. The evacuation program rested explicitly on the former ground not on the latter as the underlying legislation shows. The authority to detain a citizen or to grant him a conditional release as protection against espionage or sabotage is exhausted at least when his loyalty is conceded. If we held that the authority to detain continued thereafter, we would transform an espionage or sabotage measure into something else. That was not done by Executive Order No. 9066 or by the Act of March 21, 1942, which ratified it. What they did not do we cannot do. Detention which furthered the campaign against espionage and sabotage would be one thing. But detention which has no relationship to that campaign is of a distinct character. Community hostility even to loyal evacuees may have been (and perhaps still is) a serious problem. But if authority for their custody and supervision is to be sought on that ground, the Act of March 21, 1942, Executive Order No. 9066, and Executive Order No. 9102, offer no support. And none other is advanced. To read them that broadly would be to assume that the Congress and the President intended that this discriminatory action should be taken against these people wholly on account of their ancestry even though the government conceded their loyalty to this country. We cannot make such an assumption. As the President has said of these loyal citizens: 'Americans of Japanese ancestry, like those of many other ancestries, have shown that they can, and want to, accept our institutions and work loyally with the rest of us, making their own valuable contribution to the national wealth and well-being. In vindication of the very ideals for which we are fighting this war it is important to us to maintain a high standard of fair, considerate, and equal treatment for the people of this minority as of all other minorities.' Sen. Doc. No. 96, supra, note 7, p. 2.

Mitsuye Endo is entitled to an unconditional release by the War Relocation Authority.

Second. The question remains whether the District Court has jurisdiction to grant the writ of habeas corpus because of the fact that while the case was pending in the Circuit Court of Appeals appellant was moved from the Tule Lake Relocation Center in the Northern District of California where she was originally detained to the Central Utah Relocation Center in a different district and circuit.

That question is not colored by any purpose to effectuate a removal in evasion of the habeas corpus proceedings. It appears that appellant's removal to Utah was part of a general segregation program involving many of these people and was in no way related to this pending case. Moreover, there is no suggestion that there is no one within the jurisdiction of the District Court who is responsible for the detention of appellant and who would be an appropriate respondent. We are indeed advised by the

Acting Secretary of the Interior that if the writ issues and is directed to the Secretary of the Interior or any official of the War Relocation Authority (including an assistant director whose office is at San Francisco, which is in the jurisdiction of the District Court), the corpus of appellant will be produced and the court's order complied with in all respects. Thus it would seem that the case is not moot....

The judgment is reversed and the cause is remanded to the District Court for proceedings in conformity with this opinion.

REVERSED.

MR. JUSTICE MURPHY, concurring.

I join in the opinion of the Court, but I am of the view that detention in Relocation Centers of persons of Japanese ancestry regardless of loyalty is not only unauthorized by Congress or the Executive but is another example of the unconstitutional resort to racism inherent in the entire evacuation program. As stated more fully in my dissenting opinion in Korematsu v. United States, 323 U.S. 214, racial discrimination of this nature bears no reasonable relation to military necessity and is utterly foreign to the ideals and traditions of the American people.

Moreover, the Court holds that Mitsuye Endo is entitled to an unconditional release by the War Relocation Authority. It appears that Miss Endo desires to return to Sacramento, California, from which Public Proclamations Nos. 7 and 11, as well as Civilian Exclusion Order No. 52, still exclude her. And it would seem to me that the 'unconditional' release to be given Miss Endo necessarily implies 'the right to pass freely from state to state,' including the right to move freely into California. Twining v. New Jersey, 211 U.S. 78, 97; Crandall v. Nevada, 6 Wall. 35. If, as I believe, the military orders excluding her from California were invalid at the time they were issued, they are increasingly objectionable at this late date, when the threat of invasion of the Pacific Coast and the fears of sabotage and espionage have greatly diminished. For the Government to suggest under these circumstances that the presence of Japanese blood in a loyal American citizen might be enough to warrant her exclusion from a place where she would otherwise have a right to go is a position I cannot sanction.

Notes

1. Mitsuye Endo was born in Sacramento, California, in 1920. She did not speak or read Japanese, had never visited Japan, and had a brother serving in the U.S. Army. She was a typist in the California Department of Motor Vehicles when, after war broke out, she and dozens of coworkers were fired for being Japanese. She filed her habeas petition after she reported for internment at the Tanforan assembly center. At one point, the government offered to release her, as part of its effort to moot out the case to avoid a Supreme Court ruling on the legality of internment, but she refused so that she could continue her legal challenge. She

remained detained for another two years. Irons at 99–103; John Tateishi, *And Justice for All: An Oral History of the Japanese American Detention Camps* 60 (1984); Lori Aratani, *She Fought the Internment of Japanese Americans During World War II and Won*, Wash. Post, Dec. 18, 2019. *See also* Mina Juhn, *"Concededly Loyal": Mitsuye Endo and the Continuing Significance of Ex parte Endo*, 27 UCLA Asian Pacific Am. L.J. 99 (2023).

2. Why did the Court hold in Endo's favor on her petition for a writ of habeas corpus? How was the detention she complained about different from the detention challenged by Fred Korematsu?

3. In what ways does Justice Murphy's concurring opinion go farther than the majority's ruling? How would you say the "unconstitutional resort to racism" against Americans of Japanese descent he excoriates in *Endo* and *Korematsu* differs from racism against African Americans after the Civil War and the enactment of the Civil War amendments that made them constitutionally free and equal?

4. To what extent did politics come into play in the internment of Japanese Americans? There is some thought that even after the military agreed that there was no longer any military rationale for exclusion, President Roosevelt delayed allowing Japanese Americans to return to the West Coast for political reasons—he needed to carry California to be reelected and West Coast political leaders continued to oppose the return of Japanese Americans. On November 10, 1944, three days after he was reelected, Roosevelt agreed to allow the Japanese to return to the West Coast. *See* Brian Niiya, *Franklin D. Roosevelt*, Densho Encyclopedia (2020), *available at* https://encyclopedia.densho.org/Franklin_D._Roosevelt/. The decision was not announced until December 17, 1944, when the government declared that Japanese Americans in the camps could return home beginning January 1, 1945. *See* Stephanie Buck, *Overlooked No More: Mitsuye Endo, a Name Linked to Justice for Japanese-Americans*, N.Y. Times, Nov. 15, 2019.

5. Politics may have played a role in the timing of the *Endo* and *Korematsu* decisions. *Korematsu* was ready to be argued in the spring of 1944, and while *Endo* was a bit behind, it could also have been heard then. Instead, the Court held both cases over until the following term, even though tens of thousands of Japanese Americans were being held in the camps; both cases were decided the same day, December 18, 1944—after election day and one day after the government's announcement that the camps would be closed. *See* Yamamoto at 157–58; Buck. Some scholars believe that the Court delayed its decision in *Endo* so as not to hand President Roosevelt a defeat during a time of war and to permit the government to announce the closure of the camps before the Court could require it to do so. *See* Buck (quoting Prof. Eric Muller); Amanda Tyler, *Habeas Corpus in Wartime: From the Tower of London to Guantanamo Bay* 235–37 (2017).

6. In authorizing the detention of enemy aliens the day before Congress declared war on Japan in response to the surprise attack on Pearl Harbor, President Roosevelt

invoked the Alien Enemies Act of 1798. *See generally* Tim Balk, *A History of the Alien Enemies Act of 1798*, N.Y. Times, March 21, 2025; Kelli Y. Nakamura, *Alien Enemies Act of 1798*, Densho Encyclopedia, encyclopedia.densho.org (June 20, 2024), *available at* https://encyclopedia.densho.org/Alien%20Enemies%20Act%20of%201798/?_gl=1*1pwmab0*_gcl_au*MTg0OTA1MTUxNS4xNzUxODE4MDYy. The Alien Enemies Act ("AEA"), enacted by the Fifth Congress on July 6, 1798, gives the President certain powers regarding "alien enemies" during a declared war or when an "invasion or predatory incursion" is "perpetrated, attempted, or threatened against the territory of the United States" by "any foreign nation or government." The little-known, little-used statute has assumed international prominence after President Trump invoked it as authorization for a March 15, 2025, Executive Order to seize, detain, and deport members of the Venezuela-based criminal organization known as Tren de Aragua ("TdA"). According to the Executive Order, "TdA is closely aligned with, and indeed has infiltrated, the Maduro regime, including its military and law enforcement apparatus." The Maduro regime remains in control of the state governance organs in Venezuela, although the United States has not recognized him as the President of Venezuela since allegedly tainted elections in 2019.

Although the AEA has been invoked only three times and only during times of war—the War of 1812, World War I, and World War II—the government invoked the statute to deport 130 men accused of being TdA members to El Salvador. *See* Tim Sullivan and Mark Sherman, *The Alien Enemies Act: What to Know About a 1798 Law That Trump Has Invoked for Deportations*, Assoc. Press, apnews.com ,April 9, 2025, *available at* https://apnews.com/article/alien-enemies-trump-immigration-deportations-21a62ede23b8c493b60d00a9c125722f; Balk, N.Y. Times, *supra*. Litigation quickly followed. *See* Alan Feuer, *Appeals Court Weighs Trump's Use of Alien Enemies Act for Deportations*, N.Y. Times, June 30, 2025. Recall that the words of the statute authorize the President to act, among other things, when a "predatory incursion" is "threatened against the territory of the United States." Do you think it is plausible to invoke the Act on the government's justification that TdA is a paramilitary organ of the renegade Venezuelan government and that its drug-related activities and violence in the United States constitute a "predatory incursion" sponsored by the Maduro regime?

7. In the 1920s, long before the War and internment, Estelle Peck, a White woman, fell in love with Arthur Ishigo, a Japanese man, in California. They married in 1929—in Mexico, to avoid the anti-miscegenation laws in the United States. After the bombing of Pearl Harbor, Arthur was sent to a concentration camp. Rather than be separated from her husband of 13 years, Estelle voluntarily joined him, first at the Pomona Assembly Center in California and then at the Heart Mountain Relocation Center in Wyoming. She remained incarcerated with him for more than three years. Estelle was an artist and recorded life in the camps in hundreds of drawings and paintings. After the war, she and her husband struggled

financially, and he died of cancer at the age of 55 in 1957. She lived in poverty and received little recognition until the publication of her book *Lone Heart Mountain* in 1972. A documentary about her life, *Days of Waiting*, by the filmmaker Steven Okazaki, was released shortly after her death in 1990. *See* Dean Ryuta Adachi, *History Is Ignored: Estelle Ishigo*, Discover Nikkei (May 17, 2012), *available at* discovernikkei.org/en/journal/2012/5/17/estelle-ishigo/.

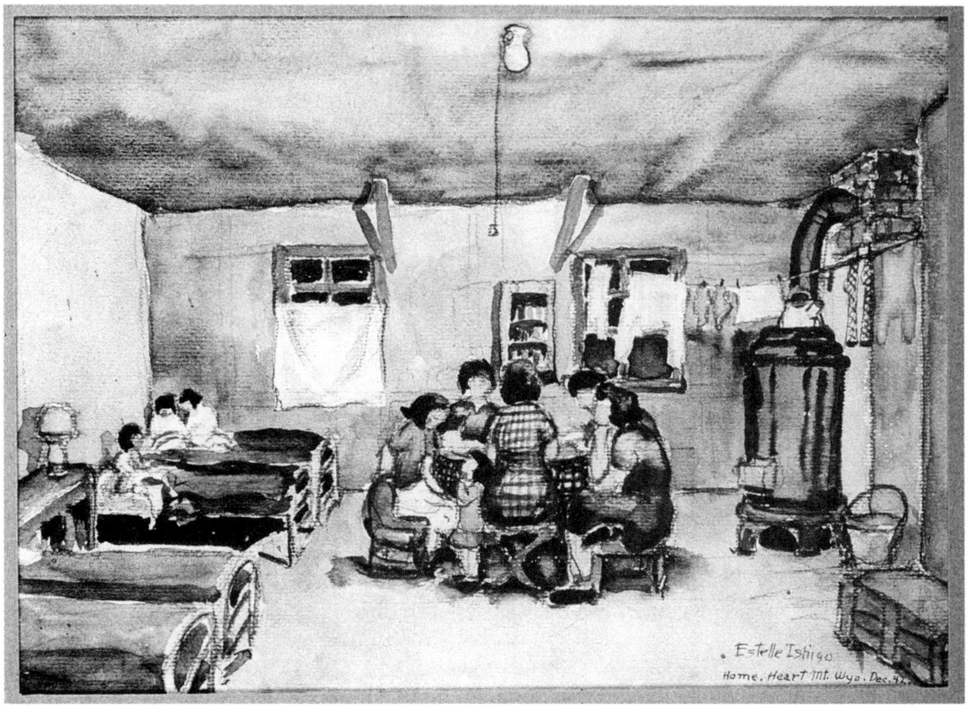

Figure 6.5 ***At Home at Heart Mountain.*** **Watercolor painting by Estelle Ishigo (December 1942). UCLA, Library Special Collections, Charles E. Young Research Library.**

8. Some 2,270 Japanese Americans were interned in Hawaii because of suspected disloyalty (often with little proof thereof). Others were rounded up and sent to internment camps on the mainland. For the most part, however, Japanese Americans in Hawaii were not treated as harshly as those on the mainland, for a number of reasons: the U.S. Navy declared martial law in Hawaii; Japanese Americans made up 37% of the population; Whites were a minority in Hawaii; Japanese Americans were the largest ethnic minority; the Japanese Americans were more established and were very much a part of the middle class, and Hawaiian society was much more integrated and diverse than was the mainland. *See generally* Nat'l WWII War Museum, *Japanese Americans and the Wartime Experience in Hawaii,* nationalww2museum.org (Oct. 15, 2021) (Stephanie Hinnershitz, contributor); Japanese Cultural Center of Hawaii, *The Untold Story: Internment of Japanese Americans in Hawaii,* hawaiiinternment.org (visited Aug. 23, 2024).

Figure 6.6 ***Estelle Ishigo at Heart Mountain Relocation Center*** **(1944). Estelle Ishigo Photographs. American Heritage Center, University of Wyoming.**

9. Japanese-American U.S. citizens were not the only ones to be interned during World War II. Some 2,200 Latin Americans of Japanese descent were deported to the United States, where they were imprisoned in concentration camps. *See* Lika C. Miyake, *Forsaken and Forgotten: The U.S. Internment of Japanese Peruvians During World War II*, 9 Asian L.J. 163 (2002); Jaime Gonzalez de Gispert, *The Japanese-Peruvians Interned in the US During WW2*, BBC News, Feb. 22, 2015, *available at* www.bbc.com/news/world-latin-america-31295270. In Canada, some 21,000 individuals—90% of all Japanese Canadians, many of whom were Canadian citizens by birth, were uprooted from their homes and sent to internment camps. *See* James H. Marsh, *Japanese Canadian Internment: Prisoners in Their Own Country*, Canadian Encyclopedia (Feb. 23, 2012; updated Nov. 28, 2016), *available at* www.thecanadianencyclopedia.ca/en/article/japanese-internment-banished-and-beyond-tears-feature. And in Alaska, some 881 Aleuts—Alaskan natives—were forcibly evacuated from their homes and relocated to camps in southern Alaska. The U.S. military then destroyed their villages, for fear that invading Japanese troops would use the homes for shelter. *See* Erin Blakemore, *The U.S. Forcibly Detained Native Alaskans During World War II*, Smithsonian

Magazine, Feb. 22, 2017, *available at* www.smithsonianmag.com/smart-news/us-forcibly-detained-native-alaskans-during-world-war-ii-180962239/.

10. Of course, the United States was also at war with Germany and Italy during World War II. Individuals of German and Italian descent in the United States were also interned, although to a much lesser extent. Some 1,600 to 3,000 Italian Americans (the estimates vary) and some 11,500 people of German ancestry were interned during World War II. *See* Paula Branca-Santos, *Injustice Ignored: The Internment of Italian-Americans During World War II*, 13 Pace L. Rev. 151, 165 (2001); Alan Rosenfeld, *German and Italian Detainees*, Densho Encyclopedia (2020), *available at* encyclopedia.densho.org/ German_and_Italian_detainees; *see also* David A. Taylor, *During World War II, the U.S. Saw Italian-Americans as a Threat to Homeland Security*, Smithsonian Magazine, Feb. 2, 2017, *available at* www.smithsonianmag.com/history/italian-americans-were-considered-enemy-aliens-world-war-ii-180962021/. There were some differences in the treatment of German and Italian Americans from the treatment of Japanese Americans. *See generally* Rosenfeld. What were some of these differences? And why was there different treatment?

11. Beginning in the fall of 1941, small numbers of Japanese, Germans, and Italians were interned at Ellis Island in New York—approximately 279 Japanese, 248 Germans, and 81 Italians. These were mostly enemy aliens who were in the United States working for foreign companies. *See* Suah Cho, *The Untold Story of Japanese Americans and Nationals Detained at Ellis Island*, Columbia Journalism School, columbianesservice.com (Feb. 29, 2024), *available at* https://columbianewsservice.com/2024/02/29/internment-in-new-york-the-untold-story-of-japanese-americans-and-nationals-detained-at-ellis-island/. A few thousand Japanese New Yorkers, mostly male, were interrogated from 1941 through 1944, and while many were released, some were repatriated and some were interned. At one point the number of Japanese held on Ellis Island grew to approximately 440 men and four women. *See Issei and Internment at Ellis Island*, Digital Museum of the History of Japanese in New York, historyofjapaneseinnewyork.org (2025), *available at* https://www.historyofjapaneseinny.org/unforgotten-stories/issei-and-internment-at-ellis-island/.

As discussed in Unit One, the Supreme Court upheld the President's Travel Ban in June 2018. In the course of doing so, the Court overruled *Korematsu*. Here are the relevant excerpts.

Trump v. Hawaii

585 U.S. 667 (2018)

ROBERTS, Chief Justice:

... The dissent invokes *Korematsu v. United States*. Whatever rhetorical advantage the dissent may see in doing so, *Korematsu* has nothing to do with this case. The forcible relocation of U.S. citizens to concentration camps, solely and explicitly on the basis of race, is objectively unlawful and outside the scope of Presidential authority. But it is wholly inapt to liken that morally repugnant order to a facially neutral policy denying certain foreign nationals the privilege of admission.

The dissent's reference to *Korematsu,* however, affords this Court the opportunity to make express what is already obvious: *Korematsu* was gravely wrong the day it was decided, has been overruled in the court of history, and—to be clear—"has no place in law under the Constitution."

SOTOMAYOR, Associate Justice:

... In the intervening years since *Korematsu,* our Nation has done much to leave its sordid legacy behind. Today, the Court takes the important step of finally overruling *Korematsu*. This formal repudiation of a shameful precedent is laudable and long overdue. But it does not make the majority's decision here acceptable or right. By blindly accepting the Government's misguided invitation to sanction a discriminatory policy motivated by animosity toward a disfavored group, all in the name of a superficial claim of national security, the Court redeploys the same dangerous logic underlying *Korematsu* and merely replaces one "gravely wrong" decision with another.

Our Constitution demands, and our country deserves, a Judiciary willing to hold the coordinate branches to account when they defy our most sacred legal commitments. Because the Court's decision today has failed in that respect, with profound regret, I dissent.

Notes

1. Much has been written about the Court's overruling of *Korematsu*. Just two days after the decision, the *New York Times* published an op-ed by Karen Korematsu, in which she wrote:

> On Tuesday, the Supreme Court got it partly right. After nearly 75 years, the court officially overruled *Korematsu v. United States*. But the court's repudiation of the *Korematsu* decision tells only half the story. Although it correctly rejected the abhorrent race-based relocation and incarceration of Japanese Americans, it failed to recognize—and reject—the rationale that led to that infamous decision.

> My father spent his life fighting for justice and educating people about the inhumanity of the Japanese-American incarceration, so that we would learn from our mistakes. Although he would be somewhat glad his case was finally overruled, he would be upset that it was cited while upholding discrimination against another marginalized group. The court's decision replaced one injustice with another nearly 75 years later.
>
> My father would still say, "Stand up for what is right."

Karen Korematsu, *How the Supreme Court Replaced One Injustice with Another*, N.Y. Times, June 27, 2018.

2. Some have debated whether *Korematsu* was really overruled. *See, e.g.*, Jamal Greene, *Is Korematsu Good Law?*, 128 Yale L.J. (Jan. 30, 2019), https://www.yalelawjournal.org/forum/is-korematsu-good-law; Neal Kumar Katyal, *Trump v. Hawaii: How the Supreme Court Simultaneously Overruled and Revived* Korematsu, 128 Yale L.J. (Jan. 30, 2019), https://www.yalelawjournal.org/forum/trump-v-hawaii; Mari J. Matsuda, *This Is (Not) Who We Are:* Korematsu, *Constitutional Interpretation, and National Identity*, 128 Yale. L.J. (Jan. 30, 2019), https://www.yalelawjournal.org/forum/ this-is-not-who-we-are; Eric K. Yamamoto and Rachel Oyama, *Masquerading Behind a Façade of National Security*, 128 Yale. L.J. (Jan. 30, 2019), https://www.yalelawjournal.org/ forum/masquerading-behind-a-facade-of-national-security. What do you think? Katyal represented the State of Hawaii in the lawsuit and was the Acting Solicitor General who, as we will see, "confessed error" on behalf of Solicitor General Fahey, who argued *Korematsu*. Yamamoto was part of the team of lawyers who represented Fred Korematsu in the coram nobis proceedings.

3. To what extent must courts defer to the Executive Branch's explanations for executive actions? Can courts go behind the stated reasons to find the "real" reasons or motivations for the government's decisions? Can courts make factual findings in this respect?

Chapter 7
The Draft Resisters

After war was declared on December 8, 1941, the United States classified all Japanese Americans as ineligible for military service. The Japanese American Citizens League led an effort for the reinstatement of the draft for Nisei, arguing that Japanese Americans would be able to best prove their loyalty on the battlefield. The War Department first responded by creating a segregated, all-Nisei unit, the 442nd Regimental Combat Team (which went on to become the most highly decorated U.S. Army combat unit in World War II for its size and length of service). *See* Key Military Unit: The 442nd Regimental Unit, U.S. Army, Mar. 15, 2025, https://www.army.mil/article/283793/key_military_unit_the_442nd_regimental_combat_team. Then, in January 1944, the War Department reinstated the draft for the Nisei; they would be reclassified by their Selective Service Boards and called for induction if physically qualified. *See generally* Eric L. Muller, *Free to Die for Their Country: The Story of the Japanese American Draft Resisters in World War II* (2001).

Induction notices were served on draft-eligible Nisei—including those interned in the camps. The vast majority reported for their physicals, but approximately 315 men among the 10 camps refused to report. These draft resisters were willing to fight for their country, but only if their rights as citizens were restored—they were not willing to report for induction while they and their families were confined in concentration camps.

The government brought criminal charges for draft evasion against the resisters. At the Heart Mountain camp, located 60 miles east of Yellowstone National Park in Wyoming, a group of internees formed the Fair Play Committee (the "FPC") and openly called for resistance to the draft. Many Nisei who received draft notices did resist and were arrested. Eventually, two indictments were filed with respect to the Heart Mountain resisters, resulting in two trials. The first was in the case of *United States v. Fujii*, as 63 draft resisters were tried together on the charge of evading the trial. The second was *United States v. Okamoto*, as seven of the leaders of the FPC as well as a newspaper columnist who had written favorably about the FPC's activities were charged with conspiracy to counsel, aid, and abet the Heart Mountain draft resisters.

Figure 7.1 ***63 members of the Heart Mountain Fair Play Committee at a court hearing in Cheyenne, Wyoming*** **(June 12, 1944). Frank Abe Collection, Densho Digital Library.**

United States v. Fujii

55 F. Supp. 928 (D. Wyo. 1944)

KENNEDY, District Judge.

The above causes are brought by indictments for violation of the Selective Training and Service Act of 1940, 50 U.S.C. Appendix, § 311. The defendants were severally arrested and arraigned before the Court upon such indictments to which all individually pleaded not guilty. The defendants were at said arraignment and at all other times in the trial of said cause represented by counsel selected by themselves. It was stipulated that the cases should be consolidated for the purpose of trial and that a jury would be waived and the cases tried to the Court without intervention of a jury, to which stipulation each individual defendant in open Court assented. The cases were thereupon set for trial on June 12, at which time the trials were commenced, and were concluded on June 19, 1944.

The proofs of the Government in support of the charges laid in the indictments show that the defendants were registrants at various local Selective Service Boards in the State of California and other western States; that they were all male citizens of the United States and within the draft age; that they were variously classified by their respective Boards in 1-A or sometimes subsequently in 4-C; that eventually they were all re-classified in 1-A and thereafter ordered to report for pre-induction physical examination. Inasmuch as defendants had been placed in a Relocation Center at Heart Mountain, Wyoming, the personal files and orders were sent to the Selective Service Board at Powell, Wyoming, for the purpose of carrying the orders of the local boards into effect as permitted by the Act and Regulations thereunder. Under an order of the Powell Board they were all directed to appear at specified times for pre-induction physical examination which order the defendants failed to obey.... Upon their failure to report for pre-induction physical examination, their names were individually reported to the United States Attorney for the District of Wyoming and their cases were presented to a grand jury resulting in the indictments upon which this prosecution is based. The defendants, upon their arrest, as is the usual custom, were fingerprinted by the United States Marshal and statements taken in connection with said fingerprinting process to which each defendant signed his name without objection. Each of the defendants was, in advance of the trial, interviewed by special agents of the Federal Bureau of Investigation and all were given the customary warning that they were being interviewed by an agent of the government, whose identity was established; that they were not required to make any statement and if they did make a statement it might be used in Court against them; that no promises or threats were made by said agents; that they were all entitled to counsel if they demanded it; and that each defendant, with one exception, freely and voluntarily made a statement to such official, some of which were taken down in writing, read over and signed by the defendant, and others made oral statements, proof of which was adduced upon the stand. There appeared to be no evidence of mistreatment either mental or physical and no coercion used in procuring such statements. There is no testimony in the record to the contrary. It appears from these statements, with the one exception heretofore mentioned, that the defendants each received his order to appear for pre-induction physical examination and that he purposely and wilfully refused to obey said order. In each instance the reason given for failure to obey said order was in the nature of a complaint that he had not been accorded his rights as an American citizen in being removed by the Military establishment from his place of former residence into a Relocation Center, that he had been previously classified as 4-C which is a class under the regulations used for enemy aliens, and that each defendant had determined on his own responsibility not to appear in response to the order for pre-induction physical examination until his rights of citizenship had been clarified. The isolated instance was in Case No. 4952—Kimura, who refused to give an interview to an agent of the Government. However, in his case it was proved that when he was arrested he had a copy of the order for him to appear upon his person. It appears from the testimony that the defendants, with many others of Japanese ancestry, were removed by the Military establishment of the Government to various relocation centers and away from the danger zones presumed to be existing along the west coast where the fear of invasion by the Japanese Government with which the United States was at war centered, and that Heart Mountain in Wyoming was one of these Relocation Centers. Here the defendants and others of their class were housed and fed in a satisfactory manner and were permitted to live in families and enjoy the ordinary family relations. A portion of the Center was surrounded by barbed wire fences and various entrances and exits were provided at which guards were stationed. No one was permitted to enter or leave the Center, whether of Japanese ancestry or otherwise, without receiving a permit from the Director. These permits were issued indiscriminately to the occupants of such Center where the reason given was a legitimate one. They were given permits upon application to seek employment outside, either permanent or temporary, and were permitted upon request to go to neighboring towns if they desired. None of the defendants in this case appears to have been refused permission to seek employment elsewhere and the permits seem to have been used as a method of keeping track of the occupants of the Center after they had been permitted to leave. Only one instance (not a defendant here) was given of an occupant of the Center of Japanese descent leaving without a permit and he was subsequently sent to Tule Lake, California. No evidence was offered by the defendants except by recalling the Assistant Director of the Relocation Center at Heart Mountain for the purpose of amplifying the method of conducting the Center in connection with the privileges extended to the occupants.

For the defense it is mildly suggested that there was no identification of each individual defendant on trial and because of the fact that the sixty-three defendants were all before the Court at the same time for trial and bearing some resemblance on account of their Japanese ancestry they could not be picked out by any Government official as being a defendant responding to the name under which he was indicted. It is true that there were several identifications of individual defendants by facial appearance but not of all. However, the answer to this suggestion is that the defendants were identified by fingerprints to which they willingly attached their signatures at or about the time of arrest. The defendants likewise identified themselves to the Government agents by responding to their names when called for the purpose of interview. They likewise identified themselves by responding to the call of the Court of their names upon the docket both at the time of arraignment and at the commencement of the trial. Finally, they now assert through the mouth of their counsel that their reasons given for failure to obey the order for pre-induction physical examination was a valid and legal excuse. Counsel argue that because of the fact that some of the defendants were ordered for induction before their respective Boards at a time while they were occupants of the Relocation Center and subsequently placed under arrest and therefore could not physically obey the order for induction that they were thereby absolved from obeying the order for pre-induction physical examination....

The defendants assert that inasmuch as they are American citizens by birth that they have been discriminated against by various acts of the Government, in classifying them in 4-C which includes enemy aliens, and removing them from their places of residence to Relocation Centers, their loyalty to the United States Government has thereby been questioned without reason and that they should not be reclassified for service in the war at least until such time as 'their status of citizenship has been clarified'—to use the expression contained in letters to their various Draft Boards and to the Government Officials. The Government regulations permit the classification of citizens of Japanese ancestry into 4-C which includes enemy aliens, at least this is the contemplation of the regulation, until their status as to being loyal citizens has been ascertained by investigation. If the Selective Service Act and the regulations thereunder permit, under the war emergency, the treatment of this class of citizens in regard to restrictions upon their personal habits in their respective communities and likewise removal to Relocation Centers, it would seem that the matter of classification for the time being in 4-C would be of relatively less importance than such other regulations mentioned. That the regulations promulgated by Congress and the President in establishing as a military necessity the Western Defense Command of Military Areas and Zones is legal has been definitely determined in Kiyoshi Hirabayashi v. United States, 320 U.S. 81. There the matter litigated was the constitutionality of the establishment of a 'curfew law' in which all Japanese-American citizens were required to report and be restricted to their places of residence during certain hours of the day. The Supreme Court in its decision of the matter bases its conclusion upon the exigencies of war existing between the United States and the Japanese Nation, calling attention to the 'sneak' attack upon Pearl Harbor, with an observation that the Japanese Diplomatic Representatives were at the same time conducting negotiations with the State Department for the purpose of settling differences between the two countries. Attention is also given in the opinion to the fact that the Japanese Government recognizes a dual citizenship and maintains that children of Japanese Nationals are citizens of the Japanese Empire whatever may be their place of birth even among persons of Japanese ancestry born in this country and therefore are citizens of Japan; that there might be logic in the conclusions that in a case of war these would hold their attachment to Japan; and that in a critical hour these could not be effectively segregated so as to relieve a menace to the National defense and safety. That Court concludes that in time of war the Nation must use measures to protect its National defense and that the Government may hit at a particular danger where it is seen. While this case does not pass upon the legality of the removal and relocation of persons under the class here before the Court, the opinion calls attention to the establishment by Executive Order of the War Relocation Authority and the right thereby afforded to effectuate a program for removal, relocation, maintenance and supervision of the persons under consideration. Our attention has not been called to any case in which the Courts have construed the constitutionality of the removal and relocation of citizens of Japanese extraction, yet it would seem that the same logic which led to the conclusion that the curfew law did not violate their constitutional rights would justify a like conclusion in regard to removal and relocation.

It is contended that there is no evidence of criminal intent upon the part of the defendants. The proof discloses, however, that they wilfully and intentionally neglected and refused to obey the order of the Board to report for pre-induction physical examination. This is a sufficient showing of intent to violate the law unless the reasons given for the failure could be determined sufficient in law to justify their actions. It has been seen that the discrimination exercised by the Government on account of their Japanese ancestry was legitimate, justified and legal as being within the power of Congress and the President in the war emergency. Kiyoshi Hirabayashi

v. United States, supra. As to the assertion that they did not desire to report until their citizenship had been clarified, this is without merit as to legal basis. The Courts have repeatedly asserted that the orders of the Boards of Selective Service have the substance of Congressional Acts and must be obeyed. It is evident that what they asserted in the matter of the clarification of their citizenship was in fact accomplished by the effect of the order which they disobeyed. After they had been segregated an investigation was undoubtedly made by the Intelligence Branch of the Military Service and in substantial numbers they were cleared of any suspicion of disloyalty and thereafter classified for military service the same as had been all other eligible classes of American citizens. No fuller exemplification of a clarification of their citizenship could be evinced than that they were recognized through the certificates of acceptability as being such a class of citizens as under regular conditions should be placed in the service of their country. Certainly it cannot be effectively contended that if they had been found disloyal to this country and still bore allegiance to the country of their ancestors they would be thought to be desirable soldiers in the branches of the service fighting for our National existence. When, therefore, they were placed in 1-A and ordered to report for pre-induction physical examination, their pure American citizenship was established beyond question....

Personally this Court feels that the defendants have made a serious mistake in arriving at their conclusions which brought about these criminal prosecutions. If they are truly loyal American citizens they should, at least when they have become recognized as such, embrace the opportunity to discharge the duties of citizens by offering themselves in the cause of our National defense.

From what has been said it is apparent that . . . the Court, under the authority delegated to it through the stipulation, must find the defendants and each of them guilty as charged in the indictments. Exceptions are reserved in their behalf.

Fujii v. United States

148 F.2d 298 (10th Cir. 1945),
cert. denied sub nom. 325 U.S. 868 (1945)

HUXMAN, Circuit Judge.

Shigeru Fujii, the appellant herein, was indicted, tried, and convicted under 50 U.S.C. Appendix § 311, for wilfully refusing and failing to report for induction into the armed forces of the United States pursuant to an order of his local draft board. He is one of 63 persons convicted under similar circumstances. By stipulation of counsel, it is agreed that the other cases shall be controlled by the decision in this case.

Appellant is an American citizen. He was born in the United States of Japanese ancestry. He registered with his local draft board in California. Thereafter, in 1942, he was removed to and confined in a relocation center at Heart Mountain Park, Wyoming. At first he was classified in IV-C. Prior to the order to report, he was reclassified into 1-A. He was still confined in the relocation center when he was ordered to report for induction.

Appellant was loyal to the United States at all times. There can be no question about this. The agent for the Federal Bureau of Investigation who investigated him after he failed to report testified that his attitude was that of being loyal to the United States, that he indicated no desire to live in Japan, and that he desired to fight for his country if he were restored to his rights as a citizen.

Appellant's entire appeal is predicated on the argument that his removal from his home and his confinement behind barbed wire in the relocation center without being charged with any crime deprived him of his liberty and property without due process of law, and that therefore he ought not to be required to render military service until his rights were restored.

Under the admitted facts as to his loyalty, he was restrained of his liberty by confinement in the relocation center. He could have secured his complete release from restraint by writ of habeas corpus at any time and could thus have been restored to freedom. This would have given him the vindication which he seeks. It would have cleared his name for all time. But this he did not do. Instead, he chose to disobey a lawful order because he claimed his rights had been invaded. Two wrongs never make a right. One may not refuse to heed a lawful call of his government merely because in another way it may have injured him. Appellant was a citizen of the United States. He owed the same military service to his country that any other citizen did. Neither the fact that he was of Japanese ancestry nor the fact that his constitutional rights may have been invaded by sending him to a relocation center cancel this debt.

Furthermore, the courts are not open to him to challenge his right to exemption from military service under the admitted facts. It is now well settled that one must exhaust his administrative remedies and must obey the order to report before he may use the courts to challenge his classification. This was definitely settled by the Supreme Court in Falbo v. United States, 320 U.S. 549. Appellant concedes this, but argues that the decision in the Falbo case is wrong. In effect, he asks us to overrule the Supreme Court. No reason, to say nothing of a cogent one, is given for this extraordinary request....

The Selective Service Act makes it a penal offense to refuse to report for induction. It was appellant's duty to report for induction and thereafter assert any claimed rights for exemption from military service by writ of habeas corpus. This he failed to do. Instead, he chose to ignore the order. As a result, he became subject to the penal provisions of the statute.

Under the stipulation of the parties, this decision is made applicable to the other sixty-two cases covered therein.

Affirmed.

Notes

1. Judge Kennedy sentenced the defendants to three years' imprisonment. The Heart Mountain draft resisters continued to serve their prison sentences until after the Japanese surrendered on August 15, 1945, and after the Heart Mountain camp closed on November 10, 1945. One resister, Fred Iriye, was killed in an accident in prison two days before he was scheduled to be released. *See generally* Muller; Yamamoto at 187–88.

2. The question in these cases was not whether internment was lawful but whether a person could be guilty of criminal conduct—willfully evading the draft—for refusing to answer the call when he and his family were locked up in an internment camp. What was the basis for the courts' decisions?

3. The Tenth Circuit cited but declined to follow *United States v. Kuwabara*, 56 F. Supp. 716 (N.D. Cal. 1944), where Judge Louis E. Goodman "quashed" the indictment and dismissed the proceedings in a similar case. Masaaki Kuwabara and 25 other defendants were indicted for refusing to report for a pre-induction physical examination when they were interned at the Tule Lake Segregation Center. Judge Goodman held:

   > While the validity and constitutionality of the Presidential order for the relocation and confinement of American citizens of Japanese ancestry is challenged by the motion, the resolution of that question is neither necessary nor proper for the determination of the motion. Defendant was at all the times with which we are concerned, in actual confinement pursuant to the President's Order. Whether such confinement is lawful or not, is beside the question.
   >
   > Certain dangers vitally imminent to the security of the West Coast motivated the President, as Commander-in-Chief of the armed forces, in promulgating the order referred to. The war powers vested in the executive may be sufficient constitutional justification therefor, just as they were so held to be in the case of curfew restrictions against Japanese-American citizens. See Kiyoshi Hirabayashi v. United States, 320 U.S. 81.
   >
   > No such dangers, however, are the basis for the prosecution of defendant for refusing to be inducted, or for refusing to undergo preinduction physical examination.
   >
   > It does not follow that because the war power may allow the detention of defendant at Tule Lake, the guaranties of the Bill of Rights and other Constitutional provisions are abrogated by the existence of war. Kiyoshi Hirabayashi v. United States, supra, concurring opinion of Mr. Justice Murphy. The defendant cannot be denied the protection of the guaranty of due process because of the war or danger to national security but only upon a

> valid declaration of martial law. Ex parte Milligan, 4 Wall 2. It is shocking to the conscience that an American citizen be confined on the ground of disloyalty, and then, while so under duress and restraint, be compelled to serve in the armed forces, or be prosecuted for not yielding to such compulsion....

The government did not appeal the ruling, but Judge Goodman's reasoning that the induction of American citizens who were confined in detention facilities was "shocking to the conscience" was not the prevailing view. Why do you think Judge Goodman ruled as he did? Was there a legal basis for his decision, under the prevailing law at the time? While Judge Goodman's ruling dismissed the criminal charges against the 26 defendants, they remained imprisoned in the internment center.

4. In the conspiracy case, the jury acquitted the newspaper columnist but convicted the other seven defendants. The trial judge sentenced four of the defendants to four years' imprisonment and the other three to two years' imprisonment. All seven were sent to the maximum-security federal prison at Leavenworth, Kansas. On appeal, however, the Tenth Circuit reversed on the basis of a recently decided Supreme Court case holding that a defendant charged with counseling another to evade the draft was entitled to a jury instruction that a person who believed in good faith that a law was unconstitutional could urge another person to bring a test case determine his status. *Okamoto v. United States*, 152 F.2d 905, 907–08 (10th Cir. 1945) (citing *Keegan v. United States*, 325 U.S. 478 (1945)).

Figure 7.2 ***The Heart Mountain draft resisters in 1993.*** **Postcard of Heart Mountain Fair Play Committee, Densho, ID ddr-densho-122-590, Frank Abe Collection.**

5. In most of the cases, the sentences ranged from two to four years. Do you think these sentences were fair for these acts of civil disobedience during World War II?

6. On Christmas Eve 1947, President Harry Truman granted the draft resisters a full presidential pardon. When some of the resisters were drafted again to fight in the Korean War, they served willingly, for they believed their rights had been clarified by President Truman's pardon.

7. How do you think the draft resisters were treated by other Japanese in the camps when they refused to report? Do you think their views changed over time?

8. Lt. General DeWitt's orders were formally rescinded on December 17, 1944. For those who remained in the camps at the end (and there were some 85,000 at the time, *see* Tyler at 237), the process of resettlement was difficult. Some were afraid to leave even after their freedom was restored. The lives of the internees, of course, had been wholly disrupted, and there remained much resentment—indeed, hatred—of Japanese Americans in the aftermath of the War. *See* Yamamoto at 192–93, 196–97. Professor Daniels described some of these sentiments:

   > In mid-December 1944 [Los Angeles] district attorney Fred N. Howser used a Bill of Rights Week speech to denounce the impending return of Japanese as "a second attack on Pearl Harbor." The *Los Angeles Times* labeled the decision allowing return "a grave mistake" and argued that the real way for Japanese Americans to show their loyalty was "by seeking homes elsewhere than on the Pacific Coast." The city's mayor, Fletcher Bowron, who had been a strong advocate of mass incarceration before it became federal policy, warned of impending "race riots" because Negro war workers had moved in to housing in what had been Little Tokyo, and called for troops to be sent in to protect white citizens.

   Roger Daniels, *The Japanese American Cases: The Rule of Law in a Time of War* 80–81 (2013).

   Only approximately half of the internees returned to the West Coast, as many resettled to other parts of the country. Yamamoto at 199. Detention would have an impact long after the camps were finally closed.

9. The first military conscription in U.S. history (commonly referred to as the "draft") was instituted by the Confederacy in 1862 during the U.S. Civil War, followed shortly thereafter by the Union. Many early Americans thought a draft was unconstitutional. For instance, Daniel Webster, then a young congressman from New Hampshire, made the following speech in 1814 in response to President James Monroe's unsuccessful attempt to institute a draft during the War of 1812:

   > The administration asserts the right to fill the ranks of the regular army by compulsion....
   >
   > Is this, Sir, consistent with the character of a free government? Is this civil liberty? Is this the real character of our Constitution? No, sir, indeed it

> is not.... Where is it written in the Constitution, in what article or section is it contained, that you may take children from their parents, and parents from their children, and compel them to fight the battles of any war, in which the folly or the wickedness of government may engage it? Under what concealment has this power lain hidden, which now for the first time comes forth, with a tremendous and baleful aspect, to trample down and destroy the dearest rights of personal liberty?

Daniel Webster, *On the Draft: Text of a Speech delivered in Congress* 6 (Dec. 9, 1814), *available at* Online Library of Liberty, https://oll.libertyfund.org/titles/webster-daniel-webster-on-the-draft-text-of-a-speech-delivered-in-congress-december-9-1814.

More than 100 years later, in 1918, the U.S. Supreme Court held that the World War I draft was constitutional, citing history from eighteenth-century England and colonial America. *See Arver v. United States*, 245 U.S. 366 (1918). Today, even non-U.S. citizen males (e.g., permanent residents, refugees, asylees) aged 18–25 must register for selective service; there have also been lawsuits challenging the exemption of women from having to register on Equal Protection grounds.

Chapter 8
The Coram Nobis Cases

In the early 1980s, with the assistance of a legal historian, Peter Irons, and a number of young lawyers, Fred Korematsu, Gordon Hirabayashi, and Minoru Yasui decided to seek relief from their convictions by bringing petitions for a writ of *coram nobis*. Irons and a researcher for the Commission on Wartime Relocation and Internment of Civilians, Aiko Herzig-Yoshinaga, discovered that the government knowingly concealed information from the courts during the criminal prosecutions and the appeals that followed their convictions. While the government had argued that the curfews, exclusion, and internment were a matter of military necessity, the factual assertions made by Lt. General DeWitt conflicted with other information known to the government. The government suppressed this information in the litigations. *See* Yamamoto at 223–46; Irons at 202–18, 278–323. The government's misconduct in withholding exculpatory intelligence was the basis for the *coram nobis* petitions.

Korematsu v. United States

584 F. Supp. 1406 (N.D. Cal. 1984)

PATEL, District Judge.

Fred Korematsu is a native born citizen of the United States. He is of Japanese ancestry. On September 8, 1942 he was convicted in this court of being in a place from which all persons of Japanese ancestry were excluded pursuant to Civilian Exclusion Order No. 34 issued by Commanding General J.L. DeWitt. His conviction was affirmed. *Korematsu v. United States,* 323 U.S. 214 (1944).

Mr. Korematsu now brings this petition for a writ of *coram nobis* to vacate his conviction on the grounds of governmental misconduct. His allegations of misconduct are best understood against the background of events leading up to his conviction.

On December 8, 1941 the United States declared war on Japan.

Executive Order No. 9066 was issued on February 19, 1942 authorizing the Secretary of War and certain military commanders "to prescribe military areas from which any persons may be excluded as protection against espionage and sabotage."

Congress enacted § 97a of Title 18 of the United States Code, enforcing the exclusions promulgated under the Executive Order. Section 97a made it a misdemeanor for anyone to enter or remain in any restricted military zone contrary to the order of a military commander....

On March 2, 1942 General DeWitt issued Public Proclamation No. 1 pursuant to Executive Order 9066. The proclamation stated that "the entire Pacific Coast…is subject to espionage and acts of sabotage, thereby requiring the adoption of military measures necessary to establish safeguards against such enemy operations."

Thereafter, several other proclamations based upon the same justification were issued placing restrictions and requirements upon certain persons, including all persons of Japanese ancestry. As a result of these proclamations and Exclusion Order No. 34, providing that all persons of Japanese ancestry be excluded from an area specified as Military Area No. 1, petitioner, who lived in Area No. 1, could not leave the zone in which he resided and could not remain in the zone unless he were in an established "Assembly Center." Petitioner remained in the zone and did not go to the Center. He was charged and convicted of knowingly remaining in a proscribed area in violation of § 97a.

It was uncontroverted at the time of conviction that petitioner was loyal to the United States and had no dual allegiance to Japan. He had never left the United States. He was registered for the draft and willing to bear arms for the United States.

In his papers petitioner maintains that evidence was suppressed or destroyed in the proceedings that led to his conviction and its affirmance. He also makes substantial allegations of suppression and distortion of evidence which informed Executive Order No. 9066 and the Public Proclamations issued under it. While the latter may be compelling, it is not for this court to rectify. However, the court is not powerless to correct its own records where a fraud has been worked upon it or where manifest injustice has been done.…

Petitioner filed his petition for a writ of *coram nobis* on January 19, 1983.…On October 4, 1983, a document entitled "Government's Response and Motion under Local Rule 220-6" ("Response") was filed. The substance of the Response consists of less than four pages. In fact, it is not an opposition to the petition, but a countermotion to vacate the conviction and dismiss the underlying indictment.…

The Petition for a Writ of Coram Nobis

A writ of *coram nobis* is an appropriate remedy by which the court can correct errors in criminal convictions where other remedies are not available. Although Rule 60(b), Fed.R.Civ.P., abolishes various common law writs, including the writ of *coram nobis* in civil cases, the writ still obtains in criminal proceedings where other relief is wanting. *United States v. Morgan,* 346 U.S. 502 (1954).…

While the government would have this court grant its motion and look no further, petitioner asks this court to look behind the conviction, view the "evidence" that has now come to light and make findings of fact. The court concludes that the first alternative, although easy, is not available; the second alternative is unnecessary.

Even were the government in a position to move under Rule 48(a) of the Fed.R.Crim.P., the court would not automatically grant dismissal. A limited review by the court is necessary, even where the defendant consents. The purpose of this limited review is to protect against prosecutorial impropriety or harassment of the defendant and to assure that the public interest is not disserved. *United States v. Cowan,* 524 F.2d at 512–13....

Ordinarily, in cases in which the government agrees that a conviction should be set aside, the government's position is made clear because it confesses error, calling to the court's attention the particular errors upon which the conviction was obtained. A confession of error is generally given great deference. Where that confession of error is made by the official having full authority for prosecution on behalf of the government it is entitled to even greater deference. *See Sibron v. State of New York,* 392 U.S. 40, 58–59 (1968). Even so, the court must conduct its own review. *Young v. United States,* 315 U.S. 257 (1942).

In this case, the government, joining in on a different procedural footing, is not prepared to confess error. Yet it has not submitted any opposition to the petition, although given ample opportunity to do so. Apparently the government would like this court to set aside the conviction without looking at the record in an effort to put this unfortunate episode in our country's history behind us.

The government has, however, while not confessing error, taken a position tantamount to a confession of error. It has eagerly moved to dismiss without acknowledging any specific reasons for dismissal other than that "there is no further usefulness to be served by conviction under a statute which has been soundly repudiated." (R.T. 13:20–22, November 10, 1983). In support of this statement, the government points out that in 1971, legislation was adopted requiring congressional action before an Executive Order such as Executive Order 9066 can ever be issued again; that in 1976, the statute under which petitioner was convicted was repealed; and that in 1976, all authority conferred by Executive Order 9066 was formally proclaimed terminated as of December 31, 1946. While these are compelling reasons for concluding that vacating the conviction is in the best interests of this petitioner, respondent and the public, the court declines the invitation of the government to treat this matter in the perfunctory and procedurally improper manner it has suggested.

On the other hand, this court agrees that it is not necessary to reopen the partially healed wounds of an earlier period in order to perform its role of conducting independent judicial review. Fortunately, there are few instances in our judicial history when courts have been called upon to undo such profound and publicly acknowledged injustice. Such extraordinary instances require extraordinary relief, and the court is not without power to redress its own errors.

Because the government has not acknowledged specific errors, the court will look to the original record and the evidence now before it to determine whether there is support for the petition and whether manifest injustice would be done in letting the conviction stand....

The Commission Report

The Commission on Wartime Relocation and Internment of Civilians was established in 1980 by an act of Congress. It was directed to review the facts and circumstances surrounding Executive Order 9066 and its impact on American citizens and permanent resident aliens; to review directives of the United States military forces requiring the relocation and, in some cases, detention in internment camps of American citizens, including those of Japanese ancestry; and to recommend appropriate remedies. Commission on Wartime Relocation and Internment of Civilians Act, Pub.L. No. 96–317, § 2, 94 Stat. 964 (1980).

The Commission was mandated to submit a written report of its findings and recommendations to Congress. It was given authority to conduct hearings, and to compel attendance of witnesses and production of documents, including documents in the possession of governmental agencies and departments.

The Commission was composed of former members of Congress, the Supreme Court and the Cabinet as well as distinguished private citizens. It held approximately twenty days of hearings in cities across the United States, taking the testimony of over 720 witnesses, including key government personnel responsible for decisions involved in the issuance of Executive Order 9066 and the military orders implementing it. The Commission reviewed substantial numbers of government documents, including documents not previously available to the public. [The Commission thereafter issued the Report of the Commission on Wartime Relocation and Internment of Civilians, entitled "*Personal Justice Denied*" (Washington, D.C., 1982) ("Report").]

In light of all these factors, the Report carries substantial indicia of trustworthiness. Indeed, as noted above, the government conceded at the March 1983 status conference that the Report was an appropriate subject of judicial notice. It acknowledged it was awaiting the final Report before formulating any policy with respect to this petition and related Japanese internment matters. After issuance of the Report, the government announced its decision to move to dismiss the charges. It appears it is relying on the Report in substantial measure for its own recommendations.

The findings and conclusions of the Commission were unanimous. In general, the Commission concluded that at the time of the issuance of Executive Order 9066 and implementing military orders, there was substantial credible evidence from a number of federal civilian and military agencies contradicting the report of General DeWitt that military necessity justified exclusion and internment of all persons of Japanese ancestry without regard to individual identification of those who may have been potentially disloyal.

The Commission found that military necessity did not warrant the exclusion and detention of ethnic Japanese. It concluded that "broad historical causes which shaped these decisions [exclusion and detention] were race prejudice, war hysteria and a failure of political leadership." As a result, "a grave injustice was done to American citizens and resident aliens of Japanese ancestry who, without individual review or any probative evidence against them, were excluded, removed and detained by the United States during World War II." *Personal Justice Denied* at 18.

The Commission's Report provides ample support for the conclusion that denial of the motion would result in manifest injustice and that the public interest is served by granting the relief sought.

Government Memoranda

Petitioner offers another set of documents showing that there was critical contradictory evidence known to the government and knowingly concealed from the courts. These records present another question regarding the propriety of judicial notice. They consist of internal government memoranda and letters. Their authenticity is not disputed. Yet they are not the kind of documents that are the proper subject of judicial notice, and they are offered on the ultimate issue of governmental misconduct.

The internal memoranda and letters may, however, be considered by the court as evidence under Rule 803(1) or 803(16). Alternatively, because they are not actually offered for the truth of the statements contained in them, but rather as evidence that the statements were made (*i.e.*, verbal conduct), they may be admitted as non-hearsay within the purview of 801(c).

The substance of the statements contained in the documents and the fact the statements were made demonstrate that the government knowingly withheld information from the courts when they were considering the critical question of military necessity in this case. A series of correspondence regarding what information should be included in the government's brief before the Supreme Court culminated in two different versions of a footnote that was to be used to specify the factual data upon which the government relied for its military necessity justification. The first version read as follows:

> The Final Report of General DeWitt (which is dated June 5, 1943, but which was not made public until January 1944) is relied on in this brief for statistics and other details concerning the actual evacuation and the events that took place subsequent thereto. *The recital of the circumstances justifying the evacuation as a matter of military necessity, however, is in several respects,* particularly with reference to the use of illegal radio transmitters and to shore-to-ship signaling by persons of Japanese ancestry, *in conflict with information in the possession of the Department of Justice. In view of the contrariety of the reports on this matter we do not ask the Court to take judicial notice of the recital of those facts contained in the Report.*

Petitioner's Exhibit AA, Memorandum of John L. Burling to Assistant Attorney General Herbert Wechsler, September 11, 1944 (emphasis added).

After revision, it read:

> The Final Report of General DeWitt (which is dated June 5, 1943, but which was not made public until January 1944) hereinafter cited as Final Report,

> is relied on in this brief for statistics and other details concerning the actual evacuation and the events that took place subsequent thereto. *The recital in the Final Report of circumstances justifying the evacuation as a matter of military necessity, however, is in several respects,* particularly with reference to the use of illegal radio transmitters and shore-to-ship signalling by persons of Japanese ancestry, *in conflict with the views of this Department. We, therefore, do not ask the Court to take judicial notice of the recital of those facts contained in the Report.*

Id. (emphasis added).

The footnote that appeared in the final version of the brief merely read as follows:

> The Final Report of General DeWitt (which is dated June 5, 1943, but which was not made public until January 1944), hereinafter cited as Final Report, is relied on in this brief for statistics and other details concerning the actual evacuation and the events that took place subsequent thereto. *We have specifically recited in this brief the facts relating to the justification for the evacuation, of which we ask the Court to take judicial notice, and we rely upon the Final Report only to the extent that it relates to such facts.*

Brief for the United States, *Korematsu v. United States,* October Term, 1944, No. 22, at 11.

The final version made no mention of the contradictory reports. The record is replete with protestations of various Justice Department officials that the government had the obligation to advise the courts of the contrary facts and opinions. Petitioner's Exhibits A–FF. In fact, several Department of Justice officials pointed out to their superiors and others the "wilful historical inaccuracies and intentional falsehoods" contained in the DeWitt Report. *E.g.,* Exhibit B and Exhibit AA, Appendices A and B hereto.

These omissions are critical. In the original proceedings, before the district court and on appeal, the government argued that the actions taken were within the war-making powers of the Executive and Legislative branches and, even where the actions were directed at a particular class of persons, they were beyond judicial scrutiny so long as they were reasonably related to the security and defense of the nation and the prosecution of the war. Plaintiff's Brief in Opposition to Demurrer before the District Court, at 11–13; Brief for the United States in *Korematsu v. United States,* in the Supreme Court of the United States, at 11–18.

Indeed, this emphasis on national security was reflected in the standard of review laid down in *Hirabayashi v. United States,* 320 U.S. 81, 95 (1943): "We think that constitutional government in time of war, is not so powerless and does not compel so hard a choice if those charged with the responsibility of our national defense have reasonable ground for believing that the threat is real." The Court acknowledged that it could not second guess the decisions of the Executive and Congress but was limited to determining whether all of the relevant circumstances "within the knowledge of those charged with the responsibility for maintaining the national defense afforded a rational basis for the decisions which they made." *Id.* at 102.

The government relied on the rationale of *Hirabayashi* in its memoranda in *Korematsu.* That rationale was adopted in *Korematsu.* 323 U.S. at 218–24.

In *Hirabayashi* and *Korematsu,* the courts at each level engaged in an extensive examination of the facts known to the Executive and Legislative Branches. The facts which the government represented it relied upon and provided to the courts were those contained in a report entitled "Final Report, Japanese Evacuation from the West Coast" (1942), prepared by General DeWitt. His evaluation and version of the facts informed the courts' opinions. Yet, omitted from the government's representations was any reference to contrary reports which were considered reliable by the Justice Department and military officials other than General DeWitt.

A close reading of the briefs filed in the District Court by the government and amicus curiae State of California shows they relied heavily on the DeWitt Report for the facts justifying their military necessity arguments.

There is no question that the Executive and Congress were entitled to reasonably rely upon certain facts and to discount others. The question is not whether they were justified in relying upon some reports and not others, but whether the court had before it all the facts known by the government. Was the court misled by any omissions or distortions in concluding that the other branches' decisions had a reasonable basis in fact? Omitted from the reports presented to the courts was information possessed by the Federal Communications Commission, the Department of the Navy, and the Justice Department which directly contradicted General DeWitt's statements. Thus, the court had before it a selective record.

Whether a fuller, more accurate record would have prompted a different decision cannot be determined. Nor need it be determined. Where relevant evidence has been withheld, it is ample justification for the government's concurrence that the conviction should be set aside. It is sufficient to satisfy the court's independent inquiry and justify the relief sought by petitioner.

Other Requirements for Coram Nobis Relief

Petitioner has met the other requirements necessary to have his petition for a writ of *coram nobis* granted. One of the factors traditionally considered relevant is generally described as "mootness," but is more specifically stated in terms of whether a petitioner who has already fully served his sentence suffers any collateral consequences such that he should be permitted to apply for a writ of *coram nobis.* At one time it was presumed that the burden was upon the petitioner to show the existence of collateral consequences. More recent cases have moved toward the view that collateral consequences are to be presumed from the fact of a criminal conviction. The Supreme Court has, in fact, stated that a "criminal case is moot only if it is shown that there is no possibility that any collateral legal consequences will be imposed on the basis of the challenged conviction." *Lane v. Williams,* 455 U.S. 624, 632 (1982) (quoting approvingly *Sibron v. New York,* 392 U.S. at 57). This articulation places the burden on the government to show that petitioner suffers no collateral consequences. Petitioner has filed a certificate setting forth the collateral consequences he believes he suffers and will continue to suffer as a result of the conviction. The government, by its "Response," has failed to come forward with evidence to overcome the presumption.

The government has also failed to rebut petitioner's showing of timeliness. It appears from the record that much of the evidence upon which petitioner bases his motion was not discovered until recently. In fact, until the discovery of the documents relating to the government's brief before the Supreme Court, there was no specific evidence of governmental misconduct available.

There is thus no barrier to granting petitioner's motion for *coram nobis* relief.

Conclusion

The Supreme Court has cautioned that *coram nobis* should be used "only under certain circumstances compelling such action to achieve justice" and to correct "errors of the most fundamental character." *United States v. Morgan,* 346 U.S. 502, 511–12 (1954). It is available to correct errors that result in a complete miscarriage of justice and where there are exceptional circumstances. *See United States v. Hedman,* 655 F.2d 813, 815 (7th Cir.1981).

Coram nobis also lies for a claim of prosecutorial impropriety. This Circuit noted in *United States v. Taylor,* 648 F.2d at 573, that the writ "strikes at the veracity *vel non* of the government's representations to the court" and is appropriate where the procedure by which guilt is ascertained is under attack. The *Taylor* court observed that due process principles, raised by *coram nobis* charging prosecutorial misconduct, are not "strictly limited to those situations in which the defendant has suffered arguable prejudice;... [but also designed] to maintain public confidence in the administration of justice." *Id.* at 571.

At oral argument the government acknowledged the exceptional circumstances involved and the injustice suffered by petitioner and other Japanese-Americans. See also Response at 2–3. Moreover, there is substantial support in the record that the government deliberately omitted relevant information and provided misleading information in papers before the court. The information was critical to the court's determination, although it cannot now be said what result would have obtained had the information been disclosed. Because the information was of the kind peculiarly within the government's knowledge, the court was dependent upon the government to provide a full and accurate account. Failure to do so presents the "compelling circumstance" contemplated by *Morgan.* The judicial process is seriously impaired when the government's law enforcement officers violate their ethical obligations to the court.

This court's decision today does not reach any errors of law suggested by petitioner. At common law, the writ of *coram nobis* was used to correct errors of fact. *United*

States v. Morgan, 346 U.S. 502, 507–13 (1954). It was not used to correct legal errors and this court has no power, nor does it attempt, to correct any such errors.

Thus, the Supreme Court's decision stands as the law of this case and for whatever precedential value it may still have. Justices of that Court and legal scholars have commented that the decision is an anachronism in upholding overt racial discrimination as "compellingly justified." "Only two of this Court's modern cases have held the use of racial classifications to be constitutional." *Fullilove v. Klutznick,* 448 U.S. 448, 507 (1980) (Powell, J., concurring and referring to *Korematsu* and *Hirabayashi v. United States,* 320 U.S. 81 (1943)). *See also* L.H. Tribe, *American Constitutional Law* §§ 16–6, 16–14 (1978). The government acknowledged its concurrence with the Commission's observation that "today the decision in *Korematsu* lies overruled in the court of history."

Korematsu remains on the pages of our legal and political history. As a legal precedent it is now recognized as having very limited application. As historical precedent it stands as a constant caution that in times of war or declared military necessity our institutions must be vigilant in protecting constitutional guarantees. It stands as a caution that in times of distress the shield of military necessity and national security must not be used to protect governmental actions from close scrutiny and accountability. It stands as a caution that in times of international hostility and antagonisms our institutions, legislative, executive and judicial, must be prepared to exercise their authority to protect all citizens from the petty fears and prejudices that are so easily aroused.

Order

In accordance with the foregoing, the petition for a writ of *coram nobis* is granted and the counter-motion of the respondent is denied.

Notes

1. Judge Patel granted Korematsu's petition for a writ of *coram nobis*. What did this mean for Fred Korematsu? What was Judge Patel's reasoning? Did she conclude that there was a miscarriage of justice here? Why?

2. The government did not disagree that Korematsu's conviction should be vacated, but filed what was essentially a "counter-motion" under Rule 48 of the Federal Rules of Criminal Procedure asking for the conviction to be vacated and the indictment dismissed. What was its strategy? Was it admitting error or wrongdoing?

3. The court relied heavily on the report of the Commission on Wartime Relocation and Internment of Civilians. Was this appropriate?

4. Judge Patel held the hearing on the petition in the court's ceremonial courtroom, which was filled with some 300 spectators, most of whom were Nisei. Fred Korematsu was permitted to speak, and he said:

> I still remember when I was arrested as a criminal here in San Francisco [and] escorted to [a] concentration camp.... The horse stalls that we stayed in were made for horses, not human beings.... As long as my record stands in federal court, any American citizen can be held in prison or concentration camps without a trial or a hearing.... I would like to see the government admit that they were wrong and do something about it so that this will never happen again to any American citizen of any race, creed, or color.

See Daniels at 171–72.

5. The government did not appeal Judge Patel's decision, but the Ninth Circuit would have other opportunities to consider the issues. Minoru Yasui also filed a petition for a writ of *coram nobis* to vacate his conviction, in the district court in Portland, Oregon. The district court, however, granted the government's cross-motion to vacate the conviction, dismiss the indictment, and dismiss the petition. Although his conviction was vacated, Yasui was not satisfied because he believed he was entitled to a finding that his constitutional rights had been violated. He therefore appealed to the Ninth Circuit. *See generally Yasui v. United States*, 772 F.2d 1496 (9th Cir. 1985) (remanding case for determination whether time to appeal should be extended). Before the proceedings could be completed, however, Yasui passed away. The Ninth Circuit granted the government's application to dismiss the appeal as moot.

6. Gordon Hirabayashi also filed his petition for a writ of *coram nobis* in the Western District of Washington in Seattle. The trial judge (Donald S. Voorhees, *J.*) held an extensive evidentiary hearing, taking testimony from a number of witnesses, including individuals involved in the proceedings in the 1940s, and reviewing historical documents. The court rendered a split decision, granting the petition and vacating Hirabayashi's conviction for violating the exclusion order but denying the petition as to his conviction for violating the curfew order. *See Hirabayashi v. United States*, 627 F. Supp. 1445 (W.D. Wash. 1986). Both Hirabayashi and the government appealed, and the Ninth Circuit finally had an opportunity to address the issues.

Hirabayashi v. United States

828 F.2d 591 (9th Cir. 1987)

SCHROEDER, Circuit Judge:

I. Introduction

Gordon Hirabayashi is an American citizen who was born in Seattle, Washington, in 1918, and is currently Professor Emeritus of Sociology at the University of Alberta. He is of Japanese ancestry. In 1942 he was living in Seattle and was therefore subject to wartime orders requiring all persons of Japanese ancestry, whether citizens or not, to remain within their residences between 8:00 p.m. and 6:00 a.m. He was also subject to subsequent orders to report to a Civilian Control Station for processing requisite to exclusion from the military area. Hirabayashi refused to honor the curfew or to report to the control station because he believed that the military orders were based upon racial prejudice and violated the protection the Constitution affords to all citizens. The Supreme Court reviewed his conviction for violating the curfew order and unanimously affirmed. In an opinion by Chief Justice Stone, the Court accepted the government's position that the curfew was justified by military assessments of emergency conditions existing at the time. *Hirabayashi v. United States,* 320 U.S. 81 (1943). Because Hirabayashi had received a concurrent sentence for violating the exclusion order, the Court affirmed that conviction as well. *Id.* at 105. The following year, a majority of what was by then a sharply divided Court applied the same military emergency rationale to uphold explicitly the exclusion of all citizens of Japanese ancestry from the West Coast. *Korematsu v. United States,* 323 U.S. 214 (1944).

The *Hirabayashi* and *Korematsu* decisions have never occupied an honored place in our history. In the ensuing four and a half decades, journalists and researchers have stocked library shelves with studies of the cases and surrounding events. These materials document historical judgments that the convictions were unjust. They demonstrate that there could have been no reasonable military assessment of an emergency at the time, that the orders were based upon racial stereotypes, and that the orders caused needless suffering and shame for thousands of American citizens. The legal judgments of the courts reflecting that Hirabayashi and Korematsu had been properly convicted of violating the laws of the United States, however, remained on their records. Petitioner filed this lawsuit in 1983 to obtain a writ of error *coram nobis* to vacate his convictions and thus to make the judgments of the courts conform to the judgments of history.

The event which triggered the lawsuit occurred in 1982, when an archival researcher discovered the sole remaining copy of the original report prepared by the general who issued the curfew and exclusion orders. This report was intended to explain the basis for those orders. War Department officials revised the report in several material respects and tried to destroy all of the original copies before issuing the final report. The Justice Department did not know of the existence of the original report at the time its attorneys were preparing briefs in the *Hirabayashi* and *Korematsu* cases.

In his *coram nobis* petition Hirabayashi contended that the original report, the circumstances surrounding its alteration, and recently discovered related documents provided the proof, unavailable at the time of his conviction, that the curfew and exclusion orders were in fact based upon racial prejudice rather than military exigency. Hirabayashi further alleged that the government concealed these matters from his counsel and the Supreme Court, and that had the Supreme Court known the true basis for the orders, the ultimate decision in the case would probably have been different.

The district court held a full evidentiary proceeding on Hirabayashi's claims. It reviewed hundreds of documents and heard the testimony of several witnesses. They included Edward Ennis, who had been the Director of the Alien Enemy Control Unit at the Department of Justice and a principal author of the government's briefs in both the *Hirabayashi* and *Korematsu* cases; William Hammond, who had been the Assistant Chief of Staff for the entire Western Defense Command; Aiko Herzig-Yoshinaga, a researcher for the Commission on Wartime Relocation and Internment of Civilians from 1981 to 1983 and the person who discovered the original version of the final report.

In a careful opinion containing detailed findings of fact, the district court confirmed Hirabayashi's contentions in virtually every factual respect. *See Hirabayashi v. United States,* 627 F.Supp. 1445 (W.D.Wash.1986). It rejected as factually and legally unsupported the government's arguments that Hirabayashi had not been prejudiced by the concealment of the newly discovered material, that Hirabayashi could and should have made the same claims years earlier, and that there was no remaining case or controversy because Hirabayashi suffered no continuing adverse consequences from the original convictions.

The district court held that Hirabayashi's conviction for violating the exclusion order resulted in a violation of due process and ordered it vacated. 627 F.Supp. at 1457. Another district court has reached the same result in the *Korematsu* case, *Korematsu v. United States,* 584 F.Supp. 1406 (N.D.Cal.1984), and there has been no appeal. The district court in this case, however, concluded as a matter of law that the curfew conviction should not be vacated. It ruled that because the curfew order less significantly infringed Hirabayashi's freedom, the Supreme Court would have distinguished it from the exclusion order and would have affirmed the conviction even if it had known the racial basis of the order. *Hirabayashi,* 627 F.Supp. at 1457.

Both Hirabayashi and the government appeal. In reviewing the district court's decision, we must uphold the findings of fact unless they are clearly erroneous, and review the legal issues de novo. *United States v. McConney,* 728 F.2d 1195, 1200 n. 5 & 1201 (9th Cir.) (en banc), *cert. denied,* 469 U.S. 824 (1984). We agree with the district court's factual and legal analysis leading to its vacation of the exclusion conviction. We disagree with the court's conclusion that the curfew conviction rests upon a legal foundation different from the exclusion conviction. We therefore hold that both convictions should be vacated.

II. Factual Background

. . .

A grand jury indicted petitioner on May 28, 1942. Count I charged that he had failed to report pursuant to Civilian Exclusion Order 57. Count II charged the curfew violation. He was tried by a jury in October 1942, found guilty, and sentenced to three months on each count to be served concurrently....

Briefing to the Supreme Court took place in the spring of 1943. In his brief, Hirabayashi argued that there was no emergency justifying a racially based classification and that the orders had been issued upon invidious racial prejudice. For example, Hirabayashi's brief stated:

> Whatever may have been the panicky notion about a Japanese invasion of the West Coast right after Pearl Harbor, it was quite evident by the time the orders here in question were promulgated that the Japanese were not easily going to be able to do this. They had not invaded Australia; had not even attacked Hawaii a second time.... The picture of Japanese paratroops hiding among the Japanese residents of the West Coast to assist at an invasion is pure fantasy. The truth of the matter is that there was no military necessity, nor even reasonable ground for belief that such necessity required either general curfew regulations or wholesale evacuation orders.

Brief for Appellant at 19, *Hirabayashi v. United States,* 320 U.S. 81 (1943) (No. 870).

The Justice Department justified the exclusion and curfew orders upon what it said was a reasonable judgment of military necessity. It argued that because of cultural characteristics of the Japanese Americans, including religion and education, it was likely that some, though not all, American citizens of Japanese ancestry were disloyal. Brief for United States at 18–32. It then argued that because of the military exigencies, the government did not wait to segregate the loyal from the disloyal. The government's brief stated:

> The classification was not based upon invidious race discrimination. Rather, it was founded upon the fact that the group as a whole contained an unknown number of persons who could not readily be singled out and who were a threat to the security of the nation; and in order to impose effective restraints upon them it was necessary not only to deal with the entire group, but to deal with it at once.

Id. at 35. Later in its brief, the government stated that "[w]hat was needed was a method of removing at once the unknown number of Japanese persons who might assist a Japanese invasion, and not a program for sifting out such persons in the indefinite future." *Id.* at 62.

The government claimed that the "operative fact" on which the classification was made was the danger arising from the existence of over 100,000 persons of Japanese descent on the West Coast. *Id.* at 63. It acknowledged, however, that the "record in this case does not contain any comprehensive account of the facts which gave rise to the exclusion and curfew measures here involved." *Id.* at 10–11. The government therefore made extensive use of judicial notice in order to convey its position that those responsible for the orders reasonably regarded an emergency situation to exist. It argued that "historical facts" and "facts appear[ing] in official documents ... are peculiarly within the realm of judicial notice." *Id.* at 11.

The government's argument that the urgency of the situation made individual hearings to determine loyalty impossible was the subject of special concern. Solicitor General Charles Fahy filed a post-argument memorandum stressing that the hearings could not have been utilized because the "situation did not lend itself, in the *unique and pressing* circumstances, to solution by individual loyalty hearings." (emphasis added).

The Supreme Court decided the case on June 21, 1943. The government's view prevailed; Chief Justice Stone deferred to the military assessment of necessity. The Court saw the racial classification as justifiable only as a matter of military expediency, and indicated that it had to accept the judgment of the military authorities that the exigencies of time required the entire Japanese population to be treated as a group. The Court concluded:

> Whatever views we may entertain regarding the loyalty to this country of the citizens of Japanese ancestry, we cannot reject as unfounded the judgment of the military authorities and of Congress that there were disloyal members of that population, whose number and strength could not be precisely and quickly ascertained. We cannot say that the warmaking branches of the Government did not have ground for believing that in a critical hour such persons could not readily be isolated and separately dealt with....

320 U.S. at 99.

The problem for the Court was stated with greater anguish in Justice Douglas' concurring opinion where he pointed out that "guilt is personal under our constitutional system. Detention for reasonable cause is one thing. Detention on account of ancestry is another." 320 U.S. at 107–08 (Douglas, J., concurring). He nevertheless rejected Hirabayashi's argument, concluding that expediency so required.

> Much of the argument assumes that as a matter of policy it might have been wiser for the military to have dealt with these people on an individual basis and through the process of investigation and hearings separated those who were loyal from those who are not. But the wisdom or expediency of the decision which was made is not for us to review.... [W]here the peril is great and the time is short, temporary treatment on a group basis may be the only practicable expedient whatever the ultimate percentage of those who are detained for cause.

Id. at 106–07 (Douglas, J., concurring)....

Hirabayashi filed this *coram nobis* proceeding early in 1983, alleging that new material had come to light in this decade which showed that the Department of War had suppressed evidence from both Hirabayashi and the Justice Department during the crucial period when the case was being presented to the Supreme Court, and that this material required the court to grant the unusual writ of *coram nobis* to vacate the convictions. The government, recognizing that the circumstances surrounding Hirabayashi's convictions may have been unjust, nevertheless asked the district court to refrain from considering the facts, and to dismiss the petition for *coram nobis*. It asked the court instead to utilize the provisions of Fed.R.Crim.P. 48, permitting termination of a prosecution by dismissal of the indictment, to vacate the conviction. The district court denied the government's motion to dismiss and held a full evidentiary hearing on Hirabayashi's claims.

The principal factual matter developed at the trial concerned the suppressed report of General DeWitt. This report set forth the basis for his promulgation of the orders of which Hirabayashi stood convicted. At the time General DeWitt issued his series of orders regarding curfew and exclusion in 1942, neither he nor the War Department provided any factual explanation of the reasons for the orders. After they were issued, General DeWitt prepared such a report. The official version of the report, *Final Report: Japanese Evacuation from the West Coast 1942*, was dated June 5, 1943, but was not made public until January 1944. Recent historical research, however, has uncovered in the National Archives a previously unknown copy of an original version of that report. That copy reflects that General DeWitt transmitted his original report to the War Department in Washington on April 15, 1943. *See Hirabayashi*, 627 F.Supp. at 1449, 1455–56 (describing circumstances surrounding discovery and transmittal).

The original version differed materially from the official version. Most significantly, the original report did not purport to rest on any military exigency, but instead declared that because of traits peculiar to citizens of Japanese ancestry it would be impossible to separate the loyal from the disloyal, and that all would have to be evacuated for the duration of the war. Other documents in the record below show that officials in the War Department were alarmed when they received the original report. The district court observed that Assistant Secretary of War John J. McCloy was "more than a little exercised because the Final Report had been printed in final form and distributed without any prior consultation by the Western Defense Command with the War Department about its contents." 627 F.Supp. at 1450.

McCloy and Colonel Karl Bendetsen, who was in charge of the Wartime Civil Control Administration of the Western Defense Command, had a number of communications with General DeWitt in order to persuade him to change the report. *Id.* at 1450–53. At first intransigent, DeWitt stated "[I] [h]ave no desire to compromise in any way govt case in Supreme Court." 627 F.Supp. at 1451 (quoting Letter of May 5, 1943, from General DeWitt to Brigadier General Barnett). He eventually capitulated. The result was that the report was changed in several substantive respects after the

War Department suggested some fifty-five alterations. The changes most relevant to this case were summarized by the district court as follows:

> Page iii, paragraph 2, second sentence: Eliminate the words "and will continue for the duration of the present war." Page iii, paragraph 2, end of the second sentence: Insert "The surprise attack at Pearl Harbor by the enemy crippled a major portion of the Pacific Fleet and exposed the West Coast to an attack which could not have been substantially impeded by defensive fleet operations. More than 120,000 persons of Japanese ancestry resided in colonies adjacent to many highly sensitive installations. Their loyalties were unknown, and time was of the essence."
>
> Page 9. Strike the following: "It was impossible to establish the identity of the loyal and the disloyal with any degree of safety. It was not that there was insufficient time in which to make such a determination; it was simply a matter of facing the realities that a positive determination could not be made, that an exact separation of the 'sheep from the goats' was unfeasible."
>
> And replace with the following: "To complicate the situation, no ready means existed for determining the loyal and the disloyal with any degree of safety. It was necessary to face the realities—a positive determination could not have been made."

627 F. Supp. at 1451–52.

The revised, official version of the report was dated June 5, 1943. The War Department tried to destroy all copies of the original report when the revised version was prepared. This record contains a memo by Theodore Smith of the Civil Affairs Division of the Western Defense Command, dated June 29, 1943, certifying that he witnessed the burning of "the galley proofs, galley pages, drafts and memorandums of the original report of the Japanese Evacuation."

Edward Ennis, the Director of the Alien Enemy Control Unit of the Justice Department and a principal author of the government's 1942 brief, testified extensively in these proceedings. He testified as to his efforts in 1943 and 1944 in briefing both the *Korematsu* and *Hirabayashi* cases, and other efforts on the part of the Justice Department to obtain the full materials from the War Department supporting General DeWitt's decisions. While preparing the government's brief in *Hirabayashi,* Ennis learned that a report had been written but when he asked for a copy, the War Department gave him only a few selected pages. The district court observed, in denying the Government's Petition for Rehearing in this case, that it found Ennis entirely credible and that it believed that had Ennis had the original report showing the true rationale of DeWitt, he would have informed the Supreme Court of its contents.

On the basis of the evidence before it, the district court entered an extensive opinion setting forth the reasons for its decision to vacate the exclusion conviction. Judge Voorhees based that decision upon the factual record developed before him. He found first, that while the Supreme Court based its decision in *Hirabayashi* upon deference to military judgment of the need for expediency, General DeWitt, the person responsible for the racially based confinement of American citizens, had made no such judgment. The district court further found that the United States government doctored the documentary record to reflect that DeWitt had made a judgment of military exigency. Finally, the court found that had the suppressed material been submitted to the Supreme Court, its decision probably would have been materially affected. The government appeals the grant of relief.

The district court refused, however, to grant *coram nobis* relief with respect to the curfew conviction. It based that decision upon its conclusion that the Supreme Court would have drawn a legal distinction between the curfew and exclusion orders. It is from that denial of relief that Hirabayashi appeals. We consider first the contentions of the government.

III. The Government's Contentions in its Appeal

The government's contentions in its appeal from the district court's decision to vacate the exclusion conviction can be classified in four general categories. They are, first, that certain factual determinations of the district court are clearly erroneous; second, that the claims are barred by laches; third, that the case is moot because Hirabayashi does not continue to suffer from any adverse consequences from the convictions; and, finally, that the district court abused its discretion in reaching the merits of the petition by not granting the government's motion to vacate the convictions pursuant to Fed.R.Crim.P. 48.

A. Factual Challenges.

We turn to the government's challenge to certain of the district court's factual findings. The government first takes issue with the district court's finding that it was General DeWitt who made the decision that exclusion of all persons of Japanese ancestry from the West Coast was required by military necessity. 627 F.Supp. at 1456. Support for the finding that the decision was General DeWitt's is abundant in this record. Secretary of War Stimson delegated his authority to General DeWitt pursuant to the power delegated to Stimson by the President. *See* Public Proclamation No. 1, 7 Fed. Reg. 2320 (1942). There has been no showing that General DeWitt even consulted with War Department officials in Washington before issuing the orders Hirabayashi refused to obey. It is now clear that DeWitt did not consult with Washington before preparing his final report. *Hirabayashi,* 627 F.Supp. at 1450. As one commentator wrote soon after the orders were issued: "The Japanese question had political and economic angles, but the President's Executive Order of February 19 treated it as fundamentally a military problem and placed responsibility squarely upon the Commanding General." Fairman, *The Law of Martial Rule and the National Emergency,* 55 Harv.L.Rev. 1253, 1299 (1942).

The government points to uncontroverted evidence in the record that there were those in the War Department who did not agree with the reasons given by General DeWitt for the order and would have justified the order on other grounds. This evidence, however, merely underscores the critical nature of General DeWitt's decision and his report. It was because General DeWitt had exercised the authority, and because his judgment was essential, that the War Department suppressed the original version of his report in the first place. Indeed, Solicitor General Fahy in his oral argument in 1944 in *Korematsu* conceded that it was the views of the Commanding General which counted, and that if his orders had been based upon racist precepts, they would have been invalid. The following colloquy took place in which Justice Frankfurter and the Solicitor General discussed the revised version of DeWitt's report without knowledge of the existence of the original version.

> MR. JUSTICE FRANKFURTER: Suppose the commanding general, when he issued Order No. 34, had said, in effect, "It is my judgment that, as a matter of security, there is no danger from the Japanese operations; but under cover of war, I had authority to take advantage of my hostility and clear the Japanese from this area." Suppose he had said that, with that kind of crude candor. It would not have been within his authority, would it?
>
> MR. FAHY: It would not have been.
>
> MR. JUSTICE FRANKFURTER: As I understand the suggestion, it is that, as a matter of law, the report of General DeWitt two years later proved that that was exactly what the situation was. As I understand, that is the legal significance of the argument.
>
> MR. FAHY: That is correct, Your Honor; and the report simply does nothing of the kind.

To support its position the government cites language in the Supreme Court's opinion in *Hirabayashi,* referring to the judgment of Congress and military authorities, in order to suggest that somehow the Supreme Court made a factual finding contrary to the district court's finding. *Hirabayashi,* 320 U.S. at 99. Neither the Supreme Court's opinion nor the record before it in 1943 supports such an argument. The district court's decision correctly reflects the historical record that the orders were the direct result of General DeWitt's exercise of the authority delegated to him. The district court's finding that it was General DeWitt who decided that the curfew and exclusion orders were required is not clearly erroneous.

The government next challenges as factually erroneous the district court's finding that the Supreme Court in 1943 would probably have reached a different result in the exclusion case if it had known the true basis for the General's decision. The government disagrees with the following portions of the district court's opinion:

> Had the statement of General DeWitt been disclosed to petitioner's counsel, they would have been in a position to argue that, contrary to General DeWitt's belief, there were in fact means of separating those who were loyal from those who were not; that the legal system had developed through the years means whereby factual questions of the most complex nature could be answered with a high degree of reliability. Counsel for petitioner could have

> pointed out that with very little effort the determination could have been made that tens of thousands of native-born Japanese Americans—infants in arms, children of high school age or younger, housewives, the infirm and elderly—were loyal and posed no possible threat to this country....
>
> Had counsel for petitioner known and been able to present to the Supreme Court the [initial] reason stated by General DeWitt for the evacuation of all Japanese, [and]... [i]f the military necessity for exclusion was the impossibility of separating the loyal from the disloyal, the Supreme Court would not have had to defer to military judgment because this particular problem, separating the loyal from the disloyal, was one calling for judicial, rather than military, judgment.

627 F.Supp. at 1456–57....

The government agrees with petitioner and the district court that the Supreme Court in *Hirabayashi* deferred to a military judgment that circumstances required the prompt evacuation of all Japanese Americans, and that there was not enough time to attempt to separate the loyal from the disloyal. The government also agrees with petitioner and the district court that General DeWitt acted on the basis of his own racist views and not on the basis of any military judgment that time was of the essence. What the government contends in this appeal is that on the basis of the record before it, the Supreme Court should have known both that General DeWitt was a racist, and that he made no military judgment of emergency. The government asks us to hold, therefore, that the Supreme Court probably would have reached the same erroneous result even if the government had not suppressed the evidence and had accurately represented to the Court the basis of General DeWitt's decision.

There are several problems with this position. First, as the district court observed when it denied rehearing, the material in the record before the Supreme Court showing General DeWitt's racism was limited primarily to a newspaper clipping. More importantly, it was principally Hirabayashi and those amici who supported him, not the government, who presented the evidence of racial bias to the Court and who argued that the decisions must have been based upon racism rather than military necessity. By contrast, the information now in the public record constitutes objective and irrefutable proof of the racial bias that was the cornerstone of the internment orders.

The basis for General DeWitt's decision was a very crucial issue which divided the government and Hirabayashi. For illustration, Hirabayashi's brief referred to testimony by DeWitt indicating that "prejudice dominated his thinking," and quoted him as stating: "It makes no difference whether the Japanese is theoretically a citizen.... A Jap is a Jap." *San Francisco News,* April 13, 1943, at 1, *cited in* Reply Brief for Appellant at 1 n. 2. Extracts from the newspaper article were reproduced in the appendix to that brief. The Amicus Brief of the American Civil Liberties Union, in support of Hirabayashi's position, also suggested that the order was based upon the racist view that it was impossible to segregate the loyal from the disloyal:

> There were those, of course, who claimed that it would have been impossible to tell the loyal from the disloyal; who said that all persons of Japanese ancestry look alike. It is a challenge to the intelligence of this nation that such childish opinions actually carried the day.

Brief for American Civil Liberties Union at 13. Similar arguments were made by the Japanese American Citizens League in their Amicus Brief in support of Hirabayashi.

The government, on the other hand, through the device of judicial notice asked the Supreme Court to recognize that the judgment made was one of exigency; the "principal danger to be apprehended was a Japanese invasion." Brief for United States at 65. It argued that the "situation did not lend itself, in the unique and pressing circumstances, to solution by individual loyalty hearings." Post-Argument Memorandum of Solicitor General Fahy. In deciding the case against Hirabayashi, the Supreme Court obviously accepted the government's view of the facts as the government presented them in 1943, and rejected Hirabayashi's.

In asking us to hold that the Supreme Court would have reached the same result even if the Solicitor General had advised Hirabayashi and the Court of the true basis for General DeWitt's orders, the government ignores the fact that in 1943 it was clearly in a better position to know that basis than was the defense. It also ignores the traditionally special relationship between the Supreme Court and the Solicitor General which permits the Solicitor General to make broad use of judicial notice and commands special credence from the Court. The record here shows that Ennis, in preparing the government's brief, felt that responsibility keenly.

The importance which the Supreme Court attached to the statements of the government regarding the factual situation at the time was brought out during the course of the proceedings in *Korematsu,* decided a year after *Hirabayashi.* By the time *Korematsu* was briefed and argued, the revised version of DeWitt's report had been made public. Justice Department attorneys with access to contemporaneous intelligence reports had had misgivings about the accuracy of even that version. This apprehension was reflected in a footnote to the government's brief in *Korematsu* limiting reliance on the report. The footnote came up during oral argument, the transcript of which is in this record. Solicitor General Fahy denied that the footnote was a repudiation of the military necessity of the evacuation and reaffirmed the government's position in *Hirabayashi.*

The Court's divided opinions in *Korematsu* demonstrate beyond question the importance which the Justices in *Korematsu* and *Hirabayashi* placed upon the position of the government that there was a perceived military necessity, despite contrary arguments of the defendants in those cases. The majority in *Korematsu* reaffirmed the Court's deference in *Hirabayashi* to military judgments. Justice Murphy's dissent highlighted the difference between his position and the majority's. He expressly faulted the majority's acceptance of the government's justification that "time is of the essence." We now know this very phrase was inserted by the War Department into

DeWitt's final report and was not a concept upon which DeWitt himself based his decision. Justice Murphy said:

> No adequate reason is given for the failure to treat these Japanese Americans on an individual basis by holding investigations and hearings to separate the loyal from the disloyal, as was done in the case of persons of German and Italian ancestry.... *It is asserted merely that the loyalties of this group "were unknown and time was of the essence."*

Korematsu, 323 U.S. at 241 (Murphy, J., dissenting) (emphasis added). Justice Jackson's dissent zeroed in on the majority's acceptance of General DeWitt's revised report. He stated:

> So the Court, having no real evidence before it, has no choice but to accept General DeWitt's own unsworn, self-serving statement, untested by any cross-examination, that what he did was reasonable. And thus it will always be when courts try to look into the reasonableness of a military order.

Id. at 245 (Jackson, J., dissenting).

The majority decision in *Korematsu* was a reaffirmation that it would defer to a military judgment of necessity in upholding first the curfew and then the exclusion orders:

> Like curfew, exclusion of those of Japanese origin was deemed necessary because of the presence of an unascertained number of disloyal members of the group, most of whom we have no doubt were loyal to this country. It was because we could not reject the finding of the military authorities that it was impossible to bring about an immediate segregation of the disloyal from the loyal that we sustained the validity of the curfew order as applying to the whole group. In the instant case, temporary exclusion of the entire group was rested by the military on the same ground.

Id. at 218–19. The claimed emergency preventing the separation of loyal from disloyal Japanese Americans was critical to the Supreme Court's decisions upholding the internment of Hirabayashi and Korematsu. This was clearly evidenced when the Court subsequently held that detention of a concededly loyal Japanese American citizen was unlawful. *See Ex Parte Endo,* 323 U.S. 283 (1944).

We cannot hold that the district court erred in deciding that the reasoning of the Supreme Court would probably have been profoundly and materially affected if the Justice Department had advised it of the suppression of evidence which established the truthfulness of the allegations made by Hirabayashi and Korematsu concerning the real reason for the exclusion order.

B. Coram Nobis Requirements: Laches and Mootness.

Hirabayashi has filed a petition for a writ of error *coram nobis* asking the court to vacate his 1942 misdemeanor convictions. In *United States v. Morgan,* 346 U.S. 502 (1954), the Supreme Court held that *coram nobis* relief is available to challenge the validity of a conviction, even though the sentence has been fully served, *id.* at 503–04, "under circumstances compelling such action to achieve justice." *Id.* at 511. As we recently explained in *Yasui v. United States,* 772 F.2d 1496, 1498 (9th Cir.1985), the *coram nobis* writ "fills a void in the availability of post-conviction remedies in federal criminal cases."...

The government contends that "ordinary misdemeanors have no 'collateral consequences' and therefore are not subject to post-conviction attack absent some special legal disability." For the following reasons, we find no support for such a per se rule and conclude that the case is not moot....

No court to our knowledge has ever held that misdemeanor convictions cannot carry collateral legal consequences. Any judgment of misconduct has consequences for which one may be legally or professionally accountable. *See Miller v. Washington State Bar Ass'n,* 679 F.2d 1313, 1318 (9th Cir.1982) (letter of admonition in attorney's permanent record for which he is professionally accountable constitutes sufficient adverse consequence for Article III).

Moreover, the government's argument here that "ordinary" misdemeanors should not carry the presumption of adverse consequences is misplaced. Hirabayashi's conviction was for no ordinary misdemeanor. His conviction was one which has been the subject of controversy for more than four decades. A United States citizen who is convicted of a crime on account of race is lastingly aggrieved.

C. The Government's Motion to Vacate and Dismiss.

The government contends that the trial court erred by denying its motion to vacate Hirabayashi's convictions and dismiss the underlying indictments pursuant to Fed.R.Crim.P. 48(a)....

Based on the record in this case we cannot find that the district court abused its discretion in denying the government's motion and considering the merits of Hirabayashi's request that an injustice be corrected.

IV. Hirabayashi's Appeal of the District Court's Refusal to Vacate the Curfew Conviction

The district court vacated Hirabayashi's conviction for violation of the exclusion order but left standing the conviction for violation of the curfew order. This was a result which neither side sought and which neither strenuously defends in this court.

The district court based its distinction on the premise that the curfew was a lesser restriction on freedom than the exclusion. It does not follow, however, that the Supreme Court would have made such a distinction had it been aware of the suppressed evidence. The Supreme Court in 1943 reviewed only the curfew order and clearly saw it as a serious deprivation of liberty. The Court therefore held that it would be justified only on the basis of a reasonable military judgment of military necessity. 320 U.S. at 99....

We have seen that Hirabayashi's two convictions were based upon simultaneous indictments, were tried together, briefed together, and decided together. In its brief to the Supreme Court, the Justice Department argued a single theory of military necessity to support both the exclusion and curfew orders....

The district court erred in distinguishing between the validity of the curfew and exclusion convictions.

Conclusion

The judgment of the district court as to the exclusion conviction is affirmed. The judgment as to the curfew conviction is reversed and the matter is remanded with instructions to grant Hirabayashi's petition to vacate both convictions.

Notes

1. The government did not seek to appeal the Ninth Circuit's decision to the Supreme Court, and so the legal proceedings concluded. The Ninth Circuit vacated both convictions. In the process of doing so, the court finally reached the merits of whether the government had engaged in misconduct. Did the decision resolve the legal question of the constitutionality of the military orders, that is, whether military necessity justified curfews, exclusion, and detention explicitly on the basis of race?

2. Both the district court and the Ninth Circuit engaged in an unusual inquiry: whether the Supreme Court would have reached a different result in *Korematsu*, *Hirabayashi*, and *Yasui* if the government had not suppressed evidence. How did they go about making this determination? Do you agree with their conclusion?

3. In the end, what did the government do wrong to warrant vacating the convictions? Do you think that kind of misconduct could happen today? What ethical issues are implicated by the conduct of the government lawyers? Should government lawyers be held to a higher ethical standard than private lawyers?

4. In May 2011, Neal Katyal, then the Acting Solicitor General of the United States, posted a "Confession of Error" on the Department of Justice website. He stated, referring to the actions of Solicitor General Charles Fahy before the Supreme Court in the *Korematsu* and *Hirabayashi* cases:

    > [T]hose decisions still stand out today as a reminder of the mistakes of that era. Today, our Office takes this history as an important reminder that the "special credence" the Solicitor General enjoys before the Supreme Court requires great responsibility and a duty of absolute candor in our representations to the Court. Only then can we fulfill our responsibility to defend the United States and its Constitution, and to protect the rights of all Americans.

Neal Katyal, *Confession of Error: The Solicitor General's Mistakes During the Japanese-American Internment Cases*, https://www.justice.gov/opa/blog/confession-error-solicitor-generals-mistakes-during-japanese-american-internment-cases. *See also* Daniels at 201–02.

5. Judge Mary M. Schroeder, the author of the opinion, would some years later describe the decision as "the opinion of my career." Mary M. Schroeder, *What Gordon Hirabayashi Taught Me About Courage*, 11 Seattle J. Soc. Just. 65, 65 (2012). What did you think of her opinion?

Figure 8.1 ***Gordon Hirabayashi, Minoru Yasui, and Fred Korematsu in 2009.*** **Photo by Steven Okazaki. Courtesy of Farallon Films.**

6. Some scholars and Asian-American activists, most notably Professor Jerry Kang, have criticized the Ninth Circuit's and Judge Patel's decisions as effectively exonerating the Supreme Court. *See* Jerry Kang, *Denying Prejudice: Internment, Redress, and Denial*, 51 UCLA L. Rev. 933 (2004). They assert that the Supreme Court majority in *Korematsu* was motivated in a significant way by racial stereotypes about the untrustworthiness and disloyalty of people of Japanese descent. The implicit assertion that the government worked a fraud on the courts, these critics suggest, does an injustice to the extent to which anti-Japanese racism has pervaded all of our institutions, including the federal courts. What do you think—has racism pervaded all our institutions, including the courts? Was the Supreme Court "exonerated" by the findings of government misconduct and fraud? What do you think was the ultimate impact of the *coram nobis* cases?

Chapter 9

Redress and Reparation

The *coram nobis* decisions achieved some measure of judicial vindication. But there were political and legislative measures as well.

In 1976, President Gerald Ford repealed Executive Order 9066. *See* Gerald R. Ford, *Proclamation 4417*, https://www.fordlibrarymuseum.gov/library/ speeches/760111p .htm.

In 1988, President Ronald Reagan signed the Civil Liberties Act, which authorized reparations of $20,000 for each surviving internee who was a United States citizen or permanent resident alien at the time of confinement. 50 U.S.C. App. §§ 1989b-4(a)(1), 1989b-7(2). The Act included a congressional apology:

> The Congress recognizes that, as described by the Commission on Wartime Relocation and Internment of Civilians, a grave injustice was done to both citizens and permanent resident aliens of Japanese ancestry by the evacuation, relocation, and internment of civilians during World War II. As the Commission documents, these actions were carried out without adequate security reasons and without any acts of espionage or sabotage documented by the Commission, and were motivated largely by racial prejudice, wartime hysteria, and a failure of political leadership. The excluded individuals of Japanese ancestry suffered enormous economic damages, both material and intangible, and there were incalculable losses in education and job training, all of which resulted in significant human suffering for which appropriate compensation has not been made. For these fundamental violations of the basic civil liberties and constitutional rights of these individuals of Japanese ancestry, the Congress apologizes on behalf of the Nation.

50 U.S.C. App. § 1989a(a). The Act created a trust fund of $1.2 billion to pay for reparations as well as for educational activities. *Id.* § 1989b-3(e). Congress later appropriated an additional $400 million, because the number of internment camp survivors had been underestimated. In the end, some 82,000 individuals received $1.6 billion in compensation. Daniels at 160, 163.

The first payments were made in 1991. In his letter transmitting the checks, President George H.W. Bush wrote:

Figure 9.1 ***Fred Korematsu in 1990*****. Photo by Shirley Nakao. Courtesy of the Korematsu Institute.**

> A monetary sum and words alone cannot restore lost years or erase painful memories; neither can they fully convey our Nation's resolve to rectify injustice and to uphold the rights of individuals. We can never fully right the wrongs of the past. But we can take a clear stand for justice and recognize that serious injustices were done to Japanese Americans during World War II.
>
> In enacting a law calling for restitution and offering a sincere apology, your fellow Americans have, in a very real sense, renewed their traditional commitment to the ideals of freedom, equality, and justice. . . .

Letter from George H.W. Bush to Japanese American Internees, www.learner.org /courses/amerhistory/interactives/sources /E7/e1/sources/5496.php.

In 1998, President Bill Clinton awarded the Presidential Medal of Freedom to Fred Korematsu, saying: "In the long history of our country's constant search for justice, some names of ordinary citizens stand for millions of souls. Plessy, Brown, Parks . . .

To that distinguished list, today we add the name of Fred Korematsu." *See* Akil Vohra, *Honoring Fred Korematsu* (February 1, 2011), https://obamawhitehouse.archives.gov/blog/2011/02/01/honoring-fred-korematsu.

In April 2012, President Barack Obama posthumously awarded the Presidential Medal of Freedom to Gordon Hirabayashi. *See* Office of the Press Secretary, The White House, *President Obama Names Presidential Medal of Freedom Recipients* (April 26, 2012), https://obamawhitehouse.archives.gov/the-press-office/2012/04/26/president-obama-names-presidential-medal-freedom-recipients. Hirabayashi had died three months earlier.

In November 2015, President Obama posthumously awarded the Presidential Medal of Freedom to Minoru Yasui as well. *See* Office of the Press Secretary, The White House, *President Obama Names Recipients of the Presidential Medal of Freedom* (November 16, 2015), https://obamawhitehouse.archives.gov/the-press-office/2015/11/16/president-obama-names-recipients-presidential-medal-freedom.

Although Gordon Hirabayashi, Minori Yasui, and Fred Korematsu all lost in the Supreme Court, they were vindicated in the end and were rightly recognized for their efforts—all three received the Presidential Medal of Freedom (Hirabayashi and Yasui posthumously). Yet, although she actually *won* her case in the Supreme Court, until recently Mitsuye Endo received far less recognition. *See* Tamiko Nimura, *Why Don't We Know Mitsuye Endo? The Layers of Silence Around a Japanese American Hero and Her Landmark Supreme Court Case*, Zocalo Public Square (May 20, 2021), https://www.zocalopublicsquare.org/2021/05/20/true-story-mitsuye-endo/ideas/essay. *See also, e.g.*, Stephanie Buck, *Overlooked No More: Mitsuye Endo, a Name Linked to Justice for Japanese-Americans*, N.Y. Times, Nov. 15, 2019; Lori Aratani, *She Fought the Internment of Japanese Americans During World War II and Won*, Wash. Post, Dec. 18, 2019. *See also* Mina Juhn, *"Concededly Loyal": Mitsuye Endo and the Continuing Significance of* Ex parte Endo, 27 UCLA Asian Pacific Am. L.J. 99 (2023). On January 2, 2025, however, Endo finally received recognition at the presidential level, as President Biden awarded her the Presidential Citizens Medal posthumously. *Mitsuye Endo Posthumously Receives Presidential Citizens Medal*, Rafu Shimpo (Jan. 14, 2025), *available at* https://rafu.com/2025/01/mitsuye-endo-posthumously-receives-presidential-citizens-medal.

Redress and reparations for Japanese-American internees resulted from the sustained efforts of many, including the scholars who conducted the research, the members of the Commission on Wartime Relocation and Internment of Civilians, the lawyers who brought the *coram nobis* cases, internment camp survivors who pressed their cause, and Japanese-American and Asian-American organizations that engaged in grass-roots organizing and lobbying. *See generally* Yamamoto at 311–12; Daniels at 136. Beyond the apologies and financial compensation, of course, there was also an important educational benefit from all of these efforts.

Notes

1. Do you think the judicial ruling, the apologies, and restitution payments were sufficient redress? How much did they help in terms of the healing process?

2. In 1983, 19 individuals—internment camp survivors or descendants of internees—brought a class action against the United States for damages based on the internment of Japanese Americans during World War II. The case was plagued by procedural problems, and in the end the district court's dismissal of the complaint on statute of limitations grounds was upheld. *Hohri v. United States*, 586 F. Supp. 769 (D.D.C. 1984), *aff'd*, 847 F.2d 779 (Fed. Cir.) (*per curiam*), *cert. denied*, 488 U.S. 925 (1988). *See generally* Daniels at 186–88.

3. Did the Japanese American redress efforts have an impact on others? Specifically, what about advocates of reparations to African Americans descended from enslaved persons? Should they be entitled to reparations, too? If not, how is their situation different?

4. There was another effort at reparations that arose out of World War II—involving Filipino war veterans. In July 1941, with the imminent threat of war with Japan, President Franklin D. Roosevelt issued a presidential order calling the Philippine Commonwealth Army into the service of the Armed Forces of the United States. *See Philippine Army and Guerilla Records*, National Archives (April 2020), *available at* https://www.archives.gov/personnel-records-center/military-personnel/philippine-army-records. The Philippines was a U.S. commonwealth at the time, and Filipinos were U.S. nationals. Many tens of thousands of Filipinos were brought into the military service of the United States. "During the Japanese invasion, Philippine soldiers fought bravely alongside other members of [the U.S. Armed Forces in the Far East]. Both Americans and Filipinos suffered the terrible Bataan death march; indeed, Philippine soldiers endured particularly cruel treatment from the Japanese." *Quiban v. Veterans Administration*, 928 F.2d 1154, 1157 (D.C. Cir. 1991) (Ginsburg, *J.*).

5. The Filipinos who served believed that they were entitled to—and indeed that they had been promised—veterans benefits. *See* Emil Guillermo, *Forgotten: The Battle Thousands of WWII Veterans Are Still Fighting*, NBC News (Feb. 18, 2016), *available at* https://www.nbcnews.com/news/asian-america/forgotten-battle-thousands-wwii-veterans-are-still-fighting-n520456; Josh Levs, *U.S. to Pay 'Forgotten' Filipino World War II Veterans*, CNN (Feb. 23, 2009), *available at* http://www.cnn.com/2009/US/02/23/forgotten.veterans/index.html. After the war ended, however, President Truman signed into law the Rescission Act of 1946—it provided for the payment of $200 million to the Philippine Commonwealth Army, but it took away many veterans benefits from the Filipinos who had served. *See*

38 U.S.C. § 107.[1] The effect of the statute was "first, to make former members of the Philippine Army and guerilla forces (and their dependents) ineligible for all non-service-connected United States veterans benefits, and second, to reduce by 50 percent the service-connected benefits that they may receive." *Quiban*, 928 F.2d at 1158; *see also Besinga v. United States*, 14 F.3d 1356, 1359 (9th Cir.), *cert. denied*, 513 U.S. 864 (1994).

6. Several cases were brought challenging the constitutionality of the Rescission Act. The D.C. and Ninth Circuits rejected the argument that the statute was subject to strict scrutiny and concluded in addition that a rational basis existed for treating Filipino veterans differently from other American veterans. *Quiban*, 928 F.2d at 1158; *Besinga*, 14 F.3d at 1359. *See also Recinto v. U.S. Dep't of Veterans Affairs*, 706 F.3d 1171 (9th Cir.), *cert. denied*, 571 U.S. 820 (2013). Given that the statute applied only to Filipino veterans, why would the courts *not* apply strict scrutiny? And what rational bases could there have been for treating Filipino veterans differently from other U.S. veterans?

7. In 2009, President Barack Obama signed into law the Filipino Veterans Equity Compensation Act. In an effort to make some amends, the law provided for a one-time lump sum payment of $15,000 for qualified Filipino veterans who lived in the United States and $9,000 for those who lived in the Philippines. *See* Guillermon, *supra*; Levs, *supra*. Many Filipino veterans, however, have had their claims for the lump sum payment denied because of insufficient or nonexistent recordkeeping (many had fought as guerillas under pseudonyms). *See* Emil Guillermo, *Thousands of Filipino-American WWII Vets Make Appeals Over Equity Pay Denial*, NBC News (Nov. 11, 2015), *available at* https://www.nbcnews.com/news/asian-america/thousands-filipino-american-wwii-vets-make-appeals-over-equity-pay-n460151. *See also Dela Cruz v. Wilkie*, 931 F.3d 1143 (Fed. Cir. 2019) (appeal from denial of claim for lump-sum payment from Filipino Veterans Equity Compensation Fund, and holding that claimant had to be given "a meaningful opportunity to challenge his service record," where Veterans Administration determined he was not listed in Reconstructed Guerilla Roster). What can be done to help these individuals while they are still alive?

---

1. The statute provides: "Service before July 1, 1946, in the organized military forces of the Government of the Commonwealth of the Philippines, while such forces were in the service of the Armed Forces of the United States pursuant to the military order of the President dated July 26, 1941, including among such military forces organized guerrilla forces under commanders appointed, designated, or subsequently recognized by the Commander in Chief, Southwest Pacific Area, or other competent authority in the Army of the United States, shall not be deemed to have been active military, naval, or air service for the purposes of any law of the United States conferring rights, privileges, or benefits upon any person by reason of the service of such person or the service of any other person in the Armed Forces, except [certain specified, service-related benefits reduced by 50%]."

The Japanese American internment cases continue to reverberate today. The cases were again raised after the 9/11 attacks, particularly with respect to the issue of profiling and the "War on Terrorism." The lawfulness and wisdom of Japanese internment became an issue again in recent political campaigns. And, of course, the issues surfaced once again with respect to President Trump's Travel Ban.

Even before the travel ban decision, *Korematsu* had largely been recognized as having been "thoroughly discredited," although it was generally considered, until the recent decision, as remaining "good law" as it had never been formally overruled. *See* Adam Liptak, *A Discredited Supreme Court Ruling That Still, Technically, Stands*, N.Y. Times, Jan. 27, 2014. Before the travel ban decision, and even as recently as a few years ago, including during the election campaigns, some individuals continued to cite *Korematsu* as support for certain proposals or actions.[2] The Supreme Court may have technically overruled *Korematsu* in the travel ban decision, but, as some have suggested, it may have revived it at the same time. To what extent—if at all—can a person's personal liberty or other rights be restricted on the basis of race, national origin, or religion when national security is at stake? Unfortunately, there may be other opportunities for the courts to consider the question.

2. *See, e.g.*, Margaret Hartmann, *Trump Supporter Cites Japanese Internment Camps As 'Precedent' for Muslim Registry*, N.Y. Mag., Nov. 17, 2016, http://nymag.com/daily/intelligencer/2016/11/trump-supporter-muslim-registry-internment-camps.html; Elie Mystal, *Korematsu Is Still Good Law, and Republicans Are Going to Use It*, Above The Law, http://abovethelaw.com/2016/11/korematsu-is-still-good-law-and-republicans-are-going-to-use-it; Matt Ford, *The Return of* Korematsu, The Atlantic, Nov. 19, 2015, www.theatlantic.com/politics/archive/2015/11/the-shadow-of-korematsu/416634.

UNIT FOUR

Contemporary Issues

We turn to contemporary issues involving Asian Americans. As we do so, the concepts and themes we discussed in the first three units provide important background and context. Some of the issues remain the same, but others have evolved.

We look first at "spies"—cases in which Asian Americans are accused of treason and espionage. In many of these cases, the accusations proved to be grossly exaggerated or outright false. Are Asian Americans being profiled? We then turn to employment and consider the question of discrimination against Asian Americans in the workplace. To a great extent, Asian Americans have prospered, but do they continue to face challenges? This takes us then to the notion of Asian Americans as the "Model Minority." Is the "Model Minority" just a stereotype or myth? And if so, what does that mean? Next, we consider education. In Unit Two we examined *Tape v. Hurley* and *Gong Lum v. Rice*, and the early efforts by Asian Americans to go to "white" schools. Today, some would argue that there are a disproportionate number of Asian Americans at highly selective colleges and universities while others contend that Asian Americans are the victims of reverse discrimination who are being held to higher admission standards in the interest of diversity. We then turn to contemporary issues involving Asian Americans in the administration of justice. Progress has been made since the era when Chinese witnesses were not permitted to testify against a White—or Black—person, as we saw in Unit 2, but other challenges have arisen. Finally, we conclude by revisiting anti-Asian violence, which still persists today, more than a century after the riots of the late nineteenth century.

Chapter 10

Spies

For many years, Asian Americans have been accused of spying for foreign governments or stealing classified information or otherwise engaging in treasonous acts and presenting national security threats. These accusations continue to be made today.

In 2018, the U.S. Department of Justice launched the China Initiative—an effort to counter "Chinese national security threats"—in particular individuals believed to be spies for China in American research and industry. *See* U.S. Dep't of Justice, *Information About the Department of Justice's China Initiative and a Compilation of China-Related Prosecutions Since 2018* (Nov. 19, 2021), *available at* https://www.justice.gov/archives/nsd/information-about-department-justice-s-china-initiative-and-compilation-china-related. A number of Chinese-American academics and scientists were investigated and prosecuted.

In 2019, the Department of Justice indicted Feng (Franklin) Tao for failing to disclose contact with Chinese institutions on conflict-of-interest forms. While he was convicted by a jury on three counts of wire fraud and one count of making false statements, *see generally* Han Zhang, *An Uncertain Future for a Chinese Scientist Accused of Espionage*, New Yorker, April 13, 2022, the trial judge vacated the convictions on three of the four counts, *see United States v. Feng Tao*, 629 F. Supp. 3d 1083 (D. Kan. 2022). On appeal the Tenth Circuit reversed the conviction on the final count, concluding that the government had offered insufficient evidence to sustain the verdict and remanding for the district court to enter a judgment of acquittal, *United States v. Feng Tao*, 107 F.4th 1179 (10th Cir. 2024). In the end, Tao prevailed on all counts. *See also* Gideon Lewis-Kraus, *Dangerous Minds: The Government Hunted Chinese Spies on Campuses, Did It Go Too Far?*, New Yorker, at 43, Mar. 21, 2022 (examining the case in detail, prior to verdict, and discussing the government's efforts with respect to espionage and China).

In 2020, Anming Hu, a mechanical engineering professor at the University of Tennessee at Knoxville, was charged with fraud, including hiding his ties to a Chinese university. He was placed on house arrest for two years and was unable to work. When the case went to trial, the jury deadlocked and the court declared a mistrial. Thereafter, however, the court granted Hu's motion for a judgment of acquittal and acquitted him on all counts, concluding that there was "no evidence" that Hu had intended to deceive or defraud the government. *United States v. Anming Hu*, No. 20-CR-21-TAV, 2021 WL 41330515, at *19 (E.D. Tenn. Sept. 9, 2021); *see generally* Marianna Bacallao,

Two Years After the FBI Labeled Him a Spy, a Tennessee Professor Returns to the Classroom, wpln.org (April 7, 2022), *available at* https://wpln.org/post/two-years-after-the-fbi-labeled-him-a-spy-a-tennessee-professor-returns-to-the-classroom/.

On January 14, 2021, at 6:30 a.m., FBI agents arrested Gang Chen, a mechanical engineering professor at the Massachusetts Institute of Technology and a naturalized U.S. citizen. Prosecutors alleged that he had omitted affiliations with Chinese governmental institutions in grant applications to the U.S. Department of Energy in 2017. A year later, the charges were dropped after the Department of Energy advised the Justice Department that there was no basis for the charges.[1]

Even before the China Initiative, there were cases brought against Chinese academics and scientists that were eventually discontinued. In 2015, Xiaoxing Xi, a world renowned physicist at Temple University who had lived in the United States for 25 years as an American citizen, was arrested by the FBI and charged with stealing technology secrets for China. The charges were dropped a few months later, with no explanation from the government other than "additional information had come to its attention."[2] On October 20, 2014, Sherry Chen, a hydrologist with the National Weather Service in Ohio who had been naturalized as an American citizen in 1997, was arrested by the FBI and charged with using a stolen password to download information about the nation's dams and lying about meeting with Chinese officials. Five months later, the government dropped the charges, with no explanation other than the exercise of "prosecutorial discretion."[3] In 2013, Guoqing Cao and Shuyu Li, two scientists with Eli Lilly in Indianapolis who also were naturalized American citizens, were arrested by federal authorities and accused of stealing trade secrets and passing them on to a competitor drug company in China. A year later, the charges were dropped, "based on a variety of factors."[4]

For all these individuals, the charges had a devastating impact, even though they were eventually dismissed. As Dr. Chen of MIT told the *New York Times*: "You work hard, you have good output, you build a reputation.... The government gets what they want, right? But in the end, you're treated like a spy. That just breaks your heart. It breaks your confidence." Ellen Barry, *'In the End, You're Treated Like A Spy,' Says M.I.T. Scientist,* N.Y. Times, Jan. 24, 2022.

---

1. Ellen Barry and Katie Benner, *U.S. Drops Its Case Against M.I.T. Scientist Accused of Hiding China Links*, N.Y. Times, Jan. 20, 2022.

2. Caitlin McCabe et al., *A Year Later, Temple Professor Haunted by Spying Allegations*, Philly.com (May 16, 2016), *available at* www.philly.com/philly/ news/20160516_A_year_later_Temple_professor_haunted_by_spying_allegations.html. *See also* Mara Hvistendahl, *Spying Charges Against Chinese-American Scientists Spark Fears of a Witch Hunt*, Post Mag., May 5, 2018, *available at* scmp.com/magazines/post-magazine/long-reads/article/2144652/spying-charges-against-chinese-american.

3 Nicole Perlroth, *Accused of Spying for China, Until She Wasn't*, N.Y. Times, May 9, 2015.

4. Jeff Swiatek and Kristina Guerra, *Feds Dismiss Charges Against Former Eli Lilly Scientists Accused of Stealing Trade Secrets*, IndyStar, Dec. 5, 2014, *available at* http://www.indystar.com/story/news/crime/2014/12/05/feds-dismiss-charges-former-eli-lilly-scientists-accused-stealing-trade-secrets/19959235/.

In 2022, the Department of Justice discontinued the China Initiative. Critics of the initiative had complained that individuals of Chinese descent were unfairly targeted. The Department adopted a new strategy that would take a broader approach, aimed at countering espionage and cyberattacks from a broader range of countries.[5] Recently, however, certain members of Congress have called for the initiative to be reestablished. *See, e.g.*, Lindsay McKenzie, *House Pushes to Resurrect China Initiative*, aip.org (Sept. 18, 2024), *available at* https://ww2.aip.org/fyi/house-pushes-to-resurrect-china-initiative; Cheyanne M. Daniels, *Democrats Warn Against Potential Reactivation of Trump-Era China Initiative*, The Hill (Jan. 23, 2024), *available at* https://thehill.com/homenews/house/4424015-democrats-warn-trump-era-china-initiative/.

On the other hand, there have been some convictions. In 2017, Szuhsiung Ho, a naturalized U.S. citizen, pleaded guilty in Tennessee to violating the Atomic Energy Act by providing unlawful aid to China to help build nuclear reactors; he was sentenced to 24 months in prison.[6] In 2019 a former CIA officer, Jerry Chun Shing Lee, a naturalized U.S. citizen who was born in Hong Kong, was sentenced to 19 years in prison after pleading guilty to conspiring to deliver classified information to China. Evidence showed that he was paid $840,000 for his deeds.[7] And in the summer of 2024, Shujun Wang, a 76-year-old Chinese American who was supposedly working with members of the Chinese community in the United States opposed to the Chinese Communist Party, was convicted of spying on Chinese dissidents in Flushing, New York, and conveying information to the Ministry of State Security in China. *See* Yudhijit Bhattacharjee, *New York's Chinese Dissidents Thought He Was an Ally. He Was a Spy*, N.Y. Times Magazine, Jan. 10, 2025.

Suspicions of espionage and disloyalty, of course, arose long before the China Initiative and more recent cases. In 1999, Dr. Wen Ho Lee, a Taiwanese-born, naturalized American citizen and a scientist at the Los Alamos National Laboratory in New Mexico, was accused of being a spy who had given U.S. nuclear secrets to China. He was arrested and detained in harsh conditions. After 278 days in custody, he pleaded guilty to one felony count of mishandling national defense information. The 58 other counts were dismissed and he was released. The presiding judge criticized the "top decision-makers in the executive branch" for the government's handling of the case, saying: "They have embarrassed this entire nation and each of us who is a citizen of

---

5. Ellen Nakashima, *Justice Department Shutters China Initiative, Launches Broader Strategy to Counter Nation-State Threats*, Wash. Post, Feb. 23, 2022.

6. Carten Cordell, *Engineer Pleads Guilty to Conspiracy to Build Chinese Reactors*, Fed. Times, Jan. 9, 2017, *available at* http://www.federaltimes.com/articles/american-engineer-pleaded-guilty-to-20-year-conspiracy-to-build-chinese-reactors; Dep't of Justice, *U.S. Nuclear Engineer Sentenced to 24 Months in Prison for Violating Atomic Energy Act* (Aug. 31, 2017), https://www.justice.gov/opa/pr/us-nuclear-engineer-sentenced-24-months-prison-violating-atomic-energy-act.

7. Zach Montague, *Ex-CIA Officer Sentenced to 19 Years in Chinese Espionage Conspiracy Case*, N.Y. Times, Nov. 22, 2019; Scott Shane, *Arrested Former C.I.A. Officer Had Ties to Chinese Spies, Ex-Colleague Says*, N.Y. Times, Jan. 18, 2018.

it."[8] In 1949, Iva Ikuko Toguri D'Aquino was tried for treason in the United States District Court in San Francisco—as the infamous "Tokyo Rose."[9] We now take a closer look at the Iva Toguri and Wen Ho Lee cases.

1. The Tokyo Rose Case

Iva Toguri was born in Los Angeles, the daughter of Japanese immigrants. She was raised a Methodist, joined the Girl Scouts, played high school varsity tennis, and graduated from UCLA with a degree in zoology. She spoke no Japanese and did not like Japanese food. In July 1941, her parents sent her to Japan to care for her sick aunt. When Pearl Harbor was attacked and war broke out, she was stranded in Japan. She refused to renounce her American citizenship, but she had to find work to support herself. Her family in America was unable to help, because they had been sent to internment camps.

Toguri began working as a typist at Radio Tokyo, a Japanese government radio station. Because of her perfect English, she was pressed into service as a disk jockey. She was one of approximately 20 women employed by Japanese radio to broadcast shows to Allied servicemen in the Pacific. They would play American music and then read scripts that were supposed to taunt and tease the servicemen, asking them, for example, "Do you know where your wife is tonight?"

Although none of the women used the name "Tokyo Rose," servicemen created a sultry, seductive siren by that name. As the government would later acknowledge, "Tokyo Rose" was "strictly a G.I. invention." Toguri used the name "Orphan Ann" and appeared on a show called Zero Hour, participating until just two days before the Japanese surrendered in August 1945. Here is a typical opening of her show:

> Hello there, Enemies—how's tricks? This is Ann of Radio Tokyo, and we're just going to begin our regular program of music, news and the Zero Hour for our Friends—I mean our Enemies!—in Australia and the South Pacific. So be on your guard, and mind the children don't hear! All set? O.K. Here's the first blow to your morale—the Boston Pops playing "Strike Up the Band!"[10]

---

8. Bob Drogin, *Wen Ho Lee Freed; Judge Scolds U.S. Over Case Tactics*, L.A. Times, Sept. 14, 2000; Lowen Liu, *Just the Wrong Amount of American*, Slate, Sept. 11, 2016, http://www.slate.com/articles/news_and_politics/the_next_20/2016/09/the_case_of_scientist_wen_ho_lee_and_chinese_americans_under_suspicion_for.html.

9. *See generally* Frederic P. Close, *Tokyo Rose/An American Patriot: A Dual Biography* (2010); Rex B. Gunn, *They Called Her Tokyo Rose* (1977; 2d ed. 2008); Russell W. Howe, *The Hunt for Tokyo Rose* (2008).

10. *See* Hans Sherrer, *Iva Toguri Is Innocent!*, 28 Justice Denied 22 (Spring 2005), http://justicedenied.org/issue/issue_28/toguri_jd28.pdf.

She would then play the Boston Pops rendition of "Strike Up the Band." She read scripts written by two Allied prisoners of war, Major Charles Cousens, an Australian, and Captain Wallace Ince, an American, and followed their instructions, as they tried to write scripts that did not serve the purported purpose of undermining Allied morale. She also brought food, medicine, and blankets to Allied POWs.

After the war ended, there was a clamor in the media to bring "Tokyo Rose" to justice. Hundreds of journalists descended on Japan, intent on finding Tokyo Rose. Two reporters for *Cosmopolitan* magazine located Toguri, who still had been unable to return to the United States. They promised her $2,000 for an exclusive interview, and she represented to them that she was "the one and the original Tokyo Rose."

Figure 10.1 ***Correspondents interview "Tokyo Rose," Iva Toguri, American-born Japanese*** **(1945). National Archives.**

Toguri was eventually arrested in Tokyo for treason—for giving aid and comfort to the enemy through her performances on the radio show. She was imprisoned. She became a celebrity, and while in prison she was asked to—and did—autograph yen notes for her G.I. prison guards, signing "Iva Toguri—Tokyo Rose." She was released after a year, when the government determined it did not have enough evidence to prosecute her.

The public remained hungry, however, for a prosecution of "Tokyo Rose." The Department of Justice eventually succumbed to the pressure, and Toguri was arrested again. She was brought home to the United States to be prosecuted. Cousens and Ince, whose scripts she read, were never fully prosecuted. Cousens was charged in Australia, but the charges were dropped before trial for insufficient evidence. Ince was never charged and, indeed, was promoted to major.

Toguri's trial commenced in San Francisco in July 1949, and continued for two and a half months. She was convicted, and the conviction was affirmed by the Ninth Circuit. Here are excerpts from the Ninth Circuit's decision.

Toguri D'Aquino v. United States

192 F.2d 338 (9th Cir. 1951), *cert. denied*, 343 U.S. 935 (1952)

POPE, Circuit Judge

Appellant was convicted of treason against the United States. The indictment charged that she adhered to the enemies of the United States giving them aid and comfort by working as a radio speaker, announcer, script writer and broadcaster for the Imperial Japanese Government and the Broadcasting Corporation of Japan, between November 1, 1943, and August 13, 1945; that such activities were in connection with the broadcasting of programs specially beamed and directed to the American Armed Forces in the Pacific Ocean area; and, that appellant's activities were intended to destroy the confidence of the members of the Armed Forces of the United States and their allies in the war effort, to undermine and lower American and Allied military morale, to create nostalgia in their minds, to create war weariness among the members of such armed forces, to discourage them, and to impair the capacity of the United States to wage war against its enemies. The indictment alleged the commission of eight overt acts. Appellant was found guilty of the commission of overt act No. 6 only, which in the language of the indictment, was: 'That on a day during October, 1944, the exact date being to the Grand Jurors unknown, said defendant, at Tokyo, Japan, in a broadcasting studio of the Broadcasting Corporation of Japan, did speak into a microphone concerning the loss of ships.'

Upon this appeal counsel for appellant have filed briefs asserting the commission of numerous errors on the part of the trial court....

5. Question of the sufficiency of the evidence.

Appellant argues that we should direct a judgment of acquittal on the ground that the evidence was insufficient to sustain a conviction. With respect to this, the record discloses that at the time of the commission of overt act No. 6, of which appellant was found guilty, she was unquestionably a citizen of the United States. She was born and educated in the United States and a few months prior to the outbreak of the war with Japan she had gone to Japan for the purpose of studying medicine. Previously she had received a college degree and had taken postgraduate work in a California university. Shortly before the outbreak of the war she applied for a passport to return to the United States and was advised by the State Department that the passport was denied on the ground that her citizenship was not proven (she had traveled to Japan upon a 'certificate of identification'). She endeavored to get clearance to board a ship scheduled to sail for the United States on December 2, 1941, but was unsuccessful. Early in 1942 she applied for evacuation through the Swiss Legation but encountering difficulties in procuring certification of her United States citizenship she abandoned this attempt. Thereafter, and throughout her period of residence in Japan and while the war continued, she was frequently invited to become a Japanese citizen but steadfastly refused. In the spring of 1945 she married D'Aquino, a Portuguese citizen. The marriage was subsequent to the date of the commission of the overt act No. 6.

After having been employed in various jobs in 1942 and in the early part of 1943, appellant sought employment at Radio Tokyo and began her work as a typist for the Broadcasting Corporation of Japan in the fall of 1943. Shortly thereafter she began her broadcast work for this corporation which was under the control of the Japanese Government. There is evidence in the record that when the appellant took her voice test and accepted employment as an announcer and broadcaster for Radio Tokyo she knew that her work was to be concerned with a program known as 'Zero Hour' which was to be beamed and directed specially to Allied soldiers in the Pacific. She was told and understood that the program would consist of music and entertainment designed to procure a listening audience among Allied soldiers, and that there was to be interspersed news and commentaries containing propaganda which was to be used as an instrument of psychological warfare. Their object was to cause the Allied troops to become homesick, tired and disgusted with the war.

Appellant participated in some 340 programs on the Zero Hour. She announced herself as 'Ann' or 'Orphan Ann'. From time to time she attended meetings of the participants in the Zero Hour program where the Japanese Army officers in command of the enterprise advised the persons present of the strategic importance of the program and urged continued efforts by the participants.

The overt act No. 6 was testified to by the requisite number of witnesses who observed and listened to the broadcast in question. One of them was a participant in the same Zero Hour program. He told the appellant of a release from Japanese General Headquarters giving the American ship losses in one of the Leyte Gulf battles and requested appellant to allude to those losses. She proceeded, as this witness and another testified, to type a script about the loss of ships. That evening, when appellant was present in the studio, the news announcer broadcast that the Americans had lost many ships in the battle of Leyte Gulf. Thereupon appellant was introduced on the radio and proceeded to say in substance: 'Now you fellows have lost all your ships. You really are orphans of the Pacific. Now how do you think you will ever get home?'

It is true that the appellant's version of her role as a broadcaster was substantially different from that which we have here summarized from the testimony of the Government witnesses. According to appellant's version of the matter, the programs were exclusively entertainment and for that purpose only, she having been informed by the officer in command that the time for propaganda would not arrive until the Japanese were having more military and naval successes. Some of appellant's witnesses testified that they were responsible for having her brought into the Zero Hour program. These persons were American prisoners of war who testified that they had been coerced into participation in this program. They testified that what they were up to was a sabotaging of the program insofar as it was designed to be propaganda to American soldiers, that they managed to inject in the program many reports of American prisoners of war and messages from them, and the appellant co-operated with them in their efforts to frustrate the purposes of the Japanese military operating through the broadcasting corporation to destroy the morale of the American soldiers.

Whether appellant's version of her activities in broadcasting should be accepted rather than that disclosed by the Government witnesses was, of course, a question for the jury. Insofar as it is contended that the program was merely one to entertain the American troops, such a version of the evidence would, we have no doubt, tax the credulity of a jury who would be hard put to imagine the Japanese military spending time and money solely for that purpose.

Appellant's counsel do not argue that we must accept her version of the testimony. They make the rather narrow point that other activities of the appellant, concerning which witnesses on both sides testified, were such as to require a conclusion that there existed reasonable doubt of appellant's intention to adhere to the enemy and reasonable doubt of her treasonable intent.

These activities were certain acts of kindness and assistance which appellant tendered to Allied prisoners of war, some of whom were working with her on Radio Tokyo, and some of whom were imprisoned at Camp Bunka. The testimony was that she brought food, cigarettes, medicine, a blanket and short wave news of Allied successes to these prisoners, and that she did this frequently at substantial risk to herself.

We are unable to perceive the force of appellant's argument in this respect. A general treasonable intent to betray the United States through the impairing of its war effort in the Pacific, might well accompany a particular feeling of compassion toward individual prisoners and sympathy for the plight in which they found themselves. If it were psychologically impossible for a person engaged in a treasonable enterprise simultaneously to furnish cigarettes and food to individual prisoners, appellant's argument upon this point might have some weight. We think that the question of the effect of these acts of kindness upon appellant's intent was one for the jury. Certainly, under the circumstances here, the court cannot declare that there must be a reasonable doubt in a reasonable mind and hence direct a verdict. The question of the existence of a reasonable doubt was for the jury....

9. Questions relating to duress.

Appellant asserts that the trial court committed numerous errors relating to the claimed defense of duress or coercion. She argues that some of the instructions given upon this subject were erroneous; that other instructions requested by her should have been given, and that the court erred in excluding numerous items of evidence which were offered in support of this defense. The court instructed the jury at length upon the defense that the criminal act was not committed voluntarily but was the result of coercion, compulsion or necessity. The instruction included the statement that 'in order to excuse a criminal act on the ground of coercion, compulsion or necessity, one must have acted under the apprehension of immediate and impending death or of serious and immediate bodily harm. Fear of injury to one's property or remote bodily harm do not excuse an offense.' It will be noted that the court's instruction was almost identical to that approved in Gillars v. United States, supra, 182 F.2d at page 976 ....

Appellant seriously contends that however correct the instruction might be in an ordinary case where a person accused of crime committed in his own country claims to have been coerced by an individual, the instruction of the court was in error particularly in its requirement of apprehension of immediate and impending death, or of immediate bodily harm, in a case where the accused person was in an enemy country, unable to get protection from the United States and where the compulsion is on the part of the enemy government itself. The contention is that under these circumstances the requirement of 'immediacy' in the court's instructions was error. Appellant makes her point by quoting from East's Pleas of the Crown (1806, pages 70 to 71), as follows: 'But if the joining with rebels be from fear of present death, and while the party is under actual force, such fear and compulsion will excuse him. It is incumbent, however, on the party setting up this defense to give satisfactory proof that the compulsion continued during all the time that he stayed with the rebels. It may perhaps be impossible to account for every day, week, or month; and therefore it may be sufficient to excuse him if he can prove an original force upon him, that he in earnest attempted to escape and was prevented, or that he was so narrowly watched, or the passes so guarded, that an attempt to escape or to refuse his assistance would have been attended with great difficulty and danger; and if the circumstances will admit of it, that he quitted the service as soon as he could: so that upon the whole he may fairly be presumed to have continued amongst them against his will, though not constantly under an actual force or fear of immediate death.'

However appropriate such quoted language might be in the case of a person impressed into military or naval service of the enemy, we think that under the circumstances here there was no occasion for departing from the ordinary rules applicable to the defense of duress and coercion. We know of no rule that would permit one who is under the protection of an enemy to claim immunity from prosecution for treason merely by setting up a claim of mental fear of possible future action on the part of the enemy. We think that the citizen owing allegiance to the United States must manifest a determination to resist commands and orders until such time as he is faced with the alternative of immediate injury or death. Were any other rule to be applied, traitors in the enemy country would by that fact alone be shielded from any requirement of resistance. The person claiming the defense of coercion and duress must be a person whose resistance has brought him to the last ditch....

When appellant began her work on the Zero Hour at Radio Tokyo, she came in contact with three prisoners of war who had broadcasted at this station for a considerable period of time before she was employed there. These were a Major Cousens, an Australian prisoner; Captain Ince, an American prisoner; and Lieutenant Reyes, a Filipino prisoner. Appellant was permitted to testify as to accounts which were given her by these prisoners of war of the manner in which the Japanese military had compelled each of them to participate in broadcasting activities and she was permitted to relate their stories to her of their harrowing experiences at the hands of the Japanese from the time they were taken prisoners. This included their accounts of torture and murder of other prisoners of war at Singapore, at Manila, and at Camp Bunka in Japan, where the prisoners whom the Japanese were using for broadcasting were kept. She testified that Cousens informed her that the Japanese were brutal and uncivilized; that they were sly and cunning and never to be trusted. Similarly, Cousens, Ince and Reyes were permitted to testify as to atrocities practiced on the prisoners of war and which they themselves related to appellant. Thus Cousens in telling appellant how he came to broadcast on the Radio Tokyo gave her an account of how the men were being starved, beaten and tortured; how an Australian prisoner had been beaten to death with a club for stealing a can of onions and a Chinese prisoner had been beaten and put to death with the water torture because he went mad with hunger and tried to seize some food. Cousens related his experience in solitary confinement, his observation of Japanese guards murdering prisoners in cold blood for trying to seize food, and how the Japanese officers told the prisoners that the punishment for disobedience would be death.

Ince and Reyes testified to telling the appellant about being compelled to broadcast for Radio Tokyo because of threats against their lives. Reyes gave accounts of the beating to death at Manila of two of his co-workers in the Manila underground radio; he told of observing Japanese soldiers at Manila bayoneting civilians for hiding food, machine gunning civilians, and of seeing Major Ince beaten.

Ince testified as to atrocities committed against the prisoners confined at Camp Bunka. In addition, the appellant was permitted to testify as to police surveillance of herself and of the suspicion with which she was regarded by other Japanese in the neighborhood where she resided. At the time this evidence was received, the court clearly indicated the theory upon which it was permitted to go in. The trial judge considered that such testimony was relevant as bearing upon the state of mind of the appellant. It is clear that the court considered and made it apparent to counsel and to the jury when the evidence was received that it had to do with the general question of whether the appellant had reasonable ground for apprehension of danger when she participated in the broadcast.

It is our view that after the court had thus received at the instance of appellant this large volume of testimony none of which disclosed any direct duress or coercion against the appellant but which was relevant only as bearing upon the question of reasonable ground for apprehension on the part of appellant, it was proper for the court to give the instruction of which complaint is made. As we understand appellant's objection to it, it is not seriously urged that this portion of the instruction did not correctly state the law, but it is contended that it had the effect of leading the jury to disregard this evidence and of preventing it from considering its cumulative effect upon the mind of the appellant. It is suggested that the primary vice in the instruction is that it 'did not tell the jury anything about the cumulative effect of the above elements or of all the elements on coercion.' It is objected that the instruction was one-sided in telling the jury that each of certain items of evidence would be insufficient without mentioning the cumulative effect of a combination of all this evidence.

It is true that the court might have told the jury about the possible cumulative effect of all this atrocity evidence. It is clear that such a comment by the court would have been a comment upon the evidence which a federal court might properly make. Yet to hold that prejudicial error resulted from a failure to make such a comment would, we think, require an improper assumption of a degree of ignorance on the part of the jury with which we think the jury cannot properly be charged. We think that the record on the whole discloses that the jury was not misled as to the significance of the atrocity evidence received and that it must have understood that the evidence was received because of its bearing upon the question submitted in the instructions as to whether the coercion or compulsion was 'of such a nature as to induce a well grounded apprehension of death or serious bodily injury if the act is not done.'...

Since we find no prejudicial error in the record the judgment is affirmed.

Notes

1. Toguri was sentenced to 10 years' imprisonment and a $10,000 fine (the equivalent of more than $132,000 today), and she was stripped of her U.S. citizenship. What do you think of the sentence?

2. Toguri read scripts written by and followed the instructions of Major Cousens and Captain Ince. Yet she was prosecuted for treason and they were not. (Cousens was initially charged in Australia but the charges were dropped.) Was this fair? Was there a legitimate distinction for these purposes? Or was a double standard applied?

3. What did Toguri argue was her real purpose in reading the scripts? What did the Ninth Circuit think of this argument?

4. Toguri presented substantial evidence at trial that she provided food, medicine, and blankets to Allied POWs, sometimes at risk to herself. She also argued that she had no choice but to do as the Japanese government demanded. What did the Ninth Circuit think of these arguments?

5. Toguri was released from prison in January 1956, after serving six years and four months, because she had accumulated enough good time credit to warrant early

release. She had been a model prisoner. She learned to take x-rays, prescribe glasses, and draw blood, and she even scrubbed up and assisted in surgery. She became a pharmacist's assistant and volunteered in the dental clinic. In her spare time she made leather goods that won her ribbons at local county fairs. When she left prison, it took four people to replace her in all her jobs.

6. In the 1970s, long after Toguri had finished serving her sentence, public opinion tilted back in her favor, in part because two critical witnesses against her, Kenkichi Oki and George Mitsushio, publicly admitted that they had committed perjury at her trial. Both asserted that they had been pressured by the U.S. government into lying and that in fact they had not actually witnessed Toguri uttering her alleged treasonous statements.. On January 19, 1977, President Gerald Ford granted Toguri executive clemency. She became the only American ever to be pardoned for treason. The pardon was certainly some recognition, many years after the fact, that Toguri had been unfairly treated. What role, if any, do you think racial bias and public pressure played in her treatment?

7. A second Nisei was convicted of treason for collaborating with the Japanese during World War II. Tomoya Kawakita was born in California but traveled to Japan in 1939—when he was 18—to visit his grandfather. He was stranded in Japan after war broke out. He eventually found employment as an interpreter at a metal processing plant in Oeyama that used Allied prisoners of war as laborers. When the war ended, he renewed his U.S. passport and was able to return to California, where he enrolled as a student at the University of Southern California. A former POW, however, recognized him at a Sears Roebuck department store—he was arrested, indicted, and prosecuted for treason, including for purportedly mistreating American POWs at the plant in Oeyama. He argued that he could not be guilty of treason because he had renounced his U.S. citizenship while in Japan. The jury rejected the defense; he was convicted and sentenced to death. *See generally* Naoko Shibusawa, *Tomoya Kawakita*, Densho Encyclopedia (2020), encyclopedia.densho.org/Tomoya_Kawakita/; *Kawakita v. United States*, 343 U.S. 717 (1952). The Supreme Court affirmed the conviction and death sentence. The death sentence, however, was later commuted to life in prison. In 1963, President Kennedy paroled him, and he was deported to Japan.

8. In 1955, the Immigration and Naturalization Service ("INS") brought deportation proceedings against a Korean immigrant named Diamond Kimm, after he had been in this country some 27 years. During the proceedings, a hearing examiner asked Kimm whether he was a member of the Communist Party; Kimm refused to answer, citing, *inter alia*, his Fifth Amendment right against self-incrimination. INS never introduced any evidence substantiating any ties between Kimm and the Communist Party, but based on Kimm's refusal to answer the question regarding Communist Party membership, INS decided to deport him. In *Kimm v. Rosenberg*, the Supreme Court upheld the deportation order, with the dissenting justices criticizing the majority for penalizing Kimm for invoking his Fifth Amendment right

against self-incrimination. 363 U.S. 405 (1960). *See generally* Cathi Choi, *Patriotism, Rebuffed*, 24 U.C.L.A. Asian Pacific Am. L. J. 17 (2020).

9. Tsien Hsue-Shen (or Qian Xuesen) left China to study mechanical engineering at MIT on a scholarship in August 1935. In 1936, he moved to the California Institute of Technology to study under Theodore von Karman, a noted aeronautical engineer. Tsien was made a temporary U.S. Army colonel and given security clearance so that he could work on classified weapons research. He became a leading expert on jet propulsion. As the Communists gained control in China, Tsien made the decision to apply for U.S. citizenship in 1949. By then, he had accepted directorship of a new center of jet propulsion research at Caltech, his wife was pregnant with their second child, and he had plans to consult for NASA's Jet Propulsion Lab and for Aerojet Corporation. In 1950, however, the FBI began investigating Tsien, claiming that several people he had befriended at Caltech in the 1930s were Communists. Although no concrete evidence ever emerged to show that he was a Communist, he was arrested by immigration authorities in September 1950 and held for two weeks at a federal prison before his colleagues at Caltech were able to arrange his bail. The government was determined to deport him, and after five years of house arrest and many hearings, he and his family left the United States and moved to China, where he received a hero's welcome.

   Tsien thereafter helped develop the Chinese rocket science program, training scientists, overseeing the launch of the first Chinese satellite into space in 1970, and helping establish China's Lunar Exploration Program. The missile program he helped develop resulted in weapons that included the silkworm missiles used against Americans in the 1991 Gulf War and in 2016 against the U.S.S. Mason, a U.S. Navy destroyer, in the Red Sea by Yemen-based Houthi rebels. Tsien died in Beijing in 2009 at the age of 98. He never returned to the United States. *See generally* BBC, *Qian Xuesen: The Man the US Deported—Who Then Helped China Into Space*, BBC News (Oct. 27, 2020), https://www.bbc.com/news/stories-54695598; Iris Chang, *Thread of the Silkworm* (1995).

2. *United States v. Wen Ho Lee*

On March 6, 1999, the *New York Times* published a front-page "special report" under the headline: "BREACH AT LOS ALAMOS: China Stole Nuclear Secrets for Bombs, U.S. Aides Say." The article reported that government sources disclosed that "American nuclear secrets" had been stolen from the Los Alamos National Laboratory in New Mexico. The article noted that "[a]t the dawn of the atomic age, a Soviet spy ring that included Julius Rosenberg had stolen the first nuclear secrets out of Los Alamos. Now, at the end of the cold war, the Chinese seemed to have succeeded in penetrating the same weapons lab." It quoted the CIA's "chief spy hunter," Paul Redmond, as saying: "This is going to be just as bad as the Rosenbergs."[11]

The article referred to a suspect, a computer scientist working in the nuclear weapons area at Los Alamos, but did not identify him by name. The description, however, fit Dr. Wen Ho Lee, and two days after the article appeared he was fired. *See* Wen Ho Lee, *My Country Versus Me* 83 (2001). The *Times* published another article a few days later about "possible espionage" at Los Alamos, identifying "a Taiwan-born American citizen, Wen Ho Lee, who was accused of security breaches and fired from his job as a computer scientist at Los Alamos." The article quoted unnamed American officials as saying Lee was "the prime suspect in the transfer of information."[12] Other articles naming Lee followed.[13]

On December 10, 1999, the FBI arrested Lee. The 45-page indictment charged him with 59 counts of violating the Atomic Energy Act and the Federal Espionage Act; most of the counts carried a maximum sentence of life imprisonment. Lee, at 201–05. Lee was remanded. He would later describe the conditions as follows:

> For my first month in detention, I wasn't allowed out of my cell except once a day, Monday through Friday, to walk 15 feet down the hall from my cell to take a shower. On weekends, I couldn't even do that. I had no idea whether it was night or day. I didn't see the sun or moon for more than a month, except for those few days in December for my detention hearings. A light stayed on in my cell at all times, even when I tried to sleep. One hour per week, I could see my family during their visiting hour—with two FBI agents standing right by us, listening to every word. Once, when Alberta [my daughter] was telling me about something new in her job, the FBI agents made her stop, just because she was talking about computers. I was also allowed out of my cell when lawyers visited, once or twice a week, to meet with them. Otherwise I stayed in my cell for 24 hours, as there was no outdoor exercise time for me during that first month. No books, no newspapers, no television, no radio, no paper, no pens, no hot water, no contact with anyone except under very restrictive conditions....
>
> I thought I was being treated like every prisoner—shackled and chained, with a 24-hour personal watch guard jotting down my every move, whether I was awake or asleep, when I showered, when I used the toilet. The guards, at least, got a break from the routine; they changed shifts every eight hours. For me, there was no letup in this degrading treatment....
>
> Not knowing my rights as an American to be free from "cruel or unusual" punishment, I accepted my treatment without question. I didn't know to

11. James Risen and Jeff Gerth, *BREACH AT LOS ALAMOS: China Stole Nuclear Secrets for Bombs, U.S. Aides Say*, N.Y. Times, Mar. 6, 1999.

12. Sandra Blakeslee, *Los Angeles Case Raises Fears of Science as Sieve*, N.Y. Times, Mar. 12, 1999.

13. *See, e.g.*, James Risen, *F.B.I. Interviews Chinese Man in Spy Case*, N.Y. Times, Mar. 27, 1999.

> complain that I was constantly cold, shivering most of the time because all I had was the red jumpsuit, undershorts, and two thin blankets. My beard grew scruffy and my fingernails became long because I didn't have a razor or nail clippers. I asked the warden if he could help me. He eventually gave me some rusty, used nail clippers. When I asked him if there was some additional clothing I could have because of the cold jail temperature, he brought in an old, beat-up pair of sweatpants—I can't imagine where he found these discarded items to give me. I tore the sweatpants so that I could put my arms through the pants legs and wear it like a jacket. It wasn't until I was later moved next to another prisoner's cell that I learned I could simply buy what I needed from the jail commissary. The FBI must have instructed Warden Romero and the guards not to give me any information or anything that would improve my dismal conditions. They wanted me to be as miserable as possible.

Id. at 245–46.

Eventually, however, it became apparent that the government had exaggerated the need to keep Lee detained. The parties commenced plea negotiations. In September 2000, they struck a deal: Lee would plead guilty to one count of mishandling information, and the government would drop the remaining 58 counts. Lee explained his decision:

> I wasn't happy about pleading guilty to the one count. I felt that I had not committed a criminal offense, and no one else who had violated security rules was ever treated this way. I was willing to stay in jail to fight it out. On the other hand, the legal costs were enormous, and my imprisonment was so hard on my family. They were suffering. When the prosecutors offered to make a plea bargain, [my lawyers] told me this: "There is a ninety-five percent chance that we will win this case if it goes to trial, but a five percent chance that we could lose. If we lose, you could face life in prison. Are you willing to take that risk?"
>
> I gave my answer: No, it was not worth the risk of spending the rest of my life in prison....

Id. at 311–12.

On September 13, 2000, Lee pleaded guilty to the one count and the remaining counts were dismissed. The court then sentenced Lee to 278 days' imprisonment—the precise number of days he had already served, which meant that he was free to go home. *Id.* at 314–16. After imposing sentence, Judge James A. Parker made the following statement:

> Dr. Lee, you have pled guilty to a serious crime. It's a felony offense. For that you deserved to be punished. In my opinion, you have been punished harshly, both by the severe conditions of pretrial confinement and by the fact that you have lost valuable rights as a citizen....

Figure 10.2 ***Dr. Wen Ho Lee with Helen Zia.*** **Photo by Corky Lee. Courtesy of Corky Lee Estate.**

The executive branch of the United States government has until today actually, or just recently, vigorously opposed your release from jail, even under what I had previously described as draconian conditions of release.

During December 1999, the then-United States attorney, who has since resigned, and his assistants presented me, during the three-day hearing between Christmas and New Year's Day, with information that was so extreme it convinced me that releasing you, even under the most stringent of conditions, would be a danger to the safety of this nation. The then-United States attorney personally argued vehemently against your release and ultimately persuaded me not to release you.

In my opinion and order that was entered Dec. 30, 1999, I stated the following: "With a great deal of concern about the conditions under which Dr. Lee is presently being held in custody, which is in solitary confinement all but one hour of the week, when he is permitted to visit his family, the court finds, based on the record before it, that the government has shown by clear and convincing evidence that there is no combination of conditions of release that would reasonably assure the safety of any other person and the community or the nation."

After stating that in the opinion, I made this request in the opinion right at the end: "Although the court concludes that Dr. Lee must remain in custody, the court urges the government attorneys to explore ways to lessen the severe restrictions currently imposed upon Dr. Lee while preserving the security of sensitive information."

I was very disappointed that my request was not promptly heeded by the government attorneys.

After December, your lawyers developed information that was not available to you or them during December. And I ordered the executive branch of the government to provide additional information that I reviewed, a lot of which you and your attorneys have not seen.

With more complete, balanced information before me, I felt the picture had changed significantly from that painted by the government during the December hearing. Hence, after the August hearing, I ordered your release despite the continued argument by the executive branch, through its government attorneys, that your release still presented an unacceptable extreme danger.

I find it most perplexing, although appropriate, that the executive branch today has suddenly agreed to your release without any significant conditions or restrictions whatsoever on your activities. I note that this has occurred shortly before the executive branch was to have produced, for my review in camera, a large volume of information that I previously ordered it to produce....

What I believe remains unanswered is the question: What was the government's motive in insisting on your being jailed pretrial under extraordinarily onerous conditions of confinement until today, when the executive branch agrees that you may be set free essentially unrestricted? This makes no sense to me.

A corollary question I guess is: Why were you charged with the many Atomic Energy Act counts for which the penalty is life imprisonment, all of which the executive branch has now moved to dismiss and which I just dismissed?...

Dr. Lee, I tell you with great sadness that I feel I was led astray last December by the executive branch of our government through its Department of Justice, by its Federal Bureau of Investigation and by its United States attorney for the district of New Mexico, who held the office at that time.

I am sad for you and your family because of the way in which you were kept in custody while you were presumed under the law to be innocent of the charges the executive branch brought against you.

I am sad that I was induced in December to order your detention, since by the terms of the plea agreement that frees you today without conditions, it becomes clear that the executive branch now concedes, or should concede, that it was not necessary to confine you last December or at any time before your trial....

> . . . In fairness, I must note that virtually all of the lawyers who work for the Department of Justice are honest, honorable, dedicated people, who exemplify the best of those who represent our federal government. . . .
>
> It is only the top decision makers in the executive branch, especially the Department of Justice and the Department of Energy and locally, during December, who have caused embarrassment by the way this case began and was handled. They did not embarrass me alone. They have embarrassed our entire nation and each of us who is a citizen of it.
>
> I might say that I am also sad and troubled because I do not know the real reasons why the executive branch has done all of this. We will not learn why because the plea agreement shields the executive branch from disclosing a lot of information that it was under order to produce that might have supplied the answer.
>
> Although, as I indicated, I have no authority to speak on behalf of the executive branch, the president, the vice president, the attorney general, or the secretary of the Department of Energy, as a member of the third branch of the United States Government, the judiciary, the United States courts, I sincerely apologize to you, Dr. Lee, for the unfair manner you were held in custody by the executive branch.[14]

Notes

1. Judge Parker's statement was remarkable—an Article III judge apologized, publicly, for the "unfair manner" in which a defendant was treated by the executive branch. What prompted him to make the apology?

2. Judge Parker also stated that the executive branch had "embarrassed our entire nation and each of us who is a citizen of it." What did the government do that Judge Parker believed was so wrong? What was the government's motivation in treating Dr. Lee as it did?

3. On September 26, 2000, less than two weeks after the guilty plea and sentencing, the *New York Times* published a statement defending its coverage of the purported breach of security at Los Alamos, but adding that "looking back, we also found some things we wish we had done differently in the course of the coverage to give Dr. Lee the full benefit of the doubt. In those months, we could have pushed harder to uncover weaknesses in the F.B.I. case against Dr. Lee. . . . The article . . . had flaws

14. *Statement by Judge in Los Alamos Case, with Apology for Abuse of Power*, N.Y. Times, Sept. 14, 2000.

that are more apparent now that the weaknesses of the F.B.I. case against Dr. Lee have surfaced."[15] What impact did the media have in this case?

4. Lee brought an invasion of privacy lawsuit against the government, alleging that the government had violated privacy laws by telling reporters details of his employment history, finances, travels, and polygraph tests. In the course of the proceedings, five reporters were held in contempt for refusing to testify and reveal the identities of confidential sources. In a highly unusual settlement, the government agreed to a settlement of $1,645,000—with five news organizations contributing $750,000 to the settlement fund even though they had not been named parties in the lawsuit. The organizations included the *New York Times*, the *Los Angeles Times*, the *Washington Post*, the Associated Press, and ABC News; they contended that they made the payments to protect the confidential sources and reporters from further sanctions.[16] Does this explanation ring true? Why do you think the media agreed to these payments?

5. Asian Americans have been concerned about the treatment of Asian Americans throughout history as national security threats.[17] Why have there been so many "spying" cases against Asian Americans that have fallen flat? Is this the result of racial profiling? Or the result of lingering concerns about the "Yellow Peril?" How does this fit in with the historical treatment of Asian Americans?

3. Asians in the U.S. Military and the MAVNI Litigation

Foreigners have served with distinction in the armed forces of the United States since the War of Independence when the Marquis de Lafayette was a key aide to George Washington. For many foreigners, service in the United States military has

15. *See* James Risen and Jeff Gerth, *BREACH AT LOS ALAMOS: China Stole Nuclear Secrets for Bombs, U.S. Aides Say*, N.Y. Times, Mar. 6, 1999 (editors' note dated Sept. 26, 2000).

16. *See* Adam Liptak, *News Media Pay in Scientist Suit*, N.Y. Times, June 3, 2006.

17. *Scientists Not Spies: Panel on Asian American Immigrants Brings Historic Perspective on Racial Profiling*, New Am. Media (Aug. 10, 2016), http://newamericamedia.org/trending/2016/08/scientists-not-spies-panel-on-asian-american-immigrants-brings-historic-perspective-on-racial-profil.php; Emily Conover, *Lawmakers Condemn Targeting of Chinese-American Scientists*, APS News (Nov. 18, 2015), www.aps.org/publications/apsnews/updates/chinese-america.cfm; Avi Asher-Schapiro, *Why Does the FBI Keep Arresting Asian-American Scientists?*, Vice News (Nov. 19, 2015), news.vice.com/article/why-does-the-fbi-keep-arresting-asian-american-scientists; Andrew Chongseh Kim, *Prosecuting Chinese "Spies": An Empirical Analysis of the Economic Espionage Act*, 40 Cardozo L. Rev. 749 (2018).

promised an expedited path to U.S. citizenship. Those serving have included many Asians such as Bhagat Singh Thind and thousands who enlisted in the U.S. Navy in the twentieth century under special programs for natives of the Philippines. Additionally, as we have seen, many U.S. citizens of Japanese descent, including Senator Daniel Inouye and other Japanese-American members of the U.S. Army's storied 442nd Regimental Combat Team, served heroically in combat even though their families were interned during the Second World War.

The U.S. armed forces have benefited greatly from recruiting persons with foreign connections or origins. First, military service members with familiarity in foreign languages and cultures may provide essential support to military operations against adversaries who share those languages and cultures. Second, and more generally, the all-volunteer U.S. armed forces often face shortages in recruitment, particularly for less-desirable specialties and ratings for enlisted service members. As with other demanding, low-paying, manual jobs in the U.S. economy, there are many foreign workers willing to fill these positions, particularly with the incentive of accelerated naturalization as U.S. citizens after a couple of years of good-conduct service.

The relevant federal statute, 10 U.S.C. § 504(b)(1), generally provides that a person seeking to enlist in the armed forces must be a U.S. citizen or legal permanent resident ("LPR"). The statute also provides, however, that the Secretary of Defense and the Secretaries of the Military Departments (Army, Navy, Air Force) have authority to enlist a non-citizen/LPR who possesses "a critical skill or expertise" that is "vital to the national interest" and will use that skill or expertise in the person's "primary daily duties" as a member of the U.S. armed forces. 10 U.S.C. § 504(b)(2). The specifications of "a critical skill or expertise" as part of "primary daily duties" are more recent additions to this statute. In 2008, the statute simply authorized the Secretaries to accept military accessions "vital to the national interest" ("MAVNI").

Invoking the prior version of this statute, the Secretary of Defense launched the MAVNI pilot program in 2008, authorizing the U.S. armed forces to enlist two categories of non-citizen, non-LPR recruits deemed "vital to the national interest": (1) healthcare professionals and (2) persons with critical foreign language skills and cultural knowledge in one of 44 designated languages, including Arabic, Chinese, Korean, Persian, and Urdu. All MAVNI recruits were required to have been lawfully present in the United States for at least two years immediately prior to their enlistment date, with no absence from the United States of more than 90 days during that period. The MAVNI pilot program was scheduled to expire in December 2009, but the Defense Department reauthorized it several times, most recently in 2016. The MAVNI program was not reauthorized in September 2017. From its inception in 2008 until its end in 2017, the U.S. armed forces recruited more than 10,000 non-citizen, non-LPRs through the MAVNI program, the great majority of whom served in the Army, far more than the Department had anticipated when they set up the pilot program. This was due in part to the fact that the Army, to meet recruitment goals, accepted many new recruits who had qualifying healthcare or language skills but assigned them to other duties, before the two current statutory restrictions noted above were passed. The majority of MAVNI recruits were from countries in South or East Asia, with China being the largest single country of origin, although there were substantial numbers of MAVNI recruits from other parts of the world, such as Russia and other countries in eastern Europe.

Seventeen individuals who became U.S. citizens through the MAVNI program brought suit to challenge aspects of the program that subjected them to greater scrutiny.

Tiwari v. Mattis

363 F. Supp. 3d 1154 (W.D. Wash. 2019)

ZILLY, District Judge.

...

Plaintiffs are seventeen (17) United States citizens who are or were, at the time trial commenced, serving in the United States Army. They each enlisted through the Military Accessions Vital to the National Interest ("MAVNI") program, which was implemented in fiscal year ("FY") 2009 to address difficulties the DoD [Department of Defense] had experienced in recruiting individuals with either proficiency in critical foreign languages or specialized healthcare training. *See* Ex. 29 at 14 & 23-24; *see also* Ex. 33 at 17. When they joined the Army, plaintiffs were not United States citizens, but rather had the requisite legal status for the MAVNI program (*i.e.*, as an asylee, a refugee, a non-immigrant alien, or a grantee of temporary protected status). Each plaintiff was naturalized as a citizen, pursuant to 8 U.S.C. § 1440, after serving honorably for some period in the Army. *See* PTO at 4-10, ¶¶ 6-22 (docket no. 179).

The parties agree that plaintiffs are currently being treated differently from other citizens in two ways: (i) plaintiffs are subject to "continuous monitoring," which requires *inter alia* a series of National Intelligence Agency Checks ("NIAC") every two years; and (ii) plaintiffs must have *inter alia* a NIAC that was performed within the last two years to be eligible for a security clearance. *See* PTO at ¶¶ 3 & 5. No person affiliated with the DoD, other than individuals who (like plaintiffs) accessed through the MAVNI program, is required, absent particularized suspicion, to undergo a biennial NIAC. Plaintiffs, however, must endure such periodic screening for the duration of their military service and even after discharge, whenever they work as a civilian for the government or an entity providing supplies or services for the DoD. *See infra* note 11.

The NIAC requirements are set forth in a memorandum issued on September 30, 2016, by then Acting Under Secretary of Defense for Personnel and Readiness Peter Levine, which states in relevant part:

> All personnel accessed through the MAVNI program since its inception in 2009 must be continuously monitored and accounted for throughout

> the duration of their affiliation with the Department of Defense (e.g. active duty, Reserve, government civilian, or contractor).
>
> ....
>
> The DoD CAF [Consolidated Adjudications Facility] is responsible for adjudicating completed personnel security background investigations to render a determination of each individual's eligibility to access classified information and may require... [a] NIAC....

Ex. 4 at 2 & 7; *see also* PTO at ¶¶ 1-5. Pursuant to the Levine memorandum, if a NIAC reveals derogatory information, a counterintelligence ("CI") security interview and/or a polygraph examination may be requested. Ex. 4 at 7. Refusal to comply with such request is grounds for separation from the military. *Id.*

Plaintiffs ask the Court to declare that the NIAC requirements unconstitutionally discriminate against them on the basis of national origin, and they seek injunctive and equitable relief. Defendant counters that the DoD's unequal treatment of citizens who were recruited through the MAVNI program survives constitutional challenge because either (i) it is premised on the manner through which the individuals enlisted in the Army rather than on those citizens' national origin; or (ii) if an inherently suspect classification is implicated, the DoD's actions are "necessary" and "precisely tailored" to achieve a "compelling" governmental interest, namely national security. *See Huynh v. Carlucci*, 679 F.Supp. 61, 66 (D.D.C. 1988) (reciting the "strict scrutiny" standard applicable to inherently suspect classifications (citing *Plyler v. Doe*, 457 U.S. 202, 217 (1982), and *In re Griffiths*, 413 U.S. 717, 721-22 (1973))).

This dispute requires the Court to balance the equal protection rights of highly qualified citizens who have served or continue to serve honorably in the military against the DoD's concerns about foreign operatives infiltrating the MAVNI program or potentially converting MAVNI soldiers into assets for our country's adversaries. It involves the constant tension between individual rights and national interests, and it reminds us that, when the asserted governmental interests appear the most compelling, courts must be the most vigilant because "grave threats to liberty often come in times of urgency, when constitutional rights seem too extravagant to endure." *See Hassan v. N.Y.C.*, 804 F.3d 277, 306-07 (3d Cir. 2015) (quoting *Skinner v. Ry. Labor Execs.' Ass'n*, 489 U.S. 602, 635 (1989) (Marshall, J., dissenting)). For the reasons explained in this Order, the Court concludes that the DoD's challenged policies discriminate on the basis of national origin, and that defendant has not carried the burden of proving that the biennial NIACs required in connection with "continuous monitoring" and security clearance eligibility, which are imposed on citizens who accessed through the MAVNI program but not on other citizens affiliated with the DoD, survive strict scrutiny.

Discussion

When this lawsuit began, plaintiffs sought relief with respect to additional aspects of the "continuous monitoring" program and the security clearance protocols applied to MAVNI personnel, but as a result of the evidence presented at trial, plaintiffs narrowed their claim to encompass only the periodic NIAC requirements of continuous monitoring and security clearance procedures. With respect to the biennial NIAC mandated for individuals who accessed through the MAVNI program and remain affiliated with the DoD, the questions before the Court are as follows: (i) whether the disparate treatment constitutes national-origin-based discrimination, and is therefore subject to strict scrutiny, or is merely related to the manner in which the soldiers entered the military (*i.e.*, via the MAVNI program), and thus, must withstand only rational basis review; and (ii) whether the MAVNI-focused policies at issue bear the requisite relationship to the government's interest (*i.e.*, national security).

A. Level of Review

The Court concludes that strict scrutiny must be applied to the challenged DoD policies. Government action that distinguishes among citizens on the basis of national origin is inherently suspect and subject to "strict scrutiny." *See Huynh*, 679 F. Supp. at 66 (citing *Graham v. Richardson*, 403 U.S. 365, 372 (1971), and *Korematsu v. United States*, 323 U.S. 214, 216 (1944), *abrogated on other grounds by Trump v. Hawaii*,——U.S.——, 138 S.Ct. 2392 (2018)). To satisfy strict scrutiny, (i) the use of a suspect classification must bear a close relationship to the promotion of a "compelling" governmental interest, (ii) the use of such classification must be "necessary" to achieve such interest, and (iii) the means or procedures used must be "precisely tailored" to serve such interest. *Id.* (citing *Plyler*, 457 U.S. at 217, and *In re Griffiths*, 413 U.S. at 721-22). The requirement that MAVNI personnel undergo NIAC screening every two years as part of either the "continuous monitoring" program or the security clearance approval process makes remaining a soldier or DoD affiliate and/or obtaining a security clearance more onerous for citizens born outside the United States than for other citizens, and therefore constitutes discrimination on the basis of national origin. *See Faruki v. Rogers*, 349 F.Supp. 723, 726-27 (D.D.C. 1972) (three-judge district court).

In *Faruki*, the plaintiff challenged a provision of the Foreign Service Act of 1946, which prohibited a person from being appointed as a foreign service officer unless he or she was "a citizen of the United States and has been such for at least ten years." *Id.* at 725 (quoting 22 U.S.C. § 910 (1970)). The *Faruki* Court concluded that the statute treated persons who were citizens at birth more favorably than and discriminated against individuals who had been born abroad and then naturalized. *Id.* at 725-27. In striking down the durational requirement of § 910, the three-judge panel warned against scenarios in which the government "grants citizenship to an immigrant and then, solely on the basis of his original foreign status, proceeds to give him second-class, more burdensome treatment." *Id.* at 729. The additional screening imposed upon plaintiffs, who gained citizenship through the MAVNI program, has the same "odor of prejudice" as the foreign service eligibility criterion held violative of equal protection guarantees in *Faruki*. *See id.* at 729-35.

1. Contemporaneous Discrimination Against Foreign Nationals

In attempting to persuade the Court to apply rational basis review rather than strict scrutiny, defendant alleges, based on classified material that was not offered or admitted as evidence at trial, *see infra* § B(1), that the MAVNI program is itself a target or magnet for our country's enemies, and that the heightened scrutiny to which plaintiffs are or will be subjected is not because of their national origin but because their means of enlistment (which is the only way, given their national origin, that they could have joined the Army) poses a potential national security threat. Defendant's assertion that national origin has played no role is contradicted by the DoD's modifications to its policies concerning another group, namely aliens who are lawful permanent residents, which were implemented contemporaneously with the current iteration of the "continuous monitoring" program. *See* Ex. 49; *supra* note 16. In October 2017, the DoD announced new protocols that prevented lawful permanent residents from entering active, reserve, or guard service until their background investigations were completed. *See Kuang v. U.S. Dep't of Defense*, 340 F.Supp.3d 873 (N.D. Cal. 2018) (issuing a preliminary injunction and requiring the DoD to return to pre-October 2017 practices for the accession of lawful permanent residents).

All military personnel must undergo background investigations (which do not involve NIACs), but the October 2017 policy treated lawful permanent residents and citizens differently, allowing the latter, but not the former, to ship to basic training before completion of the required investigations. *Id.* at 889 & 919. The DoD's stated purpose for the disparate treatment of lawful permanent residents was "to facilitate process efficiency and the appropriate sharing of information for security risk based suitability and security decisions for the accession of *foreign nationals*." *See* AR at 1 (docket no. 57 at 5) (emphasis added) in *Kuang v. U.S. Dep't of Defense*, N.D. Cal. Case No. 3:18-cv-3698-JST; *see also Kuang*, 340 F.Supp.3d at 889. Given the DoD's explicit reference to nationality in a similar policy simultaneously announced, defendant's contention that the DoD was concerned *solely* about the targeting of the MAVNI program lacks credibility. The Court concludes plaintiffs have shown all that they need to prove, specifically that national origin was "**a** motivating factor" in the DoD's disparate treatment of MAVNI recruits. *See Martin v. Int'l Olympic Comm.*, 740 F.2d 670, 678 (9th Cir. 1984) (emphasis added)....

3. Proof of Discriminatory Animus Not Required

In a different approach aimed at receiving the benefit of rational basis review, defendant asserts that, absent proof of discriminatory animus or motive, the NIAC components of continuous monitoring and security clearance protocols merely have a disproportionate impact on a protected group and cannot rise to the level of an equal protection violation. Defendant's analysis is flawed because it assumes, without demonstrating, that the continuous monitoring and more rigorous security clearance requirements are facially neutral, and it therefore relies on inapposite authorities. When the government classifies persons on the basis of race, national origin, or similar immutable characteristic, a plaintiff challenging such action in a lawsuit "need not make an extrinsic showing of discriminatory animus...to trigger strict scrutiny." *Mitchell v. Washington*, 818 F.3d 436, 445-46 (9th Cir. 2016). Moreover, strict scrutiny applies even when the reason for the differential treatment is "benign," for example, preferences in academic admissions, government contracting, election redistricting, as well as when the protected attribute is just one of several factors in a government decision. *Id.* at 444-45. Finally, a suspect classification need not be stated explicitly to warrant strict scrutiny. *See Washington v. Seattle Sch. Dist. No. 1*, 458 U.S. 457 (1982)....

4. The Evidence Establishes Any Required Animus

Under both *Mitchell* and the *Seattle School District* case, strict scrutiny must be applied in this case because the policies at issue are not facially-neutral rules that merely disproportionately impact a protected class, but rather affect every MAVNI enlistee affiliated with the DoD who is a United States citizen, and who was, by definition, born outside the United States. Even if, however, the NIAC requirements could be considered facially neutral, defendant would not be entitled to rational basis review. As recognized in a case cited by defendant, the Supreme Court has non-exhaustively outlined the sources of evidence that might reveal whether a facially-neutral governmental action was taken for invidious purposes. *See Snoqualmie Indian Tribe v. City of Snoqualmie*, 186 F.Supp.3d 1155, 1164-65 (W.D. Wash. 2016) (citing *Vill. of Arlington Heights v. Metro. Housing Dev. Corp.*, 429 U.S. 252 (1977)).

In *Arlington Heights*, faced with a challenge to the Village's denial of a rezoning request, the Supreme Court observed that, when a discriminatory purpose has been a motivating factor in a decision, the legislative or administrative body is no longer entitled to judicial deference. 429 U.S. at 265-66. Determining whether an improper animus played a role in the official action "demands a sensitive inquiry" into the available direct and circumstantial evidence, which may include whether one race (or protected group) is more "heavily" impacted than another. *See id.* at 266. This factor alone might be determinative (as in the case of the MAVNI-centric policies at issue), but if not, courts may look to other evidence. *See id.* Among other considerations of possible relevance are (i) the historical background of the decision at issue, (ii) the specific sequence of events leading up to the challenged action, (iii) departures from normal procedures, (iv) substantive departures, particularly when the factors usually considered important would strongly favor a decision contrary to the one reached, and (v) legislative or administrative history, especially statements made contemporaneously with the allegedly unconstitutional decision, meeting minutes, or reports. *Id.* at 267-68.

While raising the specter of *Arlington Heights*, defendant did not, in his trial brief or closing argument, conduct the necessary inquiries, and the Court cannot take seriously defendant's assertion that the continuous monitoring and security clearance policies at issue are entitled to the type of judicial deference accorded under rational basis review. Contrary to defendant's suggestion, even if the Court found that the challenged DoD policy is facially neutral, the equal protection analysis would not end.

Rather, the Court would proceed to evaluate whether the *Arlington Heights* factors evidence an improper motive warranting strict scrutiny.

Having performed the additional work required by *Arlington Heights*, the Court concludes that the considerations articulated by the Supreme Court do not support defendant's view that, assuming the MAVNI regulations at issue are facially neutral, they were implemented without any of the motives that would give rise to strict scrutiny. Indeed, the historical background of the biennial NIAC requirements and the sequence of events leading up to the Levine memorandum indicate that national origin was at least "a motivating factor" in the DoD's actions. The DoD's procedural and substantive departures from the protocols applicable to non-MAVNI personnel and the administrative history likewise weigh in favor of applying strict scrutiny. For all of the foregoing reasons, the Court concludes that defendant must bear the burden of proving the use of the suspect classification (*i.e.*, national origin) promotes a compelling interest, the classification is necessary, and the means at issue are precisely tailored to achieve the governmental interest. *See Johnson v. California*, 543 U.S. 499, 505 (2005).

B. Applying Strict Scrutiny

1. Compelling Interest

Plaintiffs do not quarrel with the concept that national security is a compelling governmental interest, but they have cast doubt on the value of certain evidence on which defendant has relied in alleging a threat to national security. In a declaration filed in connection with motion practice, the DoD's Chief of Personnel Security, Roger Smith, indicated that "a number of individuals accessed into the military [through the MAVNI program] based on receiving fraudulent visas to attend universities that did not exist." Smith Decl. at ¶25 (docket nos. 131-1 & 132-1). The only example Mr. Smith could provide at trial concerned the University of Northern New Jersey, *see* Tr. (Nov. 29, 2018) at 60:14-23 (docket no. 190), which was a fake school created by the Department of Homeland Security as part of a "sting" operation aimed at trapping brokers who were unlawfully referring foreign students to academic institutions for a fee, *see* Tr. (Nov. 27, 2018) at 173:10-17 (docket no. 188). The Court is unimpressed with any assertion that MAVNI recruits who were deceived by an agency of the United States into believing that they were enrolled in, or engaged in either curricular or optional practical training through, a legitimate school constituted a threat to national security.

Mr. Smith's declaration also referenced a MAVNI enlistee who said he would "voluntarily help China in a crisis situation." Smith Decl. at ¶25 (docket nos. 131-1 & 132-1). During trial, Mr. Smith agreed that this individual was the subject of a DoD PowerPoint slide, which indicated that this person declined to become a naturalized United States citizen (and thus, is not similarly situated to plaintiffs), admitted to being a communist and loving socialism, identified himself as Josef Stalin, wore old foreign military (Nazi) apparel, and was removed from campus housing and suspended from a university after a search revealed several non-functioning firearms and a bayonet. *See* Ex. 98 at 11; Tr. (Nov. 29, 2018) at 66:20-67:14 (docket no. 190). While this person (and others like him) might pose a risk to community safety, defendant has not shown how he or similar individuals would escape detection through the MAVNI, or even the more lax non-MAVNI, enlistment protocols, and thus, defendant's reliance on this example as evidence that MAVNI soldiers constitute a national security threat is unpersuasive....

2. Neither Necessary Nor Precisely Tailored

Plaintiffs contend that the "continuous monitoring" program and the enhanced security clearance protocols for MAVNI personnel are both overbroad and underinclusive, and thus, do not bear a sufficiently narrow relationship to national security. The Court agrees. The Court notes that plaintiffs, who all accessed after February 2012, already underwent investigations that were beyond what anyone else seeking the highest levels of security clearance must endure, and they did so just to enlist and obtain a favorable Military Service Suitability Determination. *See supra* note 16. Defendant has offered no statistical basis or other evidence to support a theory that a subsequent biennial NIAC (as part of a continuous monitoring system or a security clearance application) would reveal national security concerns somehow left unexposed by the SSBI/Tier 5, NIAC, and CIFSR performed upon recruitment. Moreover, defendant has provided no explanation for engaging in flagrant profiling, *i.e.*, equating MAVNI status with national security risk, rather than justifying on a case-by-case basis the heightened monitoring or screening that the DoD wishes to conduct. Indeed, as conceded by defendant's witnesses, no citizen who accessed into the Army through the MAVNI program has ever been charged or convicted of any criminal offense or been denaturalized, and defendant has offered no evidence that espionage or similar activity is so rampant among MAVNI personnel who have attained citizenship that a departure from the usual standard of particularized suspicion is necessary. *See* Tr. (Nov. 29, 2018) at 144:6-14 (docket no. 190) (indicating that the Army can "investigate anyone" it has "reason to believe" might be "involved in a national security crime").

In this litigation, plaintiffs do not question the DoD's authority to conduct additional security investigations on an individualized basis, *see* Tr. (Nov. 28, 2018) at 188:3-12 (docket no. 189), and the issues before the Court concern only whether the DoD may, without any indication of wrongdoing or cause for concern, routinely subject a group of citizens born outside the United States to a higher level of scrutiny than other citizens. More vetting and more monitoring will certainly reveal more information, *see* Tr. (Nov. 29, 2018) at 159:13-16 (docket no. 190), but the DoD's approach, which is, according to defendant's witness Stephanie Miller, to obtain the information first and then decide whether individualized review is warranted, *see* Tr. (Nov. 28, 2018) at 199:16-200:22, 201:15-18 (docket no. 189), puts the proverbial cart before the horse. Defendant simply has not shown why the DoD needs to conduct a NIAC every two years, as a matter of course, on the entire MAVNI population, and therefore, has not refuted plaintiffs' challenge of overbreadth....

Defendant has offered no reason for believing that MAVNI personnel who have successfully navigated the rigorous enlistment requirements (*i.e.*, received a favorable MSSD based on SSBI/Tier 5, NIAC, and CIFSR results), and who have become United States citizens, constitute any higher risk to national security than other members of the DoD population. Nevertheless, defendant requires all MAVNI soldiers, even those who have no access to classified information, to undergo biennial NIACs, while imposing no similar condition on the maintenance of "secret," "top secret," or even "top secret/SCI" clearance by non-MAVNI personnel. Defendant does not subject any other members of the military to the MAVNI level of monitoring, even those with equivalent or perhaps greater ties to other nations than the typical MAVNI soldier.... The Court concludes that the challenged NIAC requirement is under-inclusive and not "precisely tailored" to the interest of national security.

The imposition of a NIAC every two years displays a general lack of trust and a concomitant desire to monitor MAVNI soldiers without needing to identify a basis for suspicion. The Court agrees with plaintiffs that this stigmatizing persistent vetting protocol constitutes impermissibly unequal treatment of United States citizens on the basis of national origin. It is inconsistent with the representations made to plaintiffs upon their enlistment that they would be "treated like any other Soldier" and that they would enjoy "all the same opportunities afforded to... any other Soldier" in the United States Army, *see* Ex. 15 at §§ E & R; Exs. 69 & 90 at §§ E & Q; Ex. 71 at §§ E & P, and it violates the military's own principles against discrimination based on immutable characteristics like national origin, *see* Ex. 37 at ¶ 3(e) ("The DoD shall not discriminate nor may any inference be raised on the basis of race, color, religion, sex, national origin, disability, or sexual orientation."); *see also* Ex. 36 at § 3.1(c) (Exec. Order No. 12,968). It deals unfairly with citizens who have volunteered to serve their nation by enduring extreme hardships and lengthy deployments, during which they are often separated from family and friends, and by preparing each and every day to make the "ultimate sacrifice of their lives if necessary" to protect our country, its people, and the constitutional rights we hold so dear. *See Kuang*, 340 F.Supp.3d at 921-22 (quoting *Doe 1 v. Trump*, 2017 WL 6553389 at *3 (D.C. Dec. 22, 2017)). It is unconstitutional, and it must be enjoined....

Notes

1. The Department of Defense identified two related counterintelligence problems for its policy of delaying or withholding interim security clearance adjudications for MAVNI recruits, and for ultimately ending the program. First, it was difficult and time-consuming to verify information regarding foreign connections, preferences, or allegiances with respect to recruits who had spent most of their pre-military lives in a foreign country, particularly a country with which the United States did not have an alliance or close ties. Every member of the U.S. armed forces

is viewed as a person occupying a national security position requiring at least a SECRET security clearance. The information for rendering a clearance adjudication is self-reported on Standard Form 86, the "Questionnaire for National Security," which mandates reporting of exhaustive details regarding former residences, relatives, friends, neighbors, schooling, financial and credit history, jobs, contacts with foreign persons (especially government officials), and foreign travel, among other things. As MAVNI recruits were only required to have two years' residence in the United States (e.g., as university students), most of these details were difficult to verify.

Second, in addition to data verifiability concerns, the sheer scale of the MAVNI program resulted in dozens of actual, documented cases of MAVNI recruits who were flagged for not reporting sensitive information as required on the Questionnaire (e.g., relatives who were government officials, foreign travel, contact with foreign defense industry, or foreign intelligence or military officers). There were even some cases of actual espionage or foreign intelligence recruitment. Many of the specific details are classified, but one publicly acknowledged case involved the September 2018 arrest of a Chinese national, Ji Chaoqu. Ji had enlisted in the MAVNI program in May 2016 and had met known Chinese intelligence agents, according to the Department of Justice's criminal indictment. Ji did not report those contacts on his SF-86 form when applying for the MAVNI program and was allegedly working previously as an unregistered agent of Chinese intelligence, obtaining background checks on Taiwanese and ethnic Chinese persons working for American defense contractors. Todd Lighty, *How a Chicago College Student Ended Up in the Middle of an FBI Investigation Into Chinese Spying*, Chi. Trib., Sept. 26, 2019.

2. The vast majority of participants in the MAVNI program, however, presented no security risks. In its decision granting plaintiffs' motion for a preliminary injunction, the court described the plaintiffs as follows:

> The Plaintiffs in this lawsuit are skilled professionals who abandoned educational and professional aspirations as civilians to enlist in the U.S. Army through the MAVNI program.... Plaintiff Amandeep Singh, for example, is a native of India who came to the United States to attend a university. He graduated from Texas Tech University with a degree in electrical/electronic engineering and, prior to enlisting in the Army, worked as an engineer in the wireless and radio frequency fields for such companies as Blackberry, Ltd., Microsoft Corporation, and Honeywell International, Inc....
>
> Plaintiff Qi "Eva" Xiong is another highly qualified MAVNI recruit. Ms. Xiong is a native of China who received a Doctor of Dental Surgery from the University of Colorado. Since becoming a licensed board-certified dentist, she has worked as a dentist in both Illinois and Missouri. Ms. Xiong enlisted in the U.S. Army Reserve on November 10, 2015, to serve as a dentist through the MAVNI program. Despite enlisting as a dentist, Xiong

> has not been allowed to practice dentistry with the Army because she has not received a security clearance.... Valdeta Mehanja is a native of Kosovo who lived in extreme poverty before fleeing to Germany as a child.... Mehanja enlisted in the Army through the MAVNI program on February 27, 2015.... Like Mr. Singh, Ms. Xiong, and Ms. Mehanja, the other Plaintiffs in this lawsuit enlisted in the Army, became naturalized citizens, and serve the United States by using their specialized skills....

Tiwari v. Mattis, No. C17-242 (TSZ), 2018 WL 1737783 (W.D. Wash. Apr. 11, 2018).

3. In contrast to the courts in the World War II Japanese-American cases, the district court in *Tiwari* did not appear to defer at all to the Department of Defense's national security justifications in assessing and upholding the plaintiffs' equal protection claims. Should it have? How is the MAVNI litigation different from the World War II cases?

4. In the modern, digital warfighting space, even the lowliest private has access to Department of Defense cloud computing networks, software, and technology that would be of great interest to foreign states. To the extent that military-industrial espionage is a serious national security concern particularly vis-à-vis China, how should the federal courts balance the concern with the danger that ethnically Chinese U.S. citizen military service members might be subject to undue suspicion for such espionage?

5. *Tiwari* was, to some extent, an easy case because the plaintiffs were U.S. citizens. What if the service members denied temporary security clearances were neither U.S. citizens nor LPRs—should they have had an equal protection claim, too?

6. The MAVNI program has been discontinued, but the question of properly screening military recruits for foreign influence and preferences and possibly divided allegiance to the United States continues. Consider the following situations:

    - Naturalized U.S. citizen, born in South Korea and emigrated to the United States at age five with family;
    - U.S.-born citizen of Chinese ethnicity; 10 trips to China in the past three years to visit family and friends and study abroad in China during college;
    - U.S.-born citizen of non-Chinese ethnicity; 10 trips to China in the past three years for leisure travel; and
    - U.S.-born citizen of non-Chinese ethnicity, employed for five years by a Chinese company in Dubai.

    Would extra scrutiny be warranted in these cases? Should concerns about foreign influence justify special counterintelligence scrutiny and, if so, how should laws or regulations police the line between national security and discrimination?

Chapter 11
Employment

As we saw in Unit I, the first substantial numbers of Asian immigrants to the United States were Chinese laborers. Indeed, "[a] century ago, most Asian Americans were low-skilled, low-wage laborers crowded into ethnic enclaves and targets of official discrimination."[1] There are still countless immigrants of Asian descent in the United States who are minimum-wage laborers today. At the same time, however, many Asian Americans have attained levels of socioeconomic achievement consistent with the myth of a model minority. Employment litigation involving Asian Americans has reflected this trajectory of upward economic mobility. Our principal case in this Chapter, *Wards Cove Packing Co. v. Atonio*, involved the efforts in the 1970s and 1980s of predominantly Filipino cannery workers in Alaska to obtain higher-status, better-compensated employment.

1. The Alaskan Cannery Cases

For many years, salmon canning was a thriving industry in Alaska. The Alaskan salmon canneries operated only for a few weeks each year. At the right time each summer, after spending several years in the ocean, the salmon would return to Alaska to spawn, usually to the very riverbed where they were born. The canneries would spring into action, catching the salmon and butchering and canning them. The canneries depended on cheap, seasonal labor—the cannery workers—to butcher and can the fish.

Beginning in the 1870s, Chinese immigrants constituted the bulk of the cannery workforce, working the "gut lines" to butcher the fish quickly and efficiently. At some point, an effort was made to mechanize the butchering process with a machine that was dubbed the "Iron Chink" by its inventor. By the late 1800s, the number of Chinese workers began to decline due to the Chinese exclusion laws. At the turn of the twentieth century, Japanese Americans became a major part of the cannery work force until their numbers were reduced by immigration quota laws in the 1920s based on

1. Pew Research Center, *The Rise of Asian Americans* (Apr. 4, 2013), www.pewsocialtrends.org/2012/06/19/the-rise-of-asian-americans/.

origin-country populations in the United States that severely restricted non-European immigrants. The Philippines was by then a U.S. possession. Thus, by 1928, Filipinos had become the third-largest labor force in the Alaskan salmon industry after Whites and Native Americans.

Figure 11.1 ***Chinese men work at an "Iron Chink" salmon butchering machine at the Pacific American Fisheries cannery in the Fairhaven district of Bellingham in 1905.*** **Photo Asahel Curtis.**

By the 1970s, most of the seasonal cannery workers were of Filipino and other Asian descent, while the vast majority of the noncannery workers were White. The cannery work was considered "unskilled" or menial labor. In contrast, most noncannery workers provided "skilled" labor for much higher pay. They included, for example, carpenters, machinists, mechanics, and trainees for such positions. Some of the younger cannery workers had college degrees and had tried, unsuccessfully, to obtain noncannery, skilled positions. The cannery workers and noncannery workers also slept in different bunkhouses and ate in different dining halls, and the younger cannery workers complained that their living conditions were inferior to those of noncannery workers.

Three class actions were filed against different canneries alleging employment discrimination, including the *Wards Cove* case, which was filed in 1974. Plaintiffs proceeded on both disparate treatment and disparate impact theories of discrimination. In a disparate treatment case, a plaintiff must prove that the employer intentionally

Figure 11.2 ***Filipino cannery workers with Giant Pacific Octopus, Alitak, Kodiak Island*** **(ca. 1937). Photograph by Pabillon, M.P. University of Washington Libraries, Special Collections Chris D. Mensalvas Photograph Collection.**

treated the employee unfairly because of race—the burden is always on the employee to prove intent. In contrast, in a disparate impact case, at least as the law was interpreted for some years, a plaintiff was *not* required to prove intent. In 1971, the Supreme Court had held in *Griggs v. Duke Power Co.*, 401 U.S. 424 (1971), that employment practices that were neutral on their face, and even in their intent, were unlawful if they had an adverse impact on a class of employees, unless the employer could show an essential business justification for the practice.

The cases moved slowly, and the *Wards Cove* case was not tried until 1982. Judge Justin L. Quackenbush of the Western District of Washington heard the case without a jury. Over the course of 12 trial days, more than 100 witnesses testified, either in person or by affidavit. Judge Quackenbush ruled for the defendant canneries, rejecting both the disparate treatment and disparate impact claims. *Atonio v. Wards Cove Packing Co.*, No. C-74-145-JLQ, 1983 WL 651 (W.D. Wash. Dec. 6, 1983).

On appeal, there were complicated proceedings in the Ninth Circuit, including *en banc* proceedings. The Ninth Circuit affirmed as to the disparate treatment claim, but reversed as to the disparate impact claim. Judge Thomas Tang, one of the first Asian-American federal judges in the country, played a prominent role as he authored both a panel opinion and an opinion of the *en banc* court. The case then moved to the Supreme Court. Here are excerpts from Judge Tang's decision for the *en banc* court, his panel decision implementing the *en banc* ruling, and the Supreme Court's decision:

Figure 11.3 ***Judge Thomas Tang's 1977 Portrait*****. Cracchiolo Law Library Digital Collections.**

Atonio v. Wards Cove Packing Co.

810 F.2d 1477 (9th Cir. 1987) (*en banc* decision)

Judge TANG:

Applying the tool of disparate impact analysis to subjective practices and criteria is necessary to fully implement the prophylactic purpose of Title VII to achieve equal employment opportunity and remove arbitrary and unnecessary barriers which have operated to favor White male employees over others.

... It is essential precisely because such practices will quite often lack any discriminatory animus. Subjective practices can operate as "'built-in headwinds'" for minority groups as readily as can objective criteria, Griggs, 401 U.S. at 431, and these practices should likewise be exposed and eradicated when they cause adverse impact without proof of a redeeming business necessity. The Supreme Court has not held otherwise....

Atonio v. Wards Cove Packing Co.

827 F.2d 439 (9th Cir. 1987) (panel decision)

Judge TANG:

Race labeling is pervasive at the salmon canneries, where "Filipinos" work with the "Iron Chink" before retiring to their "Flip bunkhouse." The district court did not find the conduct laudatory but found that it was not "persuasive evidence of discriminatory intent." Perhaps not, but the court must carry the analysis further and consider whether such a practice has any adverse impact upon minority people, i.e., whether it operates as a headwind to minority advancement....

The vast majority of cannery workers live at the canneries during the season in bunkhouses provided by the companies. The plaintiffs claimed that nonwhites, particularly Filipinos, were segregated from whites and placed in inferior bunkhouses because of racial discrimination. The district court found that the factory cannery workers established a prima facie case of intentional discrimination, but that the defendants' evidence proved nondiscriminatory motivations which the class had failed to prove pretextual. Specifically, the court found that the employees were housed by their time of arrival and by crew rather than with an intent to discriminate. The record contains sufficient evidence to support the district court's conclusion that the companies articulated a nondiscriminatory reason for their practice.

Cannery workers were also fed separately from the remainder of the work force. They alleged that this was due to discrimination. The district court agreed that they had established a prima facie case of discrimination, but that the defendants met their burden of production and the cannery workers had not proved pretext. It is undisputed that the cannery worker mess halls served what is termed a "traditional" oriental menu. The district court noted that the Local 37 contract provided for a separate culinary crew, and that Filipino and Asian persons dominated the membership in Local 37. Further, the court found that the quality and quantity of food served in the respective mess halls were the responsibility of the respective cooks, and that the older cannery workers preferred the traditional menu, to which the younger workers acceded. The court concluded that complaints about the food were attributable to personal taste, and that the segregated messing arrangement was attributable to the union and not the conduct of defendants. There is support in the record for these findings, and we cannot find them clearly erroneous.

The district court also evaluated the complaints of segregated housing and messing under the impact theory and found that business necessity justified these practices. See Wambheim v. J.C. Penney, 705 F.2d 1492 (9th Cir. 1983) (impact analysis applies in employment benefits cases), cert. denied, 467 U.S. 1255 (1984). The impact is clear in this case. The segregated housing aggravated the isolation of the non-white workers from the "web of information" spread by word-of-mouth among white people about the better paying jobs. See Domingo, 445 F. Supp. 421, 435 (W.D. Wash. 1977), aff'd, 727 F.2d 1429 (9th Cir.), modified, 742 F.2d 520 (9th Cir. 1984)....

In assessing how racial labeling and segregated housing and messing facilities may cause an adverse impact we suggest that the district court consider the message that such practice conveys to the general population. As the Supreme Court has warned:

> The ["whites only"] message can be communicated to potential applicants more subtly but just as clearly by an employer's actual practices—by his consistent discriminatory treatment of actual applicants, by the manner in which he publicizes vacancies, his recruitment techniques, his response to casual or tentative inquiries, and even by the racial or ethnic composition of that part of his work force from which he has discriminatorily excluded members of minority groups.

Teamsters, 431 U.S. at 365. . . .

The judgment is VACATED and the cause is REMANDED for further proceedings consistent with this opinion.

Wards Cove Packing Co. v. Atonio

490 U.S. 642 (1989)

Justice WHITE delivered the opinion of the Court.

. . .

The claims before us are disparate-impact claims, involving the employment practices of petitioners, two companies that operate salmon canneries in remote and widely separated areas of Alaska. The canneries operate only during the salmon runs in the summer months. They are inoperative and vacant for the rest of the year. In May or June of each year, a few weeks before the salmon runs begin, workers arrive and prepare the equipment and facilities for the canning operation. Most of these workers possess a variety of skills. When salmon runs are about to begin, the workers who will operate the cannery lines arrive, remain as long as there are fish to can, and then depart. The canneries are then closed down, winterized, and left vacant until the next spring. During the off-season, the companies employ only a small number of individuals at their headquarters in Seattle and Astoria, Oregon, plus some employees at the winter shipyard in Seattle.

The length and size of salmon runs vary from year to year, and hence the number of employees needed at each cannery also varies. Estimates are made as early in the winter as possible; the necessary employees are hired, and when the time comes, they are transported to the canneries. Salmon must be processed soon after they are caught, and the work during the canning season is therefore intense. For this reason, and because the canneries are located in remote regions, all workers are housed at the canneries and have their meals in company-owned mess halls.

Jobs at the canneries are of two general types: "cannery jobs" on the cannery line, which are unskilled positions; and "noncannery jobs," which fall into a variety of classifications. Most noncannery jobs are classified as skilled positions. Cannery jobs are filled predominantly by nonwhites: Filipinos and Alaska Natives. The Filipinos are hired through, and dispatched by, Local 37 of the International Longshoremen's and Warehousemen's Union pursuant to a hiring hall agreement with the local. The Alaska Natives primarily reside in villages near the remote cannery locations. Noncannery jobs are filled with predominantly white workers, who are hired during the winter months from the companies' offices in Washington and Oregon. Virtually all of the noncannery jobs pay more than cannery positions. The predominantly white noncannery workers and the predominantly nonwhite cannery employees live in separate dormitories and eat in separate mess halls.

In 1974, respondents, a class of nonwhite cannery workers who were (or had been) employed at the canneries, brought this Title VII action against petitioners. Respondents alleged that a variety of petitioners' hiring/promotion practices—*e.g.*, nepotism, a rehire preference, a lack of objective hiring criteria, separate hiring channels, a practice of not promoting from within—were responsible for the racial stratification of the work force and had denied them and other nonwhites employment as noncannery workers on the basis of race. Respondents also complained of petitioners' racially segregated housing and dining facilities. All of respondents' claims were advanced under both the disparate-treatment and disparate-impact theories of Title VII liability.

The District Court held a bench trial, after which it entered 172 findings of fact. 34 EPD ¶ 34,437, pp. 32,822–33,836 (WD Wash.1983). It then rejected all of respondents' disparate-treatment claims. It also rejected the disparate-impact challenges involving the subjective employment criteria used by petitioners to fill these noncannery positions, on the ground that those criteria were not subject to attack under a disparate-impact theory. *Id.*, at I–102. Petitioners' "objective" employment practices (*e.g.*, an English language requirement, alleged nepotism in hiring, failure to post noncannery openings, the rehire preference, etc.) were found to be subject to challenge under the disparate-impact theory, but these claims were rejected for failure of proof. Judgment was entered for petitioners.

On appeal, a panel of the Ninth Circuit affirmed, 768 F.2d 1120 (CA9 1985), but that decision was vacated when the Court of Appeals agreed to hear the case en banc, 787 F.2d 462 (CA9 1985). The en banc hearing was ordered to settle an intra-circuit conflict over the question whether subjective hiring practices could be analyzed under a disparate-impact model; the Court of Appeals held—as this Court subsequently ruled in *Watson v. Fort Worth Bank & Trust*, 487 U.S. 977 (1988)—that disparate-impact analysis could be applied to subjective hiring practices. 810 F.2d 1477, 1482 (CA9 1987). The Ninth Circuit also concluded that in such a case, "[o]nce the plaintiff class has shown disparate impact caused by specific, identifiable employment practices or criteria, the burden shifts to the employer," *id.*, at 1485, to "prov[e the] business necessity" of the challenged practice, *id.*, at 1486. Because the en banc holding on subjective employment practices reversed the District Court's contrary ruling, the en banc Court of Appeals remanded the case to a panel for further proceedings.

On remand, the panel applied the en banc ruling to the facts of this case. 827 F.2d 439 (CA9 1987). It held that respondents had made out a prima facie case of disparate impact in hiring for both skilled and unskilled noncannery positions. The panel remanded the case for further proceedings, instructing the District Court that it was the employer's burden to prove that any disparate impact caused by its hiring and employment practices was justified by business necessity. Neither the en banc court nor the panel disturbed the District Court's rejection of the disparate-treatment claims.

Petitioners sought review of the Court of Appeals' decision in this Court, challenging it on several grounds. Because some of the issues raised by the decision below were matters on which this Court was evenly divided in *Watson v. Fort Worth Bank & Trust, supra,* we granted certiorari, 487 U.S. 1232 (1988), for the purpose of addressing these disputed questions of the proper application of Title VII's disparate-impact theory of liability.

II

In holding that respondents had made out a prima facie case of disparate impact, the Court of Appeals relied solely on respondents' statistics showing a high percentage of nonwhite workers in the cannery jobs and a low percentage of such workers in the noncannery positions. Although statistical proof can alone make out a prima facie case, see *Teamsters v. United States,* 431 U.S. 324, 339 (1977); *Hazelwood School Dist. v. United States,* 433 U.S. 299, 307–308 (1977), the Court of Appeals' ruling here misapprehends our precedents and the purposes of Title VII, and we therefore reverse.

"There can be no doubt," as there was when a similar mistaken analysis had been undertaken by the courts below in *Hazelwood, supra,* at 308, "that the . . . comparison . . . fundamentally misconceived the role of statistics in employment discrimination cases." The "proper comparison [is] between the racial composition of [the at-issue jobs] and the racial composition of the qualified . . . population in the relevant labor market." *Ibid.* It is such a comparison—between the racial composition of the qualified persons in the labor market and the persons holding at-issue jobs—that generally forms the proper basis for the initial inquiry in a disparate-impact case. Alternatively, in cases where such labor market statistics will be difficult if not impossible to ascertain, we have recognized that certain other statistics—such as measures indicating the racial composition of "otherwise-qualified applicants" for at-issue jobs—are equally probative for this purpose. . . .

It is clear to us that the Court of Appeals' acceptance of the comparison between the racial composition of the cannery work force and that of the noncannery work force, as probative of a prima facie case of disparate impact in the selection of the latter group of workers, was flawed for several reasons. Most obviously, with respect to the skilled noncannery jobs at issue here, the cannery work force in no way reflected "the pool of *qualified* job applicants" or the "*qualified* population in the labor force." Measuring alleged discrimination in the selection of accountants, managers, boat captains, electricians, doctors, and engineers—and the long list of other "skilled" noncannery positions found to exist by the District Court, see 34 EPD ¶34,437, p. 33,832—by comparing the number of nonwhites occupying these jobs to the number of nonwhites filling cannery worker positions is nonsensical. If the absence of minorities holding such skilled positions is due to a dearth of qualified nonwhite applicants (for reasons that are not petitioners' fault), petitioners' selection methods or employment practices cannot be said to have had a "disparate impact" on nonwhites. . . .

Such a result cannot be squared with our cases or with the goals behind the statute. The Court of Appeals' theory, at the very least, would mean that any employer who had a segment of his work force that was—for some reason—racially imbalanced, could be haled into court and forced to engage in the expensive and time-consuming task of defending the "business necessity" of the methods used to select the other members of his work force. The only practicable option for many employers would be to adopt racial quotas, insuring that no portion of their work forces deviated in racial composition from the other portions thereof; this is a result that Congress expressly rejected in drafting Title VII. See 42 U.S.C. §2000e–2(j); see also *Watson v. Fort Worth Bank & Trust,* 487 U.S. at 992–994, and n. 2 (opinion of O'CONNOR, J.). The Court of Appeals' theory would "leave the employer little choice . . . but to engage in a subjective quota system of employment selection. This, of course, is far from the intent of Title VII." *Albemarle Paper Co. v. Moody,* 422 U.S. 405, 449 (1975) (BLACKMUN, J., concurring in judgment).

The Court of Appeals also erred with respect to the unskilled noncannery positions. Racial imbalance in one segment of an employer's work force does not, without more, establish a prima facie case of disparate impact with respect to the selection of workers for the employer's other positions, even where workers for the different positions may have somewhat fungible skills (as is arguably the case for cannery and unskilled noncannery workers). As long as there are no barriers or practices deterring qualified nonwhites from applying for noncannery positions, see n. 6, *supra,* if the percentage of selected applicants who are nonwhite is not significantly less than the percentage of qualified applicants who are nonwhite, the employer's selection mechanism probably does not operate with a disparate impact on minorities. Where this is the case, the percentage of nonwhite workers found in other positions in the employer's labor force is irrelevant to the question of a prima facie statistical case of disparate impact. As noted above, a contrary ruling on this point would almost inexorably lead to the use of numerical quotas in the workplace, a result that Congress and this Court have rejected repeatedly in the past. . . .

The peculiar facts of this case further illustrate why a comparison between the percentage of nonwhite cannery workers and nonwhite noncannery workers is an improper basis for making out a claim of disparate impact. Here, the District Court found that nonwhites were "overrepresent[ed]" among cannery workers because petitioners had contracted with a predominantly nonwhite union (local 37) to fill these positions. See 34 EPD ¶33,437, p. 33,829. As a result, if petitioners (for some permissible reason) ceased using local 37 as its hiring channel for cannery positions, it appears (according to the District Court's findings) that the racial stratification between the cannery and noncannery workers might diminish to statistical insignificance. Under the Court of Appeals' approach, therefore, it is possible that *with no change whatsoever* in their hiring practices for noncannery workers—the jobs at issue in this lawsuit—petitioners could make respondents' prima facie case of disparate impact "disappear." But *if* there would be no prima facie case of disparate impact in the selection of noncannery workers absent petitioners' use of local 37 to hire cannery workers, surely petitioners' reliance on the union to fill the cannery jobs not at issue here (and its resulting "overrepresentation" of nonwhites in those positions) does not—standing alone—make out a prima facie case of disparate impact. Yet it is precisely such an ironic result that the Court of Appeals reached below.

Consequently, we reverse the Court of Appeals' ruling that a comparison between the percentage of cannery workers who are nonwhite and the percentage of noncannery workers who are nonwhite makes out a prima facie case of disparate impact. Of course, this leaves unresolved whether the record made in the District Court will support a conclusion that a prima facie case of disparate impact has been established on some basis other than the racial disparity between cannery and noncannery workers. This is an issue that the Court of Appeals or the District Court should address in the first instance.

III

Since the statistical disparity relied on by the Court of Appeals did not suffice to make out a prima facie case, any inquiry by us into whether the specific challenged employment practices of petitioners caused that disparity is pretermitted, as is any inquiry into whether the disparate impact that any employment practice may have had was justified by business considerations. Because we remand for further proceedings, however, on whether a prima facie case of disparate impact has been made in defensible fashion in this case, we address two other challenges petitioners have made to the decision of the Court of Appeals....

A

First is the question of causation in a disparate-impact case. The law in this respect was correctly stated by Justice O'CONNOR's opinion last Term in *Watson v. Fort Worth Bank & Trust,* 487 U.S., at 994:

> "[W]e note that the plaintiff's burden in establishing a prima facie case goes beyond the need to show that there are statistical disparities in the employer's work force. The plaintiff must begin by identifying the specific employment practice that is challenged.... Especially in cases where an employer combines subjective criteria with the use of more rigid standardized rules or tests, the plaintiff is in our view responsible for isolating and identifying the specific employment practices that are allegedly responsible for any observed statistical disparities."

Cf. also *id.,* at 1000 (BLACKMUN, J., concurring in part and concurring in judgment)....

Our disparate-impact cases have always focused on the impact of *particular* hiring practices on employment opportunities for minorities. Just as an employer cannot escape liability under Title VII by demonstrating that, "at the bottom line," his work force is racially balanced (where particular hiring practices may operate to deprive minorities of employment opportunities), see *Connecticut v. Teal,* 457 U.S., at 450, a Title VII plaintiff does not make out a case of disparate impact simply by showing that, "at the bottom line," there is racial *imbalance* in the work force. As a general matter, a plaintiff must demonstrate that it is the application of a specific or particular employment practice that has created the disparate impact under attack. Such a showing is an integral part of the plaintiff's prima facie case in a disparate-impact suit under Title VII.

Here, respondents have alleged that several "objective" employment practices (*e.g.*, nepotism, separate hiring channels, rehire preferences), as well as the use of "subjective decision making" to select noncannery workers, have had a disparate impact on nonwhites. Respondents base this claim on statistics that allegedly show a disproportionately low percentage of nonwhites in the at-issue positions. However, even if on remand respondents can show that nonwhites are underrepresented in the at-issue jobs in a manner that is acceptable under the standards set forth in Part II, *supra,* this alone will *not* suffice to make out a prima facie case of disparate impact. Respondents will also have to demonstrate that the disparity they complain of is the result of one or more of the employment practices that they are attacking here, specifically showing that each challenged practice has a significantly disparate impact on employment opportunities for whites and nonwhites. To hold otherwise would result in employers being potentially liable for "the myriad of innocent causes that may lead to statistical imbalances in the composition of their work forces." *Watson v. Fort Worth Bank & Trust, supra,* 487 U.S., at 992. . . .

Consequently, on remand, the courts below are instructed to require, as part of respondents' prima facie case, a demonstration that specific elements of the petitioners' hiring process have a significantly disparate impact on nonwhites.

B

If, on remand, respondents meet the proof burdens outlined above, and establish a prima facie case of disparate impact with respect to any of petitioners' employment practices, the case will shift to any business justification petitioners offer for their use of these practices. This phase of the disparate-impact case contains two components: first, a consideration of the justifications an employer offers for his use of these practices; and second, the availability of alternative practices to achieve the same business ends, with less racial impact. See, *e.g., Albemarle Paper Co. v. Moody,* 422 U.S., at 425. We consider these two components in turn.

(1)

Though we have phrased the query differently in different cases, it is generally well established that at the justification stage of such a disparate-impact case, the dispositive issue is whether a challenged practice serves, in a significant way, the legitimate employment goals of the employer. See, *e.g., Watson v. Fort Worth Bank & Trust,* 487 U.S., at 997–999; *New York City Transit Authority v. Beazer,* 440 U.S., at 587, n. 31; *Griggs v. Duke Power Co.,* 401 U.S., at 432. The touchstone of this inquiry is a reasoned review of the employer's justification for his use of the challenged practice. A mere insubstantial justification in this regard will not suffice, because such a low standard of review would permit discrimination to be practiced through the use of spurious, seemingly neutral employment practices. At the same time, though, there is no requirement that the challenged practice be "essential" or "indispensable" to the employer's business for it to pass muster: this degree of scrutiny would be almost impossible for most employers to meet, and would result in a host of evils we have identified above. See *supra,* at 2122.

In this phase, the employer carries the burden of producing evidence of a business justification for his employment practice. The burden of persuasion, however, remains with the disparate-impact plaintiff. To the extent that the Ninth Circuit held otherwise in its en banc decision in this case, see 810 F.2d, at 1485–1486, or in the panel's decision on remand, see 827 F.2d, at 445, 447—suggesting that the persuasion burden should shift to petitioners once respondents established a prima facie case of disparate impact—its decisions were erroneous. "[T]he ultimate burden of proving that discrimination against a protected group has been caused by a specific employment practice remains with the plaintiff *at all times.*" *Watson, supra,* 487 U.S., at 997 (O'CONNOR, J.) (emphasis added). This rule conforms with the usual method for allocating persuasion and production burdens in the federal courts, see Fed. Rule Evid. 301, and more specifically, it conforms to the rule in disparate-treatment cases that the plaintiff bears the burden of disproving an employer's assertion that the adverse employment action or practice was based solely on a legitimate neutral consideration. See *Texas Dept. of Community Affairs v. Burdine,* 450 U.S. 248, 256–258 (1981). We acknowledge that some of our earlier decisions can be read as suggesting otherwise. See *Watson, supra,* 487 U.S., at 1006–1008 (BLACKMUN, J., concurring in part and concurring in judgment). But to the extent that those cases speak of an employers' "burden of proof" with respect to a legitimate business justification defense, see, *e.g., Dothard v. Rawlinson,* 433 U.S. 321, 329 (1977), they should have been understood to mean an employer's production—but not persuasion—burden. Cf., *e.g., NLRB v. Transportation Management Corp.,* 462 U.S. 393, 404, n. 7 (1983). The persuasion burden here must remain with the plaintiff, for it is he who must prove that it was "because of such individual's race, color," etc., that he was denied a desired employment opportunity. See 42 U.S.C. § 2000e-2(a).

(2)

Finally, if on remand the case reaches this point, and respondents cannot persuade the trier of fact on the question of petitioners' business necessity defense, respondents may still be able to prevail. To do so, respondents will have to persuade the factfinder that "other tests or selection devices, without a similarly undesirable racial effect, would also serve the employer's legitimate [hiring] interest[s]"; by so demonstrating, respondents would prove that "[petitioners were] using [their] tests merely as a 'pretext' for discrimination." *Albemarle Paper Co., supra,* 422 U.S., at 425; see also *Watson,* 487 U.S., at 998 (O'CONNOR, J.); *id.,* at 1005–1006 (BLACKMUN, J., concurring in part and concurring in judgment). If respondents, having established a prima facie case, come forward with alternatives to petitioners' hiring practices that reduce the racially disparate impact of practices currently being used, and petitioners refuse to adopt these alternatives, such a refusal would belie a claim by petitioners that their incumbent practices are being employed for nondiscriminatory reasons. . . .

For the reasons given above, the judgment of the Court of Appeals is reversed, and the case is remanded for further proceedings consistent with this opinion.

Justice BLACKMUN, with whom Justice BRENNAN and Justice MARSHALL join, dissenting.

. . . Today a bare majority of the Court takes three major strides backwards in the battle against race discrimination. It reaches out to make last Term's plurality opinion in *Watson v. Fort Worth Bank & Trust,* 487 U.S. 977 (1988), the law, thereby upsetting the longstanding distribution of burdens of proof in Title VII disparate-impact cases. It bars the use of internal work force comparisons in the making of a prima facie case of discrimination, even where the structure of the industry in question renders any other statistical comparison meaningless. And it requires practice-by-practice statistical proof of causation, even where, as here, such proof would be impossible.

The harshness of these results is well demonstrated by the facts of this case. The salmon industry as described by this record takes us back to a kind of overt and institutionalized discrimination we have not dealt with in years: a total residential and work environment organized on principles of racial stratification and segregation, which, as Justice STEVENS points out, resembles a plantation economy. . . . This industry long has been characterized by a taste for discrimination of the old-fashioned sort: a preference for hiring nonwhites to fill its lowest level positions, on the condition that they stay there. The majority's legal rulings essentially immunize these practices from attack under a Title VII disparate-impact analysis.

Sadly, this comes as no surprise. One wonders whether the majority still believes that race discrimination—or, more accurately, race discrimination against nonwhites—is a problem in our society, or even remembers that it ever was. Cf. *Richmond v. J.A. Croson Co.,* 488 U.S. 469 (1989).

Justice STEVENS, with whom Justice BRENNAN, Justice MARSHALL, and Justice BLACKMUN join, dissenting.

Fully 18 years ago, this Court unanimously held that Title VII of the Civil Rights Act of 1964 prohibits employment practices that have discriminatory effects as well as those that are intended to discriminate. *Griggs v. Duke Power Co.,* 401 U.S. 424 (1971). Federal courts and agencies consistently have enforced that interpretation, thus promoting our national goal of eliminating barriers that define economic opportunity not by aptitude and ability but by race, color, national origin, and other traits that are easily identified but utterly irrelevant to one's qualification for a particular job. Regrettably, the Court retreats from these efforts in its review of an interlocutory judgment respecting the "peculiar facts" of this lawsuit. Turning a blind eye to the meaning and purpose of Title VII, the majority's opinion perfunctorily rejects a longstanding rule of law and underestimates the probative value of evidence of a racially stratified work force. I cannot join this latest sojourn into judicial activism....

I respectfully dissent.

Notes

1. In *Griggs v. Duke Power Co.*, 401 U.S. 424 (1971), the Supreme Court held:

> Under [Title VII], practices, procedures, or tests neutral on their face, and even neutral in terms of intent, cannot be maintained if they operate to 'freeze' the status quo of prior discriminatory employment practices....
>
> [Title VII] proscribes not only overt discrimination but also practices that are fair in form, but discriminatory in operation. The touchstone is business necessity....
>
> We do not suggest that either the District Court or the Court of Appeals erred in examining the employer's intent; but good intent or absence of discriminatory intent does not redeem employment procedures or testing mechanisms that operate as 'built-in headwinds' for minority groups and are unrelated to measuring job capability....

401 U.S. at 430, 431, 432. In reversing the Ninth Circuit's disparate impact analysis, the Supreme Court in *Wards Cove* thus overturned years of disparate impact law, concluding that where an employment practice has an adverse impact on a class of workers, it is still lawful if the practice merely serves, in a significant way, the legitimate employment goals of the employer. *Cf. Griggs v. Duke Power Co.*, 401 U.S. at 431 ("The touchstone is business *necessity*." (emphasis added)). Moreover, while *Griggs* had held that it was the employer's burden to prove the business justification, the Court held instead that it was the employee's burden to prove that the employer's business justification was not legitimate.

What were the employer's practices here that were of concern to the plaintiffs? How did they have, according to the plaintiffs, an adverse disparate impact? What was the employer's response?

2. As soon as the Supreme Court decision came down in 1989, the workers turned to Congress for relief. They learned that Congress was already working on a new civil rights law, and eventually the Civil Rights Act of 1991 was enacted. P.L. No. 102-166, 105 Stat. 1071 (Nov. 21, 1991). Congress codified the pre-*Wards Cove* disparate impact analysis, rolling back Supreme Court precedent in eight cases, including

Wards Cove. In addition, while previously plaintiffs were not entitled to jury trials under Title VII and could only recover back pay and equitable relief, the Act provided that they could now seek compensatory and punitive damages from a jury of their peers.

In Section 2 of the Act, Congress specifically identified the *Wards Cove* decision as an impetus for the reform, asserting that "the decision of the Supreme Court in *Wards Cove Packing Co. v. Atonio* has weakened the scope and effectiveness of Federal civil rights protections." *Id.* § 2. Congress, however, also carved out an exception with respect to *Wards Cove*: the employees of Wards Cove were unable to benefit from the Act's remedies, as the Act provided an exemption: "Notwithstanding any other provision of this Act, nothing in the Act shall apply to any disparate impact case for which a complaint was filed before March 1, 1975, and for which an initial decision was rendered after October 30, 1983." *Id.* § 402(b). Only one case fit that definition— *Wards Cove Packing Co. v. Atonio*. After years of effort, the workers lost their case in the Supreme Court when it deviated from existing law. And then when Congress passed a law to address the *Wards Cove* decision, the Wards Cove workers were expressly excepted from the protections and benefits of the law. Efforts have been made over the years to repeal the exemption, without success. Why do you think that the *Wards Cove* litigation was explicitly exempted? Do you think that Congress has the power to enact a statute changing the law but at the same time declining to change the result in a particular case to accord with the revised law?

2. The Bamboo Ceiling

The term "bamboo ceiling" refers to the perception that persons of Asian descent can only achieve so much upward mobility in American society.[2] It is similar to the idea of a "glass ceiling" preventing women from attaining the highest levels of

2. *See, e.g.*, Samantha Kubota, *What Is the 'Bamboo Ceiling'? Here's What Asian Americans Want You to Know*, Today.com (Mar. 17, 2021), https://www.today.com/tmrw/what-bamboo-ceiling-here-s-what-asian-americans-want-you-t212014; Jane Hyun, *Breaking the Bamboo Ceiling: Career Strategies for Asians* (2006); Peggy Li, *Hitting the Ceiling: An Examination of Barriers to Success for Asian American Women*, 29 Berkeley J. Gender L. & Just. 140 (2014) ("Despite increased visibility on college campuses and in elite professions, Asian Americans are rarely seen in high-ranking positions."); Grace Meng, *Corporate America's Bamboo Ceiling*, The Hill (July 18, 2016), http://thehill.com/blogs/congress-blog/economy-budget/288081-corporate-americas-bamboo-ceiling ("The time has come to break the 'bamboo ceiling' in corporate America. Similar to the glass ceiling that exists for many women in the workplace, the bamboo ceiling is felt by Asian Americans seeking leadership positions within America's most successful companies."); Stefanie K. Johnson and Thomas Sy, *Why Aren't There More Asian Americans in Leadership Positions?*, Harv. Bus. Rev., Dec. 19, 2016, https://hbr.org/2016/12/why-arent-there-more-asian-americans-in-leadership-positions ("Since the 1960s, Asian Americans have become the country's 'model minority.' . . . Yet this narrative around Asians' success obscures the

professional success. Today, both terms seem somewhat outdated; for instance, Jensen Huang, the CEO of NVIDIA, is not only one of the wealthiest but also one of the most politically powerful businesspersons in the United States if not the world. And in the legal world, Faiza Saeed has been the presiding partner of Cravath, Swaine & Moore, one of the most prominent Wall Street law firms, since 2016.[3]

At the same time, Asian Americans are still "vastly underrepresented at the leadership level" in Silicon Valley[4] and elsewhere.[5] While Asian Americans make up 13% of "working professionals" in the United States, they fill only 3% of executive and leadership positions.[6] A 2021 survey of investment managers found that 93% of respondents agreed that Asian employees are diligent workers, 85% believed that Asian employees "are good with numbers," and almost 70% thought that Asian Americans are not perceived as "good leaders."[7] As of 2020, according to the U.S. Census, Asians constitute approximately 7.2% of the U.S. population.[8] While quotas are impermissible, of course, the statistics are useful in considering whether there are significant disparities.

Different explanations have been provided for the leadership gap. The authors of a Silicon Valley study write:

> We identify three major Asian leadership gaps: a gap in awareness and expectations, a gap in role models, and a gap in behavior. Although awareness and behavioral gaps are not unique to the Asian community, social

---

fact that they are underrepresented in leadership positions, a phenomenon referred to as the 'bamboo ceiling.'").

3. *See* Michael J. de la Merced, *Faiza Saeed to Become First Woman to Lead Cravath, Swaine & Moore*, N.Y. Times, July 13, 2016; Asia Society, *Faiza Saeed: For reaching the pinnacle of corporate law and blazing a path for others to follow* (2025) ("a first-generation American of Pakistani descent"), https://asiasociety.org/asia-game-changer-awards/faiza-saeed.

4. Shawna Chen, *Tech's Troubled History with Asian Workers*, Axios (Oct. 16, 2021), https://www.axios.com/2021/10/16/tech-asian-workers-racism-equity; *see also* Cydney Posner, *New Survey: diversity on Fortune 100 and Fortune 500 Boards*, Cooley PubCo (June 9, 2021), https://cooleypubco.com/2021/06/09/board-diversityfortune500/#:~:text=Among%20the%20Fortune%20500%2C%205.7,were%20 White%20and%200.1%25%20other (representation of Asian Americans on Fortune 500 boards remains low).

5. Chris Westfall, *Battling Discrimination and the Bamboo Ceiling: The Bias Facing Asian American Managers*, Forbes.com, Sept. 14, 2021 (citing statistics in federal government, law, banking, the "C-suite," and asset management), https://www.forbes.com/sites/chriswestfall/2021/09/14/discrimination-and-bamboo-ceiling-the-unconscious-bias-facing-asian-american-managers/?sh=3801940a23dc.

6. John Wang, *Breaking the "Bamboo Ceiling at Work*, Wall St. J., May 15, 2025.

7. *Id. See also* Westfall, *supra*, Forbes.com (the "bamboo ceiling" "manifests itself in regular microaggressions—co-workers who always confuse Asian Americans on staff because they 'look alike' or a manager who expects an AAPI professional to play the role of 'model minority,' stereotypically shy or demure").

8. This number is for "Asian alone or in combination." U.S. Census Bureau, *Race and Ethnicity in the United States: 20210 Census and 2020 Census* (Aug. 12, 2021), https://www.census.gov/library/visualizations/interactive/race-and-ethnicity-in-the-united-state-2010-and-2020-census.html. In 2010, this number was 5.6%. *Id.*

> science research and our personal observations find that traditional upbringing and cultural norms can hinder many in bridging those gaps. Social science research suggests that an Asian effect is rooted in a cultural mismatch between Asian and western leadership norms which feed the western implicit stereotype that Asians have poor leadership skills.[9]

Others offer different thoughts: "Why aren't Asian Americans advancing into leadership positions? Based on the psychology literature, we believe that stereotypes about Asians contribute to the problem in two ways: Stereotypes about Asians being highly competent can make Asians appear threatening in the workplace, and stereotypes about Asians lacking social skills make them seem unfit for leadership."[10] Another has written:

> Asian Americans are perceived to be model minorities: overly competent, hardworking, educated, intelligent, and ambitious. They are viewed as a large middle-class group that has achieved "economic success without using government programs or welfare." Despite this perception, Asian Americans do suffer from discrimination—a discrimination that is different from that suffered by other disempowered groups. They are perceived to be competent, yet lacking warmth and social skills. Asian Americans are also not historically seen as leaders. These positive and negative stereotypes contribute to why Asian Americans are not adequately represented in executive-level positions.[11]

For Asian women, there is both a bamboo ceiling and a glass ceiling. "[R]esearch has found that Asian women are the least likely to ascend to positions of power when compared with Asian men and White women."[12]

What do you think? Is there a bamboo ceiling? If so, why? And what can be done to help break it?

Asian Americans have brought discrimination cases, arguing that they were denied promotions because of their race. In the law enforcement context, some years ago, 11 Asian-American police officers sued the Port Authority of New York and New Jersey under Title VII, alleging that they had been passed over for promotion to sergeant because of their race. Seven of the 11 prevailed at trial and were awarded substantial

---

9. Buck Gee et al., *Hidden in Plain Sight: Asian American Leaders in Silicon Valley,* Ascend Foundation (2015), https://c.ymcdn.com/sites/ ascendleadership.site-ym.com/resource/resmgr/Research /HiddenInPlainSight_ Paper_042.pdf.

10. Johnson and Sy, *supra.*

11. Li, 29 Berkeley J. Gender L. & Just. at 146; *see also* Chris Westfall, *Battling Discrimination and the Bamboo Ceiling: The Bias Facing Asian American Managers*, Forbes.com, Sept. 14, 2021, https://www.forbes.com/sites/chriswestfall/2021/09/14/discrimination-and-bamboo-ceiling-the -unconscious-bias-facing-asian-american-managers/?sh=289876cf23dc.

12. Ludmila Nunes, *Lessons from the Bamboo Ceiling*, Ass'n for Psych. Sci. (June 28, 2021), https:// www.psychologicalscience.org/observer/bamboo-ceiling.

damages. They asserted disparate impact and disparate treatment claims. On appeal, the Second Circuit largely affirmed. *Chin v. Port Authority of New York & New Jersey*, 685 F.3d 135 (2d Cir. 2012).

More recently, in *Finney v. Delaware Department of Transportation*, an Asian-American engineer was denied a promotion three times. He sued, alleging racial discrimination and retaliation. The court denied the employer's motion for summary judgment, concluding that plaintiff's evidence—which included the fact that five of six employees hired by the supervisor during the relevant period were White and that the supervisor made comments about plaintiff's skin color and hair texture—was sufficient to support an inference of discrimination. No. 22-1059-SRF, 2024 WL 3273497, *7 (D. Del. July 2, 2024). On the other hand, an Asian-American associate professor who was denied a promotion to full professor failed in his race discrimination claim in part because at least some of his comparators had stronger credentials and at least three were themselves Asian American. *Nelatury v. Penn. St. Univ.*, No. 21-cv-279, 2025 WL 216320, **10–11 (W.D. Pa. Jan. 16, 2025).

Not surprisingly, there have been cases brought by plaintiffs of other races who claimed they were unlawfully passed over for Asian Americans who received the promotions instead. *See, e.g.*, *Cyrus v. Bank of East Asia, Ltd.*, No. 22-cv-4115 (AMD), 2025 WL 964016 (E.D.N.Y. Mar. 28, 2025) (granting in part and denying in part discrimination and retaliation claims, including failure to promote claim, brought by African American woman who alleged, *inter alia*, that defendants "treated White and Asian American employees" more favorably because of race); *Singletary v. King Crab Boiling Seafood & Bar, Inc.*, No. 22-1591-MGL, 2024 WL 1571689, *2 (D.S.C. Apr. 11, 2024) (adopting magistrate judge's report and recommendation and, *inter alia*, denying summary judgment as to African American employee's failure to promote claim in part because plaintiff was told that if anyone was going to be promoted, it would be "one of us," meaning an Asian male). And in one recent case, a Filipino man alleged that he was discriminated against (including in the denial of promotions) in part because of "racism against Filipinos by people from Hong Kong." *Cheong v. Bank of East Asia, Ltd.*, No. 22-cv-9234 (ER), 2024 WL 1348498, *10 (S.D.N.Y. Mar. 29, 2024). The court granted defendants' motion to dismiss the complaint, noting that plaintiff relied only on his "subjective beliefs" and had failed to present any evidence that national origin was a motivating factor. *Id.*

Similar issues have existed in the legal field. In 2017, Yale Law School students and Justice Goodwin Liu of the California Supreme Court published *A Portrait of Asian Americans in the Law*. It concluded that "Asian Americans have penetrated virtually every sector of the legal profession but remain significantly underrepresented in the leadership ranks of law firms, government, and academia."[13]

---

13. Eric Chung et al., *A Portrait of Asian Americans in the Law* 3 (2017), *available at* https://static1.squarespace.com/static/59556778e58c62c7db3fbe84/ t/596cf0638419c2e5a0dc5766/1500311662008/170716_PortraitProject_SinglePages.pdf; *see also* Yale Law School, *Justice Liu '98 and Students*

In the fall of 2022, the Portrait Project was updated by Justice Liu and others, with the publication of *A Portrait of Asian Americans in the Law 2.0*.[14] The updated findings show an increased desire "to advance issues or values" and "the desire to change or improve society." *Portrait Project 2.0* at 2. It also concluded that while "[u]nderrepresentation of Asian Americans in the top ranks of the legal profession persists . . . there has been notable progress in the appointment of federal judges and in the ranks of general counsel." *Id.* at 3. Asian Americans continue to be the largest minority group at major law firms, while continuing to experience the highest rate of attrition. They have the lowest ratio of partners to associates. And they continue to lag in terms of elected prosecutors and U.S. Attorneys. *Id.*

Shortly after he was inaugurated as president for the second time, Donald Trump signed three executive orders seeking to end diversity, equity, and inclusion programs both in the public and private sectors.[15] It remains to be seen what impact these executive orders and the new policies will have on employment relations and efforts to overcome the bamboo ceiling, to the extent it still exists.

Many Asian Americans, of course, are not concerned about breaking the bamboo ceiling. Many Asian Americans still work in service industries, including, for example, restaurants, grocery stores, dry cleaners and laundries, and nail salons. They are worried about more basic concerns, not significantly unlike the challenges faced by the earlier Asian Americans.

3. Intersectionalism

Do Asian American women face particular challenges because of the combination of their race and gender? In recent years the concept of "intersectionalism" has arisen: "Women of color experience discrimination in multiple spheres that cannot be categorized as solely race-based or solely gender-based. Their experiences are a result of both their race and gender. The identities of women of color must encompass the intersection of the two." Virginia W. Wei, *Asian Women and Employment Discrimination: Using Intersectionality Theory to Address Title VII Claims Based on Combined Factors of Race, Gender and National Origin*, 37 B.C. L. Rev. 771, 771 (1996);

Present Extensive Study on Asian American Lawyers (Nov. 14, 2016), https://law.yale.edu/yls-today/news/justice-goodwin-liu-98-and-yls-students-present-extensive-study-asian-american-lawyers; *see also* Associated Press, *Few Asian-Americans Hold Top Legal Jobs, New Study Says*, L.A. Times, Jan. 15, 2017.

14. Tyler Dang et al., *A Portrait of Asian Americans in the Law 2.0* (2022), *available at* https://static1.squarespace.com/static/59556778e58c62c7db3fbe84/t/ 6366cd41b5bd85248c3b5b0a/1667681660036/Portrait+Project+2.0.pdf ("*Portrait Project 2.0*").

15. *See, e.g.*, Lara A. Flath, David E. Schwartz, and Emily D. Safko, *DEI Under Siege: A Guide to the Trump Executive Orders*, Skadden.com (Winter 2025), https://www.skadden.com/insights/publications/2025/02/the-informed-board/dei-under-siege.

see also D. Mukkamala and D.L. Suyemoto, *Racialized Sexism/Sexualized Racism: A Multimethod Study of Intersectional Experiences of Discrimination for Asian American Women*, Asian Am. J. Psych., 9(1), 32–46 accessed Aug 28, 2024, https://psycnet-apa-org.ezp-prod1.hul.harvard.edu/record/2018-11225-004.

In *Lam v. University of Hawai'i*, a woman of Vietnamese descent sued the University of Hawai'i Richardson School of Law for failing to hire her when she twice applied for a position of director of a legal studies program. She claimed she was discriminated against based on her race, sex, and national origin. The district court granted summary judgment for the university with respect to the first application and ruled in favor of the university at trial with respect to the second application. The Ninth Circuit affirmed as to the claims dismissed at trial, but reversed the award of partial summary judgment and remanded for trial as to the first application. It reasoned in part as follows:

> [T]he [district] court seemed to view racism and sexism as separate and distinct elements amenable to almost mathematical treatment, so that evaluating discrimination against an Asian woman became a simple matter of performing two separate tasks: looking for racism "alone" and looking for sexism "alone," with Asian men and white women as the corresponding model victims. The court questioned Lam's claim of racism in light of the fact that the Dean had been interested in the late application of an Asian male. Similarly, it concluded that the faculty's subsequent offer of employment to a white woman indicated a lack of gender bias. We conclude that in relying on these facts as a basis for its summary judgment decision, the district court misconceived important legal principles.
>
> . . . As other courts have recognized, where two bases for discrimination exist, they cannot be neatly reduced to distinct components. . . . Rather than aiding the decisional process, the attempt to bisect a person's identity at the intersection of race and gender often distorts or ignores the particular nature of their experiences. . . . Like other subclasses under Title VII, Asian women are subject to a set of stereotypes and assumptions shared neither by Asian men nor by white women. In consequence, they may be targeted for discrimination "even in the absence of discrimination against [Asian] men or white women." . . . Accordingly, . . . when a plaintiff is claiming race *and* sex bias, it is necessary to determine whether the employer discriminates on the basis of that *combination* of factors, not just whether it discriminates against people of the same race or of the same sex.

40 F.3d 1551, 1561–62 (9th Cir. 1994) (footnotes and citations omitted); *see also* Caitlin Ramiro, *After Atlanta: Revisiting the Legal System's Deadly Stereotypes of Asian Women*, 29 Asian Am. L.J. 90 (2022).

What do you think of the concept of intersectionality? As a practical matter, how would a plaintiff prove discrimination on the basis of a *combination* of factors?

Chapter 12

The Model Minority

What does it mean to be a "model minority?" One Asian-American academic put it this way:

> "You Asians are all doing well anyway" summarizes the model minority myth. This is the dominant image of Asians in the United States. Ever since immigration reforms in 1965 led to a great influx of Asian people, we have enjoyed an excellent reputation. As a group, we are said to be intelligent, gifted in math and science, polite, hard working, family oriented, law abiding, and successfully entrepreneurial. We revere our elders and show fidelity to tradition. The nation has become familiar with the turn-of-the-century Horatio Alger tales of "pulling yourself up by your own bootstraps" updated for the new millennium with an "Oriental" face and imbued with Asian values.
>
> This miracle is the standard depiction of Asian Americans in fact and fiction, from the news media to scholarly books to Hollywood movies. From the 1960s to the 1990s, profiles of whiz kid Asian Americans became so common as to be cliches. . . . *Time*, *Newsweek*, *Sixty Minutes*, and other media outlets have awarded Asian Americans the title "model minority." *Fortune* magazine dubbed us the "superminority." *The New Republic* heralded, "the triumph of Asian Americans" as "America's greatest success story" and *Commentary* magazine referred to Asian Americans as "a trophy population." *The New York Times* announced that we are "going to the head of the class." *The Washington Post* said in a headline, "Asian Americans Outperform Others at School and Work." Smith College sociologist Peter Rose has described Asian Americans as making a transition "from pariahs to paragons."[1]

A *New York Times* columnist wrote an op-ed titled "The Asian Advantage," asking "Why are Asian-Americans so successful in America?"[2]

1. Frank H. Wu, *Yellow* 40–41 (2002) (footnotes omitted).
2. Nicholas Kristof, *The Asian Advantage*, N.Y. Times, Oct. 10, 2015.

Asian Americans have made significant advances since the days of the historical and blatant racism we discussed earlier. Indeed, as the Pew Research Center has recognized, based on U.S. Census information:

> Asian Americans are the highest-income, best-educated and fastest growing racial group in the United States. They are more satisfied than the general public with their lives, finances and the direction of the country, and they place more value than other Americans do on marriage, parenthood, hard work and career success. . . .
>
> A century ago, most Asian Americans were low-skilled, low-wage laborers crowded into ethnic enclaves and targets of official discrimination. Today they are the most likely of any major racial or ethnic group in America to live in mixed neighborhoods and to marry across racial lines. . . .

Pew Research Center, *The Rise of Asian Americans* (Apr. 4, 2013), www.pewsocialtrends.org/2012/06/19/the-rise-of-asian-americans/.

The Pew Center reported the following median household incomes for 2020:

U.S. population	$67,521
Asians	$94,903
Whites	$74,912
Hispanics	$55,321
Blacks	$45,870

Income and Wealth in the United States: An Overview of Recent Data, Peter G. Peterson Foundation (Nov. 17, 2021), https://www.pgpf.org/blog/2021/11/ income-and-wealth-in-the-united-states-an-overview-of-data.

Still, there are many who observe that the myth of the model minority masks a history of discrimination against AAPIs and has been used as a wedge to divide Asian Americans and other groups.[3] Indeed, while recent census data shows that Asians as a whole are less likely than the overall U.S. population to live in poverty (12.1% v. 15.1%), the percentages living in poverty are higher for certain AAPI subgroups:

3. Erin Blakemore, *The Asian American 'Model Minority' Myth Masks a History of Discrimination*, Nat'l Geographic, May 27, 2021, *available at* https://www.nationalgeographic.com/culture/article/asian-american-model-minority-myth-masks-history-discrimination; Kat Chow, *'Model Minority' Myth Again Used as a Racial Wedge Between Asians and Blacks*, NPR.com (Apr. 19, 2017), *available at* https://www.npr.org/sections/codeswitch/2017/04/19/524571669/model-minority-myth-again-used-as-a-racial-wedge-between-asians-and-blacks; *see also* Robert S. Chang, *Toward an Asian American Legal Scholarship: Critical Race Theory, Post-Structuralism, and Narrative Space*, 81 Calif. L. Rev. 1241, 1258 (1993) ("This history of discrimination and violence, as well as the contemporary problems of Asian Americans, are obscured by the portrayal of Asian Americans as a 'model minority.' Asian Americans are portrayed as 'hardworking, intelligent, and successful.' This description represents a sharp break from past stereotypes of Asians as 'sneaky, obsequious, or inscrutable.'").

for example, Hmong (28.3%), Bhutanese (33.3%), and Burmese Americans (35%).[4] Indians have a median family income of $119,000, but Burmese households earn only $44,000.[5] The rate of cervical cancer, for example, is twice as high in Vietnamese women than in non-Hispanic White women, and higher rates of diabetes are found in Filipinos and South Asians compared to the non-Hispanic White population.[6]

The Center for American Progress has issued a report urging "a closer look at disaggregated data" about Asian Americans. It concludes that there is "tremendous diversity in the Asian American population" and "large shares of this population struggle economically."[7] The report states:

> The aggregate data for Asian Americans show an apparent contradiction: Unemployment rates are lower and wages and incomes are higher for Asian Americans than they are for whites, but poverty rates and the number of people without health insurance are also higher. This is likely the result of aggregating data over a larger subgroup that does comparatively well—one that has a lower unemployment rate and higher earnings and income than whites—and a smaller subgroup that has high poverty and uninsured rates. The economically vulnerable subpopulation has to be sizable or their struggles have to be very large to affect the aggregate data on Asian Americans in a noticeable way. Put differently, we can infer from the data that most Asian Americans do somewhat better than most whites with respect to unemployment and earnings, but a sizable number of Asian Americans do worse, possibly much worse, than most whites. And we have enough data on subpopulations available to know that the subpopulations that tend to do better than whites are usually those of Chinese and Indian descent, while those of Vietnamese, Cambodian, and Filipino descent tend to fare worse than whites.[8]

And another observer writes:

---

4. Thomas Le and Emma Zeng, *Data Disaggregation Shows Startling Health Disparities Among Asian Americans*, Balt. Sun, Mar. 31, 2021, *available at* https://www.baltimoresun.com/opinion/op-ed/bs-ed-op-0331-asian-health-disparities-20210331-xciw35hutzg2pmbdduv73prdm4-story.html.

5 These are 2018 statistics. Sakshi Venkatraman, *N.Y. Enacts 'Groundbreaking' Law to Change How Asian American Populations Are Counted*, NBCNews.com (Dec. 29, 2021), *available at* https://www.nbcnews.com/news/asian-america/new-york-state-disaggregate-data-asian-american-groups-rcna10237.

6. Le and Zeng, *supra. See also* Andrea Fox, *Asian and NHPI Health Equity Is Elusive Without Disaggregated Data*, Healthcare IT News (June 6, 2023), *available at* https://www.healthcareitnews.com/news/asian-and-nhpi-health-equity-elusive-without-disaggregated-data.

7. Farah Z. Ahmad and Christian E. Weller, *Reading Between the Data: The Incomplete Story of Asian Americans, Native Hawaiians, and Pacific Islanders*, Center for American Progress (March 3, 2014), *available at* www.americanprogress.org/issues/race/reports/2014/03/03/85055/reading-between-the-data/.

8. *Id.* at 14.

> The existence of the model minority myth harms Asian Americans because they are not perceived to need the same kinds of social services, and their personalities are flattened into two-dimensional caricatures. On top of this, there is dual harm where the model minority myth serves to deny the existence of racism towards and oppression of Asian Americans while legitimizing the oppression of BIPOC communities, particularly Black communities.

Nicholas Loh, *Diasporic Dreams: Law, Whiteness, and the Asian American Identity*, 48 Fordham Urb. L.J. 1331, 1347 (2021) (footnotes omitted); *see also* Erica Pandey et al., *Redefining Asian America*, Axios (May 15, 2022) ("Asian Americans hail from dozens of countries—and their experiences in America are starkly different depending on their origins."), *available at* https://www.axios.com/2022/05/15/asian-americans-diversity-education-income.

In December 2021, New York State enacted a law that requires state agencies to break down data for individual ethnic groups under the AAPI umbrella, becoming one of the few states to pass such a law. Any state department collecting information about ethnicity or ancestry will have to use different categories for each major Asian group, including Chinese, Japanese, Filipino, Korean, Vietnamese, Indian, Laotian, Cambodian, Bangladeshi, and Hmong, and also for Pacific Islander groups, including Native Hawaiian, Guamanian, Chamorro, and Samoan. The hope, among supporters of disaggregation, is that better data will help bring about a better understanding of the challenges facing lower-income, Asian sub-groups who are often lumped together with higher-earning individuals.[9]

"Asian American Pacific Islander" seems a constructed umbrella identity that does not correspond to real facts, as the disaggregation movement rightly asserts. Why, then, use it at all? To enable political voice in U.S. politics?[10] If so, is it purely instrumental or does it reflect a real cultural identity? And, in either case, isn't it better and more faithful to the melting-pot idea of the United States as one people to celebrate unity, not diversity or affinity groups to which not all Americans belong? Is it necessarily a zero-sum game? And if not, what is the right balance to strike between "Asian" and "American?

9. Venkatraman, *supra*. *See also* Molly Lao, *The Case for Requiring Disaggregation of Asian American and Pacific Islander Data*, Calif. L. Rev. (Mar. 2021) (online blog), *available at* https://www.californialawreview.org/the-case-for-requiring-disaggregation-of-asian-american-and-pacific-islander-data/.

10. While some have argued that more data will help pinpoint needs, others contend that Asians should be counted as one group. *See* Hansi Lo Wang, *"Racist Bill?" Chinese Immigrants Protest Effort to Collect More Asian-American Data*, NPR.org (Aug. 5, 2017), *available at* https://www.npr.org/2017/08/05/ 541844705/protests-against-the-push-to-disaggragate-asian-american-data.

Chapter 13
Education

As we saw in Unit Two, education has been an important concern of Asian Americans since the nineteenth century. In *Tape v. Hurley* and *Gong Lum v. Rice*, Chinese-American parents sought to educate their children in White schools, presumably with the view that their children would benefit from assimilating into the dominant White American culture. In *Tokushige* and the post-*Brown* Chinatown public school cases, Asian-American parents sought to give their children additional or basic public school education grounded in their specific cultures and languages. In the aftermath of *Brown v. Board of Education* in 1954, supermajority Chinese-American public schools in the San Francisco School District were judicially ordered to desegregate, despite the strong desires of Chinese-American parents to maintain the status quo. The saving grace was that the Supreme Court soon thereafter in *Lau v. Nichols* construed governing statutes to require meaningful provision of English as Second Language programs—a requirement that survives today to the benefit of all new Americans who were not raised in English-language-speaking homes.

For Asian Americans, a new issue arose in the 1970s around the time of *Lau v. Nichols*. Perceiving education as the key to social mobility, younger Asian Americans sought and obtained admission to outstanding colleges, universities, and graduate schools. Their numbers at these institutions grew to a level that was disproportionate to the percentage of persons of Asian descent in the general population of the United States. Simultaneously, the leadership of those same institutions of higher education perceived access as critical to achieving racially diverse student bodies reflecting the underprivileged as well as students of means. Furthermore, these elite institutions served an important credentialing function for leadership positions in every aspect of U.S. society.

To enroll such diverse student bodies, elite colleges and universities (about 20% of U.S. higher-education institutions) employed holistic admissions processes in which racial diversity was an important factor. The legal basis for such holistic admissions processes was Justice Powell's concurring opinion in *Regents of the University of California v. Bakke*, 438 U.S. 265 (1978). In the following years, lawsuits challenging the diversity rationale in the higher educational setting were filed in *Bakke*'s aftermath. Twenty-five years after *Bakke*, the Supreme Court reaffirmed student-body diversity as a compelling interest in elite colleges, universities, and graduate schools by a 5–4 vote in *Grutter v. Bollinger*, 539 U.S. 306 (2003), a case challenging race-conscious holistic admissions to the University of Michigan Law School. At the same time, the Court struck down by a 6–3 vote the race-conscious admissions process at the University of Michigan where underrepresented minorities were given plus points in the aggregate process. *See Gratz v. Bollinger*, 539 U.S. 244 (2003). Justice O'Connor's majority opinion in *Grutter* explained that racial preferences in admissions were a compelling interest at the time but must be narrowly tailored and warned that "race-conscious admissions policies must be limited in time."

More than a decade later, in November 2014, a nonprofit corporation called Students for Fair Admissions, Inc. ("SFFA") filed a lawsuit against Harvard University in federal district court in Boston. The 120-page complaint alleged that the Harvard Corporation and its Board of Overseers "have employed and are employing racially and ethnically discriminatory policies and procedures in administering the undergraduate admissions program at Harvard College in violation of Title VI of the Civil Rights Act of 1964, 42 U.S.C. § 2000d *et seq.*" SFFA alleged that, under the guise of a "holistic" program for evaluating college applicants, Harvard had discriminated against Asian Americans to keep their numbers artificially low relative to their academic and other qualifications for elite college admission. SFFA was founded by the conservative activist Edward Blum, who also backed the plaintiff in *Fisher v. University of Texas*, 579 U.S. 365 (2016). There, the U.S. Supreme Court upheld the University of Texas's 10% admissions program by a 4–3 vote. *See generally* Anemona Hartocollis and Stephanie Saul, *Affirmative Action Battle Has a New Focus: Asian Americans*, N.Y. Times, Aug. 2, 2017.

The case was tried in Boston federal district court, without a jury, in 2018, with 30 witnesses testifying over the course of 14 days. The court ruled on September 30, 2019, in favor of Harvard. *See* 397 F. Supp. 3d 126 (D. Mass. 2019). SFFA appealed, and the First Circuit affirmed on November 12, 2020. *See* 980 F.3d 157 (1st Cir. 2020). SFFA then filed a petition for certiorari to the U.S. Supreme Court, which granted the petition on January 24, 2022. *See* 142 S. Ct. 895 (2022). The Harvard case was consolidated with an SFFA challenge to the race-conscious college admissions policy at the University of North Carolina ("UNC"). Justice Ketanji Brown Jackson recused herself from the Harvard case because she had been a member of its Board of Overseers, but she participated in the UNC case. On June 29, 2023, the Supreme Court handed down its joint decision striking down the Harvard (by a 6–2 vote) and UNC (by a 6–3 vote) race-conscious admissions policies. Chief Justice Roberts wrote the majority opinion; Justices Thomas, Gorsuch, and Kavanaugh issued concurring opinions; and Justices Sotomayor and Jackson wrote dissenting opinions.

Students for Fair Admissions, Inc. v. President and Fellows of Harvard College

600 U.S. 181 (2023)

ROBERTS, C.J.:

In these cases we consider whether the admissions systems used by Harvard College and the University of North Carolina, two of the oldest institutions of higher learning in the United States, are lawful under the Equal Protection Clause of the Fourteenth Amendment....

The admissions process at Harvard works as follows. Every application is initially screened by a "first reader," who assigns scores in six categories: academic, extracurricular, athletic, school support, personal, and overall. A rating of "1" is the best; a rating of "6" the worst. In the academic category, for example, a "1" signifies "near-perfect standardized test scores and grades"; in the extracurricular category, it indicates "truly unusual achievement"; and in the personal category, it denotes "outstanding" attributes like maturity, integrity, leadership, kindness, and courage. Id., at 167–168. A score of "1" on the overall rating—a composite of the five other ratings—"signifies an exceptional candidate with >90% chance of admission." In assigning the overall rating, the first readers "can and do take an applicant's race into account." Once the first read process is complete, Harvard convenes admissions subcommittees. Each subcommittee meets for three to five days and evaluates all applicants from a particular geographic area. The subcommittees are responsible for making recommendations to the full admissions committee. The subcommittees can and do take an applicant's race into account when making their recommendations. The next step of the Harvard process is the full committee meeting. The committee has 40 members, and its discussion centers around the applicants who have been recommended by the regional subcommittees. At the beginning of the meeting, the committee discusses the relative breakdown of applicants by race. The "goal," according to Harvard's director of admissions, "is to make sure that [Harvard does] not hav[e] a dramatic drop-off" in minority admissions from the prior class. Each applicant considered by the full committee is discussed one by one, and every member of the committee must vote on admission. Only when an applicant secures a majority of the full committee's votes is he or she tentatively accepted for admission. At the end of the full committee meeting, the racial composition of the pool of tentatively admitted students is disclosed to the committee. The final stage of Harvard's process is called the "lop," during which the list of tentatively admitted students is winnowed further to arrive at the final class. Any applicants that Harvard considers cutting at this stage are placed on a "lop list," which contains only four pieces of information: legacy status, recruited athlete status, financial aid eligibility, and race. The full committee decides as a group which students to lop. In doing so, the committee can and does take race into account. Once the lop process is complete, Harvard's admitted class is set. In the Harvard admissions process, "race is a determinative tip for" a significant percentage "of all admitted African American and Hispanic applicants." . . .

In the wake of the Civil War, Congress proposed and the States ratified the Fourteenth Amendment, providing that no State shall "deny to any person...the equal protection of the laws." Amdt. 14, § 1. To its proponents, the Equal Protection Clause represented a "foundation[al] principle"—"the absolute equality of all citizens of the United States politically and civilly before their own laws." The Constitution, they were determined, "should not permit any distinctions of law based on race or color," Supp. Brief for United States on Reargument in Brown v. Board of Education, O. T. 1953, No. 1 etc., p. 41, because any "law which operates upon one man [should] operate equally upon all." As soon-to-be President James Garfield observed, the Fourteenth Amendment would hold "over every American citizen, without regard to color, the protecting shield of law." And in doing so, said Senator Jacob Howard of Michigan, the Amendment would give "to the humblest, the poorest, the most despised of the race the same rights and the same protection before the law as it gives to the most powerful, the most wealthy, or the most haughty." For "[w]ithout this principle of equal justice," Howard continued, "there is no republican government and none that is really worth maintaining." At first, this Court embraced the transcendent aims of the Equal Protection Clause. "What is this," we said of the Clause in 1880, "but declaring that the law in the States shall be the same for the black as for the white; that all persons, whether colored or white, shall stand equal before the laws of the States?" *Strauder v. West Virginia*, 100 U. S. 303, 307–309 (1880). "[T]he broad and benign provisions of the Fourteenth Amendment" apply "to all persons," we unanimously declared six years later; it is "hostility to... race and nationality" "which in the eye of the law is not justified." *Yick Wo v. Hopkins*, 118 U. S. 356, 368–369, 373–374 (1886); see also id., at 368 (applying the Clause to "aliens and subjects of the Emperor of China"); *Truax v. Raich*, 239 U. S. 33, 36 (1915) ("a native of Austria"); *semble Strauder*, 100 U. S., at 308–309 ("Celtic Irishmen") (dictum). Despite our early recognition of the broad sweep of the Equal Protection Clause, this Court—alongside the country—quickly failed to live up to the Clause's core commitments. For almost a century after the Civil War, state-mandated segregation was in many parts of the Nation a regrettable norm. This Court played its own role in that ignoble history, allowing in *Plessy v. Ferguson* the separate but equal regime that would come to deface much of America. 163 U. S. 537 (1896)....

These cases involve whether a university may make admissions decisions that turn on an applicant's race. Our Court first considered that issue in *Regents of University of California v. Bakke*, which involved a set-aside admissions program used by the University of California, Davis, medical school. 438 U. S., at 272–276. Each year, the school held 16 of its 100 seats open for members of certain minority groups, who were reviewed on a special admissions track separate from those in the main admissions pool. Id., at 272–275. The plaintiff, Allan Bakke, was denied admission two years in a row, despite the admission of minority applicants with lower grade point averages and MCAT scores. Id., at 276–277. Bakke subsequently sued the school, arguing that its set-aside program violated the Equal Protection Clause. In a deeply splintered decision that produced six different opinions—none of which commanded a majority of the Court—we ultimately ruled in part in favor of the school and in part in favor of Bakke. Justice Powell announced the Court's judgment, and his opinion—though written for himself alone—would eventually come to "serv[e] as the touchstone for constitutional analysis of race-conscious admissions policies." *Grutter*, 539 U. S., at 323. Justice Powell began by finding three of the school's four justifications for its policy not sufficiently compelling. The school's first justification of "reducing the historic deficit of traditionally disfavored minorities in medical schools," he wrote, was akin to "[p]referring members of any one group for no reason other than race or ethnic origin." *Bakke*, 438 U. S., at 306–307 (internal quotation marks omitted). Yet that was "discrimination for its own sake," which "the Constitution forbids." Id., at 307 (citing, inter alia, *Loving v. Virginia*, 388 U. S., at 11). Justice Powell next observed that the goal of "remedying... the effects of 'societal discrimination'" was also insufficient because it was "an amorphous concept of injury that may be ageless in its reach into the past." *Bakke*, 438 U. S., at 307. Finally, Justice Powell found there was "virtually no evidence in the record indicating that [the school's] special admissions program" would, as the school had argued, increase the number of doctors working in underserved areas. Id., at 310.

Justice Powell then turned to the school's last interest asserted to be compelling—obtaining the educational benefits that flow from a racially diverse student body. That interest, in his view, was "a constitutionally permissible goal for an institution of higher education." Id., at 311–312. And that was so, he opined, because a university was entitled as a matter of academic freedom "to make its own judgments as to... the selection of its student body." Id., at 312. But a university's freedom was not unlimited. "Racial and ethnic distinctions of any sort are inherently suspect," Justice Powell explained, and antipathy toward them was deeply "rooted in our Nation's constitutional and demographic history." Id., at 291. A university could not employ a quota system, for example, reserving "a specified number of seats in each class for individuals from the preferred ethnic groups." Id., at 315. Nor could it impose a "multi-track program with a prescribed number of seats set aside for each identifiable category of applicants." Ibid. And neither still could it use race to foreclose an individual "from all consideration... simply because he was not the right color." Id., at 318. The role of race had to be cabined. It could operate only as "a 'plus' in a particular applicant's file." Id., at 317. And even then, race was to be weighed in a manner "flexible enough to consider all pertinent elements of diversity in light of the particular qualifications of each applicant." Ibid. Justice Powell derived this approach from what he called the "illuminating example" of the admissions system then used by Harvard College. Id., at 316. Under that system, as described by Harvard in a brief it had filed with the Court, "the race of an applicant may tip the balance in his favor just as geographic origin or a life [experience] may tip the balance in other candidates' cases." Harvard continued: "A farm boy from Idaho can bring something to Harvard College that a Bostonian cannot offer. Similarly, a black student can usually bring something that a white person cannot offer." The result, Harvard proclaimed, was that "race has been"—and should be—"a factor in some admission decisions." . . .

Grutter [while affirming Justice Powell's concurrence in *Bakke*] concluded with the following caution: "It has been 25 years since Justice Powell first approved the use of race to further an interest in student body diversity in the context of public higher education.... We expect that 25 years from now, the use of racial preferences will no longer be necessary to further the interest approved today." 539 U. S., at 343.

Twenty years later, no end is in sight. "Harvard's view about when [race-based admissions will end] doesn't have a date on it." Neither does UNC's. Yet both insist that the use of race in their admissions programs must continue. But we have permitted race-based admissions only within the confines of narrow restrictions. University programs must comply with strict scrutiny, they may never use race as a stereotype or negative, and—at some point—they must end. Respondents' admissions systems—however well-intentioned and implemented in good faith—fail each of these criteria. They must therefore be invalidated under the Equal Protection Clause of the Fourteenth Amendment....

First, the interests they view as compelling cannot be subjected to meaningful judicial review. Harvard identifies the following educational benefits that it is pursuing: (1) "training future leaders in the public and private sectors"; (2) preparing graduates to "adapt to an increasingly pluralistic society"; (3) "better educating its students through diversity"; and (4) "producing new knowledge stemming from diverse outlooks." 980 F. 3d, at 173–174. UNC points to similar benefits, namely, "(1) promoting the robust exchange of ideas; (2) broadening and refining understanding; (3) fostering innovation and problem-solving; (4) preparing engaged and productive citizens and leaders; [and] (5) enhancing appreciation, respect, and empathy, cross-racial understanding, and breaking down stereotypes." Although these are commendable goals, they are not sufficiently coherent for purposes of strict scrutiny. At the outset, it is unclear how courts are supposed to measure any of these goals. How is a court to know whether leaders have been adequately "train[ed]"; whether the exchange of ideas is "robust"; or whether "new knowledge" is being developed? Even if these goals could somehow be measured, moreover, how is a court to know when they have been reached, and when the perilous remedy of racial preferences may cease? . . .

Second, respondents' admissions programs fail to articulate a meaningful connection between the means they employ and the goals they pursue. To achieve the educational benefits of diversity, UNC works to avoid the underrepresentation of minority groups, while Harvard likewise "guard[s] against inadvertent drop-offs in representation" of certain minority groups from year to year. To accomplish both of those goals, in turn, the universities measure the racial composition of their classes using the following categories: (1) Asian; (2) Native Hawaiian or Pacific Islander; (3) Hispanic; (4) White; (5) African-American; and (6) Native American. It is far from evident, though, how assigning students to these racial categories and making admissions decisions based on them furthers the educational benefits that the universities claim to pursue.

For starters, the categories are themselves imprecise in many ways. Some of them are plainly overbroad: by grouping together all Asian students, for instance, respondents are apparently uninterested in whether South Asian or East Asian students are adequately represented, so long as there is enough of one to compensate for a lack of the other. Meanwhile other racial categories, such as "Hispanic," are arbitrary or undefined. And still other categories are underinclusive. When asked at oral argument "how are applicants from Middle Eastern countries classified, [such as] Jordan, Iraq, Iran, [and] Egypt," UNC's counsel responded, "[I] do not know the answer to that question."

Indeed, the use of these opaque racial categories undermines, instead of promotes, respondents' goals. By focusing on underrepresentation, respondents would apparently prefer a class with 15% of students from Mexico over a class with 10% of students from several Latin American countries, simply because the former contains more Hispanic students than the latter. Yet "[i]t is hard to understand how a plan that could allow these results can be viewed as being concerned with achieving enrollment that is 'broadly diverse.'" And given the mismatch between the means respondents employ and the goals they seek, it is especially hard to understand how courts are supposed to scrutinize the admissions programs that respondents use.

The universities' main response to these criticisms is, essentially, "trust us." None of the questions recited above need answering, they say, because universities are "owed deference" when using race to benefit some applicants but not others. It is true that our cases have recognized a "tradition of giving a degree of deference to a university's academic decisions." *Grutter*, 539 U. S., at 328. But we have been unmistakably clear that any deference must exist "within constitutionally prescribed limits," and that "deference does not imply abandonment or abdication of judicial review," *Miller-El v. Cockrell*, 537 U. S. 322, 340 (2003). Universities may define their missions as they see fit. The Constitution defines ours. Courts may not license separating students on the basis of race without an exceedingly persuasive justification that is measurable and concrete enough to permit judicial review....

The race-based admissions systems that respondents employ also fail to comply with the twin commands of the Equal Protection Clause that race may never be used as a "negative" and that it may not operate as a stereotype. First, our cases have stressed that an individual's race may never be used against him in the admissions process. Here, however, the First Circuit found that Harvard's consideration of race has led to an 11.1% decrease in the number of Asian-Americans admitted to Harvard. 980 F. 3d, at 170, n. 29. And the District Court observed that Harvard's "policy of considering applicants' race... overall results in fewer Asian American and white students being admitted." 397 F. Supp. 3d, at 178. Respondents nonetheless contend that an individual's race is never a negative factor in their admissions programs, but that assertion cannot withstand scrutiny. Harvard, for example, draws an analogy between race and other factors it considers in admission. "[W]hile admissions officers may give a preference to applicants likely to excel in the Harvard-Radcliffe Orchestra," Harvard explains, "that does not mean it is a 'negative' not to excel at a musical instrument." But on Harvard's logic, while it gives preferences to applicants with high grades and test scores, "that does not mean it is a 'negative'" to be a student with lower grades and lower test scores. This understanding of the admissions process is hard to take seriously. College admissions are zero-sum....

For the reasons provided above, the Harvard and UNC admissions programs cannot be reconciled with the guarantees of the Equal Protection Clause. Both programs lack sufficiently focused and measurable objectives warranting the use of race, unavoidably employ race in a negative manner, involve racial stereotyping, and lack meaningful end points. We have never permitted admissions programs to work in that way, and we will not do so today. At the same time, as all parties agree, nothing in this opinion should be construed as prohibiting universities from considering an applicant's discussion of how race affected his or her life, be it through discrimination, inspiration, or otherwise. But, despite the dissent's assertion to the contrary, universities may not simply establish through application essays or other means the regime we hold unlawful today. (A dissenting opinion is generally not the best source of legal advice on how to comply with the majority opinion.) "[W]hat cannot be done directly cannot be done indirectly. The Constitution deals with substance, not shadows," and the prohibition against racial discrimination is "levelled at the thing, not the name." *Cummings v. Missouri*, 4 Wall. 277, 325 (1867). A benefit to a student who overcame racial discrimination, for example, must be tied to that student's courage and determination. Or a benefit to a student whose heritage or culture motivated him or her to assume a leadership role or attain a particular goal must be tied to that student's unique ability to contribute to the university. In other words, the student must be treated based on his or her experiences as an individual—not on the basis of race.

Many universities have for too long done just the opposite. And in doing so, they have concluded, wrongly, that the touchstone of an individual's identity is not challenges bested, skills built, or lessons learned but the color of their skin. Our constitutional history does not tolerate that choice.

The judgments of the Court of Appeals for the First Circuit and of the District Court for the Middle District of North Carolina are reversed.

Justice SOTOMAYOR, with whom Justice KAGAN and Justice JACKSON [for the UNC case] join, dissenting.

The Equal Protection Clause of the Fourteenth Amendment enshrines a guarantee of racial equality. The Court long ago concluded that this guarantee can be enforced through race-conscious means in a society that is not, and has never been, colorblind. In *Brown v. Board of Education*, 347 U. S. 483 (1954), the Court recognized the constitutional necessity of racially integrated schools in light of the harm inflicted by segregation and the "importance of education to our democratic society." For 45 years, the Court extended *Brown*'s transformative legacy to the context of higher education, allowing colleges and universities to consider race in a limited way and for the limited purpose of promoting the important benefits of racial diversity. This limited use of race has helped equalize educational opportunities for all students of every race and background and has improved racial diversity on college campuses. Although progress has been slow and imperfect, race-conscious college admissions policies have advanced the Constitution's guarantee of equality and have promoted *Brown*'s vision of a Nation with more inclusive schools.

Today, this Court stands in the way and rolls back decades of precedent and momentous progress. It holds that race can no longer be used in a limited way in college admissions to achieve such critical benefits. In so holding, the Court cements a superficial rule of colorblindness as a constitutional principle in an endemically segregated society where race has always mattered and continues to matter. The Court subverts the constitutional guarantee of equal protection by further entrenching racial inequality in education, the very foundation of our democratic government and pluralistic society. Because the Court's opinion is not grounded in law or fact and contravenes the vision of equality embodied in the Fourteenth Amendment, I dissent.

. . .

Two decades after *Brown*, in *Bakke*, a plurality of the Court held that "the attainment of a diverse student body" is a "compelling" and "constitutionally permissible goal for an institution of higher education." Race could be considered in the college admissions process in pursuit of this goal, the plurality explained, if it is one factor of many in an applicant's file, and each applicant receives individualized review as part of a holistic admissions process. Since *Bakke*, the Court has reaffirmed numerous times the constitutionality of limited race-conscious college admissions....

In short, for more than four decades, it has been this Court's settled law that the Equal Protection Clause of the Fourteenth Amendment authorizes a limited use of race in college admissions in service of the educational benefits that flow from a diverse student body. From *Brown* to *Fisher*, this Court's cases have sought to equalize educational opportunity in a society structured by racial segregation and to advance the Fourteenth Amendment's vision of an America where racially integrated schools guarantee students of all races the equal protection of the laws.

Today, the Court concludes that indifference to race is the only constitutionally permissible means to achieve racial equality in college admissions. That interpretation of the Fourteenth Amendment is not only contrary to precedent and the entire teachings of our history, but is also grounded in the illusion that racial inequality was a problem of a different generation. Entrenched racial inequality remains a reality today. That is true for society writ large and, more specifically, for Harvard and the University of North Carolina (UNC), two institutions with a long history of racial exclusion. Ignoring race will not equalize a society that is racially unequal. What was true in the 1860s, and again in 1954, is true today: Equality requires acknowledgment of inequality....

Answering the question whether Harvard's and UNC's policies survive strict scrutiny under settled law is straightforward, both because of the procedural posture of these cases and because of the narrow scope of the issues presented by petitioner

Students for Fair Admissions, Inc. (SFFA). These cases arrived at this Court after two lengthy trials. Harvard and UNC introduced dozens of fact witnesses, expert testimony, and documentary evidence in support of their admissions programs. SFFA, by contrast, did not introduce a single fact witness and relied on the testimony of two experts. After making detailed findings of fact and conclusions of law, the District Courts entered judgment in favor of Harvard and UNC. The First Circuit affirmed in the Harvard case, finding "no error" in the District Court's thorough opinion. SFFA then filed petitions for a writ of certiorari in both cases, which the Court granted. The Court granted certiorari on three questions: (1) whether the Court should overrule Bakke, Grutter, and Fisher; or, alternatively, (2) whether UNC's admissions program is narrowly tailored, and (3) whether Harvard's admissions program is narrowly tailored. Answering the last two questions, which call for application of settled law to the facts of these cases, is simple: Deferring to the lower courts' careful findings of fact and credibility determinations, Harvard's and UNC's policies are narrowly tailored....

The Court argues that Harvard's and UNC's programs must end because they unfairly disadvantage some racial groups. According to the Court, college admissions are a "zero-sum" game and respondents' use of race unfairly "advantages" underrepresented minority students "at the expense of" other students. That is not the role race plays in holistic admissions. Consistent with the Court's precedents, respondents' holistic review policies consider race in a very limited way. Race is only one factor out of many. That type of system allows Harvard and UNC to assemble a diverse class on a multitude of dimensions. Respondents' policies allow them to select students with various unique attributes, including talented athletes, artists, scientists, and musicians. They also allow respondents to assemble a class with diverse viewpoints, including students who have different political ideologies and academic interests, who have struggled with different types of disabilities, who are from various socioeconomic backgrounds, who understand different ways of life in various parts of the country, and—yes—students who self-identify with various racial backgrounds and who can offer different perspectives because of that identity. That type of multidimensional system benefits all students. In fact, racial groups that are not underrepresented tend to benefit disproportionately from such a system. Harvard's holistic system, for example, provides points to applicants who qualify as "ALDC," meaning "athletes, legacy applicants, applicants on the Dean's Interest List [primarily relatives of donors], and children of faculty or staff." ALDC applicants are predominantly white: Around 67.8% are white, 11.4% are Asian American, 6% are Black, and 5.6% are Latino. By contrast, only 40.3% of non-ALDC applicants are white, 28.3% are Asian American, 11% are Black, and 12.6% are Latino. Although "ALDC applicants make up less than 5% of applicants to Harvard," they constitute "around 30% of the applicants admitted each year." Similarly, because of achievement gaps that result from entrenched racial inequality in K–12 education, a heavy emphasis on grades and standardized test scores disproportionately disadvantages underrepresented racial minorities. Stated simply, race is one small piece of a much larger admissions puzzle where most of the pieces disfavor underrepresented racial minorities. That is precisely why underrepresented racial minorities remain underrepresented. The Court's suggestion that an already advantaged racial group is "disadvantaged" because of a limited use of race is a myth.

The majority's true objection appears to be that a limited use of race in college admissions does, in fact, achieve what it is designed to achieve: It helps equalize opportunity and advances respondents' objectives by increasing the number of underrepresented racial minorities on college campuses, particularly Black and Latino students. This is unacceptable, the Court says, because racial groups that are not underrepresented "would be admitted in greater numbers" without these policies. Reduced to its simplest terms, the Court's conclusion is that an increase in the representation of racial minorities at institutions of higher learning that were historically reserved for white Americans is an unfair and repugnant outcome that offends the Equal Protection Clause....

Citing no evidence, Justice Thomas [in his concurrence] also suggests that race-conscious admissions programs discriminate against Asian American students. It is true that SFFA "allege[d]" that Harvard discriminates against Asian American students. Specifically, SFFA argued that Harvard discriminates against Asian American applicants vis-à-vis white applicants through the use of the personal rating, an allegedly "highly subjective" component of the admissions process that is "susceptible to stereotyping and bias." It is also true, however, that there was a lengthy trial to test those allegations, which SFFA lost. Justice Thomas points to no legal or factual error below, precisely because there is none. To begin, this part of SFFA's discrimination claim does not even fall under the strict scrutiny framework in Grutter and its progeny, which concerns the use of racial classifications. The personal rating is a facially race-neutral component of Harvard's admissions policy. Therefore, even assuming for the sake of argument that Harvard engages in racial discrimination through the personal rating, there is no connection between that rating and the remedy that SFFA sought and that the majority grants today: ending the limited use of race in the entire admissions process. In any event, after assessing the credibility of fact witnesses and considering extensive documentary evidence and expert testimony, the courts below found "no discrimination against Asian Americans."

There is no question that the Asian American community continues to struggle against potent and dehumanizing stereotypes in our society. It is precisely because racial discrimination persists in our society, however, that the use of race in college admissions to achieve racially diverse classes is critical to improving cross-racial understanding and breaking down racial stereotypes. Indeed, the record shows that some Asian American applicants are actually "advantaged by Harvard's use of race," and "eliminating consideration of race would significantly disadvantage at least some Asian American applicants," Harvard I, 397 F. Supp. 3d, at 194. Race-conscious holistic admissions that contextualize the racial identity of each individual allow Asian American applicants "who would be less likely to be admitted without a comprehensive understanding of their background" to explain "the value of their unique background, heritage, and perspective." Because the Asian American community is not a monolith, race-conscious holistic admissions allow colleges and universities to "consider the vast differences within [that] community." Harvard's application files show that race-conscious holistic admissions allow Harvard to "valu[e] the diversity of Asian American applicants' experiences." Moreover, the admission rates of Asian Americans at institutions with race-conscious admissions policies, including at Harvard, have "been steadily increasing for decades." By contrast, Asian American enrollment declined at elite universities that are prohibited by state law from considering race. At bottom, race-conscious admissions benefit all students, including racial minorities. That includes the Asian American community....

By ending race-conscious college admissions, this Court closes the door of opportunity that the Court's precedents helped open to young students of every race. It creates a leadership pipeline that is less diverse than our increasingly diverse society, reserving "positions of influence, affluence, and prestige in America" for a predominantly white pool of college graduates. At its core, today's decision exacerbates segregation and diminishes the inclusivity of our Nation's institutions in service of superficial neutrality that promotes indifference to inequality and ignores the reality of race.

True equality of educational opportunity in racially diverse schools is an essential component of the fabric of our democratic society. It is an interest of the highest order and a foundational requirement for the promotion of equal protection under the law. *Brown* recognized that passive race neutrality was inadequate to achieve the constitutional guarantee of racial equality in a Nation where the effects of segregation persist. In a society where race continues to matter, there is no constitutional requirement that institutions attempting to remedy their legacies of racial exclusion must operate with a blindfold. Today, this Court overrules decades of precedent and imposes a superficial rule of race blindness on the Nation. The devastating impact of this decision cannot be overstated. The majority's vision of race neutrality will entrench racial segregation in higher education because racial inequality will persist so long as it is ignored.

Notwithstanding this Court's actions, however, society's progress toward equality cannot be permanently halted. Diversity is now a fundamental American value, housed in our varied and multicultural American community that only continues to grow. The pursuit of racial diversity will go on. Although the Court has stripped out almost all uses of race in college admissions, universities can and should continue to use all available tools to meet society's needs for diversity in education. Despite the Court's unjustified exercise of power, the opinion today will serve only to highlight the Court's own impotence in the face of an America whose cries for equality resound. As has been the case before in the history of American democracy, "the arc of the moral universe" will bend toward racial justice despite the Court's efforts today to impede its progress. Martin Luther King "Our God is Marching On!" Speech (Mar. 25, 1965).

Notes

1. Does the majority opinion overrule *Grutter?* What can colleges and universities that remain committed to racial diversity in their student bodies do to realize such diversity? What, if any, will be the impact of the Supreme Court's decision on Asian-American applicants?

2. If you are Asian American, were you concerned about stereotypes when you applied to college? Is there discrimination against Asian Americans if, as SFFA argued, they have higher test scores but lower "personal ratings" than similarly situated applicants? Do you agree with Justice Sotomayor's argument in dissent that race-based diversity admissions policies benefit all minorities, including Asian Americans? If so, how, exactly? What does Chief Justice Roberts' opinion for the majority say specifically regarding SFFA's argument that race-conscious admissions policies help underrepresented minorities such as Black and Hispanic applicants at the expense of Asian-American applicants?

3. Harvard's lead attorney at trial was Bill Lee, a partner at WilmerHale and one of the country's leading intellectual property lawyers. In response to a suggestion that he was perhaps chosen to try the case "because it put an Asian-American face on the team," Lee responded to the *New York Times* as follows: "When I arrived here in Boston I was the only Asian-American lawyer in the entire city.... Forty-two years later I hope I'm still doing it because I'm good at it." Anemona Hartocollis, *Lead Counsel for Harvard in Bias Trial Recalls His Run-ins with Discrimination*, N.Y. Times, Oct. 16, 2018.

4. Unlike the other affirmative action cases that reached the Supreme Court, which were decided on stipulated facts, the Harvard case was actually tried, with live witnesses. As a consequence, a rich factual record was developed. The district court's 120-page decision set forth detailed findings of fact, carefully describing Harvard's admissions process. The parties relied heavily on statistics, but Harvard admissions officers and eight former or current Harvard students testified. The students were not called by Harvard, but were permitted to testify on behalf of *amici curiae*. What do you think the live testimony added? How is it that the students testified on behalf of *amici curiae* when live testimony is generally limited to the parties to the lawsuit?

5. Do you think the Supreme Court would apply the same analysis to race-conscious admissions policies to public high schools? In the New York City public school system, there are eight specialized high schools where students are admitted solely on the basis of their scores on a standardized test. At Stuyvesant High School, more than 70% of the student body is now Asian American. In 2024, only 10 out of 744 offers of admission to the incoming freshman class were made to Black students, up from only nine the year before. Some have proposed eliminating the test, but

any such change would require a change in state law for three of the high schools (Stuyvesant, Bronx Science, and Brooklyn Tech). Efforts to address the issue over the years have failed. *See* Troy Closson, *More Black and Latino Students Admitted to New York's Elite High Schools*, N.Y. Times, June 18, 2024.

Although Black and Latino students make up nearly 70% of New York City's public school system, only 12% of the students admitted to the City's elite high schools are Black and Latino. *See id.* (12 percent of offers went to Black and Latino students, the highest number since 2013) While the City has proposed replacing the exam with a system that would admit the top students from every middle school in New York City, some have predicted that while such a system would substantially increase the number of Black and Latino students in the specialized high schools, the number of Asian students would be cut by about half. Eliza Shapiro, *This Year, Only 10 Black Students Got Into N.Y.C.'s Top High School*, N.Y. Times, Mar. 19, 2020. The question has divided Asian Americans, and some view the proposal as pitting Asian Americans against other groups. *See* Eliza Shapiro, *Racist? Fair? Biased? Asian-American Alumni Debate Elite High School Admissions*, N.Y. Times, Feb. 6, 2019.

Should the "test" be scrapped? Do we want schools that are more than 70% one race—any race? Doesn't that seem like a segregated school system in fact, even if not by design? If you agree that diverse student bodies at the top NYC specialized schools are desirable, how do we achieve such diversity without seeming to "penalize" Asians, many of whom are socioeconomically disadvantaged and perceive admission to such schools as their best opportunity for social mobility?

6. In February 2022, a judge in the Eastern District of Virginia held that a new admissions policy at the prestigious Thomas Jefferson High School for Science and Technology discriminated against Asian Americans. The court held that the new program, which the school board implemented to boost African American and Latino representation at the school, resulted in illegal "racial balancing." The new policy replaced an admissions test with a system evaluating "experience factors." In the first year under the new system, Asian-American representation dropped from 73% to roughly 54%; the Black student population increased from 2.0 percent to 7.1%; the Hispanic student population increased from 3.3% to 11.3%.

   Swayed in particular by statements by individual school officials that there were too many Asians at the school, the district court granted summary judgment in favor of the plaintiff, which is very rare. *See Coalition for TJ v. Fairfax Co. School Bd.*, No. 1:21cv296, 2022 WL 579809 (E.D. Va. Feb. 25, 2022); *see also* Hannah Natanson, *Judge calls Thomas Jefferson High Admissions Changes Illegal*, Wash. Post, Feb. 25, 2022. The Fourth Circuit granted the School Board's motion for a stay pending appeal and ruled that the School Board "may proceed with its use of the challenged admissions plan." *Coalition for TJ v. Fairfax Co. School Bd.*, No. 22-1280, 2022 WL 986994, *1 (4th Cir. Mar. 31, 2022). An application to the Supreme Court to vacate the stay was denied on April 25, 2022. *See Coalition for*

TJ v. Fairfax Co. School Board, 142 S. Ct. 2672 (2022). The denial of the motion to vacate the stay meant that the School Board could proceed—pending a resolution of the appeal on the merits—with its new admissions program. *See* Robert Barnes and Hannah Natanson, *Supreme Court Lets Thomas Jefferson High School Admissions Policy Stand*, Wash. Post, April 25, 2022. A Fourth Circuit panel then reversed the district court's grant of summary judgment and granted summary judgment in favor of the defendant school board by a 2-1 vote on May 23, 2023. The plaintiffs filed a petition for *certiorari*, which the Supreme Court denied on February 20, 2024, with Justice Alito, joined by Justice Thomas, dissenting from denial of *certiorari*. Why do you think there were not four votes by members of the Court for *certiorari*? How is the argument for student body diversity at specialized and elite public high schools different, if at all, from the argument for such diversity at elite colleges and universities? What about student-body racial diversity at preschools, elementary schools, and middle schools? How is the aim of racial diversity in these settings similar to and yet different from the interest in racial diversity in higher education or in high schools?

7. Also in February 2022, San Francisco voters recalled three members of the seven-member school board, in part because of plans to replace a merit-based admissions system with a lottery system at Lowell High School, one of the city's best public schools. The vote was overwhelmingly in favor of recalling the three board members, one of whom some years earlier tweeted purportedly racist statements about Asian Americans. *See* Peter Granitz, *San Francisco Voters Recall 3 School Board Members*, NPR (Feb. 16, 2022), https://www.npr.org/2022/02/16/1081035770/san-francisco-voters-recall-three-school-board-members.

8. While it is unclear what the long-term effects the Supreme Court's decision will have on college admissions, *see* Anemona Hartocollis, *Harvard's Black Student Enrollment Dips After Affirmative Action Ends*, N.Y. Times, Sept. 11, 2024 (noting a "dip" in enrollment of Black Students at Harvard, "smaller than the school predicted, but still significant," of 16 to 14% from the year before; Asian-American representation remained the same at 37%; Hispanic enrollment increased from 14 to 16%), many organizations—both in the private and public sectors—are rolling back or discontinuing their diversity programs. *See* Conor Murray, *FBI Shutters DEI Office: Here Are the Organizations Ending Diversity Programs*, Forbes, Jan. 17, 2025, *available at* https://www.forbes.com/sites/conormurray/2025/01/17/fbi-shutters-dei-office-here-are-the-organizations-ending-diversity-programs-full-list/ (naming, among others, the FBI, Amazon, Meta, McDonald's, Walmart, Boeing, Ford Motor Co., Harley Davidson).

Chapter 14
The Administration of Justice

In Unit Two, we saw the early challenges that Asian-American litigants faced in the courts. In *People v. Washington*, on the basis of a law prohibiting Chinese witnesses from testifying against White persons, the court held that a Chinese victim of an assault by, in the words of the court, a "mulatto" could not testify against the assailant; otherwise, the defendant's right to equal protection of the law would be violated, as a Black man was entitled to the same protections as a White man. The ruling entirely ignored the rights of the Chinese victim of the crime.

In the modern era, Asian Americans still face challenges in the administration of justice—of a different sort. We consider five cases: a murder case against a young Korean American in California in the 1970s; the criminal prosecution of a family-owned bank in New York's Chinatown in the aftermath of the 2008 financial crisis; the criminal prosecution of a Chinese New York police officer for killing a Black man; the criminal prosecution of 10 Filipino nurses and their lawyer arising from a labor dispute; and the case of Private Danny Chen, a victim of hazing.

1. *People v. Chol Soo Lee*

On June 3, 1973, about 7:00 p.m., on a crowded street in San Francisco's Chinatown, an Asian man was shot three times, once in the back of the head. He was the latest casualty in a series of Chinatown gang murders. The assailant, also an Asian man, escaped into the crowd, tossing his gun away in an alley.

Within days the police arrested Chol Soo Lee, a 20-year-old Korean immigrant. He was convicted of first-degree murder and sentenced to life imprisonment. In 1977, while serving his sentence, he fatally stabbed another inmate, a neo-Nazi, in a prison-yard fight. Despite his claim of self-defense, Lee was convicted of first-degree murder—and this time, because of his prior murder conviction, he was sentenced to death.

A third-generation Japanese-American college student, an American-born Korean community organizer, and a Korean immigrant newspaper reporter began to question the fairness of the police investigation and judicial proceedings. The case became known as "the Alice in Chinatown Murder Case." The effort to free Chol Soo Lee that followed brought together a broad coalition of Asian Americans of different generations, ethnicities, and ideologies.

Why was Chol Soo Lee arrested? How did he come to the attention of the authorities? And if he was indeed innocent, how was a jury persuaded to convict him?

There were a number of factors—shoddy police work (including a critical error in the ballistics analysis and the suppression of material evidence), the inherent unreliability of eyewitness identification testimony (particularly given the setting of a shooting on a crowded street), a suggestive line-up, uneven lawyering, and undoubtedly an element of cultural and racial bias. Chol Soo Lee was tried before an all-White jury, and the judge, prosecutor, and defense lawyer were all White as well. At trial, the arresting officer identified Chol Soo Lee as a "Chinese male"—and Lee's lawyer did not even object or point out that Lee was Korean, a significant distinction in a case involving Chinese gangs. But Lee was also at fault—he had accidentally fired a gun a few days earlier and had been visited by the police in the ensuing investigation.

Figure 14. 1 ***Chol Soo Lee, holding number 5 in police lineup.***

And so Chol Soo Lee was arrested, tried, and convicted. He was sentenced to life imprisonment and was imprisoned in the California state prison system at a time when prison gangs organized largely on racial lines dominated. There was safety in numbers, but there were few Asian-American inmates, and so Lee had to find other ways to survive. In 1977, while in prison, Lee fatally stabbed another prisoner, a neo-Nazi. Lee claimed self-defense, but he was convicted of first-degree murder and sentenced to death.

A newspaper reporter—a Korean immigrant named K.W. Lee—had taken an interest in Chol Soo Lee's case before, but the situation became more urgent once Chol Soo Lee was put on death row. K.W. Lee wrote a series of articles about the case, including a two-part feature published in January 1978. The first story focused on Lee's life after his arrival in America at the age of 12. Unable to speak English and small for his age, he was bullied, beaten up, arrested, committed to the state mental hospital, and placed in a foster home. He tried to commit suicide. In all those years, he received little support; he never met a Korean interpreter or counselor or teacher. In the second article, K.W. Lee focused on what he called "the nagging question," writing: "This young Korean, who police suspected belonged to a Chinese gang, may have been railroaded in an unreal, Alice-in-Chinatown murder case where the deck was stacked against him in an ethnocentric system oblivious to the realities and experiences of Asian ethnic groups in California.... The San Francisco police practice did little to dispel the old fear of Asian Californians who have often been plagued by the so-called 'Orientals all look alike' syndrome in criminal matters." K.W. Lee, *Alice-in-Chinatown Murder Case*, Sacramento Union, Jan. 30, 1978; *see also* K.W. Lee, *Lost in a Strange Culture*, Sacramento Union, Jan. 29, 1978.

Figure 14.2 ***Chol Soo Lee with Jay Yoo*****. Photo by Grant Din.**

With K.W. Lee's articles as a catalyst, and through efforts of other individuals who wanted to help, the Chol Soo Lee Defense Committee was created. Many Asian Americans, from different walks of life—college and law students, Buddhist monks, foreign-born and American-born Asians, Korean church communities, strangers willing to put their homes up as security for bail—came together in what many believe to be the first pan-Asian grassroots movement, to support Chol Soo Lee in his fight for justice. With the Committee's help, Lee was able to retain new counsel. They filed on his behalf a petition for a writ of habeas corpus challenging his conviction in the Chinatown murder case. In February 1979, after an evidentiary hearing, the court granted the petition, finding that critical evidence—the identity of an eyewitness—had been suppressed. *In re Chol Soo Lee*, No. 54003, Memorandum and Order (Superior Ct. Sacramento Co. Jan. 19, 1979) (granting writ of habeas corpus).

In the meantime, the trial judge in the prison yard case refused to stay the proceedings, even after the habeas petition was granted in the Chinatown case. The two cases thus moved forward in parallel. Eventually, the California Court of Appeals affirmed the granting of the habeas petition in the Chinatown case, *In re Chol Soo Lee*, 103 Cal. App. 3d 615 (1980), and in the retrial, Lee was acquitted of the Chinatown murder. Lee's conviction in the prison yard murder was also reversed on appeal, as the appellate court found that the trial judge erred in its instructions to the jury and in allowing hearsay evidence. *See* Michael Otten, *Chol Soo Lee's 2nd Conviction Reversed*, Sacramento Union, Jan. 15, 1983. On remand, Chol Soo Lee was granted bail and released. He eventually agreed to plead guilty in the prison yard case to a lesser charge of second-degree murder, without an admission of guilt, in return for a sentence of time served.

After his release, however, Chol Soo Lee's struggles continued. He was not prepared for life after prison. He eventually started using drugs and returned to prison to serve 18 months for drug possession. In 1991, in a failed arson attempt, he slipped and fell on a gasoline-soaked floor and suffered extensive burns. *See* Issacs, Matt, *Twice Burned*, SF Weekly, June 14, 2000, *available at* http://www.sfweekly.com/ news/twice-burned/. But over the years, he turned his life around, as he spoke to Asian-American groups, provided guidance to at-risk youth, and advocated on behalf of incarcerated Asian Americans.

Lee had taken copious notes in prison, and eventually his notes and recollections were compiled into a book published in 2017, with the assistance of Professor Richard Kim and students in the Asian American Studies Department at UC Davis. Chol Soo Lee, *Freedom Without Justice: The Prison Memoirs of Chol Soo Lee* (Richard S. Kim, ed. 2017). Unfortunately, Lee did not live to see his work completed, as he died in December 2014, at the age of 62, because of continuing difficulties from his injuries suffered in the arson attempt.[1]

Chol Soo Lee's fight for justice inspired many to action and drew much attention. In 1978, Asian-American musicians recorded a folk-rock song, the *Ballad of Chol Soo Lee*, to raise funds for his defense. In 1982, the ABC news program *20/20* aired an award-winning story, *A Question of Justice*. And in 1989, the movie *True Believer*, starring James Woods and Robert Downey, Jr., was released, although it focused on the two defense lawyers rather than on Chol Soo Lee.[2] Perhaps the greatest impact of Chol

1. Bob Egelko, *Chol Soo Lee, Famed for Murder Conviction and Release, Dies at 62*, SF Gate, Dec. 17, 2014, *available at* https://www.sfgate.com/bayarea/article/Chol-Soo-Lee-famed-for-murder-conviction-and-5963898.php. *See also* Richard S. Kim, *A Conversation with Chol Soo Lee and K.W. Lee*, 31 Amerasia J. 76 (2005); Richard S. Kim, *In Search of Freedom and Justice: Thirty Years After the Free Chol Soo Lee Movement*, 39 Ameriasia J. 3 (2013).

2. Matt Saincome, *Hear Jeff Adachi's 1978 Psychedelic Folk-Rock Tune: "The Ballad of Chol Soo Lee,"* SF Weekly, June 11, 2015, *available at* http://www.sfweekly.com/music/hear-jeff-adachis-1978

Soo Lee's story is the impact he had on others, including those who helped him, who were inspired to continue working to address the issues Chol Soo Lee's case raised.

Here are excerpts from the decision affirming the granting of the habeas petition:

In re Chol Soo Lee

103 Cal. App. 3d 615 (3d Dist. Mar. 21, 1980)

Justice PARAS:

In the course of examining discovery files regarding the 1974 conviction, the 1977 defense attorneys learned of an all points bulletin and a San Francisco Police Department interdepartmental memorandum, neither of which had been given to defense counsel in 1974.

A petition for writ of habeas corpus was filed alleging inter alia that defendant was denied a fair trial by the prosecution's suppression of material evidence. During the course of the habeas hearings, defense investigators used the information contained in the memorandum, the bulletin, and other documents to locate one Steven Morris, who reported to them that he had witnessed the shooting and defendant was not the attacker. He so testified at the habeas corpus hearings and added emphatically that he had advised the San Francisco police by a phone call the day after the killing that he was an eyewitness.

At the conclusion of the hearings, the trial court found that Morris in fact told [Detective] Coreris he was an eyewitness and that this crucial information was withheld from the defense to its prejudice.

The People contend Morris' testimony was inherently improbable and unworthy of belief. Irrespective of whether the testimony of Morris as to what he saw on June 3, 1973 is or is not inherently improbable, the defendant and his lawyers were still entitled to know of it so that they could judge that matter for themselves.

The judgment is affirmed.

2. *People v. Abacus Federal Savings Bank*

In 2012, the New York County District Attorney's Office indicted Abacus Federal Savings Bank along with 19 employees or former employees. Abacus and the employees were charged in a 184-count indictment with selling hundreds of millions

-psychedelic-folk-rock-tune-the-ballad-of-chol-soo-lee/; *20/20, Chol Soo Lee documentary, Part 1 of 2* (1982), *available at* https://www.youtube.com/watch?v=HudisAmMC8s.; *20/20, Chol Soo Lee documentary, Part 2 of 2* (1982), *available at* https://www.youtube.com/ watch?v=RB3PhrJq9Mk; *True Believer* (1989) (movie based on Chol Soo Lee case, starring James Woods, Robert Downey Jr., and Margaret Colin).

of dollars of fraudulent mortgages to Fannie Mae, by scheming to falsify loan applications for borrowers who did not in fact qualify for the loans.[3] More than three years later, following a three-month trial, the bank and the supervisors were found not guilty of all charges.[4] Some of the bank employees had in fact engaged in criminal conduct, and indeed 10 former bank employees had earlier pleaded guilty.[5] But the bank discovered the misconduct, fired the employees, and promptly reported the matter to the authorities. Yet the prosecutors pursued the charges against the bank and several of its officers. In doing so, they engaged in conduct that would later become the subject of scrutiny. For example, they paraded bank employees through the Manhattan Criminal Courthouse, handcuffed and chained together, in front of news cameras. They showed a lack of understanding for how the economy worked in Chinatown, where low-wage-earning immigrants had difficulty getting bank credit but still managed to save substantial sums of money.

As we saw with the early arrivers, the Chinatown immigrants worked hard, spent little, and saved a lot. In fact, there were few defaults—the bank's default rate during the five-year period covered by the indictment was 0.3%, far below the national average. McKinley, *supra*. Abacus—a small family bank run by lawyers—spent more than $10 million defending against the charges. In the aftermath of the 2008 financial crisis, Abacus was the only bank prosecuted for mortgage fraud. In 2018, a documentary about the case—*Abacus: Small Enough to Jail*—was nominated for an Academy Award for best documentary feature.[6]

3. Police Officer Peter Liang

On November 20, 2014, Akai Gurley, a 28-year-old, unarmed Black man, was killed by a ricocheting bullet when a New York City police officer discharged his drawn sidearm in a darkened stairwell of a Brooklyn public-housing apartment building. The public-housing complex was known as a dangerous area for police to patrol. The police officer, Peter Liang, had emigrated to the United States from

---

3. Karen Freifeld, *Abacus Federal Savings Bank Indicted for Mortgage Fraud*, Reuters.com (May 31, 2012), *available at* https://www.reuters.com/article/abacus-mortgage-fraud/update-2-abacus-federal-savings-bank-indicted-for-mortgage-fraud-idUSL1E8GV89520120531.

4. *See* Karen Freifeld, *Abacus Bank Acquitted of All Charges in N.Y. Mortgage Fraud Trial*, Reuters.com (June 4, 2015), *available at* https://www.reuters.com/article/us-abascus-federal-acquittal/abacus-bank-acquitted-of-all-charges-in-n-y-mortgage-fraud-trial-idUSKBN0OK21620150604; James C. McKinley Jr., *Abacus Bank Found Not Guilty of Mortgage Fraud and Other Charges*, N.Y. Times, June 4, 2015.

5. *See* Jiayang Fan, *The Accused: When a Chinatown Bank Was Investigated for Fraud, a Community's Financial Way of Life Was Put on Trial*, New Yorker, Oct. 12, 2015.

6. *See* Mark Feeney, *When Goliath Indicts David*, Bos. Globe, June 15, 2017; Elahe Izadi, *A Small Family Bank Was the Only One Prosecuted After the 2008 Crisis. 'Abacus' Tells Its Tale,"* Wash. Post, June 24, 2017; *see Abacus: Small Enough to Jail*, IMDb.com, *available at* https://www.imdb.com/title/tt5952382/awards.

Hong Kong with his parents as a child and had been on the force for only 18 months at the time of the fatal shooting. In February 2015, Liang was indicted for manslaughter and official misconduct; he was convicted in February 2016. In April 2016, the judge who presided over his trial, Justice Danny Chun, upon the recommendation of the prosecutor, reduced the charges to criminally negligent homicide and sentenced Liang to six months of house arrest and 500 hours of community service. *See* Laura Wagner, *Former NYPD Officer Peter Liang Gets Probation for Fatal Shooting*, NPR (April 19, 2016), *available at* https://www.npr.org/ sections/thetwo-way/2016/04/19/474846986/former-nypd-officer-peter-liang-gets-house-arrest-probation-for-fatal-shooting; Hansi Lo Wang, *'Awoken' by N.Y. Cop Shooting, Asian-American Activists Chart Way Forward*, Code Sw!tch (April 23, 2016), *available at* https://www.npr.org/ sections/codeswitch/2016/04/23/475369524/awoken-by-n-y-cop-shooting-asian-american-activists-chart-way-forward.

The fatal shooting and Liang's subsequent prosecution and sentencing triggered contentious debates in New York City and the country at large. On the one hand, Gurley's demise was yet another tragic instance of the use of deadly force by police officers against young Black men under circumstances indicating the use of force was excessive. Members of the New York City community, including Asian Americans, protested the pointless death. The controversial death of Eric Garner, when a White officer, Daniel Pantaleo, jumped on Garner's back and applied a fatal chokehold, occurred on April 17, 2014. Garner had shouted "I can't breathe" 11 times, but Pantaleo did not release him until he was motionless. On December 3, 2014, two months after the grand jury began reviewing evidence, it elected not to indict Pantaleo despite video footage of the incident taken by a bystander that went viral. *See* Phippen, *supra*. This happened two weeks after Akai Gurley's death.

On the other hand, in contrast to the Garner case, there was no video or other witnesses, and all the facts indicated that a negligent discharge of Liang's firearm, followed by a freakish ricochet, had caused Gurley's death. And no criminal prosecutions had been undertaken against White officers in New York City or elsewhere in analogous or more egregious instances. As one informed commenter noted, "[i]t takes a lot to indict and convict an officer in New York. The last time it happened was in 2005, with the death of Ousamane Zongo, a West African immigrant shot in a warehouse during a raid on a counterfeit CD operation.... Convictions of officers are usually restricted to extreme circumstances..., which makes Liang's case all the more surprising." J. Weston Phippen, *Why Was Officer Peter Liang Convicted?*, The Atlantic (Mar. 3, 2016), *available at* https://www.theatlantic.com/national/archive/2016/03/peter-liang-police-shooting/471687/. According to the *New York Daily News* in 2014, there were 179 fatalities involving on-duty NYPD officers in the prior 15 years; only three resulted in indictments and only one in a conviction. *See* Sarah Ryley et al., *In 179 Fatalities Involving On-Duty Cops in 15 Years, Only 3 Cases Led to Indictments—And Just 1 Conviction*, Daily News, Dec. 8, 2014. Consequently, many Asian Americans in the New York City community protested that senior police officials and political leaders had hung Liang out to dry because he was a Chinese immigrant. They believed a lenient sentence was justified as a corrective to this underlying race-based bias permeating Liang's criminal prosecution and conviction in the first place. One observer summed it up thusly:

> Both the Black and Chinese communities were angry at the New York City Police Department for different, but valid, reasons. But both groups ended up directing that justified anger at each other, showing up at each other's protests and staging shouting matches.

Frank Shyong, *A Film and Documentary Try to Make Sense of the Akai Gurley Shooting*, L.A. Times, Jan. 22, 2022.

What role—if any—do you think that race played in: (1) the grand jury's decisions to indict Liang but not Pantaleo; (2) the petit jury's decision to convict Liang; (3) the perceived lack of support for Liang by White-led police senior leadership and unions; (4) the relatively lenient sentence the judge (himself Asian American) imposed on Liang; and (5) the media's coverage of the Gurley incident as opposed to the Garner incident? What about the fact that Akai Gurley—a Black man—had been killed by police just like Eric Garner? Should it matter that the perpetrator was Asian, White, or even Black, given the scourge of gratuitous and often fatal police violence against Black persons? What if, as in the police shooting of Ashley Babbitt, a participant in the storming of the Capitol on January 6, 2021, the victim were White and the shooter were Black: do you think that prosecutors, jurors, judges, and the media would have acted differently?

4. Prosecutorial Discretion and Immunity

As we have seen, prosecutors have broad discretion in deciding whether to bring criminal charges and, if so, what charges to bring. The Department of Justice's "Principles of Federal Prosecution" note as follows:

> Under the federal criminal justice system, the prosecutor has wide latitude in determining when, whom, how, and even whether to prosecute for apparent violations of federal criminal law. The prosecutor's broad discretion in such areas as initiating or foregoing prosecutions, selecting or recommending specific charges, and terminating prosecutions by accepting guilty pleas has been recognized on numerous occasions by the courts.

U.S. Dep't of Justice, Principles of Federal Prosecution § 9-27.110 (Feb. 2018) (comment, citing cases), *available at* https://www.justice.gov/jm/jm-9-27000-principles-federal-prosecution. Too often, however, political or other external pressures come into play. In the *Toguri* Tokyo Rose case, for example, prosecutors declined to file charges at first and only succumbed after intense public pressure. In many of the

Chinese espionage cases, prosecutors brought serious charges with great fanfare only to voluntarily dismiss the charges or reduce them to minor infractions.

There are some who worry that "[t]here is an increasing sense that unrestrained prosecutors in the United States are a problem—'quite possibly the most pressing challenge in American criminal justice.'" Samantha M. Caspar and Artem M. Joukov, *The Case for Abolishing Prosecutorial Immunity on Equal Protection Grounds*, 49 Hofstra L. Rev. 315, 316 (2021). Yet prosecutors are shielded from liability for money damages in the vast majority of cases even when a defendant has been wrongfully charged, because prosecutors have absolute immunity for actions taken as prosecutors and qualified immunity for actions taken as investigators. *See, e.g., Anilao v. Spota*, 27 F.4th 855, 863–64, 865 (2d Cir. 2022).

In *Anilao*, 10 Filipino nurses who had been recruited from the Philippines to work in a nursing home on Long Island resigned in 2006 to protest what they believed to be unfair work conditions. On the advice of their lawyer (who was also Filipino), they waited until the end of their shifts to do so, and the lawyer filed a claim of discrimination on their behalf with the immigrant and employee rights office of the Civil Rights Division of the U.S. Department of Justice. The nursing home filed a complaint with the Suffolk County Police Department, but the Police Department declined to take action after investigating the matter. The nursing home then filed a civil suit in state court and sought a preliminary injunction, but the court determined that the nursing home had failed to establish a likelihood of success on the merits of their claim of patient abandonment. And the state agency with licensing authority over the nurses investigated and concluded that no disciplinary action against the nurses was warranted.

Nonetheless, the nursing home persuaded the Suffolk County District Attorney's Office (the "DA's Office") to convene a grand jury investigation and, indeed, the DA's Office indicted the 10 nurses *and* their lawyer for endangering the welfare of patients and conspiracy to do the same, and also charging the lawyer with criminal solicitation. Eventually, the Appellate Division, Second Department, took the extraordinary step of issuing a writ of prohibition to bar the DA's Office from pursuing the charges, holding that the prosecutors were "proceeding... 'without or in excess of jurisdiction.'" *Vinluan v. Doyle*, 873 N.Y.S.2d 72, 75 (2d Dep't 2009) (Eng, *J.*).

The 10 nurses and their lawyer sued Suffolk County, the District Attorney, and the lead Assistant District Attorney for damages pursuant to 42 U.S.C. § 1983. The district court dismissed the claims, holding that the prosecutors were protected by absolute immunity to the extent they were acting as prosecutors and by qualified immunity to the extent they were acting as investigators. *See Anilao v. Spota*, 774 F. Supp. 2d 457, 466–68 (E.D.N.Y. 2011) (granting in part motion to dismiss as to certain claims); *Anilao v. Spota*, 340 F. Supp. 3d 224, 250 (E.D.N.Y. 2018) (granting motion for summary judgment as to remaining claims). The Second Circuit affirmed in both respects, holding that the prosecutors were immune. *See Anilao v. Spota*, 27 F.4th at 870, 871.

The exceptions to absolute immunity for prosecutorial conduct are rare, but they do exist:

> where a prosecutor is sued under § 1983 for constitutional abuse of his discretion to initiate prosecutions, a court will begin by considering whether relevant statutes authorize prosecution for the charged conduct. If they do not, absolute immunity must be denied. But if the laws do authorize prosecution for the charged crimes, a court will further consider whether the [prosecutor] has intertwined his exercise of authorized prosecutorial discretion with other, unauthorized conduct. For example, where a prosecutor has linked his authorized discretion to initiate or drop criminal charges to an unauthorized demand for a bribe, sexual favors, or the defendant's performance of a religious act, absolute immunity has been denied.

Bernard v. County of Suffolk, 356 F.3d 495, 504 (2d Cir. 2004) (internal quotation marks and citations omitted). Hence, "where a prosecutor acts without any colorable claim of authority, he loses the absolute immunity he would otherwise enjoy." *Barr v. Abrams*, 810 F.2d 358, 361 (2d Cir. 1987); *accord Shmueli v. City of New York*, 424 F.3d 231, 237 (2d Cir. 2005).

Should the prosecutors have been immune from suit for indicting the nurses for resigning their jobs to protest unfair conditions and their lawyer for giving them legal advice and filing a charge of discrimination on their behalf? Did they have authority to charge the nurses and their lawyer for this conduct?

Here are excerpts from the dissent:

> . . . The Appellate Division, Second Department, took the extraordinary step of issuing a writ of prohibition to *bar* the DA's Office from pursuing the charges, recognizing that the nurses and their attorney were "threatened with prosecution for crimes for which they [could not] constitutionally be tried." *Vinluan v. Doyle*, 873 N.Y.S.2d 72, 83 (2d Dep't 2009) (Eng, *J.*). Indeed, as the Second Department held, "these criminal prosecutions constitute[d] an impermissible infringement upon the constitutional rights of these nurses and their attorney." *Id.* at 75. . . .
>
> . . . In my view, . . . the complaint plausibly alleged, as the Second Department found, that the nurses and their lawyer could not be prosecuted for the charged conduct and thus the immunities do not apply. In the extraordinary circumstances presented here, where the prosecutors were "proceeding . . . 'without or in excess of jurisdiction,'" *Vinluan*, 873 N.Y.S.2d at 77 (quoting N.Y. C.P.L.R. § 7803(2)), they were not protected by absolute or qualified immunity. . . .

Anilao, 27 F.4th at 875 (Chin, *J.*, dissenting).

Context is always important. Here, the nursing home (like other healthcare facilities in the United States) recruited many nurses from the Philippines and concerns had been raised as to their treatment. In fact, the nursing home in question has been successfully sued by a group of Filipino nurses in the Eastern District of New York for violations of the Trafficking Victims Protection Act, 18 U.S.C. § 1589 *et seq.*, and for breach of contract. The district court granted summary judgment in *favor* of plaintiffs on liability, *see Paguirigan v. Prompt Nursing Empl. Agency LLC*, No. 17-CV-1302, 2019 WL 4647648, at *1, *21 (E.D.N.Y. Sept. 24, 2019), *aff'd in part and appeal dismissed in part*, 827 F. App'x 116 (2d Cir. 2020) (summary order), and thereafter awarded plaintiffs compensatory damages of $1,559,099.79. *See Paguirigan v. Prompt Nursing Empl. Agency LLC*, No. 17-CV-1302, 2021 WL 2206738, at *1, *8 (E.D.N.Y. June 1, 2021). In 2022, the court approved a class action settlement providing for the defendants to pay more than $3.2 million. *Paguirigan v. Prompt Nursing Empl. Agency LLC*, No. 17-cv-1302, 2022 WL 6564755 (E.D.N.Y. April 7, 2022).

Do you think criminal charges would have been brought against the nurses and their lawyer if they had been White or if they had been American citizens? *See Anilao*, 27 F.4th at 884 (Chin, *J.*, dissenting).

5. Private Danny Chen

On October 3, 2011, U.S. Army Private Danny Chen, who was 19 years old and on his first tour in Afghanistan, was found dead in a guard tower on an American outpost[7] with a gunshot wound in his head—later described by the Army as "an apparent self-inflicted gunshot wound."[8] The "details of his story... slowly emerged, relayed by Army officials to his family":

> A group of his superiors allegedly tormented Chen on an almost daily basis over the course of about six weeks in Afghanistan.... They singled him out, their only Chinese-American soldier, and spit racial slurs at him: "gook," "chink," "dragon lady." They forced him to do sprints while carrying a sandbag. They ordered him to crawl along gravel-covered ground while they flung rocks at him. And one day, when his unit was assembling a tent, he was forced to wear a green hard-hat and shout out instructions to his fellow soldiers in Chinese.[9]

There was other physical abuse as well, including yanking him out of bed and dragging him across 50 yards of gravel as punishment for supposedly breaking a hot-water pump for a shower.

Eight men were eventually charged by the Army in connection with Chen's death: one lieutenant, two staff sergeants, three sergeants, and two specialists. They were all White and ranged in age from 24 to 35 years old. In addition to belittling him

---

7. Kirk Semple, *Soldier's Death Raises Suspicions in Chinatown*, N.Y. Times, Oct. 30, 2011; Jennifer Gonnerman, *Pvt. Danny Chen, 1992–2011*, N.Y. Mag., Jan. 6, 2012, *available at* https://nymag.com/news/features/danny-chen-2012-1/.

8. Gonnerman, *supra*.

9. *Id.*

with racial slurs, they subjected him to other physical abuse.[10] At the court-martial of one of the men, the prosecutor argued that Chen had been "ostracized" after he was deployed to Afghanistan, and that the racial harassment and hazing made him miserable.[11] One of the men, a first lieutenant, avoided trial by agreeing to separate from the Army. A sergeant, who was convicted of maltreatment and assault but acquitted of the most serious charges (including negligent homicide, hazing, and reckless endangerment), was sentenced to 30 days in prison, demotion of one rank, and forfeiture of one month's pay. Four others received demotions and short prison sentences, and two others received demotions but no prison time.[12] The Chen death was preceded just a few months earlier by the suicide, in April 2011 in Afghanistan, of U.S. Marine Lance Corporal Harry Lew, another Asian-American soldier who was subjected to brutal hazing by his fellow Marines, three of whom were charged. One pleaded guilty and was sentenced to 30 days' confinement and reduction in rank; the other two were acquitted.[13]

Unfortunately, hazing is often practiced in male-dominated military combat units in the United States and worldwide. The perception is that warfighters need to be able to withstand and persevere against physical, mental, and emotional adversity and anguish. The idea is that once a soldier, marine, sailor, or airman has proven himself, the rest of the unit will trust him. And trust is critical among warriors whose lives literally depend on each other. Does this practical reality condone or excuse race-based taunting and hazing as part of building up resilience to adversity? Even if military necessity doesn't excuse race-based hazing, does it necessarily follow that the military-justice system should severely punish the perpetrators? If the end goal is a U.S. warfighting force where race does not matter and each warrior is evaluated and valued based solely on warfighting capability, how should military leaders deal with racialized hazing?

---

10. *Id.*

11. James Barron, *Memories of a Soldier from Chinatown, by 12 Speakers*, N.Y. Times, Oct. 2, 2023.

12. Kirk Semple, *Army Officer Reaches Deal in the Suicide of a Private*, N.Y. Times, Dec. 17, 2012; Barron, *supra*.

13. Jeremy Herb, *Rep. Chu Fights for Tough Hazing Policies After Nephew's Death*, The Hill (March 23, 2012), *available at* https://thehill.com/policy/defense/109547-rep-chu-fights-for-tough-hazing-policies-after-nephews-death/; CNN Wire Staff, *Marine Pleads Guilty in Hazing-Suicide Case, Gets 30-Day Sentence*, CNN.com (Jan. 31, 2012), *available at* https://www.cnn.com/2012/01/31/us/marine-hazing/index.html.

Chapter 15

Contemporary Violence

In Unit Two, we explored historical violence—mob violence, mass murders, and rioting against early Asian Americans in the late nineteenth century. Episodic violence against persons of Asian descent in the United States did not end with the turn of the twentieth century. Even in the twenty-first century, the unsettling pattern of violence against persons of Asian descent, particularly in the wake of catastrophic events or disasters of South or East Asian origin, would continue.

1. 9/11 and the Global Pandemic

The tragic events of 9/11 triggered a wave of violence against South Asian victims and those who appeared to be South Asian. On September 15, 2001, a man in Arizona embarked on a shooting rampage. He fatally shot the Sikh owner of a gas station and then shot at but missed a clerk of Lebanese descent at another gas station. Shortly thereafter, he fired shots into the home of an Afghan family. When he was captured, he declared, "I stand for America all the way."[1] Such incidents would continue to occur long after the 9/11 tragedy. On February 20, 2017, a man fired shots at two men of Indian descent in a bar in Kansas, killing one and wounding another, as he told them to "get out of my country."[2] And on March 3, 2017, a U.S. citizen of Indian descent was shot in the arm in Seattle, by a man who shouted, "Go back to your own country."[3]

The coronavirus pandemic, with its suspected origin in China, sparked a fresh outbreak of acts of violence and harassment against Asian Americans. *See, e.g.*, Thomas Fuller, *Violent Attacks Against Asian-Americans Persist in the Bay Area*, N.Y. Times, Mar. 19, 2021; Sabrina Tavernise and Richard A. Oppel Jr., *Spit On, Yelled At, Attacked: Chinese-Americans Fear for Their Safety*, N.Y. Times, Mar. 24, 2020. On

1. Tamar Lewin, *Sikh Owner of Gas Station Is Fatally Shot In Rampage*, N.Y. Times, Sept. 17, 2001.
2. Sangay K. Mishra, *An Indian Immigrant Is Murdered in Kansas. It's Part of a Spike in Hate Crimes Against South Asians*, Wash. Post, Mar. 7, 2017; Mark Berman and Samantha Schmidt, *He Yelled 'Get Out of My Country,' Witnesses Say, and Then Shot 2 Men from India, Killing One*, Wash. Post, Feb. 24, 2017.
3. Colin Dwyer, *Sikh Man Shot Outside His Seattle Home, Told to 'Go Back to Your Own Country,'* NPR (March 5, 2017), *available at* http://www.npr.org/sections/thetwo-way/2017/03/05/ 518637650/sikh-man-shot-outside-his-seattle-home-told-to-go-back-to-your-own-country.

March 16, 2021, a gunman killed eight people at three massage parlors in the Atlanta area; six of them were Asian women. *See* Paulina Firozi et al., *Suspect Charged with Eight Counts of Murder in Killings at Atlanta-Area Spas, Authorities Say,* Wash. Post, Mar. 17, 2021. In March 2022, a 67-year-old Asian woman in Yonkers, New York, was punched more than 125 times, stomped, and spat upon while her assailant called her "an anti-Asian misogynistic slur." Ed Shanahan, *Man Hit Woman in the Head 125 Times Because She Was Asian, Officials Say*, N.Y. Times, Mar. 14, 2022. In fact, the group Stop AAPI Hate reports that almost 11,500 "hate incidents" against Asian Americans occurred between 2020 and 2022.[4] In the first three months of 2022 alone, three Asian-American women were killed in New York City—Michelle Go, Christina Yuna Lee, and GuiYing Ma.[5] And in 2024, an American man was convicted in Germany of raping and murdering a woman and attempting to murder her companion—two Asian-American women who were on a trip to Europe following their graduation from the University of Illinois. Evidence suggested that the man targeted the women because of their Asian heritage. *See* Erika Solomon, *American Man Sentenced to Life After Killing Woman at German Castle*, N.Y. Times, Mar. 11, 2024.

As a consequence of the hostility against Asian Americans during the pandemic, in 2021 President Biden signed into law the Covid-19 Hate Crimes Act. The legislation, which was sponsored by Rep. Grace Meng of New York and Sen. Mazie Hirono of Hawaii, was passed with overwhelming bipartisan support in both houses of Congress. It aimed to make reporting of hate crimes more accessible and authorized funding for local crime-reduction programs to address hate crimes. *See* Barbara Sprunt, *Here's What the New Hate Crimes Law Aims to Do as Attacks on Asian Americans Rise*, NPR (May 20, 2021), *available at* https://www.npr.org/2021/05/20/998599775/biden-to-sign-the-covid-19-hate-crimes-bill-as-anti-asian-american-attacks-rise.

There are many more persons of Asian descent in the United States in the twenty-first century than there were in the latter half of the nineteenth century. And there are prominent Asian Americans in every branch of the federal government and throughout state government, particularly on the West Coast. But why does it seem that violence against Asian Americans appears to occur disproportionately, particularly in the wake of crises like 9/11 and the coronavirus? Are the dynamics of this anti-Asian violence different from the incidents of violence in the late nineteenth and early twentieth centuries? What has changed and what are constant themes and factors? *See generally* Denny Chin and Kathy Hirata Chin, *"Kung Flu": A History of Hostility and Violence*

---

4. Stop AAPI Hate, *National Report*, *available at* https://stopaapihate.org/2023/11/14/key-findings-2023/; *see also* AABANY and Paul Weiss, *A Rising Tide of Hate and Violence Against Asian Americans During COVID 19: Impact, Causes, Solutions* (2021), *available at* https://cdn.ymaws.com/www.aabany.org/resource/resmgr/press_releases/2021/A_Rising_Tide_of_Hate_and_Vi.pdf; AABANY and Paul Weiss, *Endless Tide: The Continuing Struggle to Overcome Anti-Asian Hate in New York* (2022), *available at* https://cdn.ymaws.com/www.aabany.org/resource/resmgr/aavtf/Endless_Tide_Report_2022_FIN.pdf.

5. *See* AABANY, *Endless Tide.*

against Asian Americans, 90 Fordham L. Rev. 1889 (2022). Our two principal cases both occurred in the early 1980s in communities where Asian Americans had not been historically present in large numbers, as in Hawaii and California. We consider first a lawsuit brought by Vietnamese fishermen against Ku Klux Klan members who terrorized them in south Texas in 1981. We then turn to what has become an iconic case for Asian Americans—the murder of Vincent Chin in a Detroit suburb in 1982.

2. The Vietnamese Fishermen

In 1975, after the South Vietnamese government surrendered and the Vietnam War came to an end, hundreds of thousands of South Vietnamese fled the country, often by sea in small fishing vessels. Many Vietnamese refugees eventually relocated to the Gulf Coast of the United States, and many took up fishing and shrimping. As the number of Vietnamese fishermen grew, so did resentment on the part of established American shrimpers and fishermen. The president of the American Fishermen's Association called in members of the Ku Klux Klan, who initiated a campaign of violence and intimidation against the Vietnamese. The Southern Poverty Law Center, led by Morris Dees, brought a civil action in federal court in Houston on behalf of the Vietnamese Fishermen's Association against the Texas Knights of the Ku Klux Klan, seeking declaratory and injunctive relief based on violations of federal civil rights, anti-racketeering, and antitrust laws, as well as state tort law.

Figure 15.1 ***Emblem of the Ku Klux Klan: "Mystic Insignia of a Klansman" or "Blood Drop Cross,"*** **Wikimedia Commons.**

Vietnamese Fishermen's Ass'n v. Texas Knights of the Ku Klux Klan

518 F. Supp. 993 (S.D. Tex. 1981)

McDONALD, District Judge.

Introduction

This is an action filed on April 16, 1981 by an organization of Vietnamese Fishermen and individual Vietnamese fishermen against the Knights of the Ku Klux Klan, the Grand Dragon of the Ku Klux Klan in the State of Texas, certain unknown members of the Ku Klux Klan, the American Fishermen's Coalition, various alleged members of that coalition, and several individual American fishermen alleging violations of various federal and state statutes.

Specifically, the plaintiffs allege that the defendants have violated their rights under several civil rights statutes: 42 U.S.C. §§ 1981, 1982, 1985(c), and 1986; the Thirteenth and Fourteenth Amendments to the United States Constitution; the Sherman Act, 15 U.S.C. §§ 1, 2, 15, and 26; the Racketeer Influenced and Corrupt Organizations Act (RICO), 18 U.S.C. §§ 1962 and 1964; and the common law torts of assault, trespass to personal property, the intentional infliction of emotional distress and intentional interference with contractual relations. In addition, the plaintiffs allege in their Second Amended Complaint that defendants Louis Beam and the Knights of the Ku Klux Klan have violated their rights under Tex.Rev.Civ.Stat.Ann., art. 5780 § 6 (Vernon)....

The plaintiffs seek a preliminary and permanent injunction enjoining the defendants generally from engaging in any activity, including unlawful acts of violence or intimidation, conducted for the purpose of interfering with the rights of the Vietnamese fishermen prior to and during the shrimping season, which begins on May 15, 1981....

The plaintiffs' class of Vietnamese fishermen was certified by agreement of all parties on May 8, 1981. The class is defined as "all Vietnamese fishermen in the Galveston Bay, Texas area" and may be maintained under Rule 23(b)(2) of the Federal Rules of Civil Procedure....

The Court conducted a hearing on the plaintiffs' Motion for a Preliminary Injunction on May 11-14, 1981, during which both the plaintiffs and the defendants presented evidence and oral arguments. Upon the conclusion of said hearing, the Court issues the following Memorandum Opinion and Order.

The Factual Setting

On or about January 24, 1981, defendant Fisher was introduced to defendant Louis Beam, Grand Dragon in the State of Texas of the Knights of the Ku Klux Klan (hereinafter KKK or Klan), by defendant James Stanfield a member of the Original Ku Klux Klan of America. (Stanfield Depo. at 13) The admitted purpose for this introduction was for defendant Fisher to secure support of Louis Beam and the Klan in order to further the purposes of a group of American fishermen who were ostensibly concerned about "over fishing" in the Kemah-Seabrook area of Texas. Defendant Fisher considered that the Klan was an organization that had the "courage" to stand by their convictions and would provide needed publicity to draw the attention of various governmental agencies he felt had failed to address his concerns. This meeting resulted in a rally that was held on February 14, 1981 on the property of defendant Joseph Collins that is located in Santa Fe, Texas. Defendant Joseph Collins leased this property for that purpose for a $1.00 payment from Mr. Stanfield. Defendant Fisher testified that he contacted defendant Beam to speak at the rally. Defendant Beam brought with him to the rally approximately 13 men who he refers to as his "security force" who were dressed in military garb and he gave a speech at that rally. He stated in substance that he would give the government 90 days to rectify the situation, (referring to the presence of the Vietnamese fishermen in the Kemah-Seabrook area) and if that was not accomplished the Klan would take action stating it "may become necessary to take laws into our own hands." He admitted stating in his speech that it was necessary to "fight fight fight" and see "blood blood blood" if this country was to survive. That rally was covered extensively by the news media. At that same rally, Beam demonstrated how to burn a boat. A cross propped with the aid of a pickup truck of defendant Joseph Collins was also burned at the rally. On that evening, defendant Beam offered to train American fishermen at one of the "military camps", later referred to as "locations" during his testimony in Court.

Figure 15.2 ***Ku Klux Klan members on boat in Texas in 1981.*** **Photo by John R. Van Beekum, Southern Poverty Law Center.**

On March 15, 1981, a "boat ride" was held in the waters surrounding the Kemah-Seabrook area. The boat was owned by defendant Joseph Collins and was navigated by defendant David Collins. The boat was the shrimping boat used by defendant Joseph Collins in his business, and by his own admission it is hardly a "pleasure craft." Defendant David Collins denies that this boat ride was planned in advance and testified that it was essentially a spontaneous event taken because it was a beautiful day. However, Mr. Emery Waite, a seafood retailer and processor in Seabrook testified that he had heard about the impending boat ride a day or perhaps a week before the boat ride actually took place. Several persons who were on that shrimp boat on March 15, 1981 wore robes of the KKK, some also wore hoods and most were visibly armed. The boat was equipped with a small cannon and a figure hung in effigy. Defendant Stanfield was present on the boat and wore a Klan robe and hood. Other persons who through testimony were clearly identified as being members of the Klan were also on the boat. Defendant Beam testified that he was informed of this boat ride shortly before it occurred and gave his approval to a member of the Klan to wear robes and bear arms, but admonished the members to refrain from any violence. Defendant Fisher, however, testified that he considered being armed a threat of violence. Other persons who viewed, participated in or heard of this boat ride acknowledged that this display would be fearful and intimidating to Vietnamese fishermen. Indeed, Joanne Oliphant-Curren, a reporter who was invited by David Collins to join them in the boat ride testified that she was "scared." By way of explanation she stated that the presence of robed, armed Klansmen on the boat might incite others to respond in a violent way and acknowledged that if she were a Vietnamese fishermen she would be afraid by such a display. Not only did she testify to this effect, but she reported the account of the boat ride in the April 22, 1981 issue of the Santa Fe Express News (Plaintiffs' Exhibit No. 38). She reported that "Collins steered the boat out into the bay well past the mile marker and the Klansmen fired their small cannon (Plaintiff's Exhibit No. 38). Everybody else had their fingers in their ears, but I was snapping pictures and the cannon blast left me nearly deaf for a few moments." The account in the newspaper further related the following: "Let's hear it for the American fishermen, David Collins shouted and the fishermen cheered."

Defendant David Collins acknowledged that the purpose of the boat ride was to gain media attention, asserting "violence sells stories." Defendant Fisher testified that defendant Beam had informed him that one of the persons on this boat ride was a Klansman involved in the Greensboro, South Carolina shooting during which members of the Communist Workers Party were killed during a confrontation with members of the Ku Klux Klan.

Members of the class who testified by deposition also expressed fear because of the presence of the shrimp boat loaded with robed and armed Klansmen. Colonel Nam Van Nguyen testified that he was especially frightened by the weapons that were carried by the persons on the boat and the figure that was hanging in effigy on the boat (Nam Depo. at 54). He also testified that the boat came right to his dock and stopped there for about four or five minutes and someone on the boat gestured toward his house (Nam Depo. at 55). Colonel Nam's sister-in-law, Phuong Pham, was present in his house when the boat approached and she saw persons wearing white robes. This so frightened her that she took her infant niece and ran from the house to a nearby relative's home. Although Miss Pham had previously lived with Colonel Nam, since this incident, she testified that she is too fearful to spend the night in that house. (Pham Depo. at 7-11)

Mr. Jerry Walzel, State Game Warden for the Texas Department of Parks and Wildlife testified that "fortunately" he was not on duty on the day of the boat ride; fortunate because if he had been in the area, undoubtedly he would have received a complaint of possible violations of water safety regulations and if he had tried to board the boat it would have been "like throwing a spark on gasoline." He explained that he would be the spark and the armed Klansman the gasoline. In his opinion, the presence of armed Klansmen aboard shrimp boats would cause violence. That view was concurred in by the Chief of Police of the City of Seabrook. R. W. Kerber testified that he did not expect violence at the opening of the fishing season on May 15, 1981 because there had been no violence the previous year, but admitted that based on his 27 months service as the Chief of Police with extensive contacts with members of the community, he would have no doubt that Vietnamese fishermen would be fearful if there is Klan presence on May 15.

Chief Kerber testified further that the tension between Vietnamese and American fishermen did not stem solely from fishing conflicts. According to Chief Kerber, some American fishermen believe there are just too many Vietnamese people in Kemah-Seabrook and therefore these individuals will only be satisfied when some of the Vietnamese leave the area.

Mr. Louis Beam, the Grand Dragon of the Knights of the Ku Klux Klan of Texas testified about the history of his organization. Mr. Beam stated that the Knights of the Ku Klux Klan of Texas opened a public information center in Pasadena, Texas in 1975. Prior to that time, he originally joined the United Klans of America in and about April of 1969 immediately after returning from Viet Nam. (Beam Depo. p. 12) According to Mr. Beam's testimony, the United Klans of America was "destroyed" by "government subversion" in 1971. Consequently, in 1973, Mr. Beam helped organize the Original Ku Klux Klan in the state of Texas (hereinafter referred to as the "Original Klan"). (Beam Depo. p. 13) . . .

Mr. Beam refused to reveal the names of the current officers of the Texas Knights of the Ku Klux Klan (Beam Depo. p. 15), and ordered destroyed all records which contained any names of the members of the organization.

The record is replete with provocative statements made by various defendants in this action. Defendant David Collins testified by way of deposition and reaffirmed at trial that he planned to have an armed Klansman on his boat on May 15, 1981. (Collins Depo. at 32, 33) Jim Craig owner of the Old Harbor Seafood House testified that he has 43 boats owned by Vietnamese fishermen docked at his establishment, referred to as the "Saigon Harbor". He testified about a conversation during the Fall of 1980 with defendant Fisher. According to Mr. Craig, Mr. Fisher told him to "watch your boats they're easy to burn." At trial Mr. Fisher testified that Mr. Craig's memory of the conversation was better than his and did not deny making this statement.

It is uncontroverted that defendant Fisher stated that it would not bother him if the Klan burned all of the (Vietnamese) boats; further adding that the Klan were the only ones with the courage of their convictions. He added that a certain number of Vietnamese boats would have to be taken out of the water and destroyed. At the rally on February 14, 1981, defendant Fisher publicly stated that "we're going to help (Vietnamese fishermen) to control themselves." At trial defendant Fisher equivocated with respect to some of the statements that were attributed to him. For example, he was quoted by the press as saying that he planned to have a squadron of the American fishermen trained at the Klan's paramilitary training camp and that he currently had a group of 50 to 60 American fishermen in training. When confronted with this statement, Mr. Fisher responded that he was "lying" to the press. Mr. Fisher testified that it was "possible" that he had stated that anyone who traded or did business with or aided or assisted Vietnamese were his enemies. However, defendant Fisher did not deny announcing that his "organization" would put armed men on the boats on May 15, 1981 if requested. (Fisher Depo. at 94) It should be noted that a few of these statements were made during the taking of depositions on or about May 2, 1981 and when Mr. Fisher testified on or about May 11 and 12, he admitted making those statements but said that he no longer felt that way.

A woman who lives in the Galveston Bay area had allowed a Vietnamese fisherman to use one of her docks for approximately two years. She testified that in January, 1981 she received a card in the mail, signed by the Knights of the Ku Klux Klan which read: "You have been paid a 'friendly visit' do you want the next one to be a 'real one.'" She also received three threatening phone calls. The first asked if she knew where her children were; the second was a threat to burn her boat; the third, stated that she would die that night. Mr. Dang, a Vietnamese fisherman, testified that approximately four weeks ago an American pointed a gun at him while he was on his shrimp boat. Miss Do Thi Doi who is a shrimp seller and married to a Vietnamese fisherman testified that six weeks ago two American men drove up in a truck and pointed a gun at her. She testified that unless there is some solution to the conflict between the American fishermen and the Vietnamese fishermen her husband will not take out their shrimp boat on May 15, 1981 because she is afraid that he will be killed.

The plaintiffs have alleged that defendants Beam and the Knights of the Ku Klux Klan have operated one or more military or paramilitary training camps in the State of Texas in violation of Tex.Rev.Civ.Stat.Ann., art. 5780, §6 (Vernon). The plaintiffs introduced a videotape depicting defendant Beam instructing persons dressed in military type uniforms in the art of psychological warfare, ambush and counter ambush, reconnaissance patrol and other types of military movements. (Plaintiffs' Exhibit 35) Defendant Beam has referred to the group of persons who will receive his training as the "Texas Emergency Reserve." He testified that in addition to civilians, he trained persons who were currently members of the armed forces. The Texas Emergency Reserve has a flag which it uses as an emblem of its organization. A witness with considerable military experience testified that after viewing the entire film footage (approximately four hours of Beam's training sessions) he considers that Beam is training a viable military organization, for it has a command structure, has discipline and is being trained to act as a military unit. In his opinion, this is not the type of training that is provided for survival, but is training to act in a combat role....

Statutory Violations

42 U.S.C. § 1985(3)

Plaintiffs have alleged that the defendants have conspired for the purpose of depriving them and their class equal protection of the laws and of equal privileges and immunities under the laws and that the defendants have acted out of a class-based animus against Vietnamese persons. (Complaint, P VI, P 2)....

The defendants argue that there has been no conspiracy established. First, they would suggest that the American Fishermen's Association is not an organization but consists of only one person, e. g., defendant Eugene Fisher. That defendant indeed testified that he is an organization of one. However, he admitted that he had collected funds allegedly for the purpose of forming an organization, that he had expended funds in furtherance of the objective of this organization and that on at least one occasion he had a meeting with various American fishermen to discuss the objective of this organization which ostensibly was to file a lawsuit against the federal government. Moreover, in a press release issued by the defendant one day after this lawsuit was filed both Joseph and David Collins as well as Eugene Fisher were named as officers of the organization. Regardless of whether there was in fact a formerly established organization entitled the American Fishermen's Coalition or an organization known by another name consisting of American fishermen which was established or attempted to be established by defendant Fisher, it is clear that the named defendants have acted together and the evidence establishes that those actions have had the effect of depriving the plaintiffs of their equal protection of the laws. The specific laws that this Court finds have been violated by the defendants will be discussed herein.

42 U.S.C. § 1986

The plaintiffs have also alleged that the defendants have violated their rights by engaging in conduct made unlawful under 42 U.S.C. § 1986. Section 1986 is a companion to § 1985. It creates a cause of action against "(e)very person who, having knowledge that any of the wrongs conspired to be done, and mentioned in (§ 1985), are about to be committed, and having power to prevent or aid in preventing the commission of the same, neglects or refuses to do so." See Dowsey v. Wilkins, 467 F.2d 1022, 1026 (5th Cir. 1972); Hamilton v. Chaffin, 506 F.2d 904 (5th Cir. 1975).

The rights protected under § 1986 are those rights which are safeguarded under § 1985; no claim lies under § 1986 except on the basis of a valid claim under § 1985. By its language, § 1986 extends protection to "the party injured" and this is construed

Figure 15.3 ***Klan calling card.***

the same way the equivalent term in § 1985 is construed. Aliens are protected under § 1986, and since the language authorizes suit against "every person" there is no requirement of state action or color of law under § 1986. 1 C. Antieau, Federal Civil Rights Acts, §§ 281-282 (2d Ed. 1980).

The testimony elicited at trial clearly established that the defendants had knowledge of the wrongs conspired to be done, and neglected to aid in preventing the commission of these wrongs. David Collins testified that he informed James Stanfield that a "boat ride" had been scheduled and he solicited Stanfield's assistance in inviting people to participate on the boat ride. Mr. Beam testified that he was notified of the boat ride on the morning of its departure. Mr. Beam stated he was informed that members of the Ku Klux Klan planned to participate in the "boat ride" and he knew these members planned to wear their robes and carry semiautomatic weapons. Although Mr. Beam admonished members of the Klan not to use violence, he did not attempt to dissuade them from joining the boat ride. Both Mr. Stanfield and Mr. David Collins participated fully in the boat ride.

The evidence establishes that all of the defendants were aware that Louis Beam and the Knights of the Ku Klux Klan had been invited to lend their support to the efforts of American fishermen to see a reduction in the number of Vietnamese fishing boats in the Kemah-Seabrook area. Moreover, all of the defendants had knowledge that Louis Beam had been invited to speak at a rally held in Santa Fe, Texas on February 14, 1981 in which he stated that the Klan may have to "take laws into our own hands" if the presence of Vietnamese fishermen in the Kemah-Seabrook area had not been decreased by May 15, 1981.

42 U.S.C. § 1981

Plaintiffs have alleged that the defendants' actions have denied the plaintiff the same right to make and enforce contracts as is enjoyed by white persons, and have further deprived plaintiffs of the full and equal benefit of laws and proceedings for the security of persons, as is enjoyed by white persons, in violation of 42 U.S.C. § 1981. (Complaint, P IX). When aliens are the victims of racial or other forms of discrimination actionable under § 1981, they have standing to sue under this section. Takahashi v. Fish & Game Co., 334 U.S. 410 (1948); Guerra v. Manchester Terminal Corp., 498 F.2d 641 (5th Cir. 1974), reh. den. 503 F.2d 567; Spiess v. C. Itoh & Co., 408 F.Supp. 916 (S.D.Tex.1976).

Section 1981 is constitutionally supported by the implementing of clauses of the Thirteenth and Fourteenth Amendments. McDonald v. Santa Fe Trail Transportation Co., 427 U.S. 273 (1976), on remand 540 F.2d 219 (5th Cir.); Runyon v. McCrary, 427 U.S. 160 (1976), later app. 569 F.2d 1294 (4th Cir.), cert. denied, 439 U.S. 927. In Jones v. Alfred H. Mayer Co., 392 U.S. 409, 436 (1968) the Supreme Court indicated that the Civil Rights Act of 1866, which was the forerunner of s 1981, was designed "to prohibit all racial discrimination, whether or not under color of law ... " and as such was within the constitutional power of Congress under the Thirteenth Amendment. The rationale of the Jones case, which authorized a private cause of action for discrimination in the sale or rental of property under 42 U.S.C. § 1982, has been followed in actions under 42 U.S.C. § 1981 .... Since there is no "state action" or "color of law" requirement under 42 U.S.C. § 1981 private citizens are proper defendants in suits arising out of purely private relationships....

Section 1981 protects a panoply of individual rights the primary one being the right to contract to earn a living. E.g., Johnson v. Railway Express Agency, 421 U.S. 454, 459-60 (1975) .... In order to demonstrate a violation of § 1981, it is only necessary that the plaintiffs show that they were unlawfully denied, by the defendants, one of the rights protected by this statute. 1 C. Antieau, Federal Civil Rights Acts §§ 32, 33 (2d Ed. 1980).

The plaintiffs argue that the commercial fishing business operates by contract and that the plaintiffs' claims of interference with their ability to participate in this business, and in particular with their ability to make commercial arrangements with dock owners, gives rise to a denial of freedom of contract claim under 42 U.S.C. § 1981. The Court is of the opinion that the plaintiff class has established a substantial likelihood of success on the merits of this cause of action....

15 U.S.C. § 1

The plaintiffs allege that the defendants' actions constitute a conspiracy to prevent the plaintiffs from engaging in the commercial fishing business, a business in interstate commerce, and further have conspired to prevent other persons from trading with the plaintiffs in this business. The plaintiffs allege that by so doing the defendants have injured and will continue to injure the plaintiffs in their business, and have thereby violated title 15 U.S.C. § 1 of the Sherman Anti-Trust Act. (Complaint, P 11, § 2).

Section 1 of the Sherman Act provides that "every contract, combination . . . , or conspiracy, in restraint of trade or commerce among the several states, . . . is declared to be illegal." 15 U.S.C. § 1. Section 1 of the Sherman Act is the broadest in scope of the major antitrust acts, and was designed to protect free and unfettered competition in interstate commerce. 1 Von Kalinowski, Antitrust Laws and Trade Regulation, § 4.01 (1980). A restraint will be found to violate § 1 if the following factors are present: (1) there are at least two persons acting in concert; (2) the restraint restrains trade or commerce; (3) the trade or commerce is trade or commerce among the several states or within foreign nations; and (4) the restraint is unreasonable. Standard Oil Co. v. United States, 221 U.S. 1 (1911); Aviation v. United Technologies, 568 F.2d 1186 (5th Cir. 1978).

Under the Sherman Act any unreasonable restraint that occurs in the flow of interstate commerce or that affects interstate commerce is subject to the provisions of § 1. The terms "trade" and "commerce" have been broadly construed by the courts. 1 Von Kalinowski, Antitrust Laws and Trade Regulation, § 4.02 (1980). Practically every commercial activity that is in the flow of or affects interstate commerce constitutes the requisite trade or commerce within the meaning of § 1. See McLain v. Real Estate Board of New Orleans, Inc., 444 U.S. 232 (1980). It has been uncontested that the commercial fishing business in Galveston Bay is clearly a part of, and substantially affects interstate commerce within the meaning of § 1 of the Sherman Act. . . .

The plaintiffs allege that the defendants have conspired to force the Vietnamese fishermen class to terminate or at the very least curtail their commercial fishing business in the Galveston Bay area. The plaintiffs assert that the defendants have attempted to intimidate them into selling off sixty percent of their shrimping boats and by so doing have acted to eliminate or reduce competition for the American fishermen in the Kemah-Seabrook area. (Complaint, P V, § 2).

It is well established that joint collaborative action designed to eliminate a class of competitors ready and able to compete is a violation of § 1 of the Sherman Act. United States v. General Motors Corp., 384 U.S. 127 (1966); United States v. Parke, Davis & Co., 362 U.S. 29 (1960); United States v. Socony-Vacuum Oil Co., 310 U.S. 150 (1940). Section 1 has been held to apply to an unlawful boycott occasioned by coercion, threats and intimidation. Loewe v. Lawlor, 208 U.S. 274 (1908). Moreover, courts have found that foreclosing and eliminating competitors from a substantial portion of the market is per se illegal. See Streiffer v. Seafarers Sea Check Corp., 162 F. Supp. 602 (E.D.La.1958).

The plaintiffs argue that the actions of the defendants constitute per se violations of the Sherman Act because their actions have a "pernicious effect on competition and lack . . . any redeeming virtue." Northern Pacific Railroad Company v. United States, 356 U.S. 1, 5 (1958). Although the facts adduced at the hearing may not have established a per se illegal restraint such as price fixing or group boycott, the evidence did reveal that the defendants agreed to engage in conduct which had the stated intent of eliminating a class of competitors from the commercial fishing business in Galveston

Bay. This type of anticompetitive conduct is not likely to be condoned under Section 1 of the Sherman Act. Therefore, the plaintiffs have shown a substantial likelihood of success on the merits of their Sherman Act § 1 claim.

Tortious Interference with Contractual Relationships

The plaintiffs have alleged that the actions of the defendants constituted the tort of intentional interference with contractual relationships, i.e., interference with their commercial fishing business. (Complaint, P XIII).

It is well established that a wrongful or malicious interference with the performance or the formation of a contract or the right to pursue a lawful occupation constitutes a tort for which damages may be recovered. See 86 C.J.S. Torts, § 43 (1954); Restatement of Torts § 766 (1939). Texas courts recognize a cause of action for improper interference with contractual relationships. Clements v. Withers, 437 S.W.2d 818 (Tex.1969). Common law has well established that the reasonable expectancy of a prospective contract is a property right to be protected from wrongful interference in the same sense as an existing contract is protected. Leonard Duckworth, Inc. v. Michael L. Field & Co., 516 F.2d 952 (5th Cir. 1975) (cites omitted). Under Texas law a party has the right to be free from malicious interference with the right to conduct negotiations that have a reasonable probability of resulting in a contract. Martin v. Phillips Petroleum Co., 455 S.W.2d 429, 435 (Tex.Civ.App.1970), rehearing denied. Texas courts have also recognized a cause of action for tortious and wrongful interference with advantageous business relationships. Cooper v. Steen, 318 S.W.2d 750, 757 (Tex.Civ.App.1958).

The elements of the tort of wrongful interference with a prospective contract right are as follows: the plaintiff must show that (1) there was a "reasonable probability that he would have entered into a contractual relationship; (2) the defendant acted maliciously by intentionally preventing the relationship from occurring with the purpose of harming plaintiff; (3) the defendant was not privileged or justified, and (4) actual harm or damage occurred as a result." Duckworth v. Michael L. Field, supra at 956 (cites omitted). As the plaintiffs have stated, the commercial fishing business is essentially contractual in nature. Moreover, the commercial fishing business is a lawful occupation which the plaintiffs have a right to pursue without wrongful interference on behalf of the defendants. The evidence adduced at the hearing clearly established that the defendants acted intentionally to impede and prevent the plaintiffs from pursuing their lawful occupation. As a result of the defendants' actions, many members of the plaintiff class have agreed to sell their shrimping boats and many have been reluctant to pursue their lawful occupation. In light of these facts and the Court's earlier discussion of 42 U.S.C. § 1981, there is a substantial likelihood that the plaintiffs will prevail on this tort claim....

Conclusion

The defendants, Eugene Fisher, Louis Beam, and David Collins have admitted making statements which this Court considers to be intimidating. These uncontroverted provocative statements, coupled with such overt acts as the burning of a shrimp boat and cross at the February 14, 1981 rally, the March, 1981 "boat ride", other cross burnings, the burning of Vietnamese owned and/or operated shrimp boats, and pointing pistols at members of the plaintiff class and/or their family members convince this Court that the predictable and intended result of the defendants' actions was to interfere with the rights of the plaintiff class. Moreover, as previously noted, the statements themselves constitute intimidation and have a substantial possibility of inciting others to engage in acts of violence and intimidation directed at the Vietnamese fishermen.

The Court has heard testimony from several defendants that certain provocative and threatening statements admittedly made by them should not, for one reason or another, be taken as an expression of their true feelings. These statements, say some of the defendants, were made only for effect, to impress or deliberately mislead the press, or merely for purposes of calling attention to the problems they perceived. The defendants assert that the recently enacted "limited entry" bill, discussed above, has quelled all tension between the American and Vietnamese fishermen. This legislation may indeed ease many of the problems once perceived by American fishermen. The Court, however, remains frankly skeptical of the wholesale reversal of positions taken, in some instances, only days before their repudiation in open court....

Upon consideration of all the evidence adduced at the hearing, it is the opinion of this Court that the plaintiffs have met their burden of proving a substantial likelihood of success on the merits with respect to the following causes of action: 42 U.S.C. § 1981; 42 U.S.C. §§ 1985(3) and 1986; 15 U.S.C. § 1; and the Texas common law tort of tortious interference with contractual relationships.

The Court also finds that there is an existence of a substantial threat that the plaintiff class will suffer an irreparable injury, if the injunction is not granted. Moreover, the threatened injury to the plaintiff class outweighs the threatened harm that the injunction will cause the defendants, and the granting of the injunction will not disserve the public interest....

It is well established that victims of discrimination suffer an irreparable injury regardless of actual pecuniary damage. See, e.g., United States v. Hayes International Corp., 415 F.2d 1038, 1045 (5th Cir. 1969). See also Bean v. Southwestern Waste Management Corp., 482 F.Supp. 673, 677 (S.D.Tex.1979); Ethridge v. Rhodes, 268 F.Supp. 83 (S.D.Ohio 1967). Moreover, here the very ability of the plaintiff class to earn a living is being severely jeopardized by the defendants' alleged unlawful actions. Clearly it is in the public interest to enjoin self help tactics of threats of violence and intimidation and permit individuals to pursue their chosen occupation free of racial animus.

Notes

1. How do the actions of the Ku Klux Klan in 1981 against the Vietnamese fishermen compare with the episodes of anti-Asian violence after 9/11 and during the coronavirus pandemic?

2. The civil rights statutes the plaintiffs invoked in their lawsuit had their origins in Reconstruction-era statutes Congress had enacted to address the power and influence of the Ku Klux Klan. Accordingly, the Vietnamese fishermen's lawsuit seemed particularly justifiable from an originalist perspective. Should that have mattered in the court's analysis? How do you think the Klansmen's conduct, status, and influence in 1981 compared to their predecessors a century earlier?

3. The plaintiffs brought federal racketeering and antitrust claims. To what extent do you think economic competition and the Vietnam War (recall that Beam was a veteran of the war) were primary motivations for the Klan's involvement and actions?

4. Judge Gabrielle Kirk McDonald was the first African American appointed to the federal bench in Texas, and only the third African American female federal judge in the country. She graduated first in her class from Howard Law School, and then joined the NAACP Legal Defense & Educational Fund as a Staff Attorney. She had been a judge for only two years when the suit brought by the Vietnamese fishermen was randomly assigned to her.

5. Early in the case, the defendants moved to disqualify Judge McDonald on the grounds of personal bias. During the hearing on the motion, Beam referred to the judge as a "negress" and stated: "I no more have the ... confidence that I could get any fairer trial here in front of you than you would feel were you to go [as a defendant] before a Ku Klux Klansman who was a judge." He based this on his asserted "knowledge" of the prejudice of "your people against the Klansmen." *See Vietnamese Fishermen's Ass'n v. Texas Knights of Ku Klux Klan*, 518 F. Supp. 1017, 1019 (S.D. Tex. 1981) (quoting Beam). Despite the fact that the Ku Klux Klan is an illegitimate and racist paramilitary organization, didn't Beam have a reasonable point that a Black judge in Texas at that time could not possibly present the appearance of impartiality essential to the judicial function? Judge McDonald denied the recusal motion, relying, *inter alia*, on the decision of Judge Constance Baker Motley in *Blank v. Sullivan & Cromwell*, 418 F. Supp. 1, 4 (S.D.N.Y. 1975) (in gender discrimination case against law firm, denying motion to disqualify judge on grounds she was a woman and had previously represented plaintiffs in civil rights litigation). *See also MacDraw, Inc. v. CIT Group Equip. Fin., Inc.*, 994 F. Supp. 447 (S.D.N.Y. 1997) (Chin, *J.*) (sanctioning lawyers for questioning judge's impartiality on account of his being Asian American), *aff'd*, 138 F.3d 33, 38 (2d Cir. 1998) ("[A]ppointment by a particular administration and membership in a particular racial or ethnic group are in combination not grounds for questioning a judge's impartiality. Zero plus zero is zero.").

6. Recall that a similar issue arose in a presidential campaign some years ago when a candidate referred to the federal judge presiding over his case as the "Mexican" judge. Garrett Epps, *The Problem with Calling Out Judges for Their Race*, The Atlantic, June 5, 2016, *available at* https://www.theatlantic.com/politics/

archive/2016/06/the-problem-with-calling-out-judges-for-their-race/485732/; Opinion, *Trump and the "Mexican Judge": Why Equating Ethnicity with Judicial Bias Is So Offensive*, Wall St. J., June 5, 2016. Do you think a judge's race, gender, or professional background should ever be a consideration in determining the judge's ability to hear a case? If not, and if justice is indeed blind, why, then, is it important to have diversity on the bench?

7. At his deposition, Louis Beam, the Grand Dragon of the Texas Knights of the Ku Klux Klan, appeared wearing his white Klan robe with a gun underneath his robe. Colonel Nam, the leader of the Vietnamese fishermen, noticed the gun and advised his lawyer, Morris Dees of the Southern Poverty Law Center. If you were the lawyer, how would you have handled the issue of the witness bringing a gun to your deposition? *See* Chin and Chin, *supra*, 90 Fordham L. Rev. at 1930, 1932–33.

8. The Vietnamese fishermen were political refugees who were trying to make a living catching shrimp and fish in the Gulf. They spoke limited English and were newcomers to this country. Yet, in the face of threats and violence and acts of intimidation against witnesses, they were willing to sue the Ku Klux Klan. And they were able to do so largely because of the efforts of Morris Dees and the Southern Poverty Law Center and three Texas lawyers, John Hayslip, David Berg, and Philip Zelikow. Throughout the case, the lawyers themselves were subjected to the Klan's bizarre and threatening behavior. *See* Chin and Chin, *supra*, 90 Fordham L. Rev. at 1933–34. Once again, we see the critical role played by non-Asian lawyers as Asian Americans fought for their rights. But, at the end of the day, the only relief that the Vietnamese fishermen obtained was a judicial order against the members of the Klan not to violate the law; they won no money damages. If so, what good did the lawsuit do?

3. The Vincent Chin Case

In 1982, following an altercation in a strip club in a Detroit suburb, Vincent Chin was beaten by two White men wielding a baseball bat. He died from his injuries a few days later. The two men pleaded guilty to manslaughter in Wayne County Circuit Court and were each sentenced to three years' probation, a $3,000 fine, and court costs.

Outraged by the murder and sentence, Asian Americans joined together to seek justice for Vincent Chin. There were protests and demonstrations, and a coalition of Asian Americans persuaded the United States Department of Justice to bring a federal criminal civil rights case against the two men. The key question in the federal prosecution was whether race was a motivating factor. There was no dispute that the two men had killed Vincent, but the government was required to prove that they did

Figure 15.4 ***Portrait of Vincent Chin.*** **Courtesy of the Vincent Chin Institute.**

so *because* of Vincent's race. One of the men was acquitted, but the other—Ronald Ebens—was convicted and sentenced to 25 years' imprisonment. But that was not the end of the story. Below are excerpts from the Sixth Circuit's decision on appeal.

United States v. Ebens

800 F.2d 1422 (1986)

ENGEL, Circuit Judge.

Ronald Ebens appeals from a judgment of conviction and a twenty-five year sentence following his conviction by a jury of count II of a two count indictment charging him and his stepson Michael Nitz under 18 U.S.C. § 245(b)(2)(F) with violating the civil rights of Vincent Chin, a United States citizen of Chinese descent. Ebens had killed Chin in an altercation which occurred on June 19, 1982.

We cannot permit the judgment to stand because Ebens was denied a fair trial.

Ebens was originally prosecuted in the Wayne County, Michigan, Circuit Court and prior to trial pleaded guilty to the crime of manslaughter. When he was placed upon probation and fined $3,720, public outrage at the perceived lenity of the penalty was extensive, especially within the Chinese-American community. The case was accompanied by massive publicity at both the state and national levels and undoubtedly because of activity on behalf of the Chinese-American community, the United States Department of Justice, overruling the decision of the local United States Attorney not to prosecute, instituted proceedings under the Civil Rights Act in the United States District Court for the Eastern District of Michigan....

I.

Ebens claims that the trial court erred in failing to grant his motion for change of venue.

Ebens had originally moved the district court for an eight to twelve month continuance of the trial in order to permit the effect of the extensive publicity surrounding the case to dissipate. Before that motion was decided, Ebens on February 17, 1984, filed a motion for change of venue.

The joint appendix filed in the appellate record contains sixty-eight pages of articles from Detroit newspapers about the Chin matter. Three video tape recordings of television broadcasts were also made a part of the record. As the trial judge noted, the publicity was not only extensive but was all adverse. A Detroit attorney, Lisa Chan, formed a group known as The American Citizens for Justice, and appears to have been instrumental in publicizing the killing, the handling of the case by the Wayne County Prosecutor's office and the sentences given to Ebens and Nitz in the state court. Rallies were held and the publicity generated much television coverage including at least two special news stories on the subject and a program over national television as well. The public excoriation of the state trial judge who placed Ebens and Nitz on probation was particularly severe. The headlines can only be described as scathing. One large cartoon, appearing in *The Detroit News*, even showed the trial judge putting a baseball bat in one ear, as if it were a pencil, and sharpening it with a pencil sharpener installed in the opposite ear.

We have carefully reviewed the extensive record made of the publicity in the case and agree that it was indeed pervasive. The question of venue is made particularly difficult because of the framework in which the prosecution arose. The nearly unanimous public judgment that Ebens and his stepson should have received jail terms and the harsh criticism of the state trial judge, followed by the federal prosecution of defendants based upon the same incident, was bound to lead to a strong public impression that justice had not been done in the state court and that it was incumbent upon the federal government to right that wrong by a second prosecution. Nevertheless we are unable to hold that the trial judge committed error when she determined to proceed to impanel a jury. While it probably would have been advisable for the trial judge to have ordered a change of venue, we conclude that it was not reversible error for her to proceed to impanel the jury. A change of venue would undoubtedly have occasioned great inconvenience both to the defense and to the government. Further, the publicity was so extensive that it was not altogether certain that any location to which the trial might be removed would itself be free from the potential impact of the publicity which had already occurred and that which was bound to accompany the trial, wherever it was held....

II.

Ebens next claims that he was entitled to a directed verdict of acquittal. We disagree.

In review of such issues, the court is of course obliged to consider the evidence in the light most favorable to the government. *Glasser v. United States,* 315 U.S. 60 (1942); *United States v. Adamo,* 742 F.2d 927 (6th Cir.1984), *cert. denied sub nom. Freeman v. United States,* 469 U.S. 1193 (1985). Only if no rational jury could have convicted is it error not to grant the motion. *Jackson v. Virginia,* 443 U.S. 307, *reh'g denied,* 444 U.S. 890 (1979). Ebens' motion in this regard must be considered in the light of the elements of the crime with which he was charged. His arguments go not to the factual events of the altercation itself and of his wielding the baseball bat which caused Chin's death, but to the specific intent which is inherently a part of the statute.

Ebens was acquitted of count I of the indictment charging him with conspiracy to deprive Chin of his civil rights under 18 U.S.C. § 241. He was convicted of count II charging him with interfering with Chin's civil rights by wilfully injuring, intimidating and interfering with Chin on account of his race or national origin and because the latter was and had been enjoying the privileges and accommodations of the Fancy Pants Lounge, a place of entertainment open to the public, by threatening, beating, and assaulting Chin with the result that the latter died, all in violation of 18 U.S.C. § 245(b)(2)(F).

The incident giving rise to this litigation occurred on June 19, 1982, in Highland Park, a suburb of Detroit. Chin, then twenty-seven years old, lived with his mother in Oak Park, Michigan, another suburb of Detroit. He had come to this country from China in 1961 when he was adopted by a Chinese-American couple. He became a United States citizen in 1965.

To celebrate his upcoming wedding, Chin invited his friends Robert Sirosky and Gary Koivu to meet him at a topless bar at 7:00 p.m. that night. After about an hour there and after having several drinks the group went on to the Fancy Pants Lounge, a nude dancing establishment in Highland Park. En route they purchased a pint of vodka and it is rather apparent from the record that they were in a mood of elevated joviality in consequence. Koivu later left to pick up one Jimmy Choi, another of Chin's friends, and together they brought another bottle of vodka into the Fancy Pants. The group was laughing, tipping the dancers heavily, and generally celebrating. At that time Ronald Ebens and his stepson, Michael Nitz, were also at the Fancy Pants, sitting directly across the elevated dancing runway from Chin and his friends. Construing the evidence most favorably to the government, Ebens began making racial and obscene remarks toward Chin calling him a "Chink" and a "Nip" and making remarks about foreign car imports. It is apparent that Ebens seemed to believe that Chin was Japanese and he was quoted as having made the further comment that "it's because of you little mother fuckers that we're out of work." Ebens may not have distinguished between Orientals of Japanese and Chinese descent since there is testimony to show he made references to both. After a further exchange of words Chin got out of his chair and walked up to the stage where Ebens was sitting and there was general jostling and fighting between Ebens and Chin in which Nitz then joined. The doorman and the parking lot attendant broke up the fight. The parking lot attendant took Chin outside and the doorman took Ebens and Nitz to the men's room. The doorman got a towel and some ice for Nitz who was bleeding from a cut on the head and later escorted Ebens and Nitz outside. The quarrel resumed outside the Fancy Pants Lounge. Chin challenged Ebens to finish the fight outside, calling him names. Ebens thereupon went to Nitz's car, opened the hatchback and removed a baseball bat. Seeing Ebens with a bat, Chin fled across Woodward Avenue and was pursued a short distance by both Ebens and Nitz.

While still in the Fancy Pants parking lot, Chin's three friends had decided that Choi would join Chin across Woodward Avenue and that Koivu and Sirosky would get their car and pick him up. Ebens and Nitz drove by in their car and, seeing Sirosky and Koivu, stopped and asked where their friend was. When they said they didn't know, Ebens then saw Choi and started after him. Nitz threw a glass bottle at Choi, and Ebens and Nitz returned to their car and drove off after Choi. After driving about a block from the Fancy Pants, Sirosky and Koivu stopped the car, removed a tire iron from the trunk and headed back toward the Fancy Pants. Unexpectedly they came upon Nitz's car which was parked on Woodward Avenue. Ebens got out of the car with the baseball bat and chased Sirosky and Koivu a short distance before getting back into Nitz's car. Meanwhile, after Choi had crossed Woodward Avenue he found Chin and suggested that they should flee. The two then ran south on Woodward Avenue for a few blocks until they stopped at a McDonald's restaurant where they apparently sought protection in the crowd, also hoping that Koivu and Sirosky would find them. Choi picked up a piece of wood for protection and handed Chin an unbroken bottle. Ebens and Nitz continued to look for Chin and upon meeting one Jimmy Perry, Nitz offered Perry $20 to help him find and catch a "Chinese guy."

According to Perry's testimony Ebens and Nitz talked during the ride about catching a "Chinese guy" and "busting his head" when they caught him.

The final confrontation occurred in the lot of a supermarket next to McDonald's. Ebens and Nitz approached Chin and Choi using a parked truck for cover. Ebens was still carrying the baseball bat. Chin saw them coming and yelled "Scram." Choi escaped but Nitz grabbed Chin in a bear hug from behind. Chin broke loose and ran onto Woodward Avenue. Ebens struck Chin several times with the bat on the back and head causing Chin to fall to the ground. While the precise circumstances of the assault are in dispute, especially whether Nitz was holding Chin at the time, it is undisputed that Ebens was the aggressor. Meanwhile, the Highland Park police officers who were working as security guards at McDonald's came up, drew their guns and ordered Ebens to drop his bat.

Chin was taken to Henry Ford Hospital, losing consciousness several times en route. He suffered two lacerations on the back left side of his head and abrasions on his shoulder, chest and neck and lapsed into a severe coma. After the performance of emergency surgery his brain ceased functioning entirely. At 9:50 p.m. June 23, 1982, a ventilator which had been employed to keep him breathing was removed and he was pronounced dead.

In claiming that there was insufficient evidence to convict him of a violation of section 245, Ebens essentially admits the physical facts of the assault. He nonetheless claims that what transpired was simply a barroom brawl which got out of hand and resulted in the death of one of the participants and injuries to another. He claims that there is an absence of any evidence by which the jury could find beyond a reasonable doubt (1) that he was motivated because of the race, color and national origin of Vincent Chin and (2) that his purpose was to injure, intimidate, and interfere with Vincent Chin's right to enjoy a place of public accommodation. He disclaimed the racial nature of the remarks attributed to him and asserted that the fight arose over Chin's insulting treatment of one of the dancers. He also claimed that the actual physical contact was initiated by Chin both in the Lounge and outside when Chin waited outside for Ebens to emerge and then challenged him to a fight.

We do not agree with Ebens' initial contention that, in enacting section 245, Congress intended to limit its application exclusively to vindicate the rights of blacks and of white civil rights workers who aid blacks but not to alleged discrimination against citizens of Oriental descent by whites. Section 245(b)(2) protects any person "because of his race, color, religion or national origin" from intimidation or interference in the enjoyment of the facilities or accommodations of any "place of exhibition or entertainment which serves the public.... " Orientals come within the broad constitutional protections of the Fourteenth Amendment even though the original thrust of the amendments was primarily motivated by concern for the rights of black persons. *See Yick Wo v. Hopkins,* 118 U.S. 356 (1886)....

A jury could have concluded beyond a reasonable doubt that Ebens, in initiating the ultimate conduct by uncomplimentary remarks toward Chin, was motivated by his belief that Chin was Japanese, not Chinese. The jury could have believed that this color and race-based or national origin bias against Chin induced Ebens to make the comments he did and that he was further irritated when he saw Chin enjoying himself in the lounge and spending money freely. The jury could further have found that his remarks were intended to make Chin's remaining on the premises uncomfortable and embarrassing and to intimidate and dissuade him from remaining on the premises because of that bias.

It is true that the ultimate assault which caused Chin's demise may also have been motivated by Chin's injury of Ebens' stepson, but defense counsel acknowledges that a specific intent to violate federal law need not have been the first among several evil intents....

We find no merit in the claim that the prosecution must fail because of an absence of direct evidence that the beating in front of McDonald's restaurant related to Chin's race or the fact that he had been in a place of public accommodation earlier. A rational jury could have found that the events at McDonald's were the culmination of a single and basically inseparable incident. It was altogether proper for the jury to consider this evidence and the comments made by Ebens as bearing upon his specific intent.

III.

Ebens claims that the trial court committed reversible error in refusing to permit the admission of certain evidence which was offered by Ebens to impeach the government's witnesses. Specifically, two types of evidence are involved.

As we have stated, after the state court sentencing, Lisa Chan, a Detroit attorney, formed a group known as the American Citizens for Justice and appears to have been instrumental in publicizing the killing and the handling of the case by the Wayne County prosecutor's office. Ms. Chan traveled to Washington, D.C., to discuss the matter with William Bradford Reynolds, Assistant Attorney General in charge of the Civil Rights Division of the Department of Justice with respect to the possibility of federal prosecution. Rallies were held in Detroit, in which the protestors carried placards reading "Jail the racist killers" and "It's not fair," the latter a comment made by Chin before he lapsed into unconsciousness. It is undisputed that the events occurring after the state court sentencing received widespread publicity.

The three principal government witnesses were Choi, Sirosky, and Koivu. All testified, in one form or another, concerning the incident and the statements purportedly made by Ebens in the course of the evening from which racism could be found.

Ebens and codefendant Nitz sought to introduce into evidence tape recordings of interviews which had been conducted by Lisa Chan with these witnesses. The defense purpose was to demonstrate that the witnesses' testimony concerning Ebens' racist statements was false and that it was the result of improper coaching of them by Chan in preparation for the trial. He claimed that the tapes were admissible to show collusion, witness influence, and prior inconsistent statements. Each time the defendants sought to introduce the tapes, however, the court sustained the government objection on hearsay grounds, ruling however that the defense counsel could confront a witness who takes the stand with his own words on the tape but that the statements of Lisa Chan to the witness which elicited that witness' statement could only be introduced through her should she be called. The government concedes that these rulings were erroneous.

The government correctly notes in its brief on appeal that the definition of hearsay under the federal rules requires that the third party statement testified to by the witness in question be offered for the purpose of proving the truth of the matter asserted. Fed.R.Evid. 801(c); *United States v. Gibson,* 675 F.2d 825 (6th Cir.), *cert. denied,* 459 U.S. 972 (1982). Obviously the purpose of introducing the Chan tapes was to show the effect of Chan's statements on the testimony of Choi, Sirosky, and Koivu. Plainly, Chan's out of court utterances were admissible to show not the truth of what she said but the effect on Choi, Sirosky and Koivu as bearing on whether the witnesses' subsequent sworn testimony was coached and hence inaccurate. *See* 4 Weinstein's Evidence ¶ 801(c)[01], at 801-77 to -80 (1985). In this light, the tapes were highly relevant and important to the defense....

We unanimously conclude that a consideration of these cited factors mandates reversal.

Ebens should have been permitted to introduce into evidence the entire contents of the tapes at least insofar as they involved conversations occurring at the time the government witnesses were present. The three witnesses were the most crucial of all witnesses for the government. Each testified as to events inside the Fancy Pants Lounge and to verbal exchanges between Ebens and Chin. The Chan tapes were offered to support Ebens' claim that Choi, Koivu and Sirosky did not tell the truth when they testified that they heard the racial statements. Since the physical facts of the assault were essentially undisputed, the entire defense hung upon Ebens' claim that the fight was not racially motivated. It is true that the district court permitted the defense to elicit the statements made in interviews and did allow a few of the statements, but it was not within the province of the court's proper discretion to prevent the jury from hearing the tapes themselves and judging for themselves the impact upon the witnesses which the purported conversation had and measuring that against the statements made in court by the witnesses....

V.

The defendant next claims that the trial was interspersed with incidents of prosecutorial misconduct mandating reversal. The government defends the conduct of its prosecutor and makes the point that the defense, having failed to object contemporaneously, may not do so now.

The best starting point for an evaluation of the prosecutorial misconduct claims here, is a repair to the recently decided *United States v. Young,* 470 U.S. 1 (1985). Specifically in issue in *Young* was the extent to which it is necessary to make timely objections to the prosecutorial conduct deemed improper in order to preserve them for potential reversal on appellate review. While the effect of *Young* was to reinstate a jury verdict of guilty upon a finding that certain statements, although improper, did not amount to plain error, any government attorney, reading the opinion carefully, can have no doubt whatever of the Supreme Court's continued dedication to its historic insistence that prosecutors representing the United States in criminal prosecutions should refrain from improper conduct calculated to produce a wrongful conviction. *See Berger v. United States,* 295 U.S. 78 (1935).

We need not determine whether the instances of misconduct complained of here, which we believe are far more egregious than those examined in *Young,* would have brought about reversal on a plain error basis since the conviction must in all events be reversed. Most of the complaints of misconduct, however, are directed to the closing argument of government counsel and, as the government points out, most occurred without specific objection by the defense....

The principal message of *Young* is that in reviewing prosecutorial misconduct for plain error, it is necessary that the error be measured not within the narrow confines of the argument but against the entire record. "It is simply not possible for an appellate court to assess the seriousness of the claimed error by any other means." *Young,* 470 U.S. at 15. Accordingly, we have carefully reviewed the entire record and against the background of all of the evidence. It must be remembered at the outset that the case itself arose in an atmosphere of extraordinary publicity. The video tapes contained as part of the special record made with respect to the motion for a change of venue, demonstrate the deep sense of public outrage especially after it was perceived that the Chin incident was motivated by racial bias. Nearly every news telecast showed the pathetic figure of Chin's weeping mother making pleas for justice. There are countless photographs of marches and demonstrations in front of both the county office buildings and the federal office buildings in Detroit, some, according to the accounts, attracting over 700 persons carrying large placards. The city council of Detroit was shown awarding a memorial plaque to Chin's mother in affirmation of its dedication to a bias-free administration of justice. The mayor of Highland Park was quoted as critical of the state's investigation. There were many videotaped news recordings showing Lisa Chan and reporting particularly the claim made by her committee that the state trial judge had been deprived of essential evidence in sentencing Ebens, evidence which if known would have induced him to impose a heavier sentence.

Every stage of the proceeding was followed with great care by the media. It was even noted that the incident was prominently featured in the press as far away as San Francisco and Hong Kong. Almost nothing was said which would have been derogatory concerning Chin or which would have carried the defendant's own version of the events leading up to the ultimate tragic climax. Every element of the population was queried in the news media concerning its reaction; that reaction was almost without exception condemnatory of Ebens. There were videocasts showing purported auto workers or others in Detroit paying or making donations for the privileges of attacking Japanese-made automobiles with sledgehammers as showing some of the uncontrolled spleen directed at the competition from Japanese imports.

We mention these elements not because we conceive that there can be any justification whatever for the assault which took place nor because the government prosecutor was chargeable with any part of the massive publicity. Likewise we recognize fully that this was a public event and a matter of great and crucial importance to the Detroit metropolitan area. We do not remotely suggest that there should be any inhibitions on the First Amendment rights of the media to report matters of such great public importance. We mention these circumstances, however, only to show that a heightened sensitivity on the part of the prosecutor was necessary if the values of a fair trial under such explosive circumstances were to be preserved. Of the jurors, only three professed no knowledge of the incident at all. The others had all been exposed to one extent or another to the massive publicity which continued right up to and through the trial itself. Plainly, it seems to us, the government attorneys were under a very special burden of responsibility to make sure that their own conduct did not contribute to what was already a very great risk that the verdict would be the product not of the evidence but of public dissatisfaction with the earlier state court sentence.

The closing arguments of the government counsel began as a model of aggressive yet entirely fair advocacy. His review of the evidence was careful and made telling use of inconsistencies in the stories and arguments of the defense. It was a classic example of the hard but fair blows recognized in *Berger.* As he progressed, however, he took advantage of the rulings of the trial court to make impermissible inferences from evidence which ought either to have been kept out of the trial or, if admitted, to have been held to a limited use.

Thus while we have already held that it was error to have excluded the Chan tapes, had those tapes been played they would have indicated an effort on the part of Lisa Chan to orchestrate the testimony of the witnesses who attended the meeting so that they would appear to be sufficiently diverse in character as not to sound rehearsed and yet would include all the essential elements to prove a racial bias. The prosecutor then took advantage of the excluded testimony by making the following comment which might otherwise be entirely proper:

> Now ladies and gentlemen, this probably doesn't need to be said; but just because these witnesses heard different things at different times doesn't mean they contradict each other. Naturally, when the music was loud and their perspectives were different, when they were paying different degrees of attention, they wouldn't hear or recall the exact same things. No, they don't contradict each other. You should worry if they came in here and said, yes, I heard the exact same thing. Now they corroborate each other, because the one thing that they all heard was that Vincent Chin was never aggressive or hostile....

Had the jurors been permitted to hear the tapes of Lisa Chan's joint witness interview of May 17, they would have had at least a means to determine whether the witnesses' testimony was in fact correct or the extent to which it was coached. Excerpts from that interview are appended hereto as appendix A and show the nature of the coaching which took place.

Government attorney Mr. Merritt then proceeded with a very strong point bearing on the existence of Ebens' guilt under the federal act: the evidence that Ebens and Nitz appeared to have singled out for pursuit only the Orientals, Vincent Chin and Jimmy Choi, and to have left their white companions largely undisturbed. This evidence of Ebens' bias was further fortified by emphasis on the testimony that Jimmy Perry was offered \$20 to, as Mr. Merritt characterized, "help catch those Chinese guys." Thus the \$20 offer and the reference to Chinese guys was a very vital part of the government's attempt to show express bias against Orientals and that there was calculation which precluded any excuse of spontaneous anger centering on a fight over the dancing girls at the bar. We do not fault the prosecutor for forcefully emphasizing this evidence once it had been allowed in by the trial court. At the same time it can be seen that the successful efforts to exclude evidence concerning Jimmy Perry's initial failure to mention to the police officer anything about the $20 and the request to find "the Chinese guy" had to have at least an important bearing on the credibility of Perry's testimony. The error in restricting the cross-examination is apparent....

The government counsel also took unfair advantage, in our view, of the restrictions upon the use of the transcripts of the Lisa Chan interviews by inferring that the defense had endeavored to use only selected portions of the tapes so as to keep their impact from the jury. Thus he argued

> [t]he defense selected lines from these voluminous transcripts, lines where they may have said something different on occasion. But how many times were those lines taken out of context, when they were trying to impeach Bob Sirosky and Jimmy Choi, where they left out part of the proceedings, where there were answers on the tape, and they said there was an interruption on the tape? How many of these inconsistencies are really about minor things like whether or not he said you son of a bitch or mother fucker.

The government also chided the defense for not putting in the entire tapes while knowing it had been prevented from doing so by the court's adverse ruling on admissibility.

... In addition the prosecutor pointed out that one of the witnesses who saw Vincent Chin was herself black and later testified that she saw the defendant with a baseball bat. The obvious strategy was continued in arguments which the prosecutor then made that "this was more than some barroom fight. This was violent hatred turned lose [sic]. This was years of pent-up racial hostilities and rage unleashed. his was a modern-day lynching, but there was a bat instead of a rope."

The government prosecutor became more strident in his remarks after the defense had finished its summation. In a series of comments on the evidence, some of it disputed, the prosecutor preceded each comment with the term "We know," such as "We know that Ebens and Nitz went after Jimmy Choi and not his white counterparts ... that Ebens said that he would have gotten [Choi] too if they hadn't stopped him ... that they offered Jimmy Perry $20 to get those Chinese guys." He then went on to observe that "We're not Niggers; we're not Kikes, we're not Polaks, we're Americans. And as Americans, we must condemn this type of racial violence." He then closes by saying, "Now these defendants have had a fair trial and now it's up to you to do your duty, to hold them responsible for their actions."

The employment by the prosecutor of comments which represent his "personal impression" are, as pointed out by Chief Justice Burger in *United States v. Young*, directly violative of the American Bar Association's standards for criminal justice that "[i]t is unprofessional conduct for a lawyer to express a personal belief or opinion in his client's innocence or personal belief or opinion in the truth or falsity of any testimony or evidence, or to attribute the crime to another person unless such an inference is warranted by the evidence." *Id.* at 9 n. 7 (quoting *ABA Standards for Criminal Justice* 4–7.8(b))....

REVERSED and REMANDED for a new trial.

Notes

1. In rejecting Ebens' argument that the federal civil rights laws only protected Black persons, the Sixth Circuit held that the civil rights laws indeed applied to "Orientals," citing *Yick Wo v. Hopkins*, the Chinese laundry case. Is it surprising that Ebens was still making this argument in the mid-1980s?

2. On remand, because of all the publicity that had been generated, the district judge transferred the case to a different venue for the retrial. *United States v. Ebens*, 654 F. Supp. 144 (E.D. Mich. 1987). The case was moved from Detroit, a city with a Black majority and a history of civil rights, to Cincinnati, a city known for its Southern sensibilities. *See* Helen Zia, *Asian American Dreams: The Emergence of an American People* 79 (2000). In *voir dire*, the vast majority of the prospective jurors answered that they had never even met an Asian-American person before. Ebens was acquitted, as the jury was not persuaded that race was a motivating factor. Do you think it was appropriate for the court to transfer the case to Cincinnati?

3. How important is this case to our discussion of civil rights as a Black/White paradigm?

4. The murder of Vincent Chin occurred in 1982. Seven years later, in 1989, in a remarkably similar case, two White men—brothers—killed Ming Lai (Jim) Loo, a Chinese American, in Raleigh, North Carolina. A group of Asian Americans, including Loo, were in a pool hall when the two brothers, Robert and Lloyd Piche, approached them and started calling them names such as "slanty-eyed gooks" and "rice eaters." The brothers apparently blamed the group for Americans dying in the Vietnam War, and misidentified Loo as Vietnamese. The brothers waited for the group in the parking lot, where Robert hit Loo in the head with a pistol. Loo fell to the pavement, where a broken bottle pierced his head. He died two days later from brain damage. Both Robert and Lloyd were convicted; Robert served 10 years of a 37-year sentence for second-degree murder and assault and Lloyd served only three weeks of a six-month sentence for assault and disorderly conduct. Although the Vincent Chin case generated national outrage and sparked a civil rights movement, little seemed to have changed in the North Carolina pool hall in 1989. *See* Andrew Chin, *Hate's Harms Persist 25 Years After Raleigh Murder*, NewsObserver .com (July 26, 2014), *available at* http://unclaw.com/chin/scholarship/hatesharms .pdf. In a subsequent federal prosecution, Lloyd was convicted of federal civil rights violations and sentenced to 48 months' imprisonment—a downward departure from the advisory sentencing range calculated under the U.S. Sentencing

Guidelines. The Fourth Circuit affirmed the convictions, and remanded for resentencing, in part because the district court "unlawfully departed downward from the [sentencing] guidelines." *United States v. Piche*, 981 F.2d 706, 720 (4th Cir. 1992), *cert. denied*, 508 U.S. 916 (1993).

5. Vincent Chin's mother was so disheartened by the verdict in her son's case that she moved back to China. She remained there for 13 years, until she became ill and returned to the United States for medical treatment. In 2002, she died in Farmington Hills, Michigan, at the age of 82.

Figure 15.5 *Vincent Chin's mother, Lily Chin, with Betty Li.* Photo by Corky Lee. Courtesy of Corky Lee Estate.

6. The critical question for the jury in the Vincent Chin case was whether Ebens was motivated by race. Ebens steadfastly denied that Chin's race was a factor. How credible do you think Ebens' denial is, that is, his murderous rage was not triggered by Chin's Asian identity but by a bar fight? How exactly does a jury determine a person's motivation—what he was thinking and what was inside his mind? Ebens was not charged with a "hate crime" as exists today, but the prosecution still had to prove that race was a motivating factor. What lessons can we learn from the case for today's hate-crime prosecutions?

7. The backdrop for the Chin case was anti-Asian sentiment because of competition from Japanese auto companies. Were there similar factors at play in the early discrimination cases? What about today?

8. The Vincent Chin case had a great impact for all Americans. It sparked public discourse on the practice of Wayne County prosecutors not to appear for sentencing. The case showed how important it was for victims of crimes and their families to

Figure 15.6 ***It's Not Fair*****. Photo by Corky Lee. Courtesy of Corky Lee Estate.**

be given notice of court proceedings and an opportunity to be heard. In the years following the Vincent Chin case, plea-bargaining and sentencing procedures were altered, laws were passed giving crime victims more rights, and hate crime laws were passed. What about Asian Americans? What impact did the Vincent Chin case have for Asian Americans?[6]

As we have seen, Asian Americans continue to be at the center of many controversies that raise issues that are important for all of society. Some of the questions have evolved in the years since the first Asian Americans arrived in this country, but many remain the same. There has been much progress in many respects, but regrettably, many of the prejudices and biases of years past are still at play today.

In this Unit, we have not been able to address all contemporary issues that involve Asian Americans and the law. For example, in the area of popular culture, the Supreme Court has held that The Slants, an Asian-American rock band, has the right to call itself what some might perceive to be a disparaging name. *See* Bill Chappell, *The Slants Win Supreme Court Battle Over Band's Name in Trademark Dispute*, NPR (June 19, 2017), *available at* https://www.npr.org/sections/thetwo-way/2017/06/19/533514196/the-slants-win-supreme-court-battle-over-bands-name-in-trademark-dispute; *Matal v. Tam*, 137 S. Ct. 1744 (2017). Issues also exist with respect to redlining in

6. *See generally* Helen Zia, *Detroit Blues: "Because of You Motherfuckers,"* Asian American Dreams: The Emergence of an American People 55-81 (2000); Paula Yoo, *From a Whisper to a Rallying Cry: The Killing of Vincent Chin & the Trial that Galvanized the Asian American Movement* 124, 148–50 (2021); Roland Hwang, *Killing Spawned Asian American Civil Rights Movement*, 88 Mich. Bar J. 30 (2009); *Racial Violence Against Asian Americans*, 106 Harv. L. Rev. 1926 (1993); *see* Chin and Chin, *supra*, 90 Fordham L. Rev. at 1921–29.

Asian communities, property ownership, and discrimination in housing. *See, e.g.*, Mary Szto, *From Exclusion to Exclusivity: Chinese American Property Ownership and Discrimination in Historical Perspective*, 25 J. Transnat'l L. & Pol'y 33 (2015-16). As touched upon in our discussion of *Oyama*, alien land laws have recently resurfaced for Chinese Americans. The issue of the treatment of Asian Americans in the context of espionage continues to develop, and as tensions between this country and China and North Korea rise or fall, Asian Americans will be impacted. Likewise, as universities and schools strive to apply the Harvard/UNC decision, conflicts will continue to result in litigation, including with respect to high schools. And, of course, aspects of life beyond education are being impacted as well.

Conclusion

The history of how persons of Asian descent interacted with the law in the United States powerfully illuminates the nation's history, its legal institutions, and the evolution of its society. At the same time, the cases tell the stories of individual human beings, including persons from all walks of life, government officials, and lawyers and judges. We see that many issues—the respective powers of the federal and state governments over immigration, birthright citizenship, race-based education policies, hate crimes, alien land laws, and others—are not just historical episodes but of continuing relevance in the modern era. In the study of Asian Americans and the law, there is a strong connection between past and present.

Asian Americans have played an important role not only in the development of American law but in the development of American society. Their stories and struggles have taught us much about our Constitution and our country.

And the stories and struggles will continue to unfold.

Table of Cases

Anilao v. Spota, 381–383
Arizona v. United States, 15, 59
Arver v. United States, 269
Asakura v. City of Seattle, 191–194
Atonio v. Wards Cove Packing Co., 335–338

Baehr v. Lewin, 170, 171
Baehr v. Miike, 170, 171
Barbara v. Trump, 83
Barr v. Abrams, 382
Bartels v. Iowa, 181
Bernard v. County of Suffolk, 382
Besinga v. United States, 299
Blank v. Sullivan & Cromwell, 399
Brackeen v. Haaland, 34
Brown v. Board of Education, 181, 182, 183, 184, 357, 360, 364, 365, 368

CASA, Inc. v. Trump, 83
Castro v. U.S. Dep't of Homeland Security, 34
Chae Chan Ping v. United States, 22–32, 33–37, 63, 135, 187, 188, 194
Cheong v. Bank of East Asia, Ltd., 350
Chin v. Port Authority, 349–350
Chy Lung v. Freeman, 6, 10–17, 33, 140, 144
Coalition for TJ v. Fairfax Co. School Bd., 370–371
Cyrus v. Bank of East Asia, Ltd., 350

Dela Cruz v. Wilkie, 299

Ex parte Endo, 211, 235, 237, 246–251, 291, 297

Farrington v. Tokushige, 180–181, 183, 184
Finney v. Delaware Department of Transportation, 350
Fisher v. University of Texas, 358, 365, 366
Fong Yue Ting v. United States, 34–36, 74
Fong Yuen Ling v. Mayor & Common Council of City of Los Angeles, 115
Fujii v. United States, 264–265

Gandolfo v. Hartman, 207
Gong Lum v. Rice, 174–178, 179–181, 301, 357
Gratz v. Bollinger, 358
Griggs v. Duke Power Co., 335, 336, 344–346
Grutter v. Bollinger, 357, 358, 361–363, 366, 367, 369
Guey Heung Lee v. Johnson, 183, 184

Hawaii v. Trump, 34, 39
Hirabayashi v. United States, 167, 199, 211, 213, 214–228, 229–233, 236, 237, 243–245, 263, 266, 276, 277, 279–280, 281–294
Ho Ah Kow v. Nunan, 33, 127–134, 135, 136, 143
Hohri v. United States, 298

In re Ah Yup, 84–87, 92, 160, 185
In re Camille, 88, 92
In re Chol Soo Lee, 376, 377
In re Easurk Emsen Charr, 87, 93
In re Halladjian, 87–88
In re Hong Yen Chang, 185–186
In re Hong Yen Chang on Admission, 186–190
In re Knight, 88
In re Look Tin Sing, 81, 185
In re Takao Ozawa, 102, 103
In re Young, 88
Int'l Refugee Assistance Project v. Trump, 34, 39

Jew Ho v. Williamson, 143
Johnson v. San Francisco Unified School District, 182, 183

Keegan v. United States, 267
Kimm v. Rosenberg, 314–315
Korematsu v. United States, 62, 168, 211, 231–246, 250, 251, 255–257, 271–280, 281, 282, 286, 288, 290, 291, 293, 294, 300, 325

Lam v. University of Hawai'i, 352
Lau v. Nichols, 183, 357
Lin Sing v. Washburn, 109
Loving v. Virginia, 167–169, 361

MacDraw, Inc. v. CIT Group Equip. Fin., Inc., 399
Meyer v. Nebraska, 181
Mojica v. Reno, 3

Naim v. Naim, 169
Nelatury v. Penn St. Univ., 350

Obata v. Williamson, 143
Obergefell v. Hodges, 170, 171
OCA-Asian Pacific American Advocates v. Rubio, 83
Okamoto v. United States, 267
Oyama v. California, 195–205, 414
Ozawa v. United States, 88, 89, 91–94, 95, 101–103, 164, 194

Paguirigan v. Prompt Nursing Empl. Agency LLC, 383
People v. Abacus Federal Savings Bank, 377–378
People v. Brady, 158, 188
People v. Chol Soo Lee, 373
People v. Crenshaw, 115
People v. Hall, 113, 147, 148, 188
People v. Peter Liang, 378–380
People v. Washington, 149–158, 373
Perez v. Sharp, 159, 166, 167, 168
Pierce v. Soc'y of Sisters, 181
Plessy v. Ferguson, 135, 178–179, 182, 360

Quiban v. Veterans Administration, 298, 299

Raouf v. U.S. Dep't of State, 34
Recinto v. U.S. Dep't of Veterans Affairs, 299
Regents of the University of California v. Bakke, 357, 360–362, 365, 366
Roldan v. Los Angeles County, 160–164

Shmueli v. City of New York, 382
Shelley v. Kraemer, 207
Singletary v. King Crab Boiling Seafood & Bar, Inc., 350
Students for Fair Admissions, Inc. v. President and Fellows of Harvard College, 358, 359–369
Sun Valley Orchards, LLC v. U.S. Dep't of Justice, 34

Tape v. Hurley, 172–174, 182, 301, 357
Tineo v. Attorney General, 34
Tiwari v. Mattis, 323–332

Toyota v. United States, 103
Trump v. CASA, Inc., 64, 83
Trump v. Hawaii, 38, 39–63, 256, 257, 325

United States v. Ah Sou, 18
United States v. Anming Hu, 303–304
United States v. Bhagat Singh Thind, 91, 95–103, 164
United States v. Ebens, 401–412
United States v. Feng Tao, 303
United States v. Fujii, 259, 260–264
United States v. Iowa, 15
United States v. Kuwabara, 266
United States v. Okamoto, 259
United States v. Piche, 412
United States v. Texas, 34
United States v. Toguri D'Aquino, 306–315
United States v. Wen Ho Lee, 315–321
United States v. Wong Kim Ark, 67–82, 87

Vietnamese Fishermen v. Texas Knights of the Ku Klux Klan, 388–400
Vinluan v. Doyle, 381, 382

Wards Cove Packing Co. v. Atonio, 333–336, 346, 347
Washington v. Trump, 39, 82
Wong Wai v. Williamson, 143–145

Yasui v. United States, 211, 228–230, 271, 280, 292–293
Yick Wo v. Crowley, 142
Yick Wo v. Hopkins, 74, 136, 137–142, 144, 188, 202, 221, 226, 360, 405, 411
Yifan Shen v. Simpson, 206

Index

#

1-A, 260, 264
1790 Naturalization Act, 7, 9, 186
1866 Civil Rights Act, 71, 73, 75, 80, 158, 395
1870 Naturalization Act, 8, 19, 83, 84, 90
22 Lewd Chinese Women, 10
4-C, 260–263
42 U.S.C. § 1983, 136, 381, 382
442nd Regimental Combat Team, 205, 259, 322
9/11, 300, 385, 386, 398

A

A Portrait of Asian Americans in the Law, 350–351
AABANY, 386
Abacus Federal Savings Bank, 377, 378
ABC News, 83, 321, 376
absolute immunity, 381, 382
abstention, 169
Act of July 14, 1870, 8, 19, 83, 84, 90
Administrative Procedure Act, 83
admissions, 327, 357–371
adverse impact, 335–338, 346
Aerojet Corporation, 315
affirmative action, 358, 369, 371
Afghanistan, 383, 384
African descent, 8, 19, 73, 81, 83–87, 89, 90, 95, 185
Ah Sou, 18
Ah Wang, 149
Ah Yup, 84, 92, 160, 185
Alaska, 117, 254, 333, 338, 339
Aleuts, 254
Alice in Chinatown, 373
Alien Enemies Act of 1798, 252
Alien Fiancées and Fiancés Act, 170
alien land laws, 194–206, 209, 414
Alito, Justice, 62, 371
allegiance, 69, 73–79, 142, 200, 214, 220, 230, 233, 264, 272, 311, 332
American Bar Association, 410
American Citizens for Justice, 402, 406
American Civil Liberties Union, 53, 289, 290
American Fishermen's Coalition, 388, 393
American G.I.s, 169
Amritsar, 100, 101
anchor babies, 80
Anilao v. Spota, 381
anti-Asian violence, 301, 386, 398
anti-Chinese legislation, 17, 109, 117
anti-Chinese wall, 38
Anti-Coolie Association, 135, 207
anti-miscegenation, 158, 159, 164–168, 252
anti-Muslim animus, 53, 57, 59
anti-Oriental prejudice, 200
Appellate Division, Second Department, 381, 382
Arabic, 322
Archbald, Justice, 160
Arizona, 15, 59, 166, 216, 385
Armenians, 87, 88
Army, 5, 87, 91, 100, 119, 121, 205, 214, 215, 219, 224, 228, 229, 231, 232, 243, 244, 250, 259, 268, 298, 299, 309, 315, 322–324, 326, 329–332, 383, 384
Arnold, General Benedict, 102
Arthur, President, 19
Aryan, 88, 97, 98, 101, 102
Asakura, 191, 194
Asakura v. City of Seattle, 191
Asia, 3, 5, 10, 14, 85, 88, 92, 96, 99, 104, 162, 323,

Asian American Pacific Islander, 356
Asian Pacific American Law Students Association, 190
Asiatic Barred Zone Act, 10, 37
Asiatic Exclusion League, 123, 207
Assembly Center, 212, 213, 234, 235, 237, 245, 250, 252, 272
assimilation, 9, 55, 99, 103, 133, 220, 224, 227
Associated Press, 321
Atlanta, 352, 386
Atomic Energy Act, 305, 316, 319
Auburn, Washington, 227
Australia, 163, 283, 306, 308, 313

B

Babbitt, Ashley, 380
background investigations, 324, 326
Baehr v. Lewin, 170, 171
Baehr v. Miike, 170, 171
Bagai, Vaishno Das, 100
Bakke, Allan, 357, 360–362, 365, 366
Baltimore, 5, 192
bamboo ceiling, 347–349, 351
Bangladeshi, 356
bar admission, 184–190
baseball bat, 400, 402–404, 410
Beam, Louis, 388–391, 394, 397, 399, 400
Beijing, 315
Belgic, 22
Bellingham, 123, 334
Bendetsen, Karl, 285
Bengal, 5
Berg, David, 400
Berkeley, 89, 94,
Bhagat Singh Thind, 88, 91, 95, 100–103, 164, 322
Bhutanese, 355
Biden, President, 63–64, 297, 386
Bigler, Governor John, 4, 107, 108
bilingual English-Chinese programs, 182–183
Birth Tourism, 66, 80
birthright citizenship, 64, 65, 66, 81–83, 104, 245
Black, Justice, 203, 231, 245
Blood Drop Cross, 387
Blum, Edward, 358
Blumenbach, 85, 98, 160–163
board of health, 143, 144
Bolivar County, 174–177
bombing of Pearl Harbor, 215, 224, 252
Boston Pops, 306, 307
Bouiss, Helene 169–170
Boxer rebellion, 125
British Columbia, 5, 123
British Crown, 144
British empire, 6
Broadcasting Corporation of Japan, 308, 309
Bronx Science, 370
Brooklyn Tech, 370
Brown v. Board of Education, 181–184, 296, 357, 360, 364, 365, 368
Bryan, Secretary of State, 201
bubonic plague, 110, 143–145
Buffon, 85
Burger, Chief Justice, 410
Burlingame, Anson, 25
Burlingame Treaty, 36, 66, 118
Burmese, 161, 355
Burton, Justice, 203
Bush, George W., 49
Bush, George H.W., 295–296
business necessity, 336, 337, 339–341, 344, 346
Butler, Justice, 103, 191, 205
Butler, Lola, 166

C

California, 3, 4, 6, 10–17, 22, 23, 25, 26, 33, 37, 66, 81, 84, 89, 94, 95, 107–110, 111–113, 115, 117, 124, 127, 133, 137, 140–142, 146–148, 155, 158–162, 164–166, 169, 172, 174, 182–184, 186–190, 194, 195–207, 211–213, 219, 220, 226, 231, 236, 241, 245, 246, 249–252, 260, 262, 264, 277, 308, 314, 315, 328, 350, 357, 360, 373–376, 387
California Attorney General, 195, 204
California Constitutional Convention, 188
California Department of Motor Vehicles, 250
California Education Code, 182
California Institute of Technology, 315
California Supreme Court, 33, 109, 113, 141, 146, 148, 158, 166, 172, 190, 350
California v. Bakke, 357, 360–362, 365, 366
Cambodian, 355, 356
Camp Bunka, 310, 312
Camp Lewis, Washington, 91

Canada, 5, 6, 254
cannery workers, 333–335, 337–339
Canton, 161
Cao, Guoqing, 304
Capitol, 380
Carter, President, 46, 62
Catholics, 62, 125, 132, 135
Caucasian, 85, 88, 92, 93, 96, 97, 99, 101, 141, 147, 160, 162, 163, 175–177, 180
Center for American Progress, 355
Central Utah Relocation Center, 246, 248, 249
Chae Chan Ping, 22, 33–37, 63, 135, 187, 188, 194
Chamorro, 356
Chan, Lisa, 402, 406, 408–410
Charr, Easurk Emsen, 87
Chee Long Tong, 113
Chen, Danny, 373, 383
Chen, Gang, 304
Chen, Sherry, 304
Chew How, 174
Chin, Gabriel, 190
Chin, Judge, 111, 386
Chin, Lily, 412
Chin, Vincent, 125, 387, 400, 401, 405, 409–413
China, 5, 6, 11–13, 15–19, 22–27, 29–33, 35, 36, 66, 67, 74, 75, 77, 79, 81, 84–87, 109, 119–121, 125, 127, 134, 135, 138, 141, 155, 160, 161, 171, 174, 185–188, 190, 194, 207, 303–305, 315, 323, 328, 331, 332, 360, 385, 403, 412, 414
China Initiative, 303–305
Chinaman, 84, 115, 117, 131, 148, 149, 153, 156, 158, 160, 163, 179, 207
Chinatown, 115, 117, 119, 127, 143–145, 174, 182, 357, 373, 375, 376, 378, 383
Chinese exclusion, 4, 19, 20, 22, 34, 36, 37, 66, 67, 81, 88, 110, 117, 121, 187, 189, 190, 200, 333
Chinese laborers, 19, 20, 22, 23, 26–36, 67, 78, 80, 104, 109, 111, 118, 138, 158, 159, 333
Chinese Laundry Case, 136, 411
Chinese lawyer, 186, 190
Chinese Massacre Cove, 122
Chinese Methodist Mission, 115
Chinese Police Tax, 109, 188
Chinese Primary School, 174
Chinese testimony, 113, 148, 158
Chinese Wall, 162
Chinese Women's Home of the Presbyterian Church, 18
Choi, Jimmy, 403, 404, 406, 407, 409, 410
Chol Soo Lee, 373–377
Chu, Representative Judy, 36–37
Chun, Justice Danny, 379
CIA, 305, 316
Cincinnati, 411
Civil Liberties Act, 295
Civil Rights Act of 1866, 73, 75, 80, 150, 151, 153, 155–158, 395
Civil Rights Act of 1991, 346
Civil Rights Division, 381, 406
civil service examination, 171
Civil War, 6, 7, 14, 83, 149, 151, 251, 268, 360
Civilian Exclusion Order, 214, 216, 231, 238, 250, 271, 283
class action, 183, 298, 334, 383
class certification, 83
Cleveland, President, 19, 118–119
Clinton, President, 296
closure of camps, 251
Cockburn, Lord Chief Justice, 69, 76
coercion, 261, 310–313, 396
coffin shop, 144
Collins, David, 390–394, 397
Collins, Joseph, 389–390
Commander in Chief, 215, 218, 232, 266, 299
Commission on Wartime Relocation and Internment of Civilians, 210, 271, 274, 279, 282, 295, 297
Commissioner of Immigration, 11, 13
Committee of 100, 206
Communist Party, 305, 314
compelling interest, 328, 357, 358
concentration camps, 235, 236, 237, 252, 254, 256, 259, 280
Confederacy, 268
confession of error, 273, 293, 294
Congress, 6–10, 13–15, 17, 19–27, 29, 30, 32–39, 42, 44, 46–48, 51, 59, 60, 64, 67, 70, 71, 73–75, 81, 82, 84–88, 90, 93–95, 98–100, 104, 114, 118, 121, 125, 133, 149–157, 166, 169, 178, 185, 186, 189, 190, 200, 206, 209, 212, 214–223, 225, 226, 231–236, 242, 248–252, 263, 271, 274, 276, 277, 284, 288, 295, 305, 341, 346, 347, 360, 386, 395, 399, 405

Constitution, 6–9, 13, 14, 18, 26, 29–31, 33–35, 46, 53, 61–63, 65, 67, 69–76, 80–82, 84, 109, 131–133, 135, 137, 138, 140, 144, 147, 149–157, 162, 166, 171, 175–179, 181, 188, 189, 191, 192, 199, 202, 203, 218, 222, 223, 225, 226, 241–244, 256, 268, 269, 281, 293, 360, 361, 363–365, 388
Constitution, Article I, 7
Constitution, Article I, section 8, 7, 8
Constitution, Article II, 9–10
Constitutional Convention, 5, 162, 188
coolies, 14, 15, 73, 107, 108, 109, 115, 135, 161, 179, 188, 207
coram nobis, 211, 257, 271, 272, 277–282, 285, 287, 291, 292, 294, 295, 297
Coreris, Detective, 377
coronavirus, 385, 386, 398
Coronel Building, 112
Cosmopolitan magazine, 307
Cousens, Charles, 307, 308, 312, 313
COVID-19, 15, 144, 146, 386
Craig, Jim, 391
Cravath, Swaine & Moore, 348
Crenshaw, Curley, 113, 115
Crockett, Justice, 153
crossfire, 111, 117
Crowley, Patrick, 142
Crown of England, 69
cruel and unusual punishment, 132
Cubans, 46, 62
Cubic Air Ordinance, 127, 135, 143
curfew, 213, 215–219, 221–223, 225–233, 243–245, 263, 266, 280–285, 287, 288, 291–293
Cushing, Caleb, 23
Customs and Border Protection, 66

D
D.C. Circuit, 299
Daily Alta, 14, 111, 113
dance hall, 124, 165, 166
de Lafayette, Marquis, 321
debauched women, 10, 11, 12
Declaration of Independence, 69, 75, 76
Dees, Morris, 387, 400
deference to executive branch, 43
Denver, Colorado, 114, 115
Department of Defense, 323–330, 332
Department of Energy, 304, 320
Department of Homeland Security, 40, 41, 43, 51, 328
Department of Justice, 210, 247, 275, 276, 282, 293, 303, 305, 308, 319, 320, 331, 380, 381, 400, 402, 406
Detroit, 221, 387, 400, 402, 403, 406, 408, 411, 413
DeWitt, Lt. General John, 209, 215–217, 228, 237, 242–245, 268, 271, 272, 274–277, 285–291
disaggregation, 355, 356
disloyal, 221, 224, 233, 239, 240, 246–247, 264, 274, 283–286, 289–291
District of Columbia, 83, 135, 178
diversity, equity, and inclusion, 351
Do Thi Doi, 392
Douglas, Justice, 182, 183, 203, 223, 227, 246, 284
Downey, Robert, 376
draft, 227, 259–260, 262, 264, 266–269, 272
draft resisters, 211, 259, 266–268
Dream Team, 34
dual citizenship, 217, 220, 239, 245, 263
due process, 8, 15, 72, 132, 138, 166, 168, 180, 181, 184, 191, 195, 199, 221, 225–226, 238, 241, 243, 246, 265–266, 278, 282
duress, 267, 310–312

E
East India companies, 5
East Pasadena, 164
Eastern District of Michigan, 402
Eastern District of New York, 382
Ebens, Ronald, 401–412
ebola, 15, 145
economic pressure, 209
education, 61, 89, 100, 103, 110, 171–173, 175–177, 181–184, 190, 220, 283, 295, 301, 357, 360–362, 364–366, 368, 371, 414
Eisenhower, President, 48–49
Eleventh Circuit, 206
Eli Lilly, 304
Ellis Island, 255
Emperor of China, 11, 13, 22, 67, 74, 75, 77, 127, 138, 360
Emperor of Japan, 191, 230
Endo, Mitsuye 213, 235, 237, 246–251, 297
Eng, Justice, 381, 382
Engel, Judge, 401

English Colonies, 69, 75
English proficiency, 183
Ennis, Edward, 282, 286, 290
Episcopalian minister, 16
Equal Protection, 8, 10, 15, 33, 58, 72, 129, 131, 132, 135, 137–141, 166–168, 174, 177, 178, 180, 182–184, 190, 191, 195, 197–199, 202, 203, 221, 238, 269, 324–327, 332, 359, 360, 362–365, 367, 368, 373, 381, 393
escheat, 195, 196, 199, 201, 204, 205
espionage, 200, 210, 215, 218–224, 226, 231–233, 239–241, 246, 248–250, 271, 272, 295, 301, 303, 305, 316, 321, 329, 331, 332, 381, 414
Establishment Clause, 39, 42, 47, 49, 53, 58, 60, 63, 64
Eureka, 117
Europe, 14, 48, 70, 79, 87, 98, 104, 193, 226, 323, 386
evacuation, 196, 205, 210, 211, 214, 217, 234, 235, 237, 239, 240, 244, 247–250, 275–277, 283, 285, 286, 289, 290, 295, 309
evil eye, 140
exclusion, 3, 4, 6, 10, 17, 19, 20, 22, 31–34, 36, 37, 47, 49, 58, 62, 66, 67, 76, 80, 81, 88, 89, 93, 96, 104, 107, 110, 111, 117, 121, 123, 133, 142, 173, 187, 189, 190, 200, 204, 207, 213, 214, 216, 228, 231–240, 245, 250, 251, 271, 272, 274, 280–289, 291–293, 333, 365, 368, 414
Executive Order, 37–39, 55, 56, 63, 64, 65, 81–83, 205, 209, 214–218, 223, 228, 231, 242, 249, 252, 263, 271–274, 287, 295, 351
Executive Order 9066, 205, 209, 215, 217–218, 223, 228, 231, 249, 271–274, 295
Executive Order No. 13769, 39, 55
Executive Order No. 13780, 39

F

Fahy, Charles, 284, 288, 290, 293
Fair Play Committee, 259–260, 267
Fancy Pants Lounge, 403, 404, 407
Fannie Mae, 378
Farmington Hills, 412
Farrington v. Tokushige, 180, 181, 183, 184, 357
Federal Bureau of Investigation, 209, 210, 228, 241, 245, 281, 265, 304, 315–317, 319, 321, 331, 371
Federal Communications Commission, 277
Federal Espionage Act, 316
Federalist No. 2, 8
Federalist Papers, 8
Field, Justice, 11, 22, 32–33, 36, 81, 127, 129, 135
Fifth Amendment, 10, 180, 214, 217, 221, 226, 238, 314
Filipino cannery workers, 333, 335
Filipino nurses, 373, 381, 382
Filipino sailors, 5
Filipino veterans, 299
Final Report, 239, 274–277, 281, 282, 285, 287, 291
First Amendment, 39, 42, 47, 50, 52, 53, 61–63, 245, 408
Fisher, Eugene, 393, 397
Flip bunkhouse, 337
Flushing, New York, 305
Ford, President, 295, 314
foreign intelligence, 331
foreign language schools, 180-181
Foreign Miners' License Tax, 108
foreign nationals, 38, 39, 41, 42, 47, 49, 66, 256, 326
Fort Vancouver, 229
Founders (or Founding), 3, 36, 52, 62, 79, 80
Fourteenth Amendment, 7–8, 10, 65, 67, 70–84, 87, 132, 133, 137–140, 144, 150, 153, 158, 168, 170, 177, 178, 181, 183, 184, 191, 197, 199, 202, 203, 207, 226, 359, 360, 362, 364, 365, 388, 395, 405
Fourth Circuit, 370, 371, 412
Fox, Justice, 185
Frankfurter, Justice, 288
Franklin, Benjamin, 5
free white person, 7, 9, 19, 83, 84, 86–88, 90, 92, 94–95, 98–99, 100, 101, 103, 104, 185–186, 194
French Revolution, 70
Fujii, Shigeru, 259, 260, 264
Fuller, Chief Justice, 75

G

Gaelic, 22
Galveston Bay, 388, 392, 396
Garner, Eric, 379, 380
Geary Act, 34–37, 158
Gentlemen's Agreement, 110, 200

Germans, 213, 216, 255
Germany, 125, 205, 225, 255, 332, 386
Gibson, Reverend, 16
Gibson, William, 174
Gillett, Governor, 201
glass ceiling, 347, 349
global pandemic, 385
Go, Michelle, 386
gold, 4, 6, 10–12, 25, 33, 66, 107–109, 112, 121, 122, 148, 187
Gold Rush, 6, 10, 33, 66, 107, 109
Gong Lum v. Rice, 174–176, 179–181, 301, 357
Goodman, Judge, 266–267
Gorsuch, Justice, 62, 358
Gray, Justice, 67
Great Britain, 5, 13, 62
Greece, 53, 61, 194
Greene, Justice, 120
Greensboro, 390
grocery stores, 179, 180, 351
Grutter v. Bollinger, 357, 358, 361–363, 366, 367, 369
guerilla forces, 299
Guey Heung Lee v. Johnson, 183
Gulf Coast, 387
Gurley, Akai, 378–380

H

habeas corpus, 11, 15, 22–23, 33, 120, 150, 213, 237, 246-51, 265, 375–377
haircut ordinance, 109
half Asian half White, 88
Ham Say Naim, 168
Hammond, William, 282
Hancock, Winfield Scott, 117
Harlan, Justice, 75, 177–179
Hart-Celler Act, 10
Harvard, 352, 358, 359, 361–369, 371, 414
Hawaii, 6, 34, 38, 39, 41, 42, 63, 89, 94, 95, 102, 110, 165, 171, 180, 181, 253, 256, 257, 283, 325, 386, 387
Hawai'i Richardson School of Law, 352
Hawaii Supreme Court, 171
Hayslip, John, 400
hazing, 373, 384
hearsay, 376, 406
Heart Mountain, 252–254, 259–262, 264, 266, 267
Hells Canyon, Oregon, 121–122
Henry Ford Hospital, 404
Herzig-Yoshinaga, Aiko, 271, 282
high caste Indian, 88, 101
high schools, 89, 94, 174–177, 289, 306, 369–371
Highland Park, 403, 404, 408
Hindu, 95, 97–102, 123
Hirabayashi, Gordon, 167, 199, 211, 213, 214, 227–229, 231–233, 236, 237, 243–245, 263, 266, 271, 276, 277, 279, 280–294, 297,
Hirono, Mazie, 386
historical discrimination, 105, 107, 110
historically Black colleges, 183
Hmong, 355, 356
Ho, Szuhsiung, 305
Ho Ah Kow, 33, 127, 129, 135, 136, 143
Ho Ah Kow v. Nunan, 33, 127, 129
Hobbes, Thomas, 125
Hobson's Choice, 122
Hong Kong, 10, 22, 26, 144, 161, 187, 219, 305, 350, 379, 408
Hong Yen Chang, 184–187, 190, 191
Honolulu, 94, 103
horse stalls, 280
House of Representatives, 7, 20, 28, 29, 36
housing, 109, 124, 268, 327, 328, 337–339, 378, 414
Houston, 387
Houthi rebels, 315
Hu, Anming, 303
Huang, Jensen, 348
human trafficking, 17, 59
Hurley, Jennifer, 172–174, 182, 301, 357
Huxley, 97, 160
Huxman, Judge, 264

I

illegal restraint, 396
Illocano, 160
immigration, 3, 6, 8, 10, 11, 13, 15, 17–19, 25–27, 33, 34, 36–38, 42, 44, 45, 48, 50, 55, 58, 59, 62, 66, 67, 79, 80, 83, 86, 88, 90, 98–100, 104, 107–110, 133, 158, 159, 161, 166, 187–190, 200, 201, 204, 252, 314, 315, 333, 353
Immigration Act of 1917, 10, 37
Immigration Act of 1924, 10

Immigration and Nationality Act, 10, 38, 42, 59
Immigration and Naturalization Service, 83, 314
impact litigation, 34
In re Hong Yen Chang, 185–187
Ince, Wallace, 307, 308, 312, 313
India, 5, 6, 88, 95, 97–102, 331, 385
Indian Archipelago, 85, 160
Indianapolis, 304
Indians, 71, 73, 85, 90, 92, 100, 102, 123, 149–151, 153, 154, 157, 161, 355
indigenous Americans, 3
inoculation, 143, 144
Inouye, Daniel, 322
internment, 55, 110, 205, 207, 209–211, 213, 228, 245, 250–255, 266, 267, 271, 274, 279, 282, 289, 291, 294, 295, 297, 298, 300, 306
internment camp survivors, 295, 297, 298
internment of Germans and Italians, 213, 216, 255
intersectionalism, 351
invasion, 26, 30, 161, 211, 215, 219–222, 224, 226, 233, 236, 239, 240, 250, 252, 261, 283, 290, 298, 321
Irish Catholic, 125
Iriye, Fred, 266
Iron Chink, 333, 334, 337
Irons, Professor Peter 227–228, 229, 245, 251, 271
Ishigo, Arthur, 252
Ishigo, Estelle, 253–254
Italians, 99, 104, 209, 213, 216, 227, 240, 242, 255, 291
Italy, 95, 205, 255
Iwamura, Akira, 205–206
Iwamura, Cecil, 205

J

Jackson, Justice Ketanji Brown, 358, 364
Jackson, Justice Robert, 203, 241, 246, 291
Japan, 6, 11, 32, 37, 85, 89, 94, 103, 104, 110, 155, 160, 169, 171, 191, 202, 206, 209, 210, 214, 215, 217, 219–222, 228, 230, 231, 233, 239, 241, 245, 250, 251, 263, 265, 271, 272, 298, 306–309, 312, 314
Japanese, 6, 37, 55, 88, 89, 91, 93–95, 103, 104, 110, 124, 143, 156, 159, 161, 168–170, 180–182, 191–196, 198–207, 209–217, 219–222, 224, 226–243, 245, 246, 249–256, 259, 261–266, 268, 271, 272, 274–277, 281, 283–291, 294–298, 300, 306–310, 312–314, 322, 333, 356, 403–405, 408, 412
Japanese "Alien" Economic Cases, 191
Japanese American Citizens League (JACL), 168, 259, 290
Japanese farmers, 194
Japanese language school, 181, 220, 228, 239
Jay, Chief Justice, 8–9
Jet Propulsion Lab, 315
Jeter, Mildred, 167
Jews, 125, 132, 135
Ji Chaoqu, 331
Jim Crow, 9, 125, 190
Johnson v. San Francisco Unified School District, 182, 183
Johnson-Reed Act, 10, 37
judicial notice, 135, 236, 274–276, 284, 290
judicial power, 142, 244
jus sanguinis, 70, 79, 245
jus soli, 70, 79, 80
Justice Department, 56, 276, 277, 281, 283, 285, 286, 290, 291, 293, 304, 305

K

Kagan, Justice 61, 62, 364
Kaimuki Dry Goods, 94
Kang, Jerry, 294
Kansas, 267, 385
Katyal, Neal, 254, 257, 293
Kavanaugh, Justice, 358
Kawakita, Tomoya, 314
Kearney, Denis 117, 188
Kemah-Seabrook 389–391, 394, 396
Kennedy, District Judge, 47, 50, 54, 260, 266
Kennedy, Justice, 58, 62, 204
Kennedy, President, 314
Kennedy, Professor Randall, 204
Kerber, R.W., 391
Kim, Richard, 376
Kimm, Diamond, 314
Kimura, 261
King, Martin Luther, 368
Knights of Labor, 119, 120
Kobayashi, Richard, 212
Koivu, Gary, 403, 404, 406, 407

Korea, 6, 32, 40–42, 46, 87, 110, 171, 332, 414
Korematsu, Fred, 62, 168, 211, 213, 231, 232, 235, 236, 241–243, 245, 250, 251, 255–257, 271, 276, 277, 279, 281, 282, 286, 288, 290, 291, 293, 294, 296, 297, 300, 325
Korematsu, Karen, 256–257
Ku Klux Klan, 245, 387–392, 394, 399, 400
Kung Flu, 111, 386
Kurfurst, John, 196
Kuwabara, Masaaki, 266
Kwang-Tung, 161

L
labor, 3, 4, 6, 15, 25, 32, 36, 73, 79, 86, 107, 109, 110, 115, 117, 119–121, 123, 179, 187, 188, 194, 201, 236, 243, 324, 333, 334, 340, 341, 373
laborers, 6, 15, 19, 20, 22, 23, 25–36, 66, 67, 78, 80, 88, 104, 109, 111, 118, 119, 124, 127, 135, 138, 158, 159, 187, 314, 333, 354
Lam v. University of Hawaiʻi, 352
Lamberth, Ruby, 168
land ownership, 94, 191, 204
Laotian, 356
lascars, 5
lashkar, 5
Latin Americans, 254
Lau v. Nichols, 183, 357
Lau, Kinney Kinmon, 183
laundries, 109, 110, 115, 127, 136–138, 141–143, 351, 411
leadership gap, 348
Lebanese, 385
Lee, Bill, 369
Lee, Christina Yuna, 386
Lee, Corky 318, 412, 413
Lee, Jerry Chun Shing, 305
Lee, K.W., 374–376
Lee, Thomas, 9, 79
Lee, Wen Ho, 305, 306, 315, 316, 318
level of scrutiny, 227, 329
Lew, Harry, 384
lewd women, 12, 16
Li, Shuyu, 304
Liang, Peter, 378–380
life, liberty, or property, 8, 132, 138
Lincoln, Abraham, 33, 135,
Little Tokyo, 207, 268
Liu, Justice, 350–351
loaded weapon, 243, 246
Local 37, 337, 339, 341, 342
Lodging House Law, 135
lodging houses 127, 132, 135
longshoremen, 339
Loo, Ming Lai (Jim), 411
Look Tin Sing, 81, 185
Los Alamos National Laboratory, 305, 315
Los Angeles, 111–113, 115, 117, 160, 167, 204, 205, 220, 268, 306, 316, 321
Los Angeles Massacre, 111–113
Los Angeles riots, 111, 117
Los Angeles Times, 205, 268, 321
Louisiana, 5, 11, 72, 178, 179
Loving, Richard, 167–169
Loving v. Virginia, 167, 169, 361
Lum, Berda, 179
Lum, Martha, 174–180

M
Ma, GuiYing, 386
Maduro regime, 252
magic washer, 21
Malay, 85, 158, 160–164, 166, 210
mandamus, 137, 174–176
Mandel, Ernest, 49, 50
Manzanar, 212
marriage, 14, 16, 98, 103, 110, 124, 154, 156, 158–160, 164–171, 309, 354
martial law, 121, 218, 225, 238, 239, 241, 253, 267
Marutani, William, 168
Maryland, 5, 39, 83, 159, 164, 222
Massachusetts, 86, 103, 139, 178, 186, 304
Massachusetts Institute of Technology, 304, 315
massage parlors, 386
Matthews, Justice, 137
McCloy, John J., 285
McDonald, Judge, 388, 399
McDonald's, 371, 404–406
McDougal, John, 4
McGraw, John, 119–121
Meagles, Mary, 141
Meares, Captain John, 5
median household incomes, 354
Mehanja, Valdeta, 332

melting pot, 356
Mendocino, California, 81
Meng, Grace, 347, 386
Merritt, Theodore, 409
Mexico, 104, 252, 305, 363
migrants, 6, 10, 14, 15, 36, 43, 56, 104, 207
military accessions vital to the national interest, 321–332
Military Area No. 1, 216, 220, 234, 272
Military Commander, 214–220, 223, 225, 231, 242, 243, 271
military necessity, 216, 227, 238–241, 244, 250, 263, 271, 274–277, 279, 283, 287, 289–293, 384
military power, 244
Miller, Justice, 11, 72
Ministry of State Security, 305
Mississippi, 174–176, 178–180
Mississippi Delta, 179, 180
Mitsushio, George, 314
mob violence, 111, 125, 385
Mochida Family, 210
Model Minority, 301, 333, 347, 348, 353, 354, 356
Mongolian, 84–87, 131, 147–149, 153, 159–164, 166, 174–176, 182, 185, 187, 188, 200
Mongoloid race, 88
Monroe, President, 268
Morris, Steven, 377
Morrison, Judge, 16
Motley, Judge Constance Baker, 399
Mulatto, 146, 147, 149, 159, 373
Munger, Tolles & Olson, 190
Murphy, Justice, 199, 203–205, 225, 227, 238, 245, 250, 251, 266, 290, 291
Murray, Chief Judge, 147
Muslim Association, 41, 60
Muslim Ban, 38, 48, 55–57
Muslims, 38, 46–49, 51, 52, 54–57, 59–63

N

NAACP Legal Defense & Educational Fund, 399
Nam, Nguyen Van, 390
NASA, 315
National Government, 13, 15, 125, 156, 218
National Intelligence Agency Checks, 323–330
national security, 38, 40–42, 44, 48–52, 57, 61, 63, 64, 204, 206, 227, 256, 257, 266, 276, 279, 300, 303, 321, 324–326, 328–332
National Weather Service, 304
nationwide injunctions, 64, 82
Native Hawaiian, 355, 356, 362
natural born citizen, 7, 9, 10, 75, 76, 79
Naturalization Act of 1790, 9
naturalization proceedings, 104
Navy, 6, 215, 219, 253, 277, 315, 322
Nazi, 125, 328
negress, 399
negro, 72, 77, 85, 92, 97, 147, 150, 151, 153, 154, 158–160, 163, 268
New American Cyclopaedia, 160
New Hampshire, 83, 268
New Mexico, 166, 305, 315, 319
New York County District Attorney, 377
New York State, 8, 11, 101, 185–187, 255, 273, 355, 356, 386
New York Times, 256, 304, 315, 320, 321, 353, 369
Ninth Circuit, 18, 39, 42, 89, 100, 101, 169, 182, 183, 215, 228, 280, 293, 294, 299, 308, 313, 335, 339, 344, 346, 352
Nisei, 205, 211, 259, 279, 314
Nitz, Michael, 401–410
Nootka Sound, 5
Norfolk, Virginia, 168, 169
North America, 3, 5
North Carolina, 169, 358, 359, 364, 365, 411
North Korea, 40–42, 46, 414
Northern Monterey Chamber of Commerce, 124
Nunan, 33, 127, 129, 134, 136
NVIDIA, 348
NYPD, 379

O

Oak Park, 403
Oakland, 143
Obama, President, 297, 299
Obergefell v. Hodges, 170, 171
Oeyama, 314
Ohio, 101, 132, 192, 222, 304, 398
Okazaki, Steven, 253, 294
Oki, Kenkichi, 314

Oliphant-Curren, Joanne, 390
Oregon, 88, 95, 100, 115, 117, 120–122, 220, 228, 229, 280, 338, 339
Orphan Ann, 306, 309
Oyama, Fred, 195–199, 203, 205, 206
Oyama, Kajiro, 195–199, 205, 206
Oyama, Kohide, 195
Ozawa, George Yoshio, 95
Ozawa, Takao 88, 89, 91, 94, 102, 103

P

Pacific Islands, 10
Pantaleo, Daniel, 379, 380
Paras, Justice, 377
pardon, 268, 314
Parker, Judge, 318, 320
Pasadena, 164, 165, 391
Patel, Judge, 271, 279, 280, 294
Paul Weiss, 386
pawn shops, 191–194
Pearl Harbor, 166, 201, 209, 210, 215, 219, 220, 224, 226, 229, 240, 241, 251, 252, 263, 268, 283, 286, 306
Peck, Estelle, 252–254
People v. Washington, 149–158, 373
Perez v. Sharp, 159, 166
permanent resident, 41, 65, 82, 269, 274, 295, 322, 326
Perry, Commodore Matthew, 6
Perry, Jimmy, 404, 409–410
Persian, 322
Personal Justice Denied, 210, 211, 274, 275
petition for certiorari, 39, 42, 83, 231, 340, 358, 366, 371
Pew Research Center, 333, 354
Pham, Phuong, 391
Philadelphia, 5, 24, 168
Philippine Army, 298
Philippines, 6, 32, 55, 56, 103, 159, 160, 164-166, 210, 219, 298, 299, 322, 334, 381, 382
Philips Academy, 186
Piche, Lloyd, 411, 412
Piche, Robert, 411
Pick Handle Brigade, 115
Pigtail Ordinance, 127, 135, 143
plantation economy, 345
plea bargain, 317
plenary power, 33, 34, 36, 63
Plessy v. Ferguson, 135, 178, 179, 182, 296, 360
police officer, 16, 349, 373, 378, 379, 404, 410
police regulation, 137
politicians, 107, 200, 207
Polynesian, 98
Pomona Assembly Center, 252
Pope, Circuit Judge, 308
population, 5, 26, 33, 47, 51, 54, 66, 98, 99, 110, 111, 117, 125, 127, 143, 144, 156, 182, 188, 189, 200, 220–222, 233, 240, 253, 284, 329, 330, 334, 338, 340, 348, 353–355, 357, 370, 408
Port Authority, 349, 350
Portland, 18, 220, 228, 229, 280
Poughkeepsie, 185
Powell, Justice, 279, 358, 361, 362
Powell, Wyoming, 261
preemption, 206
pregnant tourists, 66
preliminary injunction, 15, 34, 39, 42, 52, 60, 61, 82, 206, 326, 331, 381, 388
Presidential Citizens Medal, 297
Presidential Medal of Freedom, 296, 297
Principles of Federal Prosecution, 380
prisoners of war (or POWs), 307, 310, 312–314
privileges and immunities, 132, 154, 393
Proclamation No. 9645, 38, 39, 52, 56
proficiency in English, 183
promotion, 175, 190, 325, 339, 349, 350, 368
propaganda, 48, 201, 217, 220, 230, 309, 310
property ownership, 206, 207, 414
prosecutorial discretion, 304, 380, 382
prosecutorial immunity, 381
prosecutorial misconduct, 278, 407, 408
Protestants, 62
Public Proclamation No. 1, 215–217, 272, 287
Punjab, 95, 97, 98, 100–102

Q

Qing dynasty, 109
Quackenbush, Judge, 335
qualified immunity, 136, 381, 382
quarantine, 15, 143–146
Queen of Great Britain, 13
Queen of the Pacific, 119, 120

Questionnaire for National Security, 331
queue ordinance, 131
Quint, Leander, 16
quotas, 10, 37, 89, 169, 170, 204, 333, 341, 348, 361

R

racism, 104, 105, 109, 190, 199, 202, 203, 205, 209, 238, 241, 250, 251, 289, 294, 348, 350, 352, 354, 356, 406
Racketeer Influenced and Corrupt Organizations Act, 388
Radio Tokyo, 306, 309, 310, 312
railroads, 6, 34, 119
Raleigh, 411
Rats, 145
Reagan, President, 43, 46, 62, 295
real property law, 207
Reconstructed Guerilla Roster, 299
Reconstruction, 148, 399
Red Sea, 315
redlining, 413
Redmond, Paul, 316
redress, 13, 132, 133, 137, 138, 207, 209, 211, 273, 294, 295, 297, 298
Reed, Justice, 203
Reed, William, 24
religious animus, 47, 58, 63
relocation center, 211, 212, 223, 234–236, 246–250, 252, 254, 261–265
reparation, 110, 207, 210, 211, 295, 297, 298
repeal of Chinese Exclusion Act, 19, 189, 204
Rescission Act of 1946, 298, 299
restrictive covenants, 207
reverse discrimination, 301
Reyes, Lieutenant, 312
Reynolds, William Bradford, 406
right to marry, 155, 168, 170, 171
Roberts, Chief Justice John, 38, 62, 256, 358, 359, 369
Roberts, Justice Owen, 236
Rock Springs, Wyoming, 118–119
Rogers, Marjorie, 164–165
Rohrbach, D.W., 124
Roldan, Salvador, 160, 164, 165
Roman law, 69, 76
Rome, 194
Roosevelt, President Franklin Delano, 55, 205, 209, 245, 251, 298
Roosevelt, President Theodore, 110, 200, 201
Rosedale Consolidated High School, 174–177, 179
Rosenberg, Julius, 315

S

sabotage, 215, 218–224, 226, 231–233, 239–241, 246, 248–250, 271, 272, 295
Sacramento, 246, 250, 375, 376
Saeed, Faiza, 348
sailors, 5, 384
salmon, 333, 334, 337, 338, 345
same-sex marriage, 170–171
Samoan, 356
San Diego County, 195, 205
San Francisco, 5, 10, 11, 14–17, 22, 26, 66, 67, 94, 109, 115, 117, 127, 128, 131, 135, 137, 141–144, 146, 147, 172, 182, 186, 245, 250, 280, 306, 308, 371, 373, 375, 377, 408
San Francisco Unified School District, 182, 183
San Leandro, 213, 231, 236, 245
San Quentin, 166
Santa Anita, 212
Sawyer, Circuit Judge, 84, 92, 160
Schroeder, Circuit Judge, 281, 294
Scott Act of 1888, 19, 22
scrutiny, 41, 50, 58, 168, 171, 202, 227, 231, 276, 279, 299, 323–329, 332, 344, 362, 363, 365, 367, 378
Seabrook, 389, 390, 391, 394, 396
Sears Roebuck, 314
Seattle, 82, 100, 119–121, 123, 191, 194, 213, 214, 216, 217, 220, 227, 280, 281, 294, 327, 338, 385
Seattle Anti-Chinese Riot, 119–120
Seattle Morning Times, 123
Secretary of Defense, 322, 323
Secretary of War, 209, 215, 216, 231, 237, 271, 285, 287
Selective Service, 259–261, 263–265, 269
Selective Training and Service Act, 260
sheriff, 11, 119, 120, 127–129, 134–136
Sherman Act, 388, 396, 397
shrimpers, 387, 390–391, 398

Sick Keesar, 5
sidewalk ordinance, 127
Sikh, 100-102, 123, 385
Silicon Valley, 348, 349
Singapore, 211, 219, 312
Singh, Amandeep, 331–332
Sirosky, Robert, 403, 404, 406, 407, 410
Sixth Circuit, 401, 411
slavery, 3, 9, 18, 71–73, 76, 84, 92, 139, 149–151, 155–157
Smith, Theodore, 286
Snake River, 121
Socialist Labor Party, 115
Sotomayor, Justice, 52, 62, 83, 256, 358, 364, 369
South Dakota, 117, 166
South Korea, 332
South Vietnam, 387
Southern Poverty Law Center, 387, 389, 400
Spanish-American War, 159
spies, 206, 301, 303, 305, 321
spousal privilege, 166
Sprague, Justice, 153
Spring Valley Primary School, 174
Squire, Governor, 121
Standard Form 86, 331
Stanfield, James, 388–390, 394
Stanford University, 50
State Department, 40, 59, 66, 119, 121, 125, 219, 263, 309, 356
stereotypes, 281, 294, 349, 352, 354, 362, 367, 369
Stockton Street, 144, 145
Stone, Chief Justice, 214, 228, 281, 284
Stop AAPI Hate, 386
Students for Fair Admissions, Inc. (or SFFA), 358, 359, 366, 367, 369
Stuyvesant High School, 369, 370
Suffolk County District Attorney, 381
Suffolk County Police Department, 381
Supremacy Clause, 33
Supreme Court, U.S., 6, 10, 11, 14–16, 32–35, 38, 58, 64, 80–83, 88, 95, 100, 101, 103, 110, 135, 142, 151, 164, 172, 176, 180–183, 189, 204–206, 230, 245, 250, 255–257, 263, 265, 267, 269, 274–279, 281–294, 297, 300, 314, 327, 328, 335, 336, 338, 346, 347, 357, 358, 369–371, 395, 407, 413
Sutherland, Justice 89, 94, 95, 101, 103

T

Tacoma, 116, 120
Taft, William Howard, 103, 174
Taiping Rebellion, 6
Taiwan, 305, 316, 331
Takao Ozawa, 88, 89, 91, 94, 102, 103
Takeuchi, Mamoru, 211
Tanforan, 213, 245, 250
Tang, Judge, 335–337
Tao, Feng, 303
Tape, Joseph, 172, 174
Tape, Mamie, 172, 174
Tape, Mary, 172, 174
Tape v. Hurley, 172, 174, 182, 301, 357
Temple University, 304
temporarily present foreigners, 66
Tenth Circuit, 266, 267, 303
test case, 158, 245, 267
Texas, 15, 34, 222, 331, 344, 358, 387–389, 394, 397–400
Texas Emergency Reserve, 392, 393
Texas Knights, 387, 388, 391, 399, 400
The Argument of Nationality, 116
The Bar Admission Cases, 184–190
The Chinese Must Go, 21, 111, 188
The Land Law Case, 194
The Slants, 413
Thind, Bhagat Singh, 88, 91, 95, 101, 102, 322
Thirteenth Amendment, 18, 72, 76, 78, 84, 149–151, 153–157, 388, 395
Thomas Jefferson High School, 370, 371
Thomas, Justice, 62, 358, 367, 371
time of war, 218, 219, 222, 223, 226, 234, 236, 251, 263, 268, 276
Title VI, 183, 184, 358
Title VII, 336, 339–341, 343, 345–347, 349, 351, 352
Tiwari v. Mattis, 323, 332
Tobera, Fermin, 124
Toguri D'Aquino, Iva Ikuko, 306–309, 313, 314, 380
Tokyo Rose, 306–308, 380
Tong, Dr. Gene, 111–113, 115
tortious interference, 397, 398
Toyota, Hidemitsu, 103
Trafficking Victims Protection Act, 382
Travel Ban, 37, 38, 48, 55–57, 62–64, 228, 246, 255, 300
treason, 242, 301, 303, 306–308, 310, 311, 313, 314

Treaty of Paris, 6
treaty-making power, 78, 133, 192
Tren de Aragua, 252
Truman, President, 268, 298
Trump, President Donald, 37, 39, 48, 54–57, 65, 81, 246, 252, 351, 400
Tsien, Hsue-Shem, 315
Tule Lake, 246, 249, 262, 266
Tung Hing Tong, 141, 142
Tydings McDuffie Act, 166

U
U.S. Census, 348, 354
U.S.S. Mason, 315
UC Davis Law School, 190,
UCLA, 167, 251, 253, 294, 297, 306
undocumented foreigners, 15, 66
unequal hand, 140
Union Pacific Railroad, 118
United Kingdom, 80
United Nations, 203, 219
United States v. Fujii, 259
United States v. Okamoto, 259
universal (or national) injunctions, 39, 42, 52, 64, 82
University of Alberta, 281
University of California, Davis, 190, 360
University of Illinois, 386
University of North Carolina (or UNC), 358, 359, 362–366, 414
University of Southern California, 314
University of Tennessee, 303
University of Washington, 214, 227, 335
Urdu, 5, 322

V
vaccinations, 145, 146
Vancouver, 123, 229
Venezuela, 40–42, 252
Veterans Administration, 298, 299
veterans benefits, 298, 299
Vietnamese, 352, 355, 356, 387–394, 396, 398–400, 411
Vietnamese fishermen, 387–392, 394, 396, 398–400
Vietnamese Fishermen's Association, 387, 388, 399
Vinson, Chief Justice, 195, 203
violence, 4, 24, 48, 54, 105, 110, 111, 115, 117–119, 121, 123–125, 158, 200, 203, 239, 252, 301, 354, 380, 385–388, 390, 391, 394, 398, 400, 410, 413
Virginia, 140, 167–169, 360, 361, 370, 403
Visa Waiver Program, 44, 51, 59, 60, 82
Vivian Davies, 101
voluntary evacuation, 205
von Karman, Theodore, 315
Voorhees, Judge, 280, 286

W
Waite, Emery, 390
Wallowa County, 121
Walzel, Jerry, 391
Wang, Shujun, 305
War Brides Act, 169, 170
War Department, 210, 259, 281, 285–288, 290
War on Terrorism, 300
war power, 49, 218, 221, 222, 225, 232, 244, 266
Wards Cove, 333–338, 346, 347
Wards Cove Packing Co. v. Atonio, 333, 338, 347
Warren Court, 245
Washington, 18, 21, 25, 32, 38, 39, 48, 82, 88, 91, 100, 115, 116, 119–121, 123, 135, 167, 191, 192, 214, 216, 219, 220, 227, 274, 280, 281, 285, 287, 292, 327, 335, 339, 406
Washington Post, 321, 353
Washington, George 48, 149, 321
Watsonville, 124
Wayne County, 400
Webster, 85, 160
Webster, Daniel, 268, 269
Western Defense Command, 209, 214–216, 263, 282, 285, 286
Whatcom County, 123
Wickersham, George, 88
WilmerHale, 369
Wilson, President, 201
Wo Lee, 140, 141
Wong Kim Ark, 66–68, 74, 75, 79–82, 87
Wong, Norman, 81
wooden buildings, 136–138, 141, 142
Woods, James, 376
Woodward Avenue, 404
Workingmen's Party, 115, 117, 188
Workingmen's Trade and Labor Union, 117
World War I, 88, 100, 252, 269

World War II, 55, 95, 104, 166, 169, 201, 207, 211, 252, 254, 259, 268, 275, 295–298, 314, 322, 332
Wyoming, 118, 119, 121, 166, 252, 254, 259–261, 264

X

Xi, Xiaoxing, 304
Xiong, Qi Eva, 331, 332

Y

Yasui, Minoru 211, 213, 228–230, 245, 271, 280, 292–294, 297
Yatko, Timothy, 166–167
yellow race, 85, 92, 96, 160, 175, 176, 178
Yellow Terror, 108
Yellowstone National Park, 259
Yemen, 39–41, 51, 315
Yick Wo, 140–142
Yick Wo v. Hopkins, 74, 136, 137, 140–142, 144, 188, 202, 221, 226, 360, 405, 411
Yonkers, 386
Yoo, Jay, 375

Z

Zelikow, Philip, 400
Zero Hour, 306, 309, 310, 312
Zia, Helen, 318, 411, 413
Zilly, District Judge, 323
Zongo, Ousamane, 379